D1233076

INDUSTRIAL REAL ESTATE

INDUSTRIAL REAL ESTATE

A Real Estate Study of the
Center for Real Estate and Urban Economic Studies
University of Connecticut

By

DR. WILLIAM N. KINNARD, JR., MAI, SRA

Director and Professor of Finance
and Real Estate

Manuscript Commissioned by the
S.I.R. Educational Fund of the
Society of Industrial Realtors

SOCIETY OF INDUSTRIAL REALTORS
of the National Association of Real Estate Boards
Washington, D.C.
1967

The Society of Industrial Realtors dedicates this book to NINA BARKER *in recognition of her 22 years of loyal, devoted service to the organization.*

Preface

FOR almost a decade, the Society of Industrial Realtors has been interested in the development of a book on industrial real estate. The present volume is the result of that long-held desire. It is a unique volume. As of this time, it is the only complete book on industrial real estate known to have been written.

Dr. William N. Kinnard, Jr., has authored a textbook with handbook characteristics. The book, devoted exclusively to industrial real estate, is intended for readers who are already skilled in the general subject of urban real estate principles and practices, and who seek information on the special characteristics of industrial property to add to their understanding of real estate in general. The book may be used as a textbook for a course in industrial real estate, or it may be used effectively as a major supplementary reference source for courses in real estate principles, appraising, real estate finance, and real estate administration. The author has purposely repeated important points throughout the book because of its reference or handbook aspects.

Early attempts by the Society of Industrial Realtors to sponsor the development of such a book did not materialize, largely because information on the unique characteristics of industrial real estate practices was not documented. The procedural break-through that finally resulted in the development of the present volume came in the spring of 1966.

The plan was relatively simple. An outline of the entire book was completed, and panels composed of members of the Society of Industrial Realtors were assembled to provide information and details of practice on the topics involved. Dr. Kinnard met with each of the panels, conducted interviews following the topical outlines, asked for illustrations, documentation, and examples. The contributions of members of the panels were merged with Dr. Kinnard's own manuscript to form the various chapters of this book. Each chapter draft was sent to the resource personnel for review and commentary and subsequently was returned to Dr. Kinnard for integration with other chapters and for final editing. The product is a tribute to the cooperation and accord of the executive staff, Society of Industrial Realtors; S.I.R. officers and members; and academic personnel of the Center for Real Estate and Urban Economic Studies, School of Business Administration, The University of Connecticut. The book is especially a tribute to the talents, energies, efforts, and perseverance of Dr. William N. Kinnard, Jr.

The project has been sponsored by the S.I.R. Educational Fund, which is supported by contributions from members of the Society of Industrial Realtors.

While this book is certain to be of great importance in learning or teaching about industrial real estate, its greatest contribution could be persuading those in the field to record experiences, document events, and summarize practices for use in subsequent industrial real estate treatises.

ROBERT O. HARVEY, Dean
School of Business Administration
The University of Connecticut
Storrs, Connecticut

Acknowledgments

IN the development of this book, information, advice and commentary were obtained from a large number of widely scattered sources. Published materials are acknowledged at appropriate places in the text.

Special mention must be made of the singular debt owed the writings of Dr. William M. Shenkel, formerly of the University of Florida, and currently Professor of Real Estate at the University of Georgia.

Members of the Society of Industrial Realtors throughout the United States graciously submitted to lengthy and intensive interviews with the author over a two-year period. Without their assistance, the level of accuracy and the scope of coverage of this book could not have been achieved. Among those members of S.I.R. who generously shared their experiences and views are: Arthur Balsam, Philadelphia; Vincent J. Byrnes, Paramus, New Jersey; Thomas J. Daly, New York; Max J. Derbes, Jr., New Orleans; W. W. Dillard, Arlington, Texas; Robert L. Free, Cleveland; R. John Griefen, Boston; the late James E. Hanson, Hackensack, New Jersey; Peter O. Hanson, Hackensack; Tom H. Lang, Cleveland; Bernard Manekin, Baltimore; Edmund J. McRickard, New York; B. Kent Murphy, Honolulu; C. B. O'Gorman, Riverside, California; J. Baldwin Pearson, Bridgeport; Frank A. Schlesinger, Newark; David Scribner, New York; Clinton B. Snyder, Jersey City; S. N. Tideman, Jr., Chicago; and B. H. Waterbury, Jr., Baltimore.

Robert Y. Adams, Community Planning Consultant for the American Electric Power Service Corporation, provided invaluable assistance in the development of Chapter 17. Robert E. Boley, Director, Industrial Program, Urban Land Institute, assisted in the development and review of Chapters 15 and 16.

In addition to providing necessary market information, several members of S.I.R. also commented on draft chapters in the manuscript. They included: Max J. Derbes, Jr., New Orleans; Peter O. Hanson, Hackensack; Tom H. Lang, Cleveland; William Martien, Baltimore; William W. Tanney, Birmingham, Michigan; and B. H. Waterbury, Jr., Baltimore.

Particular thanks are due Irving Korb of Oakland and David Scribne of New York City, who read the entire manuscript and offered many valuable comments throughout.

Throughout the entire process of gathering data, developing ideas and writing the manuscript, assistance and encouragement were forthcoming from the professional staff of the Society of Industrial Realtors: Mrs. Nina Barker, Executive Vice President; John G. (Jerry) Davis, Assistant Executive Vice President; and David Rutherford, Director of Education. Jerry Davis was especially helpful throughout the difficult months of writing, editing, and rewriting. Although it is far from adequate, particular thanks are extended to him here.

The physical task of typing, editing, and proofing fell to the staff of the Center for Real Estate and Urban Economic Studies at the University of Connecticut. Over a prolonged period, the exacting job of typing manuscript was completed by Pauline Drouin, Marilyn LeBlanc, Carol Lutes, Nancy Lyman, and Carol Searing. Exceptionally fine editorial assistance came from Janine Robert, Sidney Seamans, and Heather Seay. Mrs. Seay also performed admirably the unpopular but necessary task of coordinating the efforts of typists and editors.

From the inception of this project in the Center for Real Estate and Urban Economic Studies, one person was a source of constant support and encouragement. He contributed innumerable suggestions for improvement in the approach and in the writing, and continuously lent a sympathetic ear to the author's ideas and problems. Without the help of Dr. Robert O. Harvey, Dean of the School of Business Administration at The University of Connecticut, this book literally would not have been completed. His critical role in its production is gratefully acknowledged.

Despite all this assistance and advice, errors and omissions will inevitably have crept into the text. For these, and for the opinions and conclusions expressed throughout the book, only the undersigned can be responsible.

WILLIAM N. KINNARD, JR.

Storrs, Connecticut
April, 1967

Table of Contents

Exhibits

Chapter 13

PART I

The Economics of
Industrial Real Estate

1 The Field of Industrial Real Estate

THE study of real estate seeks understanding of the principles and techniques by which real estate may be most efficiently used. The most efficient use of real estate in a market economy tends to produce the greatest net returns over the long run.

The specific concern of this book is with *industrial* real estate. The basic economic and market principles applicable to real estate analysis in general are equally applicable to industrial real estate. What sets industrial real estate apart from other types of real estate is the manner in which it is used, the type of user occupying it, and the processes which it houses.

Before a meaningful discussion of principles and techniques involved in achieving the most efficient use and allocation of industrial real estate can be undertaken, it is necessary to reach an agreement on precisely what is meant by Industrial Real Estate. The field must be carefully delineated. Beyond this, a review of the general economic principles of the real estate market as they apply to industrial real estate is appropriate. Then the specific methods and techniques of behavior peculiar to industrial real estate activity can be examined meaningfully.

INDUSTRY DEFINED

The basic function of all urban real estate is to provide a site or location for human activity. Its value on the market is a direct function of the type of activity that may be conducted on the premises, and the efficiency which the realty imparts to the performance of this activity. This is the case whether one is concerned with an unimproved site or a site improved with buildings.

Industrial real estate, therefore, includes all land and buildings (often referred to as "urban space") either utilized or suited for industrial activities. "Industry" is based upon manufacturing, but is much more inclusive. The United States economy is essentially oriented toward industrial activity,

3

despite a long-term trend toward increasing emphasis on service activities. Industry embraces all activities involved in the production, storage, and distribution of tangible economic goods, rather than intangible services.

Manufacturing has been defined as "the mechanical or chemical trans-formation of inorganic or organic substances into new products." [1] This includes all activities which are involved in the creation of what economists call *form utility*.[2] In this process, physical resources are transformed, fabricated and assembled into other physical goods.

The Analytical-Functional Approach

As used in the analysis of industrial real estate, "Industry" refers to a classification of activities on some functional or logical basis. The Industrial Council of the Urban Land Institute has provided the following definition, which is probably the best available working statement of the activities included under the heading of industrial real estate:

> "Industry is the gainful activity involved in producing, distributing, and changing the form of raw materials, or of assembling components and parts, packaging, warehousing, and transporting finished products." [3]

This concept obviously includes all activities that could be regarded as manufacturing, since it involves production, changing form, assembly, and packaging. In addition, however, it also includes distribution and warehousing of the product of the manufacturing process, as well as merchant wholesaling. The bulk storage and distribution of the finished product are *incidental to* the fabricating and form-transformation process. Thus, wholesale or retail outlets essential to the distribution of manufactured goods are also included under the heading of industrial real estate.

In addition to fabrication and distribution activities, industry includes research and development or laboratory activities, whether as an integral part of a manufacturing firm or operating independently to serve the needs of manufacturing. Moreover, the facilities of transportation companies which provide terminal space and maintenance facilities as a service to industrial firms come under this classification. These include public warehousing facilities, airport terminal services, stockyards, and packing and crating activities. Finally, such business services as publishing and printing, automobile and equipment repair, and cleaning establishments are regarded as industrial activities.

To a very large extent, industrial service organizations can be identified by their concentration or "agglomeration" in the immediate vicinity of the manufacturing firms that they are best designed to serve. Many studies have revealed that such service facilities represent a significant segment

---

[1] U.S. Bureau of the Budget, *Standard Industrial Classification Manual* (Washington, U.S. Government Printing Office, 1957), p. 43.

[2] For a discussion of utility and its particular applications to real estate activity, consult American Institute of Real Estate Appraisers, *The Appraisal of Real Estate*, 4th ed. (Chicago, The Author, 1964), pp. 14–21.

[3] Quoted in William M. Shenkel, *Principles and Practices of Industrial Real Estate: A Course Syllabus,* 3rd Printing (Washington, Society of Industrial Realtors, 1963), p. 2.

of the industrial base in certain regions, and their real estate needs are most nearly consonant with those of manufacturing establishments.[4]

It is important for the broker to recognize that industry encompasses considerably more than manufacturing and directly related activities, so that he can approach the field of industrial real estate with full appreciation of its scope.

The Zoning Concept

Because zoning is a powerful land-use control that prescribes either what may be done or what may not be done—or both—in substantial areas of the United States, one way to identify "industry" is to ascertain the kind of land uses and building uses that are permitted in an Industrial Zone.[5] There are two practical difficulties with this approach, however. The first is partly terminological, because many communities use the term "Manufacturing" rather than "Industrial" in their zoning.

A much more significant limitation, however, is the fact that there is extremely wide and apparently nonsystematic variation in the range of uses that are either directly permitted or specifically excluded from Industrial Zones. This is true even when the three most widely used categories of "Light Industrial," "General Industrial," and "Heavy Industrial" are combined for purposes of analysis. While these precise titles are not always employed, they represent the usual bases of distinction.

The use of zoning ordinances to define industry is generally a pragmatic guide in any given local area, but it is too imprecise because most zoning ordinances permit at least some commercial activities in Industrial Zones. It appears that a broad conception of "Industry" is necessary for effective administration of land use regulations.

Two examples will serve to illustrate the wide range of uses that might be included in an Industrial Zone, and which could lead the industrial real estate specialist afield if he should choose to define his sphere of activities in terms of all uses permitted in Industrial Zones.

For example, the Cook County (Chicago) zoning ordinance permits the following uses in Restricted Manufacturing Districts: auto laundries, automobile service stations, and "production, processing, cleaning, servicing, testing, repair, or storage of materials, goods, or products . . . and which shall not be injurious or offensive to the occupants of adjacent premises . . ."[6] Restricted Manufacturing Districts also permit the location of building material supply houses, contractor offices, dry cleaning establishments, greenhouses, laundries, mail-order houses, medical and dental clinics, public utility uses, recreation buildings, stadiums, auditoriums, trade schools, wholesale establishments, and other similar uses.

[4] See, for example, Zenon S. Malinowski and William N. Kinnard, Jr., *The Metals Service Industry: A Case Study of a Satellite Industry* (New York, McGraw-Hill, 1960).

[5] For a fuller discussion of Industrial Zones and Industrial Zoning, see Chapter 4 of this book, or consult F. Stuart Chapin, Jr., *Urban Land Use Planning*, rev. ed. (Urbana, Illinois, University of Illinois Press, 1965).

[6] *Cook County Zoning Ordinance Adopted March 8, 1960, as Amended to January 15, 1962,* Board of Commissioners of Cook County, p. 122A.

A second example is taken from the zoning regulations of Minneapolis, Minnesota, which allows the following nonindustrial uses in Industrial Districts: [7]

Storage	Laundries
Auto laundries	Lodges
Service stations	Mail-order houses
Banks	Medical and dental clinics
Building materials	Packing and crating
Cartage facilities	Printing
Contractors	Public utilities
Community centers	Radar towers
Drug stores	Radio studios
Dry cleaners	Railroad resthouses
Dwelling units	Restaurants
Fuel sales	Signs
Garages	Stadiums
Greenhouses	Taverns
Highway maintenance shops	Trade schools

These examples indicate that industrial zones often constitute the loosest type of districting since many nonindustrial uses are allowed in the zone. Such permission not only aggravates any shortage of industrial space which may exist (and this is a problem common to many communities), but also makes the identification of the appropriate scope of activity of the industrial real estate specialist considerably more complex. The definition of industrial real estate, utilized in the course in the *Principles of Industrial Real Estate Brokerage* presented by the University of California as part of its Extension Certificate Program in Real Estate, is "any real property zone (Industrial) used for warehousing, wholesaling, distribution, assembly or manufacturing purposes where permitted to be so used under a zone variance." [8] This is a pragmatic approach fraught with potential difficulties. Since it is utilized on occasion, it must be recognized by the industrial real estate broker.

The Approach of the Professional Industrial Real Estate Broker

Another way to identify the realm of industrial real estate is to discover what kinds of properties industrial brokers handle. More significantly, the exclusions from their normal activities indicate the kinds of property that normally would *not* be regarded as industrial real estate, such as retail, some wholesale, office, consumer service, and other "commercial" activities. The industrial specialist will, of course, assist in finding an office or retail outlet (or even a residence) for a manufacturing client. Indeed, the entire effort to define and delineate the area of industrial real estate can become bogged down in attempts to achieve too high a degree of precision. For example, a major food chain in California sought the assistance of a

---

[7] Cited in Chapin, *op. cit.,* p. 303 ff.

[8] University of California—Los Angeles, Extension Division, *Principles of Industrial Real Estate Brokerage* (Los Angeles, The Author, 1962), p. 2.

member of the Society of Industrial Realtors (S.I.R.) in locating and developing a plant for its egg processing activities. This chain utilized commercial brokers for assistance in locating its retail outlets. Simultaneously, the same S.I.R. was retained by a commercial bakery to handle its real estate problems. This included both its bakery facilities and several other retail outlets. In this instance, the broker felt qualified through past experience to undertake the retail assignments as well.

The important point in the foregoing discussion is that industrial real estate encompasses land and buildings (or urban space) utilized for more than just manufacturing activities. Storage, trans-shipment, distribution, and service functions clearly associated with manufacturing are as much a province of the industrial real estate broker as are fabricating and assembly. The location and siting of these activities is functionally related to the process of delivering manufactured goods to the purchaser: consumer, retailer, wholesaler, or another manufacturer.

The Standard Industrial Classification System

For purposes of analysis and identification, industries and industrial groupings are often divided according to the Standard Industrial Classification System published by the United States Bureau of the Budget.[9] Quite apart from any assistance it might provide in indicating what "Industry" is and what it is not, the Standard Industrial Classification System (often referred to as S.I.C.) offers assistance to the industrial real estate broker on two important counts. First, it helps to define and delineate the area of concern in a particular industrial real estate problem, by indicating the kinds of products and the kinds of processes that are (in the estimation of the compilers of the S.I.C. coding system at least) closely related to one another. This is extremely important when the identification of one area of interest is a central portion of a real estate problem.

Even more important is the fact that the S.I.C. coding system helps to identify the characteristics of similar processes and related activities. The industrial real estate specialist confronted with a land use or space use problem thus has a means for ascertaining the range of probable and reasonable users. When a facility is available for sale or lease, or when a site is to be made available, a study of S.I.C. characteristics can offer insights into potential buyers and/or users of the space that is to be marketed.

This system is contained and explained in the *Standard Industrial Classification Manual* published by the Bureau of the Budget. It is a system of code identification for *all* types of economic activity within the American economy, which goes into successively more detail as the size of the activity groupings decreases. The four stages of classification and code identification are, in decreasing order of size of the component groups, the one-digit Divisions, the two-digit Major Groups, the three-digit Groups, and the four-digit Subgroups. The number of categories found in each division is illustrated in Exhibit 1.

---

[9] U.S. Bureau of the Budget, *op. cit.*

Exhibit 1

THE INDUSTRIAL DIVISIONS IN THE STANDARD INDUSTRIAL
CLASSIFICATION SYSTEM

Division Code (1-Digit)	Divisions	Number of Major Groups (2-Digit)	Number of Groups (3-Digit)	Number of Sub-Groups (4-Digit)
A	Agriculture, forestry, and fisheries	5	17	39
B	Mining	5	20	55
C	Contract construction	3	12	21
D	Manufacturing	21	148	433
E	Transportation, communication, electric, gas, and sanitary services	9	38	72
F	Wholesale and retail trade	9	54	121
G	Finance, insurance, and real estate	8	32	78
H	Services	14	62	106
I	Government	4	(1)	(1)
J	Nonclassifiable establishments	1	1	1
	Total, all divisions	79	384	926

SOURCE: U.S. Bureau of the Budget, *Standard Industrial Classification Manual* (Washington, U.S. Government Printing Office, 1957), p. 15.

(1) There are no three-digit or four-digit groups in the Government Division of the code.

Care must be exercised in the use of this system. The classification of a firm or of an establishment (one location or one plant within a multi-unit firm) is based upon the major source of income and/or employment for that firm or plant. Large, complex units will therefore be classified under one heading, even though they carry on several activities. Despite this important limitation, the S.I.C. system is an extremely useful tool for analytical purposes.

As indicated in Exhibit 1, there are 10 Divisions of one-digit Industrial Groups. A Division is a group of establishments engaged in the same or similar kinds of general economic activity. For example, Manufacturing is one Division.

Within each Division, there are two-digit Major Groups. As shown in Exhibit 2, there are 21 Major Groups within the Manufacturing Division. Major Group 19 (Ordnance and Accessories) is occasionally included with Major Group 39 (Miscellaneous Manufacturing Industries) in many reports of economic data. The Major Groups are identified either in terms of raw material used or end-product. As close a degree of similarity as possible is maintained within each Major Group to permit close comparison.

Each Major Group is subdivided into Groups identified by a three-digit code number. Using Fabricated Metal Products (S.I.C. 34) as an illustra-

Exhibit 2

THE 21 TWO-DIGIT MAJOR GROUPS IN THE
MANUFACTURING DIVISION OF THE
STANDARD INDUSTRIAL CLASSIFICATION SYSTEM

S.I.C. Code	Major Group
19	Ordnance and accessories
20	Food and kindred products
21	Tobacco manufacturers
22	Textile mill products
23	Apparel and other finished products made from fabrics and similar materials
24	Lumber and wood products, except furniture
25	Furniture and fixtures
26	Paper and allied products
27	Printing, publishing and allied industries
28	Chemicals and allied products
29	Petroleum refining and related industries
30	Rubber and miscellaneous plastics products
31	Leather and leather products
32	Stone, clay and glass products
33	Primary metal industries
34	Fabricated metal products except ordnance, machinery, equipment and supplies
35	Machinery, except electrical
36	Electrical machinery, equipment and supplies
37	Transportation equipment
38	Professional, scientific, and controlling instruments; photographic and optical goods; watches and clocks
39	Miscellaneous manufacturing industries

SOURCE: U.S. Bureau of the Budget, *Standard Industrial Classification Manual* (Washington, U.S. Government Printing Office, 1957).

tive Major Group to indicate how industries are subdivided further, Exhibit 3 shows that Fabricated Metal Products consists of nine Groups for which separate statistics are reported.

Finally, the three-digit Groups are subdivided into four-digit Subgroups. For example, Cutlery, Hand Tools and General Hardware (S.I.C. 342) are subdivided into four Subgroups: Cutlery, 3421; Hand and Edge Tools, 3423; Hand Saws and Saw Blades, 3425; and Hardware Not Elsewhere Classified, 3429.

Two examples of the use of the Standard Industrial Classification for reporting data help to point up its importance. Both of these involve manufacturing data, because most industrial real estate is found in the manufacturing area.

The United States *Census of Business* and *Census of Manufactures* reports information on employment, wages, number of establishments, gross

Exhibit 3

THE NINE THREE-DIGIT GROUPS OF
MAJOR GROUP 34, FABRICATED METAL PRODUCTS, IN THE
STANDARD INDUSTRIAL CLASSIFICATION SYSTEM

S.I.C. Code	Group Title
341	Metal cans
342	Cutlery, hand tools, and general hardware
343	Heating apparatus (except electric) and plumbing fixtures
344	Fabricated structural metal products
345	Screw machine products, and bolts, nuts, screws, rivets and washers
346	Metal stampings
347	Coating, engraving, and allied services
348	Miscellaneous fabricated wire products
349	Miscellaneous fabricated metal products

SOURCE: U.S. Bureau of the Budget, *Standard Industrial Classification Manual* (Washington, U.S. Government Printing Office, 1957).

receipts, and value added—all in terms of the Standard Industrial Classification System. Comparisons of the business and industrial mix in one region with that of another area are facilitated through the use of such information. So, too, is growth analysis within a given area.

As a second example, many state labor departments and development commissions issue periodic reports on the number of manufacturing and related establishments in existence, newly formed, and relocating within the state. Changes in the industrial population can be followed and analyzed carefully. These data ordinarily are provided according to Standard Industrial Classification, for ease of analysis.

IMPORTANCE OF INDUSTRY TO THE COMMUNITY

Despite the fact that manufacturing has been increasing less than other activities in the American economy (see Exhibit 4), the United States is still essentially an industrial nation. The industrial real estate broker must be in a position to estimate the role of industry in his particular area of activity, in part to anticipate the kinds and volume of industrial space required in the future. With appropriate forecasting, the broker can initiate actions designed to assure the future availability of adequate industrial space.

Measures of Importance

The relative importance of industrial activity within an area, whether a local community or the entire nation, can be measured in a variety of ways. The most commonly employed measure is the number of employees. For example, the general dividing line between "small" and "large" *manu-*

facturing establishments, when estimating eligibility for Small Business Administration assistance, is the number of employees, although other criteria occasionally apply. On the other hand, dollar volume of business is generally employed to distinguish "small" from "large" establishments in *retailing, wholesaling,* and *service trade.*

Among manufacturing firms, the number of employees is also a good basic guide to land and/or building area requirements. As is demonstrated in Chapter 3, several types of systematic relationships have been noted between the number of employees, and the total floor area and/or total land area occupied by manufacturing plants in various Industrial Groups.

A less common but equally simple measure of relative importance of industry in an area is the number of establishments. This has the obvious disadvantage of assuming comparability among frequently non-comparable units. However, when an analysis by number of establishments is added to a tabulation by employment-size groups, the industrial real estate specialist has a good guide to the amount and type of industrial space required in a given area. A time-series of such figures indicates trends in the demand for industrial space. This information is available in many states. For example, the state of Connecticut publishes periodic inventories of manufacturing establishments that indicate the Major Industrial Group (two-digit S.I.C.), the employee size group, and the location of every manufacturing establishment in the state. Careful comparison of these inventories over time yields considerable information about trends in industrial space requirements throughout the state.

Another direct measure of demand and trends in demand for industrial space is a periodic inventory of land and/or building area actually occupied by industrial establishments. These normally will be undertaken in connection with community planning or urban renewal programs, although local chambers of commerce and local industrial development commissions often undertake such studies as well. For example, a detailed inventory of industrial land and space use emerged as a by-product of the economic studies segment of the Hartford (Connecticut) Community Renewal Program.[10]

The role of industry in the economy may also be measured by one or more of several monetary means: wages paid to employees, profits, gross receipts or sales, and value added. Value added is particularly significant for manufacturing, and is regarded for most purposes as the best dollar measure for comparing the relative economic importance of manufacturing activity among different industries and/or among different geographical areas. Value added by manufacture is derived for each manufacturing establishment (and hence for all establishments in an Industrial Group) by subtracting goods costs (raw materials, parts, components, supplies, fuels, goods purchased for resale, and contract work) from the value of shipments (including resales). An adjustment is also made for the net change in finished goods inventory.

---

[10] Larry Smith & Co., *Economic Studies: Hartford Community Renewal Program* (New York, The Author, 1964).

Most frequently, employment is used as a measure of relative importance and growth. In the following discussions, it will be relied on most heavily.

The Role of Industry in the United States Economy

Because of the imprecise definition of "Industry," it is impossible to estimate accurately the quantitative significance of industrial activity in the American economy. However, it does exceed the importance of manufacturing alone, which *can* be measured effectively. Whether expressed in terms of employment, value added, share of national income, or wages paid, figures for manufacturing understate the importance of industry: locally, regionally, and nationally.

The share of national income generated by manufacturing remained at approximately 30 per cent between 1950 and 1965. It actually declined slightly, as the figures in Exhibit 4 show, yet manufacturing remains by far the largest single source of national income among the Industrial Divisions in the American economy. National income generated in the Manufacturing Division increased less between 1950 and 1965 than did that produced in several other divisions.

Some segment of what is regarded as industrial activity for industrial real estate purposes is included in several of the other divisions. Thus, in-

Exhibit 4

NATIONAL INCOME CLASSIFIED BY INDUSTRIAL ORIGIN: 1950 TO 1965
(Billions of Dollars)

Industrial Division	1950*	1960	1965 (preliminary)	Percentage Change 1950–1965
All industries totals	$241.1	$414.5	$559.0	+132%
Agriculture, forestry and fisheries	17.6	16.9	21.0	+ 19%
Mining and construction	17.2	26.5	34.8	+102%
Manufacturing	76.2	125.8	170.4	+124%
Transportation	13.4	18.2	22.9	+ 71%
Communication	3.3	8.2	11.2	+239%
Electric, gas and sanitary services	3.9	8.9	11.6	+197%
Wholesale and retail trade	40.9	64.4	83.6	+104%
Finance, insurance, and real estate	22.0	45.9	61.0	+177%
Services	21.8	44.4	63.0	+189%
Government and government enterprises	23.6	52.9	75.2	+219%
Rest of the world	1.2	2.4	4.3	+258%

* 1950 figures exclude Alaska and Hawaii.

SOURCE: U.S. Department of Commerce, *Statistical Abstract of the United States 1966* (Washington, U.S. Government Printing Office, 1966), p. 326.

dustry may be said to account for at least one-third of total national employment, and between 35 and 40 per cent of national payroll. Moreover, over one-third of the national income originates with activities that may be regarded as industrial.

This widespread major source of employment and income also requires substantial and increasing proportions of total urban space to house its employees (and their automobiles), its equipment, its laboratories, and its inventory. It is particularly noteworthy that the great majority of industrial establishments employs fewer than five persons. These require space just as much as the giant corporation employing thousands of persons in one plant. Their needs are obviously different, but they are often more acute. The management of such a small industrial organization frequently feels it cannot afford professional real estate assistance, even though in most instances the need for such assistance is greater.

The Impact of Industry on the Tax Base

As the largest employer among the Industrial Divisions in the American economy, manufacturing is also the largest single source of most forms of business taxes collected at the national, state, and local levels. From the point of view of the industrial real estate broker, however, as well as that of the local community, the contributions of industry to the local property tax base is most significant. In analyzing the fiscal effects of industry, however, one should judge the total impact on local government budgets rather than simply the stimulus provided to the property tax base. Although the discussion is normally expressed in terms of the impact of new industry on the local fiscal scene, the continuing role of existing industry has been found to be essentially the same.

New industry may be expected to create pressures on local governments to supply expanded services, such as protection, streets, and utilities. New industry will also definitely add to the local tax base—the "ratables" as they are called in much of the United States, or the "grand list" as it is termed in New England. For communities that subsidize industry with local revenue bonds, the local debt load is affected as well.

If the industry is new to the region and of sufficient size to attract workers from outside (new population), then very probably some of the new families will have children of school age. One of the immediate effects of new industry, therefore, may well be to increase local school budgets. Since school budgets represent a high proportion of local governmental expenditures, this effect may place an unanticipated burden on local governments.

Industrial expansion may call for additional public transportation services. Congestion on local highways, in parking lots, and even in downtown areas may be expected to increase as population expands. Extensive industrial development may also require additional facilities for truck transportation, rail, air, and related services.

Industrial demands on local facilities may strain existing water supplies and sewerage disposal systems. If these utility services are not fully adequate, new utility lines must be constructed to satisfy new industry. Where industrial sewerage and waste disposal create problems that are expensive to resolve, a community may even discourage the industry from locating there.

Added cost in supplying police and fire protection may be another consequence of new industry. Municipal departments, such as the planning department, may also find it necessary to add personnel.

The location of new industries or the expansion of existing industries will affect local tax revenues in two ways: directly, through increased assessed value of the new industrial plant and equipment; and indirectly, through stimulation of residential and commercial construction. It is normally anticipated that the beneficial effects of industry on local revenues will exceed the costs, but few studies are available to support this generalization.

New industry is often sought as a direct means to keep local taxes down. It is reasoned that the new industry will increase the local tax base, so that increased property valuation or higher levies will be unnecessary. This view may or may not be valid in any given community because of the expenses attendant on providing necessary services to both the industry and the supporting activities (including residences) it stimulates.

To the extent that new industry stimulates retail business and other activities, collections from excise taxes, license fees, sales taxes and/or income taxes may also show meaningful increases. Furthermore, an increase in salaries and wages associated with a new industry will generate increased consumption of local goods and services, which in turn creates other employment.

The particular appeal of industry, as opposed to commercial or retail activity as a local revenue stimulant, is that industry can often—at least theoretically—be attracted from outside and provide a new surge of taxable resources into the community. Commercial expansion is often limited by the buying power resident in the region.

The Multiplier Effect of New Industry

While it is by no means restricted to industrial expansion, there is a multiplier effect which is often felt in a local community when new employment or income is injected. It has been demonstrated in studies of actual experience throughout the United States that an external stimulus in the form of new or expanded industry is more likely to occur than is an autonomous increase in commercial or service trade activity. This, in turn, is the foundation of the so-called "economic base" theory most often associated with Homer Hoyt.[11] Stated in its simplest terms, the principle is that an injection of investment funds from outside the community will result in an

[11] For an exposition of Economic Base and Community Multiplier Analysis, see Ralph W. Pfouts, ed., *The Techniques of Urban Economic Analysis* (Trenton, N.J., Chandler-Davis, 1960).

expansion in economic activity substantially greater than the initial investment. Within the framework of this argument, industry is regarded as
peculiarly important as a stimulus to the local economy because most
industrial establishments tend to be net exporters of goods.

The impact may be felt on employment, on income, or on tax revenues,
as was indicated in the preceding section. There is also a multiplying effect
on population and, usually, on housing as well.

A new industry which purchases a considerable amount of its supplies
within the community will multiply the direct effects of wage and salary
payments. This is the income multiplier. Such expansion will tend to increase activity in supplying industries, or even to attract other industries
dependent on the new firm. This further increases consumer expenditures.
As a consequence, income and sales taxes may increase with expanded
business, as has been noted earlier. The effect of new investment by an
industry has led some authorities to suggest that a local income multiplier
of approximately two times the original investment exists. This means that
a new plant with a $500,000 annual payroll may be expected to cause a
total increase in local incomes of $1,000,000.

A study of the metropolitan area of Wichita, Kansas by the Federal
Reserve Bank of Kansas City led to the conclusion that the addition of one
worker to supply outside markets (i.e., an industrial worker) leads to an
increase of approximately one and one-third workers engaged in serving
local markets. This may be translated to an employment multiplier of
approximately two and one-third.[12] In other words, a new plant employing
100 workers would result in 133 additional new jobs in retailing, service
industry, government, and the like. In all, there would be 233 new jobs in
the community.

This result is representative of findings of many similar studies, in which
slight variations in the employment multiplier or income multiplier cited
here were found. In virtually every case, however, a multiplier of approximately 2.0 or greater was found to result from new industrial activity in the
community. Moreover, it appears that the multiplier effect of industrial
expansion is greater when it is combined with an increase in population
through in-migration, and when the industrial expansion occurs in a region
of nearly full employment of labor.

The United States Chamber of Commerce engaged in a study of 11
counties throughout the United States for the period between 1950 and
1960, in an effort to measure the effects of increased manufacturing employment. The study concluded that the specific effects of increased manufacturing employment on the local community will depend on the type of
industry, the labor force, and the utilization of community facilities, among
many other factors. The findings suggested a population multiplier of
approximately 3.6, and an employment multiplier of 1.65. That is to say,
a new manufacturing establishment employing 100 persons would result
in a total of 165 new jobs and 360 new residents in the community.

---

[12] See John E. Moes, *Local Subsidies for Industry* (Chapel Hill, North Carolina: University
of North Carolina Press, 1962), pp. 164–65.

The 65 new non-manufacturing jobs were divided among retailing (19 jobs); professional and related services (14 jobs); business and personal services (6 jobs); construction (5 jobs); and other industries (21 jobs).[13]

Finally, a study of six small communities in Wisconsin and a similar analysis of one small city in Arkansas both confirmed the fact that a net tax receipt gain—a property tax multiplier—was associated with industrial expansion in the communities investigated.[14]

IMPORTANCE OF REAL ESTATE TO INDUSTRY

It has already been noted that the basic function of industrial real estate is to provide a site for industrial activity, so situated and with such facilities that the industrial process housed in the real estate receives the maximum contribution to its efficiency and its profitability. Increased regional shifts in industrial activity throughout the United States, suburbanization of industry, changing technology and processes within industrial production, and changes in tastes and product importance—all have caused industrial firms to develop a substantially sharpened awareness of the significance of real estate to their particular operations. Therefore, it is useful to consider briefly some of the distinguishing ways in which real estate makes its contribution to the industrial firm.

Kinds of Industrial Real Estate

Whenever analysis of real estate is undertaken, it is usual to distinguish between land, and man's improvements on and to the land. These improvements are typically buildings. In the analysis of industrial real estate, such a distinction is especially useful.

An industrial site represents the location at which industrial activity takes place. Primarily, it offers accessibility to important resources or markets, and provides adequate space on which buildings are to be placed. The buildings or improvements should contribute directly to the success of the industrial operation by providing the most efficient environment possible.

Both industrial land and industrial buildings (or improved industrial properties) may be analyzed in terms of the degree of adaptability to more than one use. Thus, industrial sites may be classified as general purpose, special purpose, and single purpose. Single-purpose sites are rarely found, because land is generally adaptable to more than one use. There may be restrictions on the adaptability of land to many uses, however. These restrictions may be functional, based on the size, shape, or other physical characteristics of the site. They may also be legal, reflected in zoning or other land use controls.

The same three categories (general purpose, special purpose, single pur-

    [13] *What New Industrial Jobs Mean to a Community* (Washington: Chamber of Commerce of the United States, 1962), p. 6.
    [14] For details see *The Effect of an Industry on a Small Rural Community* (Little Rock: Arkansas Department of Labor, 1958); and *The Effects of Industrialization on Six Small Wisconsin Cities* (Madison, Wisconsin: Bureau of Business Research and Service, 1959).

pose) can be applied to industrial buildings. These include warehouses, offices, and other non-manufacturing structures, as well as manufacturing plants. General-purpose industrial buildings are those with a wide range of alternative uses. These are often constructed on speculation, and generally are adaptable to light manufacturing, assembly, and/or storage.

Special-purpose buildings are those with physical characteristics or facilities suitable to a restricted range of industrial processes. Heavily insulated storage facilities, for example, are usually required in only a few types of activities.

Single-purpose industrial buildings are those adaptable to only one particular process, or even one particular firm. A grain storage silo, or a petroleum refinery, for example, can be used for little else. Generally speaking, the more specifically facilities are adapted to the particular needs of a given process or firm, the less convertibility there is to other uses. Convertibility is nearly always possible at a price, however. The test of *effective* convertibility or adaptability to alternative uses is cost of conversion. The converted space must be competitive with existing space in which the alternative process or firm can operate efficiently and profitably. This is usually a severe limitation on conversion.

Characteristics of Industrial Real Estate

The peculiar characteristics of industrial real estate indicate the significance of real estate to the industrial firm.

1. *Heavy Investment.* As with all other types of real estate, industrial real estate represents a large commitment of funds or working capital. From the point of view of the user-occupant, the funds could often be utilized better in the productive processes of the firm. Therefore, various financing devices are frequently utilized to minimize the commitments of cash that are necessary to ensure occupancy of the space. This is translated to the fact that industrial real estate is very often investment real estate, with the occupant paying rent to an investor-owner who seeks a profit from the rental of the space.

2. *High Nonliquidity.* In common with other types of real estate, industrial real estate tends to be a slow-moving commodity. Generally, the more specialized the facilities, the less rapidly they will turn over. Moreover, the larger the facility, the more difficult it is to market, in most instances. This enhances the investment risk and calls for special treatment in the real estate investment market.[15]

3. *Process-Related.* The value or contribution of industrial real estate is typically interrelated intimately with the profitability of the industrial process it houses. This is especially true of more specialized industrial real estate.

4. *Customized.* The custom aspect of industrial real estate is enhanced through integration of the real estate with the machinery and inventory of the user-occupant. Indeed, it is often difficult to distinguish between plant

---

[15] For a detailed discussion of this significant point, see Arthur M. Weimer, "Real Estate Decisions are Different," *Harvard Business Review*, November-December, 1966, Vol. 44, No. 6.

and equipment, once the equipment is installed and is functioning as an integral part of the capital investment of the establishment.

5. *Innovation and Functional Obsolescence.* Technological change in industrial processes as well as in construction or design can render industrial real estate facilities functionally obsolescent quite rapidly. This both increases investment risks and requires adaptability on the part of management. It also challenges management to plan boldly into the future in an attempt to minimize these risks.

6. *Immobility.* Because moving industrial equipment and inventory is extremely expensive, most industrial organizations choose to minimize their geographic movement as much as is consistent with efficient and profitable operations. Aside from direct out-of-pocket expenses, interruption of the production process also results in a loss during the period surrounding the move. Therefore, despite pressures from changing locational factors and from obsolescence, a high degree of immobility characterizes most industrial locations. This means that the location decision is very important, even critical, in the success of the organization. Particular care must be exercised to make sure that the location is as nearly appropriate as possible. There is a strong possibility that the firm will occupy its space for a longer period of time than may be justified on the basis of productive efficiency.

Industry's Real Estate Needs

Industry needs real estate in order to house its facilities, its operations, its offices, its inventory, and its employees. Beyond this, however, industrial organizations frequently encounter peculiar real estate needs.

1. *Custom Facilities.* No matter how standardized the industrial process of a particular firm may appear, it has product, process, market, or personnel characteristics that distinguish it from all other industrial operations. If the real estate that it occupies is to contribute to the efficiency and profitability, it must be an integral part in the productive process of the firm. This means that the facilities, the space, and the location must be as nearly optimum as possible. The typical industrial firm, possibly excluding major national concerns that are so active in real estate that they have their own real estate or development departments, usually needs locational advice from the industrial real estate specialist.

2. *Financing.* Whether industrial real estate is owned or leased, the occupant's major desire is often to minimize the amount of capital invested ("tied up") in real estate. Therefore, financing and/or leasing arrangements that offer the safe release of funds which might otherwise be used for working capital or production purposes, are actively sought by the industrial firm.

3. *Location Analysis.* With the exception of the national or regional firm with many facilities, and with a relatively high turnover of locations, most industrial organizations do not enter the real estate market frequently. Consequently, their knowledge of this market is minimal. It may even be

somewhat distorted because of an attempt to transfer their experiences and impressions from the residential real estate market. Their relative immobility underscores the importance that must be attached to the selection of the proper location with appropriate facilities for the particular firm.

4. *Future Marketability.* Less often, but with increasing frequency in recent years, industrial firms also want to dispose of plants or other facilities being vacated. This may be the result of a move or a decision to abandon a particular operation. If the managements of industrial firms are generally ignorant of the procedures involved in *acquiring* industrial real estate, they are even less versed in the techniques or the market through which *disposition* of industrial facilities takes place. Therefore, the industrial firm needs a means to dispose of real estate quickly, efficiently, and reasonably in order to minimize the financial drain of unproductive investment in idle assets. The industrial real estate broker can often perform more meaningful and valuable plant disposition services to the industrial firm than he can acquisition assistance, primarily because he is filling a more pressing need.

5. *Market Advice.* The industrial firm is not usually in the real estate business. Even those organizations with active, full-time real estate departments cannot be sensitive to all regional variations or to developments in all aspects of real estate markets (e.g., finance, leasing, development, zoning). They need information and advice with respect to such developments, but even more they need seasoned insights into market conditions that assist in business decisions and their timing. Just as the industrialist turns to the financial specialist when he is seeking to raise funds, or to decide on the best method for doing so, he should turn to the industrial real estate specialist when he requires assistance in a decision with respect to the acquisition, disposition, or utilization of real estate.

FUNCTIONS OF THE INDUSTRIAL REAL ESTATE BROKER

The industrial real estate broker is basically no different from his counterpart in residential, commercial, or institutional real estate. At the same time, the peculiar characteristics of industrial real estate do lend a flavor to his activities that requires recognition and understanding.

The overriding function of the industrial real estate specialist is to promote the efficient (and hence profitable) use of industrial real estate. This will result in the highest value for the real estate, the greatest profits for the firm, and presumably the greatest overall satisfactions for society. Incidentally, it will also result in the highest fee pattern for the industrial real estate broker. In most instances he acts as an agent or consultant, and is compensated through the payment of commissions or fees, rather than acting as a principal for profit. In each of the major types of functions considered below, the particular contribution of the real estate specialist is that he is the focal point of the transaction. He is the coordinating specialist among other specialized practitioners and principals.

Finance

Financing is critical to any real estate transaction, and is particularly important in industrial real estate because of pressures to minimize cash commitments and cash outflow for real estate. Both credit (or loan funds) and equity funds must be assembled from appropriate sources. It is not sufficient for the broker or consultant to concentrate on sources of financing, however. At least as important is the question of the most appropriate form and terms of financing. In the industrial real estate field, there is a substantial volume of custom or individual financial arrangements. The coordinating, catalytic role of the industrial real estate specialist is particularly significant here.

Valuation

The techniques and methods of real estate valuation (or appraisal) are basically no different for industrial real estate than they are for other types of real estate, especially income-producing real estate. Particular emphasis must be placed on the specialized or custom aspect of the real estate in relation to the user-occupant, however. Moreover, much of what the real estate appraiser does for the potential purchaser or investor is as much investment analysis as it is the valuation of the physical real estate. Indeed, the consideration of Value in Use is in many respects as important as the estimation of Value in Exchange.

Development

The industrial real estate broker may find himself in the position of principal in a pioneering, entrepreneurial undertaking. To this extent, he is actually creating value by providing new market opportunities where previously they did not exist. The industrial specialist will more often be asked to assist the entrepreneur in developing either a single-standing facility, or an industrial park. The developmental problems are much the same, although the planned industrial district has characteristics which require specific experience and knowledge for successful development. An adjunct to development of new industrial facilities is the redevelopment or rehabilitation of existing facilities for new and (hopefully) more profitable uses. In each of these cases, the industrial real estate specialist is the catalytic agent bringing together the necessary ingredients and helping to create either new value or a pattern of new uses which will generate value.

Brokerage and Related Services

As a broker, the industrial real estate specialist is attempting to match the needs of real estate owners with those of industrial users. In many instances, he is as likely to represent the user (purchaser or tenant), as the owner (seller or landlord). The latter is more usual in most other types of real estate transactions. In bringing together owner and user, he is providing a custom service to meet the specific needs of the user. This matching of user needs with facilities tends to distinguish industrial real estate brokerage practice.

In marketing and promotional work, more specific personal contact is made, as compared with the more general market approaches of residential or commercial brokers. Similarly, leasing is more a matter of direct contact with specific potential users or with specific owners. Industrial real estate management is not as highly developed a specialty as is commercial real estate management, primarily because of the larger proportion of properties occupied by one tenant for prolonged periods.

Perhaps most important of all, the industrial real estate broker increasingly is called upon for advice or counseling. This may take the form of investment analysis, feasibility or development analysis, location analysis, or market analysis. It may also be related to community industrial development activities, involving advice on zoning, planning and/or urban renewal.

In providing various services and functions to his clients, the industrial real estate specialist must remember that he is also a businessman. To this extent, he must also maintain current working familiarity with new business management and analytical techniques that are applicable to the practice of industrial real estate. The industrial specialist should strive to operate his own business efficiently while advising others how to do so with theirs.

INDUSTRIAL REAL ESTATE ORGANIZATIONS

While the precise number of organizations involved in industrial development is unknown, one authority has estimated there are more than 10,000 local organizations of all kinds throughout the United States concerned with industrial development. The Committee for Economic Development has further estimated annual expenditures by communities and states in promoting industrial growth to be at least $200 million. This does not include expenditures by private utilities, railroads, banks, and other private organizations.[16]

The organizations discussed in this section have a common purpose: to promote industrial development and encourage the most efficient use of industrial real estate. However, their immediate interests and their methods vary. It is because of these varied interests that industry may secure special advantages from each group.

Professional and Trade Associations

Organized promotion of industrial real estate is undertaken by many private and public organizations. Three private groups deserve special mention: the Society of Industrial Realtors, the American Industrial Development Council, and the Industrial Council of the Urban Land Institute. These voluntary, nonprofit organizations perform services for business, government agencies, educators and the public.

Society of Industrial Realtors. The Society of Industrial Realtors (S.I.R.) is a professional affiliate of the National Association of Real

---

[16] From an address by Victor Roterus, U.S. Department of Commerce, before the Second Annual Governor's Conference on Industrial Development, Springfield, Illinois, March 17, 1960.

Estate Boards (NAREB). Its members specialize in marketing industrial properties, meeting the real estate needs of industry, and promoting the efficient use or allocation of industrial real estate. The Society was organized in January, 1941 from the Industrial Property Division of NAREB, with a charter membership of about 200. The Society has grown steadily to more than 1,000 members in virtually every state, Canada, and Puerto Rico.

1. *Organization Objectives.* As stated in Article II of its By-Laws, the objectives of the Society are:

1. To unite those Realtors who are engaged in buying, selling, renting, or leasing for others and for a compensation the lands, buildings, and other facilities used in the process of industry and manufacturing.
2. The fostering of knowledge, education, integrity, and quality workmanship in the field of industrial real estate.
3. The exchange of information relating to industrial real estate among members of the Society.
4. Mutual cooperation in exchange of listings and the proper and sound service to owners and users of industrial real estate.
5. The certification, identification, and qualification of experienced and competent industrial real property brokers.
6. The cooperation with all governmental (national, state, and city) departments and civic organizations, public utilities, financial institutions, and insurance companies, by proper contact.

The unique service provided by the Society is a network of cooperating member-brokers throughout North America to market industrial real estate efficiently. Cooperation among Society members from coast to coast contributes to the flow of market information for the mutual benefit of sellers and buyers of industrial real estate, which is often bought and sold in a national market.

The Society sponsors educational activities designed to increase the quality of service to clients by equipping its members better to serve industry, the public, and governmental agencies. The qualification of member industrial brokers (designated as S.I.R.'s) tends to protect industrial real estate owners and buyers from incompetence. By cooperating with national, state, and local groups, members of the Society of Industrial Realtors advance community industrial development programs.

2. *Membership Requirements.* The Society has three types of membership: active, salesman affiliate, and associate. Active members are Realtors with a record of eight or more years of successful and ethical performance as industrial real estate brokers. Advanced education may be substituted for up to three years of the required experience. A candidate for invitation to active membership must be 28 years of age, a member of a Board of Realtors or an officer of a firm that belongs to the National Association of Real Estate Boards, and sponsored by an active member. Candidates meeting these requirements must demonstrate their technical knowledge of the industrial real estate field by demonstrated history of successful experience, high quality of ethical practice, and by a comprehensive written

examination. Active members are entitled to use the professional designation "S.I.R."

Salesmen affiliates are those with creditable records in the industrial real estate field for at least five years, and are associated with active members. Associate memberships are awarded to organizations with an active interest in industrial development (public utilities, such as railroads, electric power, gas and telephone companies; manufacturers with national or international distribution; established private industrial districts; and insurance companies with major industrial mortgage portfolios). They are represented by individual officers, such as industrial development managers of railroads and other public utilities, or real estate managers of industrial corporations.

3. *Membership Services.* Because the membership is widely representative of industrial areas in the United States and Canada, the Society can furnish local plant location information within 24 to 48 hours. With a thorough knowledge of locational data in their respective areas, members can complete preliminary surveys on short notice.

The Society also maintains for exclusive use by its members an executive mailing list of some 8,000 industrialists who are responsible for plant location decisions. A monthly *Newsletter* is distributed to keep members informed of industrial real estate trends and organization activities. In addition, special studies on such topics as developing organized industrial districts, financing and appraising industrial real estate, and the marketing of warehouses are distributed periodically to the membership.

A bi-monthly *Market Letter* enables members to list plants with the entire membership, or to request facilities being sought by a client. Offers and listings of industrial real estate in the United States and Canada are included in the publication.

The Society also conducts educational and public relations activities. Regional seminars on industrial real estate are a regular part of the educational program. Frequently, these regional seminars are held in cooperation with local development organizations, public utilities, and chambers of commerce. Panels and roundtables at the Society's three national meetings each year, and activities of the Society's 30 chapters, further implement its broad educational program.

4. *Services to the Public.* Several university short courses have been undertaken by the Society as part of its educational program. The first known industrial real estate course offered for both graduate and undergraduate college credit in the United States was initiated with the sponsorship of the S.I.R. Educational Fund at the University of Florida in 1961. Since then, courses on industrial real estate have been introduced in several universities and adult evening classes with the assistance of local chapters of the Society.

The Society published and made available, to all colleges and universities offering real estate courses, a syllabus for a course in industrial real estate entitled *Principles and Practices of Industrial Real Estate.*

Sponsorship of courses, publication of the syllabus, and the development of the present volume have all been carried out through the S.I.R. Educational Fund from contributions by Society members.

Since 1949, the Society has presented an annual award to the Industrialist of the Year, chosen by an impartial board composed of business and professional leaders throughout North America.

A Professional Trophy Award is presented annually by the Society to the state or province judged to have the most effective industrial development program.

American Industrial Development Council. The Constitution and By-Laws of this organization, formed in 1925, state that members are dedicated to the exchange of information on principles and practices of industrial development.[17]

The Council establishes no policy nor does it commit a member to organization policies. Rather, the Council works in close cooperation with all organizations, public or private, in promoting their constituent area's industrial development activities.

"Categories of membership in the American Industrial Development Council are: Member, Active Member, Fellow Member and Honorary Life Member.

"Membership is held by the individual and includes anyone interested in or concerned with industrial development, regardless of country of residence. Active Membership is available to individuals who have been members for three years and who are actively engaged in the practice of industrial development.

" 'Fellows' must meet a certain rigid criteria and have prepared and published an original paper on some element of Comprehensive Industrial Development.

"Honorary Life Membership is available to active members who have, in the opinion of the Board of Directors, made a major contribution to the profession over a period of years.

"The following is a breakdown of the principle organizations retaining AIDC membership:

Civic
Area/Regional
Port Authorities
Bureau (not Chambers)
Chambers
Foundations I.D.
National Associations
Corporations

Educational
Universities
Special Schools

Government
Authority (non-port)
Authority (port)
County

Federal
Municipal
Provincial
State
Territory or Possession
International

Private
Advertising and public relations
Consultants
Developers (Parks etc.)
Realtors
Publishers
Retired
International

---

[17] American Industrial Development Council, *Constitution and By-Laws* (revised 1966).

Research	Financial Institutions
Firms	Gas Utilities
Institutes	Insurance
	Multiple Utilities
Service	Railroads
Airlines	Transportation
Communications	Other" [18]
Electric Utilities	

The AIDC provides for an informal exchange of ideas and emphasizes ethics and procedures relating to industrial development. It maintains a formal educational program directed toward professionalism in the practice of industrial development through a three-year Industrial Development Institute at the University of Oklahoma. It issues "Professional Notes" and "Technical Articles" through its by-monthly newsletter, *AID,* and its *Handbook on Industrial Development.* The *A.I.D.C. Journal* is a valuable periodical covering topics in industrial development and location activities. Membership conferences and study groups cover current issues that are of interest to members of industrial development organizations.

Industrial Council, Urban Land Institute.   The Urban Land Institute (ULI) is a nonprofit research organization formed in 1936 to promote better planning and development in urban areas. The Industrial Council is a 30-member committee of the Institute that specializes in seeking solutions to industrial development problems. Most of the work of the Council involves group consultation, research and panel studies on industrial land and feasibility problems. The activities of the Council are directed primarily to the expansion and distribution of knowledge leading to the most effective use of land by industry.

The Council uses a unique approach to specific industrial development problems, by forming a panel composed of members who have had experience in dealing with the issue in question. Problems to be investigated by the panel are first reviewed by the professional staff of ULI. Information and data bearing on the problem are assembled and forwarded to each panel member for advance study. Panel members are then briefed by local authorities, conduct a field investigation of the study area, complete interviews, assemble additional facts, and correlate their work. A final review is then made prior to submitting the panel's recommendations to the sponsor.

The Panel Study is not a substitute for the services of a technical consultant, since the panel does not make original planning or engineering studies. Its main purpose is to provide a means by which such studies can be evaluated "in the light of feasibility, practical accomplishment, and sound business judgment." Panel members selected to serve on the Industrial Council contribute their time without compensation.

Plan Analysis is another service rendered by the Council. Sustaining members of the Urban Land Institute may submit industrial development plans for review by the Industrial Council at meetings held twice each year. Plan Analysis sessions offer confidential advice from nationally known

[18] *Ibid.* (quoted in written statement to the author by Richard Preston, Secretary, AIDC, 1966).

experts on industrial development plans: e.g., plant location analysis, zoning problems, site layout, road widths, parking provisions, or land improvement problems.

The Industrial Council, with the organizational support of the Urban Land Institute, supplies a service to the industrial community ordinarily not available from other groups. The emphasis on research and publication of studies in industrial development, by the Council and by ULI, gives high acceptance to the work of the Council.

Industrial Development Organizations

The industrial development programs of railroads, electric light and power companies, natural gas companies, and other public utilities supplement the services of nonprofit organizations. Industrial development departments, because of their close relation to manufacturing firms, often are able to furnish special services to industry and the community, not available from other groups. The special attention paid industrial prospects is justified by the added business expected to be realized. Although many types of public utilities promote industrial development, the discussion here is confined to the industrial departments of railroads and electric light and power companies.

Industrial Development Departments of Railroads. The number of persons railroads employ in economic development ranges from nearly 150 on the Northern Pacific Railroad to one or two specialists with smaller carriers. More than 10 Class I railroads report 20 or more employees primarily engaged in industrial development work. The management of resources owned by railroads (i.e., oil, mineral and timber lands), in addition to their industrial development work, requires specialized industrial departments.[19]

The primary motivation for serving industry is to attract businesses that will use railroad services. In most cases, railroads own land and buildings for sale or lease to industry. It is not unusual for railroads to sponsor organized industrial districts, or to cooperate in the development of organized industrial districts. As one example, the Illinois Central Railroad disclosed that new construction and expansion among new industries locating on the railroad in 1961 represented a total investment of more than $115 million. This industrial growth increased annual freight hauls by 38,000 carloads, producing an estimated annual revenue of $5.5 million.[20] A survey of 76 railroads in the United States and Canada estimated that 667,539 new carloads and some $165,031,000 in new revenues were obtained in 1961 from new industries utilizing industrial space served by railroads.[21]

Railroad development departments differ from most private organizations in one important respect: the majority of railroads own large acreages of industrial land. All of the 76 railroads surveyed in 1961 stated that railroad-owned land was available for sale or lease to industry, and 55 were

---

[19] "Industrial Development," *Railway Age,* Vol. 153, No. 6 (August 6, 1962), p. 24.
[20] *Ibid.,* p. 32.
[21] *Ibid.*

sponsors of industrial developments or organized industrial districts. The majority of companies also indicated an interest in developing air rights over railroad yards, tracks, terminals, or existing buildings.[22]

Industrial Development Departments of Electric Utilities. The industrial development services of light and power companies are generally available throughout the distribution area of the company. Perhaps the greatest service provided to industrial prospects is the analysis of economic data and site information.

The services of industrial development departments generally go beyond the advice of industrial engineers regarding power supply and power costs of manufacturing. For example, a list of plant location services furnished by the Allegheny Power System (operating in Ohio, West Virginia, Pennsylvania, Maryland and Virginia, including the Monongahela, the Potomac Edison Company, and the West Penn Power Company) is typical of industrial departments. Staff members review locational specifications of a prospect and recommend regions or even specific sites that most nearly meet these requirements. Detailed data are collected on specific buildings or sites. They are supplemented by community data covering present industries, climate, labor force, transportation, warehousing, housing, taxes, recreation, local regulations, schools, churches, and the like. Industrial prospects are assisted by joint meetings arranged by the power company with civic and industrial groups that may assist the new firm. The company also offers assistance and advice in arranging construction, transportation, housing, and financing.

The extent to which power companies go to attract industrial prospects is illustrated by the research reports published and distributed to industrial development officials and interested prospects. The West Penn Power Company of Greensburg, Pennsylvania, for example, publishes a directory of manufacturers operating in its area. The directory identifies products, companies, and the location and economic features of industrial and consumer markets served in the area.

In addition to reporting area economic data, other utility companies sponsor special economic studies relevant to industrial prospects. For instance, the Commonwealth Edison Company of Chicago employs a full time economist to prepare economic analyses of local industrial development issues, such as a report on the O'Hare Airport and its influence on industrial expansion in metropolitan Chicago. Other studies have analyzed the effect of public improvements on industrial growth.

Maintaining extensive inventory records of industrial real estate is often an added service, with data available on sites and buildings currently for sale or lease.

Community Organizations for Industrial Development. Among the leading groups promoting local industrial development are various government agencies and community service organizations, such as local chambers of commerce. State-supported development agencies, the Small Business Administration, and the Economic Development Administration of

---

[22] *Ibid.*

the U.S. Department of Commerce also contribute greatly to industrial development activity. These federal agencies usually offer means to financial assistance, as well as advice and other services.

The promotional activities of local chambers of commerce cover most phases of industrial development. Many chambers of commerce have organized "Committees of 100," consisting of community leaders who devote time and resources to gaining new industry. Information on the local community, confidential information on industrial sites, financing of plants, and other services are arranged by these groups.

The U.S. Chamber of Commerce publishes numerous pamphlets useful to local communities, such as *The Community Industrial Development Survey; Finding Prospects for Community Industrial Development;* and *How to Create a Program of Work for Community Development.* Community advertising, industrial promotion programs and the publication of industrial development aids characterize industrial development work of chambers of commerce.

State development agencies are among the most active groups involved in industrial promotion. Their work ranges from the support of national advertising to the preparation of research reports helpful to industry and development organizations. One major service of a state development commission is illustrated by the detailed annual reports on new industrial plants published by the Florida Development Commission. These show the location of new plants by county and by industry, and give not only the number of new plants but also indicate plant expansions, the company name, principal products of the new firm, number of employees, and size of the anticipated new plant or expansion. The classification of this list by counties and by S.I.C. groups permits local community organizations to anticipate trends in industrial land use and space requirements.

Some state development commissions go even further by sponsoring research reports giving community data for industrial areas of the state and developing other types of information directed to special industries. The Connecticut Development Commission, for example, publishes a *Guide to Industrial Development* for use by local communities and industrial development groups. This guide describes major steps necessary to organize campaigns for industrial development.

The Connecticut Development Commission also publishes *Community Monographs* which summarize pertinent social and economic data for most towns in Connecticut. The Commission maintains a record of actual and potential industrial sites, with the cooperation of utilities and local groups. The work of the Connecticut Development Commission has been described as an attempt: ". . . to maintain as comprehensive a list as possible of *all* actual or potential industrial sites and vacant factory buildings in the entire state." [23] In brief, state development organizations seek to attract an industrial prospect to the state, and then act as a go-between for industry and local community groups to the extent necessary and possible.

---

[23] *Guide to Industrial Development for the Local Community* (Hartford, Connecticut: Connecticut Development Commission, 1965), p. 30.

CURRENT TRENDS AND ISSUES IN INDUSTRIAL REAL ESTATE

Perhaps the single most distinguishing characteristic of the dynamic American economy is continuous change. As any professional, the industrial real estate specialist must have the sensitivity and the skill to adjust to change, and to translate the implications of changes in the field to his clients. The major issues can be dealt with here in capsule form only. Nevertheless, they provide the framework within which the function and activities of the industrial real estate broker are analyzed throughout the remainder of this book.

Migration of Industry

Concomitant with increased geographic mobility of the American population following World War II, industry has shown a tendency to increase its mobility. There has been a marked shift from traditional centers of activity, to take advantage of new markets, new pools of labor, and new transportation facilities. Despite the pressures toward immobility that result from the extremely high cost of moving, when a move is finally decided upon, the industry often becomes "foot-loose" and may consider locations previously unthinkable. The most significant manifestation of this trend has been a shift in industrial employment and activity from the traditional concentrations in the Northeastern and North Central United States, to the South, South West, South Central, and Pacific regions. This has required many new industrial sites in the expanding areas. Moreover, considerable ingenuity has been called for to rehabilitate existing facilities in the relatively declining, mature areas. In many instances, the geographic shift in industrial activity has been one of emphasis, rather than one of overt removal or relocation. That is to say, new facilities of existing firms have been more likely to be located in the growing areas, but facilities in the Northeast and North Central regions have not been abandoned.

Suburbanization of Industry

Simultaneously with the southward and westward movement of industry, there has been a marked tendency for new establishments, and for planned expansions, to be concentrated in suburban or outlying communities, rather than in already developed central cities. Once again, while there has been some movement of established firms from central city locations to suburban or even rural sites, much of the shift has been the result of concentrating new plants outside the central city. This phenomenon is borne out by two studies of metropolitan areas in New England: Boston and Hartford.[24] Transportation developments, notably the increase in good highway access throughout most of the United States, have tended to accentuate this trend. It is also based in part upon the need for less densely developed sites containing one-story buildings.

---

[24] A. J. Bone, *Economic Impact Study of Massachusetts Route 128* (Cambridge, Massachusetts Institute of Technology, December, 1958); W. N. Kinnard, Jr., *et al, Greater Hartford Economic Climate Study* (Hartford, Greater Hartford Chamber of Commerce, June, 1963).

Transportation Changes

By far the most dramatic single change in transportation to emerge since the end of World War II has been the rapid development of highway and expressway travel. This has led to greater reliance upon, and innovation in, truck transportation. Moreover, the American worker has become increasingly automobile oriented, and has had sufficient purchasing power to utilize the automobile for commuting. At the same time, public transportation systems in metropolitan areas have not kept pace with the outward movement of population and industry. All of these developments have combined to accelerate the outward movement of freight-generating industries and large employers from congested central districts.

Meanwhile, the less mobile, less flexible railroads have suffered relative declines in importance, particularly in the more heavily concentrated regions of the northeastern United States. As truck freight has increased, the share of total freight carried by rail has decreased. Moreover, as is indicated in Chapter 2, rail facilities have become less important to many industries in their site requirements. Some industries have become extremely dependent on truck transportation.

Finally, there has been a rapid growth in air freight transport in recent years, particularly in areas of activity in which speed of delivery is the critical issue. As air freight services are expanded, industries with a market limited by the time of transport will tend to expand into more distant market areas. Locations providing air transport facilities will therefore have a great competitive advantage in attracting such activities. To the extent that air freight facilities tend to be concentrated near metropolitan centers, this will represent a partial counteraction to the tendency for industry to disperse into suburban locations. Indeed, one authority has claimed that special air freight terminal facilities in New York City means that the New York region "will maintain and even increase its advantage as a national assembly point for high-skilled talent and as a distribution point for high-value merchandise." [25]

Manufacturing Processes

The shift in locations from central areas to more outlying regions has made possible, and in turn has been accentuated by, a trend toward one-story buildings in which goods flow horizontally rather than vertically. The evidence of this trend comes from all over the United States.

In a survey of some 1,500 manufacturing establishments in Detroit as far back as 1956, 71.6 per cent occupied one-story buildings, and only 10.4 per cent occupied buildings with three or more stories. While some 28.4 per cent of the surveyed manufacturing establishments occupied multi-story plants, only 10.8 per cent of the firms expressed a preference for multi-story buildings. Moreover, in a four-year period preceding the survey, 98 per cent of all plants built in Detroit contained only one story. [26]

[25] Benjamin Chinitz, *Freight and the Metropolis* (Cambridge, Harvard University Press, 1960), p. 163.
[26] *Industrial Study,* Master Plan Technical Report, Second Series (Detroit, Detroit City Plan Commission, 1956), pp. 27–36.

A continuing study covering 13 years of industrial locations throughout the state of Connecticut confirmed these findings. In addition, it found that generally the greater the number of stories in a plant, the more likely the occupant(s) planned to move.[27]

Two basic reasons may be advanced to explain the overwhelming trend toward the one-story plant, warehouse, or industrial building. The first is the cost of construction. Not only is the cost per square foot of total building area generally lower for single-story construction, but the percentage of total space that is usable is generally greater in single-story construction. Of course, it must be borne in mind that unless large enough sites are available at reasonable prices in suburbs, the industrial establishment cannot take advantage of these lower construction costs. The feasibility of using less densely occupied sites is largely a function of accessibility.

The second major reason that most firms prefer a single-story plant is that the layout and flow of goods is considerably more flexible than is the case in multi-story structures. Production process variations are encouraged because heating and ventilation can usually be handled more efficiently. Among manufacturing establishments in particular, any one of three layout arrangements is most likely to be followed: (1) production line layout; (2) layout for job manufacturing; and (3) layout for a stationary product.[28] In each of these types of arrangements, there are strong advantages in the single-story plant.

It would be erroneous and misleading to infer that there are always net advantages in a one-story industrial building. This simply underscores the fact that the specific needs of the individual client must be carefully analyzed before action is taken. The important point, however, is that the general trend toward the one-story plant is both feasible and defensible in terms of basic economic considerations influencing efficiency of land use and profitability of industrial operations.

Technology and Automation

Technological advance typically involves changes in equipment, changes in techniques for handling goods and materials, and/or changes in the number and type of employees required for a given process. In each instance, the full advantage of technological change is often not achieved until the space within which the activity is to occur is itself changed. The custom character of much of industrial space has already been emphasized. It behooves the industrial property specialist to keep abreast of technological changes in industries with which he is familiar or has a working relationship, so that he may translate them to real estate terms for the benefit of his clients.

One segment of the broad area of technological change is termed auto-

---

[27] W. N. Kinnard, Jr., *et al, Thirteen Years of Industrial Location in the Capitol Planning Region* (Storrs, Center for Real Estate and Urban Economic Studies, University of Connecticut, 1966).

[28] Lawrence L. Bethel *et al,* 4th ed., *Industrial Organization and Plant Management* (New York, McGraw-Hill Book Company, Inc., 1962), pp. 196–98.

mation. This may mean the use of electronic data processing equipment, the continuous processing of materials, or techniques of control based on the feed-back principle. When automation is introduced into an industrial operation, replacing plant and equipment which thereby has become obsolete, a three-fold effect on space needs may be identified.

First, if a plant is organized on a job basis in which production proceeds from one machine to another for different operations, then automation may require a new building and site. For example, a new method for processing sorghum grains with automatic controls adapted to a new wet milling process led to the establishment of a new plant and location. A new plant produced the same output as the former dry milling operation, but the automated plant required a site of only 47 acres, as contrasted with the old site of 125 acres.[29] A corollary effect of the demand for new industrial land and buildings stimulated by automation is the necessity to dispose of and/or adapt vacated space for other uses or users.

A second probable effect of automation is that if the same production is maintained, floor-space requirements are usually reduced, as automation tends to result in greater efficiency in the use of floor area. Several examples of the savings thereby effected are contained in the book, *Industrial Organization and Plant Management,* by Lawrence L. Bethel.

Finally, the introduction of automation generally results in increased land requirements. The new plant is almost invariably a one-story structure, and lower densities in suburban locations are most commonplace.

Obsolescence

As a result of technological change, including automation, and of changes in manufacturing processes and product demand, many existing industrial buildings and sites have become, and will continue to become, obsolescent. This means that their capacity to meet the needs of modern industry will be considerably diminished, and they will be less efficient in their contribution to the production and profit of the occupant-users. The chief impact on industrial real estate owners, investors, and brokers has been, and will continue to be, increasing pressure to devise means for rehabilitation for reuse of the obsolescent facilities. Increasingly, inventive feasibility analyses will be called for in the older, more mature industrial areas.

Product and Demand Shifts

Another significant change that has occurred in the United States economy since the end of World War II is the combined development of new products and new patterns of tastes of both consumers and producers. This means that there has been a substantial change in the relative importance of certain goods and the industries which produce them. As new products and services have emerged and won favor on the marketplace, others have declined in importance. This pattern of change is reflected in the activities of major industrial groups in the United States. Exhibits 5 and 6 depict

---

[29] *Ibid.,* pp. 176–177.

Exhibit 5

MANUFACTURING EMPLOYMENT IN THE UNITED STATES
BY MAJOR INDUSTRIAL GROUP
(1958 and 1963)

S.I.C. Code	Major Industry Group	Thousands of Employees 1958	1963
20	Food and Kindred Products	1,718	1,643
37	Transportation Equipment	1,562	1,601
35	Machinery, except Electrical	1,350	1,459
23	Apparel, etc.	1,181	1,280
36	Electrical Machinery	1,141	1,512
33	Primary Metals	1,092	1,127
34	Fabricated Metal Products	1,061	1,082
22	Textiles	903	863
27	Printing, Publishing	865	913
28	Chemicals	699	737
24	Lumber and Wood Products	585	563
32	Stone, Clay, Glass	553	574
26	Paper	551	588
39	Miscellaneous	365	391
25	Furniture Fixtures	354	377
31	Leather	349	327
30	Rubber, Plastics	348	415
38	Instruments	286	305
29	Petroleum	179	153
21	Tobacco	84	79
	Total (All Establishments)	15,227	15,989

NOTE: Excludes Administrative and Auxiliary Facilities reported separately as Non-manufacturing. Figures may not add to totals due to independent rounding.

SOURCE: U.S. Bureau of the Census, *U.S. Census of Manufactures: 1963, Summary and Subject Statistics* (Washington, U.S. Government Printing Office, 1966), pp. 46–47.

two sets of shifts that have occurred between 1958 and 1963 among major manufacturing industry groups. Exhibit 5 shows the number of employees in each two-digit manufacturing industry group in 1958 and in 1963. For purposes of analysis, they are ranked in the order of employment in 1958. Exhibit 5 indicates clearly that there have been substantial changes in the pattern of employment among major manufacturing industries in the United States, even over as short a period as five years.

Exhibit 6 provides the same information by two-digit manufacturing industries for value added by manufacture in both 1958 and 1963. While the same ranking did not prevail in 1958, there still were substantial changes between 1958 and 1963, reflecting once again both product and demand shifts.

These developments simply accentuate the process of obsolescence of many existing industrial facilities and sites. They underscore the importance of ingenious efforts to rehabilitate and salvage existing industrial real estate, at the same time that new sites and buildings are being developed.

Exhibit 6

VALUE ADDED BY MANUFACTURE IN THE UNITED STATES
BY MAJOR INDUSTRIAL GROUP
(1958 and 1963)

S.I.C. Code	Major Industry Group	Millions of Dollars 1958	1963
20	Food and Kindred Products	17,701	21,826
37	Transportation Equipment	15,315	22,766
35	Machinery, except Electrical	12,414	17,311
28	Chemicals	12,308	17,586
33	Primary Metals	11,542	15,261
36	Electrical Machinery	10,624	17,011
34	Fabricated Metal Products	9,440	11,791
27	Printing, Publishing	7,973	10,476
23	Apparel, etc.	6,001	7,861
26	Paper	5,669	7,396
32	Stone, Clay, Glass	5,533	7,044
22	Textiles	4,870	6,123
30	Rubber, Plastics	3,277	4,654
24	Lumber and Wood Products	3,213	4,021
38	Instruments	2,781	3,992
39	Miscellaneous	2,678	3,562
29	Petroleum	2,518	3,713
25	Furniture, Fixtures	2,396	3,068
31	Leather	1,898	2,079
21	Tobacco	1,413	1,681
	TOTAL	139,584	189,221

NOTE: Figures may not add to totals due to independent rounding.

SOURCE: U.S. Bureau of the Census, *U.S. Census of Manufactures: 1963, Summary and Subject Statistics* (Washington, U.S. Government Printing Office, 1966), pp. 46–47.

Land Use Patterns and Controls

Not only have locations and location factors undergone considerable change since the end of World War II, but the organization of locations has also experienced considerable revision. In the private sphere, the most important single development is probably the planned industrial district or industrial park. This is not a postwar invention, but its emergence as a major force in industrial real estate activity postdates 1945. Planned concentrations of industrial establishments, taking advantage of the new locational amenities offered by outlying areas with excellent access, have brought to the fore the importance of external economies of scale, or so-called "agglomeration."

On the public side, two sets of developments influencing land use patterns have been particularly important. The first is the emergence of zoning as a conscious device to influence community economic growth and development, rather than to restrict and protect (almost exclusively from the viewpoint of the individual homeowner). As is discussed in Chapter 3, performance standards of zoning have been especially effective in the industrial field. The trend is toward wider use of such zoning controls. Indeed, the private restrictions and covenants found in planned industrial districts or industrial parks have increasingly followed the same general framework in recent years, shifting from specific inclusions or exclusions to standards of performance.

Industrial renewal and/or rehabilitation has been thrust upon many communities because of a declining employment and tax base. Whatever the origin of the effort, however, the programs have emphasized the desirability and need for providing some new, efficient industrial space downtown, or at least in central city locations. Because of the legal problems and the vast expense involved, in most instances this will be undertaken through federally-supported urban redevelopment or urban renewal programs.

Finally, efforts to influence land use patterns and controls are largely a reflection of the attitude of the local community toward industry and industrial use. Since the end of World War II, there has emerged a growing awareness of the advantages to a community in having both sources of employment and income, and a strong industrial tax base within the jurisdiction of the local community. Indeed, there has been some tendency to go too far in regarding *any* industry as inherently desirable. This contrasts with a widespread view of not too many years earlier that tended to consider *any* industry as inherently evil and unattractive.

The salutary effect of the new thinking and attitudes toward industry is that a new consciousness of the role of industry in the community's economic life has emerged. Decisions affecting patterns and programs of industrial real estate development and use within the community now have an opportunity to receive fuller consideration than has been the case in the past.

SELECTED REFERENCES

Bryce, Murray D., *Industrial Development* (New York, McGraw-Hill, 1960).

Calef, Wesley C. and Daoust, Charles, *What Will New Industry Mean to My Town?* (Washington, U.S. Government Printing Office, 1955).

Chamber of Commerce of the United States, *Organizing for Community Industrial Development* (Washington, The Author, 1959).

Chinitz, Benjamin, *Freight and the Metropolis* (Cambridge, Harvard University Press, 1960).

Guide to Industrial Development for the Local Community (Hartford, Connecticut Development Commission, 1961).

Handbook on Industrial Classification, BES No. R91 (Washington, U.S. Government Printing Office, 1958).

Malinowski, Zenon S. and Kinnard, William N., Jr., *The Metals Service Industry: A Case Study of a Satellite Industry* (New York, McGraw-Hill, 1960).

Mallick, Randolph W., and Graudreau, Armand T., *Plant Layout Planning and Practice* (New York, John Wiley & Sons, 1951).

Moes, John E., *Local Subsidies for Industry* (Chapel Hill, North Carolina Press, 1962).

Randall, Roland R., "Industrial Real Estate Counseling," *Proceedings*. First Annual Research and Education Workshop (Washington, Society of Industrial Realtors, 1959).

Society of Industrial Realtors, *Directory* (Washington, The Author, 1966).

U.S. Bureau of the Budget, *Standard Industrial Classification Manual* (Washington, U.S. Government Printing Office, 1957).

U.S. Department of Commerce, "Annual Income Issue," *Survey of Current Business* (Washington, July Issue each year).

U.S. Department of Commerce, *Statistical Abstract of the United States: 1966* (Washington, U.S. Government Printing Office, 1965).

U.S. Department of Commerce, Bureau of the Census, *1963 Census of Manufactures: United States Summary* (Washington, U.S. Government Printing Office, 1965).

Voris, William, *The Management of Production* (New York, Ronald Press, 1960).

Young, William A., "Meeting Industry's Real Estate Needs," *Advanced Course in Techniques of Industrial Real Estate* (Washington, Society of Industrial Realtors, 1964).

2

Industrial Growth and the Demand for Industrial Space

ONE of the major functions of the industrial real estate broker is to assist the market in producing the most efficient allocation of industrial space in any given area. The basic principle of urban land economics guiding the allocation of urban space is that it tends to be put to its highest and best (or most profitable) use in the long run. This is not necessarily true in the short run. It is the result of the operation and interaction of the forces of supply and demand on the open market.

In order to understand and react appropriately to the market, participants in industrial real estate activities must be aware of the ingredients of both the demand for, and the supply of, industrial space. In particular, S.I.R.'s and representatives of area development organizations should appreciate the origins of industrial real estate demand. Otherwise, it will not be possible to generate easily the separate, custom facilities needed by the great majority of industrial firms.

FACTORS IN INDUSTRIAL GROWTH AND DEVELOPMENT

The capacity to forecast accurately the future land and other space needs of industry in a given area will assist greatly in identifying programs of action appropriate to satisfy these needs. On one hand, local governmental action may be employed to reserve industrial land for future use. Such action can take the form of annexation to add more industrially zoned land to the municipality, or eminent domain may be employed to acquire private property for public development purposes, including, among many possibilities, urban renewal. Land may also be reserved for industrial use through regional planning (when supplemented by zoning), or it can be acquired directly through publicly owned land-development corporations.

Private investment can also be guided to meet industrial land and space requirements more fully. Selective analysis of the growth and development potential of industry in an area will identify the kinds of space in which investment is most likely to be profitable. Both overdevelopment and misdirected development can be avoided—or at least minimized.

The key to effective analysis of industrial growth—both past and potential—in any area is a comparative and selective study. It has already been noted in Chapter 1 that differential industrial growth rates have been experienced among the several regions of the United States, between central cities and suburban areas throughout the entire nation, and among different major industrial groups of manufacturing establishments. This differentiation can be extended to more refined geographic and industry categories for more meaningful analysis. Two important facts stand out: (1) industrial growth figures should be converted into percentages to compare *relative* gains or losses; and (2) percentage changes in industry should be related to other data that may serve as a meaningful standard of comparison.

Shifts in the Characteristics of Industry

Two major sets of changes noted in Chapter 1 are at work influencing the type and degree of industrial growth. In turn, they affect the amount and kind of industrial space needed in any region. The first is the continuing shift in basic growth factors that is going on in the industrial economy: changes in technology and automation; innovations in industrial methods and processes; developments in transportation; new products; and altered tastes and desires.

As the economy grows, these shifting patterns signal differential *rates* of change among industrial groups and subgroups, and even individual firms. These are often obscured when gross totals and averages for whole industries are reported. After all, an industrial average does not occupy specific sites, nor does a particular firm locate in a general region. General background analysis is important to indicate the framework within which industrial real estate activity takes place, but the ultimate task is to match a particular firm to a particular site, plant, or warehouse. This requires detail of a sort not typically found in published information. Data must be generated in accordance with the approach suggested later in this chapter.

Geographic Differences in Industrial Growth

The second major set of changes significant to a study of industrial growth or development in an area is the observed geographic shift in industry that has been going on in the United States for some years. The shifts have stemmed from significant economic, social, political, demographic, and technological changes. In an effort to indicate the character of this regional shift in industry, a recent study compared total manufacturing employment in 1929 with that in 1954, for the nine major Census regions of the United States.[1]

---

[1] Consult Victor R. Fuchs, *Changes in the Location of Manufacturing in the United States Since 1929* (New Haven, Yale University Press, 1962).

A comparison of industries that were similarly defined in both years is provided in Exhibit 7. To the extent that both old and declining, and new and expanding industries may be excluded from this comparison, the geographic shift of industry is probably understated. One further word of caution in the interpretation of Exhibit 7 is in order. Differential rates of growth do *not* necessarily reflect movement of industry from one region to another. While movement has occurred, the best evidence available indicates that growth figures more generally reflect new industry and varying expansion rates of existing industry.[2]

Exhibit 7

TOTAL MANUFACTURING EMPLOYMENT BY CENSUS
DIVISIONS IN THE UNITED STATES: 1929 AND 1954
(Similarly Defined Industries, Both Years)

Region	1929 (00)	1954 (00)	Percentage Increase
U. S. Total	96,560	150,990	56.4%
New England	12,154	13,873	14.1
Middle Atlantic	28,698	39,680	38.3
East North Central	28,267	43,363	53.4
West North Central	5,072	8,736	72.2
South Atlantic	9,388	16,943	80.5
East South Central	3,813	6,846	79.5
West South Central	3,091	6,815	120.5
Mountain	990	1,783	80.1
Pacific	5,083	12,948	154.7

SOURCE: Fuchs, Victor R., *Changes in the Location of Manufacturing in the United States Since 1929* (New Haven, Yale University Press, 1962), p. 7. Copyright Yale University Press, 1962.

Marked differences in the growth rate of the nine census divisions as contrasted with the United States rate, and with one another, are illustrated in Exhibit 7. New England shows the smallest percentage increase. However, the difficulty of relying entirely on percentage increases is also illustrated here. For instance, the Mountain region shows an absolute increase in employment from 99,000 to 178,300, resulting in an 80.1 per cent increase. In absolute terms, however, the New England region had almost the same employment gains as the Mountain region.

If the manufacturing base of a given area consists of rapidly growing industries, the area would have a favorable industrial structure and would most probably show a rate of growth above national averages. But if the industrial structure consists of more slowly growing industries, or declining industries, a relative decline of industrial growth appears. To judge the potential demand for industrial space in an area, differences in locational

---

[2] These conclusions derive from an examination of Fuchs, *op. cit.*, and *A Fortune Survey on Locating Plants, Warehouses, Laboratories* (New York, Time, Inc., 1963).

characteristics of its major industries, as well as growth statistics in employment or production, must be considered.

Victor R. Fuchs studied changes in the location of manufacturing in the United States for the period 1929–1954, and included several generalizations that help explain the redistribution of industry among the nine Census regions. The major trends identified for this period were:

(1) *The New England Region.* The relative decline in manufacturing in the Northeast was attributable partly to the relocation of textile activity from New England to the South. More recently, electronics assembly picked up some of the slack, as did the transportation equipment industry (especially defense-oriented aircraft components and shipbuilding). The westward and southward movement of both population and markets has caused many New England firms to open or expand branches closer to these markets.

(2) *The Middle Atlantic Region.* Textile and apparel industry shifts also resulted in comparative losses from the Middle Atlantic Division as these industries moved to the South Atlantic and the East South Central region. The aircraft, electrical machinery and chemical industries were growth industries that tended to expand in the Middle Atlantic. There is also evidence that a decline in net immigration of population reduced the supply of unskilled but easily trained labor willing to work for relatively low wages. The scarcity and/or high price of space in metropolitan centers for plants creating noxious gases, industrial waste, or other nuisances also tended to foster redistribution. The problem of locating "nuisance" industries is not confined to the Middle Atlantic Region, however.

(3) *The North Central Regions.* The East North Central Region grew at slightly less than the national rate after 1929. The lower rate of growth stems primarily from decentralization in certain industries. Earlier gains were associated with the rapid growth of the automotive production and related activities. More recently, new growth industries have not concentrated in the North Central areas.

The West North Central area improved its share of United States manufacturing in the 1929–1954 period by attracting large industries that require relatively high paid, highly skilled workers (for example, the aircraft industry in Kansas).

(4) *The South.* The three southern regions showed comparative gains in manufacturing employment largely as a consequence of abundant supplies of relatively cheap labor, and the availability of natural resources. The textile industry was a major force in manufacturing growth in Virginia, North Carolina, South Carolina, and Georgia. The labor released from agriculture since 1929 contributed to the growth of apparel, furniture, footwear, lumbering, and paper industries. The federal government, by expanding payrolls in the South, was another factor in attracting market-oriented industries to that region. Increasing population, the mild climate, and the rise of the motor trucking industry are other reasons for the comparative gain in manufacturing employment. The aerospace industry

has particularly benefited Florida and Texas. In the West South Central region, the growth of chemicals, aircraft, and subsidiary industries has been responsible for substantial increases in manufacturing employment.

(5) *The West.* The greatest manufacturing growth in the West was centered in Washington and California, primarily because of the expansion of the aircraft industry. The mild climate represents a major advantage along the Pacific Coast. Moreover, much branch expansion has been aimed at serving rapidly expanding consumer markets.[3]

Variables Affecting Interregional Growth Shifts

In general, manufacturing shifts since 1929 have been away from the Northeast and toward the Southwest. In his analysis of reasons for the differences in regional rates of growth, Fuchs cited 10 causes: [4]

(1) Consumer demand based on population shifts.
(2) Raw materials availability.
(3) Taxes, both property and income.
(4) Foreign trade shifts.
(5) Federal government policy on plant dispersal.
(6) Wage levels.
(7) Extent of unionization.
(8) Space (land) availability and cost.
(9) Climate.
(10) The "catching up hypothesis": states that have been experiencing rapid growth in recent years have been doing so primarily because of the low levels from which they began.

Interregional Differences in Attitudes

In a nationwide survey conducted by the editors of *Fortune* magazine,[5] 304 major industrial managements indicated that they planned a facility at a new location within five years. When asked to indicate the "Most Likely," "Second Choice" and "Third Choice" region for the facility from among the nine Census regions, their replies were distributed as shown in Exhibit 8. The figures show that the largest industrial firms do not necessarily follow the averages, since their attitudes toward the nine Census regions as new plant locations differed somewhat from past regional growth rates. In general, central locations with respect to markets, labor, and/or raw materials appear to have been most attractive—at least for future planning.

An interesting sidelight is the fact that assigning differential weights to second and third choices had absolutely no effect on the ranking of regions based on the most likely locations reported. This implies that first choices are fairly good guides when client intentions are being sought, at least for regional locational preferences.

---

[3] For a more detailed discussion of the patterns of change, see Fuchs, *op. cit.*
[4] See Fuchs, *op. cit.*, p. 253ff.
[5] *A Fortune Survey on Locating Plants, Warehouses, Laboratories, loc. cit.*, pp. 18–20.

Exhibit 8

PREFERENCES OF 304 INDUSTRIAL FIRMS TOWARD SPECIFIC REGIONS

Region	"Weighted" Attitude Rank Order	Percent	"Most Likely" Rank Order	Percent
East North Central	1	37.3%	1	27.0%
Middle South	2	33.5	2	22.4
Deep South	3	26.3	3	21.0
Pacific	4	21.6	4	18.4
Southwest	5	19.7	5	14.8
Middle Atlantic	6	18.0	6	13.2
West North Central	7	15.6	7	9.9
New England	8	5.5	8	3.9
Mountain	9	3.9	9	3.0

NOTE: Percentages may add to more than 100.0 due to multiple answers.

SOURCE: *A Fortune Survey on Locating Plants, Warehouses, Laboratories* (New York, Time, Inc., 1963), pp. 18–20.

THE NATURE OF DEMAND FOR INDUSTRIAL REAL ESTATE

The demand for industrial real estate is a derived demand. That is, it is based upon or derived from the demand for another product or service. In this case, the product or result of the industrial process—fabrication, assembly, storage, or distribution—is the primary object of demand. Industrial real estate is needed primarily because these activities must be housed.

The industrial real estate specialist must acquaint himself with the nature of industrial processes, the character of industrial growth and development in his area, and both the quantitative and qualitative space requirements of various industries. Knowledge of operations of the industry that will occupy the space is a prerequisite to estimating the amount and character of space that will be required.

The demand for industrial space is felt in a variety of ways. First, it can come from entirely new establishments, or as the result of moves from outside the area. It can also come from relocations within the area, from on-site expansion of existing establishments, or from new branches. Whatever the origin of the demand, however, several types of decisions are required: the selection of a location (or site); the selection of facilities (or building) on the site; and the choice of the form of tenancy of the facilities. These choices are largely dependent upon the specific characteristics and requirements of the individual firm. Nevertheless, generalizations about the priority of site or building factors are possible from previous studies, and from the distilled experience of industrial real estate specialists. Following a consideration of the basic characteristics of industrial space, these factors are discussed in some detail.

DEFINITIONS OF INDUSTRIAL SPACE

Industrial Plant

A plant refers to an establishment at a single location where industrial operations are performed. It includes all structures on the site. Accessory buildings not used directly in production, such as office space, power plants, repair shops, garages, warehouses, laboratories, and other structures, are considered part of the plant and are included in the total floor area.

A distinction is made between an industrial establishment or plant and an industrial firm. A firm may have one or more plant locations. An establishment is a plant at a single location, including all structures on the site.

Plant Area

The United States of America Standards Institute, in cooperation with other interested private and public groups, adopted a standard method of computing plant size:

The gross floor area of a plant is the sum of the areas at each floor level included within the principal outside faces of exterior walls, and neglecting architectural set-backs or projections.[6]

To qualify as part of the floor area, the clear standing headroom must be at least 7 feet 6 inches, regardless of use. An unenclosed ground-floor area in a multiple-story building is assumed to have the same floor area as the projected area of the floor above. Balconies and mezzanines are included in the gross floor area if they form an integral part of the building, and have a minimum width of 12 feet.

Certain other structures are not properly considered a part of the gross floor area. Structures with unroofed floor areas, unenclosed roof spaces, light wells, connecting passageways and various sheds, lean-to's, and unenclosed loading platforms and silos are all separately described. They are excepted from the gross floor area of the plant. Some authorities have suggested a minimum ceiling of 14 feet as a standard measurement, but because many existing buildings are constructed with lower ceilings, industrial specialists have not agreed on a standard ceiling height.

Industrial real estate brokers generally prefer the term "floor" rather than "story" in describing plant levels.

Plant Site (Land Area)

A plant site, expressed in either square feet or acres, refers to the total land area within the property boundaries. In defining the site area, the total land includes open space plus the area covered by buildings and struc-

---

[6] USA Standards Institute, *USA Standard Methods of Determining Areas in Industrial Buildings* (New York, The Author, 1962).

tures of all kinds, railroad sidings, landscaped sections, parking lots, reservoirs, driveways, floating docks, waste disposal ponds, and the like. The net land area excludes public easements or public roads not under private control.

Structural Density (Floor Area Ratio)

In estimating land requirements, it is often necessary to consider the ratio of building ground-floor area to land area, which is called the structural density. This figure is derived by dividing the ground area of structures by the total land area. A site of 50,000 square feet improved with buildings with a ground-floor area of 25,000 square feet has a structural density of 50 per cent. The floor area ratio is the ratio of *total* floor area of plant to site area. Thus, a three-story building containing 10,000 square feet per floor on a 50,000-square-foot site has a floor area ratio of 60 per cent.

Employment Density

To allow properly for parking areas, it is advisable to consider land needs in relation to major shift employment.[7] This term refers to the number of employees actually working at the plant site during the largest daily shift and during periods of normal plant operation. To obtain an accurate estimate of needed parking space, major shift employment refers to *all* employees, whether they serve in administrative, maintenance, or operating capacities. Employment densities are figured by relating the number of employees on the major shift to the land area. They are expressed as the number of employees per acre of land. The ratio does not include employees working on other than the major shift. In estimating parking requirements, however, an allowance for overlap in shifts is common.

Floor Space Per Employee

The ratio of total floor area to major shift employment provides an additional index for estimating industrial space needs. It is expressed in terms of square feet per employee. This varies considerably by industry, geographic region, size of firm, and age of plant, among other factors.[8]

THE ECONOMICS OF INDUSTRIAL LOCATION

In order to appreciate and act properly on the basis of demand for space by industrial firms, the industrial real estate specialist should understand the basis on which locational or site selection decisions are made. In this chapter, the general principles of location and site selection are considered. The discussion of specific factors and of techniques for attempting to measure industrial real estate demand are deferred to Chapter 3.

---

[7] For more discussion on this point, see Dorothy A. Muncy, *Space for Industry, an Analysis of Site and Location Requirements,* Technical Bulletin No. 23 (Washington, Urban Land Institute, 1954), p. 9.

[8] Unpublished survey of 3500 plant locations in Connecticut between January 1, 1953 and December 31, 1966, conducted at University of Connecticut by W. N. Kinnard, Jr.

The decision to move or expand an industrial plant must be based upon recognition of two fundamental points: (1) an industrial plant is a long-term investment that must remain competitively productive during the period of the investment; and (2) although both production and distribution techniques will assuredly change over time, the basic economics of the industry, and the fundamental economic rationale of the location, must remain compatible.[9] It is imperative that a careful, logical selection of location be made. The function of the industrial real estate specialist is to guide the industrial client to a rational, appropriate choice.

Development of Industrial Location Theory

The principles of industrial location are based on broader considerations of the location of all economic activity that have developed over more than 100 years.

One of the earliest writers on location theory was the German, von Thünen, who in 1826 considered agricultural location. In his view, agricultural production logically developed around a central market place in concentric circles. The type of production in a given location depended on its distance from the city center. Distance from the market directly affected the cost of transportation. Land near the city tended to be used for the most intensive agricultural production, such as garden vegetables. As distances and hence transportation costs increased, land prices declined because less intensive uses could be supported. Thus von Thünen's explanation of location was essentially based on transportation cost differentials. In this he was a real pioneer, but he did not consider other factors necessary for understanding the location of non-agricultural activities.[10]

Nearly 100 years after von Thünen's writings, another German economist, Alfred Weber, offered an explanation of industrial location solely on cost minimization: labor costs, transportation costs, and resource or factor costs.[11] The plant is supposed to locate at the least cost point. Weber concluded that varying combinations of transportation costs would lead plants to locate near the point of consumption, near the source of raw materials, or at intermediate points. The precise location depends on which cost is most important to the type of process in question. Products that lose weight in manufacturing would tend to pull the plant toward raw material sources, for example, as in sugar cane crushing, ore smelting, and cotton ginning. On the other hand, products that gain weight or bulk in manufacturing tend to push the plant locations near the market. Illustrations would be beverage bottling plants, which add water to syrup, and manufacturers of

[9] These ideas were presented by David Scribner in an address titled "Land Economics As It Applies To Industry's Location Requirements," delivered at the Advanced Course in the Techniques of Industrial Real Estate, sponsored by the Society of Industrial Realtors at Northwestern University, August 18, 1964.

[10] For a fuller explanation of von Thünen's views see George M. McManmon, *A Survey of the Literature on Industrial Location* (Syracuse, New York, Business Research Center, Syracuse University, 1959), pp. 7–13.

[11] See Alfred Weber, *Theory of the Location of Industries,* trans. by C. J. Friedrich (Chicago, University of Chicago Press, 1929); and Melvin L. Greenhut, *Plant Location in Theory and Practice* (Chapel Hill, North Carolina, University of North Carolina Press, 1956), pp. 8–17.

electronic products, such as television tubes, in which there are more truck-loads or carloads shipped out than received.

Weber argued further that if labor cost savings are greater than added transportation costs, then the industry would tend to locate closer to the labor supply. To the extent that increased automation reduces the amount of labor required, industry tends to change its orientation from labor to transportation, according to Weber. As automation develops, the demand for industrial property is increased in relatively undeveloped areas which attract industries that were formerly labor-oriented, but are now less labor dependent.

The general location factors noted by Weber were regarded as either concentrating ("agglomerating") or decentralizing ("deglomerating") forces. An agglomerating force or "clustering tendency" results from the fact that one type of production tends to be concentrated in one place (e.g., air frame production). Production costs are decreased as a result. Industrial services expand to meet the needs of the dominant industry, and a complex is created that attracts still other industries requiring the same services, or perhaps "foot-loose" industries. Agglomeration is also referred to as "external economies of scale." Substantial concentrations are usually necessary before related services and supporting facilities develop in any significance.

There is factual evidence of the existence of agglomerative or clustering forces in the American economy in the *Fortune* survey of plant location activities of the nation's largest industrial companies: "When a new plant is built by a large company, a number of satellite plants usually follow to provide components, and service businesses of all kinds, ranging from banking to transportation, from recreation to education, are established to support the central plant." [12]

Deglomerating forces are factors that detract from otherwise favorable locational advantages. These are termed "external diseconomies of scale." High land prices resulting from increased demand as industry expands in an area illustrate deglomerating forces. Another example could be plant obsolescence in the dominant industry. In sum, Weber has emphasized the relationship between transportation costs, labor costs, and general location factors. In his approach, the optimum or selected location is always the *least cost* location.

E. M. Hoover has explained industrial location essentially in terms of minimizing transfer costs and production costs.[13] Transfer costs include procurement and distribution costs (including added costs of servicing customers at long distances); the maintenance of large inventories; and any loss of business that results from slower service and customer dissatisfaction because the plant is distant from the market. Hoover emphasized the fact that transportation costs are not necessarily proportional to distance.

---

[12] *A Fortune Survey on Locating Plants, Warehouses, Laboratories, loc. cit.,* p. 2.
[13] For a detailed treatment of this approach, see Edgar M. Hoover, *Location of Economic Activity* (New York, McGraw-Hill Book Company, Inc., 1948).

They also depend on the type of transportation involved. For example, transportation via railroads tends to be more economical for long hauls; truck transportation with its relatively low terminal costs is more economical for short hauls.

Hoover's general conclusions are qualified somewhat by the relationship between the value of the goods and transportation charges. If the transport charge is small compared to the total cost of the delivered article, the goods are capable of bearing a high transfer cost, as in the case of high-value, low-weight goods.

The second factor introduced by Hoover involves production or processing costs. He contends that the producer will strive for that combination resulting in the least cost location. This combination includes consideration of land rents, wages, tax rates, interest rates, and the like. Accordingly, high land value may be offset by low processing and marketing costs at a given location. Similarly, low land values may compensate for higher processing costs. Therefore, selecting an industrial location involves a choice among sites that have different combinations of production and transfer costs. The advantages and disadvantages are weighed against the respective rate charges, as well as against each other.

These earlier explanations of industrial locational activity have been criticized on the grounds that site selection involves more than merely finding a location that minimizes transportation, production, raw material and wage costs. Maximum profit is involved, which includes a comparison of costs of the location, demand or income factors, and personal factors.[14]

A firm seeking to maximize profit (and it is assumed that the typical firm does so) may choose a certain city to gain a competitive advantage over other firms. Even if the selected location is not the least cost location, it can still be the most profitable location. Both cost and demand factors are involved. Therefore, Melvin Greenhut (the leading exponent of this approach) argues that the more competitive the market, the more industry will be inclined to seek and adjust to the maximum profit location. The location selected will then also depend on such demand factors as:

(1) Elasticity of product demand (its responsiveness to price changes).
(2) The location of competitors.
(3) The importance of proximity to customers.
(4) The importance of direct contacts with customers.
(5) The extent of the market area, and
(6) The relative competitiveness of the industry.[15]

Cost factors still do influence location. They include: basic land prices, labor and management costs, community facilities, housing availability, state labor laws, cost of materials and equipment, and costs of transportation. Personal management factors represent a third locational force included in the profit maximization approach. These are important operative

---

[14] Greenhut, *op. cit.*, pp. 263–72.
[15] *Ibid.*, pp. 279–80.

forces only in the case of firms in which the owner is personally involved in selecting plant locations, however.[16] They could involve interdependence among branch plants, civic pride, established community relations, or simply an area preference on the part of management.

The forces involved in any economic location decision therefore include both cost factors and demand factors, as well as the possibility of personal factors. The location selected on a rational economic basis is the one that will contribute most to the net profit of the operation of the plant in the long run. In this respect, industrial real estate has value and meaning to the extent that it is functionally productive. The best location is the most functional one.

Classification of Industry by Locational Orientation

In order to identify the kinds of factors most likely to be operative in any industrial location decision, the major types of locational orientation should be considered. The orientation of the firm means the considerations that appear dominant in rendering the location as efficient as possible, by contributing most to the profitability of the firm's operations. These are not mutually exclusive categories. They simply reflect the ingredients to which a given firm is most sensitive.

There are five basic categories of industry, in these terms: (1) industry most oriented to sales markets (both consumer and producer markets); (2) industry most oriented to raw materials resources other than labor and/or supplies; (3) industry most oriented toward transportation (facilities or costs); (4) industry most oriented toward labor (numbers or skills); and (5) non-oriented or "foot-loose" industries.

These categories stem directly from the application of the profit-maximization, optimum-location approach to site selection to the empirical evidence of actual location case studies.

1. *Market-Oriented Industry.* Industries in this category may be divided between: (1) those industries that sell products directly to consumers, e.g., beverages, bread, other foodstuffs; and (2) industries that sell to other industries, e.g., electronic firms producing electrical components, parts fabricators selling to airplane producers. In both instances, the firm is oriented to the market for *its* final product.

Producers of consumer products will tend to follow population. The demand for plant space for this group is closely associated with population growth and shifts.

On the other hand, firms that produce for other industries are affected by changes in the *demand* for those other goods. If, however, parts are manufactured for the export market, the demand for space also follows trends in international trade.

Industries oriented to consumer markets seek to reduce transportation

---

[16] See, for example, William N. Kinnard, Jr. and Zenon S. Malinowski, *Personal Factors in Small Manufacturing Plant Locations* (Storrs, Bureau of Business Research, University of Connecticut, 1962).

costs and distribution time. It has already been noted that products which add weight in manufacturing tend to be located near the market, to minimize transportation costs. Beverage bottling is a case in point.

Products that are highly perishable (for example, bakery and dairy products) will also tend to be located near the point of consumption, as will other industries that must locate near customers because of the need for personal contact and service. Printing is an example of an industry that tends to locate centrally because frequent contact with customers is necessary.

The production of certain other goods, because of their bulk and relatively high transportation cost, also tends to be located near points of consumption. Producers and suppliers of building materials require space near centers of population to reduce transportation costs.

For these reasons, most communities will have at least three types of local industry: (1) printing firms; (2) food processors; and (3) construction industries. The demand for industrial space for these industries is closely associated with population shifts.

2. *Materials and Resources-Oriented Industry.* Other industries require a location near the source of raw materials or supplies to reduce inward transportation costs. Two major types of industry may be found in this group.

First, plants that use large amounts of fuel (metallurgy), electric power (aluminum production), or a special type of fuel (natural gas in the glass industry), tend to locate near sources of fuel supply. For these industries, the cost of transporting raw materials is less important than either the cost of moving fuel or simply its availability.

Secondly, processes that lose weight in manufacturing are strongly tied to the source of raw materials or supplies. Firms in this category include furniture manufacturing, the processing of ore, and cement manufacturing.

Similarly, the reduction of bulk in the manufacturing process requires a location near a source of raw materials. Cotton ginning, which transforms unprocessed cotton in bulk form to compact bales, is an example.

A miscellaneous group of industries that ship their output in carload lots prefer locations near raw materials. Firms included in this group are grain elevators, junk dealers, freight forwarders, food processors, and similar industries.

3. *Transportation-Oriented Industry.* In dealing with effective transportation cost, more than relative freight rates must be considered. Total transportation or transfer costs also include: (1) terminal costs (characteristically high for railroads and low for truck transportation); (2) added costs of dealing with customers at a distance; (3) the cost of maintaining large inventories at more distant supply points; and (4) added costs resulting from customer dissatisfaction and loss of business because of slower service.

Those industries to which transportation or transfer costs are paramount, as is true for much of warehousing and bulk storage, tend to locate near the appropriate *type* of transportation. For example, fuel oil bulk plants tend to locate near deep water transport; and high-value instrument plants tend to locate near air freight terminals.

4. *Labor-Oriented Industy.* Industries influenced in choosing a location by labor supply are generally concerned with not only the cost of labor, but also the availability of special skills. For instance, the demand for factory space in abandoned textile mills of the Northeast has increased partly because of the availability of women for work in the apparel and electric parts industries. Some industrial areas, while having relatively high wage rates, continue to serve as manufacturing centers because of the availability of a local skilled labor supply. New Britain, Connecticut, the hardware capital of the United States, remains a center for prefabricated metal production and tool manufacturing because of the continued availability of workers trained in operating metalworking machinery.

Aircraft manufacturing is another industry centering around employment centers with skilled and semi-skilled labor supplies. Likewise, research and development companies, largely centering around electronic industries, tend to concentrate scientific and professional personnel in a given area.

Firms employing highly skilled or trained personnel often cluster in the vicinity of centers of advanced technical training. Research and development activities, among others, have developed heavily on the San Francisco peninsula because of the proximity of Stanford University and the University of California at Berkeley; in Los Angeles, near the University of California—Los Angeles, and the California Institute of Technology; and in the Massachusetts Institute of Technology–Harvard district, near Boston. This leads to a reinforcing agglomerating effect in many cases, as local educational institutions develop the capacity to serve the needs of technical industry. This applies to technical schools as well as universities. Educational and technical facilities serve to hold and attract "thought" industry.

5. *Non-Oriented or "Foot-Loose" Industry.* Certain types of activities are not strongly oriented toward any of the foregoing factors, and do not require that transportation costs on either output (products to market), or input (resources, supplies, labor) be minimized. These are often among the fastest growing industries. One example is the precision instrument industry. Relatively few employees are found in any one plant, but high levels of skills are generally required. Transportation cost is not an important ingredient in the sales price of the finished product. Few raw materials are required, especially in bulk.

The local orientation of such industry tends to be enhanced as local lenders, real estate practitioners, and others develop experience with their peculiar locational requirements. The continuity of such experience is especially important in adding to the attractions of the local area.

Levels of Location Decisions

In seeking to understand and evaluate the factors affecting plant location, it is necessary immediately to distinguish among the different levels at which location decisions take place. At least three such levels exist. Some authors identify them by referring to primary, secondary, and tertiary factors.[17]

Primary factors are those which delineate a broad region or area within which the location of the plant is limited. For example, the cost of labor may induce the management of a firm to think of five or six southern states as the broad area of plant location. As a second example, the location and the nature of the market for a manufacturer's product will often determine the general area of location. This level of decision-making typically results in the selection of the region and state in which the plant will be located.

Secondary factors are those which narrow the area of selection to one or a few communities within this broad region. Carrying through the examples already cited, tax advantages, a railroad, a major highway, or a network of highways—to mention only a few—might help to determine which town or metropolitan area will be selected within the specified group of southern states.

The third level of location decisions, involving the tertiary factors, may appropriately be called the level of *site* selection. Here the owner or manager of the firm is concerned with size and shape of site, utilities (their specifications or cost), drainage, soil conditions, road surface, parking area, room for expansion, specific neighbors, and so forth. In other words, he is actually choosing the physical locus of his plant.

Location decisions are not always consciously made at all three levels. For example, the owner-manager of a small heat treating shop, or of a custom-job machine shop, either in his original plant location or in later moves, probably does not make a conscious decision at the primary level. Because of the tremendous importance of personal contacts, and of intimate knowledge of industrial customers in the area,[18] this type of owner-operator instinctively restricts his thinking to a location within a 20 to 40-mile radius at most. Although undoubtedly there are good alternative locations in other states, such small manufacturers seldom if ever consciously consider them. Much the same is true of locally oriented distribution and warehouse facilities.

Failure to choose consciously between, say, Metropolitan Hartford and Metropolitan Baltimore does not then mean that important influences are not still operating. On the contrary, it may be precisely because of the tremendous importance of one or more primary factors that the decision is almost an automatic one. It is only when the decision-maker's attention is focused on the question of alternative regions for location that these primary factors are openly studied.

To different firms, precisely the same factors may be either primary or secondary. In some unusual cases, the same element may be important

[17] See, as one example, William N. Kinnard, Jr. and Zenon S. Malinowski, *Highways as a Factor in Small Manufacturing Plant Locations* (Storrs, Bureau of Business Research, University of Connecticut, 1963), Ch. 1, for a more detailed discussion of the three levels of location decision-making.

[18] See, for example, Zenon S. Malinowski and William N. Kinnard, Jr., *The Metals Service Industry: A Case Study of a Satellite Industry* (New York, McGraw-Hill, April, 1960).

also at the third level—that of site selection. For example, the need for a particular type of labor skill might lead the owners first to a region, then to a community, and finally to a specific site.

Moreover, location decisions in many cases are made at two or three levels simultaneously. This occurs particularly when factors at the broader level of choice tend to be approximately equal in two or more localities or regions. In such a case, a factor which would ordinarily be influential only at a lower level for the particular type of firm is consciously evaluated, and actually becomes a determinant at the higher level.

This is particularly true with respect to site selection considerations. For example, the availability of sewers, water, and other utilities may be the ultimate influence on the choice of one from among several towns under consideration in a region, because other factors are nearly equal. But rarely, if ever, do site selection considerations become the primary forces leading a firm to one section of the country.

For the industrial real estate broker, recognizing that location factors or considerations are occasionally not consciously stated can be most important in serving the needs of his clients. When studying and attempting to quantify the importance of various forces behind location decisions— especially through depth interviewing—the investigator can commit gross errors by failing to recognize the different levels cited above. In response to a simple question, "Why did you locate here?," a respondent might answer at any one of the three levels—or at more than one at the same time. The respondent himself will generally not decompose the question into its three elements and say, "I am in New England because the technical skills required are here and my greatest concentration of customers is in New England; I am in Metropolitan Hartford because it is in the approximate center of my concentrated market and I like the cultural advantages of Hartford; the firm is located in West Hartford at this particular site because a suitable building with adequate facilities for expansion over a period of at least 20 years was available and because the price was right."

In response to the unfocused question "Why did you locate here?," many respondents will immediately mention site selection factors, and neglect to state reasons for coming to the region or even to the specific locality. They cite taxes or utilities or land costs rather than market or labor factors. It is, therefore, important that the investigator focus the respondent's attention at the desired level, and probe to differentiate the forces operating at all three levels.

THE COMMUNITY EVALUATION SURVEY

As an aid to all potential parties to an industrial real estate transaction, the industrial real estate specialist should either prepare or have prepared a community survey. This provides factual information and objective commentary about the factors important to industry in selecting a plant location. While the specific items covered, as well as the emphasis given them, will vary considerably with the needs of the individual industry or firm, a general format required in any case can be an important guide for the industrial broker in assembling community data to be readily available for any client.

Much of this material is available in published form, from public or widely known private sources: Census information, tax collections, covered employment, and the like. Other information is often available in the files of local development groups, public agencies (such as planning commissions, renewal agencies or industrial development commissions), utility companies, banks and universities. Since the survey and evaluation of socio-economic information involves the application of research principles and techniques, university personnel are often an excellent source of previously conducted studies. In particular, state university bureaus of business research and/or urban studies investigate local communities on either a continuing or a contract basis.

Professional university research groups, real estate counselors, and economic or market research consultants, are generally best qualified and equipped to conduct community analyses. Industrial real estate brokers are best qualified to order their preparation (specifying items of coverage) and to apply the findings to the particular location or site selection problem. The industrial real estate specialist also performs the most important function of all: setting the standards and specifications for community surveys, so that they serve the specific needs of the industrial customer.

The industrial firm wants straight facts and honest evaluation, usually in confidence. The disinterested objectivity of an independent research organization helps in this regard. In addition, the community seeking to broaden its industrial base needs an objective appraisal of itself. It should also have an indication of what needs to be done to correct apparent deficiencies: e.g., outmoded planning or zoning, inadequate water or sewer lines. This latter role is best performed by the industrial broker. He, in turn, needs to know both what industry wants, and what the community has, in order to match them properly—or to suggest action designed to bring them together.

Functions of Cities

In order to provide standards of performance by which to evaluate a local community, industrial real estate brokers should be aware of the basic services and functions that cities ought to provide. Then they can understand better how the factors included in the survey influence and contribute to effective location of industry. The list which follows, prepared by the Regional Planning Association of New York, is by no means the only compilation of functions that is possible, but it is a useful one.

(1) There should be a wide, meaningful choice of housing types and neighborhood densities. Development programs should exist to expand this choice over time.

(2) There should be access to an increasingly wide choice of job opportunities. This is one significant standard in terms of which to define

growth. There should be advance planning in anticipation of these changes to take advantage of them.

(3) There should be a reduction in the time of necessary travel. This means both high speed highways and mass transit facilities. Here, also, advance planning is mandatory.

(4) There should be ready access to both natural open spaces and urban services and amenities. With increasing leisure available to much of the working population, facilities for recreation and entertainment become more and more significant in urban life.

(5) There should be improved cultural, educational, and recreational opportunities of broad range. These need not be free, but opportunities for expanding personal abilities, skills, and interests supplement the needs indicated above.

(6) The community's program of development should encourage optimum use of both natural and financial resources.[19]

General Area Information

Given the goals of a community survey and the objectives for effective functioning of the community, the kinds of information to be extracted from both public and private sources are then dependent on the data needs of locational decision-makers in industrial firms. Both current information and trends in economic forces (both favorable and unfavorable) should be identified and analyzed.

An industrial firm considering a community as a potential new location will generally require facts about: population, labor supply, economic base, finance, transportation services, utility characteristics, community services, living amenities, taxes, and other costs specific to the area. More than general, platitudinous information about these areas is necessary. Detailed, factual data are the only real help to plant executives in making locational decisions.

The "community" is not necessarily defined by political boundaries, for purposes of the community survey and analysis. Instead, functional, operational boundaries prevail: geographic, topographic, and economic. In particular, data in terms of the Census-defined Standard Metropolitan Statistical Area (SMSA) are very meaningful as area information for the industry engaged in location or site selection. Economic regions are often delineated by state or university groups. The Connecticut Development Commission, for example, has divided the state into some 20 economic planning regions.

Economic Base. Employment opportunities represent the basic reason for the existence of most communities, as well as the fundamental reason for growth. Therefore, the business firms—particularly the industrial establishments—already operating in a community offer a good preliminary indication of the probable direction and strength of economic development in the area. Moreover, an industrial inventory offers insights into the kinds of business that may, could, or should be induced to locate in the area in the future.

---

[19] Adapted from speech by David Scribner, *loc. cit.*

In addition, there should be some indication of the degree of industrial or economic diversification in the community. Some authorities argue that only in wide diversification is there strength. A diversified economic base is certainly an indication of economic stability in the area.

Population Data. It would probably be difficult to secure too much information on population. The size and family characteristics of the population, the age distribution, the level of incomes, occupational groups, education—and trends in each of these measures—help to describe the suitability and adaptability of the area for the proposed plant. Though some of this information may not be required in every instance, it is most helpful if details of the population are reported within at least a 10-mile radius of the proposed industrial area, or industrial site. If a suburban location is considered, the population within a 25-mile radius is important to plant executives. This is acknowledged as a reasonable commuting range. Some authorities even suggest that cities and towns outside the 25-mile limit should be studied, since some of these areas might provide supplements to the local labor supply. In fact, the labor supply deserves a separate analysis.

The Labor Supply. Describing the local labor supply involves more than a mere head count of total employment. Major manufacturing firms will need information on the competition for labor. So, to begin with, existing local industrial employment is classified by employee characteristics. To show the potential competition for labor that a new firm might encounter, some companies may ask for a list of major local industries by name. As part of this general requirement, the major products manufactured, and the employment by four-digit S.I.C. industry (male and female) are additional facts relevant to the labor supply.

Data on labor skills, training, education, and labor turnover rates are vital.

To show the potential labor costs, the average hourly earnings by type of worker, male and female, represent another area of importance. Related to this is information on the average work week. Labor organization activity, the degree of union organization—reported by company—and a history of labor-management relations in the community are other facts necessary in evaluating the labor supply. The analysis of the local labor supply depends heavily on published, official labor statistics. In addition to local sources, various governmental agencies collect and publish statistics useful to plant location studies. The following is a list of major publications on labor statistics from the U.S. Department of Labor:

Area Labor Market Trends: Bureau of Employment Security. Monthly. Current area labor supply classifications, recent labor market developments, and labor outlook for 149 major labor areas, each with a local field office. Smaller areas with relatively "substantial labor surplus" also listed. National round-up of labor market area developments and outlook.

Industry Manpower Surveys: Bureau of Employment Security. Issued as prepared (usually one each month). Analyses of manpower developments, current situation, and outlook with respect to major industries. Data based primarily upon industrial employment information collected by local offices of state agencies affiliated with the U.S. Employment Service.

The Labor Market and Employment Security: Bureau of Employment Security. Monthly. Articles and statistical data on current economic and labor market developments; special features.

Employment and Earnings: Bureau of Labor Statistics. Monthly. Basic source of current statistics on nonagricultural industries. Information on trends and levels of employment, hours of work, earnings, and labor turnover; developments in particular industries, states, and metropolitan areas.

Employment and Wages: Bureau of Employment Security. Quarterly; annual summary. Monthly employment and quarterly wages of workers covered by state unemployment insurance laws, by industry group, and by state.

Monthly Labor Review: Bureau of Labor Statistics. Monthly. Labor economics, labor-management relations, trade-union developments, and legislative changes. Statistical data on employment and payrolls, labor turnover, earnings and hours, consumer and wholesale prices, work stoppages, buildings and construction, and work injuries.

Unemployment Insurance Claims: Bureau of Employment Security. Weekly. Current information, by state, on unemployment among workers covered by various state and federal unemployment insurance programs. Monthly figures on insured unemployment, by local area, for 145 major employment centers.[20]

Transportation Services. An appropriate review of freight and passenger service will include schedules for motor lines (truck and bus), railroads, water and air transport. Some studies emphasize the elapsed freight time from the community to major market centers. Data on other local transportation services (pickups, less-than-carload delivery service, package cars, railroad and public warehouses, piggy-back service, and railway express service with service-delivery area shown) represent further kinds of information considered a part of area data essential to site selection.

In reviewing highway, trucking and bus service, it helps to identify state highways and limited access parkways serving the community. If the community is not in a metropolitan region, it is important to obtain the passenger car travel time to more heavily populated areas. New highway construction, current or planned, must also be noted.

A list of motor carriers serving the area, the location of the nearest terminal, and truck transit times to major market centers are also useful. In addition, interstate and intrastate bus service is often listed. Where applicable, there should be a description of water transportation, air transportation, and postal service. Terminal, transfer and storage facilities, if any, should be emphasized. In all cases, the service is described by giving the number of trips, travel time and the service to major market cities, as well as both passenger and freight rates.

---

[20] Office of Area Development, U.S. Department of Commerce, *Data Sources for Plant Location Analysis* (Washington, D.C., Government Printing Office, 1959), pp. 4–6.

Utility Characteristics. It is not enough to describe the mere availability of utility service in explaining site advantages. Most industrial executives need to know the *source* and *capacity* of reservoirs for water; they will also want to know the chemical characteristics and temperature of water, water treatment facilities and rates. If the site abuts a major river, the average stream flow will be required. If ground water is to be used, its quantity, depth, flow, and quality must be given.

Equally definite information is necessary in noting electric power availability: the company serving the area, the maximum demand, rated capacity of locally available facilities, number of accounts, and the rates, indicating the industrial and commercial rates that have been approved. Industrial gas, fuel oil and coal must be described in terms of the maximum available supply, present demand, and rates—and BTU content where available. In short, every means is used to report detailed data concerning utility availability. Waste disposal facilities—including a description of the sewage disposal system in the area, percolation rates, and related issues that bear on waste disposal problems—should receive the fullest possible attention.

Utilities are meaningful because they make it possible for the industrial user to operate more efficiently, and thus more profitably.

Community Services. As one example of standards for appropriate data to be gathered, the Connecticut Development Commission suggests that location studies report banking facilities, including assets and deposits of commercial and savings banks, as well as their loan policies (i.e., the attitude toward industrial prospects and construction financing). Local government services and reputation should also receive detailed treatment. Sources of tax income, tax rates, property tax assessment policies, municipal expenditures, and municipal services are an essential part of the study.

The Connecticut format, for example, suggests that community facilities covered in a location survey and evaluation include the following items:

Municipal Expenditures (Annual): schools; public works; police and fire departments; welfare; department retirement and service; other.

Anticipated Capital Expenditures.

Indebtedness and Credit Rating.

Municipal Services: fire protection service; police protection; health protection service; highway and snow removal service; sewer system; rubbish collection and garbage disposal.

Schools: high school, plant and enrollment; junior high and elementary schools, public (number and when constructed; enrollment and estimated future enrollment; new facilities contemplated; number of pupils in each type of course; number of public school teachers; teachers' salaries); parochial schools (same); vocational training schools (enrollment and yearly graduates; breakdown of trades and number studying); colleges, business schools, universities (graduate and advanced training; specialized or technical programs; extension programs).

Libraries.

Hospitals and Medical Facilities: nearest hospital, beds, clinics, staff; number of doctors and dentists with local offices.

Recreational Facilities: theaters, playgrounds, swimming pools, tennis courts; nearby state parks and beaches.
Churches (number and denominations).
Hotels, Motels, and Restaurants Serving the Area.
Newspapers, Radio and Television Stations Serving Area.
Civic Organizations and Clubs.
Other Attractions and Points of Interest.

This list covers points of primary interest to industry. With these data, the industrial real estate broker should be in a position to describe the local community and its locational characteristics to prospective industries. The community itself can also profit by adopting policies to correct conditions unfavorable to industry revealed as a result of community industrial surveys. A continuing industrial real estate operation should have facilities available for keeping this material up to date. This is the only way in which surveys can be conducted efficiently and profitably for industrial clients.

SELECTED REFERENCES

A Fortune Survey on Locating Plants, Warehouses, Laboratories (New York Time, Inc., 1963).

USA Standards Institute, *USA Standard Methods of Determining Areas in Industrial Buildings* (New York, The Author, 1962).

Chapin, F. Stuart, Jr., *Urban Land Use Planning,* rev. ed. 2 (Urbana, University of Illinois Press, 1965).

Connecticut Development Commission, *Guide to Industrial Development for the Community,* rev. ed (Hartford, The Author, 1965).

Fuchs, Victor R., *Changes in the Location of Manufacturing in the United States Since 1929* (New Haven, Yale University Press, 1962).

Greenhut, Melvin L., *Plant Location in Theory and in Practice* (Chapel Hill, University of North Carolina Press, 1956).

Hoover, E. M., *The Location of Economic Activity* (New York, McGraw-Hill, 1948).

Isard, Walter E., *Location and Space Economy* (New York, John Wiley & Sons, 1956).

Kinnard, William N., Jr., and Malinowski, Zenon S., *Highways as a Factor in Small Manufacturing Plant Locations* (Storrs, Connecticut, Bureau of Business Research and Services, University of Connecticut, 1962).

Losch, August, *The Economics of Location* (New Haven, Yale University Press, 1954).

McManmon, George M., *A Survey of the Literature on Industrial Location* (Syracuse, Business Research Center, Syracuse University, 1959).

U.S. Department of Commerce, Office of Area Development, *Data Sources for Plant Location Analysis* (Washington, U.S. Government Printing Office, 1959).

Weber, Alfred, *Theory of the Location of Industries,* trans. by C. J. Friedrich (Chicago, University of Chicago Press, 1929).

3 Site Selection and Space Requirements of Industry

THE industrial real estate specialist familiar with the general framework of location analysis, and armed with realistic community data, is in a position to serve well both the industrial client and the community by applying this analysis to the data. The result will be a specific, custom evaluation of location needs, and an identification of sites to meet these needs. This process constitutes the first important step in providing space for industry: finding its location or site.

The second step is equally important. It is to make available industrial building space of the type, and in the volume, required by industry seeking new or expanded space on the sites previously selected. Both steps must be completed successfully before the industrial establishment is properly housed.

The industrial firm usually knows what it needs and wants, although on occasion the broker can assist in clarifying these requirements. The community looking for industry, or the property owner or developer, usually can do little to change locational characteristics of available sites. However, the broker may be able to indicate means that *do* exist to enhance the attractiveness of these sites to industrial firms. To perform these advisory functions, as well as to facilitate the matching of site and building requirements with industrial space characteristics, the industrial real estate specialist must have a good working knowledge of the process and standards of selecting an industrial location. The broker must be able to gather, interpret, and present the facts to the industrial client. He must also be prepared to advise the client on the most profitable course of action to take.

THE INDUSTRIAL SITE SELECTION PROCESS

In attempting to provide a "home for industry," the broker finds that market studies are important in the process of identifying the criteria or

59

standards by which the industrial firm judges the suitability of alternative locations, sites, and industrial space. These are only general guidelines available to help in this identification. The specific needs or requirements of the individual firm are such that no "packaged" or "canned" approach can substitute for individualized, customized assistance.

The site selection process is essentially an objective, coldly analytical procedure in which personal—as opposed to market or operational—preferences play no role except in forms dominated by the owner-manager.[1] The industrial location or site selection process proceeds at successive levels. First, generally acceptable areas are identified. Specific communities within these areas are then abstracted for further study. Finally, individual sites are chosen for the final decision. Although the first two phases or levels often result from market studies conducted by either the staff of the industrial firm or by area research specialists,[2] the industrial broker should also be familiar with the procedure. He can be called on to carry out such a survey (for a separate fee) or to advise on its direction. He certainly must be able to apply its findings in aiding or advising the firm in the final site selection.

Standards Used in Selecting a Site

The actual conduct of a site selection study for or by a particular company, depends upon its site requirements. What appears to be generally a serious locational deficiency may be quite unimportant to a given firm. Conversely, a favorable locational factor of seeming importance may be irrelevant to another company. Locational projects must be related to the special requirements of the firm. As an illustration, an industrial real estate broker was recently given the assignment to locate, within four weeks, a site with a one million gallon per day supply of process water of a quality usable directly, or by normal treatment, for all purposes including boiler feed, grade A water production, cooling, component washing, and sanitary purposes. Besides the water requirement, the company sought an electric power supply of 6,000 kilowatt amperes.

To the real estate representative of the industrial firm seeking a location, the specific requirements of the firm and its processes are overriding. "The weight or emphasis to be placed upon the many factors affecting the selection of an industrial site depend upon a great many variables, such as the type of product, product market, and size of operation or facility (be it a distribution or manufacturing facility); location of competitors; and to a certain extent upon the particular political-economic conditions prevailing at the time a selection is made. The only general rule that can be set forth is that industry tries to select a site where the cost of production, overhead,

[1] See, for example, Zenon S. Malinowski and William N. Kinnard, Jr., *Personal Factors Influencing Small Manufacturing Plant Locations* (Storrs, Bureau of Business Research, University of Connecticut, 1962).

[2] See Richard D. Hileman, "Factors in Plant Location," *Advanced Course in Techniques of Industrial Real Estate* (Washington, Society of Industrial Realtors, 1964). Mr. Hileman is supervisor—Industrial Development, Real Estate Division, United States Steel Corporation.

and distribution is at a minimum—in other words, the location that will effect the greatest profit or the lowest cost." [3]

Beyond this generalization, however, some companies impose plant or site size limits: for example, 100,000 square feet of plant area. Company policy may also establish a maximum plant employment level. It would be undesirable to try to develop sites for a company if these limits were exceeded.

Company policy may also be quite definite with respect to local labor supply requirements. Corporations operating branch plants may plan the location of new plants so that the new facilities will not compete in the same labor markets occupied by their existing plants. It is also often against company policy to employ more than a given share of the local labor supply: perhaps a payroll of not more than 5 per cent of total area payrolls, or a work force not exceeding 20 per cent of the eligible working force in a given area.

As noted earlier, special attention may be given to community facilities. A proper business climate, adequate public services, educational facilities of a specific type, cultural and residential amenities, and the availability of good local transportation are among the most frequently cited requirements established by major firms.

The Preliminary Study

The preliminary study is concerned mainly with requirements of the new plant. Before judgments can be made about the type of site required, the specific needs of the plant must be identified. Certain basic questions must be answered, whatever the primary orientation of the firm. The products manufactured, for instance, will indicate the materials needed. So the first step is to locate the sources of needed materials, both the quantity and the quality required, and the transportation facilities best suited for their acquisition.

A related problem arises in regard to distributing the finished product. The major distribution points and the quantities likely to be shipped are identified, together with the most likely modes of shipment. Given this information, executives of the firm may calculate materials costs, their transportation costs, and distribution costs of the finished product, among a range of alternative locations.

Plant size is another important item: the number of square feet of floor area and the required land area. Many companies establish minimum land-to-building ratios. Once the size of plant for current needs (and provision for anticipated expansion) is estimated, the minimum required site may be calculated.

Labor requirements cannot be ignored. The specific skills needed, plus the number of male and female employees anticipated, represent another basis for judging site suitability.

Detailed requirements for utility services for the plant should be esti-

---
[3] *Ibid.*

mated. For each type of utility, the volume of use must be specified. From this estimate the minimum size of mains and utility capacities is derived: water, waste disposal, electricity, and gas. Another consideration important to site selection is the capacity of mains in relation to anticipated peak service demand, which is especially important for those firms having wide variation in demand.

If the proposed facility is large relative to the communities that are being considered, the number of housing units required by management and other key personnel will also enter into the final decision.

In summary, the purpose of the preliminary study is to establish the specific site standards applicable to a particular proposed plant. The products and processes involved determine materials-sources and the distribution of the final product. The type and volume of transportation facilities needed can determine transportation costs at each potential site. Requirements of plant size, labor force, utilities, and employee housing provide further criteria to judge the suitability of alternative sites.

Selection of the General Geographic Area

Once the preliminary study is completed, the firm can proceed to select general areas that offer the most profitable labor and transportation cost combinations. In setting boundaries that may be acceptable from the standpoint of these costs, the minimum and maximum acceptable community size must also be considered. In some instances, the company may prefer to locate near a large metropolitan center; in other cases a smaller community would be preferred.

With these broad objectives in mind, experienced executives suggest that next a few communities which appear to meet the criteria within the geographic area be selected for more intensive study. Some say that no more than half a dozen should be compared; others claim that as many as 25 should be included at this level. The next step typically is to refine data so as to reduce the number of communities under consideration.

Qualifying Selected Communities

Extracting the most preferred communities from the original group of initially qualified communities usually requires the employment of industrial location specialists. The S.I.R. and the real estate counselor are often particularly qualified to handle this assignment. Also, industrial agents of railroads, utilities, and industrial development organizations may be asked for more detailed information. From here the work proceeds almost invariably in confidence. After the most likely communities are selected, either industrial real estate brokers or others may be asked to recommend the best sites in each. When agents have identified the best sites in each of the communities, they still must be inspected by company representatives. At this point, the length of utility extensions which must be constructed at company expense, and the cost of installing access roads should be identified for each location. Also, each community will be evaluated with respect to local attitudes and policies toward new industry, planning and zoning programs, the local property tax burden, current assessment practices, and the general economic and social climate.

Selecting the Site

Next, the investigator becomes concerned with individual site characteristics. The industrial real estate broker is most likely to be hired for both assistance and advice at this stage of the process. Acquisition cost and site preparation costs for the proposed plant must be reviewed with great accuracy and considerable detail. General estimates are no longer acceptable. The cost of land preparation, the cost of extending utilities to each site, and the transportation costs, both in and out, are items of great importance in making these cost projections. Finally, property taxes (including the real property taxes and personal property taxes on inventory and equipment) and other business taxes will be estimated for the proposed plant.

Other cost items pertaining to individual sites would include the estimated monthly cost of utility services, and the topographic and geological characteristics of the site that might result in added construction expenses. The danger of flooding will be carefully reviewed where any potential hazard exists. Thus, the final estimate of site costs includes both the cost of vacant land and the cost of site preparation. Moreover, the costs of operating the plant at each site under review are carefully calculated.

By now the company will have reviewed several sites in a few selected communities, and will have estimated the initial site acquisition costs, costs of site preparation, and operating costs at each location. Thus far, emphasis has been on cost factors, in large part because they are rather readily measured. These are essentially financial or economic factors. Before the analysis is complete and the final choice made, community attitudes toward new industry, local labor-management history, and the attractiveness of the community to technical and management personnel must be rated. These are sometimes termed noneconomic factors. Certainly they cannot be measured precisely. These may be the controlling factors in plant location, especially if economic factors are almost equal. Travel convenience to national headquarters, the availability of housing, and convenience to plant customers are examples of subjective matters which can control the final selection of site.

Sources of Information

The industrial real estate broker occasionally needs help in approaching a site selection assignment, because the research nature of the undertaking may be beyond the scope of his usual pattern of activities. He can turn to one or more of a number of published sources that offer more details and insights than can be provided in an introductory statement such as the present treatment.

Several books, handbooks and guides are included among the Selected

References at the end of this chapter. Further references to specific volumes may be found in the "Industrial Property" section of *Real Estate Information Sources,* an annotated bibliography edited by Janice B. Babb and Beverly F. Dordick, and published by the Gale Research Company of Detroit, Michigan in 1963.

The most useful information of all, however, can often be found in the current reports, articles, and case studies contained in periodicals dealing with industrial location and site selection. These include, but are not restricted to:

Society of Industrial Realtors Newsletter (Society of Industrial Realtors, 1300 Connecticut Avenue, N.W., Washington, D.C. 20036).

Industrial Development and Manufacturers Record (Conway Publications, Inc., 2592 Apple Valley Road, Atlanta, Georgia 30319).

National Real Estate Investor (20 West 38th Street, New York, New York 10001).

Economic Development (formerly *Area Development*) (U.S. Department of Commerce, Economic Development Administration, Washington, D.C. 20230).

Urban Land (Urban Land Institute, 1200 18th Street, N.W., Washington, D.C. 20036).

INDUSTRIAL LOCATION AND SITE SELECTION FACTORS

From earlier discussions in this volume, it is clear that a wide variety and range of factors impinge upon the industrial location decision. Any attempt to produce a definitive catalogue of location or site selection factors generally applicable in all (or even most) cases would be an exercise in frustration and futility.

First, there is considerable divergence in the known needs and desires of industrial firms, depending upon the nature of the product and the process involved. In addition, there is substantial evidence that the factors considered during the location process vary widely with the size of the firm, the size of the plant, and the phase in the life cycle of the firm. For example, a study of some 250 manufacturing plant locations in central Connecticut over a seven-year period revealed that existing firms seeking to relocate were significantly more aware of the operation of location factors, than were new firms seeking their first sites.[4]

Even more important is the fact that specific location considerations are perceived differently by decision-makers in industrial firms. Both the level at which the factors are consciously considered, and whether they are even consciously considered at all, vary greatly among seemingly identical firms.

Despite these limitations, it is generally useful to employ some kind of checklist or form in considering site selection factors in a particular case, so that no potentially significant factor is inadvertently overlooked. If

[4] William N. Kinnard, Jr. and Zenon S. Malinowski, *Highways as a Factor in Small Manufacturing Plant Location Decisions* (Storrs, Bureau of Business Research, University of Connecticut, 1963).

system and logic are to replace guesswork and chance in site selection, a reasonably consistent method must be applied.

Studies of Site Selection Factors

Site or location factors can be divided into two major categories: general and specific. "General factors include those that are used in selecting one town or state over other towns or states and include such items as transportation facilities and costs, tax structure, zoning and land use, labor, utilities, financing, community services, housing and education, sources of material available to industry, and many other items." [5] These are the factors about which *some* standard generalizations can be made.

Specific site factors are those that pertain to judgments made about the site itself. Because they vary so widely in importance with each individual case, it is not possible to present them in any generally accepted order. However, they will normally include the following: [6]

Size and shape of the plot of land—adequacy for specific plant, and for expansion;

Physical condition of the land—topography, soil and subsoil conditions desired;

Land costs—acquisition price plus site preparation costs, financing terms;

Utilities availability—adequacy, costs of providing necessary facilities;

Transportation facilities available at the site—adequacy, frequency of service, cost;

Zoning, building codes, and other land and/or building use controls—protection to industry from residential or commercial encroachments, reasonableness of restrictions, equitable enforcement;

Taxes—rates and trends, assessment policies and trends, relative burdens;

Protection—fire, police.

Studies of the claimed importance of industrial location factors, based on interviews or surveys of industrial firms, also help in indicating what should be investigated when a client asks for assistance in seeking a site. Recent surveys of plant location patterns have emphasized factors affecting the movement of plants closer to their markets. The federal highway program has resulted in new road networks. This has sparked further decentralization of industry. For example, the practical area of labor supply attraction has increased nearly five-fold because of new highway patterns. In a study by the American Trucking Associations, the factors of plant location most frequently mentioned by industrial respondents, in order of frequency, were:

(1) Proximity to good highways.
(2) Abundant labor supply.
(3) Availability of suitable land.
(4) Proximity to markets.
(5) Availability of rail service.
(6) Availability of raw materials.

[5] Hileman, *op. cit.*
[6] Adapted from Hileman, *op. cit.*

(7) Favorable state and local tax structure.
(8) Favorable leasing or financing.
(9) Abundant water supply.
(10) Proximity to related industry.
(11) Existence of building at site.
(12) Community's cultural-recreational assets.
(13) Nearby vocational training facilities.[7]

While many similar studies have revealed essentially the same factors to be significant in plant location decisions, there has always been some substantial variation in the priority of factors, depending upon the industry, the size of the firm, or the process. For example, the *Fortune Survey* of over 400 of the largest manufacturing firms in the United States found the following factors to be most frequently mentioned as important in plant location decisions (in order of indicated importance):

(1) Availability of workers.
(2) Proximity to customers (for transportation).
(3) Proximity to raw materials, supplies, and services.
(4) Ample area for future expansion.
(5) A growing regional market.
(6) Water supply.
(7) Inexpensive power and other utilities.[8]

It is quite apparent that this listing is different—at least in emphasis and priority of factors—from that developed in the American Trucking Associations' study. Moreover, factors at several levels of location decision are rather indiscriminately intermingled, because the respondents did not themselves distinguish among the levels.

These lists may be contrasted with the indicated priority of factors derived from a survey of some 250 manufacturing plants newly located and relocated in central Connecticut between 1953 and 1959. These were predominantly small plants: i.e., less than 100 employees. Frequency of mention is still the basis for ranking the factors.

(1) Availability of the site.
(2) Suitability of the site.
(3) Proximity to (or access to) customers.
(4) Personal considerations.
(5) Cost-reducing factors (taxes, wages).
(6) Attractive price or rental.
(7) Highways (transportation facilities).[9]

It is interesting to note that there really are similarities in the three listings if allowance is made for differences in wording. The comparison is shown below for selected factors:

---

[7] For details, see *Summary of Highways, Trucks, and New Industry* (The Department of Research and Transport Economics, American Trucking Associations, July 1, 1963), p. 5.

[8] Adapted from *A Fortune Survey on Locating Plants, Warehouses, Laboratories* (New York, Time, Inc., 1963), p. 13. Only factors receiving mention by at least 30 per cent of the respondents are listed here.

[9] Kinnard and Malinowski, *op. cit.*, p. 57. Only factors receiving mention by at least 30 per cent of the respondents are listed here.

Location Factor	Rank in "All Plants Survey"	Rank in "Large Plants Survey"	Rank in "Small Plants Survey"
Highways-Transportation	1	2–3	6–7
Labor Supply	2	1	5
Site Availability-Suitability	3	4	1
Market Proximity	4	2	2–3

These findings show clearly the market, labor, and transportation orientation of modern industrial plants in the United States, and the declining significance of proximity to raw materials or to suppliers (for non-basic industry at least).

Relatively little data exist which describe variations in the importance of site selection factors by type of industry. The central Connecticut study did consider the different importance attached to highway access by broad industrial groups, however. It showed conclusively that metal fabricating establishments were, by far, most sensitive to highway proximity, and consciously sought this attribute in their locations above all other considerations.[10] Technically-oriented industrial firms were found to be particularly anxious to locate near universities with appropriate graduate programs for their scientific, professional personnel, and in "areas where there is a concentration of technical manpower." [11]

Variation is also observed in site requirements and needs (and hence in importance of factors influencing site selection) among industrial groups involving differing functions and processes. The factor lists cited thus far have all related to manufacturing site selection, primarily because nearly all published location studies concentrate on manufacturing. Some modest comparison is possible with an unpublished analysis of warehouse location factors in the Metropolitan Los Angeles area.[12] This shows somewhat different emphasis from those found in manufacturing location studies, as would logically be expected.

Since warehouses are directly related to distribution rather than to production, the greatest emphasis is placed on access to markets (or customers), and on availability of highway transportation. On the other hand, since warehousing tends to rely much less heavily on labor, the availability of, or access to, labor supply is a relatively unimportant location consideration. The most important factors found to be operating in warehouse site selection were:

(1) Size, shape and adaptability of site.
(2) Location of customers.
(3) Highway system, access, delivery cost.
(4) Traffic and congestion.
(5) Neighborhood environment, land use controls.
(6) Community protection (fire and police) services.
(7) Parking and loading facilities.

---

[10] *Ibid.*, p. 60.
[11] Richard J. Anderson, *Factors Affecting the Location of Technically-Oriented Corporations* (Washington, Society of Industrial Realtors, 1964), p. 3.
[12] The discussion of warehouse location factors is based on materials provided by C. B. O'Gorman, S.I.R., Riverside, California.

Even among warehousing and distribution operations, substantial variation will be found, based on the specific nature of the product, the need for fast delivery, the size of the typical shipment, and the like.

From the foregoing, it is quite clear that no matter how much study, investigation, analysis, and past experience go into the development of guides and checklists of site selection factors, no generally applicable formula has emerged to serve in all or even most cases. In each instance there is at least one location consideration absolutely critical to site selection. It must take precedence over all others, while the remaining factors may be considered on a more general, analytical basis. For example, despite the general trend away from reliance on public transit facilities, the availability of a public bus system was absolutely vital in the location of an electric appliance assembly plant employing large numbers of women in Manchester, Connecticut.

Plant location and site selection thus remain custom services tailored to the specific needs and desires of the individual firm.

INDUSTRIAL BUILDING CHARACTERISTICS

Site selection provides the physical space from which goods and services are provided, and on which the plant may be placed. The actual production, storage, or office functions must be housed in one or more buildings, however. The characteristics of the buildings and other improvements are as important as site characteristics to the success of a location.

For basically sound reasons, there has been a general trend toward low-density, single-story industrial buildings throughout the economy, regardless of function or process to be performed in the structure. The important point to note, however, is that the function or process *determines* the layout and construction of the building. Under most conditions, when the firm has sufficient financing available, the type of building to be constructed is decided upon *after* the floor layout is settled upon, based on the nature of the activities to be housed. This leads to more custom adaptation of industrial structures to user requirements, and incidentally to more problems of conversion when there is a change in occupants.

It would be a mistake to assume that single-story structures meet all industrial space needs effectively. For example, multiple-story plants are better adapted to industrial processes in which gravity flow is required or recommended. Also, segments of activity which should be isolated from the major functions of the establishment are often better located at a different level, rather than in a separate building. Multiple-use or multiple-occupant structures (often serving as "incubators" for small, new and growing firms) are often appropriately multiple-story buildings. Indeed, in many former mill structures in New England towns there have been conversions to such multiple-uses. These conversions are often sponsored by local industrial development commissions eager to replace the jobs lost through the removal or sharp curtailment of activity from the original mills.

Finally, multistory plants still make economic sense in locations where the cost of land prohibits low-density use. Not all industry wants to or can locate in lower-priced suburban or rural areas. Central city land is generally expensive, whether it is made available through private developers or through public agencies. When industrial land sells for $1.00 or more per square foot, pressure grows to build upward rather than outward.

Industrial buildings vary considerably with respect to many physical attributes, most of which should be related to the nature of the activities to be housed in the building. As with site requirements, building ingredients tend to be adjusted to the specific needs of the particular user. Therefore, any listing of factors in building-space development or selection must necessarily be highly generalized. It can serve only as a guide to the kinds of items that ought to be considered by a broker or consultant seeking to assist a firm in selecting industrial building space.

Among the items to be considered, aside from the amount of floor area required to carry on the functions of the establishment, are:

(1) *Type of Material.* This will vary with climate, load-bearing capabilities of the land, construction costs, span and height requirements, insulation needs, building codes, durability requirements, and desires or requirements for exterior appearance.

(2) *Foundations, Floors, Floor-Loads.* These depend on the nature of the process, coupled with the capabilities of the soil. General-purpose space tends to be slightly over-engineered so as to be more widely adaptable to alternative types of uses. The added costs involved in such a course of action usually set an effective limit to complete adaptability, however.

(3) *Structural Members.* The requirements here depend primarily on the processes or functions to be carried on in the structure. Spans and ceiling heights, for example, tend to be provided in multiples of six feet in warehouse or storage space, because pallet sizes are widely standardized at six feet.

(4) *Electrical Installations.* Many production activities require not only high voltage and heavy wattage, but also specialized levels or cycles of electrical power. It is not sufficient to have "enough" power, and lines and circuits with high enough capacities. The proper type of electrical installation represents one example of what are termed "economic" standards as opposed to "physical" standards.

(5) *Protection (Security) Systems.* The importance of this factor depends on the significance of security to the particular firm. However, protection systems and devices can be quite expensive, especially if they must be installed at a later date. One potential pitfall is to expend excessive sums in providing super-adequate fencing and other devices. This factor therefore requires particular care in its evaluation, preferably by an experienced specialist.

(6) *Fire Protection and Sprinkler Systems.* This varies with the type of activity and with local or state codes.

(7) *Elevators, Lifts, Conveyors.* Because of the expense of these items, both in acquisition price and installaton cost, as well as the space which they absorb, extreme care must be exercised to be sure that they suit the purpose for which they are intended. Correcting mistakes can be

most costly. Moreover, allowance for future expansion of production or activity has to be made.

(8) *Heating and Lighting.* Technological advances in these fields have led to opportunities and capabilities to meet a wide range of needs more efficiently than ever before.

The foregoing list illustrates the opportunities for both improvement and error that exist in providing industrial plant space for a client firm, even after settling the critical issue of how much space. Further assistance and guidance are available in a number of publications and periodicals dealing with current developments in industrial building construction. The books are included in the Selected References at the end of this chapter. The periodicals potentially useful in understanding industrial building components and specifications include:

American Builder (30 Church Street, New York, N.Y. 10007).

Architectural Record (McGraw-Hill, Inc., 330 W. 42nd Street, New York, N.Y. 10036).

Buildings (Stamats Publishing Co., 427 Sixth Avenue, S.E., Cedar Rapids, Iowa 52401).

Construction Review (U.S. Department of Commerce, Office of Business Economics, Washington, D.C. 20230).

Dodge Reports: Construction Contracts Statistics—Engineering Service (Mc-Graw-Hill/F. W. Dodge Corp., 330 W. 42nd Street, New York, N.Y. 10036).

Progressive Architecture (430 Park Avenue, New York, N.Y. 10017).

TRENDS AND VARIATIONS IN INDUSTRIAL SPACE REQUIREMENTS

The quantitative aspects of demand for industrial space have been the subject of study and analysis for many years. The aim is to derive measures that can be used to forecast land and building space needs, both for the individual firm and for communities to reserve space for industrial use. In most instances, the number of employees can be estimated independently, whether for the individual plant or for a community. As a result, the most common measure for estimating the demand for industrial space is some variant of the employment density ratio discussed in Chapter 2.

Two basic employment density measures are commonly utilized. One is the land-area/employment ratio. It is expressed either as the number of square feet of land area per employee, or as the number of employees per acre of land. This is a very useful measure because it permits a direct estimate of required land area from the forecast of major shift employment.

The second employment density guide is a floor-area/employment ratio. This permits an estimate of total building or plant area required or expected. Estimating the land area necessary, or to be set aside, requires a second conversion from the plant area forecast. In both cases, the employment figure used is the average number of employees actually working at the plant during the largest daily shift; second and/or third shift employment is not included.

Land area requirements may also be calculated from a combination of three factors. The first is the structural density, which is the ratio of building ground-floor area to land area. Next is parking area, which requires sufficient space for both major shift employment and employment on the next largest shift, customer and/or visitor parking, and loading and docking facilities. Finally, sometimes overlooked but extremely vital, there must be sufficient room for expansion. Otherwise, the problems of relocating will be encountered long before the investment in the present location is amortized.

Land Requirements

Industries may be classified by total land area required, employees per acre (the land/employment ratio), and parking area needed. Every modern industrial site must provide space for 10 types of functions, and many must provide for 14.[13] The essential 10 include:

  (1) Processing or production.
  (2) Storage of materials.
  (3) Storage of finished goods.
  (4) Offices and salesrooms.
  (5) Wash rooms, locker rooms, lunch rooms.
  (6) Heating and ventilating equipment.
  (7) Repair or tool shops.
  (8) Parking for employees.
  (9) Parking for visitors.
(10) Loading and unloading.

In addition, land area must often be provided for:

  (1) Landscaping.
  (2) Employee recreation areas.
  (3) Garages or parking for truck fleets.
  (4) Internal streets and walks (for large plants).

1. *Total Land Area Required.* For purposes of analysis, it is convenient to identify those industries seeking sites of less than 10 acres (at one end of the scale), and industries requiring sites of 100 acres or more.

Industrial establishments using less than 10 acres are generally operations offering custom service. These are called ancillary industries, largely dependent on and concentrated near major manufacturing plants. In most industry, a group of operations offering subcontracted job work, prefabrication, or custom service to larger manufacturing companies will be found. Such examples include fabricated metals, precision tools, optical instruments, manufacturing of electronic components, and the like. The so-called Metals Service Industry referred to in Chapter 2 is also a classic illustration of such small-site industries concentrated near major employers.

---

[13] This listing is adapted from Stuart P. Walsh, "Buy Enough Land," *Orange County Industrial News*, Santa Ana, California, June, 1958.

In contrast, industries requiring over 100 acres are usually activities with a relatively high capital investment: primary metals, aircraft manufacturing, transportation equipment, chemicals, and similar operations.

2. *Land-Employment Densities.* Another way of characterizing industry is to classify it by the number of major shift employees per acre. Industries with a low ratio of employees per acre are termed labor-extensive; industries showing a high concentration of employees per acre are termed labor-intensive.

A low ratio of employment per acre, i.e., 10 employees or fewer per acre, usually means that the plant must have a fairly large area. Examples of industries in this group include chemical plants, steel and aluminum plants, and other industries dealing mostly with raw material processing. Labor-extensive industries are generally capital-intensive; they have a high ratio of capital investment or equipment per employee. Warehousing and distribution activities are also labor-extensive.

The labor-intensive industries include instrument manufacturing, electronics, and other operations using highly skilled, scientific and professional personnel. Activities such as fire control instruments and impregnated fabrics are also among the few requiring as many as 75 employees per acre.

3. *Industrial Plant Parking.* Improper planning for parking can cause delay, confusion, accident expense, and even premature pressure to relocate. Parking areas must be adequate to meet the requirements of employee vehicles, visitors' vehicles, shipping (trucks), and pedestrian use.

Four basic factors control the selection and size of parking areas. First are land costs. Prohibitive land costs can discourage a plant location. Next is a consideration of the number of vehicles and the type of parking in each shift. Overlapping shifts require a direct and proportionate increase in the number of vehicles to be stored. In general, 60 per cent of a plant parking area will be used for vehicle storage, while the other 40 per cent is needed for vehicle movement. Third, the shape and contour of the land influence the layout and capacity of the lot. Generally, rectangular lots with access on at least two sides are least costly. However, other shapes and layouts are growing in favor because they offer greater convenience to employees and visitors. This is related to the fourth consideration, which is that the parking areas must be in close proximity to the plant.

Directly related to, and generally considered as a part of, parking requirements, are needs for truck loading and unloading. The Highway Research Board recommends that industrial buildings have off-street truck loading or docking facilities, except in already built-up city areas where curb loading is available and adequate. Off-street truck loading requirements depend on the size of the market area served, the activity (volume of incoming and outgoing freight) of the plant, the width of streets, the size of trucks and trailers serving the plant, and the floor area of the plant.

Parking area and loading area standards are also set in local zoning ordinances. An increasing number of communities tend to express these requirements in relation to the floor area of the plant, plant employment, or volume of activity. While specific needs vary somewhat, it is generally recommended that loading bays should be 12 feet wide with an overhead clearance of 14 feet. The recommended length is at least 45 feet. The precise length necessary depends on local and state regulations covering truck and trailer size.

Building Area Requirements

Total floor area needs can rarely be forecast simply by knowing the specific industry to be housed. This is because there are firms and establishments of all sizes in the great majority of industries occupying both central and outlying sites in both old and new buildings. Despite this limitation, some very broad generalizations are possible.

Small plants (those with less than 25,000 square feet of floor area) tend to be most concentrated in high-skill, labor-intensive activities such as machine tool accessories, drug manufacture, precision instruments, and specialty chemicals and insecticides. On the other hand, large plants (those with over 100,000 square feet of floor area) are most often associated with capital-intensive industries commonly regarded as "heavy": automotive assembly and parts, steel production, aircraft assembly, and basic chemicals.

When floor area employment densities are considered, patterns very similar to those found among land area employment densities exist. The labor-intensive industries are those requiring highly skilled labor, and producing specialty products: instruments, precision parts and tools, and the like. These typically utilize 200 square feet of floor area per employee or less. Capital-intensive industries, especially primary metals and chemicals producers, exhibit the highest ratios of floor area per employee, often in excess of 1,000 square feet.

Structural Densities

The major fact about structural densities among all industrial groups is that the land-to-building ratio has been increasing since the end of World War II. This is in part the result of the trend toward one-story structures, in part the result of increased parking needs as plants move to less central locations, and in part the result of conscious planning by industrial firms (and their site selection advisers) for future expansion needs.

While structural densities of 80 per cent and more are common among older industrial sites in central cities, common rules of thumb shortly after 1945 suggested no more than 50 per cent to be desirable. A study conducted by the Urban Land Institute in 1954 covering Dr. Dorothy Muncy's sampling of 220 plants built during World War II, plus a sample compiled by the National Industrial Zoning Committee of 150 plants built after World War II, and a ULI inventory of 180 plants built during 1953–1954, revealed that over four-fifths of the plants surveyed had structural densities of 35 per cent or less.[14] Similar tendencies have been exhibited in studies conducted in Philadelphia, Detroit, Chicago and the Hartford Metropolitan

---

[14] See Dorothy A. Muncy, *Space for Industry*, Technical Bulletin No. 23 (Washington, Urban Land Institute, 1954).

area, to cite a few examples.[15] Some authorities now recommend structural densities as low as 12 to 15 per cent. The "going" ratio of land area to building area for new general-purpose industrial buildings in most commonly between 3:1 and 4:1; this results in structural densities of 25 to 33 per cent.

Trends and Variations in Area Requirements

In general, the basic trend in American industry is toward less intensive use of land and plant area. The major exceptions are found in industrial renewal and rehabilitation areas in central cities. This means that an establishment of given size (as measured by number of employees) will usually occupy a larger plant on a proportionately larger site than was the case even before 1950.

It has already been noted that there is an identifiable pattern of variation in land and building densities by type of industry. The type of product, the nature of the process, and whether the activity is capital-intensive or labor-intensive, all impinge on this pattern.

A further indication of the general trend toward lower space densities is found in the Philadelphia, Chicago, and Hartford studies cited earlier. Each contains a comparison of floor area densities between the former location and the new plant for all those establishments which changed locations during the survey period. In all three cities, the average floor area per employee increased significantly at the new locations.

Since most of these new locations were at sites more removed from central areas than the old locations were, the changes accentuated another variable in employment densities found to exist: both employment densities and structural densities tend to decrease as the distance from the central business district of the center city increases. Moreover, larger plants tended to locate on, or relocate to, more outlying sites. Whether this is a function of land costs, or of scarcity of adequate sites in more central locations, seems to vary among metropolitan regions, but the tendency is general and widespread. Conversely, the smallest plants tended to locate near business centers. These are generally service and distribution establishments.

ESTIMATING THE DEMAND FOR INDUSTRIAL LAND

If it is known approximately how many acres will be needed to meet industrial land requirements in a given area five, 10 or more years in the future, then enough space suitable for industrial use may be reserved. In the industrial areas of the northeastern United States, many communities

---

[15] For details, refer to Institute for Urban Studies, *Industrial Land and Facilities for Philadelphia* (Philadelphia, University of Pennsylvania, 1956); Detroit City Plan Commission, *Industrial Study,* Master Plan Technical Report, Second Series (Detroit, The Author, 1956); Chicago Department of City Planning, *Industrial Movements and Expansion, 1947–1957,* Economic Base Study Series, Study No. 3 (Chicago: The Author, 1961); W. N. Kinnard, Jr. *et. al., Thirteen Years of Industrial Location in Metropolitan Hartford* (Storrs, University of Connecticut, 1966).

desiring industrial expansion have seen their supply of potential industrial land virtually exhausted. This has resulted, at least in part, from a lack of adequate planning and action.

The rate of land absorption is much higher for residential use than for industrial purposes. Potential industrial land is often taken over for residential and other competing uses. At the same time, unrealistically optimistic estimates of the demand for industrial land may result in over-zoning for industry. This is an experience common to many growing suburban communities. Land held for industrial purposes, with little chance of actually being used for industry in the long run, represents an uneconomic allocation of real estate that might better be adapted to other uses.

If the potential demand for industrial land has been overestimated, the investment in both public and private industrial districts may be misdirected to the point where the demand for industrial space does not even support the investment in public utilities. The cost of adapting unimproved land to industrial use requires care in relating new industrial facilities to a realistic estimate of industrial real estate needs. An accurate projection of the local demand for industrial space will help in achieving optimum economic development.

The methods used to estimate the future demand for manufacturing space follow a fairly standard pattern. Future land needs are based on analyses of industrial employment density trends.[16] In relating the number of employees to industrial acreage demand, all land within the boundaries of the plant site is considered: plant location, parking, driveways, railroad spurs, landscaped areas, outdoor storage areas; plus one-half the area of all drives, streets, highways, or railroad spurlines bordering the property. This gross measure is easier to apply to unsubdivided raw land in estimating future requirements.

The steps in estimating future space requirements for industry include the following:

1. *Determine the present number of manufacturing employees per gross acre, by type of industry.* This step requires a detailed inventory of existing industrial activities and plants, together with recognition of trends and variation in growth rates within each industrial group. For instance, an estimate of future land requirements of an aircraft parts manufacturer in New England would probably be more conservative than one for a similar company located in California. Similarly, the industry under examination may be highly dependent on raw materials that will be in shorter supply. It is therefore possible that future acreage requirements of an industry may be less than the present acreage being used.

2. *Estimate future industrial employment, by type of industry and size of firm.* The next step is for the investigator to estimate the future industrial employment in the various industry classifications in the area, by size category, or to obtain a reliable estimate made by an appropriate research agency such as the Bureau of Business Research of a nearby university.

---

[16] See F. Stuart Chapin, Jr., *Urban Land Use Planning,* rev. ed. (Urbana, University of Illinois Press, 1965) for a detailed discussion of the rationale for this approach.

3. *Estimate future employee densities in the light of changing trends in industrial space requirements.* Space requirements of industry are changing for several reasons discussed in preceding sections of this chapter. As industry modernizes plant and equipment, the result is usually greater output per square foot of floor space. Offsetting this is the trend toward one-story buildings on outlying sites which contain more parking area, and more room for plant expansion. Industrial densities will change as a consequence of shifts in the industrial pattern, but appear most likely to decrease if past trends continue. The point here, however, is that whatever the trends are locally, they must be identified and included in any projection of future densities in the area being studied.

4. *Estimate the future land requirements by multiplying the estimated number of employees per acre (the industrial density) by the expected industrial employment for each use as of a given date.* This is the final step in estimating future industrial land needs. However, employment estimates must relate to all industrial uses (rather than simply to manufacturing), or land needs for industrial purposes will be understated. A further adjustment may be necessary if nonindustrial uses are permitted in industrial zones. Employment density analysis would have little applicability for many commercial uses often allowed in industrial zones. While industrial land needs are estimated by this technique, the estimate cannot ignore the land use regulations of the community. Moreover, if the estimate of demand is to be useful as a guide for forming a policy on industrial land needs, a further step will be necessary.

5. *Compare the estimated demand for industrial land with an estimate of the future supply of industrial land.* Comparing the expected or potential future *supply* of industrial land directly with the anticipated future *demand* may appear adequate as the basis for future planning. However, these estimates of demand and supply do not include judgments about the type or quality of the space, or their timing. Future land requirements may, in fact, be dominated by the demand for space with a structural density of 20 per cent or less. Yet the probable supply of available space may consist in large part of scattered lots of odd sizes, or land with inadequate utilities service, and poor topography or drainage. Thus, a survey of industrial land supply, which is later related to the expected demand, must consider the quality of the industrial land which is expected to be made available. Timing is equally important.

Applications of Industrial Space Demand Projection Techniques

Generally accepted methods of projecting industrial land requirements are based on the proposition that the land area which will be needed is equal to estimated future industrial employment (by industry and plant size), multiplied by the square feet of land area required per worker (also by industry and plant size). In applying this thinking in practice, some investigators have refined the technique by dividing employee densities into several classifications, with separate projections made for each classification. This procedure was followed by the Greater Boston Economic Study Committee in estimating industrial land needs through 1980.[17]

1. *The Boston Survey.* In this study, industry was divided into three groups, classified by the number of acres required per 1,000 workers. The number of acres per 1,000 employees ["a"] was first calculated for industries classified as intensive industries ["E_i"]. Once this standard was established, the moderately intensive industries ["E_{mi}"] were identified. The land use requirements for moderately intensive industries ["b"] were estimated as 1.5 times those for the intensive industries. The last group, the moderately extensive industries ["E_{me}"] on the average required 2.5 times as much land per employee ["c"] as the intensive industries. A somewhat complex-appearing, but essentially simple, formula was derived,[18] resulting in the estimate of industrial land needs in 1980. It is really nothing more than multiplying estimated employment in each of three groups of industries by the average densities applicable to each group, and then summing the products for the final estimate.

The accuracy of the method depends on the effectiveness of the classification of industries into the three categories, the estimate of future employment, and an accurate inventory of land use densities for each group. The method also assumed that the employee densities will remain unchanged over the period of forecasting. If the investigator has grounds for believing these ratios may change, the formula should be adjusted accordingly.

2. *The San Francisco Study.* Two methods were used to estimate the amount of industrial land needed by 2020 in the San Francisco Bay Area: a map method and a statistical projection method.[19] Both methods were based on similar assumptions, but their techniques varied considerably.

a. *The Map Method* involved developing a large-scale map which showed industrial land available, and existing land uses, in the San Francisco Bay Area in 1960. New industrial areas were interpolated along or between transportation routes, and where large vacant tracts appeared feasible for industrial parks. Projections were made only for land of adequate bearing capacity with slopes of 5 per cent or less. Land needs were related to manufacturing employment by estimating manufacturing employment at 20 per cent of total employment. Total employment was forecast at 40 per cent of the population, based on detailed analysis of labor force trends in the area.

Superimposing a slope map over the industrial zone map identified areas regarded as unsuitable for industrial use. Urban growth was then projected from planning commission studies in the Bay Area, and industrial growth was assumed to be concentrated in areas abutting existing industrial use areas. Different employment densities, based on current findings, were applied to the northern and southern sections of the Bay Area.

[17] Greater Boston Economic Study Committee, *Industrial Land Needs through 1980,* Land Use Report 2 (Boston, The Author, 1961).
[18] Total land used by industry $= (E_i \times a) + (E_{mi} \times b) + (E_{me} \times c)$, where $b = 1.5a$ and $c = 2.5a$.
[19] See *Future Development of the San Francisco Bay Area 1960–2020* (Washington, D.C., Office of Area Development, U.S. Department of Commerce, 1959), Appendix D.

The map method was relatively expensive and time consuming in the amount of field work required. However, it did provide a specific means of estimating land needs in small areas where topographical or historical conditions dominated future land use.[20]

b. *The Statistical Method* helped check the reasonableness of the map method, as well as providing an independent estimate of future industrial land use needs. First, anticipated industrial employment was projected for the years under study. Next, appropriate employment densities were applied to these industrial employment projections to give an estimate of needed industrial land. Industrial densities, adapted from earlier studies in Philadelphia, were divided into four groups, as shown in Exhibit 9.

Exhibit 9

ILLUSTRATIVE TABLE OF INDUSTRIAL DENSITIES

Industry Land-Use Group	Type of Major Industry Group and S.I.C. Codes	Acres per 1,000 Employees	Employees per Acre
I	Intensive	30	33
	23 Apparel and related products.		
	36 Electrical machinery.		
	38 Instruments and related products.		
II	Intermediate-intensive	40	25
	27 Printing and publishing.		
	37 Transportation equipment.		
III	Intermediate-extensive	90	11
	20 Food and kindred products.		
	24 Lumber and wood products.		
	25 Furniture and fixtures.		
	26 Pulp, paper, and products.		
	28 Chemicals and products.		
	30 Rubber products.		
	33 Primary metal industries.		
	34 Fabricated metal products.		
	35 Machinery, except electrical.		
	39 Miscellaneous manufactures.		
IV	Extensive	375	3
	29 Petroleum and coal products.		
	31 Leather and leather goods.		
	32 Stone, clay, and glass products.		
	All industry not included above	125	2
	Public Utilities	200	5

SOURCE: *Future Development of the San Francisco Bay Area, 1960–2020* (Washington, D. C., Office of Area Development, U. S. Department of Commerce, 1959).

In order to provide for probable future increases in land requirements per worker, percentage adjustments were made to account for greater mechanization, industrial dispersal, and increased parking and service needs.

The two methods produced strikingly similar results: the map method

[20] *Ibid.*

indicated 310 square miles needed to meet industrial land requirements by 2020, compared with statistically derived estimates of 346 square miles for the San Francisco Bay Area.

3. *The Cleveland Study.* In a study of industrial land use requirements in Cleveland, the number of workers engaged in manufacturing, wholesaling, and transportation industries was divided by the number of acres of industrial land occupied by each of these uses.[21] This produced a land employment density ratio that was then applied to minimum and maximum employment estimates for the year 2000, to derive a range of industrial land use needs. A second set of land use requirement projections was based on an estimated 50 per cent reduction in the land employment density ratio by the year 2000.

SELECTED REFERENCES

A Fortune Survey on Locating Plants, Warehouses, Laboratories (New York, Time, Inc., 1963).

Chapin, F. Stuart, Jr., *Urban Land Use Planning,* rev. ed. (Urbana, University of Illinois Press, 1965).

Chicago Department of City Planning, *Industrial Movements and Expansion, 1949–1957,* Economic Base Studies Series, Study No. 3 (Chicago, The Author, 1961).

Detroit City Plan Commission, *Industrial Study,* Master Plan Technical Report, Second Series (Detroit, The Author, 1956).

Highway Research Board, *Parking Requirements in Zoning Ordinances,* Bulletin 99 (Washington, The Author, 1955).

Institute for Urban Studies, *Industrial Land and Facilities for Philadelphia* (Philadelphia, University of Pennsylvania, 1956).

Kinnard, William N., Jr., and Malinowski, Zenon S., *Highways as a Factor in Small Manufacturing Plant Location Decisions* (Storrs, University of Connecticut, 1963).

Muncy, Dorothy A., *Space for Industry,* Technical Bulletin No. 23 (Washington, Urban Land Institute, 1954).

Shenkel, William M., "Estimating the Demand for Industrial Real Estate," *The Real Estate Appraiser,* September, 1965.

Shenkel, William M., *Principles and Practices of Industrial Real Estate: A Course Syllabus* (Washington, Society of Industrial Realtors, 1963).

Thompson, James H., *Methods of Plant Site Selection Available to Small Manufacturing Firms* (Morgantown, West Virginia, Bureau of Business Research, University of West Virginia, 1961).

Yaseen, Leonard C., *Plant Location,* rev. ed. (New York, American Research Council, 1960).

---

[21] See Regional Planning Commission, Cleveland, Cuyahoga County, *Land for Industry,* Second Report of Land Use in Cuyahoga County.

4 Meeting the Demand for Industrial Space

ONCE industrial space needs in a given area are estimated, the industrial real estate specialist is still confronted with the task of identifying the appropriate space to meet that demand. The demand may be occasioned by on-site expansion of existing establishments, relocations of existing establishments, new branches or new firms. The basic task of the broker remains matching supply with demand by finding space that meets the requirements of industrial firms. If space with the proper characteristics does not exist in a desired location, then the industrial real estate broker should be able to assist in attempts to create it.

THE NATURE OF THE INDUSTRIAL SPACE SUPPLY

It is not enough simply to know what volume of industrial space is available in a given market area. This is true for building floor space, developed sites, or undeveloped acreage. Both the physical and the economic characteristics of space being sought by the client must be met. This is why the broker must make sure what the industrial firm wants in a plant. He must also make certain by careful and tactful inquiry that the stated requirements actually represent what the firm really wants and needs.

The supply of industrial space is therefore stratified or compartmentalized by type. For supply to be effective on the market, it must represent space that is in fact available to be acquired—either by purchase or by lease—at a competitive market price or rental. If it is not, then further consideration of its potentiality is meaningless, as well as a waste of both the broker's and the client's time. In many situations, the inventiveness or ingenuity of the broker can generate effective availability of space which was previously unrealistically priced or excessively restricted.

In examining and evaluating the supply of industrial space in a given area, the broker needs a knowledge of the market for the various types of space being considered. He also needs to understand the means available to alter market conditions.

Role of the Community

The local community plays an extremely important role in influencing the amount, the type, the location, and even (primarily through indirect impact) the market prices of industrial space within its political and geographic limits. Local planning and zoning activities set limits on the amount of space potentially available for industrial use in a community, as well as identifying the areas or zones in which industry can locate. Urban renewal can actually create new industrial sites in areas previously devoted to other uses. Local industrial development commissions (however titled) can often acquire and hold land—and occasionally buildings—for future development and use by industry.

All of these activities are related to the basic urge and power of the community to take positive action to enhance its economic base. These powers are generally based upon legislative authorizations provided by the state. In Connecticut, for example, the enabling statutes granting planning, zoning, urban renewal and industrial development authority to towns all carry the admonition that these powers must be directed "to preserve and protect property values, and to promote the orderly and economic development" of the local community.[1] The local industrial development program must be related to these goals.

The failure of the community to provide sufficient land or space for industry at good locations, or to protect industrial reserves, is recognized as a serious mistake. Since industry cannot operate in an economic, social or physical vacuum, "the intimate association of housing, industrial development, retailing, financing and managerial activities requires some regulation if they are to satisfactorily cohabit the same urban area for long. The overall guidance of the intimate association of these various activities is the function of urban planning—and zoning as a tool of planning." [2] It is the responsibility of real estate brokers both to understand, and to contribute to, the soundness of these regulatory activities.

Professional opinion within the Society of Industrial Realtors agrees that the broker must acquaint himself as fully as possible with planning, zoning, land and building use controls, and community development activities in his area of operation. Without this knowledge, he cannot serve industry effectively.

Components of the Supply of Industrial Space

The classification of industrial space among the major types of both land and buildings utilized by industry is examined at length in Chapters 1 and 2.

[1] *Connecticut General Statutes,* Revision of 1958, as amended through 1963 (Hartford, Secretary of the State of Connecticut, 1964).

[2] Marvin R. Springer, "Importance of Zoning and Land Use Controls," *Planning and Zoning: A Tool for Guiding Economic and Industrial Growth* (Washington, Society of Industrial Realtors, 1963), p. 1.

For purposes of relating these categories to policies and programs of the supply of industrial space, however, a brief review is in order.

1. *Industrial Land.* In fitting the supply of industrial land to projected needs, a study of the characteristics of the existing vacant land will often suggest remedial steps to be taken when the community seeks to expand industrial employment. Exhibit 10 was developed from such a study, in which the available acreage was classified by size of site. The total amount of vacant land that could be made available in each category was also ascertained.

Exhibit 10

VACANT INDUSTRIAL LAND IN PHILADELPHIA
CLASSIFIED BY THE NUMBER OF NET ACRES

Acreage Size Class	Number of Parcels	Percent of Total	Number of Acres	Percent of Total
Under 1.0	13	5.8%	7.8	0.2%
1.0– 2.4	75	33.3	123.3	2.9
2.5– 4.9	60	26.7	219.4	5.2
5.0– 9.9	36	16.0	237.7	5.6
10.0–49.9	23	10.2	469.6	11.2
50 and over	18	8.0	3,142.7	74.9
Total	225	100.0	4,200.5	100.0

SOURCE: *Industrial Land and Facilities for Philadelphia* (Philadelphia: Institute for Urban Studies, University of Pennsylvania, 1956), p. 81.

The distribution in Exhibit 10 indicates that while 65.8 per cent of the total number of parcels in the study contained less than 5.0 acres, the 148 parcels in this classification accounted for only 8.3 per cent of the total available acreage. On the other hand, the 18 parcels of 50 acres and over represented almost 75 per cent of the total vacant industrial land. A survey such as this helps identify problem areas where private and/or public action to alter the inventory of vacant industrial sites may be appropriate.

More detailed data may be necessary to pinpoint the needs in subregions of a metropolitan area. Such an analysis is contained in the work of the Greater Boston Economic Study Committee, whose findings are summarized in Exhibit 11.

Aside from size characteristics and the quantity of industrial land available on an area-wide basis, industrial sites may be classified for analytical and developmental purposes into four groups. Each type has its particular applications and limitations, which should be understood by the industrial broker so that he may better match available sites with the needs of the industrial client.

a. *Centrally Located Industrial Land.* Historically, preferred industrial locations were near railroad lines and the central business district. It was generally more economical to build multiple-story plants near the rail-

Exhibit 11

ESTIMATED INDUSTRIAL LAND NEEDS THROUGH 1980 COMPARED
WITH THE SUPPLY OF INDUSTRIALLY ZONED LAND IN 1960*

Greater Boston Subregions	Estimated Industrial Land Needs 1960–1980 (000 acres)	Land Zoned For Industry in 1960 (000 acres)		Ratio of Suitable Supply to Need (Col. 3/Col. 1)
		Total	Suitable	
	(1)	(2)	(3)	(4)
Core	.44	1.60	1.10	2.5
Route 128 Band	3.29	5.42	3.23	1.0
Lynn-Salem	.54	2.63	1.87	3.5
South Shore	.57	6.32	3.53	6.1
Northeast Coastal	.22	2.39	1.66	7.6
Merrimack	1.20	13.29	10.58	8.8
Western	1.18	11.30	8.04	6.8
Brockton-Taunton	.30	10.59	7.98	26.5
Southeast Coastal	.42	1.64	1.14	2.7
Greater Boston	8.17	55.19	39.10	4.8

NOTE: Column figures may not add to totals due to independent rounding.

SOURCE: *Industrial Land Needs through 1980* (Boston, Massachusetts, Greater Boston Economic Study Committee, 1961), p. 67.

*The data do not include land needed for extractive uses.

road; it was cheaper to move goods vertically in multiple-story buildings than to transport goods horizontally away from the railroad.

Over time, central locations have become subject to several disadvantages. Generally, land in the older industrial areas is relatively scarce. Further, the sites are often small and irregularly shaped. Moreover, traffic congestion is common in central areas. The cost and inconvenience of serving customers or attracting employees limit the utility of central industrial sites.

Probably the greatest defect of the central site is the limited amount of land available for parking, for off-street truck loading, or for expansion. If such land is available at all, it tends to be very expensive.

Available central sites may be adversely affected by surrounding uses. Dilapidated buildings, smoke, smell, and noise of the central district seriously limit prospects for modern industrial use. Relatively high property taxes are also often encountered, in part because other central-district uses normally support higher land values.

To the extent that skilled and semiskilled workers seek to live in suburban communities, the central location is poorly situated with respect to employee housing. Because of obsolescent land-use regulations, the older factory districts often contain a mixture of residential, commercial and industrial uses. Narrow lots, walk-up apartments, and deteriorated buildings surrounding major industrial areas of the central core do not attract skilled workers.

Utility service facilities in older industrial areas may not be adequate for modern industry. The street and utility plan is often more nearly adapted to residential or commercial use than to industrial use.

While many of these points are common to centrally located space, the disadvantages must be balanced against many advantages. For some industries, the importance of a central location may be overriding.

Because centrally located industrial space is generally near the central business district, it has special usefulness to industries distributing goods to downtown customers. The saving in transportation costs may justify locating warehouses and other distribution facilities in the downtown fringe area. Moreover, where customer contact is highly important, industrial space in the central area is often preferred. Industrial services and job printing, for instance, require a central location if they serve businesses in the city center. Thus, where delivery time and frequent customer contact are important, the central location is often preferred.

Relative to unimproved suburban locations, the central area may be better served by utilities. Also, municipal services in the central area are often superior to comparable services in outlying areas. Hence, the occupant of an industrial site in the central area obtains more than industrial space; he acquires the right to use existing utilities, and fire and police protection, among other municipal services.

The downtown site is often strategically located with respect to the supply of unskilled and semiskilled labor. Central locations may be surrounded by low income housing, or readily reached by public transit.

Another reason for locating in the central district is to secure industrial services readily. The proximity of professional consultants, suppliers, and subcontractors helps explain the popularity of central locations for some firms.

Transportation lines often terminate in the central business district. Central industrial areas, though limited by traffic congestion, are often advantageously placed near major transportation terminals.

Finally, for certain industries a central location improved with older buildings provides a means of securing low-cost space. Industrial buildings vacated by previous occupants may often be made suitable for new tenants. Multiple-story structures divided for rental to several occupants may attract industries that require inexpensive space. Older buildings and limited land areas may discourage large plants, but a demand for such space often exists among small, newer firms.

Existing space in the urban core area is especially suitable for a limited group of industries. Their specific needs must be discovered and met if the central space is to be utilized.

b. *Suburban Sites and Acreage.* Industrial acreage and individual sites in rural or suburban areas surrounding urban centers are often currently devoted to agricultural uses. In many instances these areas are undergoing a transition from agricultural to industrial use.

Industrial acreage is often quite remote from central urban areas. For some firms, a location inconvenient to central facilities, other businesses, or municipal services would constitute a serious limitation. A related factor concerns the availability of utilities: water, waste disposal, natural gas, and electricity. The cost of a suburban site is the cost of vacant land plus the cost of land development.

Topography and the load-bearing quality of the soil are also important determinants of whether industrially zoned land can be made into an industrial site. To the extent that the soil is not adapted to industrial use (i.e., load-bearing capacity is inadequate, or drainage is poor), outlying land has limited utility. Uneven or sloping land can add excessively to site development costs. Land use regulations tend to be relatively limited or even absent in outlying areas. This lack may reduce protection from intrusions by noise, smoke, noxious smells, or unattractive storage.

Though industrial areas outside urban centers can have marked disadvantages for individual firms, the relative advantages of the suburban location often more than outweigh its limitations.

First, land is generally available in sufficient quantity and at competitive prices. Large sites (100 acres or more) in outlying areas permit occupants to isolate their operations from adjoining landowners. Dangers from explosion, heat, glare, fire, radiation; and nuisances from noise, smell, and smoke may be minimized by purchasing sufficient acreage. Room for expansion can usually be provided economically.

Though utilities are often lacking, large plants may prefer to install their own systems. In this manner a firm may avoid the limitations of inadequate existing water lines, sewer mains, gas lines, and power sources.

A plant locating in an outlying area may preserve an open, attractive appearance. Sufficient land may be acquired for landscaping and construction of a one-story building. Relatively low land costs are encountered because industrial sites in these areas are not competing with commercial and other uses to the same extent as are industrial sites in central areas.

When most employees commute by automobile, there is a definite advantage in locating outside central cities. Not only do employees save commuting time, but the availability of housing for employees is generally superior to that near centrally located plants.

Industrial sites in outlying areas appeal to particular groups of users: (1) industries that require large tracts of land, i.e., over 100 acres; (2) land-extensive firms requiring one-story plants and room for parking; (3) larger firms that have the resources to extend utilities and develop land to a usable condition; (4) establishments that have little vital linkage with other firms; (5) industries that, because of their operations, require sites fairly remote from other land uses.

c. *Industrial Sites in Organized Industrial Districts.* The organized industrial district represents a tract of land reserved for the *exclusive use* of industry under proprietary control. Sites in these areas are developed according to a general land use plan which includes required utilities and land use controls appropriate to the district. As indicated in the detailed discussions in Chapters 15 and 16, industrial park sites are adapted to a special category of industries that prefer the planning, restrictions, and services of organized industrial districts.

Sites in industrial parks are relatively expensive compared to industrial acreage. However, higher prices are often associated with better services and superior location. The more specialized districts, especially those privately owned, may have comparatively small sites that are not suitable for large plants.

Industries that do not conform to the requirements of industrial districts are unable to utilize organized industrial district sites effectively. On the other hand, zoning and other land use problems are resolved by the industrial park sponsor. Firms locating in organized industrial districts avoid the time and expense necessary to negotiate and arrange for utility extensions with public authorities. For the most part, organized industrial districts are strategically located relative to *markets*. In comparison to uncontrolled industrial areas, the organized industrial district generally has superior highway access.

The organized industrial district represents a specialized source of industrial land primarily useful for: (1) firms that generally require less than 10 acres; (2) distribution establishments that prefer superior market access; (3) firms that require the special services and facilities of the organized industrial district; (4) industries that make intensive use of industrial land; (5) firms that can adapt to architectural and landscaping requirements.

d. *Redeveloped Land.* The older areas of many cities are being redeveloped under federal or state urban renewal programs. Frequently land of mixed uses, blighted sections, and dilapidated buildings surrounding downtown areas have been redeveloped into industrial space. In these areas, privately owned land has been acquired by local public agencies, cleared, subdivided and offered to industrial prospects for sale or lease. For many cities, this is a new source of industrial land.

Land available for industrial reuse is generally subject to highly restrictive land use controls. The buyer or tenant must use the land according to a redevelopment plan. Quite often the prospect must enter into costly and time-consuming negotiations. Building plans must be approved by the local public agency.

Sites are often odd-shaped, irregular and uneconomic in size. The land is generally expensive, at least in comparison with outlying sites. Prospects for industrial renewal may also be adversely affected by surrounding incompatible land uses that have not been eliminated.

Urban renewal space is generally convenient to urban centers, with the attendant attractions of such locations for firms seeking them. The price of land for exclusively industrial use is generally less than the price of competitive industrial sites in the same neighborhood.

Redeveloped space is primarily attractive to: (1) industries and distribution firms requiring centrally located space; (2) industries that emphasize customer service and convenience to downtown merchants, suppliers, and customers; (3) industries that must locate near labor supplies surrounding the downtown fringe area; (4) small plants and industries ancillary to major industries located in the central areas; (5) firms that can afford relatively high land prices and can comply with severe restrictions.

An example of industrial redevelopment is the Mill Creek Valley Project, consisting of approximately 460 acres west of the central business district of St. Louis. This area contained an obsolescent mixture of uses, and was characterized by traffic congestion and inadequate parking space.

Under the urban renewal plan, small ownerships were merged into marketable sites. The narrow streets were eliminated to make larger disposition parcels. A portion of the project area was reserved for industrial uses, while land in another portion was redeveloped for commercial and residential purposes. Industrial use was made compatible with surrounding uses (including residential) by adopting land use rules controlling private redevelopment. For example, the industrial area may not have billboards or open storage visible from public streets. The industrial site plan had to be approved by the St. Louis Land Clearance Authority so the character of the redevelopment would conform to the urban renewal plan.

A means of insuring a reasonable supply of industrial land was initiated by the City of Philadelphia in 1956. Some 1,200 acres of city-owned land, suitable for industrial development, was transferred to the Philadelphia Redevelopment Authority for improvement and development. The land was to be sold to private industrial firms at fair market value. Deed restrictions were introduced to provide for orderly development, and exclusively industrial use. Income from the sale of the industrial land was deposited in an industrial development fund for the *acquisition and improvement of additional industrial property*. The development agency, the Philadelphia Industrial Development Corporation (P.I.D.C.), is empowered to acquire, improve, and sell both publicly and privately owned real estate, and to rehabilitate and finance the expansion of existing plants.

The P.I.D.C. plan incorporates many of the features of urban renewal, but the transfer of city-owned land to the Redevelopment Authority actually constitutes a land bank program, reserving land for industry through public ownership.[3]

2. *Space in Industrial Buildings.* The fact that the supply of industrial land may be increased does not assure that the demands of industry will be met. The problem involves supplying both vacant land and improved real estate to meet the requirements of that industry most likely to need the increased space. This point is made clear in a study of seven types of industry in Philadelphia. In considering employment in the electronics industry, for example, it stated:

The space needs of manufacturers must be met by locations that are accessible to semiskilled production workers and close to other component producers serving the same or related markets.[4]

---

[3] For further discussion see Paul A. Wilhelm, "Industrial Development Planning," *Journal of American Institute of Planners,* Vol. XXVI, No. 3 (August, 1960), pp. 216–43.

[4] *The Usefulness of Philadelphia's Industrial Plant: An Approach to Industrial Renewal* (Cambridge, Arthur D. Little, Inc., 1960).

The survey disclosed further that electronics firms could use two-story plants with offices and engineering space on the second floor. Other needs were ceiling heights of 10 to 15 feet, floor loads of 150 to 250 pounds per square foot, and minimum space for the "incubator" firms of 5,000 to 10,000 square feet.

In the same survey, space requirements of the apparel industry were summarized:

(1) Space should be made available in multi-story buildings.
(2) Floor areas should be at least 25,000 square feet, but not more than 50,000 square feet.
(3) Bays should be as wide as possible, with at least a 20-foot spacing between columns.
(4) Ceiling heights should be at least 15 feet.
(5) Steam, plus 110 and 220 volt electricity should be available.[5]

The recommendations applying to the apparel industry were directed primarily to the rehabilitation of buildings vacated by former users. The need for *suburban* locations for warehousing, storage and truck terminals was emphasized in the same study because of their special requirements.

These studies show that every major community or metropolitan area has an industrial complex with widely varying demands, and that the supply of industrial real estate is undergoing rapid changes. To utilize industrial space to the greatest advantage, it is necessary to adapt the available local supply to those industries most likely to require space.

For analytical purposes, industrial buildings may be classified in five major categories: by plant layout, type of construction, architectural design, number of stories, and adaptability of use. Any given structure can be characterized in each category; it is the *combination* of features that must be related to the needs and requirements of industry to meet demand. Because of both the multitude of construction details that can vary among buildings, and the continuing changes evident in construction materials and methods, only general points are noted here. The sources of information noted among the Selected References offer appropriate vehicles to obtain specific data required in any given situation.

a. *Plant Layout.* When individual buildings are designed for a particular process or product, the layout of the structure is significantly affected. A *product layout* results in a building aimed at accommodating equipment arranged according to a particular sequence of operations. For example, a building organized for continuous production will be adapted to a continuous flow of materials through the plant to the finished product.

On the other hand, plants producing different but related products generally reflect *process layout,* which involves centralization of certain productive functions. As an example, prefabricated metal production, which involves grinding and buffing of several products, would require the grouping of all grinding and buffing operations in one location. This permits a higher degree of flexibility in the use of men and equipment.

---

[5] *Ibid.,* p. 26.

b. The *Type of Construction* classification generally involves three classes distinguished by degree of fire resistance and quality of materials employed. The function of the building in providing protective shelter for the occupant is the primary consideration, regardless of the nature of the activity involved.

First class buildings are usually constructed of non-flammable materials. Exterior walls, bearing partitions, roofs and floors are usually concrete, steel or aluminum, including doors and window frames. Floors are concrete with hardwood, rubber blocks, or metal strip covering. A minimum of vibration and noise transmission is involved. Alteration, building expansion, and demolition costs will be relatively high for these buildings.

A *second class building* is only partially fireproof. Here the exterior walls, bearing partitions, stairwells, elevator shafts, and doors are fireproof. Such buildings are illustrated by the mill-type structures erected in the late 1800's or early 1900's. The exterior walls are usually solid brick, constructed to a height of five or six stories. In this case, floors, interior walls, columns and all other interior construction, and the roof, are generally flammable. Consequently these buildings must be served with overhead sprinkler systems (dry or wet), fire doors, fire walls, and exterior fire escapes. In general, they are suited to light or medium, multiple-product operations.

A *third class building* is of wood frame construction, and is more flammable than the preceding types. Light-duty construction of one or two stories, a relatively low floor load-bearing capacity, and high maintenance costs are features of this type. Compared to first and second class buildings, construction costs are relatively low. Third class buildings are inexpensive to alter, expand, or remove.

c. *Architectural Design.* Industrial buildings may be classified by architectural design, in terms of ceiling heights, roof construction, column widths, building shape, and the like.

In judging building utility, it is important to relate the uses to which the building is adapted to the demand for those uses. For example, high walls with few windows are highly desirable for warehouse and general storage. On the other hand, a building with lower walls and 12 foot high windows is more suitable for assembly and similar types of manufacturing. Where climate is highly variable, masonry, brick, concrete or concrete block walls are preferred. Steel or galvanized iron walls are often used where the climate is more moderate.

Floors elevated to railroad car or truck bed levels are important for distribution purposes. Street level floors are best for tow motor use. Sloping floors, adapted to food processing, are unsuitable for most manufacturing or storage use.

Buildings with open ceilings, where rafters, trusses, and beams are exposed, are more useful for warehousing because of greater ceiling clearance.

d. *Number of Stories.* Buildings may also be classified by the number of stories. Where land is highly valuable and relatively scarce, multiple-story buildings tend to be used. For some specialized purposes, multiple-story buildings will be superior to one-story construction. In most cases, however, single-story buildings are preferred. To judge the appropriate type of construction, it is necessary to consider the specific process or activity to be housed.

e. *Adaptability of Use.* Industrial buildings may be classified by flexibility of use: single-purpose, limited-purpose and general-purpose buildings. Where possible, industrial buildings are constructed for general use, rather than for a specific type of process or product.

Management often prefers to occupy a general-purpose building because changes in industrial processes or changes in products manufactured may be accommodated more readily. A building designed for general purposes usually has a longer economic life than a structure built around a specific process, which may be subject to a high degree of functional obsolescence. The general-purpose building usually is more salable when vacated, and will normally be easier to finance.

Special-purpose buildings are illustrated by steel mills, iron foundries, oil refineries, and other types of plants built around a specific process. Initially, special-purpose buildings and equipment are constructed to give maximum efficiency at the time of construction. As a result they are less adaptable to other uses.

Characteristics of Space to be Provided

Whether it is land or improved real estate which is to be provided for industrial purposes, there are certain basic ingredients which must be considered by the broker in evaluating the space designed to meet industry's requirements. Both the land classifications and the building categories discussed above offer guides to the kinds of physical attributes that should be related to industrial space needs. It is also possible to generalize about the economic and market attributes of industrial space supply elements.

1. *Principles of Location.* The general principles relating to the location of *work areas* (as they are termed by Professor F. Stuart Chapin, Jr.) are that they:

should be located in convenient proximity to living areas where there are nearby interconnecting transit and thoroughfare routes to insure easy access back and forth, and should be in convenient proximity to other work areas where uses accessory to one another have access to interconnecting truck routes. Some work areas should be in locations accessible to heavy transportation facilities and large-capacity utility lines. Work area locations should provide sites adequate in size, economic to develop, and attractively situated for the particular uses intended.[6]

Somewhat more detailed requirements of space supply for *manufacturing areas* include:

(1) "Reasonably level land, preferably with not more than 5 per cent slope, capable of being graded without undue expense.

---

[6] F. Stuart Chapin, Jr., *Urban Land Use Planning,* 2nd ed. (Urbana, University of Illinois Press, 1965), p. 371.

(2) "Range of choice in close-in, fringe, and dispersed locations. Extensive manufacturing: large open sites for modern one-story buildings and accessory storage, loading and parking areas in fringe and dispersed locations, usually five acres as a minimum, with some sites 10, 25, 50 or 100 or more acres, depending on size of urban area and economic outlook for industrial development of extensive lines of activity. Intensive manufacturing: variety of site sizes for modern one-story or multiple-story buildings and accessory storage, loading, and parking areas in close-in and fringe locations, usually under five acres.

(3) "Direct access to commercial transportation facilities; in fringe and dispersed locations, access to railroad, major trucking routes, cargo airports, and, in some urban areas, deep water channels; and in close-in locations, for a major proportion of sites, access to both railroad and trucking routes, with the balance adjoining trucking thoroughfares or, if appropriate, port areas.

(4) "Within easy commuting time of residential areas of labor force and accessible to transit and major thoroughfare routes directly connected with housing areas.

(5) "Availability of utilities at or near the site such as power, water, and waste disposal facilities.

(6) "Compatibility with surrounding uses, considering prevailing winds, possibilities of protective belts of open space, development of 'industrial parks,' and other factors of amenity both within the manufacturing area and in relation to adjoining land uses." [7]

For *wholesale and distribution* activities, slightly different requirements prevail:

(1) "Reasonably level land, preferably with not more than 5 per cent slope, capable of being graded without undue expense.

(2) "Range of choice in close-in and fringe locations, site sizes usually under five acres.

(3) "Direct access to trucking routes and major street system for incoming goods and outgoing deliveries; frontage on a commercial street or in well-served wholesale centers essential; railroad access for minor proportion of sites or centers.

(4) "Suitability for development of integrated centers, with consideration for amenity within the development and adjoining areas." [8]

2. Location Standards. Beyond the principles that help in identifying the *areas* suitable for industrial uses, there are generally applicable standards for both evaluating and measuring the efficacy of a specific industrial location. Standards established in laws, such as zoning, are typically *minimum standards* that are regarded as necessary in the public interest. Private developments such as industrial parks, on the other hand, tend to establish *desirable* standards above the minimum. The industrial real estate broker must be aware of both the minimums set by community land and space controls, and the desirable standards appropriate to meet industry's needs.

There are *convenience* standards of time and distance beyond which industry chooses not to locate with respect to customers, employees, and sup-

[7] *Ibid.*, pp. 372–373.
[8] *Ibid.*, p. 373.

pliers. These vary by industry, firm and local conditions, but general standards offer a good first approximation. For industry, "convenience" is usually regarded as no more than 30 minutes' distance.[9]

Performance standards provide bases in terms of which the adequacy or acceptability of a particular function may be measured. Performance standards are applied to test whether industrial activity creates a hazard or nuisance through the generation of smoke, dust, noise, glare, odor, fumes, or traffic. As a tool of zoning regulation, performance standards tend to set minimum rather than desirable levels. These standards set the pattern of characteristics that firms need to qualify to locate in a given area.

Security factors are related more to national defense than to community safety. However, they are increasingly significant considerations in the location of industry, and hence in the provision of industrial space throughout the United States. Dispersion is a protective device which, coupled with low-density development, results in the need to supply extremely large sites. The CANEL atomic aircraft engine plant in Middletown, Connecticut, for example, was located on over 1,500 acres, most of which were wooded, hilly, protection "buffer" areas.

PROVIDING INDUSTRIAL SPACE

If the industrial space supply is to meet actual or anticipated demand in any given area, it will often be necessary to take action to create it. While the total supply of all land can be increased only with great difficulty and expense, industrial sites can be created by conversion from other uses (open or developed) under either private or public auspices. Moreover, industrial space in buildings can be produced through construction-development or by conversion from nonindustrial use. Finally, industrial space *of the desired type* may be developed by adapting existing industrial facilities to the requirements of the new users.

In specific undertakings, private activity is usually associated with the development of and construction on individual sites. This is considered in detail in Chapter 14. The major focus here is on activities that can be undertaken to provide industrial space to meet demand in a neighborhood, a community, or possibly a metropolitan area. While private development and financing may also play an important role in this kind of activity, the primary responsibility in area-wide efforts to provide space to meet industrial demand falls on public agencies.

One further distinction should be made between specific, individual efforts to increase supply, and the more general, broadly based programs emphasized here. The private developer usually acts in direct response to a specific stimulus from a particular user or purchaser. He may pioneer or speculate occasionally. The community effort, including planned industrial district development, increases the space *potentially* available for industrial use. Thus, it is more often permissive than creative, establishing a frame-

---

[9] See *Ibid.,* p. 377, for details.

work or atmosphere designed to be conducive to an increase in the effective supply of space in the area.

Attributes to be Provided

Given the needs and the demand for space of industrial firms, and the kinds of space and locations that can be supplied (either from the existing inventory or through the conversion-development process), the real estate broker must study the specific space alternatives confronting him to match them with needs. To help him in this task, it is useful to consider the major groups of attributes of any industrial space that must be analyzed.

(1) *Amount of space available.* This applies to both land area and building area, and to the site sizes that might be developed by assembly.
(2) *Location of available space.* This refers to specific siting (where industry is permitted) as well as to the relationship to markets, supplies, labor, and/or transportation.
(3) *Physical characteristics of available space.* This includes size, shape, topography, soil conditions of site; and size, dimensions, age, construction of buildings.
(4) *Adaptability of available space.* This indicates the flexibility of the site and/or buildings for more than one or a few uses. The feasibility of conversion from current use is one important consideration.
(5) *Suitability of available space.* This relates to the functions to be performed by the space in housing the specific activities involved: production, goods and materials storage, office use, parking, landscaping, and protection or whatever.
(6) *Availability of space.* There are three ingredients to be considered in judging whether potentially usable industrial space is in fact available for acquisition in a practical market sense: whether the use is *legal* in terms of zoning regulations, building codes, or other controls imposed under the police power; whether the *price* is essentially competitive and reasonable; and whether the space is actually *available* at any price at the time in question.

On the assumption that these characteristics can be provided in industrial space, either effectively now or potentially, the objectives to be met are:

(1) To allocate the available industrial space as efficiently as possible in terms of the present and anticipated future demand for that space;
(2) To meet the locational standards and requirements of both industry and the community;
(3) To provide industry with equitable access to, or opportunity to acquire, land suitable for development and industrial use;
(4) To anticipate and provide for industrial space needs in a growing and expanding community economy;
(5) To preserve and protect the "precious inventory" of well-located, well-adapted industrial space for future use, providing particularly for defense from encroachment by residential and commercial uses in industrial areas.

The last point—the protection and preservation of industrial areas—is particularly significant in view of the fact that "rivalry among land uses for good sites is intense, and the best sites for industry, unfortunately, can also be occupied by commercial or residential uses under most zoning ordinances. Worse still, these latter uses often outbid industry on the price of land." [10] In terms of the protection which can appropriately be afforded industry, S.I.R.'s contend that "enlightened planning for broad community growth demands that *industrial* property requirements be considered on a par with the need for parks, recreation areas, open spaces, residential subdivisions, governmental facilities, and commercial centers." [11]

Activities to Influence the Supply of Available Industrial Space

Custom industrial development activities related to individual sites do increase the supply of industrial space in an area, as does speculative development of planned industrial districts. So, too, does the conversion of multiple-story buildings to multi-tenant "incubators," or even the holding of land for future industrial use by private investors. However, these are limited in effectiveness in most areas. Usually, only the community or an agency affected with the public interest can afford to take the long-term view.

There are three basic methods available to the public agency seeking by direct action to increase the supply of industrial land: zoning, utilities extension, and outright purchase. In addition, land subdivision regulations, building codes, fire codes, plumbing codes, electrical codes, and health codes all influence the *kinds* of industrial space that may legally be provided within the community. They also determine the characteristics of industrial space that may be provided. Finally, municipal services may be extended to underdeveloped areas and thereby add to the supply of potential industrial land.

1. *Zoning.* Zoning is the major legal tool of community planning and development. It is "simply the division of a city (or community) into districts of various types, with a set of regulations that set forth the way in which each type of district may be used." [12] Generally, zoning embraces three types of control: it stipulates the *use* to which land and/or building space in a given zone may be put; it sets *bulk and height* requirements for buildings; and it limits the *density or intensity* of land use, whether measured by population density, by worker density, by structure density, or by parking density.

Zoning may add to the potential supply of industrial space in an area in a variety of ways. The most obvious method is to increase the amount of land zoned for industrial use. In addition, however, restricting or excluding nonindustrial uses in industrial zones increases the *effective* supply of in-

[10] From a speech by Victor Roterus, Assistant Administrator for Planning and Research, Area Redevelopment Administration, U.S. Department of Commerce, before the Southeastern Virginia Regional Planning Commission, Norfolk, Virginia, November 10, 1961.
[11] F. Lawrence Dow, S.I.R., "Encouraging Sound Industrial Growth," *Planning and Zoning: A Tool for Guiding Economic and Industrial Growth* (Washington, Society of Industrial Realtors, 1963), p. 4.
[12] Richard L. Nelson and Frederick T. Aschman, *Real Estate and City Planning* (Englewood Cliffs, N.J., Prentice-Hall, Inc., ©1957), p. 247.

dustrial land. Reserving land truly suitable for industrial purposes in industrial zones enchances the *quality* and hence the utility of industrially zoned land in the community. Increasing permitted structure and employee densities in industrial zones means that a wider range of industrial uses is possible.

2. *Utilities Extension.* The community can render outlying, undeveloped, industrially zoned land considerably more likely to be acquired and used by industry if public water and sewer lines, roads and highways, gas mains, and other municipal services are extended to the area. This involves an investment in capital improvements requiring substantial immediate outlays, but the overwhelming experience of communities that have made this type of expenditure is that it more than pays for itself in economic development. The only exceptions appear to be communities with fundamental locational flaws that cannot be offset by site amenities.

3. *Land Purchase and Reservation.* Buying and holding land for future industrial use is usually the function of a local industrial development commission (the precise title may vary). In some states, powers of eminent domain have been given to localities or their agencies to assist in this work. Outright purchase assures the future availability of the land for industrial use, and even affords some control over the *type* of industrial development that will occur in the area.

4. *Urban Renewal.* To a large extent, urban renewal (especially urban redevelopment) [13] represents one variant of the purchase-reservation approach to increasing the supply of industrial space. Both blighted, already built-up areas and open, undeveloped areas can be converted or adapted to industrial use (among other possible uses) with the aid of federal financial assistance. These federal funds, administered through the Renewal Assistance Administration of the Department of Housing and Urban Development, represent either two-thirds or three-fourths of net project costs. Thus the stakes in qualifying for federal assistance are quite high.

Most urban redevelopment projects have been in or near the central urban core where land is relatively expensive. Consequently, industrial activities in reuse areas have tended to be customer-oriented, land-intensive operations of the type most likely to seek sites near the central business district.

In addition, some states also offer financial aid to communities seeking to improve the local economy through better land use patterns. Statutes encouraging urban renewal are a major factor. For example, the state of Connecticut has operated a matching grant program since 1955, limited in scope of uses only by the volume of funds appropriated each biennium by the General Assembly.[14] In this program, as in several other state programs,

---

[13] For a more detailed discussion of the legal and technical aspects of urban renewal, consult: Housing and Home Finance Agency, Urban Renewal Administration, *Urban Renewal Laws: The Housing Act of 1949, as Amended* (Washington, U.S. Government Printing Office, 1965); F. Stuart Chapin, *Urban Land Use Planning*, rev. ed. (Urbana, University of Illinois Press, 1965), pp. 309–338.

[14] See *Connecticut General Statutes, Revision of 1958, as Amended* (Hartford, Office of the Secretary of State, 1965).

industrial reuse has been given particular emphasis so as to reinforce the industrial development activities of the Connecticut Development Commission.

Regardless of the source of financial assistance, the essence of urban redevelopment in creating industrial space in the community is that public powers of eminent domain are coupled with public funds to convert nonindustrial areas to needed industrial land. The industrial real estate broker can advise the community on the most needed and marketable kinds of space; he can also serve the industrial client by exploring the possible development of plants in industrial reuse projects.

5. *Codes and Subdivision Regulations.* Codes and subdivision regulations are generally limiting rather than enhancing in their effect on the local supply of industrial space. Since they are municipally enacted and administered, however, they can be important devices in the community's efforts to provide an adequate supply of industrial space. By changing the regulations that apply at any time to any type of use or construction, the community can either stimulate or discourage industrial development. The same applies to the degree of enforcement of the regulations. One important role that the Realtor can play is in advising the community of this fact, so that one arm of municipal government is not unconsciously undermining other agencies' efforts to create an environment attractive to industry.

6. *Impact on Development and Operating Costs.* One important determinant of the suitability of the supply of industrial space is its competitive attractiveness to the potential industrial user. To be competitive, the space must, among other considerations, cost no more to acquire and to occupy than does space in alternative locations. Land costs, transportation costs, and taxes have been discussed earlier. In addition, construction costs must be considered.

In particular, construction costs and related costs of development and maintenance can be significantly altered by land-use and space-use regulations. Both the content of the regulations, and their interpretation and enforcement by local authorities, can raise or lower substantially the impact that zoning, subdivision regulations, and building codes have on cost. The chief consideration from the point of view of the industrial firm seeking new space is whether the regulations or limitations appear to be *unreasonable,* and therefore add unnecessarily to costs. If this impression is created, then the space is not competitive, no matter how much is made available or how well located it is.

Regulations and controls are designed to preserve and protect property values, and to promote public health, public safety, public morals, and the general welfare. When they are written too tightly, or enforced too zealously, or allowed to become obsolete, they deter rather than encourage industrial development. For example, building codes may continue to specify construction materials or methods of construction that have become both inappropriate and unnecessary through technological advances. Requiring older methods and materials, or in effect prohibiting new ones, can add greatly to construction costs.

Newer codes have generally set standards of performance for construction materials, rather than identifying them by name or type. The advantages and limitations of performance standards as the basis for regulations are discussed at length in the detailed analysis of industrial zoning; the observations on zoning apply to building codes as well.

Similarly, excessive or unreasonable structure-density limitations, setback requirements, parking requirements, landscaping requirements, building height limits, or minimum lot sizes—all can render otherwise attractive industrial locations noncompetitive. If industry's standards and requirements are not met by space which is made available on the market, then effective supply has not been increased. Conveying this basic fact to community industrial development groups is an important function of the broker.

ZONING FOR INDUSTRY

Because of the widespread use, misuse, and abuse of zoning regulations with respect to industrial development, particular attention should be given by the industrial real estate specialist to the principles and techniques of industrial zoning. While some communities, such as Houston, have no zoning, most municipalities do.

The Importance of Industrial Zoning

Zoning involves dividing a community into land-use and building-use districts. Within each such district, or zone, the regulations may control the *use* of land and/or buildings, the *bulk and height* of buildings, and the *density* or *intensity* of use of land and buildings.

The character of industrial development is strongly affected by local zoning ordinances or regulations. They essentially control the industries permitted in controlled areas, and they identify industries that are prohibited from locating in the community. Obsolete practices, such as the use of long lists of prohibited industries, discourage firms from locating in the community. If the ordinance further imposes costly requirements in paving, landscaping, building setback requirements, parking ratios, or other similar limitations (possibly appropriate for a selected few industries but not for all), then industrial prospects may be diverted elsewhere.

Moreover, a shortage of industrial space may actually exist as a consequence of inappropriate zoning, possibly based on improper planning for industrial use. Failure to provide properly zoned future industrial sites can discourage industrial prospects. The absorption of industrial land by non-industrial users, still permitted in most zoning ordinances, further restricts the supply of suitable industrial land.

In contrast, a possible surplus of land zoned for industry can have different but equally undesirable consequences. "Over-zoning for industry" leads to mixed commercial and industrial districts, and also to haphazard development with attendant risks of incompatibility. Thus, a surplus of uncontrolled land zoned for industry can also lower the likelihood of industrial development.

The Objectives of Zoning Regulations

The land economist and the real estate broker view zoning as a means of sharing the supply of urban land among competing uses. The more urgent land uses receive the greatest protection from competing uses. To use land efficiently, certain objectives must be met.

1. *General Plan of Development.* Community planning is effective only insofar as it is supported by action arms such as zoning regulations. Zoning must reflect closely and accurately the aims of the general plan. Indeed, a zoning ordinance or regulation can be ruled invalid by the courts if it is not in conformity with the general plan of development. Zoning is therefore the legal representation of the community's expectations and aspirations for future land use patterns.

2. *Separate Incompatible Land Uses.* Most real estate brokers or operators would not regard a junkyard as compatible with a modern industrial park. Nor is the location of a truck terminal in the midst of a residential district ordinarily recommended. One of the first concerns of industrial zoning (or of any zoning) is the separation of incompatible uses. Without this control, land may be wasted. Land containing mixed, incompatible uses has limited utility or attraction for industrial purposes.

3. *Encourage Compatible Land Uses.* A community has an interest in the development of industrial areas that use related processes, products or raw materials. If hardware manufacturing is the leading source of employment, land can be developed and reserved for prefabricated metal plants and related suppliers, sub-contractors, and service industries. A trend toward industrial sites near airports can be recognized and supported in a zoning ordinance by providing for industries compatible with airport operation.

4. *Provide Space for Unattractive Uses.* Cities need space for the so-called unattractive industries: second hand machinery sales, construction industries, auto wrecking yards, bulk product distributors, raw material processors, and food processors. These and similar activities must have land reserved for their peculiar requirements. The zoning ordinance should provide for and protect them. If the community does not plan for these activities, encroachments against more intensively developed property may result. Alternatively, migration of industry to less rigidly controlled areas may occur, accompanied by serious economic loss for the area.

5. *Control Building Standards.* Structure densities, and building height and bulk regulations represent a further effort to insure through zoning the most efficient use of land, particularly industrial land. The control of *intensity* of land use within a zoning district can often encourage more industrial development.

Mechanics of Industrial Zoning

If the resources of the local community are directed to attracting new industry, creating new jobs, and stimulating new investment, then zoning policy should be compatible with these goals. To assist in meeting such objectives, standards of industrial zoning have been developed by the National Industrial Zoning Committee. The list reads like an outline of the industrial zoning process, and serves as an introductory guide for the industrial real estate broker:

"1. Most communities require a certain amount of industrial development.

"2. Zoning controls are basic tools in the reservation of space for industry.

"3. Industrial use is a legitimate land use deserving protection against encroachment.

"4. Proper zoning can make industrial and residential areas compatible.

"5. Industry will require larger land areas in the future.

"6. For zoning purposes, industry needs to be reclassified based on modern manufacturing processes.

"7. Potential industrial sites should be recognized in the zoning process.

"8. Highways should be planned to create a maximum amount of desirable industrial land.

"9. Streets in industrial zones should be constructed as needed.

"10. Zoning ordinances should be permissive rather than prohibitive.

"11. A zoning ordinance should definitely state the possible industrial uses permitted.

"12. Industrial zoning should be administered on a metropolitan basis." [15]

Zoning regulations may be analyzed in terms of land use regulations, bulk and height restrictions, and density controls. This provides the necessary background for a discussion of industrial zoning practices.

1. *Land Use Districts.* Industrial zones are frequently classified as "light" industrial and "heavy" industrial. However, the difference between light and heavy industrial districts is not always clear. A light industrial district may permit the smaller manufacturing establishments: assembly plants, jewelry manufacturing, apparel manufacturing, and the like. Wholesale, commercial, trade and light storage businesses are usually permitted in light industrial districts. Some authorities regard light industry as compatible with land uses of the general business district.[16]

The real distinction between light and heavy industrial districts seems to be based on the presumed offensiveness of heavy industrial uses. For instance, one zoning ordinance defines light industry in the following terms:

The A-1, Light Industrial District, is a district of industrial uses designed to serve the needs of the community for industrial activity not *offensive* to nearby commercial and residential uses.[17]

Heavy industries, in contrast, usually include industries using basic raw materials and bulk transportation. Steel-making, shipbuilding, oil refining and other activities related to transporting and processing of extracted raw material products are regarded as heavy industries. One community has defined a heavy industrial district as "a district of . . . heavy industrial uses

---

[15] National Industrial Zoning Committee, *Principals of Industrial Zoning* (Washington, The Author, March, 1959).

[16] See, for example, Harland Bartholomew, *Land Uses in American Cities* (Cambridge, Harvard University Press, 1955), p. 32.

[17] *Zoning Ordinance of the City of Phoenix, Arizona, Ordinance No. G—449,* Adopted by the City Council on December 28, 1961. Emphasis added.

designed to serve the needs of the community for industrial uses *which may be offensive* if located near commercial or residential uses." [18]

The problem of defining light and heavy industries can be partially avoided by using a districting procedure such as that followed in Cook County, Illinois. *The Cook County Zoning Ordinance, 1960* divides industry into four groups; restricted manufacturing (M-1), general manufacturing (M-2), heavy manufacturing (M-3), and motor freight terminal uses (M-4). The permitted uses for each of these districts are shown in Exhibit 12.

Subjective definitions of heavy and light industries are avoided with this system. Each subdistrict is identified by lists of permitted industries. In the Restricted Manufacturing district, for instance, permitted industries (besides agricultural buildings) are listed by name. In addition, special uses commonly associated with industrial districts are also allowed: airports, railroad and water freight terminals, parks, playgrounds, race tracks, sewage treatment plants, theaters, and similar uses. The Restricted Manufacturing district includes industries closely related to central business district activities: retail and wholesale functions.

In the General Manufacturing district, the number of permitted uses is increased: all uses permitted in the M-1 district are also allowed in the M-2 area. Moreover in the M-2 district, "special uses" are permitted upon application. Refuse disposal, junkyards, and raw material extraction represent less attractive industrial uses permitted in M-2 districts.

The Heavy Manufacturing districts of Cook County (M-3) allow all uses permitted in the M-2 areas. In addition, the storage of flammable gases or liquids is allowed, but only through special permit. Finally, in the Motor Freight Terminal district (M-4), some 30 industries are permitted. The M-4 district also includes certain special uses allowed only with specific permit.

In short, the Cook County ordinance illustrates two zoning techniques. First, the arbitrary description of heavy and light industry is omitted in favor of use districts defined by lists of permitted industries. Second, the zoning regulation does not treat industry as a nuisance. Lists of prohibited industries are not employed.

2. *Bulk and Height Restrictions.* Zoning regulations controlling building bulk and height include prohibitions of buildings over a given height and stipulated minimum front wall setback distances.[19] Industrial buildings in New York City, for instance, must observe the sky exposure plane, an imaginary line that defines the maximum bulk of industrial buildings measured from the front lot line. Buildings located on narrow streets are restricted to vertical front walls of not more than 60 feet, and the upper stories must be set back one foot for every 2.7 foot increase in building height. More liberal allowances are permitted for buildings on wider streets.

---

[18] *Zoning Ordinance of the City of Phoenix, Arizona, op. cit.,* Section 421. Emphasis added.
[19] See *Zoning Ordinance* with amendments through December 1, 1958, Ch. 31, Code of the City of Sarasota, Florida, p. 50; and *Zoning Resolution* effective December 15, 1961, City of New York, pp. 199–208.

Exhibit 12

INDUSTRIAL USES PERMITTED IN INDUSTRIAL ZONING DISTRICTS OF COOK COUNTY, ILLINOIS

	Restricted Manufacturing (M-1)	General Manufacturing (M-2)	Heavy Manufacturing (M-3)	Motor Freight Terminals (M-4)
Permitted Uses	Agricultural Buildings Industries listed for M-1 districts	Uses permitted in Restricted Manufacturing Districts (M-1)	Uses permitted in General Manufacturing Districts (M-2)	Industries listed for M-4 districts
Uses that Meet Performance Standards	Any industry that conforms to performance standards and that is not offensive to occupants of adjacent premises.	Any industry that conforms to performance standards and that is not offensive to occupants of adjacent premises.	Any industry that conforms to performance standards and that is not offensive to occupants of adjacent premises.	Uses that conform to performance standards of M-2 districts.
Special Uses with Permission	Listed uses, i.e., airports, railroad and water freight terminals, parks and playgrounds, race tracks, sewage treatment plants, theaters and the like.	Special uses of M-1 districts, except house trailer parks. Listed uses, i.e., garbage disposal, junkyards, extractive uses.	Special uses of M-2 districts. Storage of flammable gases or vapors.	Listed uses, i.e., heliports, parks and playgrounds and signs.

SOURCE: *Cook County Zoning Ordinance Adopted March 8, 1960, as Amended*, pp. 119A–155A.

Virtually all zoning codes control building bulk and height in some way. These controls prevent the dark canyons that might result from full coverage of industrial sites by multiple-story buildings constructed on the narrow streets of older industrial corridors. The same principle is applied to newer industrial districts and even to private industrial parks, where the emphasis is placed on openness, light and airy surroundings, and one-story buildings.

3. *Building Area and Density Regulations.* Regulation of building areas controls the intensity of use. Such zoning is justified on several grounds: it reduces traffic congestion; it offers opportunity for light and air; and it contributes to a more attractive, open appearance. Intensity of use is generally controlled in two ways: by controlling the maximum floor area per site, and by establishing minimum yard requirements.

Exhibit 13 shows the maximum floor area ratio permitted for subdistricts within the three manufacturing classifications in New York City. *The floor area ratio is defined as the total floor area on a lot divided by the lot area.* For instance, in the light manufacturing district, subdistrict one, the maximum floor area ratio is 1 to 1. A building with 10,000 square feet of floor area can be constructed on a 10,000-square-foot site. In the second light manufacturing district, the maximum floor ratio is 2.00. This means that an industrial building with 20,000 square feet of total floor area can be built on a site of 10,000 square feet.

In addition to floor area ratios, yard requirements also control the density of use. Front and side yards are not required in manufacturing districts of New York City. If open areas are provided, however, they must meet the minimum side yard and rear yard requirements. Front yard setbacks vary with street width. Building area and density controls also vary widely from one community to another. Through modification of maximum building area ratios and the density of industrial uses in the zoning ordinance, the special requirements of each community can be met effectively.

Types of Industrial Zoning Practice

Stemming historically from the common law of nuisances, zoning today is based primarily on the application of the police power to community programs to control land and building space use. To understand the operation of zoning regulations, and to appreciate the application of zoning to industrial real estate problems, it is useful for the real estate broker to know the various bases on which zoning regulations may be established. Zoning practices may be classified as:

(1) Protections of Residential Use (Hierarchical Approach);
(2) Identification Lists (Permissive vs. Prohibitory);
(3) Inclusive vs. Exclusive Districts; and
(4) Performance Standards.

1. *The Protection of Residential Uses.* The segregation or prohibition of industrial uses from residential areas is based on the principle that residential and industrial uses are incompatible. In addition, much zoning

Exhibit 13

BUILDING AREA AND DENSITY REGULATIONS FOR MANUFACTURING DISTRICTS IN NEW YORK CITY

Manufacturing district	Sub-district	Maximum Floor Area Ratio (a)	Yard Requirement if Provided (b)				
			Side Yard	Rear Yard	Front Yard		
			Minimum width of open area (in feet)	Minimum depth (in feet)	Minimum setback distance (in feet)		
					Narrow Street	Wide Street	
Light	1	1.00	8	20	20	15
	2	2.00	8	20	20	15
	3	5.00	8	20	20	15
	4	2.00	8	20	20	15
	5	5.00	8	20	20	15
	6	10.00	8	20	20	15
Medium	1	2.00	8	20	20	15
	2	5.00	8	20	20	15
	3	2.00	8	20	20	15
	4	5.00	8	20	20	15
Heavy	1	2.00	8	20	20	15
	2	2.00	8	20	20	15

SOURCE: Adapted from *Zoning Resolution*, City of New York, December 15, 1961
a) The floor area ratio is the total floor area divided by the lot area.
b) No front yards or side yards are required in Manufacturing Districts. No rear yards are required for corner lots.

activity (especially in communities outside metropolitan centers) is predicated on the presumption that residential use is somehow more desirable, or "higher," than industrial use. Commercial use is generally rated between the two: "lower" than residential and "higher" than industrial.

One means to afford protection to residences, in addition to restricting a residential zone exclusively to residential use, is to create a "buffer" zone of "light" non-residential uses between the residential zone and the more intensive industrial or commercial zone. This requires close coordination between the planning and zoning authorities.

Historically, protecting residential property from incompatible industrial uses (but not the reverse) stemmed from the common law doctrine of nuisance. One of the first instances of the control over industry restricted the location of powder houses in residential districts in Massachusetts in 1706.

The initial success of efforts to segregate hazardous and unattractive uses resulted in attempts to protect residential areas from a broader range of industrial uses. This was illustrated by the Chinese laundry cases in California between 1870 and 1890, based upon a series of regulations limiting the location of laundries to certain districts.

The desire to protect residential areas found further expression in the ordinances of Los Angeles between 1909 and 1916. Zoning at this time was therefore little more than mere nuisance control administered for the benefit of residential property.

Yet good zoning cannot be based on the common law doctrine of nuisance. Modern zoning ordinances rarely use the word "nuisance." Zoning must be more comprehensive than regulations that merely protect residential districts.

2. *Identification Lists (Prohibited or Permitted Uses).* A common but increasingly inappropriate method employed in identifying or classifying industrial districts consists of listing activities which are either prohibited or permitted in a given industrial zone. The two listing methods are essentially similar, since each prohibited or permitted activity is identified by name in the zoning ordinance. The permitted list approach is occasionally favored on the ground that it is more "positive." The difficulty, however, is that anything not specifically listed as a permitted use is therefore prohibited. This is often not the intent of the zoning authorities, but it is the effect.

The prohibited list approach is more commonly utilized. It generally identifies, for each zone classification, activities which are nuisances, unattractive or unsafe, and industries regarded as undesirable *per se.* Prohibited industries are either banned altogether, or special permission is required before they may locate in a zoned area.

Exhibit 14 illustrates such a list of prohibited industries, originally adopted in 1935, which is part of a current zoning ordinance. In using lists of prohibited industries, the danger of encroachment is presumably prevented by stating that in the district in question land and buildings may be used for any purpose *except* those industries included in the prohibited

Exhibit 14

TABLE 4. A TYPICAL LIST OF "PROHIBITED" INDUSTRIES

In an industrial district land may be used and buildings may be erected, altered or used for any purpose except the following:

PROHIBITED USES:

1. Abattoir
2. Asbestos manufacture
3. Acetylene gas . . .
4. Acid manufacture
5. Asphalt manufacture . . .
6. Blast furnaces and foundries
7. Babbit metal manufacture
8. Bronze powder manufacture
9. Burlap manufacture
10. Brick, tile or terra cotta manufacture
11. Candle manufacture
12. Carbon, lamp black or graphite manufacture
13. Coal yards . . .
14. Celluloid or pyroxylin manufacture
15. Chlorine or bleaching powder manufacture . . .
16. Coke ovens
17. Coal tar products . . .
18. Creosote manufacture
19. Disinfectant or insecticide manufacture . . .
20. Distillation of bones, coal or wood
21. Dyestuff manufacture
22. Emery cloth or sandpaper manufacture
23. Enameling, japanning or lacquering . . .
24. Fat rendering, soap, tallow . . . manufacture or refining
25. Felt manufacture ([a])
26. Fertilizer manufacture
27. Fish smoking
28. Flour milling
29. Garbage, offal, dead animals or refuse . . . reduction . . .
30. Gunpowder, fireworks or other explosive manufacture . . .
31. Gas manufacture . . .
32. Glue, size or gelatine manufacture
33. Iron or steel works . . .
34. Linoleum manufacture
35. Match manufacture
36. Nitrating processes
37. Oil cloth, oiled clothing manufacture . . .
38. Ore reduction and general smelting operations
39. Paint, oil, shellac, turpentine, size, varnish enamel manufacture
40. Paper and pulp manufacture
41. Petroleum refining
42. Poison manufacture . . .([b])
43. Potash manufacture
44. Printing ink manufacture
45. Radium extraction
46. Rock and slag crushing
47. Rolling mill, forge shop or fabricating plant
48. Rubber, caoutchaoc or gutta percha manufacture
49. Sandblasting or curring . . .([c])
50. Shoe-blacking manufacture
51. Starch and dextrine manufacture
52. Stove polish manufacture
53. Soda ash, caustic soda or washing compound manufacture
54. Stone quarry
55. Slag dump
56. Tanning, curing or storage of raw hides or skins
57. Tar distillation or manufacture
58. Tar roofing or tar water-proofing
59. Vinegar manufacture
60. Wire or rod drawing
61. Wool pulling, scouring or shoddy manufacture
62. Wood distillation
63. Yeast manufacture
64. And in general those uses which may be hazardous to health or life, noxious or offensive by reason of the emission of odor, dust, smoke, gas, vibration or noise.

SOURCE: *Zoning Ordinance* with amendments through Ordinance No. 1028, adopted December 1, 1958, Ch. 31, *Code of the City of Sarasota*, 1951, pp. 42–44.

   a) Felt manufacturing is permitted if the dust is not allowed to escape from the building.
   b) Poisons may be manufactured for pharmaceutical and medical purposes.
   c) Sandblasting is permitted where the dust is controlled.

list. Besides the industries frequently itemized in such prohibited lists, a general exclusion is generally added that reads substantially as follows:

and any other use that is objectionable because of the emission of dust, odor, noise, excessive vibration, or other nuisances. . . .[20]

Lists of prohibited industries are subject to three criticisms: (1) they are obsolete; (2) they are incomplete; and (3) they are misdirected. A review of the industries listed in Exhibit 14 shows the *obsolete* nature of industrial zoning ordinances using prohibited lists. Industries identified as "acid manufacture," "candle manufacture," or "glue manufacture" fail to recognize technological changes that often permit many "nuisance" industries to operate nonoffensively. For instance, by including "glue manufacturing" in prohibited lists, plants that manufacture glue from chemicals (rather than from animal products) are excluded. Furthermore, even if animal products were used, a glue factory *could* be constructed and operated in a nonoffensive manner.

Similarly, linoleum and paint are representative of industries that have experienced technological changes that reduce the undesirable effects of the industry. Clearly, obsolete lists based upon manufacturing techniques existing decades earlier exclude many industries that otherwise might be quite acceptable. To the extent that prohibitions are *obsolete,* therefore, they fail to carry out the objectives of zoning ordinances. It is also a known fact that zoning ordinances are often quite difficult to revise or amend. This reinforces the tendency toward obsolescence.

Prohibited industries lists are often *incomplete* compared to the number of manufacturing and related enterprises that might be offensive or dangerous to surrounding property users. Any list of prohibited industries, confined to a few dozen uses, would be quite unlikely to include other land uses that might be considered equally undesirable. Thus, even if the concept of prohibition were acceptable for zoning purposes, lists of prohibited industries usually do not include newer activities arising from new products, new techniques, new raw materials, and new machinery.

Some contend that prohibited lists are *misdirected,* arguing that compatibility is not dependent on the type of industry but on its operation. If industries listed as prohibited can be operated in a manner that would not encroach on surrounding properties, they possibly should receive encouragement. Moreover, because of variations in the *method* of operation, some firms within industries that are *not* included in the prohibited lists could seriously disturb surrounding properties.

3. *Inclusive vs. Exclusive Districts.* In part as a holdover of the view that residential use is the "highest" or most desirable use to which land may be put, traditional zoning practice has resulted in a system of progressive and successive inclusion of permitted uses. In this scheme, single-family detached residential use is at the top of the scale, while "heavy" manufacturing or general industrial zones are at the bottom. This means that in

---

[20] Dennis O'Harrow, "Performance Standards in Industrial Zoning, *Planning 1951,* American Society of Planning Officials, Chicago, p. 42.

"heavy" industrial zones all other uses may compete with industrial activity for the available space. On the assumption that incompatible uses do actually deter the most efficient allocation of industrial space, then the widespread use of increasingly inclusive zones is highly undesirable.

An alternative approach has gained increasing acceptance in zoning circles, particularly for industrial zoning. It is based on the view that incompatibility among non-complementary uses is undesirable, regardless of the zone in which they are located. Therefore, the exclusion of most or all nonindustrial uses from industrial zones should enhance the efficiency of space allocation just as much as the exclusion of industrial uses from residential or commercial zones does.

Under a system of progressively inclusive districts, there are generally two undesirable effects: (1) industry must compete with commercial or residential uses for a fixed supply of industrial land, leading to artificially high industrial land prices; (2) the industrial zone will gradually be improved with a wide variety of commercial and industrial uses, and will, in time, probably exhibit heavy functional obsolescence because of these mixed, incompatible uses. As a consequence, the land which was hopefully reserved for industry eventually becomes characterized by traffic congestion, on-street truck loading, inadequate parking and expanding nonindustrial uses. The end result is an industrial district that protects neither industry nor other activities. One observer claims that zoning should:

assure *each* land use the location which will allow it to produce its goods or services at maximum efficiency. This standard should apply whether the use in question involves a factory or a residence.[21]

Thus, continued use of progressively inclusive districts which afford industry the least protection would seem to violate the basic objectives of zoning.

This practice of permitting residential and commercial uses in industrial districts has been defended on grounds that such nonindustrial uses are only temporary land uses awaiting a future increase in the demand for industrial space. There are, however, four objections in opposition to this argument:

(1) The redevelopment of an improved area is usually too costly to justify land use succession by industry.
(2) Public improvements (e.g., streets, water mains, sewer lines) suitable for residential and commercial use are poorly adapted to industrial use.
(3) Residential and commercial property owned in small, separate parcels is difficult to assemble for industrial reuse.
(4) Mixed districts, especially districts dominated by residential improvements, soon become blighted districts which are unsatisfactory for new industry or other improvements.[22]

In view of these objections, most zoning officials recommend that residential uses be excluded from industrial districts. The prohibition of resi-

[21] Richard B. Andrews, *Urban Growth and Development* (New York, Simmons-Boardman Publishing Corp., 1962), p. 342.
[22] See, for example, Seward H. Mott and Max S. Wehrly, *The Prohibition of Residential Developments in Industrial Districts,* Technical Bulletin No. 10 (Washington, Urban Land Institute, 1948), p. 2.

dential uses in industrial districts involves recognition of the principle that industry requires the same protection from competing uses that is enjoyed by single-family dwellings.[23] Hence, the exclusion of residential uses is the first step in recognizing formally the legitimate land use requirements of industry.

4. *Performance Standards.* A relatively recent development in zoning regulations, as well as in other land use and space use controls, is the application of performance standards to industrial zoning. A performance standard provides a technique to judge an industry in terms of the effect it has on the surrounding environment. In effect, this approach emphasizes and measures what an industrial activity does rather than what it is. If any plant can meet the standards of acceptability established in the zoning regulations, then it may occupy space in that zone, regardless of the nature or the name of the operation. No industry or plant is by definition either acceptable or unacceptable under performance zoning, whereas it is when identification lists are employed.

a. *Advantages of Performance Standards.* The substitution of performance standards for prohibited lists is not, in itself, sufficient to control industry. Indeed, the enforcement of performance standards has created other problems, which are mostly administrative. But municipalities have welcomed performance standards as a needed reform in industrial zoning.

(1) *Performance standards substitute quantitative measurement for subjective qualitative judgments.*

(2) *Performance standards reduce the use of arbitrary lists of prohibited industries.* Industrial uses are not controlled by lists of prohibited activities. Performance standards are generally permissive. If prohibited industries are mentioned, the list is usually confined to activities using explosive materials, handling bulk products or processing raw materials.[24]

(3) *Performance standards represent a positive method of controlling industry.* The idea that industry is a nuisance is rejected by advocates of performance standards. In essence, municipalities using performance standards assume that *all* industry is potentially acceptable, provided performance standards are met. The problem of admitting industry is reduced to enforcing engineering standards.

(4) *Performance standards can be adjusted to meet objectives of the community.* Industries which promote the goals of the general plan can be actively sought or attracted.

(5) *Performance standards promote industrial development.* Some industries may view the existence of performance standards as an indicator of a favorable community attitude toward industry. Assuming that industries will conform to the performance standards, the potential number and range of industries is thereby increased.

(6) *Performance standards are more adapted to modern technology.* Lists of prohibited or permitted industries do not normally adjust to tech-

---

[23] For further details, see Andrews, *op. cit.,* p. 340.
[24] See, for example, *Chicago Zoning Ordinance,* 1961, Ch. 194A, *Municipal Code of Chicago* as amended to January 1, 1961, p. 44A.

nological advances, new products, new materials, and new plants. Furthermore, changing land use requirements of industry warrant changes in the concept of industrial zoning.

b. *Types of Performance Standards.* The results of industrial activity involving potential negative impacts on the surrounding environment must be carefully selected for the establishment of performance standards. Not only the items themselves but their measurement must be settled in advance.

(1) *Noise control.* What sort of noise constitutes a nuisance? An intermittent noise usually is more irritating than a continuous noise; high frequency sounds are more disturbing than low frequency sounds; a nearby noise of low intensity is more objectionable than a louder sound at a greater distance; a noise acceptable in the daytime might constitute a serious nuisance at night. Clearly requiring good judgment, performance standards have been developed by which to judge the acceptability of industry, in terms of the amount and type of noise emanating beyond the property line.

Performance standards relating to noise assume various forms. The most common method of establishing the maximum amount of permissible noise involves the measurement of sound by the number of decibels: a measure of sound pressure. Since low-pitched sounds are less irritating than high-pitched noises, louder noises are permitted with low frequencies. Decibel standards are also sometimes varied by the time of day, with lower limits prevailing for the night hours.[25]

Performance standards which set maximum acceptable limits for noises measured at the lot line are illustrated in Exhibit 15 by the standards applied in New York City.

Exhibit 15

THE PERFORMANCE STANDARD CONTROLLING NOISE UNDER
THE *ZONING RESOLUTION*, NEW YORK CITY
The Maximum Permitted Sound Pressure Level
(in decibels)

Octave band (cycles per second)	Manufacturing District		
	M–1	*M–2*	*M–3*
20 to 75	79	79	80
75 to 150	74	75	75
150 to 300	66	68	70
300 to 600	59	62	64
600 to 1,200	53	56	58
1,200 to 2,400	47	51	53
2,400 to 4,800	41	47	49
over 4,800	39	44	46

SOURCE: *Zoning Resolution,* City of New York, December 15, 1961.

[25] *Industrial Zoning Standards,* Information Report 78, September, 1955, American Society of Planning Officials, p. 10.

Industries operating within these limits conform to this section of the zoning ordinance. Here the name of the industry is immaterial; the noise level caused by the industry determines acceptability.

(2) *Smoke and particulate matter.* Industry is often associated with smoke, dirt, and dust. The emission of smoke and fly ash is one of the easiest factors to control by performance standards. The United States Bureau of Mines publishes a chart (the Ringelmann Chart) which designates five shades of darkness. Performance standards of smoke emission state that industries must not discharge smoke denser in shade than a given chart number. For instance, the acceptable limits for smoke emission in Oak Ridge, Tennessee are defined in the following terms:

The discharge into the atmosphere from any single source of emission what-soever of any air contaminant for a period or periods aggregating more than four minutes in any one-half hour which is:

(a) As dark or darker in shade as that designated as No. 2 on the Ringel-mann Chart. The Ringelmann Chart, as published by the United States Bureau of Mines, which is hereby made a part of this Code, shall be the standard.[26]

(3) *Noxious odors and fumes.* The Chicago Zoning Ordinance, 1961, controls the emission of noxious odors by prohibiting odors detectable at any point *along lot lines* when diluted in the ratio of one volume of noxious, odorous air to four or more volumes of clean air. Odorous emissions may also be controlled by establishing acceptable quantities of offensive odors measured in ounces per thousand cubic feet of air.

(4) *Toxic gases.* Noxious gases considered harmful to plant and animal life are also often prohibited. The New York City Zoning Resolution prohibits the emission *beyond lot lines* of noxious gases that endanger the public health, safety, comfort, and general welfare.

(5) *Glare and heat.* Glare and heat are controlled by providing that any operation producing intense glare or heat shall be performed within an enclosure so as not to create a public nuisance or hazard *along lot lines.*

(6) *Vibration.* Any use creating intense earthshaking vibrations (e.g., heavy drop forges or heavy hydraulic surges) may be required to be set back a substantial distance from the lot lines on all sides. Controls on vibration measure the effect on the environment *beyond the lot line.*

(7) *Fire and explosive hazards.* The storage, manufacture, or utilization of flammable materials may be restricted to buildings that are completely enclosed by noncombustible exterior walls. Buildings housing flammable materials are generally required to have greater building setbacks.

(8) *Radiation hazards.* Radiation materials in excess of certain limits may not be assembled if the quantity of materials exceeds established limits.

(9) *Discharge of industrial wastes.* Beyond lot lines.

(10) *Electromagnetic interference.* Beyond lot lines.

---

[26] Chapter 45, *Zoning Code,* as amended May 1, 1951, Oak Ridge, Tennessee.

These and other items can be and are measured to ascertain whether standards of performance are being met by industries seeking to locate, or already located, in zones regulated by performance standards.

Even aesthetic controls, such as regulations governing the size and placement of advertising signs, may be applied to industry. The major advantage of performance standards has been characterized by one of their earliest proponents as a substitution of: "A quantitative measurement of an effect for the qualitative description of that effect that we have used in the past." [27]

c. *Administration of Performance Standards.* Under some zoning ordinances, industries may locate in a given zone only if they are included in the list of permitted industries, or are allowable only by special permit. Under performance standards, certain additional administrative problems must be resolved. In judging the effectiveness of performance standards, a major issue is whether industrial zoning, as administered under the zoning code, serves community objectives. Most of the administrative problems surrounding performance standards can be grouped under four headings:

(1) *Range of performance standards needed.* The New York City Resolution even establishes maximum permitted quantities of radioactive materials that can be assembled at any one point,[28] while the County of Riverside, California [29] establishes performance standards only for the emission of particulate matter, dust, smoke, and toxic gases into the atmosphere. The performance standards required in New York City are not those needed in Riverside, California, or other areas. This is one of the advantages of performance standards: they may be adapted to the specific requirements of each local community. The selection of elements to be controlled is also a local administrative problem, however.

(2) *Types of external effects to be controlled.* The question of what performance standards to apply in a given locality is dictated largely by the local economic base, and by the character of the industries already in the area, as well as those being sought.

(3) *The measurement of industrial effects.* Highly technical equipment and personnel to measure the effects of industry are expensive. Noise measuring machines cost $1,000 or more. The measurement of particulate matter can cost over $300 per sample. If laboratory equipment is purchased, the investment involves several thousand dollars. However, if the performance standard has merit, and the municipality hopes to realize the advantages of orderly industrial development, the cost of improving zoning administration and enforcement should be warranted.

(4) *The enforcement of performance standards.* The methods used to enforce performance standards vary almost as widely as do industrial zoning regulations. For example, the City Manager of Oak Ridge, Tennes-

---

[27] O'Harrow, *op. cit.*

[28] *Zoning Resolution,* City of New York, December 15, 1961, p. 191.

[29] *Zoning Ordinance,* Ordinance No. 348 as amended to October 15, 1957, County of Riverside, California, p. 12.

see, has final responsibility for enforcing the zoning code, including the administration of performance standards.[30] But the Commissioner of the Department of Buildings, New York City, enforces performance standards and most sections of the *Zoning Resolution* of December, 1961. One widespread problem is that industry is not always certain that performance standards will be interpreted fairly or consistently. Soon after the 1961 Zoning Resolution of New York City became effective, industrialists considering New York City locations were reportedly uncertain how the performance standards would be administered. According to one observer:

The problem exists that an industrial prospect is unsure as to the use to which a specific property can be put, and when he inquires of the industrial broker, the lawyer or architect, he gets no concrete response because the professionals too are baffled. When the architect goes to the building department engineers for a definite answer, they too are uncertain as to the legal use to which a particular property can be put. As a result, the industrial prospect hesitates to sign a lease or purchase property because he does not know whether his occupancy will be acceptable to the building department.[31]

Therefore, if an industry begins an operation that later might be found to be in violation of zoning, performance standards may defeat one major object justifying their introduction. Robert E. Boley, director of the Industrial Council, Urban Land Institute, has concluded that "while in theory performance standards are desirable, practical application could be troublesome." He adds that "above all it is extremely important to the success of any zoning plan, and especially to one using performance standards, that it be competently administered." He cautions further that "overly rigid interpretation and enforcement of untried or insufficiently tested standards could prove to be a deterrent to further industrial development in the area." [32]

d. *Limitations of Performance Standards.* From the foregoing discussion and analysis, it is quite clear that performance standards are not a panacea for the problems of industrial zoning. While on net balance they offer both in theory and in practice important advantages over alternative approaches, they also have limitations that must be recognized and balanced against the gains. This represents another area of potential contribution by the industrial real estate broker: advising local authorities how industry will probably react to performance standard zoning and its enforcement in the community in question.

While most of the limitations of performance standards in industrial zoning derive from administrative problems which have already been discussed, they are reviewed here for convenience of analysis in context:

(1) Specialized, technical equipment and personnel are required to administer and enforce performance standards. These are nearly always expensive, and often not available to the community on a continuing basis.

---

[30] *Zoning Code, loc. cit.,* part VI, Chapter 9.
[31] Address by Samuel H. Kosse, to the Society of Industrial Realtors, June 11, 1962, at the Yale Club, New York City.
[32] Robert E. Boley, "Performance Standard Zoning," *Urban Land* (Washington, Urban Land Institute, Volume XIX, No. 6, 1960), p. 8.

While consultants can be and are called in to investigate specific complaints, this is no substitute for continuing local enforcement.

(2) Performance standard zoning is only as good as the enforcement and administration applied to it. A small community may find that the demands of performance standards are simply too great for its ability or willingness to support the needed programs of enforcement.

(3) Often, state, local and even federal agencies already control many aspects of industrial performance zoning. Duplication of controls and their administration can lead to conflicts and possible deterrents to local industrial development.

(4) The responsibility of enforcement is often delegated to agencies not officially interested in area industrial development or the orderly development of patterns of land use. To this extent, the goals of the community's industrial zoning program might be undermined.

(5) Performance standards, for all their relative flexibility, also can suffer from a lack of response to changing industrial technology and industrial space requirements. To this extent, they are as limited as any type of zoning.

(6) New industry often cannot be sure it will comply with local regulations without going through a long and possibly expensive application procedure. If administration of the standards is also inconsistent, uncertain or even discriminatory, industry can and will be discouraged from locating in the community.

(7) Performance standards do not eliminate the necessity to decide what items of industrial activity should be controlled, what the standards should be, and what types of industry should be encouraged (or discouraged). These hard decisions must still be made in terms of community economics and politics; inappropriate decisions cannot be offset by the mechanical measurement of certain aspects of industrial activity.

Zoning for Planned Industrial Districts

Planned industrial districts or industrial parks are land areas reserved for industrial development and use. While they are often privately developed and operated, as is noted in the detailed discussions in Chapters 15 and 16, the basic pattern of land use controls is provided by the community through zoning and related regulations. In addition, the developer (whether a private or a public organization) typically imposes additional standards for firms seeking to locate in the district. These are usually enforced as contractual obligations.

The pattern of requirements for occupancy in most planned industrial districts illustrates the difference between minimum standards (usually represented by zoning) and desirable standards (the covenants and other control devices imposed by the district developer). To a large extent, planned industrial districts have served as laboratories and testing grounds for new concepts in land and building controls. The developer, seeking to maximize his own profits, generally wants to protect both current and future occupants from inharmonious or incompatible neighbors.

The experience of planned industrial districts demonstrates the desirability of excluding nonindustrial uses. Moreover, performance standards met their first rigorous tests in industrial parks. Many more successful developments have been associated with regulations related to function (performance standards) than with those based on use or name (lists).

It therefore appears that, in general, municipal zoning techniques are constantly striving to catch up to the standard of planned industrial districts. Moreover, local zoning ordinances now reflect recognition of the advantages of planned industrial districts by creating special zones exclusively for planned industrial development. This trend represents further acceptance of the idea that industry operates most efficiently when it is protected from incompatible encroachments, regardless of the type of use associated with the incompatibility.

The Effectiveness of Zoning in Supplying Industrial Space

The basic purpose of industrial zoning is to create an environment of land and building uses that will contribute most to the orderly and economic growth and development of the community. Zoning by itself rarely can create or destroy industrial space. Rather, it provides the framework within which industrial firms are either encouraged or deterred in their search for suitable plant locations.

Zoning is a broad control which cannot be wielded with precision for the individual firm. Moreover, in encouraging certain types of industrial activity through zoning regulations, a community will ordinarily discourage others. The first major step in any program of industrial zoning is a clear-cut, conscious, well-considered identification of the community's industrial zoning objectives. Subsequent choices and judgments can then be made consistently and rationally in terms of these objectives.

Zoning is (and will probably continue for some time to be) the principal means of attempting to add to or reserve the supply of land for industrial use. It is therefore useful to recognize the major problems confronting the creators and administrators of industrial zoning regulations. Inappropriate decisions on any of them can result in less than optimum industrial development in the community.

1. *Amount of Land to Zone for Industry.* Since zoning is designed to make industrial space available to potential users, the amount of land zoned for industry can be a critical factor in the industrial development of the community. Obviously, too little land available in an area acts as a brake on industrial growth. However, too much land zoned for industry can be a deterrent as well. Overzoning for industry tends to generate scattered, uneconomic development that places excessive and unnecessary burdens on community facilities. Furthermore, pressures tend to grow to put some of the unused land to nonindustrial use, or even to change the zoning. This often occurs in a haphazard, unplanned, individual case basis with little regard for the general plan of development for the community.

A related question is what *type of land* to zone for industry. This point was considered at some length earlier in this chapter. It is mentioned again here as a reminder that industrially zoned land must be actually suitable for use by industry to be part of the effective or potential supply of industrial space in an area.

2. *Kinds of Industry Sought.* While zoning is not a precision tool, it can influence the kinds of industrial operations either attracted to or discouraged by a community. Conscious awareness of this fact must replace decision-making by default if the industrial zoning regulations are to serve the specific industrial development goals of the municipality.

3. *Degree of Restriction or Selectivity Required.* It has been argued that:

in altogether too many areas, an industrial zoning classification is the same as no zoning at all. You can build anything in an industrial zone. From the industrial development point of view, this simply does not make sense.[33]

On the other hand, excessively restrictive regulations that seek to attract only "clean, desirable" industry often preclude *any* industrial development in the community.

The degree of inclusiveness or selectivity of industrial zones must be decided carefully and consciously. The lists of permitted or prohibited uses, the performance standards, the density and bulk requirements—all must be appropriately related to an objective evaluation of the community's goals, its attractions, its facilities, and its enforcement capabilities.

4. *Kinds of Controls or Regulations Required.* Zoning regulations may be quite simple and straightforward, or exceedingly complex. Generally, as the community attempts to accomplish more with industrial zoning, the number of categories of zones and the number of regulations in each zone tend to proliferate. Performance standards have an appeal that is difficult to ignore, even in communities unequipped to apply them effectively. As complexities are introduced into the regulations, the potential industrial space user becomes more chary of a location within the area. The lesson is that there must be a real and compelling economic reason for adding such standards or controls; otherwise, being "modern" may prove excessively expensive to the community.

5. *Needed Enforcement Machinery.* If the zoning authority is not adequately staffed and financed to enforce the regulations impartially and rigorously, then the regulations may be worse than useless. They can actually detract from the area as a potential location for industrial activity because of uncertainty about their interpretation and enforcement that is created in the minds of industrial space users. This applies to granting exceptions and variances as well as to administrative interpretations.

An industrial establishment often cannot tolerate uncertainty about whether it may later expand, or may later be found to violate regulations, or may have to wait for prolonged periods to receive an interpretation of the regulations, or may encounter unexpected encroachment by undesirable and incompatible neighbors. To many families, these represent serious annoyances; to most industrial firms, they affect survival in a given location.

---

[33] Dow, *op. cit.,* p. 4.

Consistent, competent, objective enforcement and administration of the regulations is therefore the *sina qua non* of industrial zoning. To a major degree, the level and kinds of zoning regulations initiated should depend on the enforcement capability of the community.

6. *Adaptability to Change.* Zoning regulations are local laws. As such, they are often difficult to amend or alter. Indeed, there is a widespread tendency to look on zoning as a "once and for all" kind of job. To the extent that this attitude prevails in the community, serious problems can develop as the methods and requirements of industry change with technology and tastes.

Thus, on one hand, zoning regulations often become rigid and difficult to change. On the other hand, zoning regulations can be changed. They are created by agencies sensitive to political pressures. There is, therefore, always some uncertainty about whether they might be amended to the detriment of existing industrial establishments which cannot relocate easily or rapidly. Appropriate zoning control calls for steering a course between the two extremes of inflexibility and insensitivity to changing needs, and of excessive ease of change that engenders uncertainty.

7. *Variations to be Permitted.* No matter how effective or comprehensive industrial zoning regulations may be, there are always three basic and legal means to avoid their application in a specific case. Inadequate or inappropriate handling of these procedures can undermine the impact of industrial zoning on the community's industrial development programs. Such inadequacy can take the form of either too strict or too easy an interpretation of the regulations. The three means of legally circumventing the provisions of industrial zoning regulations in individual cases are: granting zoning variances, making exceptions to the application of the regulations, and permitting nonconforming uses.[34]

a. *Variances.* When inflexible application of zoning regulations to an individual parcel of land would create "undue hardship" for the owner, the regulations may be varied with respect to setbacks, minimum lot size, structure density, or even use. Hardship goes with the land, and is usually based on lot size, shape, topography, drainage, or subsoil conditions. Unrealized profits are usually not regarded by the courts (which are the ultimate arbiters in such cases) as a hardship within the definition here.

Variances are usually granted after a public hearing by the board of zoning appeals (or whatever it may be termed in the jurisdiction in question) and a finding that undue hardship does exist. The capacity to grant variances is a necessary ingredient in zoning administration. The difficulty is that the power can be misused to the point of abuse, so that in effect the board of appeals is actually carrying out spot zoning. This can quickly and effectively undermine the zoning regulations.

b. *Exceptions.* Unlike variances, which are decided individually as

---

[34] This presentation is necessarily curtailed because of limitations of space. For more detailed discussions, see R. L. Nelson and F. T. Aschman, *op. cit.*, pp. 281–286; William L. Crawford, *A Primer for Connecticut Zoning Boards of Appeals* (Hartford, Connecticut Federation of Planning and Zoning Agencies, 1960); and Null, *op. cit.*

specific hardship cases, exceptions to zoning regulations are built into the ordinance. Any potential user who meets specified requirements is entitled to a special permit to use the property in the manner requested. The point is that he must demonstrate to the satisfaction of the administering authority that the necessary conditions have been and will continue to be satisfied.

For example, a sand and gravel operation may be permitted in an industrial zone provided the applicant and operator convince the zoning administrator that facilities for minimizing offsite emission of dust and dirt are adequate. Zoning exceptions and special permits represent a simplified form of performance standard that can be applied in communities with relatively unsophisticated or modest zoning enforcement programs.

c. *Nonconforming Uses.* When an existing industrial use (or any other use, for that matter) does not meet the requirements of the zoning regulations on any count, it is said not to conform to the regulations. Because zoning regulations cannot render an existing legal use illegal retroactively, nonconforming uses (or buildings or lots) may continue to be used in the same manner, subject to conditions that vary widely among zoning ordinances and among communities.[35]

The extent to which a nonconforming use may be continued or may have to be amortized; whether it may be expanded or intensified, and by how much; whether it goes with the land or with the user; whether it may be reinstituted after discontinuance, and within what time limits; whether it may be continued after destruction of any structures—these are all important issues that can have a significant impact on the suitability of a given location for an industrial firm. Accordingly, the industrial real estate broker must familiarize himself with the regulations pertaining to nonconforming uses, and with their local interpretation and enforcement. Generalization is virtually impossible; it is necessary to go into specific detail each time.

Industrial zoning represents one approach to the provision of suitable industrial space in a community to meet the needs of industry. It is by far the most commonly utilized device available to the community in its efforts to expand the supply of industrial space. While its impact is felt primarily on land, zoning can and does also influence the amount and character of building area that is potentially available.

When appropriately administered and enforced, industrial zoning regulations can effectively reinforce the community's program of industrial development. When the regulations or their administration are improper or inadequate, however, they can be worse than nothing at all because they actively discourage desirable industry from locating in the area.

Even when they are well drawn and well administered, however, zoning regulations are effective in attracting and retaining industry only when sites

---

[35] For a comprehensive and detailed discussion of the implications of nonconforming use considerations for the industrial real estate broker, consult Richard Babcock, "The Legal Aspects of the Zoning Ordinance," *S.I.R. Newsletter Bonus* (Washington, Society of Industrial Realtors, October, 1963).

are available and served by needed community facilities. Good industrial zoning regulations, properly administered, represent a necessary but not a sufficient condition to making local sites attractive to industry.

The entire process and problem of supplying adequate space for industry has been summarized succinctly by Victor Roterus, former Assistant Administrator for Planning and Research of the Area Redevelopment Administration of the United States Department of Commerce, as follows:

"(1)   Providing adequate land for anticipated industrial use is a vital way of helping to insure a community's future economic growth.

"(2)   Although planned industrial parks are of major importance, the location and extent of these areas must be planned as part of a community's overall land use plan.

"(3)   In order to maintain a healthy economy, all new industry and locally established industry with expansion needs should have a choice of sites at good locations.

"(4)   Estimates of future land use needs should be based on the employment land use ratio of suburban plants built since 1945 (use local data when possible), with such modifications as changing technology justifies.

"(5)   If in doubt as to the area needed for industry, provide an oversupply because vacant land not used by industry always can be employed for other purposes.

"(6)   Land designated for industrial use must be protected from encroachment by competing uses. Failure to do this leaves the community with a short supply of industrial land and an impaired economic base.

"(7)   Although zoning is an important legal tool in protecting industrial land, it is essential that more positive methods, such as outright purchase of land for future industrial use . . . also be used to assure that industry—the primary job creator of a community—will have ample room to breathe." [36]

---

[36] Victor Roterus, *op. cit.*, p. 8.

SELECTED REFERENCES

Andrews, Richard B., *Urban Growth and Development* (New York, Simmons-Boardman, 1962).

Boley, Robert E., "Performance Standard Zoning—Practical Considerations," *Urban Land* (Washington, Urban Land Institute), Vol. 19, No. 6, June, 1960.

Chapin, F. Stuart, Jr., *Urban Land Use Planning,* rev. ed. (Urbana, University of Illinois Press, 1965).

Garrabrant, Robert B., "Performance Standards for Industrial Zoning: An Appraisal," *Urban Land* (Washington, Urban Land Institute), Vol. 15, No. 6, June, 1956.

Industrial Land and Facilities for Philadelphia (Philadelphia, Institute for Urban Studies, University of Pennsylvania, 1956).

Industrial Study, Detroit City Plan Commission, Master Plan Technical Report, Second Series, July, 1956.

Mott, Seward H. and Wehrly, Max S., *The Prohibition of Residential Developments in Industrial Districts,* Technical Bulletin No. 10 (Washington, Urban Land Institute, November, 1948).

Nelson, Richard L. and Aschman, Frederick T., *Real Estate and City Planning* (Englewood Cliffs, N.J., Prentice-Hall, Inc., 1957).

Null, James A., *Some Selected Administrative Problems Caused by Performance Standards in County Industrial Zoning,* Information and Educational Service Report No. 11 (Washington, National Association of County Officials, 1960).

Performance Standards in Industrial Zoning (Columbus, Ohio, National Industrial Zoning Committee, 1960).

Planned Industrial District Zoning, Information Report No. 120 (Chicago, American Society of Planning Officials, 1959).

Principles of Industrial Zoning (Columbus, Ohio, National Industrial Zoning Committee, 1959).

Ratcliff, Richard U., *Urban Land Economics* (New York, McGraw-Hill, 1949).

Shenkel, William M., "Industrial Zoning Regulations and the Demand for Industrial Space," *The Appraisal Journal* (Chicago, American Institute of Real Estate Appraisers), January, 1965.

Shenkel, William M., "The Economic Consequences of Industrial Zoning," *Land Economics,* August, 1964.

The Usefulness of Philadelphia's Industrial Plant (Cambridge, Massachusetts, Arthur D. Little, Inc., 1960).

5 Industrial Real Estate as an Investment

INDUSTRIAL real estate analysis provides a basis for developing the most efficient allocation of the industrial space available in an area. In a free, informed market, that space will tend to be put to its highest and best use over the long run. Highest and best (or most profitable) use is that use which will produce the highest net return over a given period of time. It is also the use that will produce the highest present worth of the space.

Through his analysis of the forces of supply and demand, the industrial real estate specialist helps facilitate the allocation of industrial space in terms of its highest and best use.

Despite the localization of industrial real estate services, the market for industrial real estate usually transcends local community boundaries. The basic reason for this is that industrial real estate transactions typically require substantial financing. While industrial real estate itself is necessarily fixed in location, the market for industrial mortgage funds is often national in character. To this extent, industrial real estate is competing with all other types of outlets for loan funds in the money market. The industrial real estate broker, therefore, must have a good working knowledge of the terms, conditions, and sources of industrial loan funds. These are considered in detail in Chapter 6; the investment market characteristics of these lenders represented are analyzed in this chapter.

In addition, industrial real estate also represents a form of equity investment for both users and non-users of the industrial space. Here too, the industrial real estate broker must develop an awareness of the nature of the industrial investment if he is to serve his clients adequately.

GENERAL INVESTMENT CONSIDERATIONS

It is generally presumed that all participants in an investment transaction seek to maximize the benefits or returns they receive from the transaction. This is usually, but not necessarily, equated with maximizing the flow of net income *after* taxes. The relative attractiveness of the investment depends, in the final analysis, on its potential for adding to the net cash position of the investor.

In order to advise a client appropriately, as well as to make decisions about his own investment activities, the industrial real estate broker must first understand the general principles and characteristics of investment analysis. Then he must apply them to the specific requirements and conditions of the particular proposal or transaction being considered. Only the more general investment features of industrial real estate are considered here. They may serve as effective guides to the solution of specific problems, however.

Investment Characteristics of Industrial Real Estate

Analysis of the specific investment features of industrial real estate requires skills from at least three areas: accounting, law, and real estate. It is sometimes easy to overlook the third requirement in view of the peculiar legal, accounting, and tax factors that necessarily must be included. However, it should be remembered that "from the point of view of determining the feasibility of a realty investment, the skill of the accountant or the attorney is limited. Basically, they can determine if the income-tax structure is advantageous, if the documents give adequate protection, and if rents and expense items are as represented. But it is precisely at this point that real estate analysis only begins." [1]

The major characteristics of industrial real estate as an investment are:

1. *Fixity of location of income and services* from industrial real estate means that investors (both equity and loan) must be attracted *into* the market area in most instances.

2. *Relatively large amounts of funds are required* to effect an industrial real estate transaction. This reinforces the tendency for investment funds to come from outside the local market area. The major centers of investment fund accumulations, such as New York and Chicago, represent outstanding exceptions.

3. *Special-purpose or single-purpose industrial real estate is infrequently traded.* When it is, the rate of turnover is relatively slow. Therefore, the liquidity risk associated with investment in industrial real estate is relatively high.

4. As compared with many other types of investment, particularly non-real estate investment, *industrial real estate exhibits a high degree of sensitivity to taxes and to government regulations.* This means that the industrial real estate specialist must have a particularly good working knowledge of tax impacts as well as regulatory impacts on industrial real estate.

5. *The environment of industrial real estate is highly sensitive to shifts in markets and in technology.* As a result, industrial real estate runs a high risk of functional obsolescence. Accordingly, rapid recovery of capital in-

---

[1] Sanders A. Kahn, Fred E. Case, and Alfred A. Schimmel, *Real Estate Appraisal and Investment* (New York, The Ronald Press Company, © 1963), p. 307.

vested in potentially obsolescent assets becomes a major consideration in industrial real estate investment decisions.

6. *Industrial real estate requires a relatively large commitment of funds on the part of an owner-occupant.* Consequently, tenant-occupancy and ownership by a third party (the equity investor) is common. Hence, the requirements of three rather than two groups of participants in an industrial real estate transaction must be met: the user, the equity investor, and the lender.

7. *Industrial real estate involves fixed charges (taxes and insurance at least) for the owner, whether it is occupied or not.* Therefore, the general market acceptability of the real estate, often measured by its convertibility or adaptability to other uses, is a major consideration for the equity investor, whether he occupies the space or not.

8. *Industrial real estate is commonly single-tenant real estate.* To this extent, the management of the business occupying the space is intimately related to the income generated to pay for the occupancy of the space.

9. *Single-occupancy also means that little management of the real estate itself is required by the investor.* Industrial real estate is characterized by a relatively high proportion of apparent gross income being translated into effective net income to the equity investor.

Nature of Returns on Industrial Real Estate

Given the basic characteristics of industrial real estate as an investment, attention focuses on the character of the returns normally associated with such investment. This is typically, but not exclusively, approached from the point of view of the equity investor.

Essentially, the return on industrial real estate can be divided into two separate parts: annual income flow, and capital appreciation. As a very practical matter, both income flow and capital appreciation are, and should be, considered in calculating return on investment. Investor preferences for these two types of flows vary with their particular investment goals. Nevertheless, the two together constitute the total return anticipated on the investment. Indeed, it is only after the investment has been finally disposed of that the true return, both in dollar and percentage rate terms, can be calculated.

A wide diversity of terminology is employed in the field of real estate investment income. Moreover, care must be taken to be sure that all participants to a transaction are in agreement on what terms are included in, or excluded from, a particular concept of income. This is important not simply for the several principals in an industrial real estate transaction (the user, the equity investor, the lender), but also among different advisors or specialists called in by the participants (the accountant, the attorney, the appraiser, the broker, the counselor).

Whatever the specific terminology employed, it is assumed that any participant in an industrial real estate investment transaction seeks to maximize the additions to his net cash assets at the end of the transactions. To the equity investor, this means maximizing the sum of the flow of dollar income after taxes, plus the dollar gain after taxes from the resale of the real estate. The user seeks to minimize the dollar cost of occupancy, all other factors remaining equal, over the entire period of occupancy. The lender seeks to maximize the dollar returns on the loan, provided requirements for safety of principal and stability of income have been met.

1. *Income Flow.* In most cases, industrial real estate occupancy is based upon a long-term lease, usually 10 or more years in duration.[2] The terms and conditions for the payment of rent under a lease contract normally are fixed. Lease income can therefore be used as the basis for valuation or other calculations, given the appropriate degree of risk attributed to the real estate and to the occupant. This is not to say that rental payments are necessarily constant. They may increase or decrease with the passage of time. The significant point is that the amount of the annual rental payment is usually known in advance for the period of the lease.

Moreover, the typical industrial lease is more nearly "net" to the investor, than is a commercial lease. This means that much of the risk of fluctuating operating expenses (such as property taxes) is assumed by the tenant, rather than by the owner.

Rates of rental generally vary with the quality and the economic characteristics of the industrial space. Rates of capitalization of the rental income, however, vary more with the presumed quality of the tenant, than with the character of the real estate itself.

A wide range of alternative measures of annual net income is employed in real estate investment analysis. The industrial real estate broker should be able to distinguish among these, so that he can assist his client in making appropriate calculations, and the proper investment decision.

Gross Income is the annual contract rental for the industrial space, plus any service (e.g., electricity) income. In those instances in which it is appropriate to make an allowance or deduction for vacancy, turnover, or non-collection of rent, a distinction is made between Potential Gross Income and Effective Gross Income. The latter represents anticipated actual collections of income. When there is a long-term lease on the property with a reasonably well-rated tenant, Potential Gross and Effective Gross are equal in amount.

To obtain what the appraiser calls Net Income, Operating Expenses of the real estate (but not of the business) are then deducted from Gross Income. These include both Fixed Expenses and Variable Expenses.

Fixed Expenses include anticipated charges for property taxes and liability insurance. Variable Expenses include those items borne by the owner of the real estate which are related to the operation of the real estate itself. They may include electricity, heat, sewerage charges, maintenance and repairs, janitorial service, and the like. The specific items included at this point depend on the terms and conditions of the specific lease contract. The Net Income figure, derived by subtracting Operating Expenses from Gross Income, is in reality Net Operating Income, because

---

[2] See Chapters 8 and 10 for the financing and legal characteristics, respectively, of industrial real estate leases.

no charge for depreciation or capital recovery has yet been deducted. Moreover, there has been no provision for debt service, nor any allowance for income tax liability.

In order to derive a Cash Flow estimate, which is what interests the investor, it is necessary next to deduct financing charges (interest and principal) on any debt that may be outstanding.

The interest charges are also deductible from Net Income before the income tax liability is calculated. The next deduction is for Depreciation. This is *not* an allowance for capital recapture such as is utilized by the appraiser; neither is it the individual investor's desired rate of capital recapture. Rather, it is the amount which is allowed by Internal Revenue Service regulations, and elected by the investor with the advice and consultation of his accountant, his tax attorney and quite often his real estate counselor.

Once Debt Service and Depreciation have been deducted from Net Operating Income, a figure which represents Net Income Before Income Tax Liability is derived. This is also referred to as Taxable Net Income (variously, Taxable Net or Taxable Income). After the income tax liability is calculated, it is subtracted from Taxable Net Income, and a figure representing estimated Net Income After Taxes is derived. This Net After Taxes represents the "profit" involved in operating the real estate. In many situations, it is used as the numerator in calculating the rate of return on the equity investment.

In calculating spendable Cash Flow, however, as well as the total annual return, Depreciation allowed under Internal Revenue Service regulations is added back to Net Income After Taxes. This sum represents the number of dollars actually available to the owner of the real estate each year. No investment will normally be made in a depreciable asset, unless that investment can be recovered over the period during which it is held or used. Cash Flow After Income Taxes provides an extremely useful measure for comparing alternative investments for many types of investors. It is also important to distinguish the income figures employed in investment analysis from those utilized by real estate appraisers.

The mechanics of deriving the various income and cash flow figures discussed in this section are illustrated in the hypothetical example contained in Exhibit 16. In addition, a valuable investment analysis form, which depicts the several measures discussed here, is illustrated in Exhibit 17.

It should be noted that provision for capital recapture, or depreciation, is normally anticipated by the equity investor in industrial real estate over the expected investment or holding period. This is particularly true for special-purpose or single-use buildings, which will require a considerable investment before they can be adapted to the needs or requirements of any other user.

Finally, because amortization payments increase monthly, and interest payments decrease monthly under a constant-payment mortgage loan, the figures used for interest payments in Exhibit 16 represent the annual average that would prevail if the loan were held to maturity. This point is considered further in Chapter 6.

2. *Capital Appreciation.* In addition to receiving annual net income from an investment in industrial real estate, the equity investor often anticipates capital appreciation: i.e., disposition of the realty at a price in excess of its book value at the time of sale. As a practical matter, the investor often seeks an increase in sales price or "value" that exceeds the decrease in purchasing power of the dollar during the holding period. This is one means of providing a hedge against inflation via investment in real estate.

The lender, of course, has no such protection or anticipation. Unless there is a sharp decline in interest rates and the loan is sold substantially

Exhibit 16

DERIVATION OF NET INCOME FIGURES FROM
ANNUAL OPERATING STATEMENT

Hypothetical Industrial Property Under Lease
(20-Year Straight-Line Depreciation for Tax Purposes)

Investment in Development		
Land		$ 50,000
Building and other improvements		700,000
Total Investment		$750,000
Financing of Property		
First Mortgage (5¾% interest, 20-year amortization)		$500,000
Equity Investment		250,000
		$750,000
Income Statement		
Gross Income (Annual Contract Rent)		$87,000
Less: Operating Expenses (Fixed plus Variable)		27,000
Net Income (Net Operating Income)		$60,000
Less:		
Interest (Average Annual Charge over 20 years)		−$17,126
Depreciation (5% of $700,000)		−$35,000
Taxable Net Income		7,874
Less: Income Tax Liability (Assumed Rate of 22%)		1,732
Net Income After Taxes		$ 6,142
Cash Flow		
Net Operating Income		$60,000
Less: Annual Financing Charge	$42,126	
Income Tax Liability	1,732	$43,858
Net Cash Flow After Taxes		$16,142
Average Annual Tax-Free Cash Flow		$10,000

NOTE: The amortization and useful life (for depreciation) periods are equal in this example simply to facilitate illustration of *average* annual relationships in income flows.

Exhibit 17

ESTIMATED PROJECTION WORKSHEET

REALTORS

Duncan Korb & Trimble INC.

REAL ESTATE INVESTMENTS • 151 GRAND AVENUE, OAKLAND, CALIF. 94612

ADDRESS: _____

TYPE: _____

DATE: _____

Telephone (415) 834-6230

THE FOLLOWING EXAMPLE IS BASED ON __1ST__ YEAR ANNUAL FIGURES

1	EST. ALLOC. TO LAND	1
2	EST. ALLOC. TO BLDG.	2
3	EST. ALLOC. TO PERS. PROP.	3
4	TOTAL COST	4

	LOANS	Monthly Payment	Annual Payment	Int. Rate	Annual Interest	Annual Principal	Yrs.	LOANS	AMOUNT	
5	1st.			%				1st.		5
6	2nd.			%				2nd.		6
7	3rd.			%				3rd.		7
8	Chattel			%				Chattel		8
9	TOTALS							TOTAL LOANS		9
10		"A"	"B"	"C"	"D"	"E"		EQUITY		10

IMPORTANT!

The information on this "Estimated Projection Worksheet" is intended as an EXAMPLE ONLY, to demonstrate estimated spendable income, percentage returns and possible income tax consequences. All figures and percentages shown on this worksheet are estimates only! All information, allocations and projections shown on this worksheet, while based upon information supplied by the owner or from other sources deemed to be reliable, are not, in any way, warranted by Duncan, Korb & Trimble, Inc. Independent tax counsel should be obtained concerning all income tax considerations involved.

Copyright © 1965 by DUNCAN, KORB & TRIMBLE, INC., REALTORS

11	Gross Rents	11
12	Other Income	12
13	SCHEDULED GROSS INCOME	13
14	ANNUAL EXPENSES: Prop. Taxes	14
15	Insurance	15
16		16
17		17
18		18
19		19
20		20
21	TOTAL EXPENSES	21
22	(Before Loan Payments) NET INCOME	22
23	(Line 9-D) TOTAL INTEREST	23
24	(Line 9-E) TOTAL PRINCIPAL	24
25	TOTAL LOAN PAYMENTS	25
26	CASH FLOW	26

27	BASED ON } $_____	The Cash Flow (Line 26) & "%" Return	or ____%	27
28	EQUITY OF } (Line 10)	The "Equity Increase" (Line 24) & "%" Return	or ____%	28
29		THIS YEAR'S TOTAL RETURN	or ____%	29

30	(Line 13) GROSS INCOME	30
31	INCOME TAX DEDUCTIONS: (Line 21) TOTAL EXPENSES	31
32	(Line 23) TOTAL INTEREST	32
33	(Method:) BLDG. DEPRECIATION	33
34	(Method:) PERS. PROP. DEPREC.	34
35	TOTAL DEDUCTIONS	35
36	THIS YEAR'S TAXABLE INCOME OR (TAX LOSS)	36

	SUMMARY "A" WHERE (TAX LOSS) IS SHOWN ON LINE 36	SUMMARY "B" WHERE TAXABLE INCOME IS SHOWN ON LINE 36	
37	(Line 29) THIS YEAR'S TOTAL RETURN	(Line 29) THIS YEAR'S TOTAL RETURN	37
38	EST. TAX SAVINGS (Tax Bracket × Line 36) +	Est. Tax Payable on Taxable Income (Tax Bracket x Line 36)−	38
39	THIS YEAR'S TOTAL GAIN (Incl. Tax Savings)	THIS YEAR'S GAIN AFTER INCOME TAXES	39

THIS YEAR'S SPENDABLE CASH......$ _____
(Line 26 + Line 38)

THIS YEAR'S SPENDABLE CASH......$ _____
(Line 26 − Line 38)

before maturity, the lender is committed to a return based entirely upon the interest rate.

Capital appreciation or long-term capital gain has significant tax advantages over ordinary income flows. As a result, those equity investors to whom income taxes are a major consideration generally seek to maximize the proportion of gain which takes the form of annual income flow (ordinary income). This distinction is primarily the result of definitions in the *Internal Revenue Code,* which is one reason that income tax considerations are examined in detail in this chapter.

3. *Rate of Return Calculations.* Comparisons of industrial real estate investments with one another, and with alternative outlets for investment funds (particularly equity funds), are often made on the basis of rates of return. It is important to recognize precisely what is included in the numerator (the return) as well as in the denominator (the investment) when such calculations are being made. For example, appraisal practice calls for rates which normally are calculated on the basis of net operating income before any deductions are made for depreciation (or capital recapture), interest, or income taxes. When such rates are compared with those calculated by the accountant, the tax lawyer, or the investor himself, appropriate adjustment must be made before a thorough analysis can begin. Very often the differences are obvious, but the necessary adjustments are not. It is another important task of the industrial real estate specialist to be able to make these adjustments for the client.

In most instances, cash flow is related to the equity investment in order to estimate the rate of return to the investor. Even here, however, differences exist. Some analysts utilize cash flow *before* income tax liability is deducted, while others emphasize cash flow *after* taxes. The analysis based on cash flow *before* income taxes are deducted is more commonly used, because tax liability tends to vary with the individual investor.

In advising a client, the industrial real estate specialist must recognize that he is engaged in calculations related to the specific needs or requirements of the individual or firm for whom the work is being done. Market averages are only general guides. Decisions to buy or not to buy, or to invest or not to invest, are based on a comparison of capital values, rates of return, or income flows in relation to the standards of the individual investor. His investment criteria will prevail, subject to the advice and counsel from his industrial real estate specialist, who provides insights into the prevailing market.

Finally, real estate investment analysis is approaching other types of financial analysis, in terms of the mechanics and the kind of data utilized in making investment decisions.

While it is still not common practice, many progressive investors are applying to real estate investments the methods of analysis which have been developed in financial analysis and the investment decisions of business firms. These methods enable the analyst to calculate the present value of the expected future yields. The techniques allow the investor to put all the information (involved in a present worth estimate via discounting of anticipated future cash flow) into a single yield estimate which can then be compared with the prospective investments.[3]

Investors in Industrial Real Estate

There are essentially two groups of investors in industrial real estate that must be considered in any analysis of the investment market. They are equity investors, and lenders. Basically, the lenders provide funds which are to be repaid in accordance with contractual agreements at specified times, together with contractually determined interest payments. The mortgage (or note secured by a deed of trust) is the most common instrument utilized in industrial real estate lending. It serves as the means whereby the real estate itself is pledged as collateral against the loan.

Equity investors vary more widely by type and by motivation than do lenders on industrial real estate.

An understanding of the desires, requirements, and characteristics of both classes of investors is important to the industrial real estate broker. The characteristics of the most likely participants in any particular transaction will help identify the nature of the market involved.

1. *Equity Investors.* Although the basic, underlying motive of all equity investors is to maximize gain (or conversely to minimize net loss), the means of achieving these fundamental goals tend to set investors apart into several distinct and identifiable categories.

a. *Users.* The industrial firm occupying the space may own the real estate itself. Its primary goal is to pay no more than a competitive price for the space. Generally, this type of investor seeks to minimize the cash commitment involved, because funds are usually more productive as working capital than they are invested in the real estate. As a result, there are substantial financial advantages for the user to be a tenant, rather than an owner. This is not a completely one-sided phenomenon, however, as is indicated in the discussion of leases in Chapter 8.

For the user, investment in the industrial real estate it occupies is attractive only so long as the advantages of ownership outweigh the disadvantages of leasing. For this type of decision, the industrial real estate broker must be prepared to make the proper comparisons for the client.

b. *Profit-Oriented Individuals or Groups.* Perhaps the most common type of equity investor in industrial real estate is the high-income individual or group seeking the advantages of high return, coupled with tax-free income flows. An investment group may organize as a partnership, a corporation, or a syndicate. All are concerned with a combination of income flow and capital appreciation, which takes maximum advantage of income tax factors. Such groups will typically exchange current income for greater potential capital gains in the future. Their investments are therefore more closely associated with risky transactions that offer the possibility of capital gain. Historically, they are likely to seek a turnover

---

[3] Sherman J. Maisel, *Financing Real Estate: Principles and Practices* (New York, McGraw-Hill Book Co., © 1965), p. 367. Reprinted with permission.

of ownership after 10 to 12 years. This influences the types of leases in which they are interested, the types of risks they will take, and the type of financing that is usually sought. The so-called "balloon" mortgage loan is particularly popular with such investors.

c. *Institutional Investors.* Life insurance companies, trusts, pension funds, and similar institutional investors make equity investments in industrial real estate, as well as mortgage loans. Such organizations are typically most interested in safety: of both returns and principal. They are more inclined to make large, long-term investments. Short-term liquidity rarely interests them. Instead, reduced investment portfolio turnover, and increased average size of investment mean a reduction in operating and management costs per dollar invested.

Institutional investors normally are subject to lower income tax rates than are private, profit-seeking individuals or groups. Many are tax-exempt. Consequently, they tend to emphasize the size of the annual income flow, rather than the prospect of capital gain. Thus, lower-risk, long-term leases with highly rated tenants are most likely to be found on properties owned by institutional investors. Their lower tax liability and long-run orientation, together with their generally greater accumulations of funds seeking investment outlets, often permit them to outbid profit-seeking investors.

d. *Corporate Surplus.* An increasingly important source of equity investment funds is the earned surplus of operating business corporations. As tax pressures increase on "unnecessary" accumulations of funds in earned surplus, operating corporations begin to seek alternative outlets for their funds. Both equity and loan investments in industrial real estate represent attractive alternatives to such investors. Although they are fully subject to federal income taxation, corporate investors will occasionally accept slightly lower yields on the total investment, because the alternative of a high penalty tax on the "unwarranted" surplus accumulation reduces the opportunity cost of industrial real estate investment.

e. *Real Estate Investment Trusts.* The distinguishing characteristic of the real estate investment trust that separates it from other profit-oriented organizations is that it tends to attract lower-income investors. They are generally less oriented toward capital appreciation, and more interested in the slightly higher annual returns that real estate is purported to produce. As an equity investment device in industrial real estate, the real estate investment trust is required to distribute a minimum of 90 per cent of its earnings to trust certificate holders. Hence, annual income, rather than capital appreciation, must be the primary motivation of any individual investor in the trust.

2. *Lenders.* At the outset, it is appropriate to consider the primary bases on which groups of lenders may be differentiated. The industrial real estate broker should learn which specific lenders operating in his area are seeking income characteristics of the type associated with the property he is attempting to finance.

Institutional lenders are necessarily interested primarily in safety:

safety of principal, and certainly of interest payments. Institutional lenders are fiduciary organizations that accumulate the deposits or savings of individuals and invest them on behalf of their depositors, shareholders or policy holders. Influencing the safety of the loan are such factors as the coverage of principal and interest payments (debt service) by the earnings of the real estate; the loan-to-value ratio of the loan; the amortization provisions of the loan in relation to any lease that may exist on the real estate; and the credit rating of the lessee or tenant.

In addition, institutional lenders typically favor longer-term and larger loans. This is because their overhead and management expenses per dollar of loan decrease markedly as the size of the loan increases, and as portfolio turnover decreases.

Liquidity is a major consideration for the institutional lender seeking to maintain safety of principal. All of these factors combine to create a generally lower pattern of interest rates from institutional investors, particularly life insurance companies and pension funds, than are found on loans from individuals, private associations, corporations, or real estate investment trusts. Non-institutional lenders typically make loans on higher-risk industrial transactions at interest rates generally higher, and on other loan terms generally less favorable to the borrower, than do institutional lenders.

Industrial Real Estate and the Goals of the Investor

From the foregoing analysis, it can be seen that many mixtures of investment goals and industrial real estate characteristics can be associated with either equity or loan investment. In each situation, the industrial real estate specialist must identify the characteristics of the real estate, of the lessee (if any), and of the income anticipated from the transaction. Then he must relate these investment characteristics to the particular type of equity investor and lender most likely to be attracted to such a transaction. Regardless of the specific aims of the particular investors involved, there are generally six basic questions to be answered in evaluating any investment:

"1. How safe is the principal? Will it be returned to the investor?
"2. How certain is the anticipated yield on the investment?
"3. How liquid is the investment? Can it quickly and inexpensively be converted to cash?
"4. What are the chances of capital appreciation? Can it be sold for a profit?
"5. What protection does the investment give the investor from inflationary pressures?
"6. What is the tax liability of the realty investment?" [4]

Although real estate generally ranks high as an investment with respect to all of the foregoing criteria except liquidity, the investor does not invest "in general." Rather, the specifics of each type of investment in real estate must be considered in comparison with the features of

[4] Kahn, *et al, op. cit.*, p. 307.

competing alternatives. Such comparisons are possible through the use of the tabulation in Exhibit 18, which indicates that limiting assumptions are necessary to rate investments in real estate even when they are separated into many different categories. This is particularly true of industrial buildings with one national tenant, which generally rate high as investments for institutional investors seeking long-term income. It is interesting to note that multitenant structures actually offer potentially better investments for profit-oriented investors with considerable income tax liability.

Leverage in Industrial Real Estate Investment

An equity investor borrows funds in order to complete an industrial real estate transaction for either or both of two reasons. The first reason is quite obvious: he simply may not have enough money to complete the transaction on a 100 per cent cash basis. Therefore, he turns to a mortgage loan or some other form of debt financing to accommodate his needs for the difference.

At least as important, however, is the fact that the equity investor often will not resort to 100 per cent equity financing, even if he has the cash. The reason is that most investments in real estate are normally expected to yield more than the cost of borrowing the necessary funds. In other words, the equity investor borrows funds in anticipation of earning a higher rate of return on those funds invested in real estate than the rate he will have to pay on the loan. This phenomenon is referred to as "trading on equity" or the use of "leverage." The higher the proportion of total investments represented by loan funds, the higher the leverage.[5]

The lender is typically satisfied with a lower rate of return or interest because of the greater safety and stability of his investment. An institutional lender, as noted previously, normally cannot legally, and will not as a matter of policy, engage in risk-taking. Some life insurance companies do occasionally take both an equity and a lender's position on the same industrial property, but this is not a widespread practice. The higher returns associated with investment in real estate stem largely from the rewards for risk-taking on the part of the equity investor.

In periods of prolonged prosperity and continuing inflationary pressures, trading on equity is almost invariably successful. The equity investor does in fact earn a higher rate of return on funds invested in real estate than he must pay for borrowed funds. The incremental earnings are added to his returns, thereby increasing substantially the rate of return on the equity portion of the investment. Under such circumstances, the higher the leverage, the greater the opportunity for extremely high returns or profits to the equity investor.

Conversely, trading on equity can be unsuccessful. This happens when a less-than-competitive rate of return is earned on the total investment in

---

[5] For more detailed presentations of the operation of leverage in real estate investment, together with other illustrative examples, see *Ibid.*, pp. 134–136; and Maisel, *op. cit.*, pp. 357–361.

Exhibit 18

RATINGS OF REALTY INVESTMENTS

Type of Investment	Safety of Initial Investment	Safety of Annual Earnings	Capital Appreciation	Liquidity	Income-Tax Shelter	Inflationary Protection
Apartment houses (middle income)	E	E	E	E	G	E**
Apartment houses (luxury)	F	F	F	F	G	E**
Office buildings (multi-tenant, in city)	G	G	G	E	F	E**
Office buildings (one national tenant, suburb)	F	G*	P*	E*	E	N
Office buildings (multi-tenant, suburb)	P	F	P	P	E	G
Retail property (average tenant, in city)	F	P	N	F	P	F
Retail property (one national tenant, city)	F	G*	P	E*	P	N***
Retail property (shopping centers)	F	G	G	G	E	P***
Retail property (one national tenant, suburb)	G	G*	P*	E*	E	N***
Loft buildings (multi-tenant)	G	G	F	F	G	G**
Industrial buildings (one national tenant)	G	G*	P*	E*	E	N
Gas stations (one national tenant, highway)	F	F*	P*	E*	E	P
Gas stations (one national tenant, in city)	E	G*	G	E*	F	P

Code: E—Excellent, G—Good, F—Fair, P—Poor, N—Negative
*Assume rental is at market, lease has many years to run, and purchase price is fair.
**Under free market conditions, otherwise poor.
***Unless percentage lease, then excellent.
SOURCE: Sanders A. Kahn, Fred E. Case and Alfred Schimmel, *Real Estate Appraisal and Investment* (Copyright 1963, Ronald Press Co., New York City). Reprinted with permission.

the real estate, and the equity portion earns a disproportionately lower rate of return. If the return on the total investment is equal to the interest rate on borrowed funds, then there is no advantage to trading on equity; and there is some risk, because the equity investor always has a secondary or residual claim on income and principal. The lender still has the legally protected prior position of a creditor.

The industrial real estate broker should be alert to the limitations and dangers inherent in trading on equity and high-leverage equity investment, so that he may advise his client appropriately. To this end, illustrative examples are presented here to indicate the nature of the process and its potential pitfalls.

Illustration No. 1 A property owner earning a net income of 8 per cent on a $100,000 investment in industrial real estate would receive $8,000 annually. If the property were purchased outright for cash, the rate of return on his investment would be 8 per cent. If, however, the total investment were divided equally between equity funds and a mortgage at 6 per cent interest, the rate of return on the equity portion of the investment would be substantially increased. For purposes of simplification and illustration only, amortization of the principal of the loan is ignored. This omission tends to overstate the attractions of trading on equity. Typically, the assumption is made that capital appreciation will offset the increased equity commitment over the life of the loan.

In the situation illustrated here, a non-amortized $50,000 mortgage at 6 per cent interest would require $3,000 in interest payments a year. If the interest charges are deducted from the net income of $8,000, the investor has a cash return on his equity investment of $5,000. Since the owner-investor has an equity investment of $50,000 in the property, the cash flow return on this equity is 10 per cent. To this extent the investor has increased his rate of return by using borrowed funds.

The advantages of trading on equity may increase with higher leverage. Assuming now that 90 per cent of the real estate may be financed with a 6 per cent mortgage, the rate of return on equity increases to 26 per cent ($2,600/$10,000). The figures for these three alternatives are indicated below:

Cash Purchase

Property Investment	Net Return	Rate of Return
$100,000	$8,000	8%

50% Financing

Property Investment	Net Return	Rate of Return	Less Mortgage Interest	Return After Interest	Rate of Return on Equity
$100,000	$8,000	8%	$3,000	$5,000	10% ($5,000/$50,000)

90% Financing

Property Investment	Net Return	Rate of Return	Less Mortgage Interest	Return After Interest	Rate of Return on Equity
$100,000	$8,000	8%	$5,400	$2,600	26% ($2,600/$10,000)

The introduction of a direct-reduction, constant-payment mortgage alters the composition of the flow of funds somewhat, but the principle remains exactly the same. To take the 50 per cent mortgage financing alternative as one case in point, a 20-year, 6 per cent loan for $50,000 would require monthly payments (both principal and interest) of $358.30. This would amount to annual debt service of $4299.60, of which $3,000 would represent 6 per cent interest on $50,000, and $1,299.60 would go for principal payments. The cash flow in this case would be $3,700.40, or 7.4 per cent of the $50,000 equity. The equity increase of $1,299.60 represents 2.6 per cent of the equity investment, and the total return (cash flow plus equity increase) is still 10 per cent of equity. The difference is that the investor has less immediate cash for current use. These relationships are illustrated as follows:

Net Income (Before Deducting Depreciation)		$8,000.00
Less Debt Service		
Interest	$3,000.00	
Principal Payment	$1,299.60	4,299.60
Cash Flow		3,700.40
Plus Principal Payment (Equity Increase)		1,299.60
Total Return to Equity Investment (First Year)		5,000.00

It must be reiterated that these advantages of leverage will be realized only if the total investment return (in this example 8 per cent) is greater than the mortgage rate of interest. If conditions are favorable, opportunities to trade on equity tend to make industrial property investments more attractive to equity investors.

Illustration No. 2. Changes in net income are magnified for the equity investor as leverage increases. For example, if net income increases from $10,000 to $20,000 (whatever the cause), the 100 per cent increase in total net income is amplified considerably for the equity investor. If the return to equity is $5,000 initially, a doubling of net income triples the dollar return to equity:

	Before Increased Income	After Increased Income	Percentage Increase
Net Income	$10,000	$20,000	100
Less Loan Interest	−5,000	−5,000	
Return to Equity	$ 5,000	$15,000	200

This means that an investor in industrial real estate purchasing property strategically located in a growing community will realize added benefits if rental income rises with increased real estate values. Income to the equity investor will be amplified as the proportion of borrowing increases. Debt service requirements are fixed so that increased net income accrues to the benefit of the equity investor.

A similar effect is produced by increases in capital value. The value of the equity grows proportionately more than does total property value.

Starting with a total property value of $100,000 and assuming a *20 per cent* increase, the original investment will have a value of $120,000. But if 80 per cent of the original property value has been borrowed, the $20,000 equity increases by *100 per cent* to $40,000. This relationship is shown below:

	Before Value Increased	After Value Increased	Percentage Increase
Total Value	$100,000	$120,000	20
Total Debt	−80,000	−80,000	
Equity Interest	$ 20,000	$ 40,000	100

Hence, with a general upward trend in industrial real estate values, the equity investor may expect to realize all the benefits of increased capital value.

Illustration No. 3. Further advantages may be realized when leverage is combined with leasehold financing. The advantages include both increasing the investor's rate of return and minimizing capital invested in real estate by the industrial user. One way to serve both interests is to utilize net ground leases to arrange 100 per cent financing.

To illustrate, assume that a site valued at $75,000 is available for purchase or for lease at a ground rental of $6,000 annually. If the industry requires a building costing $225,000, the property represents a total investment of $300,000. Assume further that the prospect may: (1) acquire the site and finance the building with a mortgage equal to two-thirds of total land and building value; (2) lease the land and secure a mortgage equal to two-thirds of the building cost; or (3) lease the land, with the landowner subordinating his leased fee interest to the lender. This subordination permits the lender to advance funds for building construction, and to make a loan equal to two-thirds of the total property value.

To show the relationships among these financing alternatives, a total net income of $30,000 is assumed. Given these assumptions, the possible gains are indicated in Exhibit 19. They show clearly that by combining the financial advantages of net ground leases with debt financing, the return on equity may be increased.

This simplified example is based on quite restrictive assumptions. Nevertheless, the point is clear: industrial real estate investors may gain a considerable advantage by trading on equity. Of course, it must also be assumed that there are attractive alternative outlets for the funds "saved" through borrowing. An industrial firm may desire to lease both land and buildings. An investor may lease the land, construct a building, and sublease the land and building to the industrial tenant. If the credit of the tenant is satisfactory, and if the building and site qualify as loan security, substantial gains may be earned for the investor through leverage.

Trading on equity does not always result in increased gains to the investor. When there is a decrease in net income, and a large proportion

Exhibit 19

COMPARISON OF RETURNS ON EQUITY UNDER MORTGAGE FINANCING,
AND LEASE FINANCING WITH AND WITHOUT
SUBORDINATION OF THE LEASED FEE

Investment	Acquisition by Purchase	Acquisition by Lease Without Subordination	Acquisition by Lease With Subordination
Land	$ 75,000	$ —	$ —
Building	225,000	225,000	225,000
Total Investment	$300,000	$225,000	$225,000
Mortgage (66%)	200,000	150,000	200,000
Required Equity	100,000	75,000	25,000
Net Income	30,000	30,000	30,000
Less:			
Mortgage Service (a)	18,000	13,000	18,000
Land Rent	—	6,000	6,000
Total Charges	$ 18,000	$ 19,000	$ 24,000
Net Return after Rent and Mortgage Charges	$ 12,000	$ 11,000	$ 6,000
Rate of Return	12.0%	14.7%	24.0%
	($12,000/$100,000)	($11,000/$175,000)	($6,000/$25,000)

(a) Mortgage service requirements include annual principal and interest payments of a 20-year loan, 6 per cent interest. For illustration, payments are rounded to the nearest $1,000.

of the investment in the property has been debt-financed, the owner's ability to meet mortgage payments is rapidly reduced. If the estimate of net income is too high, the equity investor runs the risk of losing his entire investment. There is also a risk that amortization may be too rapid. The owner may find that he is earning a potential or "paper" profit, but that the real estate is not generating enough cash to meet mortgage payments. This is a fairly common occurrence in equity positions with high leverage.

In brief, leverage offers the potential for substantially higher net returns on equity investments, but it is also fraught with dangers. Careful investment and market analysis are necessary before advising the client about the proper proportion of debt to equity in any industrial real estate investment.

INCOME TAX CONSIDERATIONS

Since there is a strong probability that tax factors will influence industrialists, property developers, and potential investors, understanding the relationship between income taxes and industrial real estate decisions will assist the industrial real estate specialist in interpreting market behavior. Income tax factors are important in industrial real estate investment decisions because both the federal personal income tax and the federal corporate income tax are progressive: the *rates* increase as income rises. The typical investor seeks to minimize his tax liability and thereby to maximize his cash gain. Within the federal income tax structure, there are devices whereby he may *legally* defer, reduce, or even avoid tax liability. This tax avoidance, but not evasion, is assumed to be practiced by every alert, rational, and knowledgeable investor in industrial real estate, with the advice and counsel of his tax accountant and tax attorney.

The industrial real estate broker should not practice tax law or tax accountancy. At the same time, he must know enough of the implications of income tax law to serve his client appropriately. This may well consist of knowing what questions to raise and with whom. He should certainly appreciate why it is essential to assemble a topflight team of tax lawyers and accountants in any industrial real estate investment problem.

Because federal tax laws and their interpretation by the Internal Revenue Service may change over time, the present discussion is only a general guide to the issues which industrial real estate investment problems may raise. The current *Internal Revenue Code,* as interpreted by competent tax counsel, is the final arbiter in any individual case (short of determination by the courts). There is always the risk that a given course of action, which is expected to be quite acceptable and legal, will be disallowed upon subsequent investigation by the Internal Revenue Service. Therefore, it is absolutely necessary to plan ahead and to consider the alternatives, the risks, and the potential penalties in the proposed approach. Competent professional advice is required to relate the suggestions contained in the present discussion to a specific property.

This discussion concentrates on (1) the effect of capital gains treatment of income from industrial real estate; (2) the means of ascertaining the type of income treatment likely to be given different types of industrial real estate investment; (3) the impact of the handling of depreciation on industrial real estate income and property values; and (4) the form of business organization best suited to the investor's needs.

Capital Gains Treatment of Income[6]

The personal income tax rates applicable under the 1964 revisions of the Internal Revenue Act start at 14 per cent of taxable net income and increase to 70 per cent. Depending upon the exact tax status of the individual (married filing a joint return, head of household, or single for tax pur-

---

[6] For a more detailed discussion of these problems than can be provided in this necessarily brief and somewhat superficial treatment, consult Alan R. Cerf, *Real Estate and the Federal Income Tax* (Englewood Cliffs, N.J., Prentice-Hall, 1965). See also U.S. Treasury Department, Internal Revenue Service, *Your Federal Income Tax,* Publication No. 17 (Washington, U.S. Government Printing Office, 1965).

poses), the rate at which additional income is taxed exceeds 50 per cent when taxable net is somewhere between $24,000 and $40,000. More than half the taxable income above this level in any given year is absorbed by personal income taxes.

The federal corporate income tax also increases with income, but there is only one point at which the rates jump. The so-called "normal" tax is 22 per cent of all net income. When taxable net exceeds $25,000, a surtax of an additional 26 per cent applies. Thus, all taxable corporate net income in excess of $25,000 is actually taxed at 48 per cent.

When a capital asset is sold or exchanged at a profit, a taxable gain will usually result. Unless the gain qualifies as a long-term capital gain, it is taxed as ordinary income in the year in which it is earned. It is added in full to the taxable net income of the individual or corporation, and taxed at the *incremental* tax rate.

If, on the other hand, the profit can qualify as a long-term capital gain, then only 50 per cent of the profit from the transaction is added to the taxable net income of the recipient. Moreover, both long-term and short-term capital losses ordinarily may be used as offsets to the long-term gain. The net or taxable long-term gain is subject to the appropriate rate of taxation, but only to a maximum of 50 per cent. Therefore, the maximum effective rate at which net long-term capital gains will be taxed is 25 per cent of the total long-term gain (50 per cent of the gain is taxable, and the maximum rate of taxation is 50 per cent).

For the profit from the sale of a capital asset to qualify as a long-term capital gain, the asset must have been held at least six months. In the case of real estate, however, further limitations and qualifications apply. These are discussed later in this section.

A capital gain is the difference between the sales price of the asset, and the sum of the selling expenses plus the "basis" or book value of the asset at the time of the sale. This "basis" figure is important because it is one important determinant of the size of the gain to be taxed. Depreciation charges reduce the basis of real property for capital gains treatment, and therefore influence the timing as well as the amount of the capital gain reported. Indeed, one of the major attractions of real estate as an investment is that it serves as an important vehicle for the conversion of ordinary income into capital gain, with the result that at least half the potential tax liability is saved and retained by the investor at the end of the investment period.

A major portion of the tax planning involved in industrial real estate investment consists of attempts to ensure capital gains treatment of the net proceeds of property sales; or conversely, to avoid the treatment of the net proceeds as ordinary income. The advantages are substantial, but the pitfalls along the path are many and varied.

The Classification of Income for Income Tax Purposes

The classification of the proceeds from the sale of real estate determines the tax consequences of a proposed transaction. Because of the substantial difference in treatment of receipts, these consequences cannot be anticipated until they are considered by the Internal Revenue Service, or ultimately the courts. The proceeds may be taxable as ordinary income or as long-term capital gain. In any case that may be questioned, the *purpose* for which the investor acquired or disposed of the property is the primary guide to the tax treatment of the gains involved.[7]

There are basically three categories into which the proceeds from real estate sales may be placed. Each reflects the character of the seller and his presumed motives. First, there is property held for sale to customers in the ordinary course of business. This is the motivation of the real estate dealer, who is usually a broker or developer. Second, there is property held for use in trade or business, but not ordinarily for sale. This reflects the motivation of the operator-investor in rental real estate, as well as that of the owner-occupant of industrial real estate. Finally, there is property which is held for investment. This reflects the capital gain or speculative motivation of the long-term investor.

In general, the owner of property held for sale in the ordinary course of business will be classified as a dealer, and the net proceeds of his sale will be classified and taxed as ordinary income. The sale receipts of investors, (whether passive investors or those using the real estate for the production of income) are typically treated as capital gain, provided they qualify under the rather rigid rules established by the Internal Revenue Service. All the details of these regulations and requirements for qualification cannot be provided here; only the general standards are indicated.[8]

It is important to note that one taxpayer may be classified differently with respect to different properties. Thus, he may be a broker with respect to property number one; he may be a dealer with respect to properties two and three; and he may be an investor on properties four, five and six. Extreme care must be taken in the treatment of each transaction, in order to obtain optimum advantage of the provisions of the tax laws. In this, as in all other tax considerations pertaining to industrial real estate, the expert advice of an experienced tax accountant and tax lawyer is needed.

1. *Property Held for Sale to Customers.* Real estate brokers must ascertain whether property is held for investment or for sale to customers. The latter makes its owner a dealer, and the sale of property becomes sale of inventory, which gives rise to ordinary income. There is no single test used for determining whether a person is a dealer or an investor; the determination depends on the facts in the individual situation. Certain indications may be used as guides to whether a person will be considered a dealer. These include:

(a) frequent and continuing sales of similar properties;

(b) possession of a real estate broker's license or other indication that the main business is dealing in real estate;

(c) rapid turnover of property, indicating profit rather than capital gain as a motive;

---

[7] David Altman, "Tax Factors Affecting Industrial Real Estate," *Advanced Course in the Techniques of Industrial Real Estate* (Washington, Society of Industrial Realtors, 1964).

[8] For details, see Cerf, *op. cit.,* Chapter 4.

(d) obvious or apparent intention to resell at a profit at the time of acquisition;

(e) active participation in sales and promotion by the taxpayer or his agents.[9]

Whenever motivation or intent is the underlying measure of whether a seller is a "dealer" or an "investor," there will be room for doubt. Therefore, it is imperative to maintain accurate and complete records, including transcriptions of important conversations and statements of intent. An unfavorable tax ruling can mean doubling the tax liability in a particular transaction, at the least. These stakes are high enough to warrant extreme care and extra effort on the part of the owner and the industrial real estate broker assisting him.

2. *Property Used in Trade or Business.* Real estate used in a trade or business is technically not a capital asset. It is only incidentally that the owner-investor may take advantage of capital gains treatment on any profit he may receive in the subsequent disposition of the real estate. A factory or warehouse which is owner-occupied is real estate used in a trade or business; so, too, is a factory or warehouse purchased or constructed by an investor for the express purpose of generating income.

Because such real estate is not a capital asset, the owner receives three tax benefits. First, he may deduct all expenses of care and maintenance from his operating income. Second, depreciation allowances may be deducted from net income before taxable net is ascertained. Finally, he may receive capital gains treatment on the difference between the sale price of property held for at least six months, and the basis plus selling costs at the time of sale. Losses, on the other hand, are treated as ordinary losses; this means they are direct offsets to ordinary income.

The Revenue Act of 1964 placed certain limitations on the capital gains treatment of proceeds from the resale of property used in a trade or business. These limitations reduce the proportion of gain that is treated as long-term capital gain for tax purposes, and increase the proportion regarded as ordinary income, the more the period of investment declines below 10 years.

The treatment of property used in a trade or business is specified in Section 1231 of the Internal Revenue Code. As a result, frequent reference is made to "Section 1231 Property." A person who is a dealer in real estate can also own property as an "investor" under Section 1231.

A large proportion of the investment in industrial real estate may be in equipment. The equipment utilized in an industrial operation is also subject to depreciation and capital gains treatment, but the rules and regulations are somewhat different from those that pertain to realty. It is also extremely important to have expert advice in the allocation of investment between plant and equipment. Much of what might ordinarily be regarded as equipment may be taxed as part of the realty. This can be an advantage

---

[9] For more detailed and technical discussions, consult Altman, *op. cit.;* and Cerf, *op. cit.,* pp. 73, 118–127.

or a disadvantage for the taxpayer. The admonition given earlier is still valid: Plan Ahead!

3. *Real Estate Held for Investment.* In order to qualify as a capital asset, industrial real estate cannot be used either in the trade or business of the taxpayer, or as part of the inventory of a dealer. If it is declared to be a capital asset, then *any* gain upon its disposition is by definition a capital gain.

In practice, most real estate held for investment is unimproved property. This is primarily because the Internal Revenue Service identifies any real estate on which "substantial improvements" have been made by the owner as either property held for use in a trade or business, or property for sale to others. This is a complex determination which cannot be anticipated in advance. Passivity of income is extremely important in determining whether a property is held for investment or not. Almost any overt act on the part of the owner or his agent to dispose of the property may result in his being declared a dealer. At the same time, the property owner can act to preserve his investment without losing its investment classification.

Unimproved real estate and vacant improved property qualify readily as real estate held for investment. Land which is subsequently subdivided must be treated very carefully because there are limiting rules governing the amount of improvement, the time period over which the investment must be held, and the frequency of transactions. Going beyond the limits established under these rules can result in loss of investment status. This is the so-called "Section 1237 Problem" with respect to the subdivision of land.

It is also possible that improved property "held for production of income" is neither property used in a trade or business, nor property held for sale to others. The determination of whether rental property is held for the production of income, or held for use in a trade or business, generally depends on a fine line of distinction. The general rule is that the investment must be *incidental to* the normal business of the taxpayer.[10] The chief advantage is that the taxpayer's normal business expenses are also deductible, along with the expenses of the real estate operation.

Here is an illustration of the distinction between property held for use in a trade or business, and property held for the production of income:

Let us take the situation of Dr. Schmidt, who holds an apartment as an investment and just receives a check from the property managers monthly, and compare it to that of apartment house operator Rose Armstrong, who owns, operates, and manages her apartment house. We shall assume that there is no controversy about the fact that Dr. Schmidt is an investor and that Rose Armstrong is in a trade or business.

Dr. Schmidt has an adjusted basis of $50,000 for his apartment and he sells it for $70,000. In addition, this year he sold some medical equipment that he used in his medical practice at a loss of $3,000. As he is using the medical equipment in his profession, this is a Section 1231 loss. As a result of the above transactions, Dr. Schmidt has a capital gain of $20,000 on his building, on

---

[10] This is further explained in Cerf, *op. cit.*, pp. 73–74.

which he pays a maximum tax of 25 per cent. He also has an ordinary loss of $3,000 from the sale of his medical equipment.

Rose Armstrong also has an apartment with an adjusted basis of $50,000 which she sells for $70,000. In addition this year she sold some appliances at a loss of $3,000. Because Rose is engaged in a trade or business, she has a Section 1231 gain of $20,000 and a Section 1231 loss of $3,000. These are offset, and the result is a $17,000 Section 1231 gain, which is treated as a capital gain. Obviously, Dr. Schmidt is in a better position because he gets his $3,000 loss as a deduction from other income.

When real estate is classified as used in a trade or business, it is desirable to attempt to have all the gains in one taxable year and all the losses in another taxable year. Thus, if in the example above, Rose sold the appliances in a different year, when there were no other Section 1231 transactions, she would have had a fully deductible loss. The entire $20,000 gain on the apartment in a different year (with no other capital transactions) would be treated as a capital gain. If, in the above example, Dr. Schmidt holding the property for investment sold the property at a loss, he would have a capital loss which could be applied against capital gains and $1,000 per year written off against ordinary income. Rose Armstrong, holding the property in a trade or business, would have a Section 1231 loss which (assuming there are no Section 1231 gains) is fully deductible.[11]

DEPRECIATION

For income tax purposes, depreciation is a reasonable allowance (permitted in the Internal Revenue Code) for the exhaustion, wear and tear, and normal obsolescence of property which is used in a trade or business, or which is held for the production of income. This applies to both real estate and equipment in the industrial field. A rather wide range of techniques for the recovery of an investment in a wasting asset is permitted, provided the method is consistent with recognized accounting practices. The three methods most widely employed are specifically cited in the 1954 Internal Revenue Code. They are:

(1) the straight-line method;
(2) the declining-balance method;
    (a) 200 per cent of the straight-line rate;
    (b) 150 per cent of the straight-line rate;
(3) the sum-of-the-years digits method.

Land is considered not to depreciate, and therefore no allowance is permitted. Depreciation is allowed only on property which is presumed to have a definite useful life. That is to say, it must be anticipated that in a foreseeable period of time the asset will cease to contribute to the generation of net income.

The industrial real estate broker must be aware that there are variations in the terminology employed in this field. For example, the accountant will call planned and future recovery of an investment in a capital asset

---

[11] Alan R. Cerf, *Real Estate and the Federal Income Tax*, pp. 74–75. Copyright 1965. Reprinted by permission of Prentice-Hall, Englewood Cliffs, N.J.

"depreciation." He will also refer to any such recovery which has already taken place as "accrued depreciation." In real estate appraisal or valuation analysis, the accountant's "depreciation" or "future depreciation" is termed "capital recapture" or "capital recovery." The "accrued depreciation" to which the real estate appraiser refers is based upon *reproduction* cost new today, whereas the accountant must necessarily deal with historical cost. These differences and distinctions are a source of confusion and difficulty. Nevertheless, the distinctions must be made carefully, for serious problems can arise through misunderstanding and misuse.

Whatever the terminology, the idea underlying depreciation or capital recovery is that an investor is entitled to the recovery of his investment in a wasting or depreciable asset over a specified period of time. Because the exact amount by which the asset is "used up" each year cannot readily be determined, accrual accounting spreads the recovery over a specified number of years. Through depreciation or capital recovery, the investor gets back what he put into the property in the first place. Therefore, this amount is not net income or return from the investment.

Tax Implications of Depreciation

Since depreciation represents a return *of* the taxpayer's investment, rather than a return *on* the investment, it is not taxable income. This has several important implications for the individual taxpayer.

First, depreciation is a deduction from net income before taxable net income is calculated. For example, the hypothetical income statement of the industrial property under lease, discussed earlier in this chapter, showed that the $35,000 annual depreciation charge resulted in a "tax free cash flow" of $10,000 per year. This would not be entirely an investment advantage, if it were the only result of depreciation charges. The real estate will in fact wear out economically, if not physically, over a finite number of years. The investor is looking for recovery of his capital investment. To secure the flow of "tax free cash" during the period of the investor's commitment, other tax factors must be considered.

Depreciated real estate will probably still command a price on the market at a future date. If the property is held for use in a trade or business, or for investment income, the difference between the sale price and the book value of the property at the time of sale (plus selling expenses) will normally result in a long-term capital gain.

The ability to charge depreciation against the investment in the building and other improvements produces a saving on ordinary income taxes during the period over which the property is held, and a conversion of tax liability to capital gains taxation at the disposition of the real estate. In addition, the "tax free" income is provided earlier in the investment period, while the tax liability is deferred to a later time. It is a fundamental principle of investment and economic analysis that income available in the near future is more desirable and worth more to the investor than income realized many years hence.

Eventually the improvement will be fully depreciated, or nearly so. At that time, there is no further tax saving. Indeed, there will be a dramatic increase in tax liability. Therefore, the next important consideration might be regarded as the key to the investment attractiveness of real estate from a tax standpoint. A new investor may depreciate the improvements all over again. Disposing of real estate on or before the date it becomes fully depreciated permits another investor to take advantage of essentially the same features of depreciation on the improvements. However, not every investor is equally sensitive to income tax avoidance. It is important not to assume that all investors seek to take advantage of the income tax laws.

Finally, for those investors to whom taxation at capital gains rates is an attraction, a problem often arises at the time of transfer. This has to do with the allocation of value of the real estate between land and improvements. The seller wishes to have the improvements represent as small a proportion of the transaction price as possible. It is to his advantage to demonstrate that his depreciation charges were not excessive in the past, and that the gain from the sale is legally taxable as long-term capital gain. The purchaser, on the other hand, is anxious to have the largest possible proportion of the sale price allocated to the improvements. This provides the basis for his own depreciation charges in the future. Parties to an investment real estate transfer may disagree more vehemently about the allocation of value between land and buildings than about the transaction price itself.

In the hypothetical case illustrated in Exhibit 16, the entire income pattern would have been quite different if the land were worth $250,000 instead of $50,000, and the improvements assigned $500,000 of total value, rather than $700,000. The most important obvious difference would have been the disappearance of the "average annual tax free cash flow." While tax considerations cannot convert an unsound investment into a sound one, they can influence the attractiveness of a particular investment to a given investor. Since the industrial real estate broker is dealing with an individual client, rather than with "the market" in general, he serves the interests of that individual client by maintaining an awareness of issues such as this tax consideration.

Normal Useful Life

It is not the physical life of an income-producing asset, but its normal useful life which forms the basis for the pattern of depreciation that is to be established. Depreciation guidelines are published by the Internal Revenue Service to aid the taxpayer. In investment planning, which is really the only area in which the industrial real estate broker can act without assuming a subordinate role to the tax accountant and tax attorney, the guidelines published by the Internal Revenue Service are most useful.[12] This set of depreciation guidelines has generally superseded the indicated useful lives in the earlier Bulletin "F."

Guidelines of useful lives for various types of industrial properties in-

---

[12] U.S. Treasury Department, Internal Revenue Service, *Revenue Procedures 62–21* (Washington, U.S. Government Printing Office, 1962).

clude: factories, 45 years; warehouses, 60 years; machine shops, 45 years; office buildings, 45 years; loft buildings, 50 years. Within the framework of these guidelines, the individual investor's estimate of the useful life of a particular property may be accepted if reasonable grounds for the judgment are presented.

The useful life of real estate is often termed its "economic life" by the appraiser. In addition, the appraiser is concerned with the remaining economic life or capital recapture period, from the viewpoint of the investor or purchaser. Indeed, one investment standard in establishing useful life of industrial real estate for depreciation purposes is to bring the useful life as closely as possible in line with the market-determined capital recapture period of the investor. Then only one set of accounts need be kept, and the investor can readily calculate cash flow and return on investment so as to make appropriate investment decisions.

Salvage Value

Under normal circumstances, property may not be depreciated 100 per cent during its useful life. This is because it will presumably have *some* value even when it has ceased to be a useful contributor to the net income of the owner. This is its salvage value. It must be deducted from the original acquisition cost or price in order to provide the amount which is to be depreciated during the useful life.

For example, suppose that a building costing $100,000 is estimated to have a remaining useful life of 20 years. Neither the Internal Revenue Service nor the courts will normally allow full depreciation of $100,000 over a 20-year period. There is much room for varying opinion as to whether the building will be worth anything 20 years hence, and what it will be worth. Nevertheless, perhaps 10 per cent of cost may be agreed upon just to settle the discussion. In this example, then, the salvage value would be $10,000, and the amount to be recovered via depreciation over a 20-year period would be $90,000.

Salvage value is supposed to be a realistic estimate of what the property will be worth at the end of its useful life.[13] Although this can be little more than an educated guess, there are potential penalties in underestimating the salvage value. The entire amount of depreciation charged in the year of the sale can be disallowed.

Alternate Methods of Depreciation

Any generally acceptable accounting technique may be permitted in calculating and charging depreciation. The three methods specifically noted in the 1954 Internal Revenue Code, and therefore specifically permitted, are: the straight-line method; the declining-balance method; and the sum-of-the-years digits method.

Selecting among the alternatives available to the taxpayer is an important decision, because it influences the apparent flow of income over a substantial period of time. Both the tax status and the tax motivation of the

[13] Altman, *op. cit.*

investor are significant considerations in choosing the method. There are substantial advantages for the high-income taxpayer in electing an accelerated depreciation method since there is opportunity for converting a substantial portion of income from ordinary income to capital gains tax status. On the other hand, electing to charge accelerated depreciation holds no tax advantage for a tax-exempt pension fund. Life insurance companies, with their special tax treatment, generally find it attractive to use longer-term capital recapture periods and straight-line depreciation. The Realtor must therefore ascertain the tax status of the client-investor, so that the appropriate advice about tax planning for any industrial real estate investment can be obtained.

A taxpayer need not use the same method of depreciation on all his depreciable property. Once he has chosen a particular method for a given property, however, he must use that method consistently and continuously *unless* he meets the rather strict requirements of the regulations for converting to another method.

It is occasionally desirable for a taxpayer to convert from one method to another, when it is legal to do so. A taxpayer using the 200 per cent declining-balance depreciation method may change to the straight-line method at any time without formal permission. This election must be made by the date for filing a return. Any other change in depreciation method must be approved in writing by the Internal Revenue Service before it will be allowed. Moreover, once a change is made, the investor is committed to use the new method for the duration of his investment.

1. *Straight-line Depreciation.*   Under the straight-line method of depreciation, the depreciable portion of the investment in the property is deducted from net income in equal annual installments over the established useful life. The depreciable portion is the cost or other basis of the property, less the estimated salvage value.

The effect of straight-line depreciation on a building costing $100,000, with an estimated salvage value of $10,000 and an estimated useful life of 20 years, is shown in the first section of Exhibit 20. The indicated annual depreciation charge is $4,500, or one-twentieth of the $90,000 depreciable portion of the investment.

2. *Accelerated Depreciation.*   Subject to limitations that are noted later, the recoverable portion of investments in buildings and other improvements may be depreciated more rapidly in the early years of estimated useful life than is the case under straight-line depreciation. No more is recovered in total via the various methods of accelerated depreciation than is true under the straight-line method. Indeed, the declining-balance method actually results in a lower total recovery over the full useful life than is the case with straight-line depreciation.

The advantage lies in the *timing* of depreciation charges, which are substantially larger in the early years of the investment when accelerated depreciation is employed. If this is coupled with a resale of the property on a basis which permits capital gains taxation, a substantial tax advantage has been earned.

a. *Declining-Balance Depreciation.*   Under straight-line depreciation, the annual charges are levied against the original cost, less salvage value. Thus, there is a constant base for calculating the annual depreciation charge. Under the declining-balance method, on the other hand, the base for calculating each year's depreciation charge is the balance remaining after the previous year's depreciation has been deducted. The *rate* of depreciation charge is normally higher in the first several years than that under the straight-line method, which is the appeal of the declining-balance method for the investor.

New property occupied by its original user may be depreciated under a 200 per cent declining-balance method. This is illustrated in the second section of Exhibit 20. No salvage value need be estimated under the declining-balance method, because it is impossible to depreciate 100 per cent of the original cost. The amount remaining at the end of the useful life is supposed to represent a built-in salvage value, and usually it is not deductible in the last year of useful life. However, this "tail" (as it is often called in practice) may be greater than the reasonable salvage value. If it is, the excess may be deductible in the year the property is retired.

It is possible to shift from the 200 per cent declining-balance method to the straight-line method at any time without any advance permission. Once the switch is made, however, the investor must remain with the straight-line method.

The figures in Exhibit 20 show that after the eighth year in the example illustrated, it would be advantageous for the investor to switch from the 200 per cent declining-balance method to the straight-line method. Even without such a switch, however, a total of $65,132 would have been recovered as depreciation under the 200 per cent declining-balance method at the end of 10 years, as compared with recovery of $45,000 after 10 years under the straight-line method. This is a total of over $20,000 in tax-free cash flow.

Any real estate which is occupied or owned by anyone other than the original user may not be depreciated via the 200 per cent declining-balance method. Rather, the 150 per cent declining-balance method may be employed for any such "used" property.

The flow of depreciation charges associated with the 150 per cent declining-balance method is illustrated in the third section of Exhibit 20. The figures there show that the total of $54,143 would have been recovered at the end of 10 years on the hypothetical property being examined. This is substantially less than is possible under the 200 per cent declining-balance method, but still significantly larger than the amount recoverable under the straight-line method.

If the 150 per cent declining-balance method is employed, the taxpayer cannot switch at his option to the straight-line method. Formal written permission from the Internal Revenue Service is required in advance.

b. *Sum-of-the-Years Digits Method.*   The third major method of depreciation, and an alternative to the declining-balance method for rapid or accelerated recapture of investment in depreciable assets, is the so-called

Exhibit 20

ILLUSTRATION OF BUILDING COST RECOVERY BY VARIOUS METHODS OF DEPRECIATION

	STRAIGHT LINE		200% DECLINING-BALANCE		150% DECLINING-BALANCE		SUM-OF-THE-YEARS DIGITS		
Year	Annual Depreciation	Cumulative Depreciation	Annual Depreciation	Cumulative Depreciation	Annual Depreciation	Cumulative Depreciation	Annual Depreciation	Cumulative Depreciation	Fraction
1	$4,500	$ 4,500	$10,000	$10,000	$7,500	$ 7,500	$8,571	$ 8,571	20/210
2	4,500	9,000	9,000	19,000	6,938	14,438	8,143	16,714	19/210
3	4,500	13,500	8,100	27,100	6,417	20,855	7,714	24,428	18/210
4	4,500	18,000	7,290	34,390	5,936	26,791	7,286	31,714	17/210
5	4,500	22,500	6,561	40,951	5,491	32,282	6,857	38,571	16/210
6	4,500	27,000	5,905	46,856	5,079	37,361	6,429	45,000	15/210
7	4,500	31,500	5,314	52,170	4,698	42,059	6,000	51,000	14/210
8	4,500	36,000	4,783	56,953	4,346	46,405	5,571	56,571	13/210
9	4,500	40,500	4,305	61,258	4,020	50,425	5,143	61,714	12/210
10	4,500	45,000	3,874	65,132	3,718	54,143	4,714	66,428	11/210
11	4,500	49,500	3,487	68,619	3,439	57,582	4,286	70,714	10/210
12	4,500	54,000	3,138	71,757	3,181	60,763	3,857	74,571	9/210
13	4,500	58,500	2,824	74,581	2,943	63,706	3,429	78,000	8/210
14	4,500	63,000	2,542	77,123	2,722	66,428	3,000	81,000	7/210
15	4,500	67,500	2,288	79,411	2,518	68,946	2,571	83,571	6/210
16	4,500	72,000	2,059	81,470	2,329	71,275	2,143	85,714	5/210
17	4,500	76,500	1,853	83,323	2,154	73,429	1,714	87,428	4/210
18	4,500	81,000	1,668	84,991	1,993	75,422	1,286	88,714	3/210
19	4,500	85,500	1,501	86,492	1,843	77,265	857	89,571	2/210
20	4,500	90,000	1,351	87,843	1,705	78,970	429	90,000	1/210

Assumptions:

1. Cost of Building—$100,000
2. Salvage Value—$10,000
3. Useful Life—20 years

sum-of-the-years digits method. Under this approach, reasonable salvage value must be deducted from original cost in establishing the schedule of depreciation charges. This is illustrated in Exhibit 20. Each year, a changing fraction is applied to this "basis." The numerator of the fraction is the number of years of useful life remaining, and the denominator is the sum of the numbers representing the years of the property.[14]

Using as an example the material in Exhibit 20, a 20 year estimated useful life would result in a sum of the digits of 210. This is the sum of the series 1 through 20. The figure 210 is the denominator, and 210 units of depreciation are to be recovered during the 20 year useful life of the property. In the case of the property illustrated in Exhibit 20, $90,000 is recovered over the 20 year period.

The advantage of the sum-of-the-years digits method is that larger amounts of depreciation are allowed in the early years, since the numerator of the fraction is the number of years of estimated useful life remaining. Thus, in the first year 20/210 of $90,000 is recovered. In the second year, 19/210 of $90,000 is recovered, and so on.

As can be seen by a comparison of the figures in Exhibit 20, the sum-of-the-years digits method offers the largest amount of depreciation during the first ten years, even though the basis for the depreciation is cost less salvage value. There are, therefore, considerable advantages to the use of the sum-of-the-years digits method in most instances. However, only property which is new and occupied by the original user may be depreciated by this method, and advance written permission is required to transfer from the sum-of-the-years digits method to any other method.

Advantages and Limitations of Alternative Methods of Depreciation

While it is true that more rapid early depreciation may be obtained via methods other than the straight-line depreciation method, it does not follow that accelerated depreciation is *always* preferable. This is a trap into which the unwary investor can easily fall, and the industrial real estate specialist should see that he has the proper advice in each case.

The selection of the appropriate method of depreciation depends primarily on the objectives of the investor. There are penalties for taking rapid depreciation on investment real estate which is not held for a minimum of 120 months (10 years). This feature of the Internal Revenue Act of 1964 has caused many investors, whether they are also users or not, to reconsider the turnover of investment properties. If the turnover period is to be less than 10 years, then there are advantages in straight-line capital recapture. It avoids the danger that "excessive" depreciation will be treated as ordinary income.

Since not all investors have the same income tax status or liability, what is attractive to some investors may not have any tax advantage or investment attraction to others. When investment advice is to be given, the in-

---

[14] The formula for calculating the sum-of-the-years digits or denominator is: $S = N \frac{(N+1)}{2}$ where N = number of years of estimated useful life, and S = the sum of the digits.

dustrial real estate broker must know the specific objectives and status of the individual client, and tailor his recommendations to these needs.

If the investor is tax liable at ordinary income rates, and if his investment pattern can support a commitment of approximately 10 years, then accelerated depreciation has considerable advantages. In the first place, a larger amount of the investment in depreciable assets is recovered over the first 10 years of the useful life. This means a larger net cash flow during these 10 years.

Secondly, the gain at the time of disposition of the asset will be taxed on a long-term capital gains basis, rather than as ordinary income. Cash income flow is therefore larger, and the bulk of the cash income flow is received earlier in the income period, when it is less subject to future discounting.

The 200 per cent declining-balance method requires no estimate of salvage value in advance. It is also easier to transfer from the declining-balance method, if a change in accounting methods appears advisable. On the other hand, the sum-of-the-years digits method generally results in larger total depreciation charges during the first 10 years of the investment; it also requires an estimate of salvage value in advance, and written permission to change to another accounting method. The added depreciation that normally will be allowable usually makes the sum-of-the-years digits method preferable to the 200 per cent declining-balance method.

Depreciation Recapture: The Revenue Act of 1964

The Revenue Act of 1964 introduced the idea of recapture or disallowance of depreciation on investment real estate which is disposed of prior to the expiration of its estimated useful life. Such disallowance has two important effects: (1) the taxable income during the period in question is greatly increased, and is taxable at ordinary income tax rates, and (2) any gain realized at the time of disposition may also be regarded as ordinary income and taxed accordingly.[15]

The important concept introduced by the Revenue Act of 1964 is "additional depreciation." This is the excess of depreciation charged over what would be chargeable under the straight-line method during the estimated useful life of the real estate. Reference to Exhibit 20 will provide an illustration of what is involved. Any "additional depreciation" is initially taxable as ordinary income at the time the property is sold or exchanged. However, through a system of credits, this recapture can be reduced. The amount of the reduction depends upon the time period over which the property is held: the "holding period." Additional depreciation is defined as "the amount of depreciation taken *after 1963* in excess of straight-line depreciation. The amount recaptured is the applicable percentage times the lower of the following: (1) gain; (2) additional depreciation." [16]

There are three classes of holding periods. The distinctions are:

a. *Less Than 12 Months.* If the property is sold within one year, all

---

[15] For further details and Code citations, see Cerf, *op. cit.,* pp. 109–111.
[16] *Ibid.,* p. 110.

depreciation charges of any kind (whether straight-line or accelerated) will be recaptured as ordinary income. In addition, if the real estate is sold or exchanged within this 12-month period, any gain that is realized is taxable as ordinary income, and not as long-term capital gain.

b. *12 Months but Less Than 21 Months.* After the first year, there is no recapture of straight-line depreciation. Any excess of accelerated depreciation over straight-line depreciation charges is regarded as ordinary income and taxed accordingly.

c. *21 through 120 Months.* After 20 months have elapsed, the exact amount of depreciation recapture depends upon how many more months the property is held. For each full month beyond the 20th month that the property is held, a 1 per cent reduction in the amount of additional depreciation that is recoverable and taxable as ordinary income is credited to the taxpayer. Thus, with the passage of 100 months, a 100 per cent credit is earned. No additional depreciation exists for tax purposes, and there is no recovery of depreciation.

Since 120 months constitute 10 years, it is apparent that tax-sensitive investors will plan to hold industrial real estate approximately 10 years.

Form of Organization for Ownership

The form of organization owning industrial real estate can have important tax implications. Organization to accumulate funds for both equity investment and loan purposes is considered at length in Chapters 8 and 9. The purpose in mentioning them here is to indicate that there are tax issues which involve the form of organization. Expert tax advice is of critical importance *before* any commitment to invest in industrial real estate is made, or any real estate advice is given.

All the details and implications of organization for tax planning cannot be provided here. Major issues are noted, however, with citations for seeking out further details from appropriate sources.

In addition, there is no single best form or organization for all purposes or for all investors. Rather, the specific objectives, goals, and tax position of the individual investor must be weighed against the advantages, disadvantages, and implication of each of the forms of organization.

1. *Proprietorships and Partnerships.* Income earned by proprietorships and partnerships is taxable to the individuals involved at the appropriate rates, regardless of whether the earnings are actually distributed to the individual owners. Ordinary individual income tax rates apply. There is relatively little opportunity for accumulation of capital in a proprietorship or partnership. On the other hand, unincorporated business is not subject to the "double taxation" associated with the corporation.

Simplicity and flexibility are the outstanding characteristics of the partnership and the proprietorship, insofar as tax considerations are concerned. Moreover, there are fewer pitfalls or hazards to be avoided, since the opportunities for special treatment are extremely limited.

2. *Corporate Ownership of Real Estate.* Because corporate income tax rates are generally lower than individual income tax rates for compa-

rable levels of net income, there are often advantages in utilizing the corporate form, as opposed to the proprietorship or partnership. So long as the marginal rate of taxation is lower in the corporation, it becomes possible for the owner(s) to accumulate profits and then remove them at a later date in the form of capital gains. Since the major objective is to maximize the total cash flow after taxes to the investor, this opportunity has considerable appeal. It also has several serious hazards, most of which are so complex and detailed that they can only be mentioned here: [17]

Excessive Accumulations. One serious limitation to utilizing a corporation for the accumulations of earnings is the possibility that the accumulated earnings tax may be levied on "excessive" or "unreasonable" accumulations of earnings in excess of $100,000. This accumulated earnings tax is a penalty surtax imposed on corporation income for any year in which the corporation accumulated earnings to avoid tax on its shareholders. It is not imposed on the retained earnings, but is added to the normal tax and surtax imposed on the corporation's income.

Multiple Corporation. The surtax rate does not become effective until corporate income exceeds $25,000 per year. Therefore, there is a temptation to establish several corporations under the same ownership, each of which is to net less than $25,000 per year, and thereby reduce the total tax burden on the group. There are severe limitations on this practice, and extreme care should be exercised in attempting to undertake it. As in the case of most tax avoidance efforts, the penalties of failure are quite substantial.

Collapsible Corporations. A corporation might be organized for the purpose of taking long-term capital gains through liquidation before any taxable income has been realized. This would avoid any corporate income tax liability. If such a "collapsible corporation" is found to have been formed intentionally, the entire gain may be taxed as ordinary income, rather than as capital gain. This situation must be handled with extreme care.

Thin Incorporation. This term refers to a situation in which the debt in the capital structure greatly exceeds the stock. Often stockholders are creditors of the corporation as well. What purports to be interest income, and therefore deductible by the corporations as an operating expense, may be declared to be a dividend and hence not deductible. This is analogous to the situation in which high salaries to corporate officers who are also stockholders may be declared to be excessive, if in the judgement of the Internal Revenue Service (or ultimately the courts) such payments are made to avoid the double tax on dividends.

Personal Holding Companies. Corporations may be held to be personal holding companies, in which case they are subject to an extremely high rate of taxation. This is particularly true since the passage of the 1964 Revenue Act, which has had the effect of reclassifying many industrial real estate

---

[17] For a detailed discussion of forms of Ownership Organization, consult Cerf, *op. cit.,* Chapters 12 and 13.

companies as personal holding companies. Since the personal holding company tax is a substantial tax imposed on the undistributed earnings of closely held corporations (with income primarily from passive sources), it is extremely important to be familiar with the applicable rules under the Internal Revenue Code. This requires careful study and expert advice.[18]

Changing Character of Income. The character of income flowing through the corporation is changed as it goes to the owner-investor. For example, income which is a capital gain to the corporation may still be ordinary income to the shareholder; tax-exempt interest to the corporation may still be taxable income to the shareholder.

Despite these limitations, there are many situations in which the corporate form of organization is by far the most attractive for a real estate investment project, in view of tax considerations. It remains for the characteristics of the individual undertaking to be identified, and the particular goals of the participants to be identified, so that the tax implications can be evaluated in all of their ramifications.

3. *Trusts.* The trust form of organization has a number of advantages for the real estate investor. A private individual has opportunities to build estates for his heirs by legally avoiding one level of income taxation.[19]

Much more important, however, is the Real Estate Investment Trust (REIT). This offers considerable opportunities for large numbers of investors to take advantage of many features of corporate ownership, while avoiding the double taxation of the corporate form. The REIT is to real estate what the open end investment trust (the so-called mutual fund) is to the securities investment business. The REIT is subject to a number of specific requirements to qualify for special tax treatment under Sections 856–858 of the Internal Revenue Code. Trusts which qualify have tax advantages similar to those enjoyed by regulated investment companies. The most important consideration is that income which flows through the REIT to the beneficiaries or individual investors is generally not taxed at the REIT level.

Since the requirements for qualifications are many and complex, they are not detailed here.[20] It should be noted that there are four basic groups of tests to be met. These involve status requirements, gross income requirements, investments requirements, and distribution requirements.

Status requirements are those that relate to the organizational structure of the REIT. The most important is that the ownership of shares in the trust must be evidenced by transferable certificates. In addition, there must be at least 100 shareholders or owners throughout the year; management of the trust must be vested in one or more trustees who actually hold legal title to any real property owned by the organization; and the REIT must *not* hold property ordinarily for sale to customers.

---

[18] This issue is discussed in further detail in Cerf, *op. cit.,* pp. 293–300.
[19] Altman, *op. cit.*
[20] Details may be found in Cerf, *op. cit.,* pp. 255–269.

The gross income requirements establish minimum proportions of total receipts that must come from property income, and maximum proportion that may come from sales of real property.

The investment requirements essentially limit the investments of REIT's to equity investments and loans on income-producing real estate. Moreover, the income must be essentially passive; that is to say, the trust as such must not operate or manage the real estate.

The most important requirement with respect to distribution is that at least 90 per cent of income must be distributed to shareholders or trust certificate holders each year.

In exchange for adhering to these rather severe qualifying requirements, the REIT offers an important vehicle for providing some tax shelter to the small investor seeking to participate in real estate investment activity. In addition to its tax advantages and attractions, the REIT has other features which are considered in Chapters 8 and 9, where its uses as an investment device and a source of funds for industrial real estate are explored further.

Postponement or Deferment of Income

Because the income tax schedule is progressive, there are often substantial advantages to the taxpayer in being able to alter the timing of his apparent gain (or loss), and the tax liability associated with it. A number of devices exist which can be utilized to take advantage of such adjustments in timing. Generally speaking, they involve postponing or deferring tax payments to future years.

The details of each of these alternative techniques are such that they cannot be provided here. The broad outlines of each device are noted, and reference is made to appropriate sources for further study.[21]

The first alternative available to the industrial real estate investor is one which has been mentioned earlier. Gains and losses offset each other if they are realized in the same tax year. Through appropriate planning, an investor may take long-term capital gains in one year, and then take losses which are offsets to ordinary income in another year. This is not automatic, and it requires professional and expert advice. It is an opportunity for reducing tax payments, however, which cannot be overlooked.

Installment sales result in income which is taxable as it is collected. Installment sale treatment is permitted on sales of real property when no payment is made in the year of the sale, or where payments in the year of the sale do not exceed 30 per cent of selling price. Extreme care must be taken in meeting the requirements of "selling price" and "payment in year of sale." If not, the taxpayer may be denied use of the installment sale method. The advantage of using this method is that payments are spread out over several years and the *rate* at which the additional income is taxed may be substantially lower.

If the installment sale method cannot be used, it is occasionally possible to utilize the deferred-payment sales method instead. If the deferred-

---

[21] See in particular Cerf, *op. cit.*, Chapters 7 and 8.

payment sales method is employed, the seller reports no gain until pay-ments received by him equal the cost (or other basis) for the property transferred. Once the entire basis for the property is recovered, all of the remaining payments are taxable. The problem here is that all of the tax-able income is bunched in future years. Nevertheless, there may be attrac-tions in certain situations for this particular type of approach.

Finally, the lease or sale-leaseback arrangement often has the effect of deferring or postponing income until future years. The investment ad-vantages of the lease and the sale-leaseback are discussed at some length in Chapters 9 and 10. Here the only consideration is that of taxes. For the operating company, the most important consideration is that *all* operating expenses of the real estate, which take the form of rent, may be deductible.

Effect of Income Taxes on Industrial Real Estate Investment

The basic objective of many real estate investors is to maximize the flow of cash after taxes for the duration of the investment period. A secondary consideration is to concentrate as much of the after-tax cash flow in the early years as possible, since for such investors, income receivable soon has more attraction and more present worth than income receivable in the distant future.

With this basic objective, operating within the limits of federal income tax laws and regulations, the subsidiary goals of this type of real estate in-vestor are to have as small a taxable income as possible, and to have as small a proportion of that taxable income regarded as ordinary income as possible.

This pattern of objectives, when measured against the complexities of the progressive federal income tax system, results in several major influences on the industrial real estate investment decision process.

The investor in industrial real estate may exchange property rather than sell it, and thereby defer payment of any tax. As his equity grows, the owner of property used in a trade or business acquires successively more valuable properties without any current tax liability. There may be several successive exchanges before he must pay a tax.

Tax considerations can affect the type of action that an investor takes: purchase, retain or sell; lease or buy; invest in equity or debt. Even more important, tax considerations will decidedly affect the *timing* of the action. For example, an investor sensitive to tax considerations is effectively com-mitted to approximately a 10-year involvement in investment real estate under the 1964 Revenue Act, on the assumption that he chooses to take accelerated depreciation on the improvements.

Timing the realization of losses and of gains is also seriously affected. Whether income is to be realized in full, or deferred and obtained piece-meal, is a decision basically influenced by tax considerations.

Beyond this, the type of property that is acquired is often definitely in-fluenced by tax factors. There is a strong bias toward the acquisition of new properties about to be occupied by the original user, because more rapid depreciation is permitted on such properties. For tax-liable investors seeking primarily an income flow, properties with a high proportion of value in the improvements (as opposed to non-depreciable land) have a much higher attraction.

Tax considerations influence the form of organization through which real estate investment is made, and through which industrial real estate may be held. In particular, a considerable amount of stimulus has been given to the REIT as a result of the favorable tax treatment it receives.

Careful tax planning also permits individuals to build estates for their heirs on terms which would not otherwise be possible. In particular, the use of the private trust has increased because of its income tax status.

Given all of these important influences, it must be noted that a very serious responsibility still exists for the industrial real estate broker. Many potential real estate investors will have heard of tax advantages of investment real estate, and will assume naively that these are ready at hand to anyone who would take advantage of them. It cannot be emphasized too often, or too strongly, that expert advice is necessary in order to avoid the many pitfalls and traps that exist in the Internal Revenue Code for the unwary or unsophisticated investor. Finally, the industrial real estate specialist himself should not be blinded so that he forgets that not all investors want tax advantages, or need them. There are still many different types of investors with considerably different tax liabilities, and there is no one "best" investment for all investors, even in terms of tax liabilities.

Important as they are, income tax considerations represent only one aspect of the total spectrum of factors that should be taken into account in evaluating an industrial real estate investment opportunity. Tax considerations can influence, but rarely can they secure a transaction.

REAL PROPERTY TAXES

Local real property taxes can influence industrial real estate development, as well as the value of industrial real estate. Moreover, opportunities to realize capital gains or to trade on equity are seriously affected by the property tax treatment afforded industrial real estate.

Most states require real property to be assessed according to some standard such as true value, fair value, just value, or actual cash value. In Oregon, true cash value is the standard. It is defined as ". . . market value as of the assessment date." [22] This "true cash value" standard must be applied to all properties. Thus, in Oregon all property "shall be assessed at 25 per cent of its true cash value.[23]

California tax assessors are required to value real property at its full cash value. For this purpose the term full cash value means:

". . . the amount at which property would be taken in payment of a just debt from a solvent debtor." [24]

[22] *Oregon Revised Statutes.* Including 1961 Replacement Parts, Vol. 2, Section 308.205.
[23] *Ibid.,* Section 308.232.
[24] *Revenue Laws of California,* 1961, Division 1, Section 110.

Exhibit 21

AVERAGE ASSESSMENT RATIOS BY PROPERTY TYPES

Types of Property	Number of Sales	Per Cent of Total Number	Sales Value	Per Cent of Total Sales Value	Average Assessment Ratio
Single Family Dwellings	21,230	50.9%	$177,118,651	61.8%	18.9%
Vacant Land	12,524	30.0	22,832,049	8.0	19.3
Miscellaneous Improvements	5,396	12.9	44,906,709	15.7	21.3
Rural Property	1,511	3.6	16,826,177	5.9	21.6
Retail Stores	440	1.1	9,199,945	3.2	27.1
Duplex Dwellings	256	.6	2,991,260	1.0	21.1
Multiple Family Dwellings	228	.5	8,211,791	2.9	19.3
Motels	58	.1	2,345,668	.8	19.1
Industrial Improvements	36	.1	1,769,206	.6	32.6
Warehouses	34	.1	207,341	.1	37.7
All Property	41,713	99.9%	$286,408,797	100.0%	19.6%

SOURCE: William M. Shenkel, *A Study of Real Property Tax Assessments in the State of Washington* (Seattle, University of Washington Press, 1954), p. 11.

The California Constitution provides further that "all property in the state ... shall be taxed in proportion to its value...." [25] The proportion is set by the State Board of Equalization.

In New Jersey, the assessor is required to determine the full and fair value of each parcel of real property at such price for which it would sell at a fair, *bona fide* sale.[26] The courts of the state have held that the assessor has a mandate to assess local real properties at true value.[27]

Uniformity of real property assessments is a general and basic requirement imposed on most local tax assessors. Departure from this standard may penalize industrial property development, and may distort plant location decisions. Failure to treat all property uniformly represents tax discrimination.

In practice, however, industrial real estate is frequently over-valued in relation to other types of real property. One survey of 41,713 properties in the state of Washington concluded that apparent tax discrimination was practiced against industrial improvements, as measured by sales assessment ratios. To ascertain relative degrees of uniformity in the Washington study, all real estate sales prices during one year were compared with the assessed value for each property involved. Thus, a plant selling for $100,000 with an assessed value of $25,000 would have an assessment

[25] *Constitution of the State of California,* Article XIII, Section 1.
[26] *New Jersey Statutes Annotated,* Title 54:4–54.
[27] *Ibid.,* pp. 379–383.

ratio of 25 per cent. By averaging assessment ratios by property types, the degree of apparent tax discrimination existing among property types may be measured. Exhibit 21 indicates average assessment ratios developed by property types in the Washington survey.

Single family dwellings showed an average assessment ratio of 18.9 per cent, which was the lowest average assessment ratio among the 10 property types studied. The average assessment ratio for the 36 "industrial" improvements covered is 32.6 per cent, exceeded only by the average assessment ratio for 34 warehouses. Taken together, the average assessment ratios of 70 industrial properties are the highest for any property group among the 41,713 real estate sales covered.[28]

The impact of discriminatory assessments on individual properties may be indicated by the annual taxes levied against two properties with unequal assessment. For instance, a warehouse selling for $725,300 was assessed at 46 per cent of the sales price, or $333,638. A 60 mill tax levy applied against the assessed value resulted in an annual tax of $20,018. But if the same property were assessed at 17 per cent of the sales price, which was the average assessment level in this jurisdiction, the assessed value would have been $123,301. A 60 mill levy applied against this sum would produce an annual tax of $7,398. These figures are summarized below:

Sales Price	Assessment Ratio	Assessed Value	Tax Levy (60 mills)
$725,300	46.0	$333,638	$20,018
725,300	17.0	123,301	7,398
Differential		$210,337	$12,620

This constitutes an annual tax penalty of $12,620 against the industrial warehouse. The higher assessed value given the industrial warehouse, relative to the average assessment prevailing in the county, would penalize the industrial property owner. If the $12,620 resulting from the over-assessment were capitalized in perpetuity at 8 per cent ($12,620/.08), the negative impact of the tax differential is equal to a capital sum of $157,750. This is a substantial deterrent to locating in the county in question.

Real property taxes represent one of the expenses of ownership. Negative tax differentials tend to lower the value of industrial property and the investment attractiveness of the community in question. Conversely, however, relatively low tax burdens on industrial property can encourage or even stimulate industrial investment and development in an area.

---

[28] Assessment ratios by property type is not a common basis for tax analysis; however, for similar data showing the degree of nonuniformity in assessments by property type, see Report of the Senate Interim Committee on State and Local Taxation, *Property Assessment and Equalization in California*, Part 6 (Sacramento: California Legislature, 1953 Regular Session, 1953), Appendix E, pp. 313–370.

SELECTED REFERENCES

Altman, David, "Tax Factors Affecting Industrial Real Estate." *Advanced Course in the Techniques of Industrial Real Estate* (Washington, Society of Industrial Realtors, 1964).

California Real Estate Association, *Real Estate Investment Property* (Los Angeles, The Author, 1964).

Cerf, Alan R., *Real Estate and the Federal Income Tax* (Englewood Cliffs, N.J., Prenticc-Hall, 1965).

Commerce Clearing House, Inc., *Revenue Act of 1964 with Explanation* (Chicago, Commerce Clearing House, Inc., 1964).

Floyd, J. S., Jr., *Effects of Taxation on Industrial Location* (Chapel Hill, University of North Carolina Press, 1952).

Institute for Business Planning, Inc., *Hidden Gold and Pitfalls in the New Tax Law*. A special report (New York, Institute for Business Planning, Inc., 1964).

Kahn, Sanders A.; Case, Fred E.; and Schimmel, Alfred A., *Real Estate Appraisal and Investment* (New York, Ronald Press, 1963).

Maisel, Sherman J., *Financing Real Estate: Principles and Practices* (New York, McGraw-Hill Book Co., 1965).

Philadelphia Industrial Development Corporation, *Federal Income Tax Aspects of Industrial Property Transactions,* Revised (Philadelphia, The Author, 1965).

Prentice-Hall, Inc., *A Careful Look at the New Real Estate Investment Trusts.* Special report (Englewood Cliffs, N.J., Prentice-Hall, Inc., 1962).

Prentice-Hall, Inc., *Explanation of the New Federal Income Tax Law* (Englewood Cliffs, N.J., Prentice-Hall, Inc., 1964).

Sawyer, J. D., "Industrial Property Investment Opportunities," *Advanced Course in the Techniques of Industrial Real Estate* (Washington, Society of Industrial Realtors, 1964).

PART II

Major Functions of the
Industrial Real Estate Broker

6 | Marketing Industrial Space

IF buyers and sellers cannot be brought together; if landlords and tenants cannot be induced to reach mutually beneficial agreements; if potential investors cannot reach appropriate, informed decisions; if industrial firms cannot find appropriate locations and plants for their activities—then the market will be chaotic and the entire economy, as well as the individual participants involved, will suffer.

The industrial real estate broker facilitates the marketing or merchandising of industrial space. He is the focal point in most industrial real estate transactions. There are others who participate in every industrial real estate transaction, as well as even more who are occasional participants: the buyer, the seller, the landlord, the tenant, the lender, the investor, the accountant, the attorney, the engineer, the economist, the architect, the builder or developer, the appraiser, the utility or railroad representative, the community industrial development executive, the real estate staff member of the industrial firm. Each of these has his own interests, but each has one important concern in common with all the others: the need to rely on a professional industrial real estate specialist who is knowledgeable in all the areas which impinge on the particular transaction or decision.

The industrial real estate broker is essential to every transaction. He must know more than any other single participant in the transaction about the implications and ramifications of the particular set of circumstances involved.

A Note on Terminology

A broker is a person who serves as intermediary to bring together two or more participants in a market transaction. In the field of real estate, licensing has led to a sharp distinction in the meanings of the terms "broker" and "salesman." However, since the licensing requirements vary widely from state to state, and since the *functions* performed by both "broker" and "salesman" are typically the same, no effort is made to distinguish between the two terms in this presentation.

For purposes of this discussion, an industrial real estate broker is a person who, for a fee, serves the interests of a participant in a proposed transfer of industrial space: whether site or building, and whether by sale or lease. Thus, the terms industrial real estate broker, industrial real estate salesman, industrial real estate specialist, and industrial real estate practitioner will be one, and refer to the same person. Care must be taken, however, to distinguish carefully the meaning of the term "S.I.R." Such a person is a professionally designated member of the Society of Industrial Realtors, which is an affiliate of the National Association of Real Estate Boards.

DISTINGUISHING CHARACTERISTICS OF INDUSTRIAL REAL ESTATE BROKERAGE

The characteristics that make industrial real estate brokerage a separate area of activity are differences primarily of degree and of emphasis. Nevertheless, they add up to a demanding range of requirements on the industrial real estate specialist. The basic, underlying principles of real estate brokerage still prevail;[1] the distinctions may be listed under eight major headings:

1. *More Technical Information Required.* Industrial real estate brokerage tends to be highly specialized, primarily because it is an important blend of technical knowledge and persuasive negotiation. The most persuasive salesman, however, cannot hope to succeed in the field of industrial real estate without a thorough understanding of industry's requirements for space.

2. *More Effort Involved Per Transaction.* The specific needs of both the industrial user (who may be a buyer or a tenant) and the owner (who may be a builder or an investor, or another industrial firm) must be carefully analyzed before an appropriate match of desires and conditions can be effected. Normally, this takes a considerable period of time. For example, one broker indicates that a major proportion of his business comes in the form of requests to sell or lease existing buildings for which there is no apparent buyer or no apparent tenant on the market at the time of the listing.

It is not uncommon for an industrial transaction to require between 18 months and two years from the date of listing to the actual consummation of the sale or lease. The market is quite thin for highly specialized properties, and the requirements of industrial users are themselves often highly specialized. Moreover, larger corporations often require substantial periods of time for the appropriate resolutions to pass the board of directors, following a series of recommendations on the part of administrators and officers.

---

[1] *See,* for example, the discussions in Frederick E. Case, *Real Estate* (Englewood Cliffs, N.J., Prentice-Hall, 1962); Frederick E. Case, *Real Estate Brokerage* (Boston, Allyn and Bacon, 1965); James C. Downs, *Principles of Real Estate Management,* rev. ed. (Chicago, Institute of Real Estate Management, 1959); Edith J. Friedman, ed., *Real Estate Encyclopedia* (Englewood Cliffs, N.J., Prentice-Hall, 1960).

A corollary is that most industrial listings are exclusives, which generally run from three months to a year.

3. *Time Is Often More Important.* Despite the low turnover rate for industrial property, speed is often extremely important for the industrial real estate broker in the performance of his assignment. Many industrial organizations tend to delay in making the decision to seek additional or new space. As a result, there is often a considerable amount of rush involved in the selection of a site or the acquisition of additional building space. Therefore, the broker must be prepared to act promptly without skimping on any of the necessary major steps in bringing buyer and seller (or landlord and tenant) together, for their mutual benefit and satisfaction. This requires a highly organized and systematically arranged set of files (considered in detail in Chapter 7), as well as a current and effective set of business contacts to help locate the type of space required on relatively short notice.

4. *More Specialization and More Broker Cooperation.* The necessity to move effectively and promptly generally leads to specialization on the part of industrial brokers and their organizations. They tend to become more versed in the requirements of specific industries, or in certain types of buildings, or in specific geographic areas. Since the market area for a particular type of plant may cover several regions of the United States, it is usually not possible for a single industrial broker to cover all the possibilities. As a result, industrial real estate brokerage firms tend to have several staff members. In addition, there is an extremely high degree of cooperation, referral, and joint effort among industrial brokers, and most especially among members of the Society of Industrial Realtors. This affords much wider coverage to both properties listed for sale or lease, and the needs of industrial organizations seeking additional space.

5. *More Emphasis on Serving The User.* The industrial real estate broker normally is compensated through a commission from the owner or seller of the real estate when it is sold or leased. Yet, industrial real estate brokers estimate that between 75 and 80 per cent of the total effort that they make is in behalf of *users* of industrial space, seeking to meet their locational requirements. In doing so, however, they are also serving the interests of owners who have listed their property with the broker. Meeting both sets of obligations requires a particularly good working knowledge of the space and locational requirements of individual industrial firms, as well as a technical knowledge of the patterns of industrial real estate activity.

Real estate activity often moves by industrial classifications. For example, reference to the *Standard Industrial Classification Manual* would reveal that a fabricator of insert barrels for fountain pens and ball point pens is in the same "industry" as the fabricator of conductor tubing in home appliances. Because they use the same equipment, the same raw materials, and essentially the same labor skills, they have many of the same space and locational requirements. One S.I.R. in southern California has utilized this approach most effectively in filling vacant plants, as well as in attracting new industries to existing industrial developments.

Many brokers contend that they generally have more control over the purchaser or tenant than they have over the owner. The broker's job is to "educate" the user in his needs and requirements, and then to show him listings from his inventory which meet these requirements.

6. *More "Package Deals."* The industrial real estate broker is much more likely to be the creator or the coordinator of a total package for sale or lease. That is to say, he may be called upon to assemble a site, arrange for construction, arrange for lease and/or sale, arrange financing, and arrange for management over the term of a lease. This type of activity is rare in real estate practice, with the exception of the creation of a shopping center complex in the commercial field. In order to achieve this result effectively, the broker must be skilled in a wide variety of fields, as well as being able to obtain the best possible technical assistance in each of the fields.

7. *Participation by More Public and Private Agencies.* In industrial real estate transactions, major participants often include public utility companies, railroads, community development corporations, and such public agencies as redevelopment commissions—as well as industrial firms themselves. This means that the industrial broker may be simultaneously cooperating with and competing with representatives of these organizations. Each group seeks to achieve its own particular ends. If he is to operate effectively, the broker must recognize the interests of these various participants in industrial real estate transactions, and adjust his behavior to that recognition.

8. *Emphasis on Function.* In general, it can be said that "industry buys or leases *utility or function* with all other considerations being of lesser significance. Industrial prospects are looking for the building which will accommodate the specific manufacturing or distributive use with the greatest efficiency." [2] While literature on industrial location is replete with examples of capricious decision-making on the part of industrial managements, the overwhelming opinion of industrial real estate specialists is that dollars and cents generally are considerably more persuasive than are amenities or personal considerations.

Thus, industrial real estate brokerage can be distinguished from other real estate practice on the following basis: "the sale [or lease] of industrial real estate is based on more detailed and technical facts than either commercial or residential property. The property must suit the particular needs of a specific [user], and the broker negotiating the sale [or lease] must understand how those problems can be met." [3]

CRITICAL ROLE OF THE INDUSTRIAL REAL ESTATE BROKER

Because the typical industrial real estate market is essentially uninformed, stratified, highly specialized, and usually thin, an industrial real estate broker "clears the market," or acts as a clearing house for industrial property in

---

[2] Statement by B. H. Waterbury, Jr. (Vice-President, Industrial Realty Co., Inc., Baltimore, Maryland), June 22, 1966.

[3] Howell H. Watson, "Selling Industrial Real Estate," *Real Estate Encyclopedia* (Englewood Cliffs, N.J., Prentice-Hall, Inc., © 1960), p. 175.

the interests of both buyers and sellers. Through his "inventory" of exclusive listings, he matches the requirements of buyer, seller and user.

A Further Note on Terminology

The industrial real estate broker may serve either the owner of the real estate or the potential user (or even both). It is important that the proper terms be applied to each of these individuals. The chief difficulty lies in a tendency on the part of many writers and practitioners to use the term "client" to refer to either the owner of the real estate, or the industrial firm seeking space, or both. This becomes a particular problem when the potential user of the space is called the "client," and yet the broker is looking to the owner for his compensation.

In order to avoid this difficulty, and at the same time to utilize terminology that is widely and appropriately employed in the market, the owner of the real estate is referred to here as the owner, the seller, the landlord, or the lessor. While some practitioners call this individual the "listing," this term is not included to avoid confusion between an individual and the property that he owns.

The industrial firm seeking space is variously the user, the industry, the prospect, the purchaser, the tenant, or the lessee. Some practitioners also call the user the "customer." However, that term is rather ambiguous.

If the purchaser or lessee does not intend to use the space, but is an investor instead, the terms purchaser, prospect, lessee, or investor are used.

Importance of the Broker and Brokerage

As an informed practitioner, the industrial real estate broker must be in a position to offer comprehensive service to either buyer or seller (tenant or landlord). By studying both the market and the property, he identifies who and what the occupant of the space *should be.* Then he goes about the important task of finding that occupant and bringing him to the owner. Finally, through the critical and basic process of negotiation, he brings buyer and seller, or landlord and tenant, into agreement. Industrial space usually cannot be marketed without this coordinating function on the part of the broker.

Custom Tailored Transactions

One of the outstanding characteristics of industrial real estate practice is the fact that rarely are two transactions exactly the same. The terms and conditions of the sale or lease have to be custom tailored to fit the needs and requirements of all the principals in each case. It is a highly individualized procedure, in which the central role of the broker requires ingenuity, imagination, flexibility, and adaptability. Because brokerage in essence involves solving a problem, the more resourceful the individual broker, the greater the chances that he will be successful in serving the needs of both user and owner in any given transaction.

Needed by Both Owners and Users

The services of the industrial real estate broker can result in savings to the owner by disposing of the property. Vacant industrial space is expensive to maintain or carry, and inappropriately used industrial space can result in an operating loss.

The more specialized the real estate, the more difficult it will be to attract a purchaser or user readily. In many instances, the broker must develop a program of change or rehabilitation to make the property marketable. In other cases, he must literally "create" a market for the property. This requires detailed knowledge of the uses to which the property can profitably be put.

In order to do the job effectively, the broker must have an exclusive listing, whether for sale or for lease. The point cannot be emphasized too strongly that the merchandise moves much more quickly (and generally on better terms) when the broker has an exclusive listing.

Owners of remote plants, plants or sites in small cities, highly specialized plants, and vacant space particularly need the assistance of an industrial broker. While the broker must often work to convince the owner to accept a reasonable offer, this is generally easier to do with industrial than with residential or even commercial property owners. As one authority states, "No one is as cooperative as the owner of vacant industrial real estate." [4]

Industrial firms also need the assistance of brokers in finding an appropriate site, or the most suitable type of space for their needs. As noted previously, many firms delay making a decision to seek additional space until they really need it. Then they often do not know what they really want or need, and have no idea how to go about looking for it. All they know is that they need it quickly.

This is particularly true of industrial firms making expansion moves. Often this is such a major decision that it is deferred until the need for space is beyond the critical point. As a result, the services of a broker become absolutely vital.

In addition, many S.I.R.'s state that they have a responsibility to assist small, new firms serving regional and local markets to grow and develop. This type of work is not always particularly lucrative, but it sometimes leads to repeat business when the locations are successful.

In brief, the industrial real estate broker is needed to "educate" the principals in the industrial real estate transaction. To the extent that they are convinced of the appropriateness of his work and his recommendations, substantial savings in time, effort and money can be realized by both user and owner.

FUNCTIONS OF THE INDUSTRIAL REAL ESTATE BROKER

The industrial real estate broker *executes* the principles of industrial real estate practice. Certain major areas of activity are particularly sensitive to skillful handling by a professional adviser.

The primary responsibility of the industrial real estate broker is to provide service to his clients. To the extent that he successfully markets the space, the broker serves his client.

---

[4] Statement by B. H. Waterbury, Jr. (Industrial Realty Co., Inc., Baltimore).

A list of industrial real estate functions developed by S.I.R. Richard P. Robarts includes nine areas of activity: [5]

Selling	Building	Appraising
Buying	Developing	Financing
Leasing	Managing	Advising (Counseling)

From this list, those activities which comprise the *marketing* of space are: selling, leasing, managing, and counseling. Actually, the activities of the industrial real estate broker overlap to such a degree that the preparation of lists of functions becomes a sterile task. For analytical purposes, however, it is useful to distinguish the major functions of sales, leasing, and management; and to consider what peculiar characteristics each possesses in the area of industrial real estate brokerage. Basic texts in the appropriate areas provide additional background and exposure to the basic principles.[6]

In each of these functions, it is important to recall that *negotiation* is a key role. It is through negotiation that the broker achieves his fundamental objective of marketing the industrial space.

Sales Brokerage

In carrying out the key role of negotiation for the sale of industrial space, the broker has been characterized as "the counselor between buyer and seller to effect a proper meeting of the minds between them." [7] On the assumption that he is properly and adequately compensated, the particular responsibility of the broker is to fulfill industry's need to merchandise "problem" properties. The special-purpose or single-use industrial plant; the obsolescent multistory plant with inadequate parking; the warehouse with insufficient ceiling heights; the plant with inadequate column spacing; the building with outmoded floor-bearing capacities; the superadequate reinforced concrete structure—all of these represent the real challenge for the industrial real estate broker. When he demonstrates that he can handle problems of this sort, then the "easy" jobs will tend to come his way as well.

Finding a suitable site or adequate space quickly for an industrial firm represents one challenge of sales brokerage in serving users. The major requirement here is a good "inventory" of listings or space known to be available.

In serving both his own and his customers' interests most effectively, the broker should be sure to show a potential purchaser all *known* sites or buildings that appear to serve his needs. Then the impression is created, quite properly, that the broker has the best interest of all parties in mind, and is not simply pushing properties because he happens to have them among his own listings.[8] This, incidentally, can be an important source of additional

---

[5] Mr. Robarts is associated with the firm of Paul Robarts & Co., Ltd., Windsor, Ontario, Canada.
[6] E.g., Case, *Real Estate;* Case, *Real Estate Brokerage;* Downs, *op. cit.;* Friedman, *op. cit.*
[7] Statement by Thomas J. Daly, S.I.R. (James H. Burns Co., Inc., New York City).
[8] Frank A. Schlesinger, "Techniques in the Successful Operation of an Industrial Brokerage Office," *Advanced Course in the Techniques of Industrial Real Estate* (Washington, Society of Industrial Realtors, 1964).

business, as reported in many interviews with S.I.R.'s throughout the country.

Finally, it is imperative that appropriate information be available to the broker so that he can both analyze the property, and accommodate the requirements or needs of industrial customers when they approach him for assistance in finding appropriate space. This means that good working files of data must be developed and maintained on *all* known industrial sites and industrial buildings available for sale (or lease) in the broker's market area. Exhibits 22 and 23 illustrate the kinds of forms that can be utilized for this purpose. They demonstrate that appropriate information can be maintained on a single 8½″ x 11″ sheet, for future reference and filing. While they do not provide complete coverage of all material that might be needed in any conceivable eventuality, they do represent good coverage of basic information needed by the industrial broker.

Leasing

One of the nation's leading authorities on industrial real estate leasing has characterized the marketing of space and the negotiating of a lease as the essence of industrial real estate brokerage.[9] He goes on to note that industrial leasing is based upon exactly the same principles and techniques that underlie leasing of other types of real estate. In general, "the techniques are the same, but more technical knowledge and more effort are required to negotiate the lease." [10] The unique problems which distinguish *industrial* real estate leasing are essentially: (1) leasing unimproved land; (2) leasing new structures built to suit the tenant, whether on a direct lease or on a sale and leaseback arrangement; and (3) leasing existing industrial buildings which require adaptation to new use.

The basic role of the broker in leasing is negotiation. Skillful negotiation has been characterized as the single most important ingredient among the necessary functions of the industrial broker.[11] Leasing of industrial real estate consists of: (1) examining the property to ascertain what its uses are; (2) finding a suitable tenant or tenants; (3) showing the property to prospective tenants; (4) negotiating the terms of the lease; (5) having the lease reduced to writing; and (6) having the lease signed by all parties. It is, therefore, a sales device. Leasing represents one alternative method of merchandising industrial space.

In order to do an effective job of leasing, the broker must be sensitive to the market. He must know the uses to which the property can effectively be put, and what type of tenant is most likely to be attracted to the space in question. In negotiating a lease, he must also know what elements he can afford to give up without jeopardizing the position of his principal.

---

[9] Irving Korb, "Light Industrial Properties," *Training Manual for Real Estate Salesmen,* Sacramento Metropolitan Real Estate Offices, Inc. (Lafayette, California, D. B. Campbell, 1957).

[10] Heath Angelo, "Leasing Techniques in a Surplus Market," *Real Estate Investment Opportunities* (Los Angeles, California Real Estate Association, 1965).

[11] Korb, *op. cit.*

B & F REALTY, INC.
PHONE 522-0175

FROM THE DESK OF
FRANK A. VITE

Exhibit 22

LAND INFORMATION SHEET

Description   Date:

Location:

Area:

Condition:

Zone:

Topography:

City or County:

Rail Facility:

Utilities

              Size   *Location*

Gas:

Water:

Sanitary Sewer:

Storm Water:

Other Information

Transportation:

Neighborhood:

Assess/Taxes:

Project Information Sheet

Owner: Tele:

Agent: Tele:

Price: Plat #

Remarks:

Industrial Realty Company, Inc., Baltimore.

In viewing leasing as an alternative to sale, the industrial broker must be prepared to show the advantages (if any) of leasing to both owner and user. As to the owner, he must be able to indicate the attractions of receiving a competitive rental for the space, as compared with either leaving it empty or selling outright at a loss. To the user, the broker must often overcome a prejudice against multiple occupancy. For many firms, this is simply the only possibility of obtaining adequate space. The desire to occupy modern, single-tenant industrial space is not always backed up with sufficient purchasing

Exhibit 23

IMPROVED PROPERTY INFORMATION SHEET

Louis Schlesinger Company
REAL ESTATE
901 BROAD STREET
NEWARK 2, N.J.   MARKET 2-6500

Vol.
FILE   PLATE

DATE

LOCATION   ZONE

OWNER   SEE

ADDRESS   TELEPHONE

Bldg. No.	Stories	Construc- tion	Floor Area	Sq. Ft. Area	Ceiling Height	Floor Cap.	Bays	Heat	Elevator	Window Light	Sprinkled	Power	Toilets	Blueprint	Survey

Size of Plot	Boilers	H.P.	Water	Gas
Acres	Engine	H.P.	Sewer	Wells
R.R. Siding Feet	Generators		Labor	
Waterfront			Electricity	
Depth Riparian Rights			Transit Facilities	

Remarks

When Built	Architect	Present Occupant	Rental Expiration
Tax Rate	Taxes	Ins. Building Rate Contents	Possession
Assessed Value	Building Land	Unpaid Assessments	Restrictions

Remarks:

Sale Price	Terms	Rental Price	No. of Years
First Mortgage	@ Due	Second Mortgage	@ Due
Held By		Held By	

Amortization

Remarks:

Sign	Size	Where Placed
Listed by	Inspected by	

Louis Schlesinger Company, Newark.

power. New or growing firms in particular find occupancy of a multitenant structure most feasible for them.

Tenant selection is often a major function in leasing. This is particularly true for multiple-occupancy buildings, in which several basic rules must be observed. For example, tenants affect fire insurance rates. Firms categorized as being in the furniture industry almost invariably require extremely high fire insurance rates. The leasing agent might well try to concentrate such users in one or a few buildings, rather than scattering them among all those being handled. This can produce a substantial saving in overall rates.

Similarly, special attention should be paid to zoning requirements and restrictions. The use definitions in local zoning regulations do not necessarily follow economic or business logic. It can be a source of both embarrassment and potential legal action if a tenant is restrained from using space for which a lease has already been negotiated.

Floor-weight requirements should be studied particularly carefully, because multiple-story buildings represent serious hazards if excessive weights are placed on upper stories. Tables of load-bearing capacities and weight requirements should be a basic element of every industrial broker's reference library. The leasing agent must also have some knowledge of specific business operations in order to avoid a serious floor-weight problem.

Most importantly, the leasing agent must be alert to the continuing problem of tenant compatibility. If the tenants or uses compete seriously for available facilities, or restrict the efficiency of one another's operations, then additional management problems will arise. Moreover, greater turnover and vacancy can very easily result. As an example, bookbinders tend to require a considerable amount of elevator time and use, and thus experienced leasing agents try to avoid putting them on upper stories.

In summary, the responsibility of the industrial real estate broker in leasing is to attract and select tenants who will keep the building completely and continuously occupied at competitive rentals. Once the tenants have been attracted and selected, it is his responsibility to negotiate, on behalf of the owner, leases that promise the best approximation of the owner's desires and expectations of return.

Industrial Property Management

Management has been characterized as "keeping tenants happy." With many tenants this is virtually impossible. Nevertheless, many of the activities of the industrial real estate manager are directed toward the achievement of this goal.

The management of industrial real estate is often tied in with leasing. In many instances, however, leasing may be separate from the management of the property. This is particularly, but not exclusively, true when there are multiple tenancies and an absentee landlord. In this case, the interests of the owner must be maintained *vis-a-vis* those of the tenants, and the property must be adequately and appropriately maintained.

In some areas, such as Philadelphia, a separate fee is not usually charged for management. It is included under a leasing contract. In other areas, such as Cleveland, a separate fee is usually charged for management only when there is multiple tenancy of the building. In still other areas, such as Bridgeport, Connecticut, a separate fee is normally charged for management, because management is regarded as separate from leasing.

Whatever the local arrangements or customs, there *is* a distinction between the function of leasing, which represents merchandising the space by attracting tenants and negotiating leases, and the management of the property, which consists of collecting rents and maintaining the physical condition of the real estate in accordance with the requirements and wishes of the owner.

In loft buildings which contain several tenants, management is almost always necessary. Turnover is greater, and leases typically do not require the tenant to maintain major segments of the building. Moreover, there are common or public facilities and areas for which no single tenant or group of tenants would normally assume responsibility.

Whatever the type of occupancy, however, there is one important point that should be emphasized repeatedly to any absentee (i.e., nonoccupant) landlord: a lease is meaningless unless it is enforced. This is more than simply a legal matter. In most instances, even if it could be accomplished fairly quickly, owners would prefer not to have to litigate every point on which nonperformance by a tenant is observed. They would rather identify the problem areas, and work out a continuing program of reminders to see that the building is being maintained, to see that it is not being damaged, and to see that no violations of the lease terms are being permitted or undertaken by the tenant.

The industrial real estate broker, in his capacity of manager, can enforce the responsibilities of the tenant, whether in a single-tenant building or in a multiple-tenant building. There are many conditions of leases which must be observed continuously if they are to be effectively enforced. For example, a provision that the building is not to be altered without prior approval of the owner can be more effective if periodic inspections are undertaken, than it would be if the only recourse were legal action after the fact.

In addition to enforcing the terms and conditions of the lease as they pertain to tenant responsibilities, periodic inspection and analysis of the property can provide the owner with information on necessary maintenance or repairs. This can forestall major structural difficulties. Indeed, a periodic program of inspection by a knowledgeable broker is a sound practice even for owner-occupied industrial buildings, if a program of internal inspection on the part of the firm's own engineers is not possible. Thus, the majority of industrial buildings need some professional management service. An industrial brokerage organization equipped to manage properties has both the procedures and the staff to maintain the property and to keep it in operation as an effective income-producing entity.

In addition to providing for preventive maintenance, the industrial broker can usually indicate areas in which operating costs can be cut. A distinguishing characteristic of industrial real estate, as opposed to commercial or residential real estate, is that many more aspects of the maintenance and operation of the building tend to be automated. That is to say, automatic boiler controls or self-service elevators are more prevalent in industrial buildings than in commercial or residential buildings.

Moreover, the owner of an industrial building generally has fewer maintenance problems. The hours of service of many facilities, such as heat, elevator, and the like, will be specified in the lease contract. Also, owners of multiple-tenant industrial buildings often buy utilities (especially electricity) at wholesale rates and then resell the services to their tenants at retail rates. This is a very important source of income in many multiple-tenant buildings. The services of an expert manager-broker are required to advise on the methods and pricing techniques that will maximize the benefit to the owner from the sale of utilities.

Whether it is regarded as separate from leasing or not, as far as compensation is concerned, management is an important function that the industrial real estate broker must often perform for the owner-client. It must be integrated with leasing so as to keep the building completely and continuously occupied at appropriate rental levels, thereby maximizing the gains to both the owner and the broker.

REQUIREMENTS OF THE INDUSTRIAL REAL ESTATE BROKER

The background requirements of the professional industrial real estate broker include the entire range of materials in this book. He should have a good working knowledge of each of the topic areas, as well as sufficient experience and insight to be able to apply them to the specific problems, and the specific areas, with which he is working.

Within this broad framework, however, there are specific requirements that are really basic. They are necessary if the broker is to function effectively *at all*. Knowledge of these important matters will make a good impression on the prospect as well as on the owner, in discussing their respective needs with them. At the same time, it is axiomatic that if the broker does not know the answer to a question, or have a certain piece of factual information at his disposal *immediately,* his course of action is to admit it openly. He should then immediately find the answer and supply the owner or user with it. This has two advantages. First, it does show that the broker is honest and straightforward in his dealings, and secondly it shows that he is interested enough in the problem at hand to make an extra effort to assist the party or parties involved.

Know the Market

The entire framework of economic, social, and political influences that surround the property in question should be understood by the broker. Perhaps the most important single problem is to identify precisely what the market is. That is to say, what properties are actually competing with the property in question? Furthermore, what uses or users represent the range of possible occupants (either as purchasers or tenants) of the property?

Standard Industrial Classification analysis can be extremely helpful in identifying alternative users for a particular industrial building or site.

The most important single source of information in keeping current with the market is the broker's own data file. If the information is filed and classified so that access is quick and easy, the data will indicate the type of space certain users are looking for, as well as the type of user likely to be attracted to a particular type of building or location.

If time permits, it is always recommended that the industrial broker engage in a formal feasibility study. This involves a careful analysis of the current market situation, the requirements of the particular user or users, and the competition for the particular space being considered. It will draw on listing information and other data in the files of the broker, as well as background market studies made by others: chambers of commerce, industrial development commissions, banks and lending institutions, and area universities.

The industrial broker must study the local situation to find out what agencies or groups will provide help. This would include chambers of commerce, utilities, lending institutions, and the like. From which sources is he likely to receive useful information? This is a matter of experience, but it must be gained prior to his actually being on an assignment. It can be very expensive information to obtain when trying to serve a client. Moreover, the broker must know the local policies and regulations affecting industrial real estate. These include zoning and other land use controls, the granting of exceptions for land use or building permits, and their enforcement.

Familiarity with the local scene involves knowing what is going on in the area. This can often be achieved simply through a careful reading of local newspapers, study of public and private reports that are published in and about the area, and continuing conversations with knowledgeable people. Analysis of the territory and of the local market situation should make the broker aware of the appropriate units of marketability for particular types of industrial real estate. This can be especially useful when advising a client about the disposition of a plant or warehouse. Knowing the most marketable units in an area can lead to useful and time-saving advice. For example, one S.I.R. discovered that existing industrial space in his area was most marketable in units of approximately 10,000 square feet for small fabricating establishments. As a result, he was able to move a 60,000-square-foot plant readily. After advising that it be divided into six sections (which was feasible and practicable in this instance), he leased out the six sections to compatible tenants. This simple illustration points up the necessity of knowing the appropriate merchandising units in the market area in which the property is located.

Knowledge of the market also entails an awareness of the current inventory of industrial space in the area, the sources of money and the terms of financing, and the level and trend of prices. Many industrial real estate brokers include an analysis of the market area and the market environment in forms that they utilize for gathering information about a property. Exhibit 24 gives a list prepared by one specialist indicating information which, in his opinion, the broker *must know* in order to merchandise any industrial property properly.[12]

Exhibit 24

NECESSARY INFORMATION FOR INDUSTRIAL REAL ESTATE BROKER IN ORDER TO MERCHANDISE PROPERTY PROPERLY

1. *Location*—In addition to the street address, the broker must have a legal description sufficiently complete so that it could be incorporated in a lease.
2. *Lot Size*—With all due respect to the owner (many of them are correct) a check of the block books for the exact dimensions should be made.
3. *Building Size*—Exact building size should be determined by personally measuring or pacing, and then computing the exact square footage.
4. *Construction of Building*—Is the construction of concrete, or block, or brick, or frame material? Is it a tight building? Will it retain heat?
   a. Is it a clear-span building (meaning no posts)—if there are posts, how many and where located?
   b. *Electric Service*—110V; 220V (single phase or three phase), wall plugs, etc.?
   c. *Air Conditioning*—Is there such a system in the building (most often not)?
   d. *Lighting*—Natural window, skylights, type of lighting fixtures?
   e. *Heating*—How many heaters, where located, approximate cost of heating?
   f. *Floor*—Condition, cement or other type, load factor, floor drains?
   g. *Truck Loading Facilities*—How many truck doors, what size? Will traffic be impeded by their use?
   h. *Office Space*—How many private offices, general offices, room for how many desks?
   i. *Toilet Facilities*—Is there a men's, women's; for shop as well as office?
   j. *Floor Clearance*—How many feet (exactly) clearance between the floor and the bottom of roof trusses?
5. *City or County Zoning*—Specific legal zoning; how many limitations? Many times a use is permitted within a particularly zoned area which at first appearance seems quite contrary to the zoning law. A complete familiarization of such restrictions is a must for a broker operating in this field.
6. *R.R. Spur Facilities*—Usually light industrial properties are not concerned with rail; however, there may be cases where some light industrial property owners may require rail which in most cases would put them in the so-called "heavy industrial" zoning portion of the city (but should not preclude you from working with them).
7. *Public Transportation Facilities*—Sometimes necessary, always an advantage.
8. *Parking*—Employees and customer—space off-street, how much? If not, how close and what is the cost?
9. *Convenience to Shopping*—Women employees like to be near shopping.
10. *Convenience to Restaurants*—Although many employees bring their lunch, being close to a restaurant is definitely an advantage.
11. *Sign Visibility*—Would it always be prominent, subdued, in between? (As a sidelight, oddly enough, many firms care nothing for signs as far as the public is concerned—they prefer not to be bothered by any but their own customers).
12. *Sub-leasing Privileges*—Will the owner give the tenant the right to sub-lease, if necessary?
13. *Option to Buy*—Is the owner interested in giving one, and if so, at what figure?
14. *Tax Clause*—Does the owner require tenant to pay any increase in taxes in subsequent years? On leases for longer than five years, this is becoming quite common.
15. *Repairs or Modifications*—More often than not a tenant will require some alterations, repairs, improvements before being able to utilize the space. Practically speaking the question of "Who Fixes?" turns out in many cases to be one of the major

---

[12] *Ibid.*, pp. 2–5.

stumbling blocks in negotiating a lease—or proves to be one of the big "give or take" parts of the selling negotiations.

The above information is all necessary in handling the leasing of industrial property. Should the property also be for sale, our fund of knowledge would have to be increased to include the following:

1. *Age of Building*—Check with local building department for specific date of building permit.
2. *Assessed Values and Taxes*—Do you know the *current* tax rate in your community —and the assessing practices?
3. *Amount of Insurance and Cost*—An owner's statement that "this building is *fully* insured," may mean a "70% co-insurance clause."
4. *Loans*
   a. Amount of existing loans and how payable; are they assumable?
   b. How much of a loan is obtainable, from whom, and how payable?
   c. Will owner take a low down payment and carry paper; all or part?
5. *Roof*—Type, condition, age.

The author of the foregoing list indicates that the compilation of such information, "while not necessarily all-inclusive, is fairly complete, and, immediately after being compiled, should be incorporated in whole or in part in a sales brochure." [13] This is extremely important. The information is not gathered and analyzed to satisfy the desires of the broker. Rather, it is assembled for use in serving the needs of property owners, industrial users, or both.

Know Construction

The industrial real estate broker will not be a construction specialist, unless he happens to have engineering and construction experience, or employs such talent in his organization. Nevertheless, if the industrial broker is to coordinate the development of "package deals," he must know enough about the construction business, the construction process, and construction terminology to serve as interpreter between a contractor and a client. He should know what quality construction is, and who is currently producing it in his area. Then he can hire the appropriate contractor for the particular project at hand.

The industrial broker must face the issue of how the structure in question can meet the particular requirements of the participants in the transaction in which he is currently involved. Much information about construction is provided on the typical Property Information Sheet that is prepared for listings in most industrial brokerage offices. Exhibits 23, 25 and 33 illustrate this fact.

The industrial broker should have access to good information about construction. One important source of such information is a local contractor with whom the broker can visit and work. At a more general level, bibliographies of information sources on building construction are available for inclusion in the brokerage office library.[14]

---

[13] *Ibid.,* p. 5.
[14] See, for example, Howard B. Bentley, *Building Construction Information Sources* (Detroit, Gale Research Co., 1964).

Specific information about construction components and building costs can be obtained from the publishers of construction cost manuals and services. Three of the more widely utilized manuals are produced by E. H. Boeckh Associates of Washington, D.C.; F. W. Dodge Corp. of New York City (*Dow Building Calculator*); and Marshall and Stevens Co. of Los Angeles.

Know the Property

What are the outstanding operational characteristics of the property being analyzed, whether for disposition or for use? Does it suit the purposes of the particular user? To what type of user or what type of use is it best adapted?

In order to answer these and similar questions, the industrial broker must have detailed information about the property. This includes its location, its environment, the site, and the building. In a successful industrial real estate office, the listing form or property inspection sheet will provide the necessary information about the property. The broker should utilize a listing checklist or form on which to record detailed information about the property as he inspects it. In this way, the property can be analyzed later without repeated return inspection trips.

In analyzing the property, the broker must work with the land. That is to say, he cannot alter the location of the property. Neither can he do much to change the character of the site, particularly if it is already improved with a building. What he can do is adapt the use program of the property to its highest and best use. This requires careful and detailed analysis, which depends upon thorough information about the property.

Exhibit 25 depicts the property analysis form utilized by the Binswanger Corporation of Philadelphia. Filling out this form in detail calls for a good working knowledge of the property. The information it contains provides a good picture of the property, its characteristics, and its condition, and gives important insights into the probable use and attractiveness of the building on the open market.

Know the Owner's Goals and Needs

Since every industrial real estate assignment is a problem to be solved by the broker, and since there are at least two decision-makers in each transaction (the owner and the user), the broker must understand what influences these decision-makers, and what will satisfy them. Without this information, he will often find it extremely difficult to bring about a meeting of the minds.

Leasing is an important and useful alternative to sale in most instances. There are many cases in which owners claim emphatically that they are not at all interested in anything but direct and quick sale of the property, and then accept a rental as an attractive alternative.

The broker must query the owner about his goals and needs, and analyze the answers that are given to him. He interprets the owner's objectives and translates them to a program of action. This requires good analytical ability as well as considerable tact.

The owner's objectives may vary, depending on his personal circumstances, and on whether the property is to be sold or leased. The following

Exhibit 25

PROPERTY ANALYSIS SHEET

PROPERTY ANALYSIS

_____(*Company*)

_____(*Full Address*)

Plans Available: Structural
              Architectural
              Fire Insurance

Size: (Total Sq. Ft. Area)

Number of Buildings:

Number of Floors:

Floor Areas:
  Gross (Dimensions)
  Net   (Dimensions)

Ground: (Total Area and Dimensions)
  Occupied by Building:
  Vacant:
  Type of Terrain:

Construction:
  Floors:
  Walls:
  Type of Columns (Cement, Steel,
    H Columns, or others)

Date of Construction:

Condition of Property:

Ceiling Heights:
  A) (Under Beam)
  B) (To Roof)

Column Spacing:

Remarks Re: Wall or Partition Divisions:

Elevators:
  A) Type
  B) Size
  C) Capacity
  D) Locations
  E) Maintenance contracts, if any:
  F) Are certificates posted?

Windows:
  A) Type
  B) Location
  C) Size
  D) Storm sash or screens, if any:
  E) Doors
  F) Gates

Toilet Facilities:
  A) Male (includes)
  B) Female (includes)
  C) Location
  D) Rest Rooms
  E) Condition

Lighting:
  A) Type of Fixtures
  B) To be included in sale:
      _____(Yes) or _____(No)

Roof:
  A) Type
  B) Bonded
  C) Construction
  D) Condition
  E) What year
  F) Monitors
  G) Ventilation facilities

Power:
  A) Supplied by:
  B) Voltage
  C) Phase
  D) Transformers:
      Type—Power & Lighting
      Owned by
      Number
      Capacity in KVA
      When last inspected, if oil type
  E) Panel Boards:
      Type
      Where located
      No. circuits
  F) Bus Duct

Heat:
  A) Type Boiler
  B) Age
  C) How many
  D) Are certificates posted?
  E) Horsepower
  F) High or low pressure
  G) Pressure in lbs.
  H) Heat distribution
  I) Blowers
  J) Radiators
  K) Oil storage facilities:
  L) Fuel used
  M) Approx. cost per year

N) Process steam
O) No. of personnel
P) General condition of boiler room

Water:
A) Supplied by
B) Size of main
C) Size of meter
D) Where located
E) Capacity
F) House tanks
G) Size and type
H) Pressure
I) Domestic hot water system

Sewer:
A) Supplied by
B) Size of pipe
C) Any restrictions
D) Location

Gas:
A) Supplied by
B) Size of main
C) Location

Sprinkler:
A) Wet
B) Dry
C) Size of sprinkler tank
D) Fire extinguishers

Office Facilities:
A) Size (sq. ft.)
B) General description
C) Floors
D) Ceiling
E) Lighting
F) Partitioning

Truck Loading Facilities:
A) Length of loading dock
B) Under cover
C) Tailgate
———————(Yes) or ————(No)
D) Location
E) No. of trucks that can be handled

Railroad Siding Facilities:
A) Name of railroad
B) Car Floor:
———————(Yes) or ————(No)
C) Car capacity
D) Type of agreement in effect

Fire Towers:
A) Number
B) Location

Stairwells:
A) Number
B) Location

Cranes:
A) Number
B) Size
C) Type
D) How old
E) Current

Air Conditioning:
A) Type
B) Size
C) Capacity
D) Approx. cost per year
E) Maintenance contract, if any

Cyclone Fence:

Liquid Storage Facilities:
A) Size
B) Capacity
C) Size of pipes

Zoning:

Water Rent:

Sewer Rent:

Fire Insurance Rate on Building:
Amt. presently carried

Assessment:
Land
Building
Misc.

Taxes:

Possible Financing:
Mortgage

Restrictions in Title:

Easements:

Asking Rental:

Asking Sale:

Possession:

Climate:

Labor:
A) Abundance of Male
B) Abundance of Female

Miscellaneous:
A) ADT
B) Autocall System
C) International Watch Clock
D) Muzak
E) Pictures
F) Survey—Deed Lines
G) Monorail System
H) Floor Scales
I) Previous Occupant

Transportation:
A) Highways (route numbers serving area, proximity to plant, etc.)
B) Airline Service (names of airlines, schedules, etc.)
C) Railroad Passenger Service (names of railroads, schedules, etc.)
D) Bus Service (names of companies, schedules, etc.)
E) Trucking Firms

Inspections:
A) Is plant in operation
_____(Yes) _____(No)
     If yes, will be vacant by

B) Names of plant manager, or watchman, or representative
   Name _____
   Plant phone number _____
   Home phone number _____
C) Keys:
   Can be obtained _____(Yes)
   _____(No)
   In possession of _____
D) Name of industrial development representative in area, or Chamber of Commerce secretary, etc.
   Business phone number _____
   Home phone number _____

Binswanger Corporation, Philadelphia

represent some of the alternative objectives an owner may have, if he really wishes to sell the property:

(1) Quick profit;
(2) Cash for other purposes;
(3) Capital gain (especially if depreciation and cash flow considerations dictate action);
(4) Long-term income (which means that there is no hurry in the transaction, so that a lease with option to purchase might suit this objective).

Alternatively, owners may have objectives which can best be filled by leasing. Even within this framework, it is important to know which is more important, because different types of tenants and different types of lease arrangements are necessary to satisfy the different objectives:

(1) Milk the property for as much income in as short a period as possible;
(2) Take full advantage of capital gains treatment, with an income flow in the interim;
(3) Preserve the investment in the real estate, by preserving and protecting the property;
(4) Build an estate for the future;
(5) Receive a high net income annually;
(6) Receive a steady net income annually;
(7) Receive a safe net income annually.

Many of these objectives are mutually incompatible, which means that the owner must make a conscious choice before settling on a plan of action. The broker's job is to assist the owner in making this choice by presenting the alternatives to him and explaining their implications.

Know the User's Needs and Desires

On the other side of the decision-making process is the user. The industrial firm has particular locational and space requirements. In addition to specifying the characteristics of the site and the building, the firm must also decide whether it should rent or buy space, and whether it should seek existing space or have facilities built to suit its requirements. In many instances, of course, the financial reality forces the decision for the firm. Generally speaking, the small, new, growing firm must content itself with rented space not designed for its own particular needs. It is only after the firm has grown large enough to support more expensive space, either as owner or tenant, that it can have facilities adapted to its own peculiar needs. The broker must recognize and communicate this fact as tactfully but as emphatically as possible to the management of the small or new firm.

Earlier in this discussion, the relatively low turnover of industrial space was noted. This is not simply the result of specialized function and a "thin" market. In addition, there is the fact that manufacturing establishments, at least, find moving or relocation an expensive and time-consuming process that often they cannot afford. As a result, firms often occupy unsuitable space. The direct expense plus the loss of production associated with a major move can threaten the firm's profits, and possibly its existence.

This underscores the fact that the location decision is a critical one to the manufacturing firm. Warehousing and distribution operations are not quite so committed to a specific location, and turnover and relocations of such operations are much more common. For the manufacturing establishment, however, the location decision is one that commits it to the particular site and building selected for a long period of time. This is borne out not only in low turnover statistics, but in the prevalence of long-term leases and long-term financing on manufacturing plants.

The industrial broker must therefore analyze carefully the character of the operation and its space requirements. He must "educate" the management of the user firm so that they can recognize their actual needs, in comparison with their desires. This is usually not difficult because most location decisions are made on a cold-blooded, financial basis, despite the occasional decision apparently made on purely personal grounds.[15]

To assist the broker in identifying the needs and requirements of the particular customer firm, lists of the characteristics of "ideal" industrial sites and industrial plants have been developed. They serve as a reminder of the considerations that must be taken into account in the final location decision.

Exhibit 26

LIST OF CHARACTERISTICS OF THE "IDEAL" INDUSTRIAL SITE [16]

"1. Minimum *contour*. Earth moving can be an expensive item of cost in preparing a site for industrial use.
"2. Good *soil* characteristics. Piling unstable ground can add a dollar a square foot or more to land costs.
"3. Adequate *drainage*. Standing water, in addition to being a nuisance, may cause paved areas and the building floor slab to buckle.
"4. Ample *utilities* available, such as electricity, steam, water, and sewage disposal.
"5. *Fuel,* available at competitive prices. This includes coal, gas, and oil.

---

[15] For an exposition of the relative role of these occasionally noneconomic considerations, see W. N. Kinnard, Jr. and Z. S. Malinowski, *Personal Factors Affecting Small Manufacturing Plant Location Decisions*, Small Business Management Research Report (Storrs, Connecticut, Bureau of Business Research and Services, University of Connecticut, 1961).
[16] Watson, *op. cit.,* p. 176. Reprinted with permission.

"6. Convenient access to all major types of *transportation,* including rail, highway, water, and air.

"7. Proximity to an area where skilled *labor* is available for employment.

"8. *Zoning* regulations that permit the use contemplated, and protect industry against encroachment by other uses.

"9. Sufficient *size* to provide ample room for off-street loading, parking, and expansion. Some industrial companies insist on four to six acres of land for each acre of building area.

"10. Reasonable *taxation.* This includes real estate taxes, personal property taxes, and income taxes.

"11. A local government that is financially stable, and a community that welcomes new industry.

"12. *Amenities* available in the area—cultural, recreational, and climatic."

These site factors are reminiscent of the analysis in Chapter 3. They are not ranked in any particular order of importance. However, emphasis is generally placed on items 8 through 12, because they are less susceptible to influence by the industrial firm's management.

In utilizing the foregoing list, the industrial broker can compare the needs and requirements of the customer firm with the items in the list. Then their relative importance and their significance to the decision of the firm in question can be evaluated. Similarly, the characteristics of an "ideal" industrial plant might include the following:

Exhibit 27

GENERAL CHARACTERISTICS OF AN "IDEAL" INDUSTRIAL PLANT [17]

"1. Solid, simple construction, utilizing the most efficient materials and techniques locally available, such as pre-stressed concrete that may be obtained in some areas.

"2. An adequate sprinkler and fire proofing system.

"3. Layout allowing for easy expansion, through curtain walls.

"4. Covered truck and rail docks.

"5. Attractive office space that is quiet, well lighted, and easily cleaned.

"6. Landscaping.

"7. Reasonable size. An industrial plant in excess of 50,000 square feet of building area may be difficult to sell.

"8. Adaptability. The ideal building is a multi-purpose structure, useful for many different kinds of manufacturing operations."

Know the Terminology

The industrial real estate broker should be familiar with the appropriate technical terminology. Otherwise, he cannot communicate with technicians and specialists, and in turn translate their statements and commentary to the principals. This is an important ingredient in the coordinating role of the broker: serving as the communications channel among the different participants in the industrial real estate transaction.

There is no known single source of information relating to industrial real

---

[17] *Ibid.,* p. 177. Reprinted with permission.

estate practice that will contain all of the financial, construction, and related terms that the industrial broker will encounter and will need to know. Indeed, many are not published at all, because they represent highly localized practice.

Nevertheless, certain basic sources can be referred to, and should constitute the nucleus of a reference shelf in the office of the industrial real estate broker. Members of the Society of Industrial Realtors receive publications of the organization, including its monthly *Newsletter*. In addition, any industrial brokerage reference shelf should include:

American Institute of Real Estate Appraisers, *Appraisal Terminology and Handbook,* 4th edition, Chicago, 1962.

Babb, Janice B., and Dordick, Beverly F., *Real Estate Information Sources,* Detroit, Gale Research Corporation, 1963.

Bentley, Howard B., *Building Construction Information Sources,* Detroit, Gale Research Corporation, 1964.

Boeckh, E. H., and Associates, *Boeckh's Manual of Appraisals,* 6th edition, Washington, D.C., 1963.

Clark, Donald T., and Gottfried, Bert A., *Dictionary of Business and Finance,* New York, Crowell, 1957.

Dodge, F. W., Corp., *Dow Building Cost Calculator and Valuation Guide,* New York, 1959.

Friedman, Edith J., ed., *Real Estate Encyclopedia,* New York, Prentice-Hall, 1960.

Marshall and Stevens Company, *Marshall Valuation Service,* Los Angeles, monthly.

Prentice-Hall Real Estate Staff, *Encyclopedia Dictionary of Real Estate Practice,* rev. ed., Englewood Cliffs, New Jersey, Prentice-Hall, 1962.

Society of Real Estate Appraisers, *Real Estate Appraisal Principles and Terminology,* Chicago, 1960.

Know When to Bring in Specialists

As the coordinator of the industrial real estate transaction, the industrial broker must know when a transaction calls for specialized, technical skills. The type of specialist required is determined by the demands of the particular transaction.

The most commonly needed specialists, and their probable contributions, are:

Accountant: advice in analysis of income statements; possible assistance in tax problems.

Appraiser: advice on value and possibly costs.

Architect: design skills and commentary on layout and location.

Economist: market analysis, feasibility analysis, marketability analysis.

Contractor: construction work, cost estimation, design advice.

Banker: financial advice, financing.

Mortgage broker: placing of loans.

Engineer: may be quite specialized. For example, there are soil engineers, construction engineers, industrial engineers, mechanical engineers, or electrical engineers. They provide technical advice with respect to *specific* problems that arise.

Tax specialist: may be an attorney or an accountant. In many instances, both are called in.

Attorney: necessary in every transaction. Industrial firms and title companies will have their own legal advice. The broker should have his own attorney for advice, as well as for any legal work (such as preparation of forms) that may arise in the course of the transaction. Each principal will have his own attorney, and the broker should, also.

SOURCES OF BUSINESS

The practicing industrial real estate broker must develop a continuing clientele. Business will be generated from a variety of sources. It is important for the broker to recognize these sources, so that he may take full advantage of opportunities that may present themselves in the course of his business.

In order to keep alert to changes and developments in the market area, many organizations utilize salesmen or sales trainees for much of this leg work. At the same time, the senior members must maintain appropriate contacts in order to channel information to the firm. In this way, current developments and opportunities can come to the attention of all sales personnel.

In order to merchandise industrial space, the broker needs an inventory of space to be marketed. These include the listings in his own files as well as those on which he knows he may cooperate with the listing broker. In order to obtain listings, he must maintain contact with owners of industrial real estate and their representatives. A survey of the sources of listings, conducted by a large S.I.R. firm, showed that 48 per cent of their listings were repeat business from former customers (both users and owners). Another 24 per cent of listings originated from recommendations by previous customers. Lease renewals and exercises of options to purchase represented 18 per cent of listings, and only 10 per cent were generated by new contacts, advertising, direct mail efforts, or co-brokerage arrangements. From this information, it is quite clear that a reputation of past success can be regarded as the single most important source of attracting new listings.

The industrial broker must also attract users or prospects. This requires somewhat more effort. Even here, however, reputation plays an important role. A representative of an established industrial brokerage firm has stated that "a good, established industrial broker really doesn't have any competition as long as he serves his clients well. Therefore, he should invest the time and effort to become a magnet, or a natural attraction to whom newcomers to the area would naturally turn because of his reputation." [18]

In order to assist the broker in developing and exploiting sources of new business, a list has been derived from interviews with several industrial specialists operating throughout the United States. Not all recommend the use of every method or procedure. However, the list represents the alterna-

[18] Statement of C. B. O'Gorman (W. Ross Campbell Co., Riverside, California).

tive possibilities which confront every industrial real estate broker, and which he should consider for the generation of new business. In this setting, "new business" means both listings and prospects.

1. *Past Customers and Office Files.*   This is by far the most important source of information, which is often easy to overlook. In addition to voluntary requests for assistance from previous customers, continuing contacts with them to inquire about their needs or aspirations often leads to considerable additional business. One brokerage office maintains a file of all leases that it has handled, arranged by expiration date. When the lease has one more year to run, personal contact is made with the tenant to inquire about their plans for the future, and to offer whatever assistance the brokerage firm might provide.

a. *Sales Transactions.*   Satisfied buyers can be assisted in finding branch locations or new locations as their needs expand. Institutional owners in particular can be an important source of continuing business. These would include real estate investment trusts, banks and trustees, as well as industrial firms who want to "trade up" or relocate.

b. *Counseling.*   Another important source of business is customers who have been counseled in the past. In many instances, informal "retainers" develop over prolonged periods. Brokers often provide services beyond the normal realm of industrial real estate activity. For example, one brokerage firm has made a point of assisting relocated executives of customer firms in purchasing or disposing of residences. In many instances, they receive co-brokerage commissions or fees from residential brokers. Whether they do or not, this activity is regarded as a service to a long-term customer which pays dividends far beyond the amount of time and effort expended.

c. *Tenants.*   Since today's tenant may be tomorrow's owner, many brokerage firms make a point of developing working relationships with current tenants in properties which they are managing. Brokers who manage multitenant buildings report that as much as 75 per cent of their new business comes from tenants in buildings which they manage. Often, the broker in question is the only industrial broker actually known to the firm. If he has treated them fairly and well, they rarely seem to shop around.

d. *Appraisals.*   Industrial brokerage organizations that perform appraisal services almost universally report that this is an important source of brokerage business.

e. *Unsold Listings.*   Some industrial brokers insist that owners of properties previously listed, but not sold by the firm in question, remain a potential source of business, since information about their needs and desires is already on file. Other brokers disagree, arguing that these can hardly be called "satisfied customers."

2. *Referrals.*   A frequent source of new business is referrals from previous customers. Obviously, the best way to generate business of this sort is to provide the best possible service to current customers.

a. *Reputation.*   A firm with a good reputation in an area will often be "the" broker to whom potential clients are referred by others. In particular, lenders, utility companies, and community organizations (chambers of commerce or industrial development commissions) can be important sources of leads. Here, too, the most effective route toward receiving referrals based on a good reputation is to provide effective professional service continuously.

b. *Cooperation and Co-Brokerage.* Members of the Society of Industrial Realtors, in particular, have a built-in cooperative network covering the United States and Canada. In many instances, a broker in one area will refer customers to a broker in another area. Specialists in certain types of properties or problems (e.g., rehabilitation specialists) will receive references from other members. A major advantage of membership in the Society of Industrial Realtors is the close-knit pattern of cooperation that is available to the member, and through that member to the client.

3. *Direct solicitation.* As information comes to the attention of the industrial real estate broker, and as he develops new listings, direct solicitation can take a number of forms. This usually is not a major source of new business, but it often has subsidiary effects. The most common forms of direct solicitation (which are considered in more detail in Chapter 7) are:

a. *Direct Mail.* This involves the use of mailing lists and brochures.

b. *Personal Solicitation,* particularly with public agencies and institutional investors.

c. *Form Letters Offering Assistance.* When information about either a new firm seeking a location or an owner seeking to dispose of an industrial property becomes known (often through a newspaper story or advertisement), many brokers send out a form letter similar to the one illustrated in Exhibit 28. Those utilizing such an approach regard it as a significant generator of new business.

d. *Advertising.* Most industrial real estate brokers agree that advertising is not a direct generator of much new business. Yet most employ it because it keeps the name of the firm in the public eye. It is a much more general and impersonal approach than most brokers care to use. They feel that direct contact of some sort is usually more effective. Nevertheless, newspaper advertising and signs on buildings for sale or lease are widely utilized.

4. *Market Analysis.* By keeping abreast of industrial real estate developments in his market area, primarily through direct personal inquiries and through careful reading of the local news, the broker can develop leads for new business.

a. *Newspaper Ads and Stories.* The form letter shown in Exhibit 28 is generally based on an advertisement or story that appears in a newspaper. Many industrial brokerage organizations have junior staff members or sales trainees read the newspapers carefully every day for possible leads.

b. *S.I.R. Market Letter.* Members of the Society of Industrial Realtors have the advantage of the S.I.R. *Market Letter* in which listings throughout the United States and Canada are noted.

c. *Neighbors.* Whenever an industrial real estate broker has a new listing, one of his first steps should be to study the character and the probable space needs of immediately abutting neighbors. If they are industrial firms

Exhibit 28

SOLICITATION FORM LETTER SENT TO ADVERTISERS
OF INDUSTRIAL PROPERTY

Gentlemen:

We have noted your advertisement in the _____ edition of

_____. The advertisement states _____

_____

If we may cooperate in any way in the marketing of this property, please complete and return this form. A stamped, addressed envelope is enclosed for your convenience.

Very truly yours,

(s) XXXXXXXXXXXXX

Location _____   Power Wiring _____ Capacity _____

Size: Land _____   Railroad _____

Building _____   Zoning _____

Number of Floors _____   Sale Price _____

Construction _____   Sale Terms _____

_____   _____

Heat _____   _____

Ceiling _____   Rent _____ Lease Term_____

Column Spacing _____   Assessed Value _____

Bays _____   Parking Area _____

Other Information _____

_____

_____

as well, they often represent an obvious source of new business. In many instances, they will not be aware that the property next door is for sale or lease, and a considerable amount of time and effort can be saved by contacting them early in the listing period.

d. *Signs on Buildings.*   Whenever an industrial broker sees a sale or lease sign on a building, it means that there is space available. This means that any user-customer of the broker might find this useful space. It also means that any present occupant of the space may be looking for something new. Finally, more than one broker's sign on a building means that it is not an exclusive listing, and it represents a potential sale or lease commission for an alert broker.

e. *Local Market Studies.*   Chambers of commerce, local financial institutions, and universities often report periodically on the industrial or economic base of an area. New firms entering the region, and expansions of existing firms, are further potential sources of new business.

5. *Personal Contacts.*   Many practitioners and many writers would put this directly after "Past Customers" in order of importance. Past customers

are, of course, personal contacts. In addition, while building a reputation and becoming known throughout the market area, the broker or the industrial brokerage firm must maintain personal relationships in at least three fields:

a. *Business Contacts.* In particular, bankers, contractors, investors and developers should be contacted periodically to ascertain what their needs and requirements are. To become known and respected in an area, it is often desirable (if not necessary) to join various professional or semiprofessional groups. This would include becoming at least an affiliate member of a local finance organization, the builders' group, the chamber of commerce, and possibly an appraisal organization. Through associations generated in meetings of these organizations, considerable amounts of referral business can be developed.

b. *Public Agencies.* Continuing courtesy calls should be made on the industrial development departments of all utilities and railroads operating in the territory covered by the industrial real estate broker. In addition, the local planning commission, redevelopment commission, building department, and others should be visited regularly, both to offer assistance and to inquire about new developments in the area.

c. *Social and Service Groups.* Aside from the normal desire to serve one's community, many industrial brokers find it good business to be active in one or more civic service organizations. Fraternal and social groups may generate sources of business. One large brokerage firm pays the membership fees and dues of its salesmen in country clubs or yacht clubs. The only limitation is that each member of the firm must belong to a different club. In that way, maximum coverage of potential contacts is achieved.

Whatever the source of the new business lead, it is meaningless if the industrial brokerage firm does not follow through on the lead. Therefore, many offices have formal procedures for reporting on leads. Exhibit 29 is one such form that is used by a large brokerage organization. It provides both a basis for establishing an office file for the property or the prospect, and a basis for checking on the performance of individual members of the brokerage organization's staff.

LISTINGS: THE BROKER'S INVENTORY

If the industrial real estate broker is to merchandise industrial space, he must have an inventory of such space to offer on the market. The properties that he has available for sale or lease are termed "listings." This term refers both to the property or space offered for sale or lease, and to the contractual agreement between the owner of the real estate and the broker, which makes the broker an employee (or agent) of the owner.

In order to function effectively, an industrial real estate broker must have a large number of exclusive listings in his own files, and he must know about the exclusive listings of other brokers, as well. Then he can allocate the inventory of industrial space at his disposal in the most efficient manner. Listings also mean better income opportunities because the bulk

Exhibit 29
LEAD REPORT FORM

LOUIS SCHLESINGER COMPANY
Industrial Dept.
LEAD REPORT

DATE _____

Firm Name

Address

Phone No.

Business: Firm Members _____

SIC #

Type of Property Desired

Sq. Ft.   Acreage

Location   Waterfront

Rail Siding   Buy _____ Lease _____

When Wanted   Match List _____

Present Lease Expires

D & B RATING

Origin of Lead: Letter _____ Tele _____ Personal _____

Circular _____ Reply to Ad _____

Sign _____

Rec by _____ Salesman _____ Co-Broker _____

of the broker's commissions come from owners of property, rather than from purchasers, tenants, or users.

Characteristics of Industrial Listings

In general, listings of industrial real estate are basically the same as those for any other type of real estate.[19] There are, however, some characteristics that distinguish industrial property listings from others: (1) the typical industrial property listing is longer than the average commercial or residential listing (three months to a year); (2) it normally calls for sale and/or lease of the premises; (3) it is typically an exclusive right to sell or lease; and (4) the fees, commissions, and compensable expenses owed to the broker typically represent a higher proportion of sales price or rental.

It is generally agreed that the industrial real estate broker should be

[19] For a general discussion of Listings, see Case, *Real Estate;* or Case, *Real Estate Brokerage.*

somewhat selective in accepting listings, accepting only those he thinks he can move in a *reasonable* time.

Types of Listing Agreements

However classified, industrial listing agreements are often tailored on an individual basis, to meet the requirements of the particular owner, the specific property, or the individual transaction. Thus, there are many exceptions to any standard forms that might be discussed. Within this framework of limitations, however, it is still possible to talk about general tendencies and guidelines.

1. *Open Listings.*   The term "open listing" is in part misleading and incorrect, since in most instances there is no formal written agreement or contract signed between the owner and the broker. It is simply an arrangement by which the broker is invited either directly, or by inference, to produce a purchaser or tenant. The broker who brings in an offer that is accepted by the owner is the one who is entitled to the commission.

Open listings can often be identified by a multiplicity of signs on one building or on one site. Each sign represents a broker who has been invited by the owner to attempt to sell the property. From the point of view of the owner, one major difficulty with the open listing is that placing a sign on the property often constitutes the sum total of the broker's efforts to sell the property. The broker has no particular incentive to expend time and effort in attempting to sell or lease the property, because he has no protection or guarantee that he will receive a commission if the property is sold. Also, a property on open listing is rarely advertised at the broker's expense, because the broker usually feels that he is simply encouraging business for his competitors.

A further limitation of the open listing is that oral invitations to sell a property are extremely difficult to enforce. Since there is no formal listing price recorded in any written document, the owner can often "change his mind" and simply say that the offer is not acceptable to him. While the possibility of litigation to collect a commission under such circumstances may exist, it is rarely in the interests of the industrial broker to do so. Unfortunate publicity might well be generated.

In an open listing arrangement, every broker involved is really in competition with all the other brokers to give the best terms to the purchaser, rather than to the seller. In order to secure a commission, each broker is encouraged to attempt to sell the property on the buyer's terms. In effect, competition among brokers can work against the property owner instead of in his favor. This is because the open listing arrangement does not offer either the time or the protection necessary for the broker to reach prospective buyers, and to negotiate the highest price with them.

At the same time, some owners persist in offering their properties for sale on an open listing basis only. Many still believe that listing a property with 20 brokers will result in 20 times the effort, and 20 times the coverage that an exclusive listing with one office will produce. As long as this attitude prevails, open listing will continue as a practice in industrial brokerage. However, it is generally agreed to be on the decline.

It has been noted that there are generally three broad categories of owners to whom the open listing arrangement will appeal: [20]

a. *Sophisticated Owners.* These are experienced in handling, leasing, and building industrial real estate. They include private builders, developers, and investors, as well as some public agencies such as urban renewal commissions. With such owners, any broker can bring in a customer and make a deal. There is never any question about paying a commission to the broker. The owner is accustomed to paying commissions and he recognizes their necessity. In many instances, as in the case of urban renewal commissions, the owner may simply be prohibited from granting exclusive listings.

b. *Land Owners and Developers.* Most often, these owners will also agree to pay commissions, but they usually have to be convinced in every instance. They often include some railroads and public utility companies, among whom there is a variety of attitudes and policies about paying commissions. In such cases, one S.I.R. uses a letter agreement form, which is to be acknowledged by the owner. In this way, he avoids questions about the payment of a commission, as well as how much it is to be.

c. *Inexperienced and Reluctant Owners.* Some individuals or organizations typically refuse to pay a sales commission. They are usually small-scale, part-time participants in industrial real estate activity. They generally insist that the broker look to his "customer" for a commission. Industrial firms typically do not like to deal with such owners, but often they must because of peculiar needs for specific sites.

2. *Exclusive Listings.* Exclusive listings in industrial real estate practice almost invariably involve an exclusive right to sell or lease. These are often called "Exclusive Agency" agreements, but this is almost always a misnomer. Under some exclusive agency agreements, the owner reserves the right to sell the property himself, without compensation to the listing broker. While such an arrangement is common in many areas in marketing residential properties, it is generally regarded as undesirable, or even intolerable, by industrial real estate brokers.

The typical exclusive listing for industrial real estate, therefore, is an Exclusive Right to Sell or Lease. It is almost always a right to *sell or lease,* rather than simply a right to sell. Indeed, the agreement often covers disposition of the property by exchange or gift, in which case the broker is also entitled to his commission. Under an exclusive listing, the listing broker is entitled to a commission, which is specified in the contract, if the property is disposed of by sale, exchange, lease or even gift, during the period of the contract. As Exhibit 30 shows, this is a detailed and potentially complex legal relationship between the broker as employee or agent, and the owner as principal. As noted earlier, the term typically runs from three months to a year.

---
[20] Statement by B. H. Waterbury (Industrial Realty Co., Inc., Baltimore).

Exhibit 30
S.I.R. EXCLUSIVE AGREEMENT FORMS

EXCLUSIVE AGENCY AGREEMENT
(Sale, Transfer or Exchange of Real Property)

AGREEMENT made this   day of   , 19

between

whose address is

(hereinafter called "Owner")

and

whose address is

(hereinafter called "Agent")

WITNESSETH THAT, in consideration of One ($1.00) Dollar by each party to the other in hand paid and the mutual covenants of the parties hereinafter contained,

1. The Agent certifies that it is a real estate broker, duly licensed under the laws of

and is a member in good standing of the
Society of Industrial Realtors.

2. The Owner hereby grants to the Agent the exclusive right for a period of

commencing   and ending

to negotiate the sale of and to sell the real property identified in Schedule I which is appended to and hereby made a part of this agreement, for the sale price and otherwise in accordance with the terms and conditions specified in said Schedule I; or, in the alternative, for such lesser price or on such other or different terms and conditions as Owner may hereafter approve.

3. The Owner represents that he is now the owner in fee simple of said real property and that to his best knowledge he possesses a marketable title thereto subject only to such mortgages, liens, restrictions, encumbrances and other conditions as are noted in said Schedule I. Wherever required by law or by local custom, the Owner shall furnish to the purchaser a complete abstract of title to said property, and/or a title insurance policy.

4. The Owner agrees to enter into a contract of sale with and to convey said premises by good and sufficient deed to any prospective purchaser ready, willing and able to purchase said real property during the term of this agreement for the price and on the terms and conditions stated in said Schedule I; or, in the alternative, for such lesser price or on such other or different terms and conditions as Owner may hereafter approve.

This form developed and approved by the Society of Industrial Realtors for use by its members.

5. The Agent is hereby authorized to place one or more "for sale" signs on said real property, and shall (i) afford the Owner the full benefit of the judgment, experience and advice of the members of the Agent's organization in respect to the policy to be pursued in selling the property; (ii) list the property with and solicit the active cooperation of members of the Society of Industrial Realtors and other real estate brokers who specialize in dealing with industrial properties; (iii) advertise the proposed sale in such manner and in and by such brochures, publications and other media as in the Agent's judgment will most likely present an appropriate offering; and (iv) take all such further steps as in the Agent's judgment will enhance the prospective sale of said real property. The Owner shall contribute towards the cost of advertising and the cost of preparation and distribution of any brochures, the sum of $

6. During the term of this agreement, the Owner shall refer to the Agent any and all inquiries received by the Owner from any source with respect to or concerning said property, together with the name and address of each person or corporation making such inquiry. Agent shall diligently investigate each such inquiry as well as other inquiries or offers received or directed to the Agent and will use its best skills and efforts to procure a purchaser for such real property.

7. The Agent shall be entitled to receive from the Owner commissions at the rate of   %
as recommended by the

Real Estate Board in effect at the time for transactions involving real estate sales or exchanges, in any of the following contingencies:

(i) If during the term of this agreement a purchaser ready, willing and able to purchase the property for not less than the sale price and otherwise upon the terms and conditions specified in Schedule I hereof is procured by the Agent alone or with the assistance of another broker. The earned commissions in such case shall be one full commission, computed on the sale price obtained, but shall not be payable unless and until:

(a) a written contract of sale is entered into between Owner and such purchaser, provided the failure to enter into such contract is not due to wilful default or refusal on the Owner's part; and

(b) title shall have closed, and the deed delivered, pursuant to such contract of sale, provided such events shall not have been prevented by a failure of title or a wilful default, refusal or omission on the part of either contracting party.

(ii) If during the term of this agreement the Owner sells, transfers or exchanges, or enters into a contract of sale or of exchange with respect to said real property with any person or corporation whatsoever, irrespective of the terms and conditions of sale, transfer or exchange and notwithstanding such person or corporation was not procured by the Agent but was procured by the Owner individually or through any other source. In such event the Agent shall be entitled to an amount equal to a full commission computed at the rates above mentioned upon the consideration received or to be received by the Owner, provided such consideration equals or exceeds the sale price stated in Schedule I hereof; otherwise, if such consideration is less than said sale price, then the Agent shall be entitled to an amount equal to a full commission computed at such rates upon said sale price. The aforesaid amount shall be deemed earned and be due and payable without demand as at the date of any contract covering such transaction, or, in the alternative, the date of transfer or conveyance of the property if no such contract is entered into.

8. In any transaction brought about by the Agent with the assistance of another broker, the commission shall be paid solely to the Agent who shall share the same with such other broker.

9. Agent is not authorized to enter into any contract in behalf of the Owner.

10. If at the expiration of this agreement no transaction has been effected, the Agent shall at such time furnish to the Owner in writing, by registered mail, return receipt requested, a list of prospects with whom the Agent theretofore negotiated in offering the property. If within ninety (90) days thereafter, the property or any interest therein is sold, or transferred to any such prospect or exchanged for any property owned by the latter, or is contracted to be sold, transferred or exchanged, the Agent shall be entitled to receive from the Owner an amount equal to full commission in the manner and to the same extent as provided in above paragraph 7 (ii) as if such transaction occurred prior to the termination of this agreement. If the Agent shall fail to furnish such list, however, the Owner shall not be liable for any such commission.

The foregoing constitutes the entire agreement between the parties and shall be binding on each of them and their respective successors in interest. This agreement may not be changed or modified except in writing signed by the parties or their successors in interest. Wherever used herein, words of one gender shall be construed to include all genders; the singular number shall include the plural and *vice versa*, as the sense requires.

IN WITNESS WHEREOF, the parties have executed this agreement the day and year first above written.

_____
Owner

Witness as to Owner

_____

_____
Agent

Witness as to Agent

_____

Schedule I

Real Property to be sold:

Address

Section	Block	Lot
County of		State of

Description from Deed or Title Policy:

Existing Mortgages and Terms of Payment:

Other Liens and Encumbrances, if any:

Zoning, Restrictions, Easements and other conditions of title:

Survey Readings and Variations, if any:

Personal Property Included in Sale, if any:

Existing Leases and Tenancies, if any:

Terms and Conditions of Sale:

Sale Price:

Percentage payable on contract:

Balance payable on closing title:

EXCLUSIVE AGENCY AGREEMENT
(Lease of Real Property)

AGREEMENT made this   day of   , 19

between

whose address is

(hereinafter called "Owner")

and

whose address is

(hereinafter called "Agent")

WITNESSETH THAT, in consideration of One ($1.00) Dollar by each party to the other in hand paid and the mutual covenants of the parties hereinafter contained.

1. The Agent certifies that it is a real estate broker, duly licensed under the laws of

and is a member in good standing of the
Society of Industrial Realtors.

2. The Owner hereby grants to the Agent the exclusive agency for a period of

commencing   and ending

to lease the whole or any part or parts of the building and premises known as

according to the Schedule of proposed leasing annexed hereto.

3. The Agent is hereby authorized to place one or more "To Let" signs on said property and shall (i) afford the Owner the full benefit of the judgment, experience and advice of the members of the Agent's organization in respect to the policy to be pursued in leasing the property; (ii) list the property with and solicit the active cooperation of other members of the Society of Industrial Realtors in the areas surrounding the property and other real estate brokers who specialize in the leasing of industrial properties; (iii) advertise the proposed leasing in such manner and in and by such brochures, publications and other media as in the Agent's judgment will most likely insure an appropriate offering and take all such further steps as in its judgment will enhance such proposed leasing; and (iv) negotiate such lease or leases as circumstances may require, as well as any renewals or extensions of existing leases, and submit the same for approval of the Owner. In connection with the foregoing the Owner shall contribute toward the cost of advertising and the cost of preparation and distribution of any brochures, the sum of $

This form developed and approved by the Society of Industrial Realtors for use by its members.

4. During the term of this agreement, the Owner shall refer to the Agent any and all offers and inquiries received by the Owner with respect to, or concerning said property. Agent shall diligently investigate and develop such, as well as all other, offers and inquiries received or directed to the Agent and will use its best skill and efforts to procure a suitable lessee or lessees for the building or its several parts, as circumstances may warrant. The Owner hereby reserves the right to reject and refuse to accept any proposed lessee, which right of rejection or refusal, however, shall not be unreasonably exercised.

5. The Owner, upon entering into any lease, any agreement renewing or extending any lease, or any arrangement granting additional space, to any lessee procured by the Agent, shall pay to the Agent a commission based upon the aggregate of the rent, additional rent and all other sums payable by the lessee pursuant to any such lease, agreement or arrangement and calculated at the rates recommended by the
Real Estate Board. It is understood that: (i) No commission shall be deemed earned until and unless the lease or other agreement or arrangement shall have become effective between lessee and Owner by the execution of a writing, or otherwise; (ii) In the event the Rules of said Real Estate Board do not prescribe specific commission rates chargeable on renewals and extensions, the commission payable by the Owner or the then lessor on such renewal or extension period shall be calculated as if such period were in force at the inception of the initial lease term; (iii) The grant of additional space to any such lessee shall to such extent be deemed an original letting and commissions thereon computed accordingly; and (iv) If during the term of any lease or any renewal or extension thereof, the lessee or the lessee's successors in interest shall purchase the leased property or any interest therein, the Owner, or its successors in interest, shall pay to the Agent, at the time of passing of title, a sales commission calculated at the rate recommended by said Real Estate Board. In such latter event, the leasing commission paid or payable to the Agent shall be recomputed and adjusted on the basis of a lease term expiring as of the date title passes and if the Agent has received a sum in excess of such recomputed commission such excess sum shall be deducted from the sales commission, but in no event shall the aggregate of the sales commission and recomputed leasing commission be less than the amount of the original leasing commission.

6. The terms, provisions and conditions of paragraph "5" above, shall also apply (i) to any lease or other rental arrangement of the whole or any part of the premises made or contracted for by the Owner during the term of this agreement with any person or corporation whatsoever (whether a new lessee or a tenant in possession at the date hereof) notwithstanding such person or corporation was not procured by the Agent but was procured by the Owner individually or through other sources; and (ii) to any lease or other rental arrangement of the whole or any part of the premises, or any interest therein, made or contracted for by the Owner, within ninety (90) days after the expiration of this agreement, with any person or corporation previously contacted by the Agent and whose name appears upon a list of prospects with whom the Agent had negotiated during the term of this agreement and a copy of which list has been furnished by the Agent to the Owner. If during such period the premises or any interest therein be sold or contracted to be sold to any such person or corporation, the Agent shall be entitled to receive a commission on the sale price calculated at the rates recommended by said Real Estate Board. If the Agent shall fail to furnish such list, the Owner shall not be liable for commissions.

7. In any transaction brought about by the Agent with the assistance of another broker, the commission shall be paid solely to the Agent who shall share the same with such other broker.

8. Where a lease is consummated giving the landlord the right of cancellation, a full commission for the entire term called for in the lease shall be paid by the Owner as provided by paragraph "5" hereof. Where a lease is consummated wherein it is provided that the tenant shall have the privilege of cancellation, a full commission shall be paid up to the date on which said lease may under its term be cancelled, but the Owner agrees to pay the balance of commission on any further period of the lease not surrendered or cancelled by the tenant.

The foregoing constitutes the entire agreement between the parties and shall be binding on each of them and their respective successors in interest. This agreement may not be changed or modified except in writing signed by the parties or their successors in interest. Wherever used herein, words of one gender shall be construed to include all genders; the singular number shall include the plural and *vice versa,* as the sense requires.

IN WITNESS WHEREOF the parties have executed this agreement the day and year first above written.

Witness as to Owner

_____   _____
                                                              Owner

Witness as to Agent

_____   _____
                                                              Agent

Schedule

Property to be leased:

    Address

    City and State

Building:

    Description

    Floor loads?

    Sprinklered?

    Parking Facilities?

Liens and Encumbrances:

    Subordination

    Zoning restrictions

Terms and Conditions:

    Rental (Gross or Net)

    Term (Initial, Renewal, options)

    Security, if any

The outstanding advantage of the exclusive right to sell or lease is that it affords the broker time in which to attempt to negotiate the best terms for the owner. The broker has ample opportunity to offer the property to one prospect at a time. He is also afforded the chance to advertise the property appropriately and adequately. One of the first things he does is to have the owner request other brokers to remove all signs, other than his own, from the property. An exclusive listing also allows the broker time to analyze the property carefully, and to offer both personal and professional advice to the property owner about the most appropriate method of disposition.

Industrial brokers disagree over whether they should be selective in the acceptance of exclusive listings, and how selective they should be. Many point out that it is simply impossible to accept all listings and do them justice. Therefore, the broker is best advised to list only those properties that he thinks he can dispose of in a reasonable period of time. The contrary view is that the broker (and especially the S.I.R.) has a responsibility to attempt to assist industry and owners of "problem" properties. This view considers that one of the major responsibilities of the industrial real estate broker is to maintain a sound market environment, in much the same way the specialist "makes a market" on the organized security exchanges.

There *is* agreement, however, that the broker should try to obtain an exclusive listing on every property that he feels is marketable by his organization. Despite the fact that exclusive listings on industrial real estate generally call for substantially longer terms than those on residential or commercial properties, industrial brokers are virtually unanimous in their view that the properties move much more quickly under exclusive listings than when open listings are utilized. The longer term is usually requested to provide protection for the broker, so that he can invest the time, money, and effort necessary to bring about a successful completion of the assignment.

The procedure for selling industrial real estate under an exclusive right to sell agreement is illustrated by the case of a company that wanted to dispose of a large surplus plant. The owner asked a broker to estimate the probable price for which the property might be sold, if a reasonable time were given to expose the property to the market. The broker estimated that the property would sell for approximately $2,100,000 to $2,200,000. He recommended that the owner sign an exclusive right to sell or lease agreement, and that the property be listed with an asking price of $2,400,000. The recommendation was accepted.

In answer to an advertisement that the broker ran, a prospect offered $2,100,000. This offer was conveyed to the owner, who rejected it. After a series of counter offers and proposals, the property was finally sold for $2,300,000. The broker maintained that under an open listing arrangement, he would have pressed for an immediate sale on the basis of the first offer of $2,100,000. In this case, however, the broker had the opportunity to negotiate the transaction at the higher price of $2,300,000. In other words, the exclusive right to sell or lease agreement resulted in a sale at the highest price obtainable on the market.

In the foregoing example, the broker advertised the property. The advertising expenses necessary to market industrial property often represent substantial investments by the broker. It is highly unlikely that a broker would risk substantial amounts of funds for advertising, or even much staff time, if he had no assurance from the owner that others would not sell the property while his sales campaign was in progress. The exclusive right to sell or lease protects the broker, and encourages advertising on his part.

The format of the exclusive right to sell or lease agreement may vary considerably. The actual form employed does not matter as long as the basic and important items are covered. This was illustrated in Exhibit 30. An alternative form, utilized by a firm in Oakland, California, is illustrated in Exhibit 31. It should be noted that the major items are essentially the same, and that the only differences are in matters of format or local wording.

Exhibit 31
EXCLUSIVE AUTHORIZATION AND RIGHT TO LEASE OR RENT

EXCLUSIVE AUTHORIZATION AND RIGHT TO LEASE OR RENT

In consideration of the services of DUNCAN, KORB & TRIMBLE, INC., Realtors, I hereby employ said BROKER, exclusively and irrevocably, for the period beginning _____, 19_____, and ending at midnight on _____, 19_____, to procure a party to lease or rent the property situated in the City of _____, County of _____, State of California, described as follows:

I hereby grant BROKER the exclusive and irrevocable right to lease or rent said property within said time and further authorize BROKER to accept a deposit thereon.

The offering price shall be at the rate of $_____ per month.

I hereby reserve the right to approve any and all terms and conditions, rental (including percentage rental, if any), and LESSEE'S qualifications, prior to entering into any lease or rental agreement.

I agree that if during the term hereof said property is leased or rented, whether at the above rental or any other rental or terms and conditions, to any party whose name was brought to my attention by BROKER, I will upon execution of said lease, pay BROKER a sum equal to the total of the following: % of the gross rental for the first year;   % of the gross rental for each of the second and third years;   % of the gross rental for each of the fourth and fifth years;   % of the gross rental for each of those years from the sixth through the tenth, inclusive; and   % of the gross rental for each year thereafter. In the event a percentage lease is entered into, I agree to pay BROKER, within 15 days after receipt of each said percentage rental by me, a sum equal to that commission percentage listed in the previous sentence for the year in which said percentage rental applies, and further agree to provide BROKER with all copies of LESSEE'S statements as they are received by me.

In the event LESSEE, its successors or assigns, remains in possession of said premises beyond the primary term of its lease, I agree to pay BROKER a sum equal to those same applicable commission percentages, listed in the previous paragraph, for each additional year of said possession, said amounts to be paid to BROKER within 15 days after receipt of each rental payment.

As additional consideration for BROKER obtaining any such Lessee, should Lessee, its successors or assigns, purchase the herein-described property during the term of any lease so entered into by me, or any extensions thereof or while remaining in possession thereof, I hereby agree to pay said BROKER, or assigns, upon close of such sale, a sum equal to   % of the first $50,000,   % of the next $150,000 and   % of the balance of purchase price as commission, after deducting therefrom the total sum of leasing commissions already paid to BROKER. In the event of such purchase, if the total leasing commissions already paid by me to BROKER exceeds the above described sales commission in amount, then I shall have no further obligation to BROKER.

I agree to pay BROKER the above described leasing or selling commission, as the case may be, if said property be leased, rented or sold during the term hereof through the efforts of said BROKER, or by me, or by another BROKER, or through any other source whatsoever. In the event I withdraw said property from the market or transfer same other than by sale during the term hereof and therefore preclude said BROKER from offering said property for lease or rent, I agree to pay BROKER a sum equal to a leasing commission applicable to a 15-year lease term based on the offering rental above.

Should a lease or rental agreement be made, or should I sell the above described property within one hundred eighty days after the termination of this contract of employment to any party to whom BROKER has introduced said property (and BROKER has given me written notice during the term hereof or within ten days thereafter that BROKER has introduced said party to such property) I agree to pay BROKER the leasing or sale commission fixed herein, as the case may be.

I hereby grant BROKER the exclusive right to post upon the above described real property suitable signs, at BROKER'S sole cost and expense.

Should suit be brought by BROKER to enforce any of the terms hereof and BROKER prevails, I agree to pay costs, including reasonable attorneys fees as fixed by the Court.

The terms of this contract of employment shall be binding upon the parties hereto and upon their respective heirs, executors, administrators, successors and assigns. I hereby acknowledge receipt of a copy hereof.

Dated: _____ OWNER _____

Dated: _____ OWNER _____

Dated: _____ OWNER _____

Dated: _____ OWNER _____

In consideration of the foregoing employment the undersigned BROKER agrees to use diligence in procuring a LESSEE for said property.

                        BROKER:
                        DUNCAN, KORB & TRIMBLE, Inc., Realtors
Dated: _____ 151 GRAND AVENUE, OAKLAND, CALIF. 94612
                        Telephone (415) 834–6230

          By _____

Industrial real estate brokers argue emphatically that the exclusive right to sell or lease is the *only* basis for cooperation among brokers, and for the sharing of commissions. Very often, one broker may have a listing on a property which precisely meets the requirements of a prospect being served by another broker. In most instances, an agreement between the listing broker and the broker with the potential purchaser or tenant can be negotiated. The most common basis for sharing commissions is 50–50, with other arrangements made between the cooperating brokers when the circumstances warrant an uneven division.

When there is an exclusive listing, the listing broker is protected in his efforts to advertise and market the property. In addition, the cooperating broker (the one representing the industrial prospect) is also protected. He knows he can work out an arrangement with the listing broker, and that his share of the fee or commission will be forthcoming when the transaction is completed.

There is a considerable amount of cooperation among industrial real estate brokers, and particularly among S.I.R.'s, although there is no formal Multiple Listing Service for industrial properties in most market areas such as there is generally for residential properties. The Maryland-Washington, D.C., Chapter of the Society of Industrial Realtors has a cooperative system whereby members share information about one another's listings. The information is transmitted through the use of the form which is presented as Exhibit 32.

Exhibit 32

LISTING REPORT FORM
MARYLAND-WASHINGTON, D.C., S.I.R. CHAPTER

Location _____ Area—Bldg. _____

Agent _____ Phone _____   Lot _____

Sale Price _____ G. R. _____   Zoning _____

RENTAL _____ Term of lease _____

| *IMPROVEMENTS* | *LOT* |

No. Stories _____ Dimens. _____ Grade _____

Bldg. Dimens. _____ Utilities _____

Ext. Const. _____ R. R. Facil. _____ Waterfront _____

Heat _____ Elec. _____ Transit _____

Elevator _____ Size _____ Cap. _____   *GENERAL*

Sprinkler _____ Ins. _____ Poss'n _____ Plats _____

Ceiling Ht. _____ Inspection _____

Floor Const. _____ Asses./Taxes _____

Loading Facil. _____ Remarks _____

Listing Information

Immediately upon being listed, the property should be inspected, and the information filed in the brokerage office. It should be readily retrievable for immediate presentation to a prospect. The industrial real estate broker is dealing with knowledgeable principals. The information derived at the time of the listing inspection can also be an important basis for setting the price or rental. It will also influence the terms of the transaction which the broker will recommend to the owner. Finally, analysis of the property information derived from the listing inspection can support recommendations for rehabilitation or conversion of the property and indicate the appropriate units of marketing or disposition.

To this end, a further checklist of items to be considered during inspection has been compiled from several major sources. It represents one alternative that might be effectively employed by an industrial broker.[21]

Exhibit 33

LISTING INSPECTION CHECKLIST—INDUSTRIAL PROPERTY

A. Site Information
    1. Location of the property
    2. Size and shape of lot
    3. Topography: stormwater drainage, subsoil and topsoil conditions
    4. Zoning
    5. Deed restrictions
    6. Transportation facilities: railroad siding (within switching limits); highways and access roads, location of nearest air freight terminal
    7. Parking: number of spaces, location, adequacy
B. Community Information
    1. Availability of labor; transportation for labor
    2. Amenities in area: shopping, churches, cultural facilities, schools
    3. Nature of industry in surrounding area; its effect on the subject property
    4. Utilities available
        a. Water: source of supply; capacity of mains; treatment problems
        b. Waste disposal: source of service; capacities; special disposal equipment
        c. Gas utilities: source; capacity of service
    5. Taxes and assessments
    6. Community acceptance of industry
    7. Locational economies: financing, suppliers, services
C. Building Information
    1. Number of buildings
    2. Floor space by square footage
    3. Shape or conformation of useable floor areas, including floor plan and layout
    4. Total ground area: square feet covered by buildings; square feet of paved areas; square feet or acres of vacant land
    5. Type of construction: floors, walls, columns, date of construction
    6. Ceiling heights by floors: under beams and to ceiling
    7. Floor construction
        a. Floor load ratings
    8. Column spacing
    9. Windows, casings, window sizes
    10. Expansion possibilities; ease of adaptation to other uses
    11. Condition and functional adequacy of building

---

[21] This checklist is adapted from several sources, including William M. Shenkel, *Principles and Practices of Industrial Real Estate: A Course Syllabus* (Washington, Society of Industrial Realtors, 1963), pp. 83–86; and Watson, *op. cit.*, p. 180.

D. Building Services Information
  1. Office space: number of square feet and location; air-conditioning, insulation from noise, light, etc.
  2. Truckloading facilities: size of docks; type of loading doors by size; covered or open facilities
  3. Railroad spurs: railroad lines; length of siding; car capacity
E. Building Equipment Information
  1. Condition and functional adequacy of each element
  2. Elevators (note make)
    a. Freight elevators: size; capacity
    b. Passenger elevators: size; capacity
  3. Plumbing and toilet facilities by location
    a. Number of units by type; male and female facilities
    b. Drains and taps
  4. Lighting facilities
    a. Type of fixtures
    b. Candle power
  5. Electric power
    a. Wiring
    b. Source and primary voltage
    c. Secondary voltage: number of transformers; capacity
  6. Heating Plant
    a. Type of unit; make
    b. Boiler size; capacity; pressure
    c. Availability of process steam
  7. Sprinkler system: wet or dry
    a. Pressure
    b. Supplemental fire extinguishers
  8. Air and steam lines: location and capacity
  9. Air-conditioning: location; type; capacity
  10. Overhead cranes: location; capacity
F. Miscellaneous Information
  1. Utility charges
    a. Water rent
    b. Sewer rent
  2. Insurance charges: fire; liability

Long as it is, the foregoing list is still not sufficiently comprehensive to meet every situation that an industrial broker will encounter. It does cover most contingencies, however. It is a basis for developing an appropriate form which the broker may adapt to his own needs and market area.

Setting the Listing Price or Rental

As a result of his inspection and analysis of the property to be listed, the broker will have an opportunity to discuss with the owner the appropriate price or rental at which the property should be listed, as well as the terms of sale under which it will be offered. Both of these are critical considerations, and will have a great deal of influence on the ease or difficulty with which the transaction is effected.

In order to advise the owner properly, the broker must be sensitive to the current conditions of the market. The broker should know current relative values, and he should be in a position to convince or "educate" the owner. One of the most effective means of carrying out this "educational" function is to show the property owner information on recent sales or leases of competing industrial properties. The broker will then suggest a range of prices within which the property most probably would be sold. In this way he encourages the owner to list the property realistically.

If there is difficulty in convincing the owner that the proposed price or rental is both realistic and fair, the broker should suggest an independent appraisal of the property. Under no circumstances should the listing broker perform this appraisal, no matter how competent or honest he may be, because he will be serving two functions simultaneously. Whatever he says may be suspect. It is even preferable to have someone not affiliated with the listing broker perform the appraisal. Most appropriately, it should be a professionally designated real estate appraiser (e.g., an M.A.I. or S.R.E.A.) with experience in appraising industrial properties. Many S.I.R. members are also M.A.I.'s.

It is important to be able to develop a reasonable listing price. It has been said that a property well listed is 50 per cent sold. This may be an exaggeration, but a property which is inappropriately priced can be extremely difficult to move on the market.

One of the important points that the listing broker must make with the owner is that many aspects of an existing building may not only add to value; they may actually detract from it. The owner of the industrial building may expect to recover investments in obsolete structures, useless steam plants or generating equipment, special-purpose buildings, or equipment usable only in a particular manufacturing process. The listing broker must point out carefully that these will probably not enhance the value of the property when it is exposed for sale or lease on the market, and indeed may be a detriment if the new occupant must expend money to remove or rehabilitate them.

In some instances, industrial managements are inclined to consider book value as synonymous with market value, or probable selling price. In this situation, the listing broker must be in a position to offer objective counsel. As already noted, utilizing the services of a professional appraiser is usually the most expeditious way to handle this particular problem.

The terms of sale are at least as important as the listing price or rental in influencing the marketability of an industrial property. These can seriously affect the broker's ability to procure a buyer. The broker is well advised to explain the uses of purchase-money mortgages, of long-term leasing (with or without an option to purchase) as an alternative to direct sale, and of deferred payments or exchanges, rather than cash transactions. The owner need not accept the broker's advice, quite obviously, but it is incumbent on the broker to bring these matters to the attention of the owner.

COMPENSATION OF THE INDUSTRIAL
REAL ESTATE BROKER

The industrial real estate broker typically receives his payment, or compensation for services rendered, from the owner of the real estate. When he is the listing broker, he is an agent of the owner, and must look to the owner for his commission. Occasionally, however, the owner may expect the commission to be paid by the industrial prospect.

Commissions on leasing are generally due and payable when the lease agreement is signed. However, many industrial brokers agree that staggering or spacing of the commission payments is often appropriate under a long-term lease. Otherwise, the commission will absorb most of the first year's rent, and this may discourage the owner from signing the lease. The leasing broker is also entitled to a commission, which is a stipulated percentage of the rent, if the lease is renewed.

Industrial brokerage commissions are often higher than those on residential or commercial properties. Land sales in particular command higher percentage rates, primarily because of the time and effort required in marketing industrial land. It is difficult to generalize about commission rates because they vary considerably from one part of the country to another. Local custom and practice generally dictate the level that is paid.

The level or rate of commission should be agreed upon in writing and in advance. Then there is no cause for disagreement or subsequent litigation. The broker's commission is earned and payable when he delivers a purchaser or tenant who is ready, willing and able to pay the stipulated price or rent, and whose offer is accepted by the owner. This is true regardless of the type of listing arrangement.

Commissions for rental management are normally a percentage of the rent collected. This, of course, is a matter of the terms and conditions of any management contract that exists.

If more than one broker participates in the transaction, the allocation or splitting of the commission between them is a matter of mutual agreement. This is another advantage to the owner of the exclusive right to sell or lease agreement. He is responsible to pay the stipulated commission to the listing broker only. Whatever arrangement is made between the listing broker and the broker representing the purchaser or tenant is independent of the owner. As a practical matter, industrial real estate brokers often pay finders' fees or referral fees to brokers who bring in purchasers or tenants, rather than splitting commissions. The reason is that in order to participate in a commission as a real estate broker (or salesman), the individual must be a licensed real estate broker (or salesman) in the state in which the property is located. Since it is both expensive and cumbersome to attempt to maintain licenses in all states plus the District of Columbia, cooperating brokers or real estate practitioners often receive fees for referrals rather than a percentage of the commission.

Many industrial real estate brokerage activities are compensated on a fee basis, rather than a percentage commission. This includes all counseling, in which a fee is paid for a study, advice, or recommendation. The amount of payment is in no way contingent upon what is recommended, or what the sale or rental price of the property happens to be. In the same way, a broker acting for a principal may earn a fee for making a market survey, or for the assembly of a site through options. If he performs appraisal functions, the broker *must* charge a fixed fee rather than a percentage of value.

Finally, the industrial real estate broker should take note of the fact that his is a professional service, whether it is rendered for a set fee or a percentage commission, and he should charge appropriately for it. If a fair, full fee is charged, the work is more likely to be acknowledged as professional.

SPECIAL SALES TECHNIQUES:
EXCHANGES AND AUCTIONS

In the normal course of events, industrial real estate is transferred through direct sale or through lease (most often long-term lease). There are, however, occasions when the normal procedures do not apply. The broker who wishes to offer a complete range of alternatives to his customers should be aware of two other possible methods of disposition of industrial properties: exchanges and auctions. Neither is particularly widespread, but each offers a solution to certain types of problems as they arise.

Exchanges

An exchange of real estate is commonly called a "trade." In effect, it involves the purchase and sale of two or more properties simultaneously, by owners who see mutual advantage in transferring their interests. Cash may or may not transfer as a result of the exchange.

Real estate exchanges normally are worked out by two or more brokers. Each cooperates with the other in analyzing the benefits and implications of the exchange to the principals involved. Indeed, cooperation with other brokers is absolutely essential to the effective completion of most exchanges. The broker must keep two important points in mind: (1) cooperation with other brokers who are seeking exchanges for their clients; and (2) discovering the client's motive for making the exchange.

Most industrial real estate exchanges do not begin with owners seeking to exchange real estate. In many instances, exchanges or trades materialize because a property is difficult to sell. Underlying every exchange must be the basic desire of the owner to rid himself of the property he currently owns, which is usually a more important consideration than the character or nature of the property for which he trades. There are important motivations for wishing to rid oneself of property, which need have nothing to do with its fundamental desirability.

The most common motivation is tax saving. The owner may have exhausted his depreciation (or nearly so), and may not wish to convert his property into cash with the attendant payment of taxes, even at the long-term capital gains rate. An exchange of industrial real estate, or of any real estate, can result in deferring immediate capital gains tax payment. It can also offer a continuation of tax-exempt cash flow through the depreciation of the newly acquired property.

Certain "hard to sell" properties often can be disposed of only through exchanges between owners of equally "hard to sell" properties. The basic and important point is that each principal should believe he has an advantage to gain. In most instances, both can be right.

In some trades, when the equity in a property is large, cash can be obtained only through an exchange of property by "trading down" and obtaining some cash with the "new," less valuable property. In other cases, industrial property owners may be willing to exchange property for purely personal reasons. For example, an owner may wish to retire, or move to another part of the country, and to have an income-generating property close to his new location. This represents an excellent opportunity for an exchange or a trade.

Exchanging or trading is a specialized real estate activity which requires expert technical assistance. It is one disposition alternative which might not necessarily occur to the industrial real estate broker. In the event that the property appears to offer an opportunity for an exchange, the broker would be well advised to seek the immediate assistance of a trading or exchanging specialist, such as a member of the International Traders' Club of the National Institute of Real Estate Brokers. References to their excellent and informative publications are found in the Selected References at the end of this chapter.

For industrial properties, situations in which trading or exchanging is most likely to be attractive include: cases in which the market is particularly thin, so that few if any potential buyers can be identified; cases of trading up or trading down on the part of investors; cases in which investors seek to defer the payment of taxes while maintaining some tax sheltered cash flow; and cases in which the investor wants to cash out at least part of his investment.

Auctions

When real estate cannot readily be disposed of through normal sales procedures, and often when questions may be raised about the authenticity or objectivity of a sales transaction, the auction represents a useful alternative form of disposition. It is the most public of public sales, and it may be required in order to settle pending litigation. Whatever price is realized, the owner (often an executor of an estate, or a public agency) can be certain of receiving cash. The uncertainty, of course, concerns the price level.

As with an exchange, an auction requires a specialist to handle it properly. An experienced real estate auctioneer who has familiarity with industrial real estate is normally sought by the owner. Even though the property is sold at public auction, a broker for the buyer can still earn a commission or fee by advising him and representing him successfully at the auction.

An auction cannot succeed unless it is properly advertised and promoted. This, too, requires an active campaign of solicitation by an expert.

While many brokers argue that an auction sale implies difficulty in disposing of the property through more usual channels, many courts and trustees hold that a well advertised, well attended public auction will result in the payment of fair value for the real estate. In situations in which a trustee, an executor, or a public agency is involved, protection of the fiduciary's interests is often at least as important a consideration as protection of the beneficiary's interests.

Brokers can cooperate in an auction sale in a variety of ways. First, the broker can recommend to a listing owner that a property which has not moved during the listing period be offered for sale at auction. In that case, the auctioneer and the listing broker participate in any commission that may be earned. A broker representing the successful bidder at an auction can also earn a commission. Finally, an auctioneer operating in an unfamiliar area will often pay a fee to a local broker to help him service the property for the benefit of the owner.

It is not often that an auction represents the most satisfactory resolution of the disposition problem for industrial real estate. When it does, however, the informed broker should be in a position to recognize the circumstances and the possibilities.

COUNSELING ON INDUSTRIAL REAL ESTATE

In many instances, the industrial real estate specialist is called upon to provide competent, objective and unbiased advice or professional guidance, based upon sound analysis and judgment, to either of the principals in an industrial real estate transaction. He may represent either the user or the owner in a given situation, but not both. This work is undertaken on a fee basis, and is not contingent upon either the completion of a transaction or the price at which the transaction is consummated.

A variety of diversified problems can be attacked by the industrial real estate broker in his capacity of counselor or advisor. His basic approach is to assemble the necessary data, analyze them in the light of market conditions and his own experience and judgment, and to make a series of recommendations for action. It must be recalled that every industrial real estate transaction represents a problem for the broker. His job is to attempt to solve the problem for the mutual benefit of all parties. Nevertheless, his fee is paid by only one of the parties.

As far as the owner is concerned, the broker in his role of counselor may hire technicians to help develop a program of recommendations for action. In many instances, when a listing is first proposed, the broker will study the property with a view toward recommending the most appropriate use pattern. Related to this is the development of a merchandising or marketing program, in which case the broker is a disposition consultant. He may recommend, for example, actions to make the property more salable. He may also recommend actions that will alter the highest and best use of the property, or even change the market in which it is operating.

For the user, the most common counseling service consists of a feasibility or location study. The broker assists the user in the selection of site and location, and in identifying the type of space that the firm most needs. In his "educational" role, the broker must overcome any misconceptions and preconceptions the user may have.

To a large extent, this activity consists of applied industrial real estate economics analysis. It is becoming much more scientific, with computers being used by some industrial real estate counselors in analyzing market data.

SELECTED REFERENCES

Angelo, Heath, Jr., "Leasing Techniques in a Surplus Market," *Real Estate Investment Opportunities* (Los Angeles, California Real Estate Association, 1965).

Bentley, Howard B., *Building Construction Information Sources* (Detroit, Gale Research Company, 1964).

Case, Frederick E., *Real Estate* (Boston, Allyn and Bacon, 1962).

Case, Frederick E., *Real Estate Brokerage* (Englewood Cliffs, New Jersey, Prentice-Hall, 1965).

Friedman, Edith J., ed., *Real Estate Encyclopedia* (Englewood Cliffs, New Jersey, Prentice-Hall, 1960): especially Part III: "How to Sell or Exchange Real Estate":
   Chapter 9:   "Selling Industrial Property," Howell H. Watson
   Chapter 12: "The Real Estate Salesman," Clinton B. Snyder
   Chapter 13: "Exchanges of Real Estate," Stanley Sotcher
   Chapter 14: "Auction Sales of Real Estate," R. C. Foland
   See also Part VII: "How to Lease Real Property"
   Chapter 32: "Broker's Role in Leasing Commercial Property," Robert P. Boblett.

Gates, Niles, "Industrial Property Investments," *Developing, Selling and Syndicating Real Estate Investment Property* (Los Angeles, California Real Estate Association, 1964).

International Traders' Club, National Institute of Real Estate Brokers (National Association of Real Estate Boards, Chicago).
   Planning the Exchange (July, 1965; sponsor: J. David Huskin).
   Tax Implications in Exchanging (March, 1966; sponsor: Maurice C. Iddings).
   Techniques of Investment Property Exchanging (March, 1965; sponsor: Sheldon F. Good).

Korb, Irving, "Light Industrial Properties," Chapter 38 of *Training Manual for Real Estate Salesmen,* prepared for Sacramento Metropolitan Real Estate Offices, Inc. (Lafayette, California, D. B. Campbell, 1957).

National Institute of Real Estate Brokers (National Association of Real Estate Boards, Chicago):
   Be a Dynamic Salesman (September, 1965; sponsor: Cliff Brisbois).
   Guide to Commercial Leasing (December, 1965; sponsor: Clifford A. Zoll).
   Learn to Trade (June, 1959; sponsor: Clinton B. Snyder).
   Real Estate Specializations (June, 1962; sponsor: Winfred O. Mitchell).
      "Industrial Real Estate": F. G. Binswanger, Jr.; LeRoy D. Owen; Clinton B. Snyder.
      "Counseling": C. D. Askew; Robert S. Curtiss.
   Solving Salesmen's Slumps (March, 1965; sponsor: Rich Port).

Prentice-Hall Real Estate Staff, *Encyclopedic Dictionary of Real Estate Practice* (Englewood Cliffs, New Jersey, Prentice-Hall, 1962).

Shenkel, William M., *Principles and Practices of Industrial Real Estate: A Course Syllabus* (Washington, Society of Industrial Realtors, 1963).

Sherman, Arthur B., *Selling Business Real Estate* (Englewood Cliffs, New Jersey, Prentice-Hall, 1955).

Society of Industrial Realtors, *Advanced Course in the Techniques of Industrial Real Estate,* Northwestern University (Washington, The Author, 1964)
"Techniques in the Successful Operation of an Industrial Brokerage Office," Frank A. Schlesinger.
"Techniques in the Rehabilitation and Marketing of Problem Properties," Frank G. Binswanger, Jr.

Society of Industrial Realtors, *Marketing Warehouse Properties; Selling Industrial Real Estate* (Washington, The Author, 1952).

7 | Industrial Real Estate Office Operation and Management

INDUSTRIAL real estate practice, and particularly brokerage, is a service business. Its basic service is to facilitate the efficient and prompt allocation of the inventory of industrial space among interested potential users. It is a business because its practitioners are performing the services for a fee. The industrial real estate brokerage office serves its customers best when its services are provided in an efficient and businesslike manner, through a well-organized and properly managed business establishment.

The industrial real estate office must be geared to the problems of industry, and must be prepared to solve every problem that industry may present, through intelligent and effective application of a combination of knowledge, integrity, and hard work. The industrial real estate brokerage organization will market space more effectively and more promptly by knowing as much as possible about the needs of the industrial user.

Whatever the organizational form of the industrial real estate business, and whatever its size, the same basic principles of business operation and management apply to it that apply to every service organization in the United States economy.[1] The emphasis here is on the distinguishing characteristics of *industrial* real estate business activity and management. The focus is on the most efficient means and methods to market industrial real estate.

ORGANIZATION OF THE INDUSTRIAL REAL ESTATE OFFICE

As in the case of most business organizations, the industrial real estate

---

[1] For discussions of these basic principles, see, for example, California Real Estate Association, *Real Estate Office Administration* (Los Angeles, The Author, 1963); Frederick E. Case, *Real Estate* (Boston, Allyn and Bacon, 1962); Frederick E. Case, *Real Estate Brokerage* (Englewood Cliffs, N.J., Prentice-Hall, 1965); Edith J. Friedman, ed., *Real Estate Encyclopedia* (Englewood Cliffs, N.J., Prentice-Hall, 1960), especially Chapters 2, 6, 52; Pearce C. Kelley and Kenneth Lawyer, *How to Organize and Operate a Small Business*, 3rd ed. (Englewood Cliffs, N.J., Prentice-Hall, 1961).

brokerage office is most likely to be efficient in providing its services when it is specialized. A survey of S.I.R. organizations throughout the country revealed the fact that the majority either specialized exclusively in *industrial* real estate, or had a separate industrial department. Despite the apparent similarity in activities, few firms provide both industrial and commercial real estate brokerage services through the same personnel. The types of users served and their space requirements are so different that there is little carry-over between industrial and commercial brokerage. Greatest emphasis in industrial real estate brokerage is placed upon the technical knowledge of the salesmen.

Within the industrial brokerage firm, specialization is generally carried further, especially as the size of the firm increases. Partnerships and corporations are found more frequently among industrial real estate brokerage firms than they are among residential or even commercial brokerage firms. Generally, as the size of the organization increases, it moves from a sole proprietorship, to a partnership, to a corporation. The specific decisions about the form of organization are made in the light of the particular requirements of the members of the firm. This requires competent legal advice. Since every industrial real estate brokerage firm will have its own attorney or law firm available for such advice, the decision will be made on the basis of the attorney's recommendations.

Many of the more highly developed specializations and forms of organization are applicable only to larger organizations, which can exploit departmentalization. Yet participants in smaller firms can improve their own industrial brokerage services by learning from the experience of the larger firms.

Organizational Principles for the Industrial Real Estate Office

Based upon the experience of successful offices throughout the United States, the most representative pattern of development of an effective industrial real estate brokerage establishment will include the following:

1. *Select a manageable area of specialization and grow within it.* Too often, the ambitious industrial broker will try to take on all comers, and to serve every industrial prospect in every conceivable area from the outset. A small organization simply cannot afford to dissipate its limited energies in this fashion.

Experienced S.I.R.'s agree that from the outset the firm should specialize in the industries it serves and in the territory it covers. As experience and skill increase, and as the size of the staff expands with successful operations —within a limited range of industries and in a limited geographic area— then, and only then, should the horizons of the establishment be expanded. Indeed, there are some organizations which find that continued narrow specialization represents the most effective means of serving their clients, and of earning truly professional fees for their work.

2. *Specialize within the office as well.* As the organization grows, greater efficiency is generally achieved when additional specialists in industries, or

areas, or particular functions, are added. Larger brokerage organizations, for example, add their own appraisers, engineers, construction supervisors, or location economists as the need for these types of skills grows with their business activity. The existence of these skills, and their successful application to the problems of previous customers, will tend to generate additional business along the same lines. Nevertheless, it is important to note that the successful industrial real estate organization is a blending of skilled specialists, rather than a conglomeration of individual generalists.

The most common direction that diversification initially takes is the addition of an appraisal department. Since the industrial broker-salesman must know something about market value and valuation processes, appraising is an important adjunct to the major activity of marketing industrial space. Most industrial brokerage firms report that as the volume of their business increases, specific individuals within the firm tend more and more to make the appraisals. The largest and most successful firms have members whose primary function is to handle the appraisal business of the office.

3. *Infrequently needed and highly specialized skills are best hired from outside, rather than being added to the firm.* It is foolish as well as unprofessional for an industrial real estate salesman-broker to attempt to engage in engineering or design work, or to conduct a location study without appropriate training, or to draw up legal papers (even without charging a fee for the function), or to attempt to serve as a general contractor or construction superintendent. All of these activities, and many more, are much better hired out or subcontracted as the need for them arises in each specific case. The firm that does not have its own staff attorney or legal department must have a good working relationship with a competent, experienced law firm. Similarly, professional engineering, economics, or construction skills should be hired rather than added, unless the volume of business clearly warrants their addition.

There will be certain kinds of skills needed that will rarely be found among the staff. For example, one S.I.R. member's firm has a food chemist at a nearby university on retainer because the industrial brokerage organization has a substantial volume of business with firms in the food processing industry. The members of the staff do not attempt to render judgments about food chemistry. Rather, they turn to a skilled technician who can provide the answers more quickly and more appropriately.

At least as important as technical skills are business management skills. For example, few industrial brokerage offices are large enough to be able to support an in-house public relations or advertising specialist. Yet promotion and advertising represent a substantial segment of industrial real estate brokerage effort. A retainer arrangement with an advertising or public relations firm is often the appropriate solution to this particular problem. The same can be said for accountants or systems analysts.

4. Just as industrial clients of the industrial brokerage organization require appropriate siting in order to carry out their functions most efficiently, *the industrial real estate brokerage office should be well located* in order to

perform *its* functions and to serve *its* customers most effectively. There is general agreement that the proper location for the industrial real estate brokerage office is in a central area, close to financial institutions, corporate offices, title companies, the local Board of Realtors, law offices, and service organizations such as advertising agencies. In such a location, proximity to clubs and business organizations is also significant because of the ease of entertaining clients in an appropriate atmosphere.

5. *The sales or leasing function must be carefully distinguished from the administration of the industrial brokerage office.* It is the responsibility of the salesman to develop business for the firm. Within the framework of the organization, the salesman should be permitted to build his own business without worrying particularly about "housekeeping" activities. Clerks and order takers are considerably less expensive to hire, primarily because they are considerably less productive. The successful firm permits the salesman (who may in fact be a licensed broker, but who is not a principal) to grow without restraint. In this way, he serves both himself and the industrial brokerage firm most effectively.

RECRUITING AND TRAINING INDUSTRIAL REAL ESTATE SALES PERSONNEL

The term "salesman" is used here to refer to a member of the sales staff of the industrial real estate brokerage firm. He may well be a licensed broker. He is called a "salesman" simply to distinguish him from the executive of the organization who has administrative responsibilities within the firm.

The selection, apprenticeship, and training of industrial real estate sales personnel is at best a haphazard process. It is often handled on an *ad hoc* basis without any systematic planning or effort in advance. Although it is an absolutely vital function for the success of the industrial real estate organization, too often it is neglected or assigned a very minor role in the activities of the organization. The salesman is a most important ingredient in the success or failure of the industrial real estate brokerage office. He is expected to be self-sufficient, and to develop business for the firm. Moreover, he represents the firm in his dealings with the outside world. His job is exactly the same as that of the principal or "broker," except that he has no formal administrative responsibility. The industrial real estate salesman is supposed to know the market, know the property, know the owner's needs and requirements, and know the user's needs and requirements. Yet there is no recognized basic source to which he can turn for the acquisition of this information.

Knowledgeable and experienced brokers recognize that "the care and feeding of this salesman . . . is something that time has to be spent on. You just cannot pick a man off the street, get him a license and send him out into the world to represent your firm." [2] The selection and compensation

---

[2] Frank A. Schlesinger, "Techniques in the Successful Operation of an Industrial Brokerage Office," *Advanced Course in the Techniques of Industrial Real Estate* (Washington, Society of Industrial Realtors, 1964).

of sales personnel indeed represents a major part of the organization of the sales staff.

S.I.R. Frank A. Schlesinger argues, "We are in a service business, and service is the most important product that we have to sell. Unless your representatives are representing you and are a prototype of you, I think this becomes the weakest link in your chain." [3]

Recruiting and Selecting Personnel

Representatives of industrial real estate organizations rarely appear on college or even high school campuses recruiting for personnel. They rarely compete with other business organizations in their efforts to attract the promising young men and women emerging from educational institutions. Most commonly, men (rarely women) with successful real estate sales experience, or industrial administration experience, are recruited. The difficulty is that the new recruit (occasionally regarded as a trainee) is left largely to his own devices to find out about industrial real estate and its peculiarities. Moreover, if he lacks any of the appropriate background in economics, real estate, law, finance, accounting or construction, the responsibility is his to acquire it where and as best he can.

A few industrial real estate brokerage firms have formally recognized that a solid foundation in education will stand a man in good stead regardless of the actual field he enters. They are therefore recruiting at colleges and universities, particularly among majors in business administration, land economics, industrial engineering, and civil engineering.

One of the difficulties tending to deter expansion of this type of recruiting is that industrial brokers are far from agreement over what the appropriate attributes of a successful industrial salesman should be. Forecasting the success of the recruit is virtually impossible under present industry conditions.

Nevertheless, a modest trend toward greater emphasis on young trainees has been noted. They have a firm grounding in the analytical skill areas that will be required in industrial brokerage, and can more readily acquire, absorb and comprehend the experience that they gain in trainee programs. It appears highly unlikely that there will be a formal degree program for the industrial real estate broker in American colleges and universities in the near future. The ideal recruit for industrial real estate brokerage will still be the college-trained technical specialist who can deal effectively both with analytical problems and with people. The broker must still determine what sort of training program is to be established in order to make most effective use of this recruit.

Training Programs

Almost the only major point on which there is general agreement among S.I.R. firms concerning the training of new sales personnel is that there is no single way of handling the problem which has proved more effective than others. To a very large extent, the process involves adaptation of the man

---

[3] *Ibid.*

and of the firm to each other. It is largely a matter of local concern, in terms of the local market and of the specific organization.

Although "most firms do consider a training program necessary, in no sense of the word are any of these programs formal ones." [4] This statement is based on a survey conducted by the Research and Education Committee of the Society of Industrial Realtors. The typical training program lasts from three to six months, and is a part-time program. Generally, it represents little more than an indoctrination of the recruit in the methods, approach, and thinking of the employer firm. Familiarity with the various forms and systems utilized in the recording and reporting of information is emphasized, rather than techniques, functions, or general approaches.

Nearly all such training programs are necessarily informal. Few industrial brokerage offices are large enough to be able to support formal training programs with lectures, either by senior members of the staff, or by outside experts and specialists. One large industrial brokerage firm does run a weekly breakfast "seminar" for its entire sales staff (rather than only trainees), and outside speakers are brought in to keep the staff current with developments of importance in their market area. This is for only a few hours every week, however, and it is not concentrated on the new members of the staff. Moreover, it is quite an exception.

In most instances, therefore, the trainee is expected to learn by doing. Several firms assign the trainee to an experienced salesman who is expected to take the newcomer "under his wing." The neophyte accompanies the senior salesman to look at listings, to talk with customers, and to establish contacts. He sits in on discussions, negotiations, and closings. In brief, he observes the activities of an experienced salesman. He is expected to absorb what he sees, and to ask the right questions when he does not understand what is happening. This is at best an informal, personalized, and possibly haphazard approach to developing a highly specialized set of skills.

Many offices put trainees on a salary, or a salary plus a draw. In this way, there is considerably less pressure on the newcomer to generate commission income while he is a trainee. This means that he can spend more time learning the business, and less time worrying about how he is going to pay his bills over the next few months.

If learning by doing is the primary approach to sales training, the firm should have a formal and systematic program of introducing different materials to the trainee. One major S.I.R. firm assigns data-gathering tasks to its trainees. They are first required to read periodicals and the local newspapers, and to clip out all articles that seem to be pertinent to the business of the firm. One of the principals of the organization also reads the same periodicals and newspapers, and comments on what should have been noted, so that the trainee will have a better idea of what to look for.

Next, the trainee is assigned to answer classified ads about industrial space or industrial needs. The trainee is expected to fill out a Lead Report Form, such as is illustrated in Chapter 6, for each classified ad that he answers. In this way, he begins to learn what information is needed, and he

---
[4] *Ibid.*

also begins to learn that it is embarrassing to have to call back a second or third time if pertinent information is overlooked the first time.

The trainee is then taken to various major sources of market information and introduced to the records in each. These records may be the files of the firm itself, the local assessors' records, the files of a local title company or lending institution, or a local chamber of commerce or industrial development commission. The trainee is then sent to each of these organizations to obtain data necessary to fill out sections of the various property report forms.

The trainee is encouraged to look around as he travels through an area. He is instructed to take a different route each morning and each afternoon on his way to and from his home. In that way, he begins to learn something of the area, and to recognize the role and character of industrial space in that area.

Finally, he is assigned the task of filling out listing sheets, examples of which are given in Chapter 6, entirely on his own and without direction. A further type of form that the trainee should know how to complete is shown here as Exhibit 34. Ultimately, he will be expected to develop the pattern of information that is illustrated in the complete listing sheet for a manufacturing plant that constitutes Exhibit 47 at the end of this chapter.

Essentially, the type of training program outlined here is designed to introduce the salesman to sources of information, and to attempt to implant good work habits. Both of these are important considerations, particularly in view of the necessity to develop complete files of information for use with clients. Nevertheless, it is still a far from satisfactory program for developing technically trained industrial real estate sales personnel.

Some opportunities for formal training are open to the newcomer to the industrial real estate field, but they require considerably longer than three to six months to complete. For example, many colleges and universities now offer courses in industrial real estate practice, either in non-credit extension (usually available in the evenings) or as part of the regular degree program. Courses are available in such widely diversified institutions as the University of California at Berkeley and at Los Angeles, Pace College in New York City, and the University of Florida at Gainesville. In addition, many S.I.R. chapters sponsor courses and workshops on specific aspects of industrial real estate practice. Other groups such as chambers of commerce, public utilities and city or state development commissions sponsor similar short-term programs on related topics. Finally, university extension programs typically offer courses in the principles of real estate, salesmanship and advertising, accounting, economics and land economics, finance and mortgage lending, land planning, construction and construction cost estimating.

The difficulty is that the individual must usually develop his own program because there are few systematic curricula established to meet the specific needs of the industrial real estate salesman. Nevertheless, particular emphasis should be placed on the fact that there *are* many courses of instruction available to both the long-term practitioner and the newcomer in the field.

Whatever training program is established for the newcomer, however, the

Exhibit 34

PROPERTY INFORMATION SHEET

C. B. Snyder Realty Inc.
550 SUMMIT AVENUE
JERSEY CITY, N. J. 07306

Salesman_____

Exclusive_____

Lead_____

Address_____

Date_____

Available_____

Rent [ ]   Sale [ ]

Bldg.	Floor Area	Dimensions	Stories	Construction	Type	Ceiling Heights	FLOORS.		Bays Col. Spacing
							Material	Capacity	
Total									

OWNER:

Address

Phone

Lawyer

RENTAL:

Terms

SALES PRICE:

Cash

Mort.

EXISTING MORT: $

Int.   Amort.   Exp.

Held by:

REMARKS:

GENERAL:

Zone

Recent Use

Labor Supply

Transportation

LAND & SERVICE:

Size of Plot

R.R. Siding

Nearest Freight Station

Street Frontage

Water Front

Electricity   Gas

Water   Sewer

Parking

EQUIPMENT:

Heating

Plumbing

Toilets (M)   (F)

Sprinkler   A.D.T.

Wiring

Elevators

Platforms: Truck   R.R.

Loading:

Boilers   Fuel

Horse Power   Pressure

Process Steam

EXPENSES:

Insurance Rate

Assessed: Land   Bldg.

Taxes   T. Rate

Water   Power

Fuel

EXISTING TENANTS:

Floor	Space Occ.	Tenant	Rental	Lease Exp.

Form 143

management of the industrial real estate brokerage firm must recognize that it cannot in conscience ask or require an individual to take a series of courses, or engage in a prolonged training program, without some form of compensation. Since surveys have revealed that the great majority of Realtors compensate their salesmen on a commission basis only,[5] there appears to be room for significant improvement in the industrial real estate field. The principals of an industrial brokerage firm must recognize that a salary is essential during the period of training, if appropriate young people are to be attracted to the business and then retained to develop into effective, skilled salesmen. Some firms even discourage their trainees from making transactions early in their careers. They prefer to put them on salary during the training period, and to work them gradually into the position of being able to serve customers. Another important training device is to start the salaried trainee on the smaller transactions. Often more can be learned in attempting to place a firm seeking 5,000 square feet of floor area, or to sell or lease a small plant, than in handling a million dollar transaction.

COMPENSATION OF PERSONNEL

The primary consideration in the compensation of industrial real estate sales personnel is whether they should be paid on a straight commission basis, or given a salary or draw. Opinion is sharply and widely divided on this issue. In this presentation, the views of both sides are presented. The reader can reach his own conclusions as to the most effective approach to his own particular problems.

There is rather less disagreement with respect to the compensation of trainees, as indicated in the preceding section. It is generally agreed that some form of salary or draw against future commissions should be provided during the training period. Otherwise, the firm cannot require the salesman to spend time in courses or training sessions, however informal, when he might be out seeking commissions. Since the typical training period lasts only three to six months, however, this is a relatively minor consideration in the total picture of compensation of salesmen.

A study conducted by the National Association of Real Estate Boards revealed that over 75 per cent of some 839 Realtors throughout the United States paid their salesmen only a flat percentage of brokerage commissions.[6] This survey included all lines of real estate activity, not only industrial real estate. The basic impression is confirmed, however, by a study subsequently conducted by the Research and Education Committee of the Society of Industrial Realtors. This revealed that most offices of S.I.R. members also paid neither salaries nor advances once the training period was completed.[7] Next to a straight commission, the most common combination is a commission with bonus, or commission with limited draw privileges.[8]

The majority of S.I.R. member firms (over 75 per cent) split commissions

---

[5] This point is borne out by the findings reported in National Association of Real Estate Boards, Department of Research, *Real Estate Salesmen: Qualifications, Compensation, Advancement* (Washington, The Author, 1962).

[6] *Ibid.*

[7] Schlesinger, *op. cit.*

[8] *Ibid.;* National Association of Real Estate Boards, Department of Research, *op. cit.*

evenly between the salesman and the employing broker.[9] If there is a split of the total commission with another office, as would be the case if organization *A* were the listing broker and organization *B* produced a buyer, the listing salesman in organization *A* receives half of his firm's share of the commission, or 25 per cent of the total. Exactly the same arrangements prevail for sharing leasing commissions in almost every instance.

The second most common split of commission between the salesman and the employing firm is 60–40, with the salesman receiving 60 per cent. This is more likely to occur among smaller industrial brokerage offices, which have less overhead and which generally offer fewer services to the salesman.

The industrial brokerage firm typically bears the expenses of day-to-day operations and overhead (rent, utilities, secretarial staff, telephone), record and data services, and supporting services. In addition, approximately 75 per cent of S.I.R. member firms pay for all of the advertising expense that is not borne by clients. A few firms ask the salesman to participate in advertising those properties on which he has the exclusive listing.

A majority of the firms pay for entertainment of customers, as well as business organization and club dues. There is some variation here, with a few firms paying the initiation fee only, and others paying all of the club expenses. It was noted in Chapter 6 that one organization pays all the expenses of each member of the sales staff in country clubs, with the proviso that each must belong to a different club so as to obtain maximum potential customer coverage. It is a fact of business life that a considerable amount of business is actually conducted on the golf course. Industrial brokerage firms recognize this, and make it possible for their members to participate in this form of sales activity, as well.

Most firms regard the automobile as one of the salesman's tools, and as a normal, everyday business expense of any salesman. Therefore, his automobile is generally the salesman's own responsibility.

Arguments for Straight Commission Compensation

The primary arguments in favor of paying salesmen solely on a commission basis are that it is a stimulus or incentive to the salesman, and that it rewards production. It is a form of piecework philosophy, coupled with the idea that the industrial real estate salesman is, to a degree, an independent contractor. As such, he is supposed to operate best with a minimum of supervision, and to be most productive for the firm as well as for himself when he feels a financial incentive to produce.

Finally, there is the further contention that a commission approach tends to eliminate the incompetent, simply by denying them compensation over any prolonged period of time.

Whatever the arguments, the straight commission basis remains the most prevalent method of paying industrial real estate salesmen. Some observers argue that this is also the origin of much of the recruiting and personnel difficulty encountered in the industrial real estate brokerage business.

---

[9] Schlesinger, *op. cit.*

Arguments in Favor of Salary-Type Compensation

Despite the overwhelming weight of evidence in favor of straight commission payments, an increasing number of leading firms appear to prefer salaries and advances against commissions, as opposed to straight commission compensation. They argue that it tends to create a more cooperative and more relaxed atmosphere within the industrial brokerage firm, with teamwork emphasized rather than competition among the firm's salesmen. One major firm attempts to keep at least a base flow of income over the peaks and troughs of business activity. Because a large amount of time and effort is often involved in a single industrial real estate transaction, the time between commissions actually earned may be substantial. Income is also likely to fluctuate widely, and many employers argue that maintaining a more nearly regular flow of income benefits both the employee and the firm. The employee's gains from regular income are obvious: he is better able to project his living and expenditure patterns on a relatively normal basis. From the point of view of the firm, the salesman is less likely to worry about keeping up with payments on debts and maintaining his plane of living if he has a reasonably steady flow of income.

Intra-office competition is reduced when compensation is on a salary or draw or bonus basis. The members of the office staff are encouraged to work as a coordinated team. In handling exclusives, members of the sales staff have less time pressure on them. Hence, they are more inclined to seek to work for the best offer, rather than to obtain a first offer for the listing. This also encourages an exchange of information within the office, and enables the organization to emphasize service to its customers.

From the point of view of management, men on salary can more easily be asked to cooperate and assist one another, and to work for the good of the firm. Moreover, the employing broker can exercise better control and better supervision over the activities of his salesmen.

Whatever the decision about methods of compensation, it can safely be said that no one system will work for every firm. Moreover, varying combinations of arrangements make sense in different circumstances. For example, trainees almost invariably will favor a salary or draw. On the other hand, some more experienced salesmen prefer a straight commission arrangement. It is incumbent upon the management of the industrial real estate brokerage firm, therefore, to study its own situation carefully, and to establish a system of compensation that appears to be most nearly consistent with its circumstances and objectives.

Sharing or Splitting Commissions

Within the office, salesmen on commission are encouraged to negotiate their own arrangements for splitting fees or commissions earned. The most common arrangement found is a 50–50 split. Employing brokers usually prefer to have splits only between actual participants in the sale, rather than as compensation for "help."

BUSINESS AND SALES MANAGEMENT OF
INDUSTRIAL REAL ESTATE OFFICES

In order to become an effective business organization, the industrial real estate brokerage office must have a systematic method for dealing with business that comes to its attention, as well as a system of internal checks to record progress in the handling of that business. This involves managerial planning. Planning, in turn, requires that there be conscious efforts to forecast future developments, both in the market and within the firm, and to establish appropriate policies of action on the basis of these forecasts.

The factors of managerial planning for real estate brokerage offices have been classified under three headings for purposes of planning analysis. There are first those which are noncontrollable, which means that the management of the real estate brokerage organization can exert little or no influence on them. These factors must simply be taken as given, and the firm's policy adjusted to expectations about their future. They include such matters as business and economic trends; real estate market trends; population changes and population characteristics; the pattern of real estate ownership versus leasing; government financial policies; and trends in money and mortgage markets.

Partially controllable factors are those which must be taken as essentially given, but which the management of the real estate organization can influence somewhat within their own market areas. These include the level and character of competition among the firms operating in the local real estate market; branch and expansion operations; and the development and utilization of new technological innovations within real estate firms.

Finally, there are those factors which are controllable by the management of the firm. Planning is particularly significant here because it involves more than merely reacting to anticipated external circumstances. It represents a realm within which the management of the firm can actually create a portion of its own destiny. These factors include the business and selling experience of the staff; the capital structure and financial stability of the organization; the sources of gross income or commissions; trends in sales, expenses and personnel; and the image and reputation of the business. Controllable factors are the ones with which the management of the industrial brokerage firm must particularly concern itself in planning for the future.[10]

Inside this framework of analysis, an intra-office system is needed to provide the support that the industrial real estate salesman requires to do his job effectively. Since industrial real estate salesmen are specialized practitioners, they cannot perform their jobs properly unless appropriate supporting facilities are available.

In addition, the application of business management principles provides the firm with the means to analyze its reports at the end of the year. Management can ascertain where listings have come from; what the cost of sales has been; what advertising and other expenses have been; what types of

---

[10] For a further discussion of the handling of controllable factors, consult Case, *Real Estate Brokerage*, p. 57.

property have been sold or leased; how much time it has taken on the average to complete a transaction; and where customers or users of leased and sold space have come from. In brief, it permits a review of the sales program, and stimulates efforts to make it more effective.

Data Records System

In addition to systematic analysis of the results of past activities for future planning purposes, there must also be an effective system of record-keeping. It is essential to have quick and easy access to listing data and other property information. One leading S.I.R. has stated that if the industrial real estate salesman can answer the first five or six questions that a prospective client or customer asks, then he generally has the prospect on his side, and can work effectively with him.[11] A well-organized and efficient data-retrieval system will permit such a performance in most instances. All data forms must be compatible with one another so that the information is maintained in a similar, systematic fashion, and kept constantly up to date. Otherwise, the confidence of prospective clients in the accuracy of the system and of the information provided will be considerably shaken.

One effective means for maintaining information on a current basis is the Change of Listing Status form utilized by the Maryland-Washington, D.C., Chapter of S.I.R., which is shown as Exhibit 35. This form is a supplement to the Listing Form illustrated in Chapter 6. It permits recipient firms to stay continually current on the status of all listings; and to remove properties from the "active" file as they are sold, leased, or otherwise withdrawn from the market.

Internal Information for Sales Management and Control

Operating records and forms can be as important for internal control by management as they can be in providing service to customers. One important rule, whatever the use of the information, is that records should be maintained only as long as they are helpful in developing successful sales programs.[12] The most successful industrial real estate brokerage offices are usually those in which all sales staff members are most informed about what is going on in all phases of the business. Within this framework, every salesman should know a particular area, and specialize in it.

Office records are important aids to specialization. Good files make it possible for clerical staff members to channel leads to the appropriate salesmen as they are received, depending on the area, the industry, the type of firm, the type of plant, or the type of owner involved.

Leads are developed from various sources, as indicated in the discussion of sources of business in Chapter 6. With good working records being maintained in the office by staff personnel, it is possible to keep salesmen out in the market visiting, talking, listening, and discussing current developments with their contacts.

In order to keep everyone within the office informed about new business,

---

[11] Schlesinger, *op. cit.*

[12] This point is developed further in Case, *Real Estate Brokerage*, p. 161.

Exhibit 35

CHANGE OF LISTING STATUS FORM

DATE _____

LOCATION: _____

AGENT: _____

_____ SOLD   _____ WITHDRAWN

_____ LEASED   _____ LISTING EXPIRED

CHANGE IN LISTING INFORMATION: _____

_____

_____

_____

_____

one major industrial brokerage firm distributes to all salesmen and all executives a daily report form on leads.[13] These are translated to data sheets to be inserted in each salesman's fieldbook, as illustrated in Exhibit 36.

The data sheet illustrated in Exhibit 36 provides capsule information for each salesman on new leads and new listings that daily come to the office. In addition to keeping the sales staff informed about new business opportunities, it also provides a check against any erroneous assignment of leads to salesmen not interested in the property in question.

In order to maintain an "open house" environment, in which everyone in the office is kept informed on what everyone else is doing, many firms have either report forms or memo forms that are regularly filled out and distributed to the entire staff. In addition to providing immediate information to the sales staff, these report forms constitute part of the permanent record maintained in the files, both for active listings, and for changes in listing status. Exhibit 37 depicts an intra-office report form for use in recording a sale or lease which has occurred. This permits all staff members to adjust their personal fieldbooks and active files, as well as the central office files. Finally, the information provides the basis for market analysis, or comparable sales or lease analysis, in the event that appraisals are undertaken by the office.

Since two or more salesmen in the same office may often be working on the same transaction or property, it is particularly important for them to be aware of what is happening. On occasion, one salesman may know the property or the owner and concentrate on selling or leasing the listing; another

---

[13] Schlesinger, *op. cit.*

Exhibit 36

DATA SHEET FOR SALESMAN'S FIELDBOOK

LOCATION:—

OWNER:—

AGENT:—

TYPE:—

DIMENSIONS:—

AREA:—

HEAT:—

RENT:—

SALE:—

POSSESSION:—

FLOOR PLAN NO.

REMARKS:—

Industrial Realty Company, Inc., Baltimore.

may be working with a user who finds that the listing suits his purposes. Since salesmen are out in the field continually, it is only through written communication that information about changes in the status of a particular property can reach everyone. Within the "open house" environment, a communications gap adversely affecting marketing efforts is less likely to result. The closed deal report form (see Exhibit 38) is a further aid to avoid either gaps in information or overlaps of activity.

Sales Controls

Many industrial brokerage firms encourage area and industry specialization by their salesmen, and protect the exclusive listings of those salesmen who are able to obtain them. They also conduct weekly staff meetings, during which both the activities and the problems of each individual salesman are discussed. With a large staff, this can be a rather lengthy meeting. Nevertheless, it provides one designated time each week when everyone becomes fully aware of what is happening throughout the entire organization. It serves to supplement and amplify the written record that is produced through forms and memoranda.

There is varied opinion as to the best or most appropriate time to hold a weekly sales meeting. There are important collateral considerations to keep in mind. One firm, for example, always holds its weekly sales meetings from 5 to 7 P.M., because calls and inquiries into the office decrease significantly

Exhibit 37

INTRA-OFFICE REPORT ON SALE OR LEASE

The Joseph J. Garibaldi Organization

DATE:..

GRANTOR or LESSOR..GRANTEE or LESSEE...

ADDRESS ....ADDRESS ....

ADDRESS OF PROPERTY..

NO. SQ. FT. ....

NO. TO BE EMPLOYED..

TYPE OF BUSINESS...

TERMS ....

PRINCIPLE OFFICERS FOR BOTH COMPANIES...

....

LAWYERS FOR GRANTOR OR LESSOR..

LAWYERS FOR GRANTEE OR LESSEE..

CHECKED FOR COPY OF CONTRACT............................CHECKED FOR PUBLICITY..

CHECKED FOR INSURANCE..CHECKED FOR SIGNS..

DATE OF CLOSING...

SALESMAN ....AMT. OF COMMISSION PAYABLE.................................

DIVISION OF COMMISSION..COMMISSION COLLECTED...

....

....

RENEWALS OR OPTIONS...

....

....

REMARKS: ....

....

....

....

....

after approximately 4:45 P.M., and most clients or potential customers do not like to be bothered or visited after approximately 5 P.M. The 7 P.M. closing time permits the sales staff to eat at home, and does not seriously interfere with their family lives.

Exhibit 38

CLOSED DEAL REPORT FORM

Louis Schlesinger Co.
CLOSED DEAL REPORT

City	Deal #_____
Street Address	Date _____
Seller—Landlord	Listing #_____
Attorney	Lead #_____
Buyer—Tenant	Area Bldg. _____
Attorney	Area Land _____
Date of Sale—Lease	Rent per sq. ft. _____
Title to Close	
Sales Price	

Rent per year   for   years, from   to

Total Rental

Rate Commission

Total Commission

L.S. Co.

Salesmen

Co-Broker

Commission Agreement

Option to Purchase   at $
                                      Notice to be given before

Renewal Privilege   from   to
                                     Notice to be given before

Publicity (Now)
         (On Title)   Expiration Cards

Remarks   _____

                                     _____

                                     _____

                                     Processed by _____

In addition, one firm found that its regular Wednesday afternoon meeting, which was selected carefully to provide middle-of-the-week reporting, had to be changed between May and September. Wednesday afternoon was Golf Day for most of the industrialists in the area! Because of the volume of business transacted on the golf course, staff members felt that the weekly meeting was seriously infringing upon selling time. Accordingly, the weekly sales meeting was changed during the golf season.

As a further control over the activities of sales personnel, weekly report forms summarizing each salesman's activities are submitted on Monday morning in one major brokerage firm. The form is shown here as Exhibit 39. These are analyzed by the principals, and then commented upon at the weekly sales meeting. They permit identification of who is doing what, and identification of which salesmen require special treatment or consultative assistance from management.

Exhibit 39

SALESMEN'S WEEKLY ACTIVITY REPORT FORM

Louis Schlesinger Co.
SALESMAN WEEKLY ACTIVITY

Leads (Out)   *Leads (Saw)*   *Leads (Phone)*

Canvassed (Person)   *Canvassed (Phone)*   *Canvassed (Letter)*

Properties Inspected   *Properties Listed*

Remarks:

INDUSTRIAL REAL ESTATE RECORDS AND FILES

The industrial real estate broker is a holder of inventory. His inventory consists of all industrial sites, buildings, users, and owners known to be on the market, or *potentially* on the market, at any given time. He has information about these properties and users, as well as his own listings. The files of data about available properties, about the market, and about users have been characterized by many as the lifeblood of the industrial real estate brokerage business.

The data must be reliable and complete. That is why brokerage organizations work long and hard on their listing information sheets, and on their property information sheets. Generally speaking, the more detailed and complete the information, the more effectively the property can be marketed. The completed illustrative listing sheet, Exhibit 47 at the end of this chapter, appeared in the January–February, 1966 issue of the *S.I.R. Market Letter*.

Ease of Access

If information is on file in the records of the industrial brokerage office, and it cannot be pulled out immediately for a prospect, then there is something wrong with both the records system and the procedures of the office. It is not enough for the information merely to be complete and accurate. It must also be quickly and easily retrievable. Industrial firms often wait until nearly the last minute to begin an active search for a new location. Under these conditions, expeditious action is absolutely necessary if the broker is to serve the needs of the prospect adequately. It is only through prompt action that immediate requirements can be met. Moreover, repeat business will often be generated as a result.

A continuing information flow is necessary to keep the files current. Active files are also used as "tickler" files, with reminders about such things as expiration dates of leases, anniversary dates of locations of previous customers, and expiration dates of known listings. These latter are administrative rather than sales considerations, but they are important sources of leads for the sales staff.

Nearly as important as these current files are what might be termed the reference files. These cover properties which have been sold or leased, and contain the types of information provided in Exhibits 37 and 38. The various listing information sheets are also filed as reference information once a property is disposed of by the office in question, or by a competitor. These must also be kept up to date so that the possible needs of past customers can be *anticipated,* and new leads developed. For example, files of past sales and leases are important because the broker can follow the growth and development of the firms involved. He can then anticipate their probable needs, and come to them at a time when they are beginning to think about additional space.

Types of Data Systems

There is no one "best" data system for an industrial brokerage office. What is feasible in a particular case will depend on a number of factors, including the scale of operations of the firm, the type of customers or properties in which the firm specializes, and the geographic scope of its activities. There are some choices and alternatives in available data systems, however. Generally speaking, they all are based on the presumption that the material is fully complete and accurate. It does not matter what specific forms are used if the system works quickly and accurately.

When the problem of establishing a data retrieval system is faced by the industrial brokerage office, it is often advisable to retain a systems analyst as consultant to develop the most appropriate system for the particular operation.

1. *File Folders.*   The simplest and easiest system is one in which the

property file folders themselves become the data file through which the searcher moves in attempting to seek out information. Manila folders or envelopes are filed by number, by location, alphabetically by street name, or by some other previously designated system that enables a searcher to find the information quickly and easily. It is possible to have several sub-classifications—one file cabinet can represent a major classification, each file drawer can represent a sub-classification, and individual properties can be filed according to yet another classification system within each drawer.

While this is a simple and easy system, it is also cumbersome for more than a few hundred case folders. It is probably best for the small office just starting in business, which cannot yet afford a more complex system.

2. *Card Index System.*   Under this arrangement, the individual file folders are much the same as they are under the simpler, direct access system. The difference is that each is assigned a code number or folder number which may or may not be then classified on a color or space basis. For example, all land listings may be located in one file cabinet, while all improved property listings are located in another. Similarly, land listing folders may have white tabs, while property listings have pink tabs. The same general kinds of classifications can be provided for leads, sold or leased properties, and so on.

The essence of the card index file is that the properties represented by each file folder are cross-indexed according to their major characteristics. For example, floor area size category might be one basis for classification (e.g., 0 to 4,999 square feet; 5,000 to 9,999 square feet; etc.). A separate index file of 3 x 5 or 4 x 6 cards is maintained for each major category or classification. Each new listing and each new lead is assigned one card for each classification category. Therefore, if the properties are cross-indexed by six different categories, then six card index files must be maintained, and six separate cards must be made up for each new entry.

This illustrates both the strength and the weakness of the card index system. It does provide for considerably more flexibility, and handles a much larger number of information folders than does the simple direct folder filing system. At the same time, the amount of work involved in entering each new piece of information is much greater, and it increases proportionately as the number of cross-classifications increases. So long as each folder is assigned a number or other identification, the cross-index permits much faster access to the information than does the simple folder system. It is more expensive to insert the information into the system in the first place, but it is much easier and much faster to retrieve it later.

3. *Salesmen's Workbooks.*   Rather than being a separate system, this is an adjunct to others that might be utilized for central files. Exhibit 36 illustrated a data sheet for a salesman's fieldbook. It is utilized in many offices to provide field representatives with uniform information. Within the notebook, the sheets can be tabbed or classified according to major categories or characteristics: land or improved property; community; sale or lease; and the like. Moreover, as long as there is a property number or other identification assigned each listing or entry, and as long as that identification

is placed on each of the summary sheets in the salesman's fieldbook, then he can quickly gain access to the central office file if a prospect is interested in further details.

4. *Map-File Site Analysis System.* One S.I.R. member's firm has assembled a large wall map depicting the major metropolitan area within which the bulk of its listings and business are located. This map measures some six by nine feet, and is assembled from United States Coast & Geodetic Survey base maps of the area. The outstanding physical features of the area are highlighted with marking pens. These include waterways, highways, rail lines, and other boundaries.

Starting at a point in the downtown core of the central city, the map has been marked off into geographic quadrants, and a quadrant numbering system has been developed. Every known listing of an industrial site in the area, whether an exclusive with the firm or a listing with another broker, is indicated with a colored tack on the map. Each colored tack is numbered, and there is a property folder that corresponds to that numbered tack in the central active file in the office. Different colors are utilized for different situations: exclusive listing, sale, lease, or whatever. Any prospect, broker, utility company or industrial development representative can walk into the brokerage office in question and see at a glance where sites are currently known to be available.

The usefulness of this system depends largely on its comprehensive coverage, its reliability, and its currency. From a preliminary visual evaluation of the situation, reference can be made directly to the files to provide detailed information on the site in question. The office maintains several copies of a data sheet in each folder so that any inquiry can be answered immediately, and the prospect or broker can receive a copy of the listing data sheet.

Aside from providing useful information which is carefully catalogued and readily accessible, the preparation of this map and the task of keeping it up to date have made the staff members in charge of it more sensitive to the local real estate market and the characteristics of site requirements of industry in the area. As a by-product of the application of this system, the sales staff of the firm has learned to separate basically attractive sites and listings from those which are probably marginal in the current market. It provides a one-stop service for potential customers, and a system of logical analysis of sites.

5. *Mechanical Sorting Cards.* Greater flexibility is provided, but more time and effort are required to prepare mechanical sorting cards. These are usually 5 x 8 cards with a series of holes drilled around their edges. These holes are so located that they can be coded for information that is typed directly on the face of the card. A coding system must be developed, and each new entry must be properly coded and punched before it is filed.

Once the coding system has been established, it is extremely important to develop a set format for the presentation of the data on the face of the card. This makes it easier for the coder, the checker, and the user. Once the card has been coded, a special wedge-shaped punch is utilized to punch out all of the marked holes. For example, hole number 17 across the top of the card may be designated as the indicator of whether the property is owner-occupied or tenant-occupied. If the property is owner-occupied, then no mark is made on hole number 17. If it is tenant-occupied, on the other hand, then a mark is made on hole number 17, and the hole is punched out. Subsequently, when cards are being sorted as between owner-occupied plants and tenant-occupied plants, a skewer-like device is run through all of the cards in the deck at hole number 17. Gently shaking the deck on the skewer releases all of those which are tenant-occupied, and retains all those which are owner-occupied.

An alternative method might be to assign one hole to each characteristic. Therefore, owner-occupied plants might be coded for hole number 16 across the top, while tenant-occupied properties would be coded for hole number 17. The important point is that through mechanical search and sorting, properties with varying characteristics can be identified. A wide variety of information can be placed on one card, and with a few sortings the individual cards representing properties that meet the specifications of the particular search can be identified quite rapidly.

The basic advantage of this system is its great flexibility. The cards do not have to be kept in any particular order. They simply have to be placed in the deck for future use. The system permits almost limitless cross-classifications and cross-tabulations, without complex additional effort in programming or otherwise coding the data. It simply requires one pass of the "skewer" for each classification to be tabulated. The cards can be machine-sorted rather than by hand with the "skewer." A sample card, showing the format used in an industrial location survey conducted by the Center for Real Estate and Urban Economic Studies at the University of Connecticut, is shown as Exhibit 40.

A final advantage of the mechanical sorting system is that a search or tabulation is usually quick, and can be conducted by anyone who can read the coding sheet. It does not require a highly trained expert to conduct the sorting "search."

On the other hand, there are serious limitations to this procedure. First, it is quite expensive in time and effort to establish an appropriate coding system. Second, several verification steps are necessary before a coded card can safely be placed in the deck. A high degree of skill is not required, but extreme care is. It is time-consuming and therefore expensive. The cards themselves are not particularly expensive, but they are rather more expensive than ordinary file cards or electronic data processing punch cards.

A further limitation of this system is that it does become cumbersome and awkward to use if more than 1,000 cards are included in any file or deck. Of course, gross sorts can in effect be made by keeping land or site listings in one deck and improved property listings in another. Unfortunately, there is a practical limitation to the size of the workable file that can be developed with this system. In addition, the coded and punched cards have a tendency to tear and fray with repeated use. Nevertheless, this system represents a significant improvement over ordinary file systems, in that it offers almost limitless flexibility.

Exhibit 40

KEYSORT CARD—INDUSTRIAL LOCATION

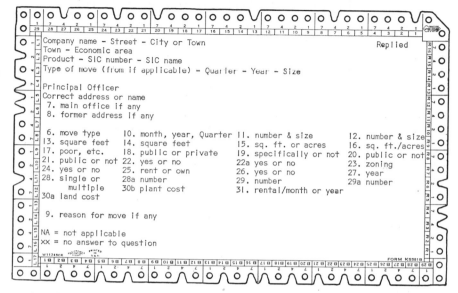

6. *Electronic Data Processing.* The use of electronic data processing equipment (often erroneously referred to as computers) presents by far the most flexible but also the most expensive method for establishing a data retrieval system. The greatest costs lie in the initial preparation of a data format and a card format, a coding system for the cards, the keypunching of the basic set of cards, and the machine instructions for sorting the cards and tabulating the information.

Since most of the effort in this type of process is data retrieval, without any further analysis or manipulation of the data, relatively simple and un-sophisticated sorting and tabulating equipment can be utilized. Therefore, a large investment in programming skills is not necessary, and expensive EDP equipment need not be utilized.

Data storage space is considerably reduced with an electronic data processing system. Extremely fast data retrieval is usually possible, although a large number of passes in a sorting machine can take quite a bit of time. This system is warranted when several thousand units are going to be processed. It is possible to include a considerable amount of detail on the cards. The number of classifications is limited only by the amount of data that can be inserted into the system. This is illustrated in Exhibit 41.

The information contained in the list which constitutes Exhibit 41 was all coded and available on one keypunch card for each listing. In fact, there were several columns remaining for adding further information. Exhibit 41 represents simply one possible alternative for providing information via electronic data processing. The data can be coded and filed in relatively little space, and information can be recalled in a wide variety of forms very

Exhibit 41

LIST OF INFORMATION CONTAINED ON
ILLUSTRATIVE EDP PROPERTY LISTING CARD

Property number (identification)
Quadrant
Site Information
  Size (Acres)
  Conditions
  Zoning Information
  Topography
  Exposure
  Access
  Railroad Facilities
  Waterfront
  Utilities
    Gas
    Water
    Storm Water
    Sanitary Sewer
  Address

Building Information
  Area (Square Feet)
  Number of Floors Available
  Elevator
  Heat
    Warehouse
    Office
  Sale: Price Indication
  Rent: Rental per annum
  Loading
  Ceiling Height
  Office Space Area (Square Feet)
  Floor
  Sprinkler

promptly. Provided the volume of business of the office warrants the initial expenditure and the cost of maintaining the system, it is by far the most effective for client service.

Mailing Lists

Every industrial real estate brokerage office of any magnitude maintains (and often jealously guards) its own mailing list of industrialists, industrial landowners, industrial brokers, utility and railroad representatives, and industrial development commission representatives. These generally cover the range of the total market area in which the firm considers itself to operate. For members of the Society of Industrial Realtors, for example, the industrial brokerage list will normally include all other members of the Society. In addition, S.I.R. has available to its members a selected mailing list of more than 8,000 key executives of major manufacturing and industrial firms.

The mailing list of the industrial real estate brokerage office must be maintained as a current, complete and accurate compilation of the appropriate prospects or sources to which the firm wishes to direct its campaigns. Beyond this, the larger the list, the more sensitive it should be to selectivity. Most addressing machines have means for coding or otherwise identifying categories into which each of the address plates will fall. By inserting a precoded instruction panel or program into the addressing equipment, a more selective list can be developed.

As with electronic data processing of property records and files, automated mailing equipment and coded mailing lists are practicable only for the large volume firm, which can afford both the initial costs and the continuing overhead for a higher degree of selectivity.

Management Control Files

Internally generated records and files of sales activity, staff activity, listings turnover, expenses, income, sources of business, and sales prices or rentals are all invaluable guides to management in analyzing past performance, and in planning for future activity. They are significant in setting standards or quotas for future periods. They also serve as important checks to identify sources of strength and weakness in the firm's sales effort. They provide a basis for cost control, and indicate the direction for major promotions.

In short, complete and accurate records of the past performance of the firm and its staff are as valuable a tool in the operation of the industrial real estate office as are listing and lead data for sales.

INDUSTRIAL REAL ESTATE PROMOTION AND ADVERTISING

The basic function of the industrial real estate salesman or broker is to market industrial space. In order to achieve this objective, he must often resort to advertising and other promotional devices. He must insist upon complete control of the handling of the promotional efforts under any exclusive arrangement.

The purpose of any promotional campaign is to create interest in the industrial real estate, and thus facilitate its marketing—either sale or lease.

Development of a Promotional Program

The development of the promotional program for any industrial listing requires careful analysis and a selection of the proper approach. The decision may become almost an automatic one with the passage of time, but a serious trap for the unwary is to assume that there is one "best way" to promote every industrial listing. Even if properties themselves do not change, market conditions and tastes do. The time, effort, and money expended in promoting sales are too valuable and too scarce to waste.

1. *Decide on What Is Likely to Be Most Effective.* The first important step is to ascertain what the potential market is for the property in question, and who or what the most likely purchaser or tenant should be. In addition, it should be determined whether to promote the property for sale or for lease. This does not mean that one or the other must be selected exclusively, but an initial decision must be made over which is to be stressed because it is the more likely. The property must be studied carefully, the market closely analyzed, and the particular set of conditions surrounding the listing carefully evaluated.

2. *Obtain the Necessary and Appropriate Skills.* Most industrial real estate brokerage organizations will not have experienced or qualified public relations, advertising or promotional personnel on their staff. Having once written copy for an advertisement that resulted in the sale or lease of an industrial plant does not qualify a member of the sales staff as an expert or

specialist in industrial real estate promotion. The most highly skilled technical efforts in listing and analyzing the property can be undermined by an amateur "do-it-yourself" sales promotional effort. It is generally agreed that it is desirable to hire a specialist or consultant for the development of standard procedures and forms, and that it is imperative to do so on major jobs.

The new or small organization should obtain an evaluation of the effectiveness of its overall promotional program, together with recommendations for improvement, from an outside advertising or public relations consultant.

At the very least, the industrial real estate firm should consult the existing published materials on specialized guidance and advice, available from such organizations as the National Institute of Real Estate Brokers of the National Association of Real Estate Boards,[14] or the Society of Industrial Realtors.

3. *Establish a Proper Budget in Advance.* The costs of advertising can rapidly become seriously disproportionate to the results that they generate. Major difficulties can be avoided if there is a clearly defined, written agreement between the broker and the owner *in advance* specifying how much effort is to be expended in advertising the property, and whether the owner will either underwrite or share in the cost of any advertising or promotional effort. Most firms do not usually ask the owner to share in this cost, but some regard this as a normal expense to be borne by the owner. Whatever the arrangement, it should be clarified in advance of any expenditure.

If the owner does participate in the cost of the advertising program, he will undoubtedly want to participate in the development of the program as well. This consideration is often serious enough to deter the broker from the practice.

There is one situation which may require specific treatment in each instance. If there is to be no advance from the owner to cover advertising expense, what happens if the property is neither sold nor leased during the period of the exclusive listing? Under these circumstances the broker may be reimbursed for all or a portion of the advertising and promotional expenses he has incurred. There are no fixed rules or standards on this practice, but it is another issue to be clarified at the outset of any agreement.

Methods and Techniques of Industrial Real Estate Promotion

A variety of alternatives is available to the industrial real estate broker for the promotion of industrial listings. Each has its advantages and its disadvantages, and each has its particular uses. It is up to the broker or salesman to decide which technique is appropriate to his circumstances.

1. *Advertising.* Most industrial brokers agree that advertising should be specific rather than general. "Listings wanted" advertising is neither stimulating to business nor professional in appearance. Newspaper advertising in general is not regarded as a major generator of business. Few brokers ignore advertising entirely, however. They seem to agree that it keeps the name of the firm in the public eye, and that it is good for public relations purposes.

---

[14] See the National Institute of Real Estate Brokers pamphlets referenced at the end of this chapter; see also Friedman, ed., *op. cit.*, especially Chapters 2 and 52; and Case, *Real Estate Brokerage.*

Advertising is recommended in selected publications that industrialists are most likely to read, such as *The Wall Street Journal,* major metropolitan dailies, and occasionally such periodicals as *Business Week, The National Real Estate Investor,* and *The Industrial Property Guide.*

Advertising copy generally should be quite specific and particular about the property being offered for sale or lease. One national brokerage organization, whose principal doubts the efficacy of advertising as a means of promoting industrial real estate sales, indicates that they advertise "when and how we have to." Single-use properties are not usually advertised. They are promoted through a highly selective and screened mailing list. On the other hand, a nonexclusive listing is occasionally advertised if it is judged by the broker that advertising a particular property will produce inquiries.

Even the skeptics admit that prospects do occasionally read newspaper advertisements. One S.I.R. related the story of a telephone call he received from an industrial organization inquiring about a particular property that his firm had advertised. A quick search of the files revealed no such active listing, and there was no record of the advertisement in the files. The broker was about to issue various inflammatory edicts to several members of his staff, when it developed that the caller had seen the advertisement two years previously! He had remembered the name of the industrial broker, and developed into a prospect, although not for the particular property in question.[15]

2. *Mailings and Mailing Lists.* Many industrial real estate brokers believe that direct mail is the most effective method of soliciting business for listings. There are two important ingredients in direct mail promotion: the enclosure and the mailing list.

Nearly every industrial brokerage organization has a mailing list which it has developed over the years. In promoting a particular property, only a selective segment of the mailing list may be contacted. It is not good advertising for obviously unsuitable properties to come to the attention of potential industrial prospects. There is general agreement that a brochure or letter addressed to a specific individual is more likely to be read than is one addressed to "Real Estate Manager," or some other such title.

In addition to industrialists, mailing lists include other industrial brokers and representatives of utility companies, railroads, and public industrial development corporations. Exhibit 42 is a form letter which is sent to industrial brokers by one firm announcing its appointment as exclusive agent for a property, and enclosing a brochure.

In similar fashion, Exhibit 43 illustrates a letter that is sent to utilities, railroads, and public industrial development corporations. This is another example of a selective mailing from a screened mailing list.

3. *Brochures.* The most common method of promoting an industrial listing is to prepare a brochure and distribute it to selective prospects and other brokers. The precise contents of a brochure will vary considerably with the nature of the property, the advertising budget that is available, the amount of sales effort that is expected to be required, and the philosophy of

---

[15] Schlesinger, *op. cit.*

Exhibit 42

EXCLUSIVE AGENT APPOINTMENT LETTER

REALTORS

BINSWANGER CORPORATION

1420 WALNUT STREET, PHILADELPHIA 2, PENNA., PEnnypacker 5-0202, CABLE-ADDRESS: BINSREAL

Dear

                              RE:

We were most anxious to call to your immediate attention
our recent appointment as exclusive agent for the very fine
property situated in (or at)_____.

We are enclosing herewith a complete physical analysis of
the property for your information and will forward the
new brochures immediately upon completion.

Naturally, we would welcome not only your cooperation but
any suggestions you may wish to make regarding the property's
disposition.

Awaiting word.

                    Cordially,

                    BINSWANGER CORPORATION
                    Frank G. Binswanger, Jr.

                    Frank G. Binswanger, Jr.
                    President

/pas

Exhibit 43

TRANSMITTAL LETTER TO UTILITIES

REALTORS

BINSWANGER CORPORATION

1420 WALNUT STREET, PHILADELPHIA 2, PENNA., PEnnypacker 5-0202, CABLE ADDRESS: BINSREAL

To Utilities, State, Railroads, etc.

We are enclosing herewith brochure and other merchandising material concerning the property located in _____, formerly occupied by _____, for which we have been appointed the exclusive real estate agent.

We would appreciate your adding the information concerning this property to your files and would, of course, appreciate your referring all inquiries concerning the property to us where possible.

If you have thoughts or suggestions as to who possibly would be interested we naturally would welcome your call.

Cordially,

BINSWANGER CORPORATION

Frank G. Binswanger Jr

Frank G. Binswanger, Jr.
President

FGBjr
Encl.

SPECIALISTS IN INDUSTRIAL AND COMMERCIAL REAL ESTATE • NEW YORK CITY, CHARLOTTE, N.C.

the listing broker. Whatever the format and appearance of the brochure,[16] there is general agreement that all or nearly all the information gathered on the listing information sheet should be included in the sales brochure.[17] It has been argued that any time a prospective customer is sent a piece of paper with information on it, it is a brochure. The problem is to make the brochure both attractive and informative, so that the prospect will read it and be interested. An illustration of a single sheet promotional brochure is provided in Exhibit 44.

The contents of a brochure should include factual data, maps, and photographs. The precise information included will vary depending on whether the property is offered for sale, for lease, or both. The important point is to aim the brochure at the anticipated needs of the prospect. One authority has written: "Think the thoughts of your prospect, and you can't go wrong." [18] An example of a four-page brochure is given in Exhibit 45.

There are some reservations about the unlimited use of brochures, however. While the effective distribution of a brochure does develop leads and inquiries, and generally generates interest on the part of potential buyers or users, "the only thing that we have never done by sending out a brochure is to sell the property that we have advertised. . . . We sell *other* properties from the brochures." [19] Nevertheless, there is almost unanimous agreement that the most effective single means of promoting the sale of industrial space is through the judicious distribution of well-prepared, attractive, and informative brochures.

4. *Personal Contacts.*   Personal contacts were noted as one of the most important sources of leads and new business in the discussion in Chapter 6. Many brokers prefer personal contacts, or at least telephone solicitation, in attempting to promote and merchandise listings that they develop. In many instances, they find it is more effective to deliver a brochure in person, or at least to have it sent by messenger, than to send it through the mail. The major objective is to encourage the prospect at least to look at the brochure. With the near flood of promotional materials crossing the desk of the typical industrial real estate department staff member, some means must be found to attract his attention.

Beyond this, the fact remains that the best public relations and the best advertising come from the comments of satisfied customers. Therefore, they represent the best potential single source of new sales or new leases. In any event, while direct mail distributions may cover a large geographic area, personal contacts supplement this coverage with very specific and very particular emphasis on individuals.

5. *Cooperation with Other Industrial Brokers.*   For members of the

---

[16] For further discussion of the use and effectiveness of brochures, see National Institute of Real Estate Brokers, *Pictorial Advertising at Work* (Chicago, The Author, December, 1962), pp. 17–61.

[17] For example, see the discussion of this point in Irving Korb, "How to Prepare Selling Brochures for Light Manufacturing Buildings," *Training Manual for Real Estate Salesmen*, Prepared for Sacramento Metropolitan Real Estate Offices, Inc. (Lafayette, Calif., D. B. Campbell, Inc., 1957), p. 1.

[18] *Ibid.*, p. 4.

[19] Schlesinger, *op. cit.*

Society of Industrial Realtors, the promotion of industrial listings is facilitated through the *S.I.R. Market Letter,* a bi-monthly publication distributed to all members. A brochure on the property is frequently enclosed with this publication.

Some listings contained in the *Market Letter* are quite detailed, and provide an excellent insight into the nature of the property, even for distant

Exhibit 44

ILLUSTRATION OF TWO-PAGE BROCHURE

COULD YOU USE THIS FINE PRODUCTION FACILITY?

IN THE BEAUTIFUL FOX RIVER VALLEY

AURORA, ILLINOIS . . .

On the New Expressway just 39 miles west of Chicago

103,000 sq. ft., ten year old building, on 9.74 acres

Sprinklered

Depressed loading for five cars on C B & Q

Depressed, under cover loading for twelve trucks

Immediate possession

All information furnished regarding property for sale or lease is from sources deemed reliable; but no warranty or representation is made as to the accuracy thereof and same is submitted subject to errors, omissions, change of price, rental, or other conditions, prior sale or lease, or withdrawal without notice.

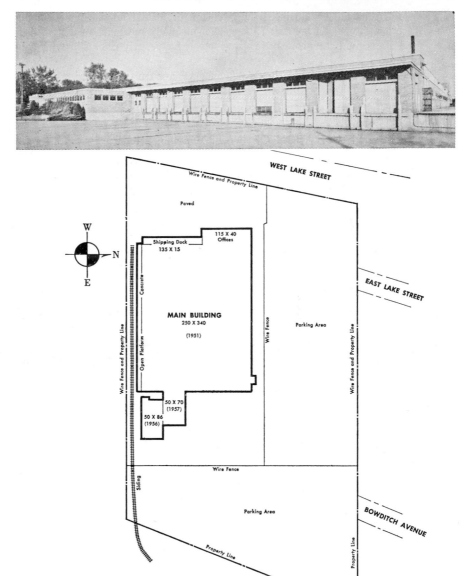

brokers. Exhibit 47 in this chapter is a copy of one such listing which appeared in the January–February 1966 issue of the *S.I.R. Market Letter.* The information can be provided in systematic fashion in relatively little space, as well as illustrating the types of information that should be gathered during a listing inspection, and accumulated on a listing information sheet.

6. *News Releases.* To the extent possible, news stories and publicity releases should be prepared whenever anything that might be considered noteworthy occurs in the sale, leasing, or other handling of industrial prop-

Exhibit 45

ILLUSTRATION OF FOUR-PAGE BROCHURE

FOR SALE ALL ONE STORY BUILDINGS BUY ANY OR ALL

37,500 SQ. FT.

26,400 SQ. FT.

TWO BLOCKS FROM NEW EXPRESSWAY CLOVERLEAF

63,900 SQ. FT.

MANUFACTURING ZONED   POSSIBLE LEASE ARRANGEMENTS

23,500 SQ. FT.

18,000 SQ. FT.

PORTABLE ELECTRIC TOOLS, INC.
is moving to a larger facility

All information furnished regarding property for sale or lease is from sources deemed reliable; but no warranty or representation is made as to the accuracy thereof and same is submitted subject to errors, omissions, change of price, rental, or other conditions, prior sale or lease, or withdrawal without notice.

THIS IS THE TYPICAL BUILDING

ALL ARE LESS THAN TEN YEARS OLD

QUICK POSSESSION

DO YOU NEED GOOD LABOR?

The best skilled and semi-skilled labor in the Chicago Area is here . . . we'll prove it!

DO YOU NEED A COMPLETE MANUFACTURING FACILITY?

Each building has very heavy power wiring, gas and air lines well distributed. Bus-Duct wiring, air compressors, evenly distributed lighting—Every building has excellent ventilation and air circulation for employee comfort, ample toilet facilities for men and women, parking for all, CTA transportation to the door, modern air-conditioned offices—

JUST 15 MINUTES TO CHICAGO'S LOOP

ONE BUILDING HAS A 20 FEET HIGH CRANE SECTION

erty by a broker. In large developments, progress reports might be treated as news. The broker should write out the release in detail, mentioning as many participants in the transaction as possible. The more names that are mentioned, generally speaking, the more likely the story is to be regarded as news by local editors. Publications such as *The National Real Estate Investor* are replete with such news stories, which do bring the successful endeavors of industrial brokers into public light.

Exhibit 46 is a reproduction of a news story, based on the sale of a large manufacturing facility in the Midwest.

7. *Signs.* Signs are regarded as important advertising devices. The first rule in their use is that an exclusive broker should ask the owner to have the signs of all others removed. Many industrial brokers will refuse to put their own sign on a building if the signs of others remain. It is important to obtain maximum exposure without a cluttered appearance.

Signs not only advertise what is for sale or for lease, but they advertise the effectiveness of the broker's efforts when a building is sold or leased. The phrase "For Sale By" is altered to read "Sold By"; the phrase "For Lease By" is altered to read "Leased By." One S.I.R., who manages multitenant buildings, maintains large signs on all buildings for which he is the rental agent. Rather than remove a sign when all of the space in the building has been leased, he changes it to read "100% Occupied," and then indicates that other desirable space is for lease by his firm elsewhere.

Perhaps the most significant aspect of the advertising impact of signs is that they reach the potential user at the point of use.

Preparation of Promotional Materials

There are two important rules in preparing promotional materials about which there is widespread agreement among industrial brokers. First, the materials should be made as nearly personal as possible. One writer argues that each individual brochure mailed out should have a personalized cover containing the phrase "prepared especially for. . . ." [20] It is important to make the appeal as personal and as direct as possible. After all, individuals make decisions, not departments or organizations.

The second major point on which there is general agreement is that whatever the normal procedure in the preparation of materials, a major listing requires the assistance of an outside specialist or consultant. It is on such efforts that the reputation of the firm is often made, and no opportunity to achieve success should be overlooked.

Summary Steps in a Promotional Program

The steps in a promotional program for an industrial listing have been outlined effectively by Dr. William Shenkel of the University of Georgia.

---

[20] Korb, *op. cit.*, p. 1.

Exhibit 46

NEWS RELEASE

SPECIAL NEWS BULLETIN

REALTY ᴀɴᴅ BUILDING

THE ECONOMIST • FOUNDED 1888

Issued Every Saturday at 12 East Grand Avenue, Chicago

February 26, 1962

J. I. Case Co. Plant in Churubusco, Ind., Sold for $1,050,000

J. J. Harrington & Co., Chicago real estate firm, represented by S. N. Tideman, Jr., was the exclusive agent and broker in the sale of the J. I. Case Co. plant in Churubusco, Ind., to the Victor Manufacturing & Gasket Co.

J. J. Harrington & Co., 22 W. Monroe St., Chicago, announces the sale of the J. I. Case Co. plant in Churubusco, Ind., for $1,050,000. The property comprises a one-story building, completed in 1958, of 251,000 sq. ft., on 90.5 acres of land. It will be occupied by Victor Manufacturing and Gasket Company as a merchandising and distribution facility, replacing their present operation located on South Iron St. in Chicago. Victor plans to be installed in the Churubusco plant by the end of the year, with about 200 employees.

Victor manufactures and distributes gaskets, oil seals, and various packing materials for all types of internal-combustion engines and vehicles, tractors, heavy equipment, etc.

G. S. McBurney of Sidley, Austin, Burgess & Smith, Chicago, and Walter S. Davis of Robertson, Hoebreckx & Davis, Milwaukee, were the attorneys.

S. N. Tideman, Jr., of J. J. Harrington & Co., was the agent for J. I. Case Co. and the broker in the transaction.

This outline provides both an excellent summary and an effective checklist for an industrial promotional campaign: [21]

A. Estimate the potential market.

    1. Analyze the property to find the type of industry and the most likely products for which the plant is adapted.

[21] William M. Shenkel, *Principles and Practices of Industrial Real Estate: A Course Syllabus* (Washington, Society of Industrial Realtors, 1963), pp. 88–89.

      a. Plant layout.

      b. Plant size.

   2. Geographic location of prospective plants.

B. The sales campaign.

   1. The preliminary campaign.

      a. Staff orientation.

      b. Complete local mailing list (records of local chamber of commerce).

      c. Other mailing lists.

         (1) State-wide list.

         (2) Specialized lists developed from trade sources or from direct mailing services.

      d. Prepare announcement advertisements for local papers.

      e. Place signs on property.

   2. The major sales campaign.

      a. Program the advertising budget.

         (1) One page flyers.

         (2) Announcement advertisements.

         (3) Brochures.

         (4) Trade magazine and newspaper classified advertisements.

         (5) Display advertisements.

         (6) Direct mailing.

      b. Select advertising media.

         (1) Newspapers: national; regional; local.

         (2) Trade magazines for more selective group.

      c. Direct mail campaigns.

         (1) Personal letter.

         (2) Brochures to selected prospects.

BROKER COOPERATION AND PROFESSIONAL SOCIETIES IN INDUSTRIAL REAL ESTATE PRACTICE

The effective operation of an industrial real estate brokerage office requires the widest possible distribution of information on its listings, and the widest possible coverage of prospects. One of the important means for achieving both of these objectives is broker cooperation. While this is neither formal nor systematic, and is certainly not required, it is particularly prevalent among the professional industrial real estate practitioners who comprise the membership of the Society of Industrial Realtors.

Broker cooperation is the strength and the lifeblood of the Society of Industrial Realtors. While seeking to market their own listings, S.I.R.'s are inclined to push the listings of others as well. They cooperate whenever it is in the best interests of the client (whether owner or prospect). Through his Society membership, the S.I.R. has a very wide geographic spread, which covers both his listings and his search for suitable space.

One of the important contributions of the S.I.R. is helping the owners of "problem" properties, and users with peculiar requirements. Because of the greater coverage and the greater variety of experience afforded members of S.I.R. through their cooperative activities, the possibilities of helping both owners and users with highly specialized requirements are much greater. Such cooperation is possible only when exclusive listings are utilized. This is true whether cooperation is among S.I.R.'s or among industrial brokers in general. Both the listing broker and the broker representing the prospective purchaser or tenant can be protected only when there is an exclusive listing.

The S.I.R. shares his exclusives with other brokers. There is, in effect, a multiple listing arrangement, although it is rarely as systematic and as organized as the Multiple Listing System found in many local Boards of Realtors, particularly for residential properties.

Through mutual inclusion in one another's mailing lists, as well as the Society's *Market Letter,* S.I.R.'s keep abreast of what space is available, and what others are seeking to market. Industrial brokers frequently refer customers (both owners and users) to other brokers for maximum efficiency in marketing the space that they are handling. Generally, the split of a commission or the fee to be paid is negotiated *after* the transaction is completed, rather than before. Indeed, most S.I.R.'s report that their practice is to let the other broker decide what his share should be.

Therefore, through the utilization of referrals and broker cooperation, both the owner seeking to sell or lease space, and the user seeking to acquire space are much more effectively served, because all brokers know that they will be protected through the exclusive right of the listing broker. This is one extremely important way in which the imperfections of the local real estate market are overcome and the market for industrial space becomes truly national in character.

Exhibit 47

COMPLETED LISTING SHEET FOR MANUFACTURING PLANT ILLUSTRATING INFORMATION NECESSARY FOR FULL REPORTING TO PROSPECTIVE OCCUPANTS AND COOPERATING BROKERS

Size:	Approximately 69,595 Sq. Ft.	
Number of Buildings:	Three (& Misc. Buildings, i.e. Boiler House, Guard House & Sewage Disposal)	
Number of Floors:	One	
	Unit 1	51,400 Sq. Ft.
	Unit 2	10,635 Sq. Ft.
	Unit 3	5,110 Sq. Ft.
		67,145 Sq. Ft.
	Misc. Boiler House	1,800
	Guard House	300
	Sewer Disposal	
	Plant	350
	Total	69,595 Sq. Ft.
Ground:	Total Area—9.333 Acres *	
	Occupied by Buildings	69,595 Sq. Ft.
		336,820
	Total	406,415 Sq. Ft.

* An additional 100 acres—may be purchased by separate negotiations with adjacent property owners.

Construction:		*Unit 1*	*Unit 2*	*Unit 3*
	Floors—	6" Concrete	Concrete	Concrete
	Walls—	Cement Block	Cement Block	Cement Block
	Columns—	Clear Span (except some block wall separations)	Clear Span	Clear Span

Date of Construction: 1952–1960

Condition of Property: Excellent

Ceiling Heights:

	Unit 1	*Unit 2*	*Unit 3*
Under Beam	14' to 20'	20'	18'6"
To Roof	20' to 27'	20' to 30'	18'6" to 27'

Column Spacing: Clear Span

Windows: Unit 1—Corregate plexiglass 11' to 14' high
Units 2 & 3—Steel casement

Toilet Facilities:

        Male
Unit 1 *Office*
       1 lavatory containing 9 toilets, 5 urinals, 2 bradleys, 1 wash basin
      Shop
       1 lavatory containing 4 toilets, 4 urinals, 4 showers
      Misc.
       1 lavatory containing 1 toilet, 1 wash basin
Unit 2 1 lavatory containing 3 toilets, 2 urinals, 3 showers
      Female
Unit 1 1 lavatory containing 2 toilets, 2 wash basins

Lighting: Fluorescent

Roof: Units 1, 2 & 3 Pitched, builtup steel roof, asbestos layer with tar paper surface (office area—flat wood builtup with tar and gravel surface)

Power: Supplied by Public Service Gas & Elec. Co.
   4160 volts primary—reducing to two banks,
   i.e. (1) 500 KVA—3 phase to 120/208V–4 wire
       (2) 500 KVA—3 single phases of 167 KVA each
            —to 120/208V–4 wire
   Total 1000 KVA—Panel Boards scattered

Heat: One "Cleaverbrook" low pressure oil fired, 200 H.P. boiler —1 yr. old
One "Cleaverbrook" low pressure oil fired, 100 H.P. boiler —6 yrs. old (Standby)
Both boilers are oil fired in winter and gas (off-peak) fired in summertime and provide heat to buildings through unit heaters. Part of Unit 1 (60' x 300') is heated by individually controlled gas fired unit heaters; and offices are heated by forced warm air (converted from steam)
5000 gallon underground oil storage tank. No. 2 oil used.

Water: Supplied by Rocky Hill Borough
   12" Main; 2–6" Lines

Sewer: Supplied by Rocky Hill Municipal Supply 12" pipe; however, plant has its own sewage disposal system.

Gas: Supplied by Public Service Gas & Electric Co.
   4" Main

Office Facilities:

Unit 1

Approximately 13,000 sq. ft. of modern air-conditioned office space containing a reception area, conference room, general office, 6 executive offices and 54 private offices.

Truck Loading Facilities:

Eight areas as follows:

Unit 1—East Side (North) One under cover motor driven metal 10' x 12' drive-in overhead door.

East Side (South) One metal 10' x 12' drive-in overhead door.

South Side (West) One metal 10' x 12' drive-in overhead door.

South Side (North) One under cover tailgate platform with 12' x 12' metal overhead door.

Unit 2—North Side (West) One metal 10' x 12' overhead drive-in door.

North Side (East) One metal 10' x 12' overhead drive-in door.

South Side (East) One metal 10' x 12 'overhead drive-in door.

*Unit 3—West Side—*One metal 10' x 12' overhead drive-in door.

Cranes:		*Length of Rail*	*Width of Rail*	*Height Under Hook*	*Name*	*Type*
	Unit 1	300'	60'	14'	Winterer	10 ton bridge; with 2–5 ton cranes
	Unit 1	300'	60'	14'	Winterer	Two bridges;—1–5 ton crane on each
	Unit 1	30'	—	—	—	2 ton trolley
	Unit 2	100'	60'	14'	Winterer	1 bridge—2–5 ton cranes
	Unit 3	60'	60'	14'	Winterer	10 ton bridge—2–5 ton cranes

Air Conditioning:

Unit 1 Two 7½ ton "Carrier" units (plant area)

One—15 ton "Carrier" unit (office area) with absorption unit in boiler room.

Cyclone Fence: Completely around property.

Zoning: Industrial

Water Rent: Rates for water use per quarter meter—First 30,000 @ 44¢ per 1000 gallons.

All gallonage over 30,000 gallons is 37¢ per 1000 gallons.

Fire Insurance on Building: Property is self insured. Estimated rate .05¢ per $100.00 per year.

Assessment:

Land	$ 7,500.00
Buildings	372,000.00
Total	$379,500.00

Taxes: $18,101.15

Miscellaneous: Cafeteria

Unit 1—Built-in freezer capacity to zero—includes compressor

Boiler Room—One 100 CFM "Ingersoll Rand" compressor (100# P.S.I.)

Paging system—12 stations

"Burns" protective agency used for security.

Source: *S.I.R. Market Letter*, No. 1, January–February, 1966, pp. 4–7; Listing S.I.R. firm; Binswanger Corporation, Philadelphia, Pa. Property: Hercules Powder Co., Rocky Hill, N.J.

SELECTED REFERENCES

California Real Estate Association, *Administration of Real Estate Brokerage Offices* (Los Angeles, The Author, 1964).

California Real Estate Association, *Real Estate Office Administration* (Los Angeles, The Author, 1963).

Case, Frederick E., *Real Estate* (Boston, Allyn and Bacon, 1962).

Case, Frederick E., *Real Estate Brokerage* (Englewood Cliffs, N.J., Prentice-Hall, 1965).

Friedman, Edith J. (ed.), *Real Estate Encyclopedia* (Englewood Cliffs, Prentice-Hall, 1960), Particularly Chapter 2: "The Modern Real Estate Office" (Jean G. Murray). Chapter 6: "Office Records of Listings" (Roger B. Conant). Chapter 52: "Public Relations in the Real Estate Business" (Robert E. Whitmer).

Kelley, Pearce C., and Lawyer, Kenneth, *How to Organize and Operate a Small Business,* 3rd ed. (Englewood Cliffs, N.J., Prentice-Hall, 1961).

Korb, Irving, "How to Prepare Selling Brochures for Light Manufacturing Buildings," *Training Manual for Real Estate Salesmen,* Prepared for Sacramento Metropolitan Real Estate Offices, Inc. (LaFayette, Calif., D. B. Campbell, 1957).

Korb, Irving, "Light Industrial Properties," *Training Manual for Real Estate Salesmen,* Prepared for Sacramento Metropolitan Real Estate Offices, Inc. (LaFayette, Calif., D. B. Campbell, 1957).

National Association of Real Estate Boards, Department of Research, *Real Estate Salesmen: Qualifications, Compensation, Advancement* (Washington, D.C., The Author, 1962).

National Institute of Real Estate Brokers (Chicago, National Association of Real Estate Boards)
>   *Business Building: Letters and Forms,* March, 1961 (Sponsor: Harold J. Schuyler)
>   *Increase Efficiency: Cut Expenses,* September, 1963 (Sponsor: Ron J. Burns)
>   *Pictorial Advertising at Work,* December, 1962 (Sponsor: L. Allen Morris)
>   *Real Estate Advertising,* June, 1961 (Sponsor: Herbert T. Jackson)
>   *Solving Salesmen's Slumps,* March, 1965 (Sponsor: Rich Port)

Schlesinger, Frank A., "Techniques in the Successful Operation of an Industrial Brokerage Office," *Advanced Course in the Techniques of Industrial Real Estate* (Washington, Society of Industrial Realtors, 1964).

Shenkel, William M., *Principles and Practices of Industrial Real Estate: A Course Syllabus* (rev. ed.) (Washington, Society of Inudustrial Realtors, 1963).

Society of Industrial Realtors, *S.I.R. Market Letter* (Washington, Society of Industrial Realtors, bi-monthly).

PART **III**

....

Supplementary Industrial Real Estate Activities

8 | Industrial Real Estate Credit

CREDIT is nearly always used to finance an industrial real estate purchase or ownership. Purchasers frequently cannot pay all cash, and even when the cash is available, it is usually uneconomic to invest the funds in real estate rather than in the business. The underlying reasons for this are explored in detail in Chapter 5. Whatever its origin, real estate credit supplements the purchaser's equity investment.[1]

Without proper debt financing of its real estate, the industrial firm may find its liquidity and even its stability jeopardized. Working capital can be reduced to a dangerous level if all cash is paid, or if other current assets are converted to purchase real estate.[2]

Perhaps even more significant is the fact that industrial firms and investors can usually put equity money to work more productively in their business than in their real estate.[3] In fact, one of the major bargaining or negotiating points in developing a credit financing program for industrial real estate is leverage. The purchaser-investor is interested in maximizing leverage so as to maximize the potential effectiveness of his equity investment. The lender, on the other hand, is anxious to see a "reasonable" equity in the property so that a higher degree of safety is present in the loan.

Finally, debt financing is often utilized in order to reduce or defer tax liability, particularly federal income tax liability. This was also noted in

[1] For details of the uses and characteristics of real estate credit in general, see, for example, Willis R. Bryant, *Mortgage Lending*, 2nd. ed. (New York, McGraw-Hill, 1962); Henry E. Hoagland and L. D. Stone, *Real Estate Finance*, rev. ed. (Homewood, Illinois; Richard D. Irwin, 1961); Sherman J. Maisel, *Financing Real Estate: Principles and Practices* (New York, McGraw-Hill, 1965).

[2] Carey Winston, "Mortgage Financing of Industrial Construction," *S.I.R. Newsletter* (Washington, Society of Industrial Realtors, May, 1966), pp. 1–4.

[3] For further discussion on this point, consult Maisel, *op. cit.*, p. 322; Robert O. Harvey, "Real Estate Finance," Ch. 26 of *Financial Handbook*, 4th ed. (New York, Ronald Press, 1964), p. 26–8; Niles Gates, "Industrial Property Investments," *Developing, Selling and Syndicating Real Estate Investment Property* (Los Angeles, California Real Estate Association, 1964), p. 90. Also, see the discussion in Chapter 5.

Chapter 5. As a tax consideration, particular emphasis should be placed on the role of refinancing presently mortgaged properties by their current owners. By increasing the amount of debt on the real estate, the owner is able to "cash out" immediately any equity he may have built up through the amortization of the existing loan. In addition, if the value of the real estate has increased beyond its book value, refinancing based upon a current appraisal enables the owner to enjoy the benefits of a capital gain immediately, without paying any federal income tax. Another possibility is refinancing during periods of reduced interest rates, so that debt service charges are reduced and net income increased accordingly. These last two possibilities are simply possibilities. Nevertheless, they represent situations of which the industrial real estate broker should be aware if he is to advise his client properly.

THE ROLE OF INTERMEDIARIES IN INDUSTRIAL REAL ESTATE LENDING

Although there is not universal agreement on terminology, a variety of intermediaries in industrial real estate mortgage market activity operate to facilitate the flow of loan funds from lender to borrower. Whatever else they do, this is one of their major functions. These participants are:

Industrial Real Estate Broker: He seeks to arrange for financing of industrial real estate, often to complete a sale or lease transaction and thereby earn his fee from the owner.

Mortgage Broker: He brings the lender and the borrower together for a fee, without reference to the transfer of real estate. He does not service loans.

Mortgage Banker: He writes commitments and makes loans, on his own account and with his own funds (whether equity or borrowed). He then sells the loans to the ultimate investor. This is called "laying off." The mortgage banker almost always services the loans that he makes, and he may or may not participate in the loan.

Mortgage Correspondent: He acts as an agent for lenders, places the loans in their name, and services the loans for them. He does *not* use his own funds.

Mortgage Company: It buys and sells mortgage paper, making a market for existing loans in particular. Such companies operate mostly in the midwestern states.

This classification identifies the various functions to be performed. The same individual or organization may perform several different functions. For example, an industrial real estate broker may very well also be a mortgage correspondent, a mortgage broker, or a mortgage banker. The difference between the industrial real estate broker and the mortgage broker in any given transaction is essentially the source of the fee. In fact, the same individual or organization might be both in the same transaction.

Industrial Real Estate Broker

The industrial real estate broker is primarily concerned with maintaining an adequate flow of loan funds to users of industrial space. Therefore, he must know about the availability of funds. He should know who has money to invest, and who has it now. He must know where to obtain money, and how. He must know and understand the functioning of the mortgage market. Most importantly, at this stage generalities no longer help; very detailed specifics are needed. It is not enough to know that life insurance companies normally lend on properties of the type that he is trying to finance. He must know, for example, that the Equitable Life Assurance Society is currently willing to consider loans on this type of property and on precisely what terms.

The broker must also know something about the policies of lenders so that he can direct his inquiries to the proper source. He should know which lenders are willing to make loans on special-purpose properties, and which ones are active, in the Kansas City market, for example. He must be aware of their standards. The broker also should know the best sources of information, particularly in his own area. Nationally, there are many publications which can provide him with some information about the current functioning of the market, such as *The Wall Street Journal, The National Real Estate Investor, The Federal Reserve Bulletin, Housing Statistics,* and *The Tally.*

In essence, the industrial real estate broker must know enough to help his client with the lender. He should be able to assist with the loan presentation. This includes the description and analysis of the property, maps and photographs, history and financial statements of the company, and a community and location analysis. He should recognize the custom character of industrial financing, and work with the lender or financing source to develop a loan agreement that accommodates the needs of both his client and the lender. Lenders appreciate this, as many of their spokesmen have indicated publicly.

Mortgage Broker

The industrial mortgage broker normally performs a wide variety of functions. Indeed, the mortgage brokerage specialist is also a mortgage banker in many instances. His function is to serve as an intermediary between borrower and lender for a fee. He is not directly involved in the sale or lease transaction, so that he can offer objective as well as expert advice on financing.

The borrower often pays the mortgage broker's fee. In this case, the transaction is net to the lender. The mortgage broker will cooperate with industrial real estate brokers, and a large volume of his business consists of shared commissions or fees. Working with the sales broker, the mortgage broker works up the detailed proposal for presentation to a lender.

Acting as the buffer between borrower and lender, the mortgage broker concentrates on, and earns his fee through, negotiation.

Mortgage Banker

The services of the mortgage banker are generally more necessary in industrial real estate than in other areas of real estate activity. "The more sophisticated the process, the more the mortgage banker is needed and used." [4] The basic role of the mortgage banker is to bring all of the variables

---

[4] Interview with David Scribner, S.I.R., New York City.

together, and to tailor the mortgage to the borrower's needs. For his work, the mortgage banker usually charges a service fee of approximately one-half per cent of the outstanding balance of the loan, per year. He also often receives a fee or a discount from the purchaser when he sells the loan. As an incidental source of income, the interest received on the loans that he originates often exceeds the interest rate that he must pay on the short-term financing he has obtained via mortgage warehousing from commercial banks. This is not always the case, however. If he must pay a higher rate, he does so because his real profit is in the turnover of funds, rather than arbitrage in the short run.

Mortgage Correspondent

This is usually a brokerage firm which acts as agent for the correspondent financial institution. The money is the institution's, and the standards of the lending company must be followed. The mortgage correspondent usually services the loan for the lending institution, receiving a servicing fee for this activity.

Mortgage Company

Although this organization is often characterized as being a mortgage banker under a different name, the primary distinction lies in the greater participation of the mortgage company in secondary market activity. The mortgage company may on occasion actually buy existing mortgages, rather than being simply an originator and seller of mortgages. Therefore, it earns profit on differentials between purchase price and sale price, as well as fees for the sale and servicing of mortgages it has originated.

CHARACTERISTICS OF INDUSTRIAL REAL ESTATE CREDIT

In order to serve his clients properly, the real estate broker must be in a position either to facilitate the extension of industrial real estate credit or to summon the assistance of a skilled professional in this field. The broker must know the needs of industry, the availability of equity funds, the policies of lenders, and the functions of mortgage intermediaries. Although the general principles underlying the negotiation and placement of mortgage loans are the same as those for residential or commercial properties, there is a much wider range of variation and possibility in the specific characteristics of the individual industrial real estate credit transaction. This represents considerably more challenge to the real estate broker.

In general, the conventional mortgage is the most prevalent instrument of industrial real estate finance. It is a collateral loan secured by a pledge of real estate, which is extinguished when the loan is repaid. However, there are also alternatives which often are not available or feasible in the financing of other types of real estate.

For example, the trust deed, which has effectively replaced the mortgage in virtually all real estate transactions in the state of California, is often used in other states when large principal sums are involved. Under this arrangement, title is conveyed to a third party (the trustee) who holds it in trust until the payment of the obligation by the borrower to the lender (the beneficiary under the trust). In addition, bonds are occasionally utilized to finance industrial real estate instead of mortgages. This possibility rarely exists in the residential or multi-family housing field, but it is a meaningful alternative in many industrial real estate transactions.

Some writers have also argued that an exchange is a form of "financing" if the objectives of the parties to the transaction are met. It is certainly a means of conserving, through substitution, the cash of the parties involved. An exchange is more likely to be recommended by an experienced broker when hard-to-sell, special-purpose industrial properties are involved.

Distinguishing Features of Industrial Real Estate Credit

1. *Individualized Loans.* The great variety of alternatives and possibilities in the specific circumstances surrounding industrial real estate transactions usually results in tailor-made loans. The terms and conditions of the loan will vary with the size of the transaction, the risk involved, the use of the premises, the character of the property itself, the location of the property, and the financial strength of the user and/or owner. There is simply no stereotyped or standard pattern of lending and loan terms that the lender or the broker can follow.[5]

2. *Wider Range of Lenders.* In any given transaction, the *possibilities* for mortgage or credit financing of industrial real estate are much wider and considerably more diverse than is true of loan sources for other types of real estate. These sources range from highly specialized, regular participants in the industrial real estate lending market, through lending institutions which consider industrial properties along with others as security for their loans, to sporadic and sometimes unintentional sources of credit who need considerably more advice and assistance than do the borrowers.

3. *Larger Loans.* Most original lenders on industrial real estate are relatively large, as measured by financial resources. This is partly because the typical industrial transaction is a relatively large one so that substantial sums of money are necessary to finance it. The average size of an industrial loan sets it well apart from residential and most commercial mortgages. Because the sums involved are large, the market is often thinner, with fewer effective sources available for any one transaction, even though the potential range of alternatives is quite large.

4. *More Complex Legal and Market Arrangements.* The wider variety of potential lenders on industrial real estate, most of which are financial institutions or fiduciaries subject to some form of public regulation, means that the real estate broker must have access to highly skilled technical advice on approaching any given lender in a particular case. Both statutory and regulatory limitations on the lending abilities of specific lenders vary

[5] Thomas F. Murray, "Financing Industrial Real Estate," *Advanced Course in the Techniques of Industrial Real Estate* (Washington, Society of Industrial Realtors, 1964).

significantly from state to state, and occasionally from transaction to transaction within the same state. More technical knowledge is required in financing industrial real estate than for most other types of real estate.

Coupled with legal limitations and regulations are the varying policies of individual lenders within groups. Because the amounts of money involved are so large, the number of specific lenders to which a particular proposal would be attractive is relatively limited. Brokers must have knowledge of the policies of these individual organizations in order to avoid wasting time and effort. For example, certain life insurance companies will not consider a loan of less than $200,000, while others will not lend on multiple-tenant industrial buildings. Some lenders place paramount emphasis on the credit rating of the borrower and/or the tenant occupying the industrial building under a long-term lease, while others are more inclined to emphasize the marketability of the real estate which serves as the collateral for the loan. The broker must consider both the regulatory and the policy restraints that influence industrial real estate loan decisions by specific lenders.

The larger size of the typical industrial loan also influences lender cooperation in the market. There is considerably more participation or sharing in industrial loans among lenders, and much greater secondary market activity, than are generally associated with residential mortgages or most commercial property loans.

5. *Greater Emphasis on Credit.* There is a widespread belief that there is more "inherent" risk in industrial real estate than in other types of real estate.[6] Since industrial real estate tends to be more specialized in use and to have a more limited market in many instances, lenders seeking to maintain safety of their investments are inclined to place heavy reliance on the character and the identity of the borrower or the user of the industrial space, or both. The credit of the owner of the real estate is often a major consideration in granting an industrial real estate loan; so is the credit of the tenant under a long-term lease, when leases are assigned to the lender.

Even the method for estimating the value of industrial real estate, on which the amount of the loan is based, relies most heavily on the income generated by occupancy of the real estate and the degree of risk in that income. To a very large extent, industrial real estate lending is more credit-oriented than real estate-oriented.

A corollary consideration is that the small industrial firm is much less likely to be able to own the real estate it uses. The small or growing firm without a high credit rating and a strong background of earnings often finds it extremely difficult, if not impossible, to obtain loan funds on a competitive basis. It is therefore common to find such a firm occupying space as a tenant in a multiple-user building.

6. *Investment-Oriented Borrowers.* The borrower on an industrial real estate loan is much more likely to be a non-user investor. The viewpoint of the investor influences the types of financing and the terms of financing sought. Reducing, deferring, or avoiding income taxes is a major determinant

---

[6] For a discussion of this belief, see Sanders A. Kahn, Frederick E. Case, and Alfred Schimmel, *Real Estate Appraisal and Investment* (New York, Ronald Press, 1963), p. 372.

of the pattern of financing that is requested in many instances. For example, efforts are commonly made to establish a mortgage amortization pattern that fits best with the depreciation that is permitted in the given circumstances.

The industrial investment market is extremely sensitive to changes in terms and conditions of financing. It is important for the industrial broker to understand the impact of financing terms and conditions on net income and profit flows to the borrower-investor.

7. *Long and Complex Negotiations.* The period of time from the initiation of negotiations to the completion of loan arrangements is generally much longer for industrial real estate transactions than for the financing of other types of real estate. Just as industrial sales or leasing transactions consume considerable periods of time, the agreement to loan also requires a substantial period of time. In addition, the number of participants in an industrial financing "package" may be quite substantial. This is especially true if multiple ownership or multiple sources of equity funds are utilized, as discussed in Chapter 9. For industrial development or construction transactions, the sources of money are frequently different. Hence, different types of loans are often negotiated for each of the various stages in the development of the same property. There may be a land or site development loan, a construction loan and, finally, "permanent" financing—all stemming from different lenders who specialize by type of lending.

TYPES OF LOANS

Most industrial real estate credit is extended on the basis of direct mortgage loans, under which the real estate itself is pledged as collateral until the debt is extinguished. Even with the complicating peculiarities surrounding the negotiations which are part of an industrial real estate transaction, the great majority of industrial mortgages are relatively straightforward and relatively standardized. The problem confronting the industrial real estate broker and his colleagues (the mortgage broker and the mortgage banker) is to decide whether a straightforward, conventional mortgage loan is most suited to the needs of all parties involved, or whether one of the several variants on the basic theme is more appropriate. In order to make this determination, the technical specialists must be aware of the range of alternatives that exist, their uses, their applications and their limitations.

First Mortgage Loans

The first mortgage loan on industrial real estate typically represents a lien against both capital value and the income generated by the real estate. Leased industrial real estate can rarely be financed without an assignment of the owner's rental income to the lender. The lender normally requires this as further security for his loan.

1. *Conventional Loans.* These represent the most common type of mortgage loan, containing what might be termed "normal" rights and obligations on the part of both parties. There is still substantial variation from

one state to another, and from one lender to another, as to exactly what is "normal," but the basic characteristics are essentially the same. This is also by far the simplest arrangement to negotiate.

2. *Construction Loans.* Conventional or long-term mortgage loans are often referred to as "permanent" financing. For new construction, builders or developers usually seek to obtain a commitment for this "permanent" financing prior to the start of construction. This commitment is normally not operative until the building is completed and occupied, and rent payments actually begin. In fact, many institutional lenders require that a Certificate of Occupancy be filed with them before the permanent loan funds are made available.

While the lender on the permanent loan may occasionally advance construction financing as well, particularly in periods of easy money, long-term lenders usually do not make construction loans. Construction financing is not necessary if the payments under the permanent financing are staged so that the builder or developer receives progress payments during construction. This arrangement is relatively rare among long-term lenders on industrial real estate, however. So is 100 per cent equity financing of industrial construction by the builder or developer. Therefore, interim financing is usually necessary from the start of construction to the time that the "take-out" commitment becomes effective.

Construction financing is almost always short-term financing, most often provided by commercial banks. It is usually based on a commitment for a take-out loan. Despite the existence of a take-out commitment with another lender, however, further safeguards are usually insisted upon in the construction loan. They include, first, the stipulation that the amount of construction financing usually will not exceed 80–90 per cent of the permanent financing commitment, or 75 per cent of market value when completed; and second, that the borrower-developer file a performance or completion bond with the lending institution.[7]

In certain market areas in which a large volume of industrial construction is under way, and in which general-purpose properties tend to move readily, it may occasionally be possible to obtain construction financing for a speculative building. The terms are substantially more strict than those for contract construction in which there is a known buyer or tenant as the basis for a permanent commitment. Maturities are quite short, loan ratios are low, and interest rates are ¼ to ½ per cent higher, but still the money is made available.

Construction financing means that the builder-developer does not necessarily need enough equity to pay for the land outright, and to still carry construction through its early stages. "There is less emphasis on the strength of the builder-developer, and more on the real estate and the market." [8]

3. *Development Loans.* In addition to construction financing, development financing or land financing is also occasionally possible. This involves

[7] While there are technical differences between a performance bond and a completion bond, their effect is the same in this instance.
[8] Interview with Peter O. Hansen, S.I.R., Hackensack, New Jersey.

a loan for site improvements to convert raw land to a usable, marketable, and (usually) more valuable site. One difficulty with this type of financing is that very often a large proportion of the expenditures are for improvements which are physically removed from the site itself. For example, water and sewer lines may have to be brought to the site, and a road may have to be brought in as well. Many lenders do not like this type of loan, and simply refuse to become involved in one. There are, however, a number of specialists in this field. They are large organizations, and they tend to concentrate their efforts on large developments. As a result, the individual builder-developer often finds that this type of financing is effectively denied him, while the large corporate developer may be able to obtain development financing from such major financial institutions as the Irving Trust Company in New York City, the Republic National Bank of Dallas, or the First National Bank of Chicago.

In addition, there are Real Estate Investment Trusts, public corporations, and private syndicates that make a point of lending for development and construction purposes. They invariably make short-term loans at premium rates. Many of the private investors also take back a portion of the equity of the development firm as an additional "kicker" or "sweetener." [9] To a large extent, this reflects the relative competitive positions of borrower and lender in this particular market.

4. *Purchase-Money Mortgages.* When a seller takes back a mortgage note from the buyer as part payment for the real estate in question, the mortgage instrument involved is known as a purchase-money mortgage. Its use varies widely in industrial real estate transactions, but it is most commonly found on sales of existing properties in which the seller finds it necessary to extend credit to the buyer if he (the seller) is to receive his price. The purchase-money mortgage is often necessary if the property is to be disposed of advantageously.

Quite frequently, the purchase-money mortgage is a second or junior mortgage, subordinated to the first mortgage that the buyer is able to obtain from an institutional lender. This saves the transaction for the seller. He defers some income and assumes what he hopes is a modest risk that there will be default, in exchange for the certainty that he will have to accept a lower price if the junior purchase-money mortgage is not granted.

Whether it is a first or a junior lien, the industrial purchase-money mortgage is usually relatively short-term, and generally has relatively modest amortization during its term, with a large "balloon" or lump sum payment at maturity.

5. *High Credit Lease Loan.* In order to increase the amount of loan that can be made on a given industrial property (as well as commercial property), particular emphasis is placed on high credit leases with rents assigned to the lender.

In New York State, for example, the "adequately secured loan" arrangement makes it possible for a New York life insurance company to make a 90 per cent loan. The pledge of the property must be validated by a long-

---

[9] Interview with David Scribner, S.I.R., New York City.

term lease to high-credit (typically Moody's Aa or better) industrial tenants. For practical purposes, the lease must be a net lease, because a gross lease is acceptable under the law only if it is fully escalated. Moreover, the lease must be non-cancelable, and the mortgagor must be a corporation. Ninety per cent of the principal must be repaid during the first term of the lease. If all these conditions are met (as well as some minor ones), then 90 per cent of the appraised value of the property may be loaned. This is one example of a strong underlying lease being used to reinforce the attractiveness of industrial real estate to an institutional lender.[10]

6. *Rehabilitation and Conversion Loans.* These loans differ little from ordinary mortgage loans, or possibly from construction loans, except that they represent an advance of funds to rehabilitate and/or to convert existing industrial buildings, and thereby make them more nearly competitive on the current market. They may involve either speculative or contract construction. Contract loans are similar to construction financing with a take-out commitment at the end. These loans may be made on single-user or multiple-occupant properties. The major point of distinction is that the specific factors considered by the lender are somewhat different. Few lenders are willing to make this type of loan. Therefore, the industrial real estate broker must often expend considerably more energy finding a source of rehabilitation or conversion loan funds.

7. *Incentive Loans.* In more risky situations, lenders often ask for, and borrowers often offer, stock options or detachable warrants to purchase stock in the corporation as a "sweetener." Such incentives are particularly useful for financing growing firms with substantial future potential, but little history of profit. The types of lenders to which this arrangement is most likely to appeal are private profit-seeking groups, rather than fiduciary institutions. For example, Small Business Investment Companies and Real Estate Investment Trusts frequently engage in this type of lending. They are, in effect, risk-taking organizations whose compensation is the prospect of participating in profit if the borrowing corporation succeeds. In some instances, a portion of the land owned by the borrowing organization (often a land development corporation) will be purchased by the lender at a low price, in anticipation of capital gain when the development succeeds. This is referred to as a "tail-end take-out." [11]

One variant of this particular procedure, that is not mortgage lending at all, deserves brief mention. Some organizations incorporate as land holding companies, and then sell stock. This has a dual advantage. First, there is no limit on the percentage of the value of the real estate that can be financed this way. At least there is no *legal* limit; the effective limit is market acceptance. The second favorable consideration is that the borrowing capacity of the corporation is not impaired. If the development is successful, institutional lenders might then be attracted to the endeavor. This is very speculative, however, and is mentioned only as one other alternative that the

---

[10] For further details, consult Murray, *op. cit.*
[11] Interview with David Scribner, S.I.R.

industrial real estate broker might consider in analyzing possibilities for a particular client.[12]

Junior or "Secondary" Financing

Junior mortgages represent liens against both the value of the real estate and the income generated by the real estate, which are subsidiary or subordinate to those of the first mortgagee. In many instances, there can be several layers of claim against the realty, depending upon the requirements of the circumstances, the ingenuity of the brokers arranging the transaction, and the willingness of lenders to participate in such an arrangement.

Purchase-money mortgages represent one frequent means of junior mortgage financing in the industrial real estate field. Most of the junior mortgage lending on industrial real estate comes from individuals or business corporations, usually at high rates. This is not always the case, however. For example, state or local industrial development corporations often fill the gap between the equity of the industrial firm, and the amount of first mortgage financing available. Materials and equipment suppliers often become junior mortgagees by deferring their claims for payment, and taking back a junior lien on the real estate.

A representative of a major life insurance company reports: "I was amazed to find that there are so many different ways to get secondary financing." One example was a plant in Ohio which cost $270,000:

We advanced $175,000 and a local development fund raised $50,000 through a stock issue, and sold a debenture issue of $45,000. In addition, they sold another debenture issue of $50,000, which provided part of the machinery costs in that plant. You have both property financing and equipment financing by this local development fund. . . .[13]

Further, he notes that another instance involved:

a major plant in Dallas, Texas, where we provided the major financing in the form of a $6,500,000 mortgage (just to show we go from little to big). On this $6,500,000 financing, the concrete supplier agreed to defer $300,000, to be paid out of income; the contractor agreed to defer $200,000; the local distributor deferred $300,000; and other miscellaneous suppliers deferred $200,000. All of these, together, provided another million dollars, in addition to our $6,500,000. They agreed that this entire million dollars was to come out of income from the property, which was rented.[14]

Such arrangements normally do not adversely affect the first mortgagee, since the positions of the junior mortgagees are subordinate to his. The one possible limitation is that the mortgagor should not be permitted to assume a burden of debt which cannot appropriately be supported by either his operations or the income from the property.

---

[12] For a discussion of this procedure, see Edmund J. McRickard, "Mortgage Investments," *Proceedings: First Annual Workshop* (Washington, Society of Industrial Realtors, 1959), p. 22.
[13] Murray, *op. cit.*
[14] *Ibid.*

Leasehold Financing

When land is leased under a long-term ground rent to a developer who then constructs a building on the land, the financing of the construction and/or ownership of that building is referred to as "leasehold financing." The developer is a lessee on the land, and his interest in the realty is only a leasehold interest. He may in turn rent out space in the building; indeed, this is the most usual procedure. Financing the building is normally based upon the stabilized income anticipated from the rental of the space in the building, or from a long-term lease on the building.

Ground leases are growing in popularity and significance throughout the United States. Because this represents a departure from what might be called standard mortgage lending practice, there is a thinner, tighter market for industrial leasehold financing than there is for loans against the fee interest in similar industrial properties.

The provisions of the ground lease that underlie a leasehold mortgage are extremely important. They determine precisely what the rights and responsibilities of the lessee are, and what the protections to the leasehold mortgagee will be. This is a legal as well as a financial consideration, and requires specialized technical advice.

Leasehold mortgages often represent a higher percentage of the value of the security than is true of mortgages on the fee. It is legally possible, in most states, for 100 per cent of the value of the building or improvements to be loaned by the leasehold mortgagee, since the security for the lien is a combination of the mortgagor's rights in the building, his rights to rental income, and his right to occupy the site for the duration of the ground lease.

Real Estate Bonds

Until the end of World War II, real estate bonds had a long and undistinguished record of unfortunate experience in the United States. Originally popular during the 1920's, they were almost always direct mortgage bonds, which might represent first or junior liens against the underlying property. In the depression of the 1930's, default and foreclosure on real estate bonds was particularly heavy.

Since 1946, however, two distinct trends in real estate bond financing have been noted. First, there have been real estate mortgage bonds, which are similar in legal appearance to those of the 1920's. Second, debentures have been utilized increasingly by industrial corporations specifically to finance real estate acquisitions and ownership.

1. *Mortgage Bonds.* Mortgage bonds are often issued by industrial corporations short of capital. It is usually possible to obtain more money through the sale of mortgage bonds than through direct mortgage placement, *provided* the bonds can be sold on the market. A small corporation can have difficulty in marketing its bonds, because there is no particular reason why investors should want to acquire them.

On the assumption that the bonds are attractive on the market, a first mortgage bond issue is created when the real estate is assigned to a trustee, who holds a mortgage against the property for the benefit of the bond holders. The bonds are then sold in more readily marketable denominations. One of the arguments for the use of a bond issue is that it tends to broaden the base of participation. In thousand dollar units, they have somewhat more marketability and liquidity than does a single lump-sum mortgage note.

Substantial limitations are usually placed on the issuing firm through the use of restrictive covenants. These are designed to protect the interest of the bond holders, and to assure the "proper" use of the funds by the borrowing corporation. The range of restrictive covenants that is possible is almost limitless, but three common provisions are: the "After-Acquired Clause," which states that any other real estate acquired by the corporation subsequent to the issuance of the mortgage bonds also becomes security for the bonds until they are retired; a limitation on dividend payments until sufficient funds are built up to assure continued payment of interest and principal on the bonds; and a requirement that minimum working capital ratios be maintained. Offsetting these restrictions, the chief advantage of the mortgage bond issue to the issuing corporation is that bonds may offer a way to avoid the legal limits on mortgages that affect some lenders. It may be possible to borrow 100 per cent of the value of the property. The costs of issuing the mortgage bond issue are considerably higher than those in placing a mortgage, however, and the effective minimum amount for a mortgage bond issue is approximately $250,000.

As an example of the effectiveness of the mortgage bond issue as a device for attracting funds and broadening the base of lender participation, the Bush Terminal in Brooklyn was financed with a $7,000,000 mortgage bond issue, and four life insurance companies participated in the loan.

2. *Debentures.* Debentures are simply promissory notes of a corporation secured by a loan agreement. There are two types of debentures that can be used to finance real estate acquisitions. First, highly rated industrial corporations may utilize their own credit on the financial markets to issue debentures, the proceeds of which pay for the acquisition of real estate. In a strict technical sense, this is not real estate finance at all. It depends almost entirely on the financial strength and credit rating of the issuing corporation. It does have the advantage of being less expensive, because the interest rate on debentures of high-credit corporations is usually lower than the rate on mortgage bond issues.

At the other end of the scale, small corporations which need funds for physical expansion often issue convertible debentures. These carry the right of conversion into stock of the issuing corporation, either directly or through the use of warrants or options that may be attached to the debentures. This is a "sweetener" designed to overcome the fact that the issuing corporation represents a relatively high risk at the time of issuance, and it offers the prospect of sharing in the success of the corporation (assuming that success is in fact forthcoming). This is a variant of the incentive loan discussed earlier. The chief difference is a legal one, since the debenture comes under the heading of "securities," while the mortgage is simply a "loan." The same types of risk-taking investors or lenders are most likely to be attracted to convertible debentures, however, especially Small Business Investment Companies and Real Estate Investment Trusts.

3. *Equipment Trust Certificates.* A rarely utilized but possible alternative to financing equipment and fixtures, which technically may be regarded as part of the realty, is the issuance of equipment trust certificates. These are a form of chattel mortgage, and are unusual enough to require the advice of a technical specialist.

LOAN TERMS

The terms of industrial real estate mortgage financing vary so widely that it is almost impossible to discuss detailed patterns of lending. There are some broad outlines which can be noted, however, to help define the general character of the market.

Much more important than details of the specific terms of lending is recognition of the fact that there is more than one term. The total "package" is made up of interest rate, loan-value ratio, maturity (or mortgage term), and amortization provisions. These determine the impact of financing on the net income of the real estate.

Each of these terms is susceptible to negotiation and adjustment between borrower and lender. The industrial real estate broker must recognize what the impact of concessions may be on each of the parties involved, and which terms each party should strive to improve for himself. A borrower may very well be willing to pay an extra 0.25 per cent in interest, if he can offset this with a longer term and hence lower annual financing charges.

Since this package of terms can vary considerably, a combination of bargaining strength and negotiating skill determines precisely where it falls in each instance. The limits within which it can vary are set by the forces of the market at any one time.

The terms of mortgage lending are interrelated. It is not possible to talk about the interest rate only, or the amortization provisions only. Each is important in the context of the others, and only the pattern of terms taken as a group has real meaning for both borrower and lender.[15]

The terms of mortgage lending influence both the value of the real estate securing the loan, and the risk involved in the loan; they are also determined by both the value of the real estate and the risk of the loan. Excessively severe mortgage loan terms, for example, can so seriously limit the ability of the borrower to carry the loan that risk is considerably increased. The value of the real estate is the basis for ascertaining how large a loan can be granted; at the same time, the amount of the loan influences leverage, and hence the present worth of the real estate.

Interest Rate

The most obvious and, generally speaking, the most powerfully influential loan character is the rate of interest charged for the use of money. It varies with the risk perceived by the lender, and with general money market condi-

---

[15] For detailed discussions of the role of mortgage terms in real estate financing, see Maisel, *op. cit.;* and Kahn, Case and Schimmel, *op. cit.*

tions. The competition for funds from other types of uses will have a direct and immediate effect on the availability of mortgage loan funds, and therefore on their price. The sudden increase in mortgage rates and the sharp decline in the availability of mortgage funds that occurred in 1966 clearly illustrate the sensitivity of mortgage interest rates to general money market conditions.

The interest rate also tends to vary by type of loan. For example, construction money generally costs one-eighth to one-quarter of a per cent more than does conventional mortgage money. Junior liens generally command a higher rate than first liens. Longer maturities have a tendency to require slightly higher rates, and larger equities generally result in slightly lower rates. All of these are functions of risk, as measured by the lender, and should be understood by the industrial broker.

Negotiation over interest rate is generally not particularly fruitful in most industrial loan transactions, however. The broker is usually better advised to look to the other terms of lending, or to seek to reduce risk directly and then approach the lender for a reconsideration of the interest rate.

Loan-To-Value Ratio

The loan-to-value ratio is the percentage figure that the principal amount of the loan represents to the appraised value of the property securing the loan. Neither cost nor sales price is the basis for the determination of how much loan can be granted on the real estate. Rather, an estimate of market value by a qualified appraiser sets the standard.

The loan-to-value ratio establishes the amount of mortgage loan that the lender either can or will grant on the particular property. The difference between the amount of the loan and the purchase price, or cost to the borrower, is the amount of down payment or equity money that he must raise. The higher the loan-to-value ratio, given the appraised value of the real estate, the smaller the equity investment required of the borrower, and the higher the leverage that the borrower will have in the real estate. With higher leverage, there is generally more risk to the lender, which is one reason that high loan-to-value ratios are sometimes associated with high interest rates. This represents compensation for the additional risk entailed.

From the point of view of the borrower, particularly in terms of income or investment real estate, the prospect of paying a slightly higher interest rate is not nearly as much of a deterrent as the requirement to invest more cash in the transaction. It is always possible to anticipate that *future* income will cover the additional interest charges; it is less easy to create additional cash *immediately*.

Conventional industrial real estate mortgages usually carry loan-to-value ratios between 66⅔ and 75 per cent of estimated market value. As a matter of policy, lenders may choose to require a higher down payment. On the other hand, there are legal limits beyond which fiduciary and other regulated lenders cannot go. It is incumbent on the industrial real estate broker to familiarize himself with these limits in any area in which he is seeking to arrange financing for a client.

There are also certain exceptions. For example, New York State insurance companies loan up to 90 per cent of value on "adequately secured loans." Construction loans usually allow for 80–90 per cent of the take-out commitment for permanent financing. Alternatively, a construction loan may be granted for 75–80 per cent of certified construction costs. A development loan might go to 60 per cent of development costs. In either case, the value of the land does not enter into the cost base.

The limitations imposed by mortgage loan-to-value ratio often make leasehold financing or bond financing attractive. Both of these techniques conserve on the cash of the borrowing firm, with the result that funds are available for other purposes; and leverage in the investment in industrial real estate is considerably increased.

Mortgage Loan Maturity

The maturity or the term of the mortgage is often referred to as the pay-out period. This is the period of time over which the loan is granted, and at the end of which the outstanding balance becomes due and payable.

While there is considerable variation among property types, loan types, and lenders, a new industrial building might normally carry a loan term between 15 and 30 years, while an older existing building might command only a 10- to 15-year maturity. These are standard ranges of loan terms among banks and insurance companies for mortgages based on the real estate, rather than on the underlying lease.

If long-term leases are the basis for the loan, with the rents assigned to the lender, substantially longer maturities *may* be permissible. It depends, however, on the term of the lease at the time the loan is granted.

To a large extent, leases tend to set the maturity of the mortgage. In order to provide coverage and safety for the lender, it is generally specified that the term of the mortgage will not run much beyond the term of the lease. In New York State, an "adequately secured loan" must mature with no more than a 10 per cent balance outstanding, upon the expiration of the *first* term of a lease on a single-tenant building, or the expiration of the *shortest* lease in a multitenant building.

If underlying leases have really long terms (e.g., 35–40 years), are non-cancelable, and are made to high credit tenants, then the term of the mortgage can and will be extended accordingly. When the real estate is the fundamental collateral, rather than the credit of the occupant or tenant, shorter terms are usually dictated by the lender's considerations of safety.

Amortization

Amortization involves the periodic repayment of a portion of the principal during the term of the loan. The lender will normally prefer to have the mortgage fully amortized over its term, although this can vary considerably. It is one matter which is often subject to negotiation.

For internal financial reasons, a borrower may desire to make accelerated payments early in the period of the loan, with repayment of equity at a reduced rate in the later years. For protection, a lender might also want accelerated amortization in the early years.

Conversely, an investor will often seek reduced amortization, so that there would be a lump sum payment, or "balloon," due at the end of the mortgage term. There are a number of reasons for this desire, based on the investment considerations contained in the discussion in Chapter 5. By having amortization less than depreciation charges, an investor can generate a flow of tax-free income for a number of years. If his expectation is that the value of the real estate will increase by the expiration of the mortgage, or if he anticipates refinancing the mortgage loan when it matures, then it is to his advantage to have a loan which is not fully amortized over its term.

Suppose, for example, that a 25-year, 6.5-per cent mortgage in the amount of $50,000 is granted. Suppose further that the amortization schedule is based upon a 30-year payout. When the loan matures at the end of 25 years, a balloon payment of $15,800 will be necessary. At the same time, the borrower will have paid $3,793.20 per year in mortgage principal and interest, which is $259.20 less per year than he would have had to pay if the loan were fully amortized over a 25-year period. Assuming that he has more productive uses for his money in the interim, there is a net advantage in deferring the lump sum payment to the end.

Lenders, on the other hand, ordinarily would like to see amortization proceed more rapidly than the depreciation on the buildings. If the value of the land is substantial enough, this can be accomplished at the same time a balloon loan is negotiated.

At the beginning of the loan period, many lenders insist that there be no prepayment of principal for a stipulated period, such as five years. Institutional lenders argue that placing a loan is an expensive process. They usually want long-term investments. They do not want their calculations upset by unforeseen and uncontrollable prepayments.

One large institutional lender insists upon a closed period at the beginning of the loan, during which no prepayment is permitted. A maximum term loan for this lender would be five years "standing" (that is, no payment of principal), and then full payout over the next 25 years, for a maximum term of 30 years.[16] This is simply one example from an almost limitless variety of patterns that could be developed.

The Mortgage Constant

The net impact of the pattern or package of mortgage loan terms on the borrower can be expressed in terms of the annual carrying charges on the loan. These carrying charges include both interest and principal, and are usually called "debt service." While they may vary slightly in some cases, they are normally a steady or constant annual amount, since the direct-reduction, constant-payment loan is most widespread among industrial mortgages. This annual payment, when expressed as a percentage of the face amount of the mortgage, is the mortgage "constant." Many investors

---

[16] For further details, consult Murray, *op. cit.*

think in terms of this mortgage constant when evaluating the attractiveness of a loan proposal, and particularly when comparing it with the anticipated annual rate of return on their required equity investment. The industrial real estate broker, therefore, should understand this measure and be able to use it in analyzing the income flow to an industrial property.

The impact of a change in interest rates on the mortgage constant is obvious. If the rate goes up, so does the cost of carrying the loan. Similarly, if the rate goes down, the cost of carrying the loan also goes down.

It is also generally appreciated by investors and brokers that extending the term of the mortgage reduces the annual payment, even though the sum total of payments increases; while reducing the term of the mortgage increases the annual requirements.

All other things remaining equal, an increase in the loan-to-value ratio increases the amount of the loan, and therefore increases the annual payment required to extinguish the loan. Conversely, a decrease in the loan-to-value ratio, or an increase in the down payment, reduces the amount of the loan, and hence the average annual payment required to pay off the loan.

Partial amortization with a balloon payment reduces the annual carrying charges. An accelerated rate of amortization would, on the other hand, increase carrying charges until the loan was completely paid off.

These four factors thus combine to establish a pattern within which the objectives of both borrower and lender can usually be met. The borrower is interested in paying as little as possible, particularly on an annual basis. He also is interested in minimizing his equity investment, both to conserve on his limited supply of cash, and to take maximum advantage of leverage. The lender, on the other hand, wants to receive as high a return for his money as possible, which means a high interest rate, consistent with required safety for his investment. If he cannot do so by increasing the down payment required, then he might shorten the maturity. The borrower is interested in a lengthened maturity, however, to keep his annual payments down. A compromise can be reached by having a shorter maturity with partial amortization based on a longer payout period.

In the example provided in the preceding section, the mortgage constant for a 25-year payout or fully amortized loan would be 8.105 per cent; the mortgage constant for the partially amortized loan is 7.586 per cent.

REAL ESTATE VERSUS CREDIT AS SECURITY

Industrial real estate loans are secured by an interest in real estate (whether fee or leasehold), the credit of the owner or tenant, or both. In each specific instance, greater emphasis will be placed upon one or the other of these ingredients; the result will be a unique combination of terms and conditions. Within the framework of analysis undertaken by the lender, an industrial loan may be classified as a "real estate" loan, or a "credit" loan, depending on which of the two is emphasized more in making the decision to grant the loan. "Credit and real estate must balance out, and you

... can make a loan on almost any kind of property, provided one or the other is present in adequate strength." [17]

As a general rule, a high-credit owner or tenant converts the transaction to a "paper deal," while it is a real estate transaction with a merely satisfactory or good tenant. In addition, "we can say there is a spectrum which goes from highly generalized to one-use real estate. As we move from the more general to the more specific, the emphasis in lending shifts from the real estate to the user and his credit." [18] A shift from emphasis on the real estate to emphasis on the credit of the tenant often is advantageous to the borrower and/or the lender. For example, one S.I.R. reported that in northern New Jersey, adjacent to New York City, a "paper deal" would result in an appraised value of between 20 and 25 per cent above the value of the identical property under a "real estate deal." This is by no means a universal tendency, but it does illustrate the important difference that high credit underlying the mortgage loan can make.

Real Estate Analysis

Institutional lenders in particular evaluate both the location and market environment of the property to be financed, as well as the property itself. This analysis is one of the ingredients in the decision whether to make the loan, based on the policies and objectives of the lender.

1. *Location and Market Analysis.* Representatives of lending institutions consistently report that locational factors are important in making the loan decision. It is felt that even with a high-credit firm, a poor location can ruin both the loan and the firm. As one example, the case of a manufacturing plant located in an isolated community was cited. After three years, the tenant firm concluded that the location was completely unsuitable, and abandoned the plant. The rent continued to be paid, and payments were kept current on the mortgage. When the mortgagee insurance company on the mortgage discovered this, however, it arranged a prepayment of the loan so that the tenant firm could buy the plant at the owner's cost. The manufacturing firm then resold the plant at a loss of nearly $200,000, which was still less than its remaining obligation under the long-term lease.[19]

Accordingly, many lenders are simply not interested in properties located outside strong, central industrial areas. One large life insurance company has devised a property classification system in which all properties proposed for mortgage collateral are graded in four classes, which represent the estimated marketability of the property. This includes the type and quality of the property, as well as the location. In most instances, a "country" property would be placed in Class 4—the least desirable—and would require extremely good credit on the part of the owner or tenant in order for the loan to be made. On the other hand, a modern, well-located, adaptable plant that attracts many users may be financed almost irrespective of the

---

[17] *Ibid.*

[18] Interview with David Scribner, S.I.R.

[19] Murray, *op. cit.*

owner or the tenant. Of course, with good credit reinforcing a loan on such a property, the terms would be even more favorable to the borrower.[20]

2. *Types of Property.* Although an almost endless classification could be established to categorize and analyze industrial properties, most analysis on the part of mortgage lenders concentrates on five major groupings. Indeed, one of these cuts across the other classifications, but is often an important consideration in the deliberations and determinations of lenders. In analyzing industrial properties, most of the emphasis is placed on the type of building and on its apparent utility in the market.

a. *General-Purpose Buildings.* A general-purpose building, which by definition has a variety of alternative uses and users, is almost always valued as real estate, regardless of the tenant. Because of its greater flexibility it is highly marketable, and is more likely to be regarded as a Class 1 property. Not only the type of construction, but the size or character of space in the building is extremely important. What constitutes general-purpose property varies substantially from area to area. For example, it is most likely to be loft space in multistory, multitenant older buildings in New York City; it may well be a one-story, one-occupant new building in the range of 40,000 to 70,000 square feet in the Cincinnati area; in many markets in California, general-purpose buildings are rarely larger than 20,000 square feet. Therefore, the lender must know what is marketable in the area in question. The industrial real estate broker has an opportunity to serve his own client by advising and assisting the lender on this point.

b. *Specialized or Special-Purpose Buildings.* As the name implies, these buildings are less general in character and hence less readily marketable. The more specialized the industrial building, the more difficult it is to obtain financing on the real estate alone. This is because of the limited marketability of the basic underlying security for the loan in the event of default. Therefore, the emphasis usually shifts more to the credit of either the tenant or the owner, or both.

c. *Multi-Tenant Buildings.* These are most frequently older buildings in central areas of cities, often containing several stories. Very often they have been converted from single-tenant use because of changing technology and changing locational requirements of the original tenant. Such buildings may very well represent general-purpose property in major cities, such as loft space in Philadelphia or New York City. There may also be a very active and strong local market for such space. Nevertheless, institutional lenders typically do not rate such properties highly. One large insurance company regards all old, multistory buildings as Class 4 properties. As a result, loans are made on such properties by this particular insurance company only when there is high credit on the part of either the borrower, or the tenants on long-term leases, or both.

d. *New Construction Versus Existing Buildings.* Generally speaking, institutional lenders prefer to make loans on new industrial structures, and generally place greater emphasis on the credit of the borrower and/or

---

[20] This view is derived from Society of Industrial Realtors, *Attitudes Toward Industrial Mortgages* (Washington, The Author, 1964).

tenant if "used" properties are offered as collateral. On the other hand, new construction which is built on speculation is not easily financed, unless it does in fact represent the ideal Class 1 property and is regarded by the lender as highly marketable.

e. *Land.* Many institutional investors (life insurance companies, banks, savings institutions) are severely limited in their ability to lend on unimproved real estate. Clients must be advised accordingly.

Credit Analysis

Industrial real estate is either owner-occupied or tenant-occupied. If it is owner-occupied, then the emphasis in credit analysis is on the income and credit rating of the owning corporation. If it is tenant-occupied, the primary emphasis in credit analysis is placed on the tenant, rather than on the owner. Secondarily, the status of the investor-borrower may still be considered. However, it usually represents much less legal or financial support to the transaction than does the credit of the tenant. This presumes, of course, that there is an assignment of rents to the mortgagee.

1. *Credit as Support for Industrial Real Estate Loans.* Emphasis is placed on the credit aspects of the transaction when the real estate to be pledged represents a special use, is a multitenant building, is a "used" building, or is in less than a prime location. The credit of the borrower and/or user is utilized to reinforce the security offered the lender by the collateral real estate. The existence of highly rated credits on the mortgage note or on long-term leases on the real estate makes some kinds of loans possible that would otherwise not be considered. For example, the "adequately secured loan" permitted New York State life insurance companies is possible only when there is a great deal of high credit underlying the loan.

The risk to the borrower in lending on industrial real estate that might not be classified as Class 1 may be either reduced or compensated for through other means as well. For example, the addition of stock warrants or the convertibility of debt instruments into equity securities illustrate features of the incentive loan already considered that can reinforce the property itself as collateral for the loan. Adding a chattel mortgage or equipment trust certificates to cover fixtures and equipment may also enhance the credit status of the loan. If the credit of the tenant is to offer effective support to carrying the mortgage, the lease or leases should be net rather than gross.

The importance of credit is underscored by the results of a survey conducted by the Society of Industrial Realtors in 1964 among major financial organizations lending on a national basis. Most respondents reported that they would consider loans with national credits only. All but a very few indicated that they would not consider a loan which was not supported by high-quality local credit, at the least.

The absence of good credit makes it very difficult to finance real estate ownership for small or new industrial firms. One basic need which presents a severe challenge to the industrial real estate broker is for financing of space for small firms with a good potential, but relatively little current or past history of financial strength. Few lenders are willing to take this sort of risk, with the result that such firms either must seek rental space in older, multitenant buildings, or must turn to high-rate lenders, who usually require incentives in the form of a share in the equity of the firm.

2. *Major Bases of Credit.* The three major bases for credit support of the industrial mortgage loan are the owner-occupant, the investor-owner, and the tenant-occupant. Although greater emphasis is placed on the status of occupants in credit analysis by mortgage lenders, the financial status of the investor-owner is not ignored. In some cases, the analysis of credit is classified in terms of the real estate interests of the parties. The owner-occupant is considered the holder of the unencumbered fee; the investor-owner is the holder of the leased fee; and the tenant-occupant is the holder of a leasehold estate.

a. *Owner-Occupant.* When the owner is also the occupant, the analysis will be detailed or brief, depending upon the character of the property itself. A blue-chip national credit as owner will always command favorable terms. If the owner-occupant is a good local risk, then there may be some financial covenants attached to the loan agreement to control the intrusion of undesirable elements. These would include such restraints as a limit on future borrowing by the corporation until the mortgage is paid off; the establishment of working capital ratio standards; or a limitation on the distribution of profits while the mortgage loan is outstanding.

b. *Owner-Investor.* Relatively little emphasis is placed on the credit standing of the owner-investor, primarily because there is often little effective recourse against him in the event of default. The trend among institutional lenders on industrial real estate, at least, is for the notes to be endorsed without personal liability on the part of the owner. Therefore, in the event of default, the property and/or the tenant represent the basis for any recovery by the lender. The property is the ultimate security; it may be sold to satisfy the obligation to the lender. More importantly, the lender will endeavor to have the tenant continue paying rent, but directly to the lender under an assignment agreement.

If the owner-investor is a leaseholder on the land, he will be asked to pledge his rights as a lessee, as well as assigning the rents due him from the tenants in the building(s). Many institutional lenders who are precluded from lending on unimproved property may lend on leaseholds without the land being pledged. In this situation, the real security for the mortgage is the credit of the tenants.

c. *Tenant-Owner.* Any lease on industrial real estate will ordinarily be assigned to the lender. Therefore, the mortgagee will normally expect the tenant to continue paying rent in the event of default by the mortgagor. As a further safeguard, the loan agreement will normally provide for subordination of any penalty clause or condemnation clause that the lease contains. This offers protection against legal risks rather than business risks, but counsel for lending institutions normally insists upon such subordination. Generally speaking, the better the credit rating of the tenant, the more favorable the terms that the borrower can receive, and the more emphasis is placed on credit rather than real estate. A net lease to a responsible tenant is a great asset to a property, and is reflected in the mortgagability of that property.

3. *Types of Credit Evaluation.* The lending institution normally pursues two avenues of investigation in evaluating the credit of either the owner-occupant or the tenant-occupant. In the case of a highly rated national firm, all of the steps of the analysis need not be undertaken. In order to provide an insight into the quality of a firm whose status is not so readily apparent, both the economic status of the firm in its industry and the financial status of the firm are investigated.

a. *Economic Analysis of the Firm and Industry.* The credit quality of either a tenant or an owner-occupant depends in part on the industry in which it is operating, and its place in that industry. The future prospects of the firm, its earnings record, and the quality of its management are all considered by the lender as well. In addition, the continuity of management, particularly the retention of critical skills, is carefully studied in terms of both succession and stability. The history of the company's operations will normally be requested, so the broker should be prepared to provide this information.[21]

b. *Financial Analysis of the Firm.* Within the framework of its industry and its history, the credit quality of a tenant or owner-occupant firm also depends upon its financial characteristics. A variety of ratios (working capital, dividend payout, capitalization) is utilized to evaluate the stability and the strength of the company. Its past record in meeting its obligations is particularly noted, together with the stability of its earnings and the use to which those earnings are put. The real estate broker should be prepared to assist his client in developing and providing this vital information to the lender for an evaluation of the loan request.[22]

SOURCES OF INDUSTRIAL REAL ESTATE LOAN FUNDS

The financing of industrial real estate is more diversified than is the financing of any other type of property. The sources of loan funds vary by lender policy, and by law, from area to area. Regulations and laws set the limits; within these limits individual variation is found among different types of lenders, from lender to lender in the same group, and even from loan to loan by the same lender.

The wide diversity in the industrial real estate field has led to the development of many alternative sources of debt funds to supplement the equity that the purchaser either can or will invest. A variety of different situations is often encountered in the same transaction, and there may be several different sources of funds for different stages in the development of the same property.

[21] For a detailed consideration of the factors involved, see William M. Shenkel, *Principles and Practices of Industrial Real Estate: A Course Syllabus* (Washington, Society of Industrial Realtors, 1963), pp. 53–55.

[22] For a detailed discussion of the factors involved, see *Ibid.*, pp. 55–57.

It is important for the industrial real estate broker to know specifically what is happening in the market so that he may go to the proper sources with the proper documentation and proposal. Beyond this, the broker should be aware of the possibilities for handling unusual or unforeseen eventualities that might arise in the course of his practice.

In the presentation here, all of the usual and some of the less common sources of mortgage loan funds are noted. The emphasis is solely on their role as lenders on *industrial* real estate. More comprehensive texts on real estate finance contain further details of the operations of these lenders.[23]

1. *Life Insurance Companies.* Life insurance companies are by far the most important single source of first mortgage money on industrial real estate. Not all life insurance companies make such loans, but in the aggregate they hold a larger volume of industrial mortgages than any other group of lenders.

Life insurance companies generally prefer loans in excess of $100,000. Except in unusual circumstances, they usually can lend between 66⅔ and 75 per cent of the appraised value. The maturities they offer are among the longest granted on industrial mortgages. Life insurance companies prefer high-credit loans with long-term leases. They are precluded by law in most states from making loans on unimproved property (land loans). Life insurance companies operate nationally, and often buy existing loans from mortgage bankers or mortgage companies. They also are important purchasers of real estate bonds.

2. *Commercial Banks.* Although they are also important sources of "permanent" financing on industrial real estate, commercial banks are particularly significant lenders of short-term construction money in the industrial field. In some areas, commercial banks tend to avoid long-term industrial mortgages, making them available only as an accommodation for important depositors.

Commercial banks are extremely active in mortgage "warehousing." They represent the most important source of short-term or interim financing available to the industrial real estate field.

3. *Savings Institutions.* Mutual savings banks (which are concentrated primarily in the northeastern United States) and federally chartered savings and loan associations are occasionally important sources of long-term industrial mortgage funds, but only to good risks with relatively large down payments. Except in a few national financial centers, most savings institutions are not large enough to be able to handle major industrial loans alone. As a result, they commonly participate with larger-scale lenders.

4. *Mortgage Companies and Mortgage Bankers.* Although there are differences in these two groups of organizations, as noted earlier in this chapter, they have many similar characteristics. Using their own funds, or "warehoused" funds advanced from commercial banks on a short-term basis, they initiate mortgage loans on their own account. They then sell these loans to major financial institutions, particularly life insurance companies, usually retaining the servicing of the loan. These intermediaries

---

[23] See, for example, Maisel, *op. cit.,* Harvey, *op. cit.;* Kahn, Case and Schimmel, *op. cit.*

play an extremely important role, particularly in the western two-thirds of the United States, in channeling major institutional funds into otherwise remote mortgage market areas. They are the primary sellers on the secondary market for industrial mortgages. They almost invariably make first mortgage loans on industrial real estate, because the purchasing financial institutions are rarely interested in junior liens.

5. *Industrial Firms.* Industrial organizations are themselves often important sources of industrial real estate credit, although cash does not usually pass from lender to borrower.

Industrial firms owning real estate often find it necessary to accept a purchase-money mortgage as part payment for a property that is being sold. Thus, the seller becomes a mortgagee of the purchaser. In many instances, these purchase-money mortgages are junior liens, subordinate to financing that the purchaser has been able to arrange with an institutional lender. The junior purchase-money mortgage fills the gap between the primary financing available from the lending institution, and any equity that the purchaser has in the transaction.

Another increasingly important source of mortgage loan funds is a group of industrial organizations which for purposes of diversification makes loans on industrial real estate. This is particularly true of building materials producers, although not all are in this category. When they *are* suppliers, they often accept junior liens in order to assist in the utilization of their materials. Such organizations as United States Plywood, United States Steel, Great Lakes Carbon and Coal, and Shell Oil have been active in this area. They tend to concentrate their efforts on major buildings.

6. *Individuals and Others.* Affluent individuals, acting either alone or in groups, are often important sources of junior mortgage financing in particular. They are usually interested in high rates of return, and are willing to assume risks that institutional lenders normally cannot or will not accept to achieve this objective. They are more likely to be equity investors than lenders, but in some instances they will lend, particularly on an incentive basis with stock options or other opportunities to acquire a "sweetener."

In some instances, it has been reported that industrial tenants have advanced funds to owners to assist in the purchase or retention of a particular property. These miscellaneous sources represent sporadic and occasional lenders to whom the industrial broker should turn only in unusual circumstances.

7. *Pension Funds.* Pension funds represent the most rapidly expanding group of lenders on industrial real estate. Most pension funds have historically avoided investment in industrial real estate, either as purchaser or lender, because their managements are not familiar with the intricacies of industrial real estate financing. Despite their phenomenal growth, therefore, they represent a largely untapped source with vast potential for the industrial real estate field.

Pension funds have a decided competitive advantage over most other lenders, in that they are exempt from federal income taxation. Therefore, they can compete effectively with other major lenders by offering slightly lower rates which are net to them. They are not hampered by the same lending restrictions that affect life insurance companies, for example, and there are no limits to the loan-value ratio on pension fund industrial loans, other than the "prudent man" rule.[24] They are most likely to be equity investors in a sale-leaseback or direct purchase transaction. To the extent that they do lend on industrial real estate financing, however, pension funds make *large loans,* especially if they are bank-administered or insurance company-administered.

There are essentially three types of pension funds, which are differentiated on the basis of their administration: by banks, insurance companies, or the funds themselves. Bank-administered funds are non-insured. They are handled by bank trust departments. Often pension funds are commingled. This means that money from several different funds will be merged into one loan. The Chase Manhattan Bank and the Morgan Guaranty Trust Company are examples of banks which administer large funds.

Insurance company-administered funds are more likely to engage in real estate investment or lending, because the investment personnel of life insurance companies are more familiar with real estate as an investment outlet.

On the other hand, self-administered funds, such as the General Electric fund, have rarely made real estate loans of any type. This is primarily because the investment personnel in these funds are essentially credit-oriented, and unfamiliar with real estate financing.

8. *Other Tax-Exempt Organizations.* Estates, private trusts, and university endowment funds are occasional sources of high-credit, long-term industrial mortgage loans. With the passage of time, the investment personnel of large university endowment funds in particular have become more sensitive to the attractions of industrial real estate investments. They insist upon extremely high-credit loans, however.

9. *Real Estate Investment Organizations.* These include public corporations, private syndicates, and real estate investment trusts. Generally, these organizations are more active as equity investors than lenders, but there are a few real estate investment trusts which make a point of granting mortgage loans. For example, Continental Mortgage Investors, one of the largest real estate investment trusts in the United States, provides a large volume of interim financing for construction and development. Real estate investment trusts rarely make long-term mortgage loans, however.[25]

10. *Suppliers, Developers and Builders.* A variety of circumstances can lead to the extension of credit to the purchaser of a new industrial building. The builder, developer, or supplier(s) may defer collection of obligations incurred during the development and construction of the building. When they are granted, such deferments are often secured by a junior lien against the real estate. This is not usually planned, however. The mortgagee must be in a relatively strong financial position to be able to engage in this activity other than involuntarily.

---

[24] Interview with David Scribner, S.I.R., and Edmund J. McRickard, S.I.R.
[25] *Ibid.;* see also Harvey, *op. cit.;* Continental Mortgage Investors, *Annual Report, 1965.*

11. *Small Business Investment Companies.* Small Business Investment Companies (SBIC's) are private organizations, licensed by the U.S. Small Business Administration, which are specifically empowered to make equity investments in, or long-term secured loans to, "small business." The definition of "small business" has expanded with the United States economy, so that many firms of substantial size may receive relatively large loans from SBIC's.[26]

Secured loans of SBIC's are generally made to growth firms which, in the opinion of the management of the SBIC, offer promise of success in the future. In most instances, SBIC makes "incentive" loans, with convertible debentures or stock warrants included.

Because they ordinarily demand premium rates and equity participation of lenders, SBIC's usually serve borrowers that cannot qualify for mortgage loans from financial institutions. Accordingly, they supplement rather than compete with banks, insurance companies, or pension funds.

12. *Public Agencies.* Most public agencies, whether at the federal, state, or local level, generally offer advice and assistance to industrial firms and industrial developers, but usually do not make loans. They are more likely to be stimulators of real estate transactions than lenders. To a very large extent, their good intentions and laudable objectives are not fully supported with public loan funds.

One notable exception at the federal level is the Small Business Administration. Any manufacturing establishment with fewer than 250 employees is an eligible "small business," and in some industries the limit is even higher.[27] As a general rule, the Small Business Administration will extend long-term credit secured by industrial real estate only if it is unavailable from private sources. SBA may make a direct loan to the borrowing firm, or it may participate in a loan by a private lender. Participation loans of SBA may involve either immediate participation, in which SBA agrees to advance a stipulated proportion of the total amount of the loan at the time that it is granted by the private lender; or it may be a deferred participation, in which the private lender initiates the entire loan, supported by SBA's agreement to advance a stipulated amount on demand.

SBA is also authorized to advance funds to SBIC's. A substantial portion of the total available from SBIC's is actually in the form of federal funds advanced through SBA.

State and local industrial development commissions (whatever their precise title might be) frequently advance funds for plant construction or acquisition, particularly when private sources do not provide as much as is needed by the industrial firm purchasing the plant. This credit is most commonly in the form of junior liens, with relatively low interest rates and very favorable amortization provisions.

Mortgage loan funds available from public agencies to finance industrial

---

[26] For details see U.S. Small Business Administration, *SBIC Financing for Small Business,* Bulletin No. OPI-13 (Washington, U.S. Government Printing Office).
[27] For details see U.S. Small Business Administration, *Loan Sources in the Federal Government,* Bulletin No. 52 (Washington, U.S. Government Printing Office).

real estate are nearly always noncompetitive with private funds. They are generally available only to borrowers who might not otherwise qualify for an industrial loan from a private source. To this extent, public agency funds enhance the prospects and the possibilities for financing industrial real estate ownership and use.

LENDER POLICIES AND STANDARDS

With the great diversity of sources of industrial mortgages, it is impossible to catalog all of the variations in policies, loan terms, and requirements that the industrial real estate broker may find confronting him when he sets out to seek loan funds for his client. At the same time, it is important to understand the reasons for variations in loan terms and loan fund availability, as well as the characteristics in which the terms of industrial mortgages will vary. It is also important to understand the factors that determine whether a loan will be granted, what type of property specific lenders prefer or avoid, the amount of loan that may be obtained, and the terms of repayment.

Legal and Policy Requirements

The requirements of the lender and his loan decisions are the result of legal limitations on his ability to lend, coupled with broad policies established for his lending program. Because they hold the funds of others in trust, fiduciary institutions (banks, life insurance companies, savings institutions, pension and endowment funds, trusts) are limited by state or federal legislation (or both) in the terms and conditions of their mortgage lending. For example, every financial institution has legal limits on the loan-value ratio that it may grant on any particular type of loan. Moreover, the method of ascertaining the "value" which is the basis for the loan is usually specified. Mutual savings banks and savings and loan associations have limitations placed on the geographic area within which they may originate mortgage loans; beyond that area they may operate only as participants. There are limitations placed on the absolute size of mortgage loans that many institutions may make, and in many states there are also legal ceilings on the interest rate that may be charged. The maximum permissible term of a mortgage loan is frequently specified in the law, and the manner of amortizing loans is often dictated as well.

Beyond this, there are limits on the *type* of property that may be mortgaged with certain institutions. For example, life insurance companies in New York State may not lend on unimproved land. A working knowledge of these limitations is extremely important for the industrial real estate broker, so that his proposal will not be rejected out of hand by a potential mortgagee.

Within this legal framework, individual institutional policies are set, depending upon the objectives of the institution and the skill and experience of the personnel available to carry out the policies of the organization. These policy limits may be long-term, continuing ones, such as the avoidance of industrial real estate loans by self-administered pension funds; or they may be temporary limitations dictated by considerations of the current status of the investment portfolio, or the availability of funds to lend. The necessity to be currently aware of these policies and changes underscores the importance of either specializing in mortgage financing or acquiring specialized technical advice in all but the most straightforward industrial financing problems.

Areas of Influence

Through their policies, lenders on industrial real estate exert considerable influence on a number of areas of industrial real estate activity. It may be willful or it may be unintentional. The standards established by institutional lenders in particular affect significantly the direction of industrial real estate practice.

Industrial lenders tend to influence the character and construction of industrial buildings. Their preference for one-story, single-occupant buildings means that these will more likely be built if there is any choice, because they can be more readily financed. A building which is more readily financed is also more readily marketed. This means that the criterion of marketability that leads the lender to set the standard in the first place is in part self-fulfilled. Some institutional lenders have a preference for increasing ceiling heights, often in excess of 20 or 22 feet. Their willingness to grant financing more readily on such buildings means that there has been an increase in ceiling heights among industrial buildings in areas in which these lenders are active. Moreover, patterns of development and staging of industrial construction have been altered by lender requirements. When a major life insurance company indicates that it gives a higher rating for mortgage purposes to a "modern, one-story, substantial, high-ceilinged, low-density building," it is not surprising to discover that these tend to be what builders and purchasers also begin to prefer.[28]

Similarly, major industrial mortgagees influence the type of locations given priority for industrial development. Life insurance companies tend to prefer properties located in established industrial centers over "country" properties, because of their presumably greater marketability. In addition, many lenders rate regions, communities, and neighborhoods, and often decline to lend any money at all in low-rated areas. This cannot fail to influence adversely the future development of those already poorly regarded areas.

The terms and conditions of leases are often controlled by mortgage lenders. An owner may consider himself better off with short-term leases if he believes that rents are likely to increase, but an insurance company may force him into longer-term leases to obtain financing. Moreover, lenders usually insist upon net leases (or fully escalated gross leases), and these have become considerably more important to lessors as a result.

By deciding which borrower shall receive funds, and which shall be denied them, lenders are in effect determining who owns industrial real estate, and who is virtually forced into a tenant occupancy position.

---

[28] See Murray, *op. cit.*

Implementation of Investment Goals of Mortgage Lenders

Particularly if it is a fiduciary institution, a mortgage lending organization is concerned with safety: safety of principal, and safety of interest income. Secondarily, the institutional lender is interested in a maximum rate of return, consistent with the basic safety of the investment. These two major goals are at the foundation of most lender policies. An analysis of policies in terms of their contribution to these goals will result in an appreciation of the objectives that the policies serve. The policies may not seem any more attractive to the industrial real estate broker or to his client, but at least they become comprehensible. Moreover, if the broker understands the objectives of the lender, he may on occasion be able to develop alternative means to the same end, which are acceptable to the lender and which at the same time *are* attractive to his client.

1. *Coverage of Debt Service (Safety).* The ratio of net income on the real estate to the total annual debt service is a measure that many institutional lenders regard as quite important to assure them of the safety they seek. Net income before deducting depreciation charges must be a specified number of times larger than debt service, in order for a loan to be acceptable, or in order for a favorable interest rate to be allowed. Careful preparation of the loan proposal is necessary so as to highlight this type of information effectively for the lender.

2. *Low Risk of Default Through High Credit Rating (Safety).* The emphasis of major life insurance companies and pension funds on national credits as either borrowers or tenants under assigned leases is another manifestation of the importance of safety to institutional lenders. They look to the income and financial stability of the occupant firm as a supplement to the income from the real estate itself to carry the loan.

If a borrower turns to a secondary source for junior mortgage financing, the primary lender is not necessarily worried, provided the financial status and income of the borrower or tenant indicate that the total volume of debt can be carried with safety and convenience.

3. *Terms of Lending (Safety).* Mortgage loan terms are designed in large part to provide safety for the lender, as well as enhancing the chances that the borrower will pay off the debt as specified in the loan agreement. For example, the loan-to-value ratio is adjusted to provide additional safety to the lender. Generally speaking, the higher the risk involved in the loan from the lender's viewpoint, the higher the down payment that will be required if a loan is to be made at all. Amortization provisions can enhance safety to the lender by requiring repayment of principal at a rate greater than the depreciation charged against the property. In this way, the book equity of the borrower in the property is increased. The argument is that the greater the equity of the borrower in the property, the greater the incentive to protect his interest in the property.

The maturity of the loan can often lower the over-all rate or constant, even when interest rates are higher. Therefore, lengthening the term of the loan may reduce rather than increase risk.

Insistence on one particular term of lending may result in an unbalanced and therefore potentially unsafe loan for the lender. The industrial real estate broker should recognize and emphasize this fact. "Loan officers should be more cautious about becoming so enamoured of the high rates, that the value of the collateral [i.e., safety] becomes secondary. Further, they should not lose a choice loan by being too arbitrary about obtaining a high rate." [29]

4. *Performance and Completion Bonds (Safety).* Many lenders will insist that a performance bond or completion bond be filed by the borrower under a construction loan. This provides further protection for the lender in the event of default. Beyond this, many institutional lenders will require receipt of a formal Certificate of Occupancy before they will release funds on a permanent loan for which a commitment is outstanding. In both cases, the consideration is safety for the lender. In both cases, these considerations raise the total cost of financing to the borrower. This is important in planning the budget for a construction or development program.

5. *Covenants and Limitations in Loan Agreements and Leases (Safety).* Many lenders require specific loan covenants designed to enhance the ability of the borrower to meet the terms of the loan obligation. For example, if the borrower is an owner-occupant, limitations on future borrowing, acquisition of additional real estate, or working capital ratios will often be included in the body of the loan agreement.

The loan agreement may also specify lease terms on tenant-occupied properties. Leasing industrial real estate can become heavily lender-influenced. For example, in order to provide coverage of the service charges on the loan, a lender may insist on a long-term lease, even though the owner may prefer a short-term lease because rents are expected to rise in the area. The lender will generally want a penalty lease subordinated to the mortgage, and will often insist on a noncancellation provision, as well as protection under a condemnation clause. Moreover, lenders can require a net lease or a fully escalated gross lease, so that stability of income can be anticipated for coverage of debt service. These limitations and requirements will often influence the *amount* of rental that the owner can obtain, because he must often make concessions to the tenant in order to obtain lease terms required by lenders.

6. *Marketability of the Collateral Property (Safety).* Since industrial real estate securing a mortgage loan or mortgage bond represents the ultimate protection to the lender in the event of default (after foreclosure and forced sale of the property), the institutional lender in particular is concerned with the marketability of that property. Some lenders have classification systems for collateral property, and rate most highly those properties which represent the highest degree of anticipated marketability in the area in which they are located. This is why general-purpose properties of a size which are anticipated to meet heavy demand on the market are given most favorable treatment on real estate-oriented loans. Moreover, it explains why lenders put increasing emphasis on the credit of the *occupant* when the property is more specialized, or is anticipated to have a thinner market.

Many lenders also evaluate both the location and the community care-

---

[29] Interview with Edmund J. McRickard, S.I.R., New York City.

fully: what might in many areas be a highly marketable general-purpose property, might find little or no market acceptance in a small community with little demand for industrial space, or in an area in which a very specialized type of industrial construction prevails.

7. *Cost Reduction* (*Income*). Because they cannot often directly influence interest rates through their own internal policies, many lenders on industrial real estate seek to increase their net incomes by reducing costs. One important cost reduction device is the requirement that the mortgage loan be at least a minimum size. This spreads loan placement costs over a larger sum, and reduces unit costs. For example, many lenders will not consider a mortgage of less than $50,000, and most life insurance companies will not consider a loan smaller than $100,000. Pension funds have even larger minimum sizes, because they are usually operating on thinner margins. There is rarely market acceptance of a mortgage bond issue of less than $250,000.

8. *Rate of Return* (*Income*). The interest rate is, of course, an important consideration to the lender. Higher risks will result in higher rates of interest, if the loan is granted at all. Junior liens will normally call for premium rates of interest, as will construction loans and loans to lower credit borrowers.

Loans made with emphasis on the real estate normally carry higher interest charges than do those based on the credit of the borrower or the tenant. The terms of the lease influence the investment attractiveness of the loan to the potential mortgagee. Safety is attractive to the lender as an income protection as well. Institutional lenders in particular are interested in a completely net investment, and therefore especially favor net leases. This reduces the management problems for the lender, as well as enhancing the safety of the loan.

Institutional lenders are also interested in keeping their money invested continuously. Turnover of the investment portfolio is expensive, and reduces the net return to the lending institution. Therefore, many permit no prepayment of mortgage principal for a specified period (commonly five years), while others charge a substantial premium for any prepayments of mortgage principal. In this way, their investment departments may anticipate portfolio and the net rate of return on that portfolio.

SUPPLEMENTARY MARKET ACTIVITIES

Direct lending from mortgagee to mortgagor with the security of industrial real estate (and possibly the assignment of rents as well) is the normal pattern of industrial real estate loans. Behind such lending on the primary market is a trio of supporting activities designed to ease the flow of mortgage funds from lender to borrower, and from one market area to another. Funds which are potentially available for industrial mortgage lending are often not appropriately distributed among lenders or geographic areas to meet the local demand for new loans. As a result: (1) an informal but highly effective secondary market structure has arisen; (2) lenders in one area often participate in loans initiated in other areas; and (3) short-term funds are made available to support long-term debt through the procedure known as mortgage warehousing. These three supplementary market activities are considered here only in terms of their impact on industrial real estate financing.[30]

Secondary Market Activity

When real estate mortgages are originated, they constitute primary mortgage market activity. The secondary mortgage market consists of all transactions involving the sale or transfer of existing mortgages. In the industrial real estate field, there is no systematic or organized market for existing mortgages. Nevertheless, there is an extremely active business involving the purchase and sale of such mortgages.

The greatest volume of activity at the secondary market level for industrial loans involves the sale of mortgages originated by mortgage companies or mortgage bankers to life insurance companies. Pension funds and large mutual savings banks are also active purchasers on the secondary market for industrial mortgages.

Mortgage companies or mortgage bankers originate loans on their own account. They are local organizations which have the necessary familiarity with the real estate, the local market, the borrower and the tenant (if any), to make a judgment about the attractiveness and acceptability to a customer life insurance company or pension fund. After having originated the loan, the mortgage company or mortgage banker then sells the loans to the ultimate lender. This may involve an advance commitment by the institutional lender, or it may have been a speculative venture by the originator of the loan. In either case, the originating lender charges a fee for the placement and sale of the loan, and usually retains the servicing of the loan as well.

Servicing a loan consists of collecting the payments for the ultimate lender, and insuring that the borrower meets all of the requirements of the loan agreement. In those instances in which these requirements are not met, servicing also involves taking action to protect the interests of the lender. The annual fee for servicing is quite commonly one-half per cent of the outstanding balance of the loan, on an annual basis.

Because there is little formal organization of the secondary mortgage market for industrial loans, the flow of information about its activities is sporadic and not always reliable. Notices of the availability of funds and/or loans may be found in such trade publications as *The National Real Estate Investor*. Secondary market activity will not normally involve the industrial real estate broker, but a knowledge of its existence will permit him to understand better the functioning of the industrial mortgage market.

Mortgage Loan Participations

Mortgage participations originate from two general sets of causes. First, many lenders may seek participation by others because the initiating institu-

---

[30] For further details and explanation of these methods, consult Maisel, *op. cit.*, pp. 232–237; Harvey, *op. cit.*

tion either cannot or will not extend the full amount of the required loan. Many saving institutions have limitations on the size of loans that they may make, as well as restrictions on the geographic area within which they may originate loans. They often find it necessary to seek another lender or lenders to share in the loan. This is participation. Lenders share the risks and the profits in proportion to the amount of money each puts into the loan.

Saving institutions in large metropolitan centers, notably New York City and New England areas, often participate in industrial mortgage loans outside their areas. They represent a good supplementary source for financing, particularly for properties in communities in which the local lending institutions are not substantial enough or sophisticated enough to be able to handle the loans by themselves. Mutual savings banks and savings and loan associations are likely candidates as industrial loan participants, and life insurance companies are also often willing to participate.

The second major cause for a participation being sought is that a lending institution is seeking to maintain an equity position, while at the same time serving a customer. The procedures are exactly the same, even though the motivations may be different. In this instance, the participation interest is in an existing loan. This is not secondary market actvity, since the originating lender still retains a significant portion of the loan. The same types of lenders are found on these partcipations. In addition, originating mortgage companies are often expected to remain as participants on industrial loans purchased by life insurance companies.

A variant on the basic idea is the junior participation. Some authorities contend that junior participations are more popular and more widely used in financing industrial real estate than is junior mortgage financing. A junior participation could be part of a purchase-money mortgage; an equity owner can be a junior participant in a loan; and mutual savings banks or savings and loan associations often participate on this basis when they cannot put up enough money themselves. Mortgage bankers are often asked by the primary or ultimate lender to remain on the loan as a junior participant, in part to insure care on the part of the mortgage banking firm in making and disposing of its loans.

The junior participant has a position which is subordinate to that of the primary participant. Because it is a first mortgage lien, however, it is legal for fiduciary institutions. It is an important device for encouraging the flow of loan funds from one market area to another.

Mortgage Warehousing

Mortgage companies and mortgage bankers initiate industrial real estate loans on their own account, and with their own funds, in anticipation of selling the loans to ultimate lenders: life insurance companies, pension funds, savings institutions. These mortgage originators need additional funds for two reasons. First, their own equity structures are limited. In addition, they thrive on turnover, and must occasionally wait until a loan is accepted by the ultimate lender before receiving funds to reinvest.

In part on their own credit, but primarily on the basis of the mortgage loans which they "own" (with or without formal commitments to buy from the ultimate institutional investors), mortgage companies and mortgage bankers borrow short-term funds from commercial banks. They offer groups of mortgages as general security for the notes, or on occasion they sell individual mortgages to the commercial bank with an agreement to repurchase at a stipulated price. In either event, this device provides the interim financing which is needed between the date of origination of loans by the mortgage company and their sale to the ultimate lender.

In general, mortgage companies and mortgage bankers have outstanding borrowings equal to six to eight times their equity funds. Banks usually attempt to retain a high degree of safety by having the right to foreclose any loan assigned to them. This is short-term financing, however, and foreclosure rarely is a serious consideration.

SELECTED REFERENCES

Brooks, Harvey & Co., *Creative Financing* (New York, The Author, 1965).

Bryant, Willis R., *Mortgage Lending,* 2nd ed. (New York, McGraw-Hill, 1962).

Cerf, Alan R., *Real Estate and the Federal Income Tax* (Englewood Cliffs, N.J.; Prentice-Hall, 1965).

Friedman, Edith J., ed., *Real Estate Encyclopedia* (Englewood Cliffs, N.J.; Prentice-Hall, 1960), Especially Part IV: "How to Finance Real Estate Transactions"; Ch. 15: "Broker's Role in Financing Real Estate Transactions," James Andrews; Ch. 18: "Commercial Property Financing," J. F. Hott.

Gates, Niles, "Industrial Property Investments," *Developing, Selling and Syndicating Real Estate Investment Property* (Los Angeles, California Real Estate Association, 1964).

Harvey, Robert O., "Real Estate Finance," Ch. 26 of *Financial Handbook,* 4th ed. (New York, Ronald Press, 1964).

Hoagland, H. E., and Stone, L. D., *Real Estate Finance,* rev. ed. (Homewood, Illinois, Irwin, 1961).

International Traders Club, National Institute of Real Estate Brokers, *Tax Implications in Exchanging* (Chicago, The Author, March, 1966).

International Traders Club, National Institute of Real Estate Brokers, *Techniques of Investment Property Exchanging* (Chicago, The Author, March, 1965).

Kahn, Sanders A., Case, Frederick E., and Schimmel, Alfred, *Real Estate Appraisal and Investment* (New York, Ronald Press, 1963).

Kinnard, William N., Jr., "Investment and Financing Considerations," *Appraising Apartments: Instructor's Manual* (Chicago, Society of Real Estate Appraisers, 1963).

Korb, Irving, and Trimble, Harold G., Jr., *Real Estate Sale-Leaseback: A Basic Analysis* (Washington, Society of Industrial Realtors, 1966).

Kratovil, Robert, *Real Estate Law,* 4th ed. (New York, Prentice-Hall, 1964).

Lewis, Bertram, *Profits in Real Estate Syndication: A Guide for the Investor* (New York, Harper & Brothers, 1962).

Maisel, Sherman J., *Financing Real Estate: Principles and Practices* (New York, McGraw-Hill, 1965).

McMichael, Stanley L., and O'Keefe, Paul T., *How to Finance Real Estate,* 2nd. ed. (Englewood Cliffs, N.J., Prentice-Hall, 1953).

McRickard, Edmund J., "Mortgage Investments," *Proceedings: First Annual Workshop* (Washington, Society of Industrial Realtors, 1959).

Melnyk, Stephen L., "Opportunities In Older Properties," *Real Estate Investment Opportunities* (Los Angeles, California Real Estate Association, 1965).

Murray, Thomas F., "Financing Industrial Property," Special Supplement, *S.I.R. Newsletter,* July, 1963.

National Institute of Real Estate Brokers, *Ground Leases* (Chicago, The Author, December, 1965).

National Institute of Real Estate Brokers, "Mortgage Banking," *Real Estate Specializations* (Chicago, The Author, 1962).

Pease, Robert H., and Kerwood, Lewis O., eds., *Mortgage Banking,* 2nd. ed. (New York, McGraw-Hill, 1965).

Ricks, R. Bruce, *Recent Trends in Institutional Real Estate Investment,* Research Report 23, Center for Real Estate and Urban Economics (Berkeley, University of California, 1964).

Shenkel, William M., *Principles and Practices of Industrial Real Estate: A Course Syllabus* (Washington, Society of Industrial Realtors, 1963), Ch. 6.

Smith, Burt, "Real Estate Syndicates," *Developing, Selling and Syndicating Real Estate Investment Property* (Los Angeles, California Real Estate Association, 1964).

Society of Industrial Realtors, *Advanced Course in the Techniques of Industrial Real Estate* (Washington, Society of Industrial Realtors, 1964).
　　"Tax Factors Affecting Industrial Real Estate," David Altman;
　　"Financing Industrial Real Estate," Thomas F. Murray;
　　"Industrial Property Investment Opportunities," J. D. Sawyer.

Swesnik, Richard H., "Multiple Ownership of Real Estate," *Real Estate Investment Opportunities* (Los Angeles, California Real Estate Association, 1965).

Twerdal, Margaret, "Approaches to Financing," *Techniques of Investment Property Exchanging* (Chicago, International Traders Club, National Institute of Real Estate Brokers, March, 1965).

U.S. Department of Commerce, Economic Development Administration, *Handbook of Federal Aids to Communities* (Washington, U.S. Government Printing Office, 1966).

U.S. Office of Economic Opportunity, *Catalog of Federal Programs for Individual and Community Improvement* (Washington, U.S. Government Printing Office, December, 1965).

U.S. Small Business Administration, *Loan Sources in the Federal Government,* Bulletin No. 52 (Washington, U.S. Government Printing Office).

U.S. Small Business Administration, *SBIC Financing for Small Business,* Bulletin No. OPI-13 (Washington, U.S. Government Printing Office).

Winston, Carey, "Mortgage Financing of Industrial Construction," *The Appraisal Journal,* October, 1965 (Reprinted in the May 1966 issue of the *S.I.R. Newsletter*).

9   Non-Credit Financing of Industrial Real Estate

THOUGH the bulk of industrial real estate financing is in the form of mortgages or other credit instruments, there are several additional techniques and devices with which the broker should also be familiar. First of all, unless 100 per cent debt financing is available, some equity funds will be required. It is obvious from a review of the market and from the materials in Chapter 8 that 100 per cent debt financing is rarely available.

From a strict technical point of view, the assembly of equity funds may not necessarily be regarded as "financing." Semantics notwithstanding, however, it is important to be able to gather together enough cash or enough value in the owner's equity to make up the difference between the sale price of the property and the debt financing available. In many instances, substantial effort and special organizational structures are required to assemble sufficient equity to complete the transaction.

Secondly, the credit of borrowers may be enhanced if a highly rated agency will underwrite or guarantee the payment of the loan. This has the effect of making loan funds available which otherwise would not be, and of reducing the lender's compensation for risk. No actual transfer of funds is contemplated by the guarantor in most instances. Thus, this is also a non-credit technique for financing the transfer and use of industrial real estate.

Finally, the long-term lease is extremely important in facilitating the use of industrial space. To this extent, it can be said to represent a form of "financing," even though no credit as such is extended to the user.

EQUITY STRUCTURES

The equity of the owner is the difference between the price or value of the real estate and the amount of credit financing that is available. This may take the form of cash, or may be the imputed value of the owner's residual interest in the real estate. Whatever form the equity takes, the industrial real

297

estate broker must be alert to the implications and possibilities of completing a transaction with different types of equity arrangements.

Single Ownership

Industrial real estate is owned either to provide space for the owner's activities or to provide income and profit for the investor. The reasons for investor ownership are becoming more pervasive and persuasive. The investor is seeking to maximize his net return, consistent with either long-term income or capital gain, and with an acceptable degree of safety of his investment. An important means to this objective is trading on equity through maximum allowable leverage. A minimum equity, however, may represent hundreds of thousands or even millions of dollars in an industrial real estate transaction.

The traditional source of equity funds is a single owner or investor. As the size of industrial real estate transactions has increased, equity investments have also increased in size. This has meant that the private individual is less likely to be the predominate investor in industrial real estate. Institutional investors or organizations specifically designed to accumulate the funds of many individuals have become more significant.

1. *Individuals.* There are still private individuals with large accumulations of cash available to invest in industrial real estate. In fact, one of the distinguishing features of industrial real estate transactions is that purchasers frequently have a considerably larger proportion of cash available to invest. Profit possibilities exist in industrial investments for high-income individuals such as physicians, attorneys, or business executives. When the individual has sufficient amounts of cash available to make a meaningful equity investment in industrial real estate, there are considerable tax advantages in individual ownership. It offers managerial flexibility as well.

Much of the equity of the individual investor or developer is frequently the value of land on which the industrial building is to be placed. When land values have increased significantly, even though the historical cash investment of the investor is relatively low, the current value of the real estate the individual owns unencumbered may be substantial enough to serve as the down payment for long-term financing. Industrial brokers have an excellent opportunity in such cases to develop one of several alternative financing arrangements that enable the landowner to take full advantage of its value, while at the same time minimizing his current tax liability.[1]

Similarly, condemnees who are in effect forced to reinvest the funds received from the condemning agency in real estate in order to avoid paying high taxes represent an important source of equity funds for industrial real estate transactions. Their real estate equity is converted into cash, but tax pressures may be strong enough to offer an excellent opportunity for the

---

[1] See, for example, discussions in Sherman J. Maisel, *Financing Real Estate: Principles and Practices* (New York, McGraw-Hill, 1965), Ch. 15; Robert O. Harvey, "Real Estate Finance," Ch. 26 of *Financial Handbook,* 4th ed. (New York, Ronald Press, 1964); Byron Trerice, Jr., sponsor, *Ground Leases* (Chicago, National Institute of Real Estate Brokers, December, 1965).

alert industrial broker.[2] The owner of real estate who wishes to exchange or "trade in" his property because his tax advantages have been virtually exhausted is in essentially the same position. He is a ripe candidate for an exchange involving industrial property.

While these opportunities do exist among private individuals, it should be recognized that the growing average size of industrial transactions has placed increasing emphasis on institutional or organizational investors.

2. *Industrial Corporations.* While these might not be regarded technically as "individuals" from an operational point of view, they are distinguished from real estate corporations or syndicates in the sense that the ownership decision is made by the management of the corporation. Moreover, the ownership of, or investment in real estate is incidental to the fundamental business of the corporation.

The most obvious form of individual equity investment by a corporation is the ownership of its own industrial space. In such circumstances, brokers have observed that the surplus of the corporation often represents the equity in the real estate, and effective 100 per cent financing is thereby available. This represents another means of utilizing valuable assets which can be pledged to the lender. The alert real estate broker should be aware of this possibility, which is increasing in importance.

In addition, many industrial firms, especially producers of building materials, have become equity investors in industrial real estate developments. As noted in Chapter 8, they frequently make loans on new industrial space in order to provide diversification of their own activities. In some instances, particularly when demonstrations of the effectiveness of new building materials are involved, they also develop the properties themselves and then lease them out to appropriate users.[3]

3. *Financial Institutions.* Life insurance companies and pension funds have become substantial equity investors in industrial real estate. The number of such institutional investors actively investing in industrial real estate equities is small, but it is growing. As awareness develops of the gains to be received and the relatively low risks inherent in well-managed, long-term lease arrangements with high-credit tenants, an effective opportunity for potential expansion of investment activity is emerging.

Life insurance companies and pension funds are particularly involved as equity investors in build-lease or sale-leaseback transactions, which are discussed in the final section of this chapter. The favorable tax treatment afforded the long-term investment income of life insurance companies, and even more of pension funds, permits them to become equity investors at highly competitive rates.[4] Life insurance companies are proscribed from

---

[2] For an indication of the framework of tax pressures at work on the investor, see Alan R. Cerf, *Real Estate and the Federal Income Tax* (Englewood Cliffs, N.J., Prentice-Hall, 1965). This view is also based on an interview with Frank A. Schlesinger, S.I.R., Newark, N.J.

[3] Interview with David Scribner, S.I.R., and Edmund J. McRickard, S.I.R., both of New York City.

[4] Thomas F. Murray, "Financing Industrial Real Estate," *Advanced Course in the Techniques of Industrial Real Estate* (Washington, Society of Industrial Realtors, 1964).

owning unimproved land; pension funds do not have any such limitation.

Some life insurance companies make equity investments in industrial real estate, and then borrow on the maximum mortgage loan that is available from another insurance company or bank. In this way, they are maximizing their own leverage, and receiving an arbitrage between the equity rate received and the loan rate that must be paid.[5]

4. *Public Development Agencies.* Particularly for "new" firms attracted to an area, local (and occasionally state) development agencies will often construct a plant and make it available to industrial firms on favorable lease terms. The incentive is to attract industry to an area which is seeking to expand or diversify its economic base. Sometimes these are general-purpose plants built on speculation, and sometimes they are built specifically for the tenant under a long-term lease arrangement.[6]

The industrial real estate broker can often, but not always, generate a commission by locating a firm in such a publicly owned plant. The policy of state and local development agencies varies with respect to the payment of commissions, and some expect the broker to collect whatever fee he can from the industrial firm being located.

Both public and private money are often found in industrial development commissions. They are much more likely to lend or guarantee loans, however, than to make equity investments. Nevertheless, public agency ownership is a possibility which can be considered realistically in many circumstances.[7] For example, the Danbury (Connecticut) Industrial Development Corporation acquired land and built several plants in what emerged as a successful effort to attract new industry when the manufacturers of men's felt hats curtailed operations in the area. Similar programs have been undertaken in such communities as Scranton, Pennsylvania, and Haverhill, Massachusetts.

Multiple Ownership

With the expanded size of the typical industrial real estate transaction has come the necessity to accumulate ever larger amounts of cash for equity investments. Operating corporations and institutional investors, such as life insurance companies and pension funds, usually encounter little difficulty in meeting this demand. On the other hand, private individuals have found it increasingly difficult to participate as equity investors in industrial real estate transactions without pooling their funds with those of others. To provide for such pooling, many organizational structures have emerged on the scene. The industrial real estate broker must be aware of the existence of these organizations, their uses in given circumstances, and their policies.

Each of the methods has as its fundamental objective broadening the base

---

[5] Interview with David Scribner, S.I.R., and Edmund J. McRickard, S.I.R.

[6] Harvey, *op. cit.,* p. 26–11. For additional discussions on this point, see also New York State Department of Commerce, Division of Economic Research and Statistics, *The Use of Public Funds or Credit in Industrial Location,* Research Bulletin No. 6 (Albany, The Author, October, 1963); Joseph L. McAuliff, "State Economic Development Programs," *AIDC Journal,* Vol. 1, No. 2, April, 1966.

[7] Murray, *op. cit.*

of investor participation in equity investment. The major basis of distinction among the organizations is in their method of providing income to the participating investor, as well as the legal requirements and organizational structures that influence their operation. They also differ according to the income tax liability of both the organization and the individual investor. Each tends to appeal to separate groups of individuals with diverse investment objectives and different tax status.

"A large number of methods has been devised for raising equity capital. Each of these techniques gives a different mixture of risks, potential liabilities, and control. . . . Which method of raising capital will be used is determined by the manner in which it influences management and control, the safety of the investment, the individual liabilities of the participants, and the net return after taxes." [8] In the discussion that follows, these different types of organizations are considered only in terms of their impact on the professional behavior of the industrial real estate broker. Details of their operation and guidelines to their organization may be found in more specialized publications.[9]

1. *Syndicates.* A group of investors brought together for the particular purpose of investing in one or more properties is called a "syndicate." It may take the form of a partnership, a corporation, a trust, a limited partnership association, or a joint venture.[10] However it is organized, the syndicate has the important feature of spreading the base of ownership, and thereby appealing to a much larger potential market. Private individuals who either do not have sufficient cash available to be equity investors in industrial real estate on their own, or who lack the technical and managerial skills to undertake such an investment, can still participate in the higher rates of return and the tax shelters provided by equity real estate investment. Moreover, some hedge against inflation is offered, as in the case of all equity investment in real estate. Finally, since most prime industrial real estate leases are net leases, the investor has a closer approximation to a guaranteed flow of income over time. This can be extremely important to high-income individuals in planning their investment programs.

Whatever the legal form of ownership, the syndicate typically has some form of professional management. In many instances, this represents an important opportunity for the experienced industrial real estate broker, particularly in a partnership or joint venture arrangement. Most individual investors are perfectly willing to hire others to manage the real estate, and to accept a "passive" role in the ownership of the real estate. Indeed, it is only through this passive role that the investor in a limited partnership associa-

[8] Maisel, *op. cit.*, p. 390.

[9] For example, see Maisel, *op. cit.*, Ch. 15; Cerf, *op. cit.*, Ch. 9–11; Niles Gates, "Industrial Property Investments," *Developing, Selling and Syndicating Real Estate Investment Property* (Los Angeles, California Real Estate Association, 1964); Bertram Lewis, *Profits in Real Estate Syndication; A Guide for the Investor* (New York, Harper & Brothers, 1962); Burt Smith, "Real Estate Syndicates," *Developing, Selling and Syndicating Real Estate Investment Property, loc. cit.*; Richard H. Swesnik, "Multiple Ownership of Real Estate," *Real Estate Investment Opportunities* (Los Angeles, California Real Estate Association, 1965).

[10] For details on organizational, legal and operational aspects, see Cerf, *op. cit.*, Ch. 10–11; see also Smith, *op. cit.*, pp. 111–114.

tion, trust, or corporation form of syndicate may enjoy the benefits of limited liability. Moreover, their identities as principals need not be revealed. An industrial real estate broker often serves as "front man" for an anonymous group of investors without the necessity of having a prospectus. The "front men" make themselves known to brokers and owners of properties to be acquired, while the sponsors remain in the background.[11]

Because of the diversity of their organizational form, syndicates will appeal to a substantial range of types of investors. The syndicate is usually formed after a property has been found which looks attractive and meets given investment objectives. Then the equity money is sought. Experienced brokers who have served as syndicators report that "investors cannot be classified by any given types or attitude patterns. There is no 'typical investor.' They vary from the very conservative to the more speculative. . . . The Realtor-syndicator must develop an ability to determine the proper type investment for a given individual investor at a given time. A thorough understanding of an investor's portfolio will help the syndicator in his counsel to the investor." [12] The participants in a syndicate are almost invariably private individuals with cash who want to participate in industrial real estate investment as *owners*.

The industrial real estate broker dealing with a syndicate, whether representing the syndicate or the property owner, should recognize that certain types of properties lend themselves more readily to syndicate investment than others. Although there may be some joint ventures or partnerships which are organized to "take a flyer" in industrial properties, Realtor-syndicators argue that the type of property most suitable for syndicate acquisition is one which can be financed through a large institutional lender, such as a life insurance company. This means that both the property and the transaction must meet the mortgage terms of such lending institutions.

These Realtor-syndicators indicate further that the industrial property most suitable for syndication is one which is relatively large, new or relatively new, either subject to strong potential market demand (general-purpose) or subject to long-term leases with highly rated tenants, and located in a geographic area where the management of the syndicate can conveniently and effectively service the property. This last point is particularly important, because it is likely to be overlooked by uninformed investors. This is a major responsibility of the broker participating in a syndicate. If he or his organization does not have the appropriate management skills, then they must be obtained on a contract basis from an experienced management organization. The gains from leverage should be tempered with considerations of safety, and relatively large equities should be arranged in financing the industrial property.

A major limitation to the attractiveness of a syndicate share for many potential investors in industrial real estate lies in the fact that the liquidity or marketability of the share may be severely restricted. There are no organized markets or systematic market mechanisms for the transfer of syndicate

[11] Interview with David Scribner, S.I.R.
[12] Smith, *op. cit.*, pp. 105–106.

shares in most instances. On occasion, syndicators themselves "make a market" for the shares in their syndicates, but this is often done on an *ad hoc, individual* basis. Since a syndicate may be organized for the specific purpose of owning and operating a particular industrial property, the gains from participating in the syndicate may not be realized until the property is disposed of by the organization. This is a potential deterrent to many investors. As a result, alternative methods of accumulating the savings of individuals for equity investment in industrial real estate have been devised.

2. *Real Estate Investment Trusts.* As a result of the passage of the *Real Estate Investment Trust Act* in 1960 as an amendment to the Internal Revenue Code of 1954, the trust form of multiple ownership of real estate acquired preferential federal income tax status.[13] REIT's may own real estate for investment purposes, as well as lending on investment real estate. If the requirements and standards of the law are followed, a qualified trust pays federal corporate income tax on its retained earnings only.

The qualifying requirements are extensive and complex.[14] The general requirements are:

1. The trust must distribute 90 per cent or more of its ordinary income to shareholders.
2. There must be at least 100 beneficiaries or shareholders; no five shareholders may own, directly or indirectly, more than 50 per cent of the trust.
3. The trust must be managed by one or more trustees, who may not operate the actual real estate owned by the trust.
4. An independent contractor must be employed to manage the property; the contractor may not be related, directly or indirectly, to the trustees.
5. At least 75 per cent of the total income of the trust must come from real estate assets, cash items, and government securities.
6. No more than 30 per cent of income can come from the profit on the sale of trust-owned real estate held for less than four years.
7. Shares in the trust must be freely transferable.

Although originally anticipated to become a major factor in real estate investment markets, REIT's have not approached the scale originally expected. After the law had been in effect for five years, fewer than 50 major REIT's had been organized. Those in existence, however, have become significant investors in industrial real estate, to the extent that their resources have permitted.[15]

There are several opportunities for the industrial real estate broker in working with a real estate investment trust. First, the REIT is a potential purchaser for long-term, high-quality investment industrial property. Second, there are also opportunities for experienced real estate management specialists to serve the trust. The REIT is likely to become an increasingly significant source of equity funds because of the advantages in owning its shares in comparison with those of the syndicate. A major advantage is that REIT

---

[13] For details, see Cerf., *op. cit.*, Ch. 11; see also Harvey, *op. cit.*, p. 26–10; and Smith, *op. cit.*, pp. 111–112.

[14] For a detailed discussion, see Cerf, *op. cit.*, Ch. 12.

[15] See, for example, the *1965 Annual Report* of Continental Mortgage Investors.

shares are more readily transferable on the open market, and some are quoted at the national market level.

3. *Condominiums.* The condominium is a form of joint or multiple ownership of real estate in which each owner has an undivided interest in his own space, as well as a share in a corporation which has title to the common space. It is designed primarily for owner-occupants. Each individual owner-occupied unit can be financed separately, once the basic organization has been established for the entire structure.

The condominium has rarely been used in industrial properties, and yet it offers an opportunity for owner-occupancy of reasonably specialized space by relatively small industrial firms which otherwise would have to be tenants in more general-purpose space.

The condominium form of ownership has been particularly widespread in Latin America, and some industrial condominiums have been developed in Puerto Rico. Some 40 states have passed legislation permitting institutional lenders to participate in condominiums. This form of multiple ownership offers a further opportunity for the alert industrial real estate broker to solve a particular problem, especially if the individual loans are not too small to interest institutional investors.

4. *Real Estate Corporations.* The real estate corporation, real estate investment corporation, or "public corporation" has been likened to a syndicate in corporate form. However, its purpose is to own and trade in a variety of properties, and to continue to own and trade in investment properties over a prolonged period of time. It is more general than the syndicate, and usually has a much broader base of investors or owners.

The public real estate corporation is particularly, although not exclusively, found in New York City. Many of the larger organizations operate on a nationwide basis, and their securities are traded on organized exchanges.[16]

S.I.R.'s contend that public offerings are much more likely to be used to accumulate equity funds in the future.[17] Because they must offer attractive returns to attract a continuing flow of investment funds from the market, these organizations are constantly on the lookout for investment properties. The alert broker will recognize that such investment organizations are more likely to be attracted to large, somewhat speculative properties, or "deals" that offer the prospect of a higher rate of return than the institutional investor seeks. They represent a potential source of funds for the special circumstance, and they can be extremely important in that special circumstance when it offers the prospect of a premium rate of return. Participations in major development programs, such as industrial parks or planned industrial districts, represent one type of special situation to which the public real estate corporation might be attracted. Such organizations as United States Land Corporation, General Development Corporation, and Gulf States Development Corporation are examples. In order to keep abreast of this market, the broker would be well advised to read regularly such publications as *The National Real Estate Investor.*

---

[16] For example, the Uris, Tishman, and Webb & Knapp organizations.
[17] Interview with David Scribner, S.I.R., and Edmund J. McRickard, S.I.R.

PUBLIC GUARANTY AND DEVELOPMENT AGENCIES

Federal, state, and local governmental agencies may make direct loans on industrial properties, primarily to stimulate economic development or to retain sources of employment in given areas. This is discussed in Chapter 8. Local agencies are also potentially important sources of equity investment, primarily to stimulate local economic development. In many instances, public credit is either substituted for, or added to, the credit of the borrowing corporation. This generally has two effects.

First, the terms under which loan funds are made available by institutional lenders to the borrowing corporation are usually more favorable to the borrower, since there is added protection to the lender in the underwriting or guaranteeing of at least a portion of the loan by a higher credit—the public agency. Second, loans are often granted on the underlying credit of the public agency, which would not otherwise be extended. By the end of 1965, some 18 states had state-wide development agencies "authorized to make direct loans to industry, provide assistance through local development commissions, or guarantee industrial loans made by conventional financial institutions." [18] These state-wide agencies are variously termed state development authorities, state industrial finance authorities, or state development credit corporations.

Among these state industrial finance authorities, there are two distinct types of programs. One includes "direct loans of state funds to local development corporations to aid in the financing of industrial projects," [19] while the other involves a guarantee on the part of the state industrial finance authority that all or part of a mortgage loan made by a private lender will be repaid in the event of default by the borrower. This latter is referred to as the "New England type" of state development credit program, primarily because the idea originated in New Hampshire in 1955. Five of the six New England states have such a program, and only one is found outside New England. [20]

Although most state industrial finance authorities have not been operative long enough to allow evaluation of their effectiveness, they do offer some prospect for alternative sources of funds, particularly for a firm which represents less than a good commercial risk. Notable success has been achieved in individual cases in Maine, Pennsylvania, and Connecticut. Industrial real estate brokers have been able to earn commissions by stimulating such arrangements. It is not a particularly important alternative source, in the view of many brokers, partly because of rate restrictions on guaranteed loans, and partly because of the frequent restriction of such guarantees to "new" firms to the state. Guaranty does make some mortgages more attractive to lenders, however, and it can be quite important for smaller, riskier firms.

Underwriting industrial loans is restricted to state governments and state agencies. The federal government restricts its loan guaranty activities to

---

[18] McAuliff, *op. cit.*, p. 35.
[19] New York State Department of Commerce, *op. cit.*, p. 1.
[20] *Ibid.*, pp. 3–4. These industrial finance authorities were found in Maine, New Hampshire, Connecticut, Rhode Island, Vermont, and Pennsylvania.

housing; local communities do have the legal authority to engage in such activity.

As a further stimulus to industrial development, public agencies often issue securities in order to finance development programs for industrial sites. The proceeds of these bond issues are most commonly utilized to provide additional sewer and water facilities, as well as access roads, to community-sponsored industrial areas. This means that the industrial firms attracted to the area will not have to expend capital funds in order to obtain these services for themselves. This is regarded in many circles as unfair competition, since tax-exempt securities are utilized to provide facilities specifically for the new firm being attracted to the area. It means that such a firm is able to obtain its site at a competitive advantage over others which must purchase or rent space from private owners in the open market.

Regardless of this viewpoint, however, the full faith and credit of either the municipality or the state are often employed as backing for the bonds which finance site development. By the end of 1965, there were 26 states which permitted political subdivisions to issue such industrial development bonds.[21] In many instances, only certain communities are authorized to issue bonds, which may be revenue bonds rather than full faith and credit bonds. Whatever the specific terms, there is an advantage to the firm which can utilize a site served with facilities financed by local bonding.

FINANCING THROUGH LEASES

Under a lease of industrial property, whether on land or improvements, or both, the net effect of the transaction is to lend the use of the space to the tenant (lessee) for a stipulated period of time, provided he makes payments in accordance with the contract to the landlord (lessor). The lease is a contract, and each party has enforceable rights under the contract.

The fundamental role of the industrial real estate broker is to bring lessor and lessee together, and to negotiate the terms of the lease on behalf of his client, whichever it may be in the given circumstance. Negotiation is regarded as a skill at least as specialized and demanding as appraisal or management. As the coordinator or pivotal character in the lease negotiation, the broker must decide when technicians should be called in, and what questions must be asked of them. The attorney, the tax accountant, the architect, and the engineer all play at least as important a role in lease negotiation as in the negotiation of a sale or a mortgage.

The important difference between leasing and purchasing space (whether land, buildings, or both) is that the lessee does not have to worry about financing a major capital outlay. Rather, he makes periodic payments over the term of the lease. A long-term lease is therefore often regarded by the user as the equivalent of 100 per cent financing of the property subject to the lease. The contractual and legal characteristics of industrial real estate leases are considered at some length in Chapter 10. Here, the lease is discussed as an alternative to mortgage, equity, or other capital financing.

---

[21] McAuliff, *op. cit.*, p. 35.

Just as the credit rating of the tenant influences the financing that the lessor is able to obtain from a mortgagee, so the credit of the tenant influences the lease "factor." In most industrial real estate lease transactions, especially those involving new or proposed construction, the annual rental is expressed as a percentage of cost to the lessor. This percentage is the lease factor.

Leasing Versus Owning

In the decision of whether to own or lease, there are basic considerations that must be taken into account by the operating industrial firm. The decisions must ultimately be made by the management of the firm. However, the Realtor can assist in the decision-making process by indicating the implications of alternative courses of action, as well as raising the issues clearly and directly for the management of the firm.

In essence, any industrial firm which owns its own real estate is actually engaged in two businesses: (1) the business of conducting its industrial operations; (2) the business of investing in real estate. "While the owning of real estate may not generally be regarded as a business, the fact remains that capital is invested in the operation of the enterprise. As one result of the differences in these yields, a question which such an owner inevitably faces is, 'Should I continue to be in both of these businesses or only in one?' " [22]

In an effort to answer this basic question, the pros and cons of owning and leasing must be analyzed carefully and comprehensively. As one guide to an answer to the fundamental question of whether to own or lease, a list of basic premises has been developed:

(1) Every industrial firm requires space in which to operate.
(2) The acquisition, disposition and/or use of real estate carries with it a concurrent income tax consequence.
(3) Any investment of capital in real estate deserves a yield.
(4) The operation of an industrial firm does not necessarily require that the organization own the industrial space it must occupy.
(5) Because so many factors must be taken into account, an analysis comparing ownership versus leasing can be extended to infinite degrees.
(6) Any decision to lease or own must be made in the light of all factors pertinent to the question, including human or emotional elements (e.g., pride of ownership) on the part of the decision-makers.
(7) In comparing leasing to owning, the dollar cost of leasing will generally exceed the dollar cost of owning real estate if no other considerations (such as alternative use of the funds "saved") are applied.[23]

Within this framework the decision to lease or to own must be made in each individual case.

The Lease as a Financing Device

The outstanding feature of the long-term lease in the industrial real estate field is that it conserves on cash for the user of industrial space. Thus,

---

[22] Irving Korb and Harold G. Trimble, Jr., *Real Estate Sale-Leaseback: A Basic Analysis* (Washington, Society of Industrial Realtors, 1966), p. 4.
[23] This list is adapted from Korb and Trimble, *op. cit.*, p. 4.

it plays the same role over the term of the lease that long-term financing performs.

The management of the industrial firm must satisfy itself that the advantages of leasing outweigh the advantages of ownership (financial, legal, tax, and personal) before it makes sense for the firm to become a lessee. Similarly, the investor or owner of industrial real estate must be convinced that it is to his advantage to lease rather than sell, before he makes the decision to become a lessor. That there are decided advantages in leasing to both lessor and lessee is borne out by the fact that most industrial properties are utilized on a lease basis. In some instances, the total property is leased; in others only the land is leased.

The industrial real estate broker must recognize that leases should be adapted to the needs of both the lessor and the lessee. "A lease suitable for one set of circumstances would be poorly adapted to owners or tenants with other development objectives." [24] Moreover, the tenant industrial firm can and should exert the same control over the design and construction of the plant that it would if it were to own it.

1. *Advantages and Disadvantages to the Lessee.* As compared with owning real estate, leasing has several important advantages and some serious drawbacks for the lessee. While the specific points may vary from one case to another, there is general agreement on the following:

a. Advantages
1. Conservation of working capital. Leasing is in effect 100 per cent financing, which releases funds which would otherwise be invested in real estate for use as working capital in the business. One author has studied the situation and concluded that net gains of over 30 per cent might be achieved with added working capital in many manufacturing firms.[25] Moreover, if the need for cash is acute in the firm, this may make the difference between success and failure.
2. Rental payments are fully deductible for income tax purposes. This means that the firm need not worry particularly about depreciation schedules. Moreover, the value of the land is in effect depreciable as part of the rental payments.
3. There is a superficial improvement in the balance sheet of the tenant firm, in that a long-term lease is not regarded as a liability in the same sense that a mortgage or other long-term debt is. This is a somewhat spurious advantage, however, because increasing emphasis is being placed on long-term lease obligations in the footnotes and other analytical commentary that accompany financial statements prepared by professional accountants. Nevertheless, experienced practitioners in the industrial real estate field continue to cite this as an advantage of leasing, an advantage which one authority in the real estate tax field has labeled "questionable." [26] It certainly is true that often the future borrowing power of the corporation will be less impaired with a long-

---

[24] William M. Shenkel, "The Effective Use of Development Leases," Byron Trerice, Jr., sponsor, *Ground Leases* (Chicago, National Institute of Real Estate Brokers, December, 1965), p. 37.

[25] Gates, *op. cit.*, p. 82 ff.

[26] Cerf, *op. cit.*, p. 178.

term lease obligation than it would be with a long-term debt obligation of the same amount.

"The present practice is to footnote the balance sheet by listing rental obligations of the corporation under existing leases. The pitfall here is that credit analysts, unfamiliar with real estate, may construe this to be an obligation or liability to the extent of the dollars involved in the rentals. This, however, is not so. To reflect the liability properly, a further remark as to the market value of the space under lease may well prove a substantial offset to, or an amount in excess of, the actual rental being paid. The corporation may be paying a lease rental that reflects its credit and which rental may be substantially under the amount for which the leased premises could be sublet to an alternate user.

"For example: One of New York's leading banks had a 15-year lease for first floor banking space on Park Avenue at a rate of $7 per square foot, or approximately $70,000 per annum. When they moved to a larger office, this space was sublet at $15 per square foot, or $150,000 per annum. This demonstrates that the liability implied by a footnote could possibly be an asset. Of course, the market rental also could be below the amount of the rental obligation, but in any event there is some rental value in every instance." [27]

4. In many cases, leasehold improvements may be amortized rapidly, resulting in a larger flow of "tax-free" funds than would be true under an ownership arrangement.
5. Restrictions on the lessee under a lease are often less severe than those on a mortgagor under a mortgage of debt indenture. As a result, there is somewhat more freedom of action for the industrial lessee in the conduct of its industrial business.

b. Disadvantages
1. The lessee will not share in any capital gains that may be experienced as a result of rising values with the passage of time.
2. At the expiration of the lease, the lessee has no further claim on the real estate. Its "investment" is 100 per cent amortized, and all claims and rights revert to the lessor.
3. There may be serious restrictions on the ability of the lessee firm to improve an undesirable situation if its powers to alter or add to the building are limited. Moreover, it may have difficulty in financing leasehold improvements, unless there is substantial protection to the lender through subordination of the claims of the lessor.

2. Advantages and Disadvantages to the Lessor.

a. Advantages
1. Rental income as a rate of return on the investment is usually higher than the overall rate of return on comparable loans. For approximately the same risk, a higher rate of return is received.
2. The property reverts to the lessor at the expiration of the lease. This normally includes any leasehold improvements made by the lessee.
3. Industrial leases, particularly to high-credit tenants, are more likely to

---

[27] Statement by Edmund J. McRickard, S.I.R., New York City.

be net rather than gross leases. If they are gross leases, they are usually fully escalated. In either event, this means that increased operating expenses, such as insurance rates or tax rates, are borne by the tenant. The landlord can therefore plan on a reasonably steady net income. This has particular appeal to institutional investors seeking stability of income for planning purposes.

4. In the great majority of cases, the tax liability of the owner at the time the property is disposed of will be based on long-term capital gain rather than ordinary income. In addition, the accelerated depreciation available under most circumstances can result in a tax free flow of income.

5. The "basic urge of ownership" is satisfied. No precise dollar value can be placed on this, but it is undoubtedly important for many participants in industrial real estate transactions.

b. Disadvantages
1. In the event of an economic decline in the area, the lessor will suffer the entire loss that may be incurred.

2. In the event of a rising market, the lessor is committed to the long-term use of his property by a tenant paying a fixed rental.

3. Unless the lease is net or fully escalated, increasing costs of taxes and insurance, in particular, can seriously reduce the anticipated net income to the lessor over time.

3. *Tax Considerations in Leasing.* Almost no industrial real estate transaction occurs without serious attention to the income tax implications. This is certainly true of long-term leasing, whether it involves a straight lease arrangement, a sale-leaseback, or a ground lease with leasehold improvements.

In addition to the implications of long-term capital gains treatment and of deducting depreciation charges (which have already been considered at length in Chapter 5), one further important tax consideration should be added. In a leasing transaction, the deductibility of rents paid by the lessee are tantamount to the ability to depreciate the land. Because this is an extremely valuable advantage, particular care must be taken not to jeopardize the income tax deductibility of full rental payments. The Internal Revenue Service may seek to have all or a portion of the rental payments disallowed under given conditions, with a resultant serious loss to the lessee (and quite possibly the lessor as well). "A combination of one or more of the following conditions in any lease will invite questions as to full deduction of rents:

"(a) Part of the rental is specifically applied to purchase price;

"(b) After a stated amount is paid in rental, title of the property passes automatically to the lessee;

"(c) Early rents are extremely high, particularly in comparison to the option price or the percentage specified in the contract;

"(d) Rental payments materially exceed fair rental value of the property;

"(e) The indicated option price or percentage is nominal in amount;

"(f) The option price is relatively small compared to the total amount of rental which is to be paid;

"(g) Part of the rent is specifically designated as interest or is readily recognized as an interest charge;

"(h) The total amount of rental paid during the lease, plus the option price,
equals the fair market value of the property plus an interest and carrying charge factor." [28]

Because of all these important technical considerations, and the wide
range of possible pitfalls, it is absolutely imperative that any industrial real
estate lease transaction be completed with appropriate legal and tax advice,
as well as professional industrial real estate brokerage assistance.

When all of the foregoing considerations are taken into account, the fact
remains that the majority of industrial space transactions in the United
States involve rental rather than sale. To be fully effective, the broker must
recognize the implications of the advantages and disadvantages of leasing
to both lessor and lessee, if he is to advise his client appropriately. Moreover,
without knowing what each party stands to gain and/or lose because of
particular lease provisions, he cannot negotiate effectively on behalf of his
client.

Major Categories of Lease Financing of Industrial Real Estate

There are essentially four major types of leasing arrangements which facilitate the use of industrial space. They are: (1) the conventional or straight
lease, in which space is simply and directly leased in an existing building
from the owner; (2) the build-lease arrangement, whereby a developer-
lessor builds a plant to the specifications of the user, and then leases the
space to that user upon completion of the building; (3) the sale-leaseback,
in which a user-owner sells its real estate to an investor, while simultaneously
leasing back the property on a long-term lease basis; and (4) the ground
lease, under which the owner of land leases it to an industrial user or developer, who then proceeds to construct a building on the land. These improvements become the property of the lessor of the land, upon the expiration of the ground lease.

All four types of leasing arrangements, with minor variations on the basic
themes, are found in industrial real estate practice. The latter three are particularly and peculiarly suited to industrial real estate activity, and require
both knowledge and care on the part of the broker seeking to merchandise
space through their use. The applications of these alternative methods of
leasing are discussed here on the assumption that the "own-or-lease" decision has been made in favor of leasing.

1. *Straight Lease.* Whenever an owner or purchaser of industrial space
seeks to lease the property, whether it is already in existence or has been built
new as a general-purpose building, a straight or direct lease arrangement
results. This always occurs in the case of multitenant buildings. It is termed

---

[28] Edmund J. McRickard, "Industrial Sale-Leaseback," Speech before Commercial Property Clinic, Chicago, May 8, 1964, p. 4.

a "straight lease" because there is nothing to distinguish its general form, or the general character of the transaction, from a long-term lease on any other type of real estate.

Negotiation of the rental and other payment considerations under the lease is still required, as well as such matters as assignment of rents to a lender (to reinforce the credit of the borrower, as discussed in Chapter 8), or subordination of the claims of the lessor to those of the lender. Moreover, lessor and lessee must agree over the responsibilities of each of the parties. In this regard, the broker, acting as agent for the lessor in enforcing the terms of the lease, performs an extremely critical function.

Further details of these considerations can be investigated in articles relating specifically to commercial and industrial leasing.[29]

2. *Build-Lease.* This arrangement is also termed "build to suit," and refers to one of two general types of situations. There is first the case in which a property owner-developer already owns a building site in which a prospective tenant is interested, and the owner constructs a building to suit the tenant. Alternatively, an investor may have an arrangement with a prospective tenant to construct a building specifically for the tenant, and must find and purchase a suitable site on which the building is to be constructed.

By definition, the building in a "build-lease" transaction is a special-purpose or special-use structure. These leases, therefore, always involve the credit of the tenant-user. As in the case of all credit-oriented industrial real estate transactions, the higher the credit rating of the tenant, the better the bargaining position of the tenant. The lessor can utilize the credit of the tenant in negotiating more favorable mortgage financing. The lender will, of course, insist upon an assignment of rents from the lessor.

A "build to suit" transaction is often referred to as a "package deal." It is described as starting with "a tenant for whom no existing building is available or suitable, and who is willing to *enter into extended negotiations* with an investor who will build a building 'to suit' the tenant on a site" selected by the two.[30]

In analyzing such situations, a leading authority on industrial leasing has commented: "The key to the successful consummation of this type of transaction is the *tenant.* If the tenant is a so-called 'National' type of firm and is willing to pay the fair going market rental, the scramble on the part of investors for such an investment is on the 'wild' side. . . . Unfortunately, there is not a preponderance of such prospects, and the broker must content himself with trying to negotiate these transactions with less strong (financially) tenants. The investor, in judging the merits of such a deal, is usually guided by the standards set up by lending institutions."[31] The writer goes on to recommend that the broker ally himself with an experienced specialist or

---

[29] E.g., David I. Wendel, "Commercial-Industrial Leases," *Real Estate Investment* (Los Angeles, California Real Estate Association, 1963); and Robert P. Boblett, "Broker's Role in Leasing Commercial Property," *Real Estate Encyclopedia* (Englewood Cliffs, N.J., Prentice-Hall, 1960).

[30] Korb, *op. cit.,* p. 13 [emphasis added].

[31] *Ibid.*

developer because of the countless details and many fine points involved in such a transaction.

Because a build-lease arrangement requires suiting the needs of the user, the negotiation team will often include (in addition to the two principals and the industrial broker) a plant engineer, one or more attorneys, and an architect with general industrial and lessee service background. It is extremely important that the *physical* aspects of the lease arrangement be as carefully attended to as the legal and financial aspects. If a company is going to be the single occupant of an industrial plant, whether as tenant or owner, that firm should in its own interests directly control the planning and construction of the plant.

3. *Sale-Leaseback.* "The sale of a parcel of real estate (either land, or building, or both) by its owner-user who, simultaneously with the sale, enters into a lease (with the buyer) for the seller's continuing use of the property just sold" is a sale-leaseback. In other words, "any real estate transaction in which an owner-user sells to an investor and at the same time leases back the property for his own or his company's use, constitutes a sale-leaseback." [32]

The sale-leaseback carries with it the same essential advantages and disadvantages to lessor and lessee that leasing in general provides. In fact, from the standpoint of the investor owning leased property, there is little distinction. From the standpoint of the user, however, some considerations are missing when the using firm is not already owner. Under the sale-leaseback transaction, a systematic analysis of the advantages and disadvantages of owning versus leasing must be conducted in light of the fact that the proposed tenant is now an owner. This requires more detail and care in the analysis.

A major distinguishing characteristic of the sale-leaseback transaction is the tax status of the proceeds of the sale. This can be the determining factor in the potential seller's decision whether to go through with the sale-leaseback. It is imperative to have competent and experienced legal and tax counsel available to the seller (often through the assistance of the industrial real estate broker) to advise in this important decision.

The buyer-lessor under a sale-leaseback transaction is most likely to be a financial institution or pension fund. Indeed, one of the major stimuli to the growth of sale-leaseback during the 1950's and 1960's in the United States was the fact of favored (i.e., reduced) tax status of life insurance companies, pension funds, university endowment funds, and trusts. These have historically been the major participants in sale-leaseback arrangements as buyer-lessors. It is not necessary to the success of sale-leaseback for the lessor to be a tax-favored or tax-exempt organization, but it does add considerably to the attractiveness of the rates that such investors are able to charge. Lessees are also much more likely to be high-credit organizations. Institutional lessor-purchasers are more interested in "paper deals" than in real estate transactions. For the investment personnel of pension funds and

---

[32] Korb and Trimble, *op. cit.*, p. 3.

university endowment funds, sale-leaseback is readily understandable because it is "based primarily upon credit and the risk can be measured by a method familiar to them: credit analysis." [33]

Because income tax considerations represent important factors in the decision whether to enter into a sale-leaseback arrangement, special care must be exercised to assure both parties that the favorable income tax treatment anticipated is in fact received. There are several pitfalls which must be particularly avoided. One is the danger that a sale-leaseback with a repurchase option may be held by the Internal Revenue Service to be an installment sale, and treated accordingly for tax purposes. The same danger underlies setting a rental either "too high" or "too low," relative to market standards developed by IRS in its evaluation of the transaction. Moreover, leases with close affiliates can also result in adverse tax rulings, as, for example, when the buyer-lessor is the employee retirement fund of the seller-lessee company. This is not by definition a dangerous situation, but extreme care is required to set it up properly. This calls for expert legal and tax advice. [34]

Although emphasis is usually placed on the high-credit sale-leaseback transaction involving large financial institutions or funds, the sale-leaseback can also be an effective device for smaller industrial firms. It can be a real estate as well as a credit transaction. The following three examples serve to illustrate this important point: [35]

Case No. 1: A metal supply company, which was a post World War II business, was doing fairly well in an extremely competitive market; however, because of the vagaries of this market (the building construction industry), it was continually in need of working capital. Its primary asset, the real estate in which it operated, was encumbered with two loans totaling $35,000. Its total financial situation was in stifling condition, and borrowing capacity at its bank was exhausted. It could either go on as it had for the past 12 years or make a major adjustment in its financial structure. The principals of this closely held corporation chose to sell the real estate rather than re-finance, because the amount of additional cash borrowing capacity over the existing loans was negligible.

After sounding out the market, a sale was effected and a sale-leaseback consummated. The selling price of $95,000 resulted in the following:

A long-term capital gains tax of $12,000 was paid to Internal Revenue.

The existing loans were paid off.

The seller-lessee entered into a 10-year firm lease at a net-net-net rental of 11 per cent to the buyer-lessor.

The seller-lessee was immediately able to add $43,000 to its current assets and operating account.

Among the other advantages accruing to this Seller-Lessee (in addition to fulfilling its primary motive of obtaining additional working capital) was its ability to project a savings of over $7,000 in the first year by programming its purchasing and discounting its bills.

Case No. 2: The owner of a one-story brick building, in which he operated

---

[33] McRickard, *op. cit.*, pp. 1–3.
[34] See Cerf, *op. cit.*, pp. 197 ff. for details and further discussion.
[35] These examples are quoted from Korb and Trimble, *op. cit.*, pp. 10–11.

his tool and die business, had an opportunity to take on some extensive and valuable contracts. Up to this time his operation was a modest one, which did not require any financial assistance beyond his own personal funds; therefore, he had not built up any banking connections which would suddenly finance his contemplated expansion.

If he could not raise approximately $25,000 in cash, he would have to forego this opportunity which was potentially highly remunerative.

His decision was to sell his property, which was free from any loans, and lease it back. He sold for $25,000 in cash and entered into a five-year lease with the buyer-lessor. In this instance there were no options to extend, and the buyer-lessor received a rental of $3,000 per year while paying for all taxes, insurance, and repair.

Case No. 3: The owner of a successful steel fabricating company, who had managed his business on a most conservative basis for 20 years, decided to expand his operation by taking his sons into the business with him.

The physical facilities were large enough to accommodate such growth—the only problem was that of funding the expansion with an adequate backlog of working capital, which this owner did not possess.

While the capacity of the business to borrow these funds was manifest, upon analysis, it was determined that bank borrowing necessitated short-term repayment which would inhibit the desired growth pattern called for in the expansion program.

Other than inventory, the largest asset of this family was the real estate which it owned and from which it conducted its business. It was determined that a sale-leaseback provided the most practical solution to this problem.

A 10-year lease was entered into concurrently with the sale of the property for $95,000. The net-net-net lease rental was 11.50 per cent annually.

Subsequent to this transaction and the freeing of this $95,000 (less sales and legal fees), this company did embark on an expansion program which has proven to be highly profitable.

The sale-leaseback, therefore, is an important and valuable financing device, which offers a high degree of flexibility for many industrial real estate users and investors. It also requires a very high level of technical competency, which requires highly skilled specialists as advisers and participants in the transaction. However, it is not axiomatic that all industrial real estate or business problems can be solved by the use of the sale-leaseback device.

4. *Ground Leases.* When an industrial real estate broker encounters substantial obstacles in his efforts to complete a sale involving a parcel of land, an alternative which is often acceptable to both owner and user is the long-term ground lease or land lease. Under this arrangement, the land is subject to a long-term lease, and the lessee utilizes his leasehold estate to finance construction of buildings on the land. In effect, the land is "lent" for a fee, and the lessor receives both the land and the building at the expiration of the lease. During the period of the lease, the lessee has the advantage of full depreciation of his building, as well as deduction of the entire rental payment on the land for income tax purposes. "A fundamental reason for the increasing use of ground leases is the fact that the high price of land often makes a purchase prohibitive since no one would be allowed to claim de-

preciation for land he bought, whereas he can claim 100 per cent deduction for the ground rental that he pays the owner." [36]

A long-term ground lease transaction is a complicated one. It involves specific agreement between lessor and lessee regarding the responsibility for buildings currently owned by the lessee, but in which the lessor has a residual or contingent interest. The lessee usually mortgages his leasehold interest in order to obtain financing for the construction of his building or buildings. In most instances, the mortgage lender will insist on protective provisions in the mortgage loan, including subordination of the fee to the mortgage. It is essential, therefore, that such leases be drafted by experts who pay careful attention to applicable law, and give due weight to the desires and needs of the lessor, lessee, and lender.

Land leases are generally highly individualized, reflecting the desires and needs of the participants in the transaction. A land lease is often easy to sell, once the proper type of investor has been found. Institutions not seeking tax benefits from depreciation charges, but interested rather in a steady, safe, and usually substantial return on their invested capital, are logical buyers of land leases. They are also appropriate lessors under ground-lease transactions. So, too, are retired individuals.

Perhaps the most important single consideration with respect to ground leases is subordination. When the leasehold financing is based primarily on the real estate, then the mortgage lender will normally require that the lessor subordinate the real estate to a construction and/or take-out loan that is to be granted on the premises by the tenant. Under these circumstances, particular care must be taken to protect the rights of both lessor and lessee.

In some instances, when the credit of the lessee is high enough, lending institutions will not necessarily insist upon subordination of the land. This is often a matter of negotiation among the parties. A representative of one institutional lender, commenting on the financing of ground-lease leasehold transactions that his organization had handled in the past, stated that "in many cases, under those circumstances the owner of the land has permitted a pledge of his land as security for the loan on the property. We think that that does not really penalize the land owner too much. However, many estates and some trusts just will not permit their land to be pledged, and in that case we will figure out what we can do to make a loan on the leasehold without the land being pledged." [37]

The importance of ground leases as a financing device is illustrated by the following example, developed by Professor William M. Shenkel of the University of Georgia: [38]

One of the main advantages of net ground leases arises from the opportunity to increase the rate of return above the rates earned by owner-development of the fee. To show the effect of long-term leases, assume that land under lease has a market value of $75,000, and that the tenant proposes a land improvement of $225,000 and agrees to an annual rent of $6,000. Assume further that

---

[36] Byron Trerice, Jr., sponsor, *Ground Leases* (Chicago, National Institute of Real Estate Brokers, December, 1965), p. 9.
[37] Murray, *op. cit.*
[38] Quoted from Shenkel, *op. cit.*, p. 30.

mortgage financing for 20 years, at 6 per cent, is available to finance improvements under a loan-to-value ratio of 66⅔ per cent.

Under these assumptions, leasehold financing, compared to mortgage financing of the fee, will show a higher return on equity. Leasehold financing is compared to mortgage financing of the fee in the example in the following table:

LEASEHOLD FINANCING COMPARED TO CONVENTIONAL FINANCING

Item	Mortgage Financing	Leasing Without Subordination	Leasing With Subordination
Minimum loan	$200,000	$150,000	$200,000
Equity	100,000	75,000	25,000
Net income to tenant	30,000	30,000	30,000
Ground rent	—	6,000	6,000
Mortgage service (20 years, 6 percent, rounded)	17,437	13,078	17,437
Total charges	17,437	19,078	23,437
Net after rent and mortgage service	12,563	10,922	6,563
Return on equity	12.6% ($12,563/ $100,000)	14.6% ($10,922/ $75,000)	26.3% ($6,563/ $25,000)

With a proposed property value of $300,000 (land, $75,000; land improvements, $225,000), the maximum loan under the assumed conditions would be $200,000. To show the return on equity after mortgage service and ground rent, it is necessary to assume a net return of $30,000 on land and buildings. Under these circumstances a first mortgage of $200,000 would require an annual deut service of $17,437, resulting in a net income after mortgage payments of $12,563—a return on the $100,000 equity of almost 12.6 per cent.

If, on the other hand, the site is leased without subordination, a loan of $150,000 would be necessary (⅔ of $225,000). Net income to the tenant would be computed after rent ($6,000) and mortgage service requirements ($13,078). After rent and mortgage service requirements, the tenant would earn a net return of $10,922 or a return on equity of 14.6 per cent.

With subordination of the leased fee, the lender would regard land and building as security, which would permit a maximum loan of $200,000. After deduction of ground rent and debt service of $23,437, a net income of $6,563 remains, which represents a return of 26.3 per cent on a $25,000 equity.

In short, by leasing an investor reduces the amount of cash required for property development and at the same time increases the rate of return on invested capital in comparison to conventional mortgage financing. In effect, leasing the site is equivalent to a loan equal to 100 per cent of the land value.

SELECTED REFERENCES

American Industrial Development Council, "Guide to Federal Development Legislation: 1965," Special Issue of *A.I.D.C. Journal,* Vol. I, No. 2, April, 1966.

American Institute of Architects, Committee on Industrial Architecture, *A Guide to Better Industrial Building Leasing* (Washington, The Author, August, 1963).

Cerf, Alan R., *Real Estate and the Federal Income Tax* (Englewood Cliffs, New Jersey, Prentice-Hall, 1965).

Federal Reserve Bank of Boston, "New War Between the States," Parts I–IV, *New England Business Review,* October, 1963, December, 1963, July, 1964, October, 1964.

Gates, Niles, "Industrial Property Investments," *Developing, Selling and Syndicating Real Estate Investment Property* (Los Angeles, California Real Estate Association, 1964).

Harvey, Robert O., "Real Estate Finance," Chapter 26 of *Financial Handbook,* 4th ed. (New York, Ronald Press, 1964).

International Traders Club, National Institute of Real Estate Brokers, *Tax Implications in Exchanging* (Chicago, The Author, March, 1966).

International Traders Club, National Institute of Real Estate Brokers, *Techniques of Investment Property Exchanging* (Chicago, The Author, March, 1965).

Kahn, Sanders A., Case, Frederick E., and Schimmel, Alfred, *Real Estate Appraisal and Investment* (New York, Ronald Press, 1963).

Kinnard, William N., Jr., and Malinowski, Zenon S., *The Metals Service Industry: A Case Study of a Satellite Industry* (New York, McGraw-Hill, 1961).

Kinnard, William N., Jr., and Malinowski, Zenon S., *Use of External Assistance by Small Manufacturing Firms,* Small Business Management Research Report (Storrs, Conn.; University of Connecticut, 1961).

Korb, Irving, and Trimble, Harold G., Jr., *Real Estate Sale-Leaseback: A Basic Analysis* (Washington, Society of Industrial Realtors, 1966).

Lewis, Bertram, *Profits in Real Estate Syndication: A Guide for the Investor* (New York, Harper & Brothers, 1962).

Maisel, Sherman J., *Financing Real Estate: Principles and Practices* (New York, McGraw-Hill, 1965).

McMichael, Stanley L., and O'Keefe, Paul T., *How to Finance Real Estate,* 2nd ed. (Englewood Cliffs, New Jersey; Prentice-Hall, 1953).

National Institute of Real Estate Brokers, *Ground Leases,* Byron Trerice, Jr., sponsor, (Chicago, The Author, December, 1965).

New York State Department of Commerce, Division of Economic Research and Statistics, *The Use of Public Funds or Credit in Industrial Location,* Research Bulletin No. 6 (Albany, New York; The Author, October, 1963).

Ricks, R. Bruce, *Recent Trends in Institutional Real Estate Investment,* Research Report 23, Center for Real Estate and Urban Economics (Berkeley, University of California, 1964).

Shenkel, William M., *Principles and Practices of Industrial Real Estate: A Course Syllabus* (Washington, Society of Industrial Realtors, 1963).

Smith, Burt, "Real Estate Syndicates," *Developing, Selling and Syndicating Real Estate Investment Property* (Los Angeles, California Real Estate Association, 1964).

Society of Industrial Realtors, *Advanced Course in the Techniques of Industrial Real Estate* (Washington, Society of Industrial Realtors, 1964).
    "Financing Industrial Real Estate," Thomas F. Murray. "Industrial Property Investment Opportunities," J. D. Sawyer.

Swesnik, Richard H., "Multiple Ownership of Real Estate," *Real Estate Investment Opportunities* (Los Angeles, California Real Estate Association, 1965).

U.S. Department of Commerce, Economic Development Administration, *Handbook of Federal Aids to Communities* (Washington, U.S. Government Printing Office, 1966).

U.S. Office of Economic Opportunity, *Catalog of Federal Programs for Individual and Community Improvement* (Washington, U.S. Government Printing Office, December, 1965).

Wendel, David I., "Commercial-Industrial Leases," *Real Estate Investment* (Los Angeles, California Real Estate Association, 1963).

10 | Industrial Real Estate Leases

AN industrial real estate lease is a contract between two parties for the use of industrial space over a specified period of time in return for the payment of a specified rental. It is the document which spells out the terms of the contract between the parties: the owner or lessor, and the tenant or lessee. The distinguishing characteristics of the industrial real estate lease are found in the highly individualized terms and conditions of the contractual agreement. They are negotiated between lessor and lessee through the intermediary services of an industrial real estate broker, assisted by legal, tax, accounting, engineering, and architectural technicians. To be effective in these negotiations, the broker must be aware of the impact of the various terms and conditions on each of the parties involved.

Although the broker is concerned primarily with the financial or economic aspects of the industrial real estate transaction, the lease arrangement is created within a legal framework. That legal framework must be developed with the advice of competent legal counsel. The discussion in this chapter concentrates on the legal aspects of the industrial lease, to complete the considerations initiated in the analysis of leasing techniques in Chapter 6, and continued in the analysis of leasing as a financing technique in Chapter 9.

Despite the diversity of practice from one area to another, and despite the highly individualized character of industrial lease terms as a result of negotiation, a broad general framework can be provided for the analysis of leases. Two illustrative examples of industrial lease forms are provided as Appendix A and Appendix B to this chapter. Throughout the present discussion of lease terms, reference will be made continually to these two illustrative leases. The reader may then follow the precise wording and the application of lease terms in context.

Since an industrial real estate lease is a contract between lessor and lessee, the identification of each is an important first step in the analysis of any lease agreement. This identification is provided in the Introduction to the lease which is Appendix A, and in Clause No. 1 of Appendix B.

ECONOMIC AND MARKET CONSIDERATIONS

For purposes of analysis, the terms and conditions of industrial leases are separated between those which may be regarded as essentially economic or financial in character, and those which are primarily legal. These represent differences of emphasis only. Lease terms involving "economic and market considerations" are those which have a direct influence on the use of industrial space (analyzed in Chapters 2 and 3), the value of that space (considered in detail in Chapter 12), and the financing of that space (discussed in Chapters 8 and 9). These three major sets of influences in turn determine the allocation of industrial space among alternative uses and users. Since the fundamental function of the broker is to assist in the efficient allocation of industrial space, it is a matter of considerable concern to him to recognize those lease terms and conditions which have a direct bearing on the use, financing, value, and hence the allocation of industrial space.

Some lease terms are negotiable, while others basically are not. Speaking very broadly, those which have an economic or financial basis are much more susceptible to adjustment through negotiation than are lease terms dictated primarily by legal considerations, as the latter are less directly sensitive and responsive to market pressures.

Classification of Industrial Leases

"The lease (while sometimes carrying a heading 'Lease') is never entitled or named in such a way as to indicate, at a glance, the 'type' of lease it is. The making of a judgment as to the contents of a lease without reading every word can be a dangerous thing. . . . Each lease is specially designed (or should be) for each situation." [1] Once the reading of the lease has been completed, however, it can be classified by term or length, by whether it is a net or a gross lease (its "netness"), and by the type and use of property or space being leased.

1. *Term.* The term of the lease is generally specified early in the document. It is Clause No. 1 in Appendix A and Clause No. 3 in Appendix B. Industrial leases generally provide for longer terms than do leases on most other types of real estate. In part, this is because the user (particularly a manufacturing firm) often finds it expensive and most inconvenient to have to move over relatively short periods of time. The lessor is also typically interested in a long-term lease, because it can supplement the value of the real estate by supporting mortgage financing. In any situation in which the credit of the tenant is part of the lender's decision to grant a mortgage loan, the term of the lease generally tends to set the mortgage payout period. All other things being equal, the longer the term of the lease, the "safer" the loan for the mortgage.

---

[1] Irving Korb and Harold G. Trimble, Jr., *Real Estate Sale-Leaseback: A Basic Analysis* (Washington, Society of Industrial Realtors, 1966), p. 9.

2. *"Netness."* A "gross" lease is one which calls for the owner to pay for basic real estate taxes, insurance on the building, as well as sidewall, roof and structural maintenance and repairs. The owner may also provide certain utilities (water, sewer service, gas, and/or electricity) under a gross lease. At the other end of the scale, a completely net lease (often termed "net-net-net") is one under which the tenant assumes full responsibility for real estate taxes, pays all liability and property insurance premiums, maintains all parts of the structure in good repair, pays for all utilities, and must restore the structure if it is destroyed from *any* cause. These costs and expenses are all in addition to the rental for the use of the space.

Within this range of possibilities, the following common variations are found:

"Net Lease: A lease situation wherein the lessee, in addition to his obligation under all the other terms and conditions of the lease, is also obligated to pay for the real estate taxes and/or assessments of other nature (either in whole or in part).

"Net-Net Lease: In addition to the statement applying to net lease above, the lessee is also obligated to pay for the insurance premiums (either in whole or in part) applicable to that insurance coverage which has been agreed to in the negotiation.

"Net-Net-Net Lease: In addition to the above statements applying to net lease and to net-net lease, the lessee is also obligated to pay for the items of repair and maintenance (either in whole or in part), the extent of which has been agreed to in the negotiation." [2]

Another form of "net" lease is the fully escalated gross lease. Under such an arrangement, the tenant agrees to pay the *additional* charges for taxes, insurance and/or maintenance above a specified level, below which the lessor continues to pay.

Examples of provisions in leases specifying which party shall bear the various expenses involved are found in Clauses 4, 6, 10, and 12 in Appendix A, and in Clauses 6b, 6c, 6d, 8a, and 8c of Appendix B. With such a wide range of possibilities, this is one important area which is subject to considerable negotiation. Speaking generally, the lessee prefers to have as "gross" a lease as possible, while the lessor prefers to have as "net" a lease as possible. Each party is anxious to minimize the risk of increased expenses (particularly unforeseen ones) in the future.

The printed lease forms in Appendix A and B call for a high degree of "netness." This is not surprising, since they are prepared for use by industrial brokers on behalf of the lessor-client. What is printed in the standard form lease is not necessarily utilized, however. Rather, "what is netted depends on the bargaining ability of the two parties." [3]

3. *Type and Use of Property.* The type of property being leased, and the use to which it is to be put, will definitely influence the clauses that should be included, as well as the terms and conditions about which there will most likely be negotiation between lessor and lessee.

---

[2] *Ibid.*, p. 5.
[3] Interview with James E. Hanson, S.I.R., Hackensack, New Jersey.

The lease agreement will normally specify the uses to which the leased property may be put, stipulating further that any changes require approval by the lessor. This is illustrated in Clause 3 of Appendix A, and Clauses 2 and 9a of Appendix B. The amount of flexibility allowed the tenant is generally a matter of bargaining between the two parties. In addition it is usually the responsibility of the lessee to obtain required legal clearances, such as zoning permits, use permits, or licenses.

The type of property involved will often affect the character of the lease. A ground lease, for example, will contain substantially different provisions from a lease on improved property. Such matters as maintenance and repair are of little significance under a ground lease, but critical in a lease of building space. Similarly, subordination of the fee for mortgage lending purposes on the leasehold estate is exceedingly important in a ground lease, but generally inapplicable on an improved property lease. The lease for space in a multitenant structure will contain substantial reference to the use of, and access to, common facilities, while the lease on special-purpose or single-occupant industrial buildings will much more likely emphasize subordination of the lease to any mortgage that may be placed on the property.

Payment Provisions of Industrial Leases

The rental and purchase provisions in industrial leases have the most direct and immediate economic impact on both lessor and lessee. They also influence the mortgagee's decision to lend on the property. These provisions represent one area in which the industrial real estate broker can influence the negotiating parties, in part by reporting authoritatively on current market rates and conditions.

Rental rates have particular interest to industrial space users "because in most cases they are primarily interested in the use of real estate, rather than in making a profit by investing in real estate." [4] Some authorities maintain that payment provisions are more important to the lessor, because they influence the investment attractiveness of the lease agreement, and of the real estate.[5] In any event, the payment provisions of industrial leases affect the availability of financing. Thus, the mortgagee will also pay close attention to rental, renewal, and purchase option provisions.

The industrial real estate broker is particularly important in the negotiations over these provisions of the lease, because "between the two major considerations of (1) prevailing market conditions, and (2) those unique conditions and circumstances pertaining to the [lessor and lessee], there exists a broad range of points which ultimately must be agreed to by the parties involved." [6]

1. *The Rent Clause.* Every industrial real estate lease must have a clear and unequivocal statement of how much rent is to be paid, over what

[4] William M. Shenkel, *Principles and Practices of Industrial Real Estate: A Course Syllabus* (Washington, Society of Industrial Realtors, 1963), Chapter 6.
[5] Niles Gates, "Industrial Property Investments," *Developing, Selling and Syndicating Real Estate Investment Property* (Los Angeles, California Real Estate Association, 1964), p. 76.
[6] Korb and Trimble, *op. cit.*, p. 9.

period, and in what manner. This is illustrated in Clause 2 in Appendix A, and in Clauses 4 and 6 of Appendix B. Any payments for taxes, maintenance, or insurance to be borne by the lessee will be added to the basic rental payments.

While the rate of rental, either on a monthly or an annual basis, will always be spelled out in the lease, it is generally recommended that the total amount of rent payments to be made over the entire term of the lease also be specified.[7] Then there can be no question what the obligation and rights of the two parties are with respect to the rental payment.

The method and timing of payment will also normally be specified. There are many variations in the types of payment schedules that may be developed. Payments may be made monthly, quarterly, semi-annually, or annually. They may be made at the beginning or the end of the period (payment at the beginning is much more common). They may be level throughout the term of the lease, or they may call for periodic renegotiation, based on standards which should be clearly established in advance, and included in the lease. They may call for upward or downward adjustment upon renewal of the lease. They are all matters which are subject to negotiation.

The annual rental or "rent factor" is usually calculated as a percentage of the cost to the investor: construction cost plus land value in the case of new buildings, and market value of the property in the case of existing construction. This annual "factor" represents the gross rate of return on the lessor's investment. The rental factor that the broker negotiates for the lessor is a combination of going rates on the market, the credit of the tenant, and the relative bargaining strength of lessor and lessee. A longer term lease may well call for a slightly lower rent factor because it provides the basis for a longer period of mortgage amortization, thereby reducing the regular loan payments, which in turn results in retention of more "spendable-now" dollars on the part of the lessor.

The tenant, on the other hand, is not interested in the "rent factor"; the tenant is interested in the rent. Given the facts of the case, the broker must be able to indicate the "rent factor" to the lessor, and the unit rental to the lessee, often simultaneously while proposals and counter-proposals are being exchanged. Neither the "rent factor" nor the annual or monthly rental per square foot of floor area is included in the lease document, however. Only the total amount of rent to be paid over the term of the lease, and the rate of rental are specified.

2. *Renewal and Purchase Option.* Many industrial leases will carry provisions for renewal on specified terms, with the decision of whether there shall be renewal left to the determination of the tenant. This is a true option, since the right is unilateral. Only the owner is bound to observe the conditions of the option; the tenant remains free to exercise or to forfeit the right.

Similarly, a lease may carry an option to purchase the property within a specified period of time, usually at a specified price. Both the option to

---

[7] Interview with Tom H. Lang, S.I.R., Cleveland; and Bernard Manekin, S.I.R., Baltimore.

purchase and the option to renew must be at "reasonable" prices.[8] If the option is interpreted by the Internal Revenue Service as a subterfuge for a conditional sale or mortgage, the rental received by the lessor may be taxed as part of the proceeds of a sale. Deductions by the lessor for depreciation on the leased property may therefore not be allowed. Moreover, the rent paid by the lessee would then be considered to represent payments on a sales contract, and therefore not deductible as an operating expense.

The renewal rental and the purchase price (or repurchase price on a sale-leaseback) should both be specified clearly in the lease, to avoid subsequent controversy. If this is not possible at the time that the lease is signed, then a method for reaching an agreement over purchase price or renewal rental should be specified in detail in the lease. It should be binding on both parties. Otherwise, if an option is exercised subsequently without agreement between the parties, the general law may prevail. The parties could find that a court will determine what is a "reasonable" payment.[9]

These income tax considerations should not be interpreted to mean that it is not possible to grant a favorable renewal or purchase option to a high-credit tenant in order to attract the firm as a lessee. One authority has indicated, for example, that a renewal option on a 20-year lease to a prime tenant might call for an annual rental of approximately 60 per cent of the original rate over the first 10-year renewal, 50 per cent for the second 10 years, and 50 per cent for the third 10 years. "It is important to let the tenant share in the profitability of the location and of the real estate. In this way, he becomes a good tenant." [10]

Renewal options and purchase options are often found under the "Miscellaneous" sections or clauses of industrial leases. They are illustrated in part in Clause 17 of Appendix A, and Clause 24 of Appendix B.

Objectives of the Participating Parties

The broker should discover the general types of objectives that each of the three participants (lessor, lessee, and mortgagee) in most industrial real estate transactions share. Within this broad framework, he must then ascertain goals of each of these participants in the particular case at hand. Then it becomes possible, through a combination of critical analysis and persuasive negotiation, to develop a set of specific terms and conditions that will meet agreement from all parties.

1. *Objectives of the Lessor.* The owner-investor-lessor generally wants a net lease which will provide him with a high level of income, coupled with a high degree of income stability and safety over time. He generally wants a long-term lease, but unless the tenant is a high-credit firm, he usually does not want to permit either renewal options or purchase options, particularly

---

[8] For a more detailed consideration of this important problem, see Alan R. Cerf, *Real Estate and the Federal Income Tax* (Englewood Cliffs, N.J., Prentice-Hall, 1965), Chapter 8; see also David I. Wendel, "Commercial-Industrial Leases," *Real Estate Investment* (Los Angeles, California Real Estate Association, 1963).

[9] Wendel, *op. cit.*, pp. 59–60.

[10] Interview with James E. Hanson, S.I.R.

at a reduced rental or price favorable to the tenant. The lessor is interested in lease terms that protect both his capital investment and his net income over the term of the lease.

The lessor wants to maximize his net return on his investment through optimum use of leverage, so he is often willing to make concessions to high-credit tenants who will permit him to obtain more favorable financing. He knows that the use to which his property is put will affect its value. If it is abused or used harshly, or if it is not maintained in good repair, his building will decrease in value. The use of the rented space may also result in higher insurance rates. It can lead to higher property assessment and increased property taxes. In a multitenant building, one incompatible use or user may seriously jeopardize the rental income from the remainder of the space in the building. Accordingly, the lessor will insist that the use of the space be specified in the lease, and that any changes must receive his approval.

Similarly, the lessor will seek to protect the safety of his income over the term of the lease by prohibiting assignment or subletting of the rented space without his prior written approval. Ordinarily, the lessor will not permit an assignment or sublease without the prime tenant remaining liable for the performance of the terms of the lease as well. However, if the assignee or subtenant is a firm with a credit rating as high as the prime tenant's (or higher), the lessor may grant an unrestricted assignment or sublease.

The lessor will want a "Waiver of Subrogation" on insurance from the lessee.[11] As a matter of fact, the lessee will want a similar waiver from the lessor. Moreover, the lender will insist on such a waiver from each to the other before mortgage financing will be granted, in most instances. This mutual waiver of subrogation is illustrated in Clause 11 of Appendix A.

2. *Objectives of the Lessee.* The lessee typically is interested in protected but flexible occupancy at the least possible cost. He is therefore usually seeking a gross lease. Moreover, the lessee normally would prefer occupancy on a short-term basis, with several irrevocable renewal options, preferably at reduced rentals. In brief, the lessee generally wants to be the party that decides whether the tenancy shall be continued.

The tenant firm will normally seek the unrestricted right to assign or sublet the space, preferably without any continued liability to the lessor as a result of such assignment or sublease.

If the lessee is liable for all or part of real estate taxes, then he will want the right to contest any increased assessment, whether the lessor-owner chooses to do so or not. Similarly, the lessee will want the right to protest or appeal rate or value decisions made by insurance companies that may result in higher insurance premiums, if he is responsible for the payment of those increased premiums. The lessee should also insist on a waiver of subrogation on insurance from the lessor.

3. *Objectives of the Lender.* A mortgagee on industrial space which is subject to a lease, or on which a lease is proposed, has a vested interest in

---

[11] For a detailed discussion of this significant technical point, see Wendel, *op. cit.,* pp. 54–55.

the terms and conditions of that lease. Anything that is likely to lead to default, financial difficulty on the part of either the lessor or the lessee, or litigation between the parties will have an adverse impact on the lender. Therefore, the lender will strive to see that the terms and conditions of the lease help each party fulfill his obligations to the other, as well as to the mortgagee.

Ordinarily, a mortgage lender will insist on an assignment of rents under the lease. "This usually causes no problem because, in effect, it does not mean very much unless it is a present assignment. The ordinary assignment is a future assignment, which means that the tenant recognizes the loan and agrees, in effect, if demanded or requested to do so, to pay the rent to the lender." [12] This is a normal pattern of lender protection, and typically will be a condition for granting the loan.

The lender will usually want the lease subordinated to the mortgage.[13] For example, an option to purchase a property may permit the property to be delivered to the tenant-purchaser without first paying off the mortgage. Many mortgagee institutions will not agree to such an arrangement, and will insist on a subordination clause. Such a subordination provision is illustrated in Clause 22 of Appendix A, and Clause 23 of Appendix B.

The lender is also anxious to have both lessor and lessee waive subrogation under insurance policies. This helps avoid a serious upset of the lease arrangement stemming from a suit by an insurance company against one of the parties.

To protect both principal and interest payments on the mortgage, a lender may insist upon long-term leases. As further protection of its interests, a mortgagee institution may object to a clause which provides for automatic termination of the lease in the event of default by the lessee. The mortgagee may well be adequately protected with a lessee in default on the property, especially as opposed to a vacant property.

In brief, the lender is looking for safety: safety of principal, and safety of the interest income on the loan. This safety can be provided by terms and conditions which protect the interest of the lender, both in the property and in the credit of the tenant.

Tax Considerations

The federal income tax implications of industrial real estate transactions in general are discussed in Chapters 5 and 9. Here, the focus is on the peculiar considerations related to industrial leases.

The first major influence is on the basic decision to own or lease (for the user), or to sell or lease property already owned (for the investor). Leasing can often be an effective device for deferring tax liability when there has been an increase in value of real estate already owned. The lessor can take advantage of the increased value through higher rental receipts, as well as

---

[12] Thomas F. Murray, "Financing Industrial Real Estate," *Advanced Course in the Techniques of Industrial Real Estate* (Washington, Society of Industrial Realtors, 1964).

[13] There are cases, however, in which institutional lenders prefer not to have subordination. The Equitable Life Assurance Society often does not require subordination in cases with a "high credit" lessee, for example.

through refinancing based on the higher current value. On the other hand, an owner can often obtain a greater net advantage by selling, paying a capital gains tax, and reinvesting the remainder in a property with a higher annual depreciation benefit.

As between owning and leasing,

the major consideration lies in the difference between the deductions available to an owner or to a lessee as compared in each case with the cost or cash outlay. For instance, an owner's cash outlay is generally the down payment and then the monthly or yearly mortgage amortization payments plus interest, but his deductions may include depreciation and interest. On the other hand, a lessee must pay rent and his deductions are limited by the amount of rent he pays (which in a net lease would include realty taxes, insurance, maintenance, etc.). Where the tax deductions for an owner will be less than his cash outlay, it is generally better to lease, but if the deductions are greater, it results in a deferral of taxable income, making it more advantageous to own.[14]

Once a decision to lease has been made, there are general guidelines to whether the rental payments can actually be deducted as operating expenses.

The rent payment must represent a fair market rental. Moreover, the rental on any renewals must be "reasonable," and not nominal. If there is an option to purchase the property (or to repurchase under a sale-lease-back) then the purchase price must also be "reasonable."

Unfortunately for the broker and the parties to a long-term lease, there are no absolute standards or criteria by which the Internal Revenue Service's reactions can be forecast. There are danger signals, however, that can be utilized as indications of what should definitely be avoided:

1. If an option to purchase permits the lessee to reduce the option price by part or all of the rental payments previously made under the lease contract, the arrangement is likely to be regarded as a conditional sale.
2. If the total rental payments under the lease exceed the lessor's allowance for depreciation plus the value of the property (less the option price), the transaction may well be treated as a conditional sale.
3. If an option price is "nominal" in relation to the reasonable value of the property, a negative reaction from the Internal Revenue Service is likely. This measures "the probability or ease with which the lessee can acquire (or reacquire in a sale-leaseback) the property. If the lessee either automatically or for a nominal sum can obtain title to the property, in all probability there has been a purchase rather than a lease." [15]
4. If the intent of the parties and their good faith in setting up the rental or purchase option amount seem doubtful to the Internal Revenue Service in the light of economic circumstances at the time the lease was executed, the transaction is likely to be considered a conditional sale. However, "the true intention of the parties is crucial, as is showing a sound business reason for the lease. Where these can be shown, they do tend to offset the other potentially disqualifying factors." [16]

---

[14] David Altman, "Tax Factors Affecting Industrial Real Estate," *Advanced Course in the Techniques of Industrial Real Estate* (Washington, Society of Industrial Realtors, 1964).
[15] *Ibid.*
[16] *Ibid.*

Particular care should also be exercised to avoid the impression that the lease is a subterfuge for a mortgage.

There must also be careful treatment of any security deposit required by the lessor to insure the return of the property in acceptable physical condition at the expiration of the lease. The Internal Revenue Service could treat this payment as part of taxable income. The last paragraph of Clause 2 in Appendix A is an illustration of careful use of the phrase "Security Deposit" to avoid this particular pitfall.

Real property taxes as well as income taxes can be affected by lease terms. For example, a leasehold improvement may result in an increased assessment on land subject to a ground lease. Similarly, an addition or improvement to an existing structure by a tenant may increase the lessor's tax assessment. In anticipation of such an eventuality, there should be a specific agreement between lessor and lessee indicating which party is to bear this additional tax expense, or precisely how it is to be allocated between the two parties if they are to share it. Moreover, under either a net lease or a fully escalated tax clause arrangement, the tenant should reserve the right to protest or appeal any increased tax assessment, whether the lessor chooses to do so himself or not.

Applications to Major Categories of Lease Transactions

The significance of specific economic and market considerations to individual lease negotiations varies, depending on whether the transaction is credit-oriented or real estate-oriented. If the greater emphasis is on the real estate rather than on the credit of the tenant, there are further analytical distinctions to be made among different types of property.

1. *Credit-Oriented Lease Agreements.* If the transaction is credit-based, the financing available from most mortgagees will reflect a higher credit rating of the tenant, through more favorable loan terms to the lessor-mortgagor. Aside from helping the lessor, the higher credit of a "national" tenant generally translates to more favorable lease terms for that tenant.

For example, a member of S.I.R. indicated that in his area of operations, a "national" tenant might well pay only 65–70 cents per square foot in space that a "local" tenant might be required to pay 90 cents per square foot to rent. Moreover, the renewal option of the "local" tenant would more commonly call for the same rental. The "national" tenant, on the other hand, would often have a renewal option at perhaps 70–80 per cent of the original rental. The difference is that "a good tenant, rather than a truly outstanding one, means that the deal is a real estate deal rather than a credit deal." [17] An additional protection to the "national" tenant is that it can probably sublease at no loss, because its credit has been utilized to gain a favorable rental.

In markets in which "national" credits pay the rent based on a factor of 7.0 to 7.5 per cent of cost on 25-year leases, "local" credits obtain leases for

---

[17] Interview with James E. Hanson, S.I.R.

virtually identical space at 10 per cent of all costs on a 15- to 20-year basis.[18]

Regardless of credit rating, tenants typically pay lower rentals or "factors" as the term of the lease increases. High-credit tenants in particular will normally pay *less* annual rent on a 25-year lease than on a 10-year lease, for example. The reason is that the lessor can use the 25-year lease for much more effective financing than he could if the same tenant were leasing the same space for 10 years.[19]

2. *Property-Oriented Lease Agreements.* When primary emphasis is placed on the real estate, the type of lease and the type of property involved bear considerably more analysis and investigation. Since new, general-purpose, single-occupant industrial properties are most readily marketable, the owner-lessor of such property will generally have the better of negotiation. Similarly, owners of well located industrial land will be in a strong bargaining position vis-à-vis the local developer or contractor seeking to become a lessee under a ground lease.

On the other hand, the owner of a special-purpose property, the owner of a "used" property subject to some obsolescence, the owner of multitenant property, and the owner of a less favorably located industrial site all are in a relatively disadvantageous bargaining position. The terms and conditions of the leases negotiated by these different groups of owners reflect their relative bargaining position.

The straight lease is most commonly found on existing properties, whether for single or multiple occupancy. They are much more likely to be gross leases on relatively short terms, with renewal options.

A build-lease transaction will always involve some emphasis on credit because the requirement of construction on the part of the owner will necessitate either the investment of his own funds or the borrowing of other funds. The key to the precise terms of the lease is provided by the tenant and his credit status. Since "national" tenants are not available for all such properties, "the broker must content himself with trying to negotiate these transactions with less strong (financially) tenants. The investor, in judging the merits of such a deal, is usually guided by at least some of the standards set up by lending institutions which concern themselves with:

"1. The net worth of the tenant (after deducting all obligations);
"2. History of business experience of the tenant;
"3. Character of the principals involved;
"4. Amount of business now being done and expected in the future;
"5. Value of land and building involved." [20]

The sale-leaseback is feasible for small firms as well as for large, "national" credits. However, there is considerably more emphasis on the value

---

[18] Interview with James E. Hanson, S.I.R.; interview with Tom H. Lang, S.I.R.
[19] Interview with Tom H. Lang, S.I.R.
[20] Irving Korb, "Light Industrial Properties," Ch. 38 of *Training Manual for Real Estate Salesmen,* prepared for Sacramento Metropolitan Real Estate Offices, Inc. (Lafayette, Calif., Duncan B. Campbell, 1957), p. 13.

and the marketability of the real estate when the lessee is a local organization. The property is much more likely to be general purpose in nature. Moreover, rentals are higher and leases are more likely to be net leases when the seller-lessee is a local credit.

Under a ground lease, the owner of land who wishes to exploit its maximum value may have to make concessions in order to achieve his desired results. For example, it is possible that relaxing some lease conditions during the early years of the ground lease, while the lessee is in the process of developing the property, may actually enhance the prospects of success and the capacity of the lessee to pay rent regularly in later years. This is one type of special condition that can be developed to accommodate the needs and desires of both lessor and lessee. As a further protection to both lessor and lessee, the lease may provide that each has first refusal to buy the other party's interest in the event that a *bona fide* offer is made to either by a third party.

Both to encourage staging of the development of a substantial parcel of land, and to permit separate development and financing in the event that more than one subtenant appears, a ground lease may provide for severability. This means that the lessee has the right to mortgage the property in sections. This has frequently proved to be an effective device for the development of industrial property, especially when the lessee on the ground lease is a local developer.[21]

LEGAL CONSIDERATIONS

The typical industrial lease is a long and complex document. Its format and wording are dictated primarily by considerations of law, although the substance of the contractual agreement that it represents is the result of the interplay of industrial real estate market forces. Detailed analysis of the legal rationale of industrial real estate leases, and of the meaning and derivation of the many clauses that both law and custom demand be included, may be found in more comprehensive treatments focusing primarily on the legal characteristics of the lease.[22]

The industrial real estate lease is developed jointly and cooperatively by a skilled and experienced industrial broker, and a skilled and experienced real estate attorney. "Both the broker and attorney are striving toward the same objective—the consummation of the transaction with the certainty that their client is protected." [23] The industrial real estate broker brings to lease negotiations a background of practical experience and market expertise which may be beyond that of the attorney. Nevertheless, "it is imperative to emphasize the importance of having competent legal counsel on both sides

---

[21] F. F. Phillips, "Proposals Involving Variables," *Ground Leases,* Byron Trerice, Jr., sponsor (Chicago, National Institute of Real Estate Brokers, December, 1965), p. 10.

[22] See, for example, Korb and Trimble, *op. cit.;* Wendel, *op. cit.;* Robert Kratovil, *Real Estate Law,* 4th ed. (Englewood Cliffs, N.J., Prentice-Hall, 1964), Chapter 29, "Landlord and Tenant"; Clifford A. Zoll, *Guide to Commercial Property Leasing* (Chicago, National Institute of Real Estate Brokers, December, 1963).

[23] Wendel, *op. cit.,* p. 50.

of the transaction when lease negotiation is being undertaken." [24] If the broker has done his job effectively and well, the task of the attorney is considerably eased and facilitated.

In addition to the attorney, other technicians will often help develop the content and the wording of many clauses of the lease. For example, the Committee on Industrial Architecture of the American Institute of Architects argues that after review and approval by legal counsel, the architect's specifications will usually include some dozen detailed features which in effect constitute lease covenants.[25] Moreover, because of the extreme importance of insurance coverage to both lessor and lessee (and to the mortgagee as well), "once the lease is executed, pertinent provisions should be sent to the client's insurance broker in order to make certain that the proper coverage is afforded." [26]

Protection of Interests of Participating Parties

"Few documents generally used in business today become as complicated in form and content as the legal contract called a 'lease' which, with respect to time, is occasionally effective for a period as long as 99 years. Even for the relatively common 10- to 20-year lease term, the conditions to which the parties agree have implications which are far-reaching in effect and which are binding to the successor-in-interest of each party for as long as the lease is in effect." [27] This complex document is developed essentially to provide for the mutual protection of all participants in the industrial lease transaction: the lessor, the lessee—and often the lender.

While no classification of lease clauses is universally accepted by all authorities, the protection of the parties involved *can* be analyzed under six main headings:

1. *Income and Expenses.* After all other ingredients have been considered, the most important and most basic factor is financial. The clauses in the lease which affect the lessor's income and the expenses of both lessor and lessee would include: the rent clause; the clause relating to the length of the lease; and clauses dealing with responsibility for the payment of taxes, insurance premiums, maintenance expense, and utilities. In addition, provisions for escalation of operating expenses, payment of the broker's commission, obligations of the parties in the event of fire or any other natural disaster (insured or uninsured), and options to renew or purchase —all affect income as well as expenses.

The ability to assign or sublet is important to the income of both the lessor and the lender, as is the assignment of rents to the lender.

Of particular interest is the eminent domain clause, or condemnation clause, as it is sometimes called. This outlines the parties' responsibilities, obligations and rights if there is a public taking of all or part of the property. There are two major financial issues here. First, there is the question

---

[24] Interview with Tom H. Lang, S.I.R.
[25] American Institute of Architects, Committee on Industrial Architecture, *A Guide to Better Industrial Building Leasing* (Washington, The Author, August, 1963), pp. 4–5.
[26] Wendel, *op. cit.,* p. 54.
[27] Korb and Trimble, *op. cit.,* p. 25.

of allocating any award that may be made by a condemning agency to the lessor. Under most eminent domain laws, the condemnor is required to compensate the fee holder directly. Any division of that compensation between lessor and lessee is a matter of agreement between the parties. If the lease is silent on this point, then the statute law of the jurisdiction in which the taking occurs will prevail. Unless the parties are well informed about the law in their specific case, unpleasant surprises may be in store for either or both.

The other issue relating to condemnation deals with the responsibility of the tenant in the event of a partial taking. There should be a detailed statement of the method for determining whether continued occupancy is feasible, and what the remedies of the parties might be.[28] Examples of wording frequently employed in condemnation clauses are found in Appendix A (Clause 20) and Appendix B (Clause 22).

2. *Use.* Since the use of the property ultimately determines its value, this is a matter of considerable concern to both lessor and lessee. The Use Clause will normally specify the uses to which the lease premises may be put. It will also indicate procedures for granting exceptions. The Fire Clause and Subletting Clause will also affect the use of the property. (See Clauses 3, 8, and 9 of Appendix A, and Clauses 2 and 9 of Appendix B.)

The use of the premises is also affected by the nature of the property. Therefore, the description of the premises in the clause which identifies them can be quite important, as shown in the Introduction of Appendix A and Clause 2 of Appendix B. Moreover, a construction clause in a build-lease transaction should carry specifications for construction, the provision for a certificate of completion, and an estoppel certificate.

3. *Financing.* Several clauses affect the ability of the lessor to obtain financing. A Subordination Clause may be required by a lender, as well as an assignment of rents. This is illustrated in Clause 22 of Appendix A and Clause 23 of Appendix B. Moreover, the terms and conditions for renewing the lease, or for an option to purchase, may affect the ability of the lessor to obtain financing. The lender will insist upon a Waiver of Subrogation, as indicated in earlier discussions; and he will be most concerned with the ability of the lessee to assign rights or to sublet, particularly if the credit of the prime tenant is an important consideration in granting the mortgage loan.

4. *Tax Liability.* The Tax Clause (A–12 and B–6) indicates which party is responsible for the payment of property taxes, and what the allocation (if any) between the parties is to be. Moreover, the security deposit clause (A–2) can influence the income tax liability of the lessor, if it is not properly worded. The terms and conditions of options to renew or purchase can have a very serious impact on the income tax liability of both lessor and lessee, as well as the income tax treatment of the entire transaction.

5. *The Property.* Many clauses in the industrial real estate lease are

---

[28] Wendel, *op. cit.,* pp. 60–62; Kratovil, *op. cit.,* Ch. 29.

designed specifically to provide protection for the physical property. Most of these are particularly significant for the lessor, who will have both possession and use of the reversion at the expiration of the lease. The use clause normally carries a prohibition against wasting of the asset, and calls for protective action by the tenant. Moreover, repairs and maintenance are often an obligation of the tenant, under a repairs or maintenance clause (B–13a). To assist in enforcing the terms and conditions of the lease as they pertain to preservation of the property, a clause providing for entry and inspection of the premises by the lessor or his agent is usually included (A–7 and B–10a). Insurance clauses are designed to provide protection of the property (A–10 and B–6c). There is usually a further provision that the lessee is obligated to return the premises to the lessor in the same condition as they were when the lessee took possession. In some instances, this could entail the removal of a considerable amount of construction undertaken by the lessee, and may involve substantial expense to the lessee.

6. *Lessor's Estate: Technical Legal Factors.* A wide variety of technical clauses is also included in the typical industrial lease. The attorney(s) involved will determine what should be included. These clauses are partly a function of the law of the jurisdiction in which the lease is operative, partly a function of the legal custom in the area, and partly the specific design of the attorney to provide the protection for his client, deemed necessary in the specific circumstances. The rights of the various parties under such actions as default, abandonment, destruction, sale of the premises, or litigation are spelled out in these clauses. Moreover, formal technical details such as the procedure for surrender of the lease or the form of notice to be given by either party will be included as the attorneys in the case prescribe.

A Lease Checklist for Industrial Real Estate Brokers

Leases for industrial property vary widely in content and form. In fact, one of the basic recommendations of the lease as a device for allocating industrial space is its flexibility and adaptability to the unique requirements of specific industrial tenants and industrial property owners. Local practices tend to complicate further the analysis of industrial leases. However, certain common subjects are covered in practice in most long-term leases on industrial space.

In an effort to provide a foundation on which a superstructure of specific individual variation might be built, a checklist is provided in Exhibit 48 which illustrates recommended clauses or sections which should be covered by any industrial lease.

As illustrations of detailed applications of the general framework provided in Exhibit 48, Appendix A and Appendix B to this chapter offer two standard industrial lease forms. They are used by firms of two S.I.R. members in widely separated market areas, which serve substantially different industrial clienteles. They are presented for illustrative purposes only, and the reader is cautioned against the dangers of attempting to lift bodily, or to adapt for his own purposes, materials from these illustrative lease forms.

Exhibit 48

INDUSTRIAL LEASE CHECKLIST

1. Identify premises unequivocally.
2. Specify term of lease precisely.
3. Indicate amount, method of payment, and method of calculation of rent.
4. Specify use of premises.
5. Provide waiver of subrogation of insurance.
6. Establish protection of asset against waste.
7. Require compliance by tenant with local ordinances.
8. Establish responsibility for alterations.
9. Establish ownership of trade fixtures.
10. Provide for subordination of and right to extinguish liens.
11. Establish rights in event of abandonment of premises.
12. Establish responsibilities to repair damage, and enforcement.
13. Establish standards for acceptance of premises.
14. Establish type, amount and evidence of lessee's insurance coverage.
15. Specify maximum amount of insurance.
16. Agree to hold harmless.
17. Establish covenant not to sue.
18. Provide for entry on roof.
19. Specify responsibility for utilities.
20. Specify liability for taxes, amount, and right to protest (by lessee).
21. Provide lessor's (or agent's) right of entry.
22. Establish rights and obligations in event of condemnation.
23. Specify rights and limitations under assignment and subletting.
24. Provide for subordination of lease to mortgage.
25. Establish parties' responsibilities in event of total or partial destruction.
26. Provide for rights in event of lessee's bankruptcy.
27. Provide for remedies in event of breach by lessee or lessor.
28. Provide for surrender of premises.
29. Provide for attorney's, broker's and manager's (if any) fees.
30. Specify amount and character of security deposit.
31. Provide for holding over and renewal, including terms.
32. Specify amount and terms of purchase option.
33. Provide for waiver of terms or clauses.
34. Establish method for modifying terms.
35. Establish method for adjudication of disagreements.
36. Establish standards for erection of signs and for auctions.

The only appropriate way to develop a lease in a given transaction is to work with one's attorney from the outset.

When we are considering premises already constructed, to be leased for a short term at a small rental, a form lease may be very satisfactory but even then, some of the so-called 'standard form' leases do not adequately solve the future problems which could arise between the landlord and the tenant . . . One of the real problems with so-called form leases is that many of them are too brief. They leave out essential provisions, and in most instances the parties are unaware of what the general law of the state provides to fill the void. *Unless the parties are aware of the general law, they may be signing a document which differs radically from their intent.* In addition, almost every printed form favors the landlord to such an extent that if the tenant is negotiating from any strength whatsoever, many provisions would be completely unacceptable . . . Lastly, the 'standard form' lease is an attempt to meet all situations, with the result that it rarely is applicable to the particular situation involved.[29]

It is often tempting to take the easy route and omit a potentially complicating factor, either on the grounds that agreement about it cannot be reached between the parties, or that the event is highly unlikely to occur. Whenever a lease is silent on a point, and the eventuality then arises, the general law will prevail. Both parties may be abrogating their rights and privileges to the courts, which will make a final determination.[30]

The literature in the field of industrial leasing is replete with examples of individual exceptions to "general rules." It is therefore imperative for the industrial real estate broker to see that any lease he negotiates is customized to meet the specific and particular needs and requirements of the parties involved—and especially of his client. The broker himself, however, should studiously avoid lease preparation. The broker should not go beyond the preparation and presentation of a "memorandum" to the appropriate attorney, summarizing the peculiarities of the transaction from the point of view of the broker and his client.

Appendix A

REALTORS

Duncan
Korb &   REAL ESTATE INVESTMENTS
Trimble   • 151 GRAND AVENUE, OAKLAND, CALIF. 94612
INC.

ACCREDITED
Telephone (415) 834-6230

C. J. Duncan, *President*

Irving Korb, *Executive Vice President*
Certified Property Manager
Member Society of
Industrial Realtors

Harold G. Trimble, Jr.
Vice President-Secretary

OAKLAND REAL ESTATE BOARD

STANDARD FORM LEASE
Copyright 1965 Oakland Real Estate Board

THIS LEASE made this_____day of _____, 19_____, between

_____ as "Lessor,"

and _____

_____ as "Lessee."

For and in consideration of the rents, covenants and agreements hereinafter agreed by Lessee to be paid, kept and performed, Lessor leases unto Lessee and Lessee hires from Lessor the

---

[29] Wendel, *op. cit.*, pp. 50–51 [emphasis added].
[30] *Ibid.*, pp. 59–62.

following described premises, together with appurtenances, situated in the City of _____ _____, County of _____, State of California:

Said hiring and letting is upon the following terms and conditions:

1. TERM; POSSESSION.

(a) The term of this lease shall be for a period of _____ commencing on the _____ day of _____, 19 _____ and ending on the _____ day of _____, 19_____.

(b) Lessee agrees that in the event of the inability of Lessor to deliver possession of the premises at the commencement of the term as hereinbefore specified, Lessor shall not be liable for any damage caused thereby nor shall this lease be void or voidable but Lessee shall not be liable for rent until such time as Lessor offers to deliver possession of the premises to Lessee, but the term hereof shall not be extended by such delay. If Lessee, with Lessor's consent, takes possession prior to the commencement of the term, Lessee shall do so subject to all of the covenants and conditions hereof and shall pay rent for the period ending with the commencement of the term at the same rental as that prescribed for the first month of the term, prorated at the rate of 1/30th thereof per day.

2. RENTAL.

As rental for the demised premises Lessee hereby agrees to pay to Lessor without deduction, set-off, prior notice or demand, the sum of _____ _____ Dollars ($_____), per month in advance on the _____ day of each month in lawful money of the United States of America, commencing on the _____ day of _____, 19 _____ and continuing throughout the balance of the term. Monthly rental for any partial month shall be prorated at the rate of 1/30th of monthly rent per day. Rent shall be paid to Lessor at _____ _____ or at such other place or places as Lessor may from time to time direct.

In consideration of Lessor executing this lease, Lessee hereby agrees to pay Lessor the sum of $_____, receipt of which is hereby acknowledged. Lessor agrees that $_____ of said sum shall be applied as the rental due for the first month of the term hereof. Lessor further agrees that if, at the time, Lessee is not in defaut of any of the terms, covenants and conditions contained herein, the sum of $_____, constituting a security deposit, shall be repaid to Lessee upon termination of this lease or any extension thereof.

3. USE.

The premises are hereby leased to Lessee upon the express condition that Lessee shall use said premises for

and for no other purpose without the written consent of Lessor first obtained.

Lessee agrees that the said Lessee's business shall be established and conducted throughout the term hereof in a first class manner; that Lessee will not use the demised premises for, or carry on or permit upon said premises any offensive, noisy or dangerous trade, business, manufacture or occupation or any nuisance, or anything against public policy, nor permit any auction sale to be held or conducted on or about said premises; that Lessee shall not commit, or suffer to be committed, any waste upon the premises; that Lessee will not do or suffer anything to be done upon said premises which will cause structural injury to said premises or the building of which same form a part; that said premises will not be overloaded and that no machinery, apparatus or other appliance shall be used or operated in or upon the demised premises which will in any manner injure, vibrate or shake said premises or the building of which it is a part; that no use will be made of the demised premises which will in any way impair the efficient operation of the sprinkler system (if any) within the building containing the demised premises; that Lessee will not leave the said premises unoccupied or vacant during the term hereof; and that without the written permission of Lessor, no musical instrument of any sort, or any noise making device will be operated or allowed upon said premises for the purpose of attracting trade or otherwise. Lessee further agrees not to use or permit the use of the demised premises or any part thereof, for any immoral or other purpose prohibited by law or which will increase the existing rate of insurance upon the building in which said demised premises may be located, or cause a cancellation of any insurance policy covering said building or any part thereof. If any act on the part of Lessee or use of the premises by Lessee shall cause, directly or indirectly, any increase of Lessor's insurance expense, said additional expense shall be paid by Lessee to Lessor upon demand. No such payment by Lessee shall limit Lessor in the exercise of any other rights or remedies, or constitute a waiver of Lessor's right to require Lessee to discontinue such act or use. No use shall be made or permitted to be made of the demised premises or any part thereof and no acts done therein which may disturb the quiet enjoyment of any other tenant in the building of which the demised premises are a part. Lessee, at Lessee's sole cost and expense, agrees to do all things necessary to maintain the demised premises, including sidewalks adjacent thereto, in a clean, neat and sanitary manner and to alter, repair and maintain the demised premises in compliance and conformity with all laws and ordinances, municipal, state, federal and/or any other governmental authority and any and all lawful requirements or orders of any properly constituted municipal, state, federal or other governmental board or authority, present or future, in anywise relating to the condition, use or occupancy of the demised premises throughout the entire term of this lease and to the perfect exoneration from liability of Lessor. The judgment of any court of competent jurisdiction or the admission of Lessee in any action or proceeding against Lessee, whether Lessor be a party thereto or not, that Lessee has violated any such law, ordinance, requirement or order in the use of the premises, shall be conclusive of that fact as between Lessor and Lessee.

4. **ACCEPTANCE AND SURRENDER OF PREMISES; REPAIRS.** Lessee accepts the premises as they are now and agrees that the premises are now in a tenantable and good condition. Lessee agrees at its own cost and expense to maintain, repair and keep the interior and exterior of the demised premises and each and every part thereof, and all appurtenances (including without limitation, sidewalks fronting thereon, wiring, plumbing, sewage system, heating and air cooling installations, all glazing in or bordering the premises and any store front), excepting only the roof, exterior walls, foundations and other structural portions of the premises, in good condition and repair during the term of this lease, damage thereto by fire, earthquake, act of God or the elements alone excepted. In the event Lessee should fail to make the repairs required of Lessee forthwith upon notice by Lessor, Lessor, in addition to all other remedies available hereunder or by law, and without waiving any said alternative remedies, may make same and Lessee agrees to repay Lessor the cost thereof as part of the rental payable as such on the next day upon which rent becomes due, and failure to pay same shall carry with it the same consequences as failure to pay any installment of rental. Lessee waives all rights to make repairs at the expense of Lessor as provided for in any statute or law in effect at the time of execution of this lease or any amendment thereof or any other statute or law which may be hereafter enacted during the term of this lease and agrees upon the expiration of the term of this lease or sooner termination hereof to surrender unto Lessor the demised premises in the same condition as received, ordinary wear and tear and damage by fire, earthquake, act of God or the elements alone excepted. Lessor agrees, after written notice of the necessity therefor, and should the same not be caused by Lessee or by reason of Lessee's occupancy, to make necessary repairs to the roof, exterior walls (excluding painting thereof and repair of glazing), foundations and other structural portions of the premises, within a reasonable time. Lessee agrees during the full term of this lease, at its own cost and expense, to make all repairs and replacements of whatever kind or nature, either to the exterior or to the interior of said premises rendered necessary by reason of any act or omission of Lessee or its agents, servants or employees.

5. **ALTERATIONS; LIENS.** Lessee agrees not to make any alterations of, changes in or addition to the demised premises without the prior written consent of Lessor. Lessee agrees that should Lessor give said written consent all alterations, additions and improvements, including fixtures, made in, to or on the premises, except unattached movable business fixtures, shall be the property of Lessor and shall remain upon and be surrendered with the premises, except that Lessee will ascertain from Lessor within thirty (30) days before the end of this term whether Lessor desires to have the premises or any part or parts thereof, restored to their condition when the premises were delivered to Lessee and if Lessor shall so desire, Lessee shall so restore said premises or such part or parts thereof before the end of the term of this lease, entirely at Lessee's own cost and expense.

Lessee agrees that if any such alterations, changes or additions are to be made, same shall not be commenced until two days after receipt of the written consent of Lessor required by this paragraph, in order that Lessor may post appropriate notices to avoid any liability on account thereof. Lessee agrees to indemnify and save harmless Lessor from all liens, claims or demands arising out of any work performed, materials furnished, or obligations incurred by or for Lessee upon said premises during said term, and agrees not to suffer any such lien or other lien to be created.

6. **UTILITIES.** Lessee agrees to pay for all the water, fuel, gas, oil, heat, electricity, power, materials and services which may be furnished to or used in or about said premises during the term of this lease.

7. **ENTRY AND INSPECTION.** Lessee agrees that Lessor and his agents may enter upon the demised premises at all reasonable times to inspect the same, to submit them to a prospective purchaser, or to make any changes or alterations or repairs which Lessor shall consider necessary for the protection, improvement or preservation thereof, or of the building in which the demised premises are situate, or to make changes in the plumbing, wiring, meters or other equipment, fixtures or appurtenances of the building, or to post any notice provided for by law, or otherwise to protect any and all rights of Lessor; and Lessor shall have the right to erect and maintain all necessary or proper scaffolding or other structures for the making of such changes, alterations or repairs (provided the entrance to the demised premises shall not be blocked thereby and that such work shall be completed with diligence and dispatch) and there shall be no liability against Lessor for damages thereby sustained by Lessee, nor shall Lessee be entitled to any abatement of rental by reason of the exercise by Lessor of any such rights herein reserved. Nothing herein contained shall be construed to obligate Lessor to make any changes, alterations or repairs. Lessee further agrees that at any time after sixty (60) days prior to the termination of this lease, Lessor may place thereon any usual or ordinary "To Let" or "To Lease" signs.

8. **ASSIGNMENT AND SUBLETTING.** (a) Lessee shall not assign or mortgage this lease or any right hereunder or interest herein and Lessee shall not sublet the premises in whole or in part or suffer any other person (the agents and servants of Lessee excepted) to occupy or use the said premises, or any portion thereof, without the prior written consent of Lessor. Any such assignment, mortgage or subletting without such consent shall be void and shall, at the option of Lessor, be deemed a breach of this lease. No consent to any assignment or mortgage of this lease or any subletting of said premises, shall constitute a waiver or discharge of the provisions of this paragraph except as to the specific instance covered thereby.

(b) Lessee agrees that neither this lease nor any interest herein shall be assignable or transferable by operation of law, and it is agreed that in the event any proceeding under the Bankruptcy Act, or any amendment thereto, be commenced by or against Lessee (or should there be more than one, then any Lessee) or in the event Lessee (or should there be more than one, then any Lessee) be adjudged insolvent, or makes an assignment for the benefit of creditors, or if a writ of attachment or execution be levied on the leasehold estate created hereby and be not released or satisfied within ten (10) days thereafter, or if a receiver be appointed in any proceeding or action to which Lessee is a party, with authority to take possession or control of the demised premises or the business conducted therein by Lessee, this lease at the option of Lessor shall immediately end and terminate and shall in nowise be treated as an asset of Lessee after the exercise of the aforesaid option, and Lessee shall have no further rights hereunder; and Lessor shall have the right, after the exercise of said option, to forthwith re-enter and repossess itself of said premises as of its original estate.

9. **HOLD HARMLESS.** This lease is made upon the express condition that Lessee agrees to keep, save and hold Lessor free from all liability, penalties, losses, damages, costs, expenses, causes of action, claims and/or judgments arising by reason of any injury or damage to any person or persons, including without limitation, Lessee, its servants, agents and employees, or property of any kind whatsoever and to whomsoever belonging, including without limitation, Lessee's, its servants', agents', and employees', from any cause or causes whatsoever, including leakage, while in, upon or in any way connected with said demised premises, or its appurtenances, or the sidewalks adjacent thereto, during the term of this lease or any occupancy hereunder, Lessee hereby covenanting and agreeing to indemnify, protect and save Lessor harmless from all liability, loss, costs and obligations on account of or arising out of any such injuries or losses however occurring.

Lessee, as a material part of the consideration to be rendered to Lessor, hereby waives all claims against Lessor for damages to goods, wares and merchandise in, upon or about said premises and for injuries to Lessee, his agents, or third persons in or about said premises from any cause arising at any time, including, without limiting the generality of the foregoing, damages arising fom acts or omissions of other tenants of the building of which the demised premises are a part and from the failure of either party to make repairs.

10. INSURANCE. Lessee further agrees to take out and keep in force during the life hereof at Lessee's expense, public liability and other insurance in companies acceptable to Lessor to protect against any liability to the public, whether to persons or property, incident to the use of or resulting from an accident occurring in or about said premises, the sidewalks adjacent thereto and such other areas which Lessee, its officers, servants, agents, employees, contractors and invitees shall have the right to use under the terms hereof during the term of this lease or any occupancy hereunder, in the amount of $_____ to indemnify against the claim of one person and $_____ against the claims of two or more persons in any one occurrence, and property damage insurance in an amount of not less than $_____ per occurrence. The said policy shall also insure the contingent liability of Lessor. Lessee further agrees, during the term hereof, to carry full coverage plate glass insurance on said demised premises in the joint names of Lessor and Lessee, and to pay the premiums therefor.

Lessee agrees that every insurer shall agree by endorsement upon the policy or policies issued by it, or by independent instrument furnished to Lessor, that it will give Lessor ten (10) days written notice at the address where rental is paid, before the policies in question shall be altered or cancelled. Either the originals or certified copies of said policies or a certificate of insurance shall be placed with or furnished Lessor.

11. WAIVER OF SUBROGATION. Lessor hereby releases Lessee, and Lessee hereby releases Lessor, and their respective officers, agents, employees and servants, from any and all claims or demands for damages, loss, expense or injury to the demised premises, or to the furnishings and fixtures and equipment, or inventory or other property of either Lessor or Lessee in, about or upon the demised premises, as the case may be, which be caused by or result from perils, events or happenings which are the subject of insurance carried by the respective parties and in force at the time of any such loss; provided, however, that such waiver shall be effective only to the extent permitted by the insurance covering such loss and to the extent such insurance is not prejudiced thereby or the expense of such insurance is not thereby increased.

12. TAXES. Lessee shall be liable for all taxes levied against personal property and trade fixtures on or about the demised premises, including, but without prejudice to the generality of the foregoing, shelves, counters, vaults, vault doors, wall safes, partitions, fixtures, machinery, printing presses, plant equipment and atmospheric coolers, and if any such taxes on Lessee's personal property or trade fixtures are levied against Lessor or Lessor's property, and if Lessor pays the same, which Lessor shall have the right to do regardless of the validity of such levy, or if the assessed value of Lessor's premises is increased by the inclusion therein of a value placed on such property of Lessee and if Lessor pays the taxes based on such increased assessment, which Lessor shall have the right to do, regardless of the validity thereof, Lessee, upon demand shall, as the case may be, repay to Lessor the taxes so levied against Lessor, or the proportion of such taxes resulting from such increase in the assessment.

In addition to the rental herein provided for and during the term hereof, Lessee agrees to pay _____% of any increases in real property taxes and special assessments levied or assessed against the building of which the demised premises are a part and the land upon which said building is located and appurtenances thereto, over and above those real property taxes and assessments levied or assessed against said premises and appurtenances for the fiscal tax year (of the government agency levying said property taxes) in which the term hereof commences (or, if the foregoing percentage has not been specified, then that portion of any such increase as the total net rentable area within the demised premises bears to the total net rentable area within the building or buildings, including the demised premises, which are included in the unit so taxed or assessed by said taxing authorities). The amounts provided for in this paragraph shall be paid by Lessee within ten (10) days after written notice therof from Lessor.

13. DEFAULT. This lease is made upon the express condition and Lessee hereby agrees that:
(a) Should Lessee fail to pay the rental herein reserved, or any part thereof, or any other sum required by Lessee to be paid to the Lessor at the times or in the manner herein provided; or
(b) If Lessee shall abandon or vacate said premises or violate the provisions of paragraph 8(b) hereof; or
(c) If default should be made in any of the other covenants or conditions on Lessee's part herein contained, and not be cured within ten (10) days after written notice by Lessor or Lessor's agent to Lessee of such default,
such default, breach or act shall give Lessor, or Lessor's agents and representatives, with or

without terminating this lease, the right to re-enter the demised premises or any part thereof, either with or without process of law, and expel, remove and put out Lessee or any person or persons occupying said premises and remove all personal property therefrom, using such force as may be necessary to again repossess and enjoy said premises as before this demise, without prejudice to any remedy which might otherwise be used for arrears of rent or preceding breach of covenant or condition, and without liability to any person for damages sustained by reason of such removal. No such re-entry or taking of possession of said premises by Lessor shall be construed as an election on his part to terminate this lease unless a written notice of such intention be given Lessee, said notice being given as provided herein. Lessor may likewise, at Lessor's option, but at the cost of Lessee and in addition to any other remedies which Lessor may have upon such default or failure or neglect and without notice to Lessee, petition the Superior Court of the State of California for and be entitled as a matter of right to the appointment of a Receiver and said Court may appoint such Receiver and vest in him such powers and authority as may be necessary or proper to fully protect all the rights herein granted or reserved to Lessor.

Lessor may likewise, at Lessor's option and in addition to any other remedies which Lessor may have upon such default, failure or neglect, let and relet said premises in whole or in part, altering, changing or subdividing the same as in its unqualified judgment may accomplish the best results at such rental and upon such terms and for such length of time, whether less or greater than the unexpired portion of the term of this lease, as Lessor may see fit, and Lessee shall be liable unto Lessor for any deficiency between the rentals so procured by Lessor for the period of said letting or reletting, not to exceed, however, the balance of the original term hereof, after deducting therefrom the cost of such letting or reletting (including the cost of any such alterations or other changes), and the rental herein reserved for a period or periods identical with the term of said letting, or reletting, and Lessor may institute action for the whole of such deficiency immediately upon effecting any letting or reletting and shall not thereafter be precluded from further like action in the event such letting or reletting shall not embrace the whole unexpired portion of the term hereof, or Lessor may monthly, or at such greater intervals as it may see fit, exact payment of said deficiency then existing, and the Lessee agrees to pay said deficiency then existing unto Lessor from time to time when called upon by Lessor so to do, and should this lease not be terminated, Lessor may, notwithstanding such letting or reletting, at any time thereafter elect to terminate it; or should this lease, prior to he expiraion of the term hereof, be terminated by Lessor by reason of any breach hereof by Lessee, Lessor shall thereupon, at its option, be entitled to recover from Lessee the worth at the time of such termination of the excess, if any, of the amount of rent and charges equivalent to rent reserved in this lease for the balance of the term hereof, over the then reasonable value of the premises for said period.

14. **ABANDONMENT.** If Lessee should abandon, vacate or surrender said premises or be dispossessed by process of law, in addition to all other remedies of Lessor, Lessor at its option may deem that any personal property belonging to Lessee left on the premises is abandoned and/or Lessor may at once enter upon said premises and remove therefrom any and all equipment, fixtures and merchandise therein and may sell said fixtures, equipment and merchandise at public or private sale at such price and upon such terms as Lessor may determine, without notice to or demand upon Lessee. Out of the proceeds of such sale, Lessor may reimburse itself for the expense of such taking, removal and sale and for any indebtedness of Lessee to Lessor and the surplus, if any, shall be accounted for to Lessee.

15. **DESTRUCTION; RENEWAL.** (a) In the event of damage or destruction of the demised premises during the term hereof from fire, earthquake, act of God or the elements, Lessor shall forthwith repair the same, provided such repairs can be made within sixty (60) days under the laws and regulations of State, Federal, County or Municipal authorities, but such destruction shall in nowise annul or void this lease, except that Lessee shall be entitled to a proportionate deduction of the monthly rental while such repairs are being made, such proportionate deduction to be based upon the extent to which the making of such repairs shall interfere with the business carried on by Lessee in said premises. If such repairs cannot be made in sixty (60) days, Lessor may, at its option, make same within a reasonable time, in which event this lease shall continue in full force and effect and the monthly rental shall be proportionately abated as aforesaid in this paragraph provided. In the event that Lessor does not so elect to make such repairs which cannot be made in sixty (60) days, or such repairs cannot be made under the laws and regulations, this lease may be terminated at the option of either party.

In respect to any damage or destruction which Lessor is obligated to repair or may elect to repair under the terms of this paragraph, the provisions of Section 1932, Subdivision 2, and of Section 1933, Subdivision 4 of the Civil Code of the State of California are waived by Lessee. In the event that the building in which the demised premises may be situated be damaged or destroyed to the extent of not less than 33⅓% of the replacement cost thereof, Lessor may elect to terminate this lease, whether the demised premises be injured or not.

Should the parties hereto be unable to agree in writing as to the time required for repair of any such damage or destruction to the demised premises or as to the percentage of damage to the building of which the same are a part, within five (5) days after the happening of said occurrence, or to the extent, if any, of reduction of rental during the period of repair within fifteen (15) days after the happening of said occurrence, each shall within five (5) days following written notice from either party to such effect, provided such party is not in default of this lease at such time, select an arbitrator and notify in writing the other of the name and address of the arbitrator so selected. Within five (5) days thereafter the two so selected shall appoint a third arbitrator and notify in writing within said last mentioned time the Lessor and Lessee of the name and address of said appointee, or of their inability to agree upon said appointee, if such should be the fact. In the latter event the selection of the third arbitrator shall be committed to the Presiding Judge of the Superior Court of the State of California, of the County in which the demised premises are located, and such appointment shall be invoked by written request addressed to said Judge signed by Lessor or by Lessee, or their respective counsel, within five (5) days after receipt by the Lessor and Lessee of said notice of inability from said two arbitrators. The appointee of said Presiding Judge shall be accepted by said two arbitrators and Lessor and Lessee. When the three arbitrators have been selected in either of the ways above set forth, they shall forthwith convene and determine the issue or issues submitted unto them, and the written determination under the signatures of a majority of said arbitrators shall be final, binding and conclusive upon the parties hereto. Should either party refuse or fail to select an arbitrator within the time as above provided and notify the other party thereof, the arbitrator selected by such other party shall be the sole arbitrator and his decision shall have the same effect as if rendered by a majority of three arbitrators. Save as modified hereby, the provisions of Title IX of Part III of the Code of Civil Procedure of the State of California dealing with the subject of arbitration, shall apply. The costs of any arbitration shall be borne equally by the parties except in the instance of refusal of a party to abide thereby, in which event, and should the award be confirmed by judicial order in conformity with the said provisions of said Title, all costs, including those incurred in the court proceeding, shall be assessed against and borne by the disaffirming party.

(b) Notwithstanding anything herein to the contrary, if, at any time during the term hereof, any governmental agency having jurisdiction over the premises demised or the building of which the said premises are a part shall require the making of any repairs, improvements or alterations to said building or premises and Lessor determines to demolish said building or premises rather than to make said repairs, improvements or alterations, or allow same to be made, Lessor, upon at least ninety (90) days written notice to Lessee shall have the right to terminate this lease. Upon the date specified in such notice, this lease shall reminate and Lessor shall have no further liability to Lessee except that: (i) Lessor shall refund to Lessee any unearned rentals and shall return any security deposit, and (ii) in the event Lessor had theretofore given written consent to any leasehold improvements upon the premises made by Lessee and had agreed, in writing, as to the cost thereof to Lessee, Lessor shall pay to Lessee upon such termination that percentage of such cost to Lessee as the number of full calendar months remaining in the original term of this lease bears to the total number of calendar months in said original term.

16. **COSTS OF SUIT.** Lessee agrees that if Lessor is involuntarily made a party defendant to any litigation concerning this lease or the demised premises or the premises of which the demised premises are a part by reason of any act or omission of Lessee and not because of any act or omission of Lessor, then Lessee shall hold harmless the Lessor from all liability by reason thereof including reasonable attorneys' fees incurred by Lessor in such litigation and all taxable court costs. If legal action shall be brought by either of the parties hereto for the unlawful detainer of the premises, for the recovery of any rent due under the provisions of this lease, or because of the breach of any term, covenant or provision hereof, the party prevailing in said action (Lessor or Lessee as the case may be) shall be entitled to recover from the party not prevailing costs of suit and a reasonable attorney's fee which shall be fixed by the Judge of the Court.

17. **HOLDING OVER.** Should Lessee hold over the term hereby created with the consent of Lessor, Lessee shall become a tenant from month to month at the monthly rental payable hereunder for the prior six (6) months, and otherwise upon the covenants and conditions in this lease contained, and shall continue to be such tenant until thirty (30) days after either party hereto serves upon the other written notice of intention to terminate such

monthly tenancy. Should such termination occur on any day other than the last day of any rental month, any unearned prepaid rental shall, immediately following surrender of the demised premises by Lessee, be refunded unto him.

18. SALE OF PREMISES. In the event of a sale or conveyance by Lessor of the building containing the demised premises or assignment of the Senior Lease (if any), the same shall operate to release Lessor from any future liability upon any of the covenants or conditions, express or implied, herein contained in favor of Lessee, and in such event Lessee agrees to look solely to the responsibility of the successor in interest of Lessor. If any security be given by Lessee to secure faithful performance of Lessee's covenants in this lease, Lessor may transfer the security, as such, to the purchaser of the reversion and thereupon Lessor shall be discharged from any further liability in reference thereto.

19. APPOINTMENT OF RECEIVER. In the event a receiver be appointed at the instance of Lessor in any action against Lessee, the receiver may take possession of any personal property belonging to Lessee and used in the conduct of the business of Lessee being carried on in said premises and Lessee agrees that the entry or possession by said receiver shall not constitute an eviction of Lessee from the demised premises or any portion thereof, and Lessee hereby agrees to indemnify and hold Lessor harmless from any claim of any character by any person arising out of or connected with the entry by said receiver and taking possession of the demised premises or said personal property. Neither the application for the appointment of such receiver, nor the appointment of such receiver, shall be construed as an election on Lessor's part to terminate this lease unless a written notice of such intention is given by Lessor to Lessee.

20. CONDEMNATION. If any part of the demised premises or of the building of which same are a part (even though no part of the premises be taken) be condemned for a public or quasi-public use by right of eminent domain, with or without litigation, or transferred by agreement in connection with such public or quasi-public use, this lease, as to the part so taken, shall terminate as of the date title shall vest in the condemnor, and the rent payable hereunder shall be adjusted so that Lessee shall be required to pay for the remainder of the term only such portion of such rent as the value of the part remaining after condemnation bears to the value of the entire premises at the date of condemnation; but in either such event Lessor shall have the option to terminate this lease as of the date when title to the part so condemned vests in the condemnor.

All compensation awarded upon such condemnation or taking shall belong and be paid to Lessor and Lessee shall have no claim thereto, and Lessee hereby irrevocably assigns and transfers to Lessor any right to compensation or damages to which Lessee may become entitled during the term hereof by reason of the condemnation of all or a part of the demised premises.

21. SENIOR LEASE. Lessee agrees that in the event Lessor holds the demised premises or the premises or the building of which the demised premises are a part by virtue of any lease or tenancy (herein referred to as the "Senior Lease"), Lessee will not suffer any act or omission on the premises which will violate any of the terms and conditions of the said Senior Lease, Lessee hereby admitting knowledge of and familiarity with the terms and conditions of the said Senior Lease. In the event the Senior Lease is terminated for any cause then this lease at Lessor's option shall forthwith terminate and Lessor shall not be under any responsibility or liability therefor to Lessee.

22. SUBORDINATION. Notwithstanding anything herein to the contrary, Lessee agrees that this lease is and shall be subordinate to any mortgage, deed of trust or other instrument of security which have been or shall be placed on the land and building or land or building of which the demised premises form a part, and such subordination is hereby made effective without any further act by Lessee. Lessee agrees that at any time or from time to time upon request by Lessor to execute and deliver any instruments, releases or other documents that may be required in connection with subjecting and subordinating this lease to the lien of said mortgage, deed of trust or other instrument of security. Lessee hereby appoints Lessor as Lessee's attorney in fact, irrevocably, to execute and deliver any such instruments.

23. SIGNS. Lessor reserves the right to the use of the exterior walls and the roof of the demised premises and of the building of which the demised premises are a part. Lessee agrees not to inscribe, paint or affix any signs, advertisments, placards or awnings on the exterior or roof of the demised premises or upon the entrance doors, windows, or the sidewalk on or adjacent to the demised premises without the written consent of Lessor first obtained. Any signs so placed on the premises shall be so placed upon the understanding and agreement that Lessee will remove same at the termination of the tenancy herein created and repair any damage or injury to the premises caused thereby, and if not so removed by Lessee then Lessor may have same so removed at Lessee's expense. Lessee shall not be allowed to use the name of the building in which the demised premises are located, or of the owner of such building, or words to such effect in connection with any business carried on in said premises (except as the address of the Lessee) without the written consent of Lessor. Lessor reserves the right to change the name and title of the building at any time during the term of said lease. Lessee hereby expressly agrees to such change at the option of Lessor and waives any and all damage occasioned thereby.

24. **SURRENDER OF LEASE.** No act or conduct of Lessor, whether consisting of the acceptance of the keys to the demised premises, or otherwise, shall be deemed to be or constitute an acceptance of the surrender of the demised premises by Lessee prior to the expiration of the term hereof, and such acceptance by Lessor of surrender by Lessee shall only flow from and must be evidenced by a written acknowledgment of acceptance of surrender by Lessor. The voluntary or other surrender of this lease by Lessee, or a mutual cancellation thereof, shall not work a merger, and shall, at the option of Lessor, terminate all or any existing subleases or subtenancies, or concessions, or may at the option of Lessor, operate as an assignment to him of any or all such subleases or subtenancies or concessions.

25. **NOTICES.** It is agreed between the parties hereto that any notice required hereunder or by law to be served upon either of the parties shall be in writing and shall be delivered personally upon the other or sent by registered or certified mail, postage prepaid, addressed to the demised premises, in the instance of Lessee, and to the place where rental is paid as provided in paragraph 2 hereof, in the instance of Lessor, or to such other address as may be from time to time furnished in writing by Lessor to Lessee or by Lessee to Lessor, each of the parties hereto waiving personal or any other service than as in this paragraph provided for. Notice by registered or certified mail shall be deemed to be communicated forty-eight (48) hours from the time of mailing.

26. **CUMULATIVE REMEDIES; NON-WAIVER.** The receipt by Lessor of any rent or payment with or without knowledge of the breach of any covenant hereof shall not be deemed a waiver of any such breach and no waiver by Lessor of any sum due hereunder or any provision hereof shall be deemed to have been made unless expressed in writing and signed by Lessor. No delay or omission in the exercise of any right or remedy accruing to Lessor upon any breach by Lessee under this lease shall impair such right or remedy or be construed as a waiver of any such breach theretofore or hereafter occurring. The waiver by Lessor of any breach of any term, covenant or condition herein contained shall not be deemed to be a waiver of any subsequent breach of the same or any other term, covenant or condition herein contained. All rights, powers, options or remedies afforded to Lessor either hereunder or by law shall be cumulative and not alternative and the exercise of one right, power, option or remedy shall not bar other rights, powers, options or remedies allowed herein or by law.

27. **MISCELLANEOUS.** (a) It is agreed by and between the parties hereto that all the agreements herein contained upon the part of Lessee, whether technically covenants or conditions, shall be deemed conditions for the purpose hereof, conferring upon Lessor, in the event of breach of any of said agreements, the right to terminate this lease.

(b) Lessee agrees at any time and from time to time within ten (10) days of written request from Lessor, to execute, acknowledge and deliver to Lessor a statement in writing certifying that this lease is unmodified and in full force and effect (or if there have been modifications, that the same is in full force and effect as modified, and stating the modifications), and the dates to which the rent and other charges have been paid in advance, if any, it being intended that any such statement delivered pursuant to this paragraph may be relied upon by any prospective purchaser, mortgagee or assignee of any mortgagee of the premises.

(c) Lessee and Lessee's Guarantor, if any, agree to deliver to Lessor, within thirty (30) days from written request therefor but not more frequently than once each calendar year, a balance sheet prepared and certified by a Public Accountant or Certified Public Accountant showing the true and accurate net worth of Lessee and said Guarantor, if any, as of the close of Lessee's and said Guarantor's last accounting period.

(d) In case there is more than one Lessee the obligation of Lessees executing this lease shall be joint and several. The words "Lessor" and "Lessee" as used herein shall include the plural as well as the singular. The covenants and agreements contained herein shall be binding upon and be enforceable by the parties hereto and their respective heirs, executors, administrators, successors and assigns, subject to the restrictions herein imposed on assignment by Lessee.

(e) Time is of the essence of this lease and of each and every covenant, condition and provision herein contained.

(f) The paragraph headings of this lease are inserted only as a matter of convenience and for reference and in no way define, limit or describe the scope or intent of this agreement or any provision thereof or in any way effect this agreement.

IN WITNESS WHEREOF, the parties hereto have subscribed their names, and if corporations, executed this lease by officers thereunto duly authorized by resolution of said corporations, in duplicate the day and year first hereinabove written.

LESSEE: **LESSOR:**

_____

_____

_____

Copyright 1965 Oakland Real Estate Board

Appendix B

LEASE

Lanard and Axilbund, Inc., Agents

Real Estate   Management

21 SOUTH 12th STREET
PHILADELPHIA 7, PA.

LOcust 3-1252

This Agreement, MADE THE _____ day of_____
1. one thousand nine hundred and _____(19_____), by and between LANARD AND AXILBUND, Inc., Agents (hereinafter called "Lessor"), of the one part, and _____

(hereinafter called "Lessee"), of the other part.
2.   **WITNESSETH THAT:** Lessor does hereby demise and let unto Lessee all that certain

_____
_____
_____
_____

in the _____ of _____ , State of Pennsylvania, to be used
and occupied as _____
_____ and for no other purpose, for the term of _____

3. beginning the _____ day of _____ one thousand nine hundred and _____
(19_____) and ending the _____ day of _____ one thousand nine
hundred and _____ (19_____)

4. for the minimum _____ rental of _____ Dollars ($_____)
lawful money of the United States of America, payable in monthly installments in advance during the said term of this lease, or any renewal hereof, in sums of _____
_____ Dollars ($_____)

on the _____ day of each month, rent to begin from the _____
day of _____ , 19_____ the first installment to be paid at the time of signing this lease.

5.   If Lessor is unable to give Lessee possession of the demised premises, as herein provided, by reason of the holding over of a previous occupant, or by reason of any cause
beyond the control of the Lessor, the Lessor shall not be liable in damages to the Lessee
therefor, and during the period that the Lessor is unable to give possession, all rights
and remedies of both parties hereunder shall be suspended.

6.   (a) Lessee agrees to pay as rent in addition to the minimum rental herein reserved any
and all sums which may become due by reason of the failure of Lessee to comply with
all of the covenants of this lease and any and all damages, costs and expenses which the
Lessor may suffer or incur by reason of any default of the Lessee or failure on his part
to comply with the covenants of this lease, and each of them, and also any and all damages to the demised premises caused by any act or neglect of the Lessee.

(b) Lessee further agrees to pay as rent in addition to the minimum rental herein
reserved _____ of all taxes assessed or imposed upon the demised premises and/or
the land and buildings of which the demised premises is a part during the term of this
lease or any renewal thereof in excess of and over and above those assessed or imposed
for the year of _____ . The amount due hereunder on account of such
taxes shall be apportioned for that part of the first and last calendar years covered by
the term hereof. The same shall be paid by Lessee to Lessor on or before the first day of
June of each and every year.

(c) Lessee further agrees to pay to Lessor as additional rent all increase or increases in
fire insurance premiums upon the demised premises and/or the buildings of which the
demised premises is a part, due to an increase in the rate of fire insurance in excess of
the rate on the demised premises at the time of making this lease, if said increase is
caused by any act or neglect of the Lessee or the nature of the Lessee's business. Lessee
further agrees to comply, at its own cost and expense, with any recommendation, rule
or regulation of any authorized insurance rating bureau which will enable the Lessor to effect a reduction in the Fire Insurance rate on the building of which the herein demised
premises is a part or on the contents therein.

(d) Lessee further agrees that in the event Lessee uses water for any purpose other
than sanitary or drinking, or that the premises herein demised is an entire building,
Lessee will pay as additional rent, upon presentation of bills by Lessor, all charges for
sewer rental and for water consumed upon the demised premises, whether metered or
otherwise, and will also promptly install and connect a meter for the demised premises,
if required to do so by Lessor at any time during the term of this lease or any renewal
thereof, and Lessee will also keep any water meter for the premises in repair, whether
such repairs are made necessary by ordinary wear and tear, freezing, accident, or other
causes, and when necessary, will replace the same. In the event the premises herein
demised are part of a larger premises or a multi-tenant building, Lessor agrees to provide
Lessee with water for drinking and sanitary purposes only free of charge, and Lessee

further agrees to pay for all other water consumed upon the herein demised premises and sewer rental as provided for herein.

Lessee shall not install any air-conditioning or refrigeration equipment in the herein demised premises without the written consent of the Lessor. If Lessor, at Lessor's sole option, shall grant such consent, Lessee agrees to pay for all water consumed in the operation of said water-cooled air-conditioning or refrigeration equipment.

7. All rent shall be payable without prior notice or demand at the office of Lessor—21 South 12th Street, Philadelphia 7, Pa., or at such other place as Lessor may from time to time designate by notice in writing.

8. Lessee covenants and agrees that he will without demand, during the term of this lease or any renewal hereof:

(a) Pay the rent and all other charges herein reserved as rent on the days and times and at the place that the same are made payable, without demand, and if Lessor shall at any time or times accept said rent or rent charges after the same shall have become due and payable, such acceptance shall not excuse delay upon subsequent occasions, or constitute or be construed as a waiver of any of Lessor's rights. Lessee agrees that any charge or payment herein reserved, included, or agreed to be treated or collected as rent and/or any other charges or taxes, expenses, or costs herein agreed to be paid by the Lessee may be proceeded for and recovered by the Lessor by distraint or other process in the same manner as rent due and in arrears.

(b) Keep the demised premises clean and free from all ashes, dirt and other refuse matter; replace all glass windows, doors etc., broken; keep all waste and drain pipes open; repair all damage to plumbing and to the demised premises in general; keep the same in good order and repair as they now are, reasonable wear and tear and damage by accidental fire or other casualty not occurring through negligence of Lessee or those employed by or acting for Lessee alone excepted. The Lessee agrees to surrender the demised premises in the same condition in which Lessee has herein agreed to keep the same during the continuance of this lease.

(c) Properly insure all plate glass, if any, in the demised premises and immediately replace same, if damaged or broken, at Lessee's own cost and expense.

(d) Comply with any requirements of any of the constituted public authorities, and with the terms of any State or Federal statute or local ordinance or regulation applicable to Lessee or his use of the demised premises, and save Lessor harmless from penalties, fines, costs or damages resulting from failure so to do.

(e) Use every reasonable precaution against fire.

(f) Comply with rules and regulations of Lessor promulgated as hereinafter provided.

(g) Peaceably deliver up and surrender possession of the demised premises to the Lessor at the expiration or sooner termination of this lease, promptly delivering to Lessor at its office all keys for the demised premises.

(h) Give to Lessor prompt written notice of any accident, fire or damage occurring on or to the demised premises.

(i) In the event that all or a portion of the demised premises is at street or pavement level, Lessee shall be responsible for the condition of the pavement, curb, cellar doors, awnings and other erections in the pavement during the term of this lease or any renewal hereof, shall keep the pavement free from snow and ice, and shall be, and hereby agrees that Lessee is solely liable for any accidents due or alleged to be due to their defective condition, or to any accumulations of snow and ice.

(j) The Lessee agrees that if, with the permission in writing of Lessor, Lessee shall vacate or decide at any time during the term of this lease, or any renewal thereof, to vacate all or a portion of the herein demised premises, prior to the expiration of this lease, or any renewal hereof, Lessee will not cause or allow any other agent to represent Lessee in any sub-letting or re-letting of all or a portion of the demised premises other than Lanard & Axilbund, Inc., and that should Lessee do so, or attempt to do so, the Lessor may remove any signs that may be placed on or about the demised premises by such other agent without any liability to Lessee or said Agent, the Lessee assuming all responsibility and liability for such action. It is further agreed that Lanard & Axilbund, Inc., shall have the exclusive right to act as Agent of the Lessee for such sub-letting and shall be entitled to the usual commission for sub-letting or re-letting and shall be entitled to the usual commission for obtaining tenants regardless of whether such sub-letting is accomplished by Lanard & Axilbund, Inc., or any other broker or by Lessee directly.

(k) Comply with all obligations undertaken by Lessee or any other entity of which Lessee is the successor under any prior lease for the demised premises.

9. Lessee covenants and agrees that he will do none of the following things without the consent in writing of Lessor first had and obtained:

(a) Occupy the demised premises in any other manner or for any other purpose than as above set forth.

(b) Assign, mortgage or pledge this lease or under-let or sub-lease the demised premises, or any part thereof, or permit any other person, firm or corporation to occupy the demised premises, or any part thereof; nor shall any assignee or sub-lessee assign, mortgage or pledge this lease or such sub-lease, without an additional written consent by the Lessor, and without such consent no such assignment, mortgage or pledge shall be valid. If the Lessee becomes embarrassed or insolvent, or makes an assignment for the benefit of creditors, or if a petition in bankruptcy is filed by or against the Lessee or a bill in equity or other proceeding for the appointment of a receiver for the Lessee is filed, or if the real or personal property of the Lessee shall be sold or levied upon by any Sheriff, Marshal or Constable, the same shall be a violation of this covenant.

(c) Place or allow to be placed any stand, booth, sign or show case upon the doorsteps, vestibules or outside walls or pavements of said premises, or paint, place, erect or cause to be painted, placed or erected any sign, projection or device on or in any part of the premises. Lessee shall remove any sign, projection or device painted, placed or erected, if permission has been granted, and restore the walls, etc., to their former conditions, at or prior to the expiration of this lease. In case of the breach of this covenant (in addition to all other remedies given to Lessor in case of the breach of any conditions or covenants of this lease) Lessor shall have the privilege of removing said stand, booth, sign, show case, projection or device, and restoring said walls, etc., to their former condition, and Lessee, at Lessor's option, shall be liable to Lessor for any and all expenses so incurred by Lessor.

(d) Make any alterations, improvements or additions to the demised premises. All alterations, improvements, additions, or fixtures, whether installed before or after the execution of this lease, shall remain upon the premises at the expiration or sooner determination of this lease and become the property of Lessor, unless Lessor shall, prior to the determination of this lease, have given written notice to Lessee to remove the same, in which event Lessee will remove such alterations, improvements and additions and restore the premises to the same good order and condition in which they now are. Should Lessee fail so to do, Lessor may do so, collecting, at Lessor's option, the cost and expense thereof from Lessee as additional rent.

(e) Use or operate any machinery that, in Lessor's opinion, is harmful to the building or disturbing to other tenants occupying other parts thereof.

(f) Place any weights in any portion of the demised premises beyond the safe carrying capacity of the structure.

(g) Do or suffer to be done, any act, matter or thing objectionable to the fire insurance companies whereby the fire insurance or any other insurance now in force or hereafter to be placed on the demised premises, or any part thereof, or on the building of which the demised premises may be a part, shall become void or suspended, or whereby the same shall be rated as a more hazardous risk than at the date of execution of this lease, or employ any person or persons objectionable to the fire insurance companies or carry or have any benzine or explosive matter of any kind in and about the demised premises. In case of a breach of this covenant (in addition to all other remedies given to Lessor in case of the breach of any of the conditions or covenants of this lease) Lessee agrees to pay to Lessor as additional rent any and all increase or increases of premiums on insurance carried by Lessor on the demised premises, or any part thereof, or on the building of which the demised premises may be a part, caused in any way by the occupancy of Lessee.

(h) Remove, attempt to remove or manifest an intention to remove Lessee's goods or property from or out of the demised premises otherwise than in the ordinary and usual course of business, without having first paid and satisfied Lessor for all rent which may become due during the entire term of this lease.

(i) Vacate or desert said premises during the term of this lease, or permit the same to be empty and unoccupied.

(j) Use or permit to be used on the demised premises any handtrucks, dollies and/or any other wheeled vehicles unless they are equipped with rubber tires.

(k) Keep in or affix in any manner to the demised premises any goods, chattels or equipment in which a third party has a security interest which exempts such goods, chattels or equipment from distraint for rent due hereunder.

10.   Lessee covenants and agrees that Lessor shall have the right to do the following things and matters in and about the demised premises:

(a) At all times by itself or its duly authorized agents to go upon and inspect the demised premises and every part thereof, and/or at its option to make repairs, alterations and additions to the demised premises or the building of which the demised premises is a part.

(b) At any time or times and from time to time to make such rules and regulations as in its judgment may from time to time be necessary for the safety, care and cleanliness of the premises, and for the preservation of good order therein. Such rules and regulations shall, when notice thereof is given to Lessee, form a part of this lease.

(c) To display a "For Sale" sign at any time, and also, after notice from either party of intention to determine this lease, or at any time within three months prior to the expiration of this lease, a "For Rent" sign, or both "For Rent" and "For Sale" signs; and all of said signs shall be placed upon such part of the premises as Lessor may elect and may contain such matter as Lessor shall require. Prospective purchasers or tenants authorized by Lessor may inspect the premises at reasonable hours at any time. If, however, Lessee prohibits or refuses to permit Lessor or its agents or any prospective purchasers or tenants authorized by Lessor to inspect the demised premises as hereinabove mentioned, in that event Lessee shall be held responsible for any loss of rent that may be incurred by Lessor, particularly by reason of the fact that Lessee shall have prohibited Lessor or its agents, prospective purchasers or tenants from inspecting the herein demised premises as hereinabove set forth.

(d) The Lessor may discontinue all facilities furnished and services rendered by Lessor or any of them, not expressly covenanted for herein, it being understood that they constitute no part of the consideration for this lease.

11.   Lessee agrees to be responsible for and to relieve and hereby relieves the Lessor from all liability by reason of any injury or damage to any person or property in the demised premises, whether belonging to the Lessee or any other person, caused by any fire, breakage or leakage in any part or portion of the demised premises, or any part or portion of the building of which the demised premises is a part, or from water, rain or snow that may leak into, issue or flow from any part of the said premises, or of the building of which the demised premises is a part, from the drains, pipes, or plumbing work of the same, or from any place or quarter, whether such breakage, leakage, injury or damage be caused by or result from the negligence of Lessor or its servants or agents or any person or persons whatsoever.

Lessee also agrees to be responsible for and to relieve and hereby relieves Lessor from all liability by reason of any damage or injury to any person or thing which may arise from or be due to the use, misuse or abuse of all or any of the elevators, hatches, openings, stairways, hallways of any kind whatsoever which may exist or hereafter be erected or constructed on the said premises, or from any kind of injury which may arise from any other cause whatsoever on the said premises or the building of which the demised premises is a part whether such damage, injury, use, misuse or abuse be caused by or result from the negligence of Lessor, its servants or agents or any other person or persons whatsoever.

12.   (a) In the event that the demised premises is totally destroyed or so damaged by fire or other casualty not occurring through fault or negligence of the Lessee or those employed by or acting for him, that the same cannot be repaired or restored within a reasonable time, this lease shall absolutely cease and determine, and the rent shall abate for the balance of the term.

(b) If the damage caused as above be only partial and such that the premises can be restored to their then condition within a reasonable time, the Lessor may, at its option, restore the same with reasonable promptness, reserving the right to enter upon the demised premises for that purpose. The Lessor also reserves the right to enter upon the demised premises whenever necessary to repair damage caused by fire or other casualty to the building of which the demised premises is a part, even though the effect of such entry be to render the demised premises or a part thereof untenantable. In either event the rent shall be apportioned and suspended during the time the Lessor is in possession, taking into account the proportion of the demised premises rendered untenantable and the duration of the Lessor's possession. If a dispute arises as to the amount of rent due under this clause, Lessee agrees to pay the full amount claimed by Lessor. Lessee shall, however, have the right to proceed by law to recover the excess payment, if any.

(c) Lessor shall not be liable for any damage, compensation or claim by reason of inconvenience or annoyance arising from the necessity of repairing any portion of the building, the interruption in the use of the premises, or the termination of this lease by reason of the destruction of the premises.

13.   (a) The Lessor has let the demised premises in their present condition and without any representations on the part of the Lessor, its officers, employees, servants and/or agents. It is understood and agreed that Lessor is under no duty to make repairs or alterations at the time of letting or at any time thereafter.

(b) It is understood and agreed that the Lessor does not warrant or undertake that the Lessee shall be able to obtain a permit under any Zoning Ordinance or Regulation for such use as Lessee intends to make of the said premises, and nothing in this lease contained shall obligate the Lessor to assist Lessee in obtaining said permit; the Lessee further agrees that in the event a permit cannot be obtained by Lessee under any Zoning Ordinance or Regulation, this lease shall not terminate without Lessor's consent, and the Lessee shall use the premises only in a manner permitted under such Zoning Ordinance or Regulation.

(c) No contract entered into or that may be subsequently entered into by Lessor with Lessee, relative to any alterations, additions, improvements or repairs, nor the failure of Lessor to make such alterations, additions, improvements or repairs as required by any such contract, nor the making by Lessor or its agents or contractors of such alterations, additions, improvements or repairs shall in any way affect the payment of the rent or said other charges at the time specified in this lease.

(d) It is expressly understood and agreed that the said Lanard & Axilbund, Inc., notwithstanding its designation herein as "Lessor," shall act as agent and shall not in any event be held liable to the owner or to Lessee for the fulfillment or non-fulfillment of any of the terms or conditions of this lease; for the return to Lessee upon termination of this lease or under any other circumstances, of rent or other sums received by it as Lessor hereunder; or for any errors of omission or commission of the Agent or its employees in the general management of said premises or for any action or proceeding that may be taken by the owner against Lessee, or by Lessee against the owner.

(e) It is hereby covenanted and agreed, any law, usage or custom to the contrary notwithstanding, that Lessor shall have the right at all times to enforce the covenants and provisions of this lease in strict accordance with the terms hereof, notwithstanding any conduct or custom on the part of the Lessor in refraining from so doing at any time or times; and, further, that the failure of Lessor at any time or times to enforce its rights under said covenants and provisions strictly in accordance with the same shall not be construed as having created a custom in any way or manner contrary to the specific terms, provisions and covenants of this lease or as having in any way or manner modified the same.

(f) This lease is granted upon the express condition that Lessee and/or the occupants of the premises herein leased, shall not conduct themselves in a manner which the Lessor in its sole opinion may deem improper or objectionable, and that if at any time during the term of this lease or any extension or continuation thereof, Lessee or any occupier of the said premises shall have conducted himself, herself or themselves in a manner which Lessor in its sole opinion deems improper or objectionable, Lessee shall be taken to have broken the covenants and conditions of this lease, and Lessor will be entitled to all of the rights and remedies granted and reserved herein, for the Lessee's failure to observe any of the covenants and conditions of this lease.

(g) In the event of the failure of Lessee promptly to perform the covenants of Section 8 (b) hereof, Lessor may go upon the demised premises and perform such covenants, the cost thereof, at the sole option of Lessor, to be charged to Lessee as additional and delinquent rent.

(h) Lessor shall not be liable to Lessee, under the terms of this lease or otherwise, for any loss or damage to Lessee's property or interest in the event that Lessee is insured against such loss or damage.

14.   If the Lessee

(a) Does not pay in full when due any and all installments of rent and/or any other charge or payment herein reserved, included, or agreed to be treated or collected as rent and/or any other charge, expense, or cost herein agreed to be paid by the Lessee; and/or

(b) Violates and/or fails to perform or otherwise breaks any covenant or agreement herein contained; and/or

(c) Vacates the demised premises or removes or attempts to remove or manifests an intention to remove any goods or property therefrom otherwise than in the ordinary and usual course of business without having first paid and satisfied the Lessor in full for all rent and other charges then due or that may thereafter become due until the expiration of the then current term, above mentioned; and/or

(d) Becomes embarrassed or insolvent, or makes an assignment for the benefit of creditors, or if a petition in bankruptcy is filed by or against the Lessee or a bill in equity or other proceeding for the appointment of a receiver for the Lessee is filed, or if proceedings for reorganization or for composition with creditors under any State or Federal law be instituted by or against Lessee, or if the real or personal property of the Lessee shall be sold or levied upon by any Sheriff, Marshal or Constable, then and in such event or events, there shall be deemed to be a breach of this lease, and thereupon at the option of the Lessor,

(1) The rent for the entire unexpired balance of the term of this lease, as well as all other charges, payments, costs and expenses herein agreed to be paid by the Lessee, or at the option of Lessor any part thereof, and also all costs and officers' commissions including watchmen's wages and further including the five percent chargeable by Act of Assembly to the Lessor, shall, in addition to any and all installments of rent already due and payable and in arrears and/or any other charge or payment herein reserved, included or agreed to be treated or collected as rent, and/or any other charge, expense or cost herein agreed to be paid by the Lessee which may be due and payable and in arrears, be taken to be due and payable and in arrears as if by the terms and provisions of this lease, the whole balance of unpaid rent and other charges, payments, taxes, costs and expenses were on that date payable in advance; and if this lease or any part thereof is assigned, or if the premises or any part thereof is sub-let, Lessee hereby irrevocably constitutes and appoints Lessor Lessee's agent to collect the rents due by such assignee or sub-lessee and apply the same to the rent due hereunder without in any way affecting Lessee's obligation to pay any unpaid balance of rent due hereunder; or in the event of any of the foregoing at any time at the option of Lessor;

(2) This lease and the term hereby created shall determine and become absolutely void without any right on the part of the Lessee to save the forfeiture by payment of any sum due or by other performance of any condition, term or covenant broken; whereupon, Lessor shall be entitled to recover damages for such breach in an amount equal to the amount of rent reserved for the balance of the term of this lease, less the fair rental value of the said demised premises, for the residue of said term.

15. In the event of any default as above set forth in Section 14, the Lessor, or anyone acting on Lessor's behalf, at Lessor's option:

(a) May without notice or demand enter the demised premises, breaking open locked doors if necessary to effect entrance, without liability to action for prosecution or damages for such entry or for the manner thereof, for the purpose of distraining or levying and for any other purposes, and take possession of and sell all goods and chattels at auction, on three days' notice served in person on the Lessee, or left on the premises, and pay the said Lessor out of the proceeds, and even if the rent be not due and unpaid, should the Lessee at any time remove or attempt to remove goods and chattels from the premises without leaving enough thereon to meet the next periodical payment, Lessee authorizes the Lessor to follow for a period of ninety days after such removal, take possession of and sell at auction, upon like notice, sufficient of such goods to meet the proportion of rent accrued at the time of such removal; and the Lessee hereby releases and discharges the Lessor, and his agents, from all claims, actions, suits, damages and penalties, for or by reason or on account of any entry, distraint, levy, appraisement or sale; and/or

(b) May enter the premises, and without demand proceed by distress and sale of the goods there found to levy the rent and/or other charges herein payable as rent; and all costs and officers' commissions, including watchmen's wages and sums chargeable to Lessor, and further including a sum equal to 5% of the amount of the levy as commissions to the constable or other person making the levy, shall be paid by the Lessee, and in such case all costs, officers' commissions and other charges shall immediately attach and become part of the claim of Lessor for rent, and any tender of rent without said costs, commissions and charges made after the issue of a warrant of distress shall not be sufficient to satisfy the claim of the Lessor. Lessee hereby expressly waives in favor of Lessor the benefit of all laws now made or which may hereafter be made regarding any limitation as to the goods upon which, or the time within which, distress is to be made after removal of goods, and further relieves the Lessor of the obligation of proving or identifying such goods, it being the purpose and intent of this provision that all goods of Lessee, whether upon the demised premises or not, shall be liable to distress for rent. Lessee waives in favor of Lessor all rights under the Landlord & Tenant Act of 1951, and all supplements and amendments thereto that have been or may hereafter be passed, and authorizes the sale of any goods distrained for rent at any time after five days from said distraint without any appraisement and/or condemnation thereof. The Lessee further waives the right to issue a Writ of Replevin under the Act of April 19th, 1901 (P.L. 88), of the Laws of the Commonwealth of Pennsylvania, or under any other law previously enacted and now in force, or which may be hereafter enacted, for the recovery of any articles, household goods, furniture, etc., seized under a distress for rent or levy upon an execution for rent, damages or otherwise; all waivers hereinbefore mentioned are hereby extended to apply to any such action; and/or

(c) May lease said premises or any part or parts thereof to such person or persons as may in Lessor's discretion seem best and the Lessee shall be liable for any loss of rent for the balance of the then current term.

16.   If the rent and/or charges hereby reserved as rent shall remain unpaid on any day when the same ought to be paid Lessee hereby empowers any Prothonotary or attorney of any Court of Record to appear for Lessee in any and all actions which may be brought for rent and/or the charges, payments, costs and expenses reserved as rent, or agreed to be paid by the Lessee and/or to sign for Lessee an agreement for entering in any competent Court an amicable action or actions for the recovery of rent or other charges or expenses, and in said suits or in said amicable action or actions to confess judgment against Lessee for all or any part of the rent specified in this lease and then unpaid including, at Lessor's option, the rent for the entire unexpired balance of the term of this lease, and/or other charges, payments, costs and expenses reserved as rent or agreed to be paid by the Lessee, and for interest and costs together with an attorney's fee of not less than One Hundred Dollars or more than 5%, whichever shall be the greater. Such authority shall not be exhausted by one exercise thereof, but judgment may be confessed as aforesaid from time to time as often as any of said rent and/or other charges reserved as rent shall fall due or be in arrears, and such powers may be exercised as well after the expiration of the original term and/or during any extension or renewal of this lease.

17.   When this lease shall be determined by term, covenant or condition broken, either during the original term of this lease or any renewal or extension thereof, and also when and as soon as the term hereby created or any extension thereof shall have expired, it shall be lawful for any attorney as attorney for Lessee to file an agreement for entering in any competent Court an amicable action and judgment in ejectment against Lessee and all persons claiming under Lessee for the recovery by Lessor of possession of the herein demised premises, for which this lease shall be his sufficient warrant, whereupon, if Lessor so desires, a writ of habere facias possessionem may issue forthwith, without any prior writ or proceedings whatsoever, and provided that if for any reason after such action shall have been commenced the same shall be determined and the possession of the premises hereby demised remain in or be restored to Lessee, Lessor shall have the right upon any subsequent default or defaults, or upon the termination of this lease as hereinbefore set forth, to bring one or more amicable action or actions as hereinbefore set forth to recover possession of the said premises.

18.   In any amicable action of ejectment and/or for rent in arrears, Lessor shall first cause to be filed in such action an affidavit made by it or someone acting for it setting forth the facts necessary to authorize the entry of judgment, of which facts such affidavit shall be conclusive evidence, and if a true copy of this lease (and of the truth of the copy such affidavit shall be sufficient evidence) be filed in such action, it shall not be necessary to file the original as a warrant of attorney, any rule of Court, custom or practice to the contrary notwithstanding.

19.   Lessee expressly agrees that any judgment, order or decree entered against him by or in any Court or Magistrate by virtue of the powers of attorney contained in this lease, or otherwise, shall be final, and that he will not take an appeal, certiorari, writ of error, exception or objection to the same, or file a motion or rule to strike off or open or to stay execution of the same, and releases to Lessor and to any and all attorneys who may appear for Lessee all errors in the said proceedings, and all liability therefore. Lessee expressly waives the benefits of all laws, now or hereafter in force, exempting any goods on the demised premises, or elsewhere from distraint, levy or sale in any legal proceedings taken by the Lessor to enforce any rights under this lease. Lessee further waives the right of inquisition on any real estate that may be levied upon to collect any amount which may become due under the terms and conditions of this lease, and does hereby voluntarily condemn the same and authorizes the Prothonotary to enter a fieri facias or other process upon Lessee's voluntary condemnation, and further agrees that the said real estate may be sold on a fieri facias or other process. If proceedings shall be commenced by Lessor to recover possession under the Acts of Assembly, either at the end of the term or sooner termination of this lease, or for nonpayment of rent or any other reason. Lessee specifically waives the right to the three months' notice required by the Act of December 14, 1863, and to the fifteen or thirty days' notice required by the Act of April 3, 1830, and agrees that five days' notice shall be sufficient in either or any such case.

20.   The right to enter judgment against Lessee and to enforce all of the other provisions of this lease hereinabove provided for may, at the option of any assignee of this lease, be exercised by any assignee of the Lessor's right, title and interest in this lease in his, her or their own name, notwithstanding the fact that any or all assignments of the said right, title and interest may not be executed and/or witnessed in accordance with the

Act of Assembly of May 28, 1715, 1 Sm. L. 99, and all supplements and amendments thereto that have been or may hereafter be passed and Lessee hereby expressly waives the requirements of said Act of Assembly and any and all laws regulating the manner and/or form in which such assignment shall be executed and witnessed.

21.   All of the remedies hereinbefore given to Lessor and all rights and remedies given to it by law and equity shall be cumulative and concurrent. No determination of this lease or the taking or recovering of the premises shall deprive Lessor of any of its remedies or actions against the Lessee for rent due at the time or which, under the terms hereof, would in the future become due as if there had been no determination, or for sums due at the time or which, under the terms hereof, would in the future become due as if there had been no determination, nor shall the bringing of any action for rent or breach of covenant, or the resort to any other remedy herein provided for the recovery of rent be construed as a waiver of the right to obtain possession of the premises.

22.   In the event that the premises demised or any part thereof is taken or condemned for a public or quasi-public use, this lease shall, as to the part so taken, terminate as of the date title shall vest in the condemnor, and rent shall abate in proportion to the square feet of leased space taken or condemned or shall cease if the entire premises be so taken. In either event the Lessee waives all claims against the Lessor by reason of the complete or partial taking of the demised premises, and it is agreed that the Lessee shall not be entitled to any notice whatsoever of the partial or complete termination of this lease by reason of the aforesaid.

23.   This Agreement of Lease and all its terms, covenants and provisions are and each of them is subject and subordinate to any lease or other arrangement or right to possession, under which the Lessor is in control of the demised premises, to the rights of the owner or owners of the demised premises and of the land or buildings of which the demised premises are a part, to all rights of the Lessor's landlord and to any and all mortgages and other encumbrances now or hereafter placed upon the demised premises or upon the land and/or the buildings containing the same; and Lessee expressly agrees that if Lessor's tenancy, control, or right to possession shall terminate either by expiration, forfeiture or otherwise, then this lease shall, at the option of Lessor, thereupon immediately terminate and the Lessee shall, thereupon, give immediate possession; and Lessee hereby waives any and all claims for damages or otherwise by reason of such termination as aforesaid.

24.   It is hereby mutually agreed that either party hereto may determine this Lease at the end of said term by giving to the other party written notice thereof at least _____

_____ prior thereto, but in default of such notice this lease shall continue upon the same terms and conditions in force immediately prior to the expiration of the term hereof as are herein contained for a further period of

_____ and so on from _____

_____ to _____
unless or until terminated by either party hereto, giving the other _____

_____ written notice for removal previous to expiration of the then current term; PROVIDED, however, that should this lease be continued for a further period under the terms hereinabove mentioned, any allowances given Lessee on the rent during the original term shall not extend beyond such original term, and further provided, however, that if Lessor shall have given such written notice prior to the expiration of any term hereby created, of its intention to change the terms and conditions of this lease, and Lessee shall not within ten days from the date of such notice notify Lessor of Lessee's intention to vacate the demised premises at the end of the then current term, Lessee shall be considered as Lessee under the terms and conditions mentioned in such notice for a further term as above provided, or for such further term as may be stated in such notice.

In the event that Lessee shall give notice, as stipulated in this lease, of intention to vacate the demised premises at the end of the present term, or any renewal or extension thereof, and shall fail or refuse so to vacate the same, on the date designated by such notice, then it is expressly agreed that Lessor shall have the option either (a) to disregard the notice so given as having no effect, in which case all the terms and conditions of this lease shall continue thereafter with full force precisely as if such notice had not been given, or (b) Lessor may, at any time within thirty days after the present term or any renewal or extension thereof, as aforesaid, give the said Lessee ten days' written notice of its intention to terminate the said lease; whereupon the Lessee expressly agrees to vacate said premises at the expiration of the said period of ten days specified in said notice. All powers granted to Lessor by this lease may be exercised and all obligations imposed upon Lessee by this lease shall be performed by Lessee as well during any extension of the original term of this lease as during the original term itself.

25.   All notices required to be given by Lessor to Lessee shall be sufficiently given by leaving the same upon the demised premises, but notices given by Lessee to Lessor must be given by registered or certified mail, and as against Lessor the only admissible evidence that notice has been given by Lessee shall be a registry return receipt signed by Lessor or its agent. In the event that Lessor shall mail notice to Lessee, the date of mailing shall be the valid date of service.

26.   It is expressly understood and agreed by and between the parties hereto that this lease and the riders attached hereto and forming a part hereof set forth all the promises, agreements, conditions and understandings between Lessor or its Agent and Lessee relative to the demised premises, and that there are no promises, agreements, conditions or understandings, either oral or written, between them other than are herein set forth. It is further understood and agreed that, except as herein otherwise provided, no subsequent alteration, amendment, change or addition to this lease shall be binding upon Lessor or Lessee unless reduced to writing and signed by them.

27.   In the event Lessee, or any one acting on Lessee's behalf or on behalf of any member of any firm, corporation, partnership, or other entity affiliated with Lessee hereunder, shall purchase the property occupied under this tenancy, Lessor's principal agrees to pay Lanard & Axilbund, Inc., a commission on the gross purchase price in accordance with the schedule prescribed by the Philadelphia Board of Realtors.

In consideration of the services of Lanard & Axilbund, Inc., in procuring the tenancy created in this lease, or any renewal or extension of said tenancy or the leasing of additional space in the building of which the herein demised premises is a part or any contiguous or adjacent property, the Lessor's principal hereby acknowledges there is due to Lanard & Axilbund, Inc., commissions, as prescribed by the Philadelphia Board of Realtors; however, in lieu thereof, it is hereby agreed that Lanard & Axilbund, Inc., shall for the full term or the renewal thereof or the continuation of the tenancy in any way collect the rent, or rents due or to become due thereunder, or any other charges as may be therein provided for, and to deduct and retain from said collections a leasing commission, in accordance with the schedule of and in the manner prescribed by the Philadelphia Board of Realtors, and to deduct and retain further sums for collecting such rents and any other charges, and for managing the premises, as is prescribed in the schedules and rules of the Philadelphia Board of Realtors for such service.

If Lanard & Axilbund, Inc., is collecting rent for their principal, Lanard & Axilbund, Inc., shall retain this lease in their possession during the term of this lease or any renewal or renewals thereof under lien for their services. Lanard & Axilbund, Inc., having a beneficial interest in this lease to the extent of any deferred leasing brokerage and commission due them hereunder, their principal is entitled to receive only the net amounts due hereunder after deduction thereof. No grantee, assignee, receiver, trustee, encumbrancer, or other person or official shall adopt or receive the benefits of this lease without paying the brokerage and commission hereinabove set forth or making provision for such payment. Lanard & Axilbund, Inc., shall be entitled to deduct from any funds of their principal in their hands arising from this lease or from any other transaction and apply them to the payment of the brokerage and commission due hereunder and of any sums advanced by them in connection with the management of the demised premises, including insurance premiums.

The agency of Lanard & Axilbund, Inc., shall not be terminated during the term of this lease, or any renewal thereof, until and unless any commissions due on any unexpired term shall have been paid to Lanard & Axilbund, Inc., in the amount prescribed by the Philadelphia Board of Realtors, and any assignment of this lease shall be binding upon the assignee as to the agency in the like manner as Lessor's principal is now bound. Any reservation in this lease whereby the Lessor may terminate the lease at an earlier time than the expiration date herein mentioned shall not release the Lessor's principal, or his assignee, from any responsibility for any commission due for the full term of this lease and any renewal thereof, as prescribed by the Philadelphia Board of Realtors.

In case a lease is renewed or continued, either by express or implied agreement, in any manner whatsoever, for any further period after the expiration of the term hereof, then in any such event Lanard & Axilbund, Inc., shall further receive, as additional commission at the time of such renewals or continuances or the entry into any such lease or agreement, a commission as prescribed in the schedule of commissions and charges of the Philadelphia Board of Realtors on the rentals to accrue under the terms of such renewal or continuance or under the terms of such other lease or agreement, and so on, thereafter up to a period not exceeding five years from the expiration of the original lease to all intents and purposes as if such continuances, renewals and leases were within the original term of said lease.

In the event Lanard & Axilbund, Inc., shall be collecting the rent, it shall have the right to collect the deferred leasing brokerage as fixed by the Philadelphia Board of Realtors, payable upon the termination of its agency upon the happening of any of the following:

(a) If an encumbrancer takes possession of, or a foreclosure is commenced on any encumbrance on, the demised premises; or

(b) If any execution is issued against, or a petition in bankruptcy is filed against, or a Receiver appointed for, or an assignment for the benefit of creditors is made by, principal; or

(c) If principal sells or leases, or permits any other person than Lanard & Axilbund, Inc., to rent or offer for rent the property, or any portion of it, of which the demised premises are a part, or instructs Lanard & Axilbund, Inc., to remove its signs from the same; or

(d) If prinicpal in any way alters this lease by agreement with Lessee without the approval of Lanard & Axilbund, Inc., or,

(e) If this lease is a sub-lease and principal or its Lessor, or trustee in equity, or bankruptcy, cancels or disaffirms the paramount lease without the approval of Lanard & Axilbund, Inc., or,

(f) If this lease is terminated for any reason, or,

(g) If Lanard & Axilbund, Inc., elects to cease collecting the rent hereunder.

28.   It is agreed that Lanard & Axilbund, Inc., in the event of the employing of any person or persons to maintain the building mentioned in this lease or to provide any kind of service to the said building, does so only as agent of its principal and such persons although chosen by Lanard & Axilbund, Inc., and paid by Lanard & Axilbund, Inc., shall at all times be considered employees, agents and servants of the said principal. But nothing in this paragraph shall obligate Lessor or Lessor's principal to furnish the said things or services to Lessee except as herein agreed. The said Lessor's principal agrees at all times to maintain Workmen's Compensation Insurance at the principal's own cost and expense and agrees to and does hereby save harmless and indemnify Lanard & Axilbund, Inc., of all liability by reason of all claims, charges, counsel fees, costs, suits, damages or workmen's compensation which might be required to be paid to or which may be claimed by any of the said employees, agents or servants or their legal representatives or dependents or by any other persons for injuries or damages sustained or claimed to be sustained to the person or any property and for any contractual obligations or expenditures in the operation of said premises.

29.   All rights and liabilities herein given to, or imposed upon, the respective parties hereto shall extend to and bind the several and respective heirs, executors, administrators, successors and assigns of said parties; and if there shall be more than one Lessee, they shall all be bound jointly and severally by the terms, covenants and agreements herein, and the word "Lessee" shall be deemed and taken to mean each and every person or party mentioned as a Lessee herein, be the same one or more; and if there shall be more than one Lessee, any notice required or permitted by the terms of this Lease may be given by or to any one thereof, and shall have the same force and effect as if given by or to all thereof. No rights, however, shall inure to the benefit of any assignee of Lessee unless the assignment to such assignee has been approved by Lessor in writing as aforesaid.

30.   Any headings preceding the text of the several paragraphs or sub-paragraphs hereof are inserted solely for convenience of reference and shall not constitute a part of this lease nor shall they affect its meaning, construction or effect.

31.   In the event the Lessor is furnishing any of the following services and/or utilities to the building of which the demised premises is a part, Lessor hereby agrees to supply the following services and/or utilities to the Lessee, as hereinafter provided, during hours and times to be determined by Lessor, in common with the other tenants in the building of which the demised premises is a part, during the term of this lease and any renewal thereof:

(a) At no additional charge therefor: heat, and service and/or use of the passenger and freight elevators.

(b) Electric current at the rate of _____ provided, however, that if Lessee should desire electrical service beyond that available at the demised premises at the time of the execution of this lease, Lessee shall pay the cost of installing all equipment required for that purpose.

(c) Process steam at the rate of $_____ per 1,000 pounds consumed, as recorded upon the meter to be installed, properly maintained and calibrated twice yearly by Lessee, at Lessee's own cost and expense.

(d) Sprinkler system supervisory service at the rate of $ _____ per month.

The charges in (b), (c) and (d) above shall be deemed to be additional rent hereunder and shall be payable within 10 days after presentation of bills therefor. The above rates are based on the cost to Lessor prevailing at the time of execution of this lease, and may, at Lessor's option, be increased to offset any increase in such cost.

In the event this lease is a renewal lease of an existing tenancy, Lessee agrees not to install any additional equipment consuming electricity on the herein demised premises over and above the present-connected electrical equipment as of the date of execution of this lease. If, however, the herein-created lease is a new lease, Lessee agrees not to install any electrical equipment on the herein demised premises with a total consumption in excess of _____ amps. Should Lessee, in either instance, desire the installation of any additional equipment consuming electricity, Lessee shall first notify Lessor and receive its written approval before such equipment shall have been installed.

The Lessor shall not be held responsible or liable for its inability to furnish heat, service and/or use of the passenger and freight elevators, electricity, steam, water, sprinkler system and/or any other service and/or utility supplied by Lessor, due to any breakdown or failure of the apparatus supplying same and/or while undergoing repairs and/or through any rule or order of any of the properly constituted authorities and/or through any other cause of whatsoever nature.

32.   This lease is subject to the approval of Lessor's principal, to be obtained within _____ days of the date of execution by Lessee.

Clauses _____ to _____, inclusive, contained on the rider attached hereto are hereby incorporated in and made a part of this lease prior to the execution hereof.

In Witness Whereof, the parties hereto have executed these presents the day and year first above written, and intend to be legally bound thereby.

SEALED AND DELIVERED IN THE   LANARD & AXILBUND, Inc. Agents
PRESENCE OF:

_____   By _____ (Seal)

_____   _____ (Seal)

_____   _____ (Seal)

_____   LESSEE

                          _____ (Seal)

                          _____ 19_____

_____, Owner, hereby accepts and approves of the foregoing Agreement of Lease made by LANARD & AXILBUND, Inc., Agents in pursuance of the Authority given it by WITNESS AT SIGNING:

_____   _____ (Seal)

_____   _____ (Seal)

SELECTED REFERENCES

Cerf, Alan R., *Real Estate and the Federal Income Tax* (Englewood Cliffs, N.J., Prentice-Hall, 1965).

Friedman, Edith J. (ed.), *Real Estate Encyclopedia,* Part VII: "How to Lease Real Property" (Englewood Cliffs, N.J., Prentice-Hall, 1960).

International Traders Club, National Institute of Real Estate Brokers, *Tax Implications in Exchanging* (Chicago, The Author, March, 1966).

Kahn, Sanders A., Case, Frederick E., and Schimmel, Alfred, *Real Estate Appraisal and Investment* (New York, Ronald Press, 1963).

Korb, Irving, "Light Industrial Properties," Ch. 38 of *Training Manual for Real Estate Salesmen,* Prepared for Sacramento Metropolitan Real Estate Offices, Inc. (Lafayette, Calif., Duncan B. Campbell, 1957).

Korb, Irving, and Trimble, Harold G., Jr., *Real Estate Sale-Leaseback: A Basic Analysis* (Washington, Society of Industrial Realtors, 1966).

Kratovil, Robert, *Real Estate Law,* 4th ed. (Englewood Cliffs, N.J., Prentice-Hall, 1964).

Maisel, Sherman J., *Financing Real Estate: Principles and Practices* (New York, McGraw-Hill, 1965).

Ricks, R. Bruce, *Recent Trends in Institutional Real Estate Investment,* Research Report 23, Center for Real Estate and Urban Economics (Berkeley, University of California, 1964).

Shenkel, William M., *Principles and Practices of Industrial Real Estate: A Course Syllabus* (Washington, Society of Industrial Realtors, 1963).

Society of Industrial Realtors, *Advanced Course in the Techniques of Industrial Real Estate* (Washington, Society of Industrial Realtors, 1964):
  Altman, David, "Tax Factors Affecting Industrial Real Estate";
  Murray, Thomas F., "Financing Industrial Real Estate";
  Sawyer, J. D., "Industrial Property Investment Opportunities."

Trerice, Byron, Jr., sponsor, *Ground Leases* (Chicago, National Institute of Real Estate Brokers, December, 1965).

Wendel, David I., "Commercial-Industrial Leases," *Real Estate Investment* (Los Angeles, California Real Estate Association, 1963).

Zoll, Clifford A., sponsor, *Guide to Commercial Property Leasing* (Chicago, National Institute of Real Estate Brokers, December, 1963).

11 | Rehabilitation and Conversion of Industrial Real Estate

WHEN industrial real estate is no longer competitive on the market in terms of price, rent, or investment return, it is a "problem" property. The best course of action for the owner or investor is to turn to an experienced professional industrial real estate broker for advice and counsel. There are four basic alternative choices open to the owner: sell the property "as is"; rent the property "as is"; rehabilitate or convert the property; or do nothing. Unfortunately, the fourth alternative is too often chosen, with disastrous financial results.

If the "problem" property is sold or leased "as is," the purchaser must also decide what to do with it. Here, too, one of the alternative courses of action to be studied is rehabilitation and/or conversion of the property.

Not all "problem" properties result from the same causes. Each represents a unique case to be studied in order to develop an appropriate plan of action that appears most beneficial to the broker's client. In his analysis, the broker should first appreciate the basic reasons leading to the development of the problem. "The older the neighborhood, the more numerous the problem properties. They have become problem properties for any one or combination of the following:

"1. Obsolescence in the structure and/or neighborhood.
"2. Physical deterioration.
"3. Mismanagement.
"4. Deleterious change from original usage.
"5. Deterioration of a neighborhood in terms of desirability of the people (social level, income level, etc.).
"6. Overly burdensome financing or taxation.
"7. Illegal conversions or usages compounded by governmental condemnation or action." [1]

---

[1] Stephen L. Melnyk, "Opportunities in Older Properties," *Real Estate Investment Opportunities* (Los Angeles, California Real Estate Association, 1965), p. 92.

358

While rehabilitation and/or conversion represent one alternative program of action in each case, the broker and all other participants in the proposed transaction must recognize that not all existing industrial properties can be successfully rehabilitated, modernized, remodeled, converted —or whatever other term is applied to the process of reversing the direction of obsolescence and of value decline. It is necessary to identify and to analyze the conditions under which renovation of an existing building is likely to be successful or feasible, and when it is not. Private rehabilitation will be undertaken *only* if a profit or return commensurate with the risk and effort involved appears likely for the developer-investor-entrepreneur. The critical role of the broker in this decision-making process is to provide the basic analytical materials that will enable the investor to make the proper decision in the light of the facts of the particular case.

The only real constant in the entire analysis is the *location* of the real estate. This fixed location influences the type of approach that the analyst must take in attempting to ascertain whether a proposed rehabilitation or conversion program is financially feasible and economically sound.

THE NEED FOR REHABILITATION AND CONVERSION OF INDUSTRIAL REAL ESTATE

In all real estate investment analysis, it is agreed that depreciation results from three basic sets of causes: physical deterioration, functional obsolescence, and economic obsolescence.[2]

Physical deterioration generally includes the wearing out of the structure or of its components, caused by use, wear and tear, action of the elements, or pest infestation. Functional obsolescence entails decreased capacity of the structure to perform the function for which it is intended *in accordance with current market standards*. A physically "good" or sound structure may experience increased operating expenses, and a less than competitive net return. Often, either technological advance or a change in tastes and standards will lead to a decrease in the market acceptance of existing industrial space. When this happens, that space loses market value, and functional obsolescence is basically the cause.

Finally, economic obsolescence is the result of changes in the neighborhood or market area surrounding the property itself, which in turn influence adversely the value of the property. These are largely beyond the control of the individual property owner (even though cooperative neighborhood efforts often work out well). He must take them essentially as given, and adjust to them.

In identifying and evaluating the forces leading to any loss in market attractiveness, it is necessary to engage in a detailed analysis of both the prop-

---

[2] For a more detailed consideration of the causes and measurement of depreciation on industrial real estate, see American Institute of Real Estate Appraisers, *The Appraisal of Real Estate,* 4th ed. (Chicago, The Author, 1964), Ch. 13; William N. Kinnard, Jr., *A Guide to Appraising Apartments,* 2nd ed. (Chicago, Society of Real Estate Appraisers, 1966), p. 30; and William M. Shenkel, *A Guide to Appraising Industrial Property* (Chicago, Society of Real Estate Appraisers, 1967), pp. 63–78.

erty and its market environment. The type of inspection checklist illustrated in Chapter 6 for listing purposes is equally useful in this type of study.

Neighborhood and Location Changes: Economic Obsolescence

Since World War II, there has been a much-heralded and much-studied
"suburbanization of industry" in the United States. Major cities especially
have recorded out-migration of existing industry, while there has also been a
marked increase in locations of new and branch plants in suburban areas.
Both relatively and absolutely, central city sites have generally declined in
importance and attractiveness as locations for manufacturing and distribution activities.[3] In particular, the one-story industrial building on a low-
density suburban lot has dealt a severe blow to the demand for older, multistory structures in central city locations. This shift in industry suggests
three points:

"(1) The available industrial space in urban areas is quite inadequate.
"(2) The changing composition of industries in urban areas requires rehabili-
      tation of buildings for city-oriented industry.
"(3) Industrial buildings, vacated by the original occupant, can often be
      rehabilitated to supply low-cost industrial space or to supply additional
      commercial space." [4]

The revolution in living and commuting patterns caused by the automobile has substantially undermined the advantage of a central city location
with respect to employee convenience. Moreover, the older industrial neighborhood in the central city is much more likely to be characterized by a
high density of land use and a mixture of land uses. This creates both an
unfavorable environment for continued industrial use, and serious difficulty
in the acquisition of space for expansion by existing firms.

To a large extent, industry has found it more economical to locate or
relocate on suburban sites with good highway access, rather than to compete with other urban land uses in the central city, especially in view of the
prices and rents that are paid for retail and office use.[5] This has been especially true of large-scale manufacturers which find one-story production
lines highly conducive to efficiency and increased profit; distribution operations also find highway access generally more profitable than a "central
location."

Moreover, mixed land and building uses in the older industrial areas of
cities often result in advanced deterioration and decay in the entire neighborhood. This is further deterrent to continued occupancy of the industrial
space by firms whose employees are reluctant to travel in the area, or to
park their cars unattended, either on the street or in lots. Many firms em-

---

[3] William M. Shenkel, *Principles and Practices of Industrial Real Estate: A Course Syllabus*
(Washington, Society of Industrial Realtors, 1963), p. 116; see also William N. Kinnard, Jr.
and Zenon S. Malinowski, *Highways as a Factor in Industrial Plant Manufacturing Location
Decisions*, Small Business Management Research Report (Storrs, Connecticut, University of
Connecticut, 1962).
[4] Shenkel, *Principles and Practices of Industrial Real Estate*, p. 117.
[5] *Ibid.*, pp. 118–119; Kinnard and Malinowski, *op. cit.*, Ch. 1.

ploying women find it difficult to retain their employees when the neighborhood declines markedly in character.

Finally, such neighborhoods are often characterized by narrow streets and congested traffic. This results in more expense for both shipping and receiving, because of the greater time required to pick up and deliver goods shipments in the clogged streets of the "central location."

Yet its location is often the most important single asset that the older industrial building in a central city still possesses. The difficulty is that this location is an advantage only under certain market and environmental conditions, and then only if the property is put to a new and different use. With the impetus provided by the suburbanization of industry, additional pressures have developed to reconsider the use of existing industrial properties in the light of changed conditions. This is only one set of considerations, however, and the feasibility of any proposed rehabilitation or conversion program can be assessed only after the property itself has been carefully analyzed.

Functional Obsolescence

There are two basic kinds of difficulties confronting the Realtor concerned with the best means of disposition of space in an obsolescent industrial plant. The first involves reaction to a general change in the standards (including locational requirements) of the type of uses or users for which the property was originally intended. A related issue is how the details of the structure meet the requirements of different industrial uses or users. Thus, the analyst first ascertains what types of uses the existing building may serve *at all,* and then measures *how well* the structure might serve the needs and requirements of those uses.

The market which the industrial building currently serves will have a direct impact on the operating costs, the rental income, the insurance rates, the occupancy, and finally the profits in owning and operating the building. In the analysis of the structure, emphasis must be placed on the *function* of the bricks and stones, rather than on the bricks and stones themselves. "Realtors are faced with perplexities in finding uses for obsolete buildings that were originally constructed to meet needs that have since changed. . . . Because most commercial and industrial properties were built to serve specific purposes, it is more difficult to adapt these properties to new uses." [6] However, "most of them can be adapted to serve *today's* needs. . . . We are continually looking for unwanted, outdated properties because we are convinced that most of them can be adapted so that the properties are again useful." [7]

The obsolescence of multistory industrial buildings is especially critical. The design of the building makes it difficult to remodel the structure to the needs of the occupant, especially if those needs are now expressed in terms of one-level goods and process flows. "Multiple-story buildings were gener-

---

[6] Harold Rosen, "Versatile Adaptations," *New Uses for Old Properties,* Henry S. Miller, Jr., sponsor (Chicago, National Institute of Real Estate Brokers, June, 1966), pp. 9–10.
[7] *Ibid.,* pp. 10–11.

ally constructed between 1890 and 1920 in the United States. These buildings were constructed to accommodate industry that used processes, machinery, and techniques considered obsolete today. Therefore, when the original occupant relocates, extensive rehabilitation is required to adapt the building for other uses." [8]

Exhibit 49

EXTERIOR VIEW OF MULTISTORY WAREHOUSE

Photo: A. L. Junken

The many aspects of functional obsolescence often found in combination in one multistory industrial building in a central location are well illustrated in Exhibit 49. This is an exterior view of a multistory warehouse occupying approximately 100 per cent of its site. The loading area encroaches on the sidewalk and the street, creating serious hazards to pedestrian and vehicular traffic alike, as well as inefficiency in the loading and unloading process. The overhead rails above the loading platform support an outmoded and inadequate loading crane, and access to the freight elevators to the upper floors is difficult and time-consuming. The upper stories of the building have such low ceilings that storage is limited to three layers of pallets, thereby increasing unit handling and storage costs even further. The first floor level is below grade. In brief, this is an inefficient storage-warehouse by modern

---

[8] Shenkel, *Principles and Practices of Industrial Real Estate*, p. 118.

standards. It suffers from substantial functional obsolescence, which is reflected in below-market rentals for the use of the space.

In most older, multistory buildings, inadequate plumbing and lighting facilities represent serious deterrents to employee morale. Moreover, specific structural limitations often render industrial buildings functionally obsolescent. As an illustration of the types of items that the industrial real estate broker would ordinarily consider and evaluate in the light of current standards and usage, the following listing of frequently encountered elements of functional obsolescence has been developed:

"1. Floor load capacities are too limited for automated machinery.
"2. Ceiling lights may permit only three layers of pallets when five-pallet heights may be required for economical storage. [Ceiling heights may be excessively high for office or manufacturing areas, on the other hand, resulting in increased heating cost.]
"3. Narrow column spacing may limit the building for alternative industrial purposes.
"4. Loading docks are usually inadequate for modern requirements.
"5. Freight and passenger elevators may not be adapted to current industrial needs.
"6. The mechanical equipment of the building usually requires renovation.
   a. The heating system is obsolete.
   b. Power wiring must be adapted to modern machinery.
"7. The design of the industrial space may make remodeling extremely difficult." [9]

Many of these features are illustrated in Exhibit 50, which shows a typical floor view of the interior of the Hoosac Mills in New Bedford, Massachusetts. The wood floors, fire hazards, relatively low load-bearing capacity, low ceilings, narrow column spacing, and obsolescent lighting fixtures are all characteristic of the functional obsolescence of mill buildings in the northeastern United States.

Physical Deterioration

In addition to the capacity of the industrial building to serve as a site for industrial activity adequately and competitively, the physical characteristics of that space represent important considerations from the point of view of the potential renovator-developer. In attempting to estimate the feasibility of a proposed rehabilitation or conversion program, the industrial broker and his client should examine the "3 C's": condition, components, and configuration.

The condition of all parts of the structure should be carefully studied, particularly in terms of the probable costs involved in bringing the structure and its facilities to a state that will be acceptable to potential users in the market. The type of inspection checklist illustrated in Chapter 6 can be an invaluable aid to the broker in identifying the condition of the various parts of the structure. This information can provide an important basis for estimating the probable costs involved in rehabilitating the structure.

---

[9] *Ibid.*, p. 119. (The added element in brackets is the present author's.)

Exhibit 50

INTERIOR VIEW, TYPICAL FLOOR, HOOSAC MILLS, NEW BEDFORD, MASS.

Photo Courtesy R. M. Bradley & Co., Boston

Investigating the components of the structure means paying particular attention to the mechanical equipment and service facilities. This includes heating systems, wiring, elevators, plumbing fixtures and facilities, fire protection systems, and the like. Their condition and suitability for present use will provide an important guide to the cost of renovation. They will also indicate what is necessary to enhance the functional utility (or offset the functional obsolescence) of the structure.

The configuration of the structure refers to the size and shape of the space to be made available for use. For example, in what units is the floor space of the building now available, and what could be done to alter this? This is a matter of physical measurement, together with an evaluation of the prospects for removing partitions and other dividers. The field inspection that an industrial broker would undertake for a property that he is listing should bring this information to light.

The physical condition and characteristics of the structure will have an impact on its operating costs, the rents that can be obtained, and ultimately on profits. Moreover, the basic decision to go ahead with further consideration of a proposed rehabilitation or conversion program will be influenced by the cost and construction analysis. "If there are serious defects in the fundamental structure, it would be wholly unjustified to attempt renovation. Many older buildings are very strongly and solidly constructed; they have good foundations, thick walls, and good load-bearing characteristics. These are better risks for renovation than newer buildings which, through age or original faults in construction, lack the strength to withstand continued use and the occasional strains resulting from major renovation." [10]

CHARACTERISTICS OF INDUSTRIAL REHABILITATION AND CONVERSION

A variety of terms is used to describe the process of "reversing obsolescence." It is useful to distinguish among different *categories* of corrective programs and the results that they are aimed at achieving. Since there is a variety of terms applied to each process, the industrial real estate broker must attempt to be precise and clear about the idea that he is trying to convey to his client. One widely accepted set of terms is:

"Rehabilitation is restoration to satisfactory condition without changing plan, form, or style. ['This is also termed *Restoration*. Physical usefulness is prolonged; economic life is not affected.']

"Modernization is the replacement in modern style of outmoded aspects of the structure and/or equipment. ['The work improves the building and makes it conform to present usage, style, and taste. Economic life is usually extended as a result.']

"Remodeling is changing the plan, form, or style to correct functional or economic deficiencies. ['This prolongs the economic life as well.'] [11]

"Conversion consists of changing space from one use to another. ['A new highest and best use with a new and generally longer economic life emerges.']" [12]

Stated slightly differently, rehabilitation involves an effort to correct physical deficiencies and to bring the property up to a competitive level of condition and appearance. It means making repairs to the property. It may prolong the useful physical life of the structure, but it does not in any way extend its economic life.

Modernization and remodeling, on the other hand, are both intended to extend the economic life of the industrial space by making it competitive with newer, more functional space. In this sense, they involve "improving" the property.

Conversion changes the use of the space, based on an analysis which concludes that the highest and best use of the property has changed, or must be changed, in response to market pressures. It entails changing the property so that it may be put to this new highest and best use.

To avoid confusion in the use of terminology, "renovation" is used throughout the remainder of this discussion to mean the collective changes that arise from rehabilitation, modernization, remodeling, or conversion.

---

[10] Statement of Frank G. Binswanger, Jr., S.I.R., Philadelphia.

[11] American Institute of Real Estate Appraisers, *op. cit.,* p. 360. The statements in brackets are from Alan M. Purling, "Modernization of Real Estate," *Real Estate Encyclopedia,* Edith J. Friedman, ed. (Englewood Cliffs, N.J.; Prentice-Hall, 1960), pp. 1236–1237.

[12] Purling, *op. cit.,* p. 1237.

Components of Renovating Activity

In addition to recognizing the characteristics and meaning of the alternative types of programs designed to correct the effects of accrued depreciation, the industrial real estate broker should also be able to identify the kinds of specific action that each embodies.

1. *Rehabilitation.* This involves repairing and altering existing components of structures, including cleaning and decorating. Occasionally, decorating, painting, and cleaning alone will provide a satisfactory solution to a rental problem. Rehabilitation is almost invariably included within any program of renovation, but it is rarely sufficient by itself to provide a complete offset to accumulated deterioration and obsolescence.

2. *Modernization.* This consists primarily of replacing mechanical equipment or other components of the structure, which may not have worn out, but which do not provide the function currently required of industrial structures. For example, modernization commonly includes replacing a high-pressure steam heating system with a low-pressure system with automatic controls, especially in a multitenant building. Aside from reducing hazards of explosion, maintenance costs, and insurance rates, this usually lowers operating costs as well by curtailing sharply the maintenance personnel required.

Ventilating fans and duct-work will be examined for replacement with newer and larger units, as will the electrical service and hot-line equipment. Replacing obsolescent wiring with modern sheathed cables, and increasing the amperage of the electrical service are frequently other aspects of modernization.

Elevators often require serious study under a modernization proposal. This involves consideration of size, load-rating, and speed for providing acceptable service in both freight and passenger elevators. Plumbing fixtures and facilities, especially toilet and washroom facilities for employees, are commonly replaced and enlarged. Whether in manufacturing, warehousing or office space, lighting fixtures are typically replaced in a modernization program. New lighting fixtures are particularly significant, both from a practical and from a promotional point of view. "America has become illumination conscious, due in part to many years of promotion by local utility companies, and because of functional requirements of many types of tenants. New lighting has, therefore, opened another avenue in which modernization can be accomplished at relatively low cost." [13]

Architectural changes are also incorporated in modernization, although they often require what is really remodeling. However, "both major and minor architectural changes to *exterior* facades have been made with remarkable results. In some instances, the appearance of a building has been completely changed by removal of an overhanging ledge, replacing it with a straight line parapet, steam cleaning the street elevations, and painting window sash. In a more extensive modernization program, an entire new

---

[13] Purling, *op. cit.*, p. 1242.

skin of stainless steel panels has given the outward appearance of a new modern structure." [14]

Exhibit 51

BEFORE AND AFTER PHOTOGRAPHS OF EXTERIOR OF MULTI-STORY INDUSTRIAL BUILDING, SHOWING EFFECTS OF MODERNIZATION OF FACADE

From Harold Rosen, "Versatile Adaptations." *New Uses for Old Properties* (Chicago, National Institute of Real Estate Brokers, 1966), pp. 10–11.

[14] *Ibid.*, p. 1239.

The substantial visual impact of relatively simple exterior changes is vividly illustrated by the comparison of photographs in Exhibit 51. These show the same multistory industrial plant in Louisville, Kentucky, before and after renovation. The cleaner, simpler lines of the building's exterior facade give it a considerably more "modern" appearance.

A combination of modernization and rehabilitation will often result in an economical and profitable renovation program for industrial space. Essentially the same uses or users will occupy the renovated space as did before the program was undertaken. In part, the extent of the rehabilitation or modernization program will depend on the strength of the market demand for space in older buildings. "In the East, the demand for real estate continues so strong that the older buildings are receiving far more attention than they have had for many years. As a result, the only reconversion of an older building is often limited to improving the electric wiring, painting the exterior and interior, installing a new heating system and, sometimes, truck facilities and loading docks." [15]

3. *Remodeling.* Changing the floor plan or the division of the space and otherwise altering the *interior* architectural design of the structure comprises remodeling. This has also been termed "functional remodeling," and may be regarded as any change which increases the operating efficiency of the building. This would include such changes as the relocation of an awkwardly placed entrance, flooring over open light court areas in a large building, relocating loading docks and storage space, and redividing the space on each floor into new and different units.

In some instances, remodeling will also require razing outbuildings or a portion of the main building in order to provide easier vehicular access, improved circulation of traffic within the lot, better loading and unloading, and more parking area. "One of the problems of older buildings has been the lack of provision for parking and loading. Where the demand for a building has been strong, we have found that by sacrificing, for instance, a section of the building—200 feet by 100 feet—sufficient space for truck docking and parking can be made available. This, in turn, so revitalizes the building's use that it is worth more than before the alterations, in spite of the interior being smaller, because a functional layout is a major asset, often valued more than size and location." [16]

One illustrative example of a successful combination of rehabilitation, modernization, and remodeling is provided by Realtor Harold Rosen of Louisville, Kentucky, who writes:

During World War II, the federal government built for use as an aluminum extrusion operation a one-story plant of 183,000 square feet on a seven-acre tract close to the downtown area. Abandoned after the war, the property was sold at auction in 1949. The purchasers tried in vain to sell or lease the property, 'as is.' It was turned over to us in 1952. After making many alterations, including structural and exterior changes, we divided it into several units. Within six

---

[15] Frank A. Schlesinger, "Variation in Conversion," *New Uses for Old Properties,* Henry S. Miller, Jr., sponsor (Chicago, National Institute of Real Estate Brokers, June, 1966), p. 18.
[16] Schlesinger, *op. cit.,* p. 18.

months, we leased the entire property to four tenants; it became the local warehouse for a major appliance manufacturer, the site of a steel-cutting operation for a national steel company, a steel warehouse for one of the 'big four' steel companies and for a steel cartage company. The first two tenants still occupy their premises; the remaining two areas have been further divided into three. These are now occupied by a wholesale paper company, an air-filter manufacturer, and one of the five big furniture manufacturers that needed storage space. The investors are earning about 25 per cent net on this property.[17]

4. *Conversion.* A combination of rehabilitation, modernization, and remodeling may be necessary to change the uses or users in the existing structure. There may be building demolition to provide for additional parking, with the basic structure remaining the same. There may also be complete removal of the existing building in order to make way for an entirely new and different land use which represents, in the opinion of the developer and his advisers, the highest and best use of the land.

The primary consideration in converting an existing structure is that a change in demand has occurred which makes the type of space into which the existing structure can reasonably be converted a feasible, alternative use. In identifying this new use program for his client, the industrial real estate broker earns his fee.

In older central-city industrial areas, existing plants have been turned into "incubators" for new, small firms. These are general-purpose, multi-tenant structures that have been created from older, single-occupant buildings that often were highly specialized. The mill building in the northeastern United States has proved particularly susceptible to conversion to multi-firm use. The former main plant of the Fuller Brush Company in Hartford, for example, was purchased by an investor-developer, and converted into an in-town "industrial park."

Another illustration of an old mill complex that was converted into multiple occupancy by a diversified group of manufacturing and warehousing firms is provided in Exhibit 52. This shows the Jackson Mills, formerly owned by the Textron Corporation, and now owned and operated by a local industrial development commission in Nashua, New Hampshire.

Conversion from manufacturing to nonmanufacturing use is particularly effective when the building is in the central core of a major city, and the location itself represents an attraction to the other uses. For example:

Loft buildings that enjoyed some of the best locations in Chicago were slowly vacated. Obviously 'location' was the one asset that these properties still possessed, but only if it related to a new and higher use. . . . It was time to suggest upgrading by remodeling, or by a completely different use to maintain the values of a particular property, thereby raising the prestige of an entire neighborhood. Our appraisal of the loft buildings disclosed that some of those old, well-constructed ones have large floor areas, which, if remodeled, would appeal to people needing office space. Another factor was that the outmoded shipping facilities of loft buildings had caused many manufacturing tenants to seek locations else-

[17] Rosen, *op. cit.,* p. 10.

Exhibit 52

AERIAL PHOTO OF JACKSON MILLS, NASHUA, N.H.

Photo: Fairchild Aerial Surveys, Inc.

where, but did not discourage clients who were seeking office space at a lower rental than that of typical office buildings.[18]

One striking conversion along these lines is illustrated in the "Before" and "After" views that constitute Exhibits 53 and 54.

This building, a few blocks from the center of Denver, was originally constructed for wagon manufacturing in 1915, but now serves as the home office of the Woodmen of the World Insurance Company. The Realtors in the project, Fuller & Company, Denver, estimate that a similar new structure equally near downtown would have cost at least $20 per square foot. This conversion, including acquisition, was completed for about $15 per square foot.

Special-purpose industrial buildings are generally more difficult to adapt to new uses than is true of more general-purpose buildings.

One case of effective conversion from manufacturing to warehousing and storage use is provided in the following description of the disposition and conversion of a multi-building manufacturing complex.

---

[18] Thomas F. Seay, "New Lives For Old Lofts," *New Uses for Old Properties*, Henry S. Miller, Jr., sponsor (Chicago, National Institute of Real Estate Brokers, June, 1966), p. 23.

Exhibit 53

EXTERIOR, WOODMEN OF THE WORLD INSURANCE
COMPANY HEADQUARTERS, DENVER

Contractor: Judd Construction Co. Photos: Kenneth D. Watson
Courtesy Fuller & Company, Denver

Exhibit 54

INTERIOR, WOODMEN OF THE WORLD BUILDING

Courtesy Fuller & Company, Denver

The three four-story buildings were sold to one investor, who leased two of them to two moving-and-storage companies and the third to a furniture store chain for storage. The properties yielded 15 per cent net to the investor. These buildings have since been sold to the occupants. The two-story building was sold to another investor, and we leased it to four tenants: a national paper company, a floor-covering wholesaler, a discount furniture operation, and a national paper manufacturer. The net return on this property is about 15 per cent. The three one-story buildings were leased as a warehouse to a national carpet manufacturer and were then sold to an investor who was earning 13 per cent on his investment.[19]

In this case, relatively little rehabilitation, remodeling, and modernization were necessary because the space requirements of the new users were closely allied with those of the original occupant. The new firms needed relatively large floor areas, and they were attracted to the property because of less-than-market rentals.

Conversion of use often requires eliminating some or all of the buildings on the site. This is because the land is more valuable for an alternative use than for continued industrial use. The location still remains, and it often can be exploited for higher values if the conversion is a dramatic and complete one.

Of course, not all old buildings lend themselves to conversion for multitenant use, and there are examples of foolish efforts by amateurs to handle conversion. This is where 'professional know-how' is important. We must learn to evaluate and to advise accordingly. We were recently asked our opinion on a building located in a congested area; after determining that the cost of conversion was greater than the after-result would warrant, we came to the conclusion that this building was beyond salvage, had to be demolished, and that the site would return a better yield as a parking lot.[20]

In similar situations, "sometimes a neighborhood has sufficiently changed to make the value of the land exceed that of the building, however extensively it might be remodeled." [21] The problem of a large, old building in a mixed residential and industrial neighborhood, in which the residents had to travel a considerable distance to do their shopping, led to the following solution:

The result was that we demolished the building and converted the site into a three-acre shopping center for a supermarket and smaller installations—a drug store, a dry-cleaning establishment, and a bank. This proved a fine solution for the property.

Similar experiences have led us to make a point of assessing the potential value of the land and the factor of location, quite apart from the possible advantages in renovating the actual building which in many cases is secondary.[22]

[19] Rosen, *op. cit.*, p. 11.
[20] Arthur Balsam, "Rehabilitation, Operation and Management of Older Multi-Story Mill Buildings," paper presented at Society of Industrial Realtors Regional Seminar, Atlantic City, N.J., October 5, 1962, p. 4.
[21] Schlesinger, *op. cit.*, p. 18.
[22] *Ibid.*

PHYSICAL ASPECTS OF
INDUSTRIAL PROPERTY RENOVATION

In assessing the potential of an industrial property for rehabilitation, modernization, remodeling, or conversion, the Realtor must first examine critically the present physical condition and characteristics of the building. Next, he must estimate the changes necessary to meet the use requirements of the types of organizations for which the space will be designed. In order to perform this function, he must have a good operational familiarity with the terminology and the techniques of construction. Moreover, he should have a good working relationship with one or more contractors who specialize in renovation, because this is different from "scratch" construction. It is not necessary to become an expert in construction, so much as it is to know what questions to ask, and how to become a translator or communicator between the owner and the contractor.

It is also important for the broker to recognize that study of condition and appearance is not enough. The physical aspects of renovating industrial properties consist of more than redecoration, painting, and cleaning. "Just because an older property is in immaculate condition, with pride-of-ownership quality of maintenance, does not mean that it may not be subjected to citations [from code enforcement authorities] of major significance, requiring changes such as the following (to cite but a few examples):

"1. Enclosing stairwells with one-hour fire resistant material;
"2. Complete rewiring of the building because the old system is overloaded;
"3. Installation of vents for plumbing (where none were installed originally);
"4. Installation of syphon-breakers on all toilet flush valves." [23]

Replacement of Equipment

When modernization is all that is required to achieve the objectives of a renovation program, replacement of equipment will constitute the bulk of the developer's activity. A number of key elements will almost always be replaced in older buildings, particularly if they are to be converted from single to multiple occupancy.

First, lighting and ventilation must be examined and evaluated carefully. Most older industrial properties are inadequately lighted by modern standards. High ceilings in mill-type buildings can often be camouflaged by dropping modern lighting fixtures that provide ample illumination. This effectively "screens" the high-ceilinged areas above the lighting fixtures, and reduces the capital outlay required for renovation. At the same time, it improves the lighting of the floor area that is to be used.

Elevators represent a second important element of equipment that typically will require replacement. Both passenger and freight elevators in most older industrial buildings are too small in size, too slow, and have too light a load capacity to meet modern standards. Moreover, automatic self-service elevators can represent a considerable saving in labor costs. "A freight elevator can be converted to what we call constant-pressure push-button opera-

---

[23] Melnyk, *op. cit.,* pp. 108–109.

tion, which does not require an attendant. . . . This conversion pays for itself in labor savings in approximately one year." [24] Moreover, the installation of additional elevators (for example at the end of a rectangular building, opposite from the end already containing elevators) makes it possible to divide space on several floors of a multistory building and still provide necessary services to prospective tenants. Such an action may effectively double the prospects for leasing the space by enhancing the number of loading docks and platforms available to prospective tenants in the building.

A third important element of equipment that must be replaced in most renovation programs is the electrical wiring system. This is particularly important when conversion from single to multiple occupancy occurs. It is also commonly required in any modernization, since the demands of modern manufacturing and office users have created increasing pressures on electrical service.

The heating system will also usually have to be replaced. Many older industrial buildings have a high-pressure steam heating system. This is not economically feasible for multiple occupancy, unless the owner sells steam to the tenants, and can therefore include in the cost of this service the expense of keeping an operative engineer on duty at all times.

Even with a high-pressure system in which steam is sold to the tenants, it is still necessary to cut down pressure at night, utilizing a by-pass, unless one or more watchmen can be supported by the operation when the regular operative engineer is not on duty. Most industrial real estate management firms recommend that the boiler be converted to automatic operation, and that the heating system be revamped to low-pressure to provide more efficient operation. This will reduce both labor and fuel costs.

For heating, wiring, and other service facilities, it is very important to have stand-by systems throughout the building because the owner cannot afford to have a breakdown.

Structural Renovation

The renovation of the structure itself takes two forms. There is first decorating, cleaning, and the general brightening of appearance. This should not be minimized in its impact on the prospective tenant or purchaser, despite the earlier admonition about the dangers of placing sole reliance on superficial rehabilitation. In this respect, merchandising is an important consideration. The space should be clean and bright, and have eye-appeal. The improvements should be well made. "This dress-up factor cannot be stressed too strongly. . . . It has been our experience that floors that have been painted and cleaned up rent much more readily than those that we wait to do after the tenant has been obtained." [25]

In addition to merchandising considerations, however, it must be possible to provide the flexibility of space that is essential for industrial renovation to be successful. Many authorities agree, for example, that there should be one large unit to attract a major tenant, if at all possible. Whatever the actual

---

[24] Balsam, *op. cit.*, p. 3.
[25] *Ibid.*, p. 3.

division, the alterations should be undertaken with certain knowledge of what is currently marketable or rentable.

The broker must also be aware of what is permitted, as well as what is required, under local zoning ordinances and building codes. One serious problem that must be considered is the possibility of the "dangerous practice of applying retroactively every change in the building code. . . . What was built legally under permit should not become illegal because of a revision in the building code. For example, if three-foot minimum width stairways are legal today and the code is changed tomorrow to four feet, the change should not be enforced retroactively and owners required to enlarge or widen them to four feet at prohibitive cost." [26] Since the possibility does exist, the policies and requirements of the local building authorities should be checked carefully before structural renovation is undertaken.

Access and Parking

Industrial users require good access to and from highways for supplies, employees, and the distribution of their products. Moreover, adequate space for loading and unloading, docking, and materials handling on the site are increasingly significant. This is in addition to needed parking facilities for employees and visitors. Shipping and receiving are extremely expensive items for most industrial organizations, and anything that can expedite the handling of materials will enhance the profitability of the operation.

Therefore, any program of conversion or rehabilitation will, if possible, include a provision for additional space for parking, and for loading and unloading. This can help offset the competitive disadvantage of the multistory building as opposed to the outlying one-story industrial building. "Naturally, a one-story building has more appeal to the manufacturer or distributor, but by enlarging and improving the loading docks and the access to them, installing new elevators, and creating better access to both, we can wipe out part of the appeal." [27]

Materials handling is regarded as absolutely critical to the success of an industrial operation. Thus, it is often suggested that "excess" buildings be demolished to provide additional space on the site for parking, loading docks, and access to both. This may even include a section of the main building.

Where conversion from single occupancy to multiple occupancy is underway, loading facilities should be made available for each section or unit being created in the new pattern in the building. This involves a combination of loading facilities at ground level, with elevators to the upper floors.

Proposals to demolish buildings require careful study of the construction of those buildings or sections to be razed. Very strong construction, such as steel-reinforced concrete, is extremely difficult and expensive to demolish. Unforeseen demolition costs can jeopardize the financial practicability of the conversion project.

Although primary emphasis in renovation and conversion projects is

---

[26] Melnyk, *op. cit.,* p. 109.
[27] Balsam, *op. cit.,* p. 3.

placed on private investment by developers, urban renewal provides a possible source of additional sites for expansion. If existing industrial properties fit into the planned reuse pattern for the neighborhood, the space on the site on which the building is located can be conserved by providing additional land for parking and access on adjacent parcels.

Relationships Between Physical Characteristics and Uses

The industrial real estate broker must know enough about construction and construction costs to be able to estimate when a proposed project is feasible. The measure of feasibility is an expected profit in excess of anticipated costs. For the project to be profitable, the new space must be competitively marketable. Therefore, the broker should understand the appeal of major structural components to possible users.

As an example, a significant rehabilitation-conversion project in Chicago owed much of its success to the broker's recognition of one outstanding characteristic of the building as a potential attraction for a new user. In this case, there was the added peculiarity that the conversion of use was from nonmanufacturing to manufacturing:

A warehouse of 300,000 square feet, with railroad and river siding had direct access to the Kennedy Expressway [in Chicago], making location the prime consideration. Each floor had a 300-pound floor load and 50,000 square feet. At the time of purchase, a warehouse operator was renting space to multiple tenants, with a return so small that the building could not be kept in repair.

The floor load and location captured the imagination of the purchasers of the property. Their faith was shared by a printing company that net-leased the entire building for 25 years, with two five-year options thereafter.[28]

This is one case in which knowledge about physical characteristics and the requirements of certain types of users made it possible for a broker with imagination and understanding to complete a transaction. In the listing that follows, an effort is made to relate the requirements of particular groups of users of industrial space to major structural features. This listing is by no means all-inclusive, but it does indicate the range of considerations available to the alert broker.

1. *Walls.*
    a. High walls with few windows are good for warehouse uses, especially when the bottoms of the windows are six feet or higher from the floor.
    b. Lower walls containing many windows are good for assembly or manufacturing uses; they should still be at least 12 feet high, however.
    c. Smooth walls, such as finished concrete or plastered brick, are particularly suitable for food processing operations.
    d. Masonry walls (brick, concrete or concrete block) are preferred when protection from the elements is particularly important.
    e. In extremely high hangar-type buildings where heating and cooling are not important considerations, steel or galvanized iron walls will suffice.

---

[28] Seay, *op. cit.,* p. 24.

2. *Floors.*
   a. Floors which are tail-gate high or railroad-car high are desirable for warehouse or distribution uses; alternatively, lowered docks or ramps providing tail-gate level docking facilities will suffice.
   b. Street-level floors are attractive when tow-motors are used to transport materials directly between the interior of the building and the street.
   c. Level floors are essential for most assembly or engineering operations.
   d. Sloping floors with floor drains are necessary when the industrial use requires washing down the floors, as in food processing.

3. *Ceilings and Roofs.*
   a. Flat ceilings are most useful when the user is a food processor, an office, or an engineering department, and where wide spans without posts are not required; if wide spans are needed, a false flat ceiling can be installed.
   b. Open ceilings which leave rafters and trusses or beams exposed provide more height between posts, and are more usable for warehousing and distribution uses.
   c. When a more finished appearance is desired, as in the case of engineering or assembly operations, lower open ceilings can be provided through tapered steel beams.
   d. Open ceilings provide more cubic space within a given structure, making uses that require "stacking" of goods more feasible.
   e. Open ceilinged space is easier to cool without air conditioning, but more difficult to heat and light.
   f. Uses requiring cranes, hoists, or monorails necessitate emphasis on the load-bearing capacity of ceilings and roofs.

4. *Electrical Requirements.*
   a. Warehouse and distribution uses usually require minimal lighting, and little or no additional power installation; they are compatible with the open ceiling despite the greater difficulty in heating it.
   b. Assembly and manufacturing uses require much better lighting, and emphasize power wiring. Power panels are important for most users, because each will want to distribute its machinery differently. Therefore, the location of the actual conduits is not usually a basic or fundamental consideration.
   c. Power wiring distribution can be very costly; installing power wiring on "speculation" is quite hazardous financially.

5. *Plumbing Requirements.*
   a. The number of toilet facilities will vary directly with the number of employees, and will be further influenced by the sex distribution of the employees. The number of personnel in the operation, rather than the size of the building or floor area occupied, is a basic determinant of plumbing requirements.
   b. Warehouse and distribution uses normally have few employees, and require few toilet and washroom facilities; manufacturing, office and assembly operations, on the other hand, have relatively high plumbing requirements.
   c. If the manufacturer-user of the industrial space uses water in the process, plumbing requirements will increase significantly.

6. *Office and Personnel Requirements.*
   a. Office sizes and needs are determined by the number and type of office personnel, and by the number of outside visitors.

b. Requirements for parking facilities, restaurant facilities and related activities are directly determined by the number of personnel and visitors.[29]

Armed with information indicated by the foregoing, especially if this information is tailored to his own market area, the broker can effectively advise an owner-client about the most appropriate renovation program for a "problem" industrial property.

MARKET ASPECTS OF INDUSTRIAL REAL ESTATE RENOVATION

The decision whether to renovate an existing industrial building is an investment decision which must be based on careful analysis of the current forces of market supply and demand. The demand analysis consists of first identifying the prospective users of the particular type of space. Next, the needs and requirements of those users must be carefully noted and evaluated. Finally, the industrial broker must indicate to his client what course of action is required to develop market acceptability for the space in question.

Demand Analysis: Identification of Prospective Users

When renovation has been proposed, the industrial real estate broker must consider the property in the light of three basic groups of characteristics: its location, which cannot be changed, although access to the site can be improved; the building(s) on the site, which can be altered or even removed, usually at considerable expense; and the facilities and equipment in the structure, which can be replaced most readily and at least cost.

A consideration of location reveals first that most "problem" industrial properties are in central city locations. Indeed, this is part of the "problem." It may also be part of the advantage of the property, provided the proper use can be found. Central locations are usually found in concentrations of good labor, along public transportation lines, and convenient to large shopping districts. "Buildings located in such areas provide an advantage to the tenants in competing for skilled labor in certain industries, such as: the garment trade, graphic arts, and electronic assembly, where a high percentage of women are employed. Women, more than men, will seek employment first in areas close to home, where they have good shopping facilities and convenient public transportation." [30] Moreover, the relative safety and reputation of the area are important for activities employing women. Since many office activities often employ large numbers of women, a safe and convenient central location enhances the prospects for successful conversion of industrial loft buildings.

"Owners whose loft buildings are in a location attractive to office tenants can consider conversion to office occupancy. In most instances where such conversion has been made, the owner is enjoying a high percentage of oc-

---

[29] This list was adapted from several sources, including university extension course outlines used throughout the United States.
[30] Balsam, op. cit., p. 2.

cupancy, with substantially higher rentals." [31] At the same time, when a multistory industrial building is renovated for multiple occupancy, it usually rents for substantially less than new, one-story space. There can be an important comparative rent advantage on the side of the loft building renovated for office use.

In addition, not all companies are high enough credits to support a build-lease or special-purpose transaction. These users must turn to lower priced space. There are also well-rated companies who wish to be located near centers of transportation and labor supply, while keeping their overhead down. Such firms are prime prospects for loft or mill-building space converted to multiple occupancy.

Some companies can still take advantage of gravity processes. Because of vandalism, there are also others who do not want to be located on the first floor. Multistory, multiple-occupant buildings appeal to such users.

Finally, activities with space requirements similar to those of industrial uses are often prime candidates for occupancy in converted industrial space. For example, converted industrial space can be particularly attractive to moving-and-storage companies, and to warehousing or storage operations:

A multiple-story textile mill (160,000 square feet) was rehabilitated and leased to a furniture dealer for his showroom, two moving-and-storage companies, and a magazine distributor. A wholesale grocery complex (four-story and one-story) was sold to a liquor distributor, who took the first floor of the four-story building. The remaining three stories of this building were then leased to a department store as storage. The one-story structure was subdivided and leased to a publisher, a trucking company, and a manufacturer of component parts for the automobile industry.

[Another example is] a food-preserving plant (a five-story and a one-story building) that was sold to an investor who leased it to a moving-and-storage company. The tenant recently bought the property.[32]

Analysis of User Requirements

Most users who will be attracted to converted or rehabilitated space in existing industrial buildings will find a particular advantage in the lower rentals that are associated with older buildings, particularly in comparison with rentals in new, outlying locations.

Large space users generally find that extensive areas of high-ceilinged floor space, with wide column spacing, are most suitable and adaptable to their needs and purposes. Generally, the higher the ceiling heights and the wider the column spacing, the more marketable the renovated space will be.

In conversions, particular attention should be paid to retaining ground floor area, because this is often easiest to rent. At the same time, industrial brokers should "give thought to a new look at what you now consider your multistory 'dogs' which you cannot sell and consider them in the light of single tenancies of big floor areas. There really is no difference whether the

---

[31] Purling, *op. cit.*, p. 1245.
[32] Rosen, *op. cit.*, p. 11.

space is on the third floor or on the ground floor if the other amenities are there and you can guarantee privacy." [33]

Another important consideration in analyzing the requirements and needs of users is that there must be compatibility among uses and users. The goal of the owner (and of the broker) in maximizing tenancy and income can be defeated through careless or thoughtless selection of tenants. It is not enough that each individual tenant find the space suitable for his needs; each must not interfere with the appropriate use of the space by the others.

Developing Marketing Acceptability

Having identified the most likely users of the industrial space to be renovated, and having further identified their space needs and requirements, the broker is in a position to recommend an appropriate course of action to his client, designed to meet those needs and requirements. If specific tenants have not been found for the space before renovation begins, then the process is speculative. The best advice the broker can give his client is to make the space as generally acceptable and as generally marketable as possible. This means creating the largest units that the building will permit (preferably one unit of occupancy per floor), with the highest ceiling heights and the widest column spacing that the structural characteristics of the space will allow.

More specifically, providing access and parking represents a major aspect of any renovation program. Ease of access and utilization by truckers, in particular, must be improved. Enlarged parking and turnaround areas will make it easier for trucks to get in and out. This will, in turn, reduce expensive turnaround and handling time, and related charges to the tenants of the building. As noted earlier, this can often be accomplished through the demolition of sheds and other outbuildings. Shipping and receiving are extremely expensive for most industrial organizations, and anything in a location that reduces these expenses will make that location considerably more attractive to prospective tenants. "The ability to get materials in and out quickly and easily can make the difference between getting a tenant or not. This is important for manufacturing activities, and is even more significant for wholesaling and distribution." [34]

Materials handling entails good loading docks and platforms, preferably at least one for each separate section of the building. Loading platforms at tail gate height (often provided by raising the platform or scooping out the ramp) and enlarged materials handling and loading docks, covered for all-weather ease in loading and unloading, will substantially enhance the attractions of the building for industrial users. This is often expensive renovation, but it usually pays off in continued, steady occupancy.

The transfer of goods between shippers and loading docks is still only one aspect of the total materials handling problem. Goods must be brought into the building and shipped out as well. A combination of conveyor facilities

---

[33] J. D. Sawyer, "Industrial Property Investment Opportunities," *Advanced Course in the Techniques of Industrial Real Estate* (Washington, Society of Industrial Realtors, 1964).
[34] Interview with Arthur Balsam, S.J.R., Philadelphia.

and elevators is extremely critical here. These also represent substantial investments, but they pay off handsomely in improved tenancy when there is basic market demand in the first place. One S.I.R., reporting on a case handled by his firm in Philadelphia, stated that "we recommended the demolition of several nonbearing walls to increase the open areas, the opening of walls between buildings to provide larger units, installation of one additional passenger elevator, the converting of one existing freight elevator to combination passenger and freight service, and the installation of one new freight elevator." [35] In the same case, "we advised the demolition of some small sheds and buildings so as to afford better access to the loading docks, which were inadequate for multitenant use, and also suggested the enlargement of the existing and creation of additional loading docks, adjacent to the various elevators." [36] Thus, access, parking, loading docks, and elevators all constitute important segments of the effort to solve the materials and goods handling problem. If this can be dealt with effectively, a major advantage is gained in the proposed industrial renovation program.

In addition to creating an appropriate environment for materials handling, a renovation program for an industrial building must concern itself with the space units being created. The preceding quotation indicated that nonbearing walls were removed, and walls between buildings opened in order to provide larger units. This is one example of acceptance of the earlier statement that the larger the unit that can be provided, the more marketable the space is likely to be. Equally important, however, is the basic question of whether the space is so arranged that it is likely to be leased once the improvements are made.

If the process is speculative, the broadest market is usually served by rehabilitation or conversion for one occupant per floor. Then it is possible to adapt and adjust the space later as tenants are signed. As an alternative, it is recommended that a building be set up for the use of one specific major tenant, and then the remainder of the space made as generally marketable as possible for future rental.

The *conformation* of the building determines the pattern of development of each floor, and quite possibly the feasibility of rehabilitation or conversion at all. That is to say, the floor plan must lend itself well to conversion, and to multiple use. For example, a building with passenger elevators at each end, and freight elevators in a bank in the middle, is much more likely to be adaptable to multiple occupancy than is a building with both types of elevators all concentrated at one end.

Market acceptability also depends upon the rent at which the space can be made available to tenants. One of the attractions already noted for renovated multiple-occupant buildings is that they usually rent for less per square foot than do comparable one-story, single-occupant industrial plants. In contemplating a rehabilitation or conversion program, the developer and his broker must consider carefully the rents that they will be required to charge in order to make the project pay. Although rentals are generally low on

---

[35] Balsam, *op. cit.*, p. 3.
[36] *Ibid.*

converted loft or mill space, a well-conceived and properly merchandized development program can still result in high occupancy rates and good returns over time.

One means of making rentals relatively low is to reduce operating costs as much as is consistent with the maintenance of appropriate and necessary building services. Automatic equipment provides one solution to this problem, even though it may involve a larger capital outlay at the beginning. This applies to elevators, heating systems, alarm systems, and the like.

FINANCIAL AND INVESTMENT ASPECTS OF INDUSTRIAL RENOVATION

The experience of industrial brokers and their clients over the years demonstrates conclusively that there are excellent investment opportunities in acquiring and renovating older buildings. The risks are high, but so are the returns, provided the program is undertaken with proper planning and appropriate professional advice.

Each building and each case is unique. All that can be provided for the broker or the developer is a guide which details what to look for, as well as what to avoid. Perhaps the most important ingredient in successful investment in properties for rehabilitation and conversion is imagination, or flexibility in thinking and planning. For example, one S.I.R. helped convert a basement into what became, in effect, a covered loading dock. A lack of loading facilities at ground level was circumvented, and direct, inside loading and unloading into the freight elevator was made possible. In some instances, it is important to know that conveyors can handle a given load more rapidly than can elevators. As further examples of flexibility of thought, scooping out a basement area or tearing out a second floor have both proved effective on occasion in providing required ground-floor ceiling heights.[37]

Feasibility Analysis

If it is possible to acquire or to convert space more cheaply than it can be built, then the space can be rented for less than the going market rate and still produce a large net return. This is the goal toward which most developers strive in undertaking industrial rehabilitation or conversion. A project appears to be feasible when the anticipated net returns (rental and service income, less operating costs) are high enough to represent adequate compensation for the risk involved and for the expenditure of time, effort, and money to create the new space.

Feasibility analysis consists essentially of asking the questions: Will it pay? Does it make economic sense for the investor-developer to embark on the proposed program, or has functional obsolescence reached such a level that it cannot be offset effectively?

In this phase of the analysis of a proposed rehabilitation or conversion project, the services of a professional industrial real estate appraiser, experienced in the analysis of renovations, can be extremely helpful. His approach

[37] Interview with Arthur Balsam, S.I.R.

is essentially to estimate the value of the property on a "before and after" basis. That is to say, he estimates the value of the property prior to the start of the renovation program, "as is." He then estimates the value that the property will have after the project is completed, based upon anticipated rentals and operating expenses.

The anticipated net return is capitalized to a present worth estimate, utilizing the analytical techniques explained in Chapters 12 and 13. The difference between the estimated value before the renovation program, and the estimated value after its completion, represents the increase in value that will be created as a result of the expenditure of time, effort, and money on the part of the developer. After his development expenses are deducted, it then remains to decide whether the anticipated profit is adequate to compensate for his effort and risk-taking. This cannot be predetermined. It is based upon the facts of the individual case, and on the projected income and operating expense estimates. However, since there is relatively high risk involved in rehabilitation and conversion, the returns required by developers to make such an investment attractive are also relatively high.

Market Standards

Until a feasibility analysis is completed, the appropriateness of embarking on any given rehabilitation or conversion program is uncertain. At the same time, there are standards and guides which have been developed by experienced practitioners in the field. Each has his own specific guides as to whether or not a particular property is susceptible to successful rehabilitation. Because of differences in terminology and emphasis on the part of the individual writers, some minor variations will be found from one listing to another. All have certain basic components in common, however. These are presented in generalized form here. Many sources of specific lists are cited for further analysis.[38]

1. *Location.* In order for an industrial property to warrant serious consideration for rehabilitation or conversion, it must be well located in a stable area. The zoning in the area must permit the uses that are proposed. It is desirable for the property to be centrally located, with good access to highway transportation. A central location provides access to a large labor pool, as well as to public transportation. Because many employees are likely to be female, proximity to good shopping is a decided advantage, as is safety of the environment.

2. *Site.* There should be good on-site access to loading facilities. Those loading facilities should be adequate to meet the needs of the most likely tenants. As indicated in the preceding section of this chapter, materials and goods handling facilities can be more important than any other single consideration in attracting appropriate tenants to the property. There should also be adequate parking, at least for visitors and for shippers, on the site.

3. *Structure.* The building must be well built and structurally sound. Both the physical condition of the structure and the condition and type of

---

[38] See, for example, Melnyk, *op. cit.,* pp. 96–99; Purling, *op. cit.,* pp. 1237–1238; Shenkel, *Principles and Practices of Industrial Real Estate,* pp. 120–121.

equipment are also important. A building which is structurally sound, but which contains outmoded equipment, can still be a prime candidate for rehabilitation or conversion. A structure which can be converted readily to large units of open space on each floor has a decided competitive advantage over a building which must remain divided into many small segments on each floor.

4. *Financial Considerations.* If it is to be purchased by an investor for subsequent renovation, an industrial property must be available at a low price. Often this is the only reason many industrial renovations are feasible. When a building can be acquired at a price "below the market," low rents are possible. This is necessary to attract potential users in a competitive market. Adequate financing must be available to the developer, or the project will not be feasible. Since institutional mortgage funds are generally denied developers of renovation projects, a relatively high proportion of equity capital is required, unless purchase-money mortgage financing can be arranged. Purchase-money financing on favorable terms can be the most attractive inducement to the creation of a feasible project.

5. *Costs.* A project is much more likely to be feasible if the costs of conversion are low in comparison with the purchase price of the property, and in comparison with the rentals that are anticipated in the first year or two. The lower the capital costs, the greater the prospect for profit for any given level of rental income. Thus, the project in which conversion or rehabilitation can be achieved most readily is the one most likely to be feasible.

6. *Marketability.* The more marketable the rehabilitated or converted space appears, the more feasible the project will appear to the investor (and to his sources of financing). A large proportion of floor area should be on the ground floor; ceiling heights should be relatively high; and column spacing should be relatively wide. The units of floor area should be large and the use of the space highly flexible. These components make an especially attractive combination for light industrial uses.

Investment Returns

The returns on industrial renovation projects are relatively high because there are high risks involved. Most projects are at least partly speculative, and many are entirely so. In addition, the equity funds of the developer are often tied up for as much as three years during construction and the subsequent leasing period. The compensation for having equity funds immobilized so long must be fairly substantial.

The returns to the investor-developer take two forms. First, there is the prospect of a high annual rate of return, as measured by the ratio of net operating income to the investment of the owner. The other ingredient in profit is the capital gain that is often anticipated when the renovated property has been completely rented or "leased up," and is then sold on the open market. This prospect is enhanced if properties susceptible to renovation can be acquired at relatively low prices. In Chicago, for example, "the increasing vacancies in loft buildings had brought prices low enough to make it become economically feasible to purchase them and plan a remodeling program, provided the location justified it. Since remodeling programs can be very expensive, the buildings must be 'bought right' if large-scale renovations are planned." [39]

The relatively high rates of return expected on rehabilitation or conversion projects must be derived from relatively low rentals. While rentals are low, so are vacancy rates. This means that the effective gross to the owner is fairly strong and stable. Moreover, an appropriate renovation program will result in substantially reduced operating costs. As one example, a complex of four-story mill-type buildings totaling 600,000 square feet was sold for $500,000. "When all our prices were in, we found that the total cost for all the improvements and those projected to be done, floor by floor, as tenants were obtained, would be approximately $250,000. However, in addition to making the space rentable, we would be able to cut our labor costs from $40,000 to $16,000 [per year], a considerable saving. . . . We estimated that we would be able to cut our fuel bill by approximately $8,000, so that our total saving was estimated at $37,500." [40] While not all anticipated savings may be as dramatic as those indicated in this example, there are real savings to be effected through an appropriate and carefully planned program of modernization, rehabilitation, and/or remodeling.

Annual rates of return approximating 15 per cent are not uncommon for successful renovation projects. Revenues include not only rentals, but also the sale of utilities in many instances. Whatever the origin of the revenues, the cases from Harold Rosen of Louisville, Kentucky, cited in earlier sections of this chapter, showed net returns to investors on their expenditures of 25, 15, 15, 13 and 15 per cent. [41] As a final example, another case in the Chicago area is cited:

> Prior to the remodeling program, the monthly income of this property was $1,275 per month, $15,300 annually. After remodeling, the annual income rose to $43,320. The average annual rental per square foot jumped from $.96 (not serviced) to $2.52 (limited service). The $75,000 expended on exterior work and $75,000 interior work, brought the total cost of conversion to $150,000. The return on the cost of conversion is about 17 per cent. [42]

Investment Characteristics

Industrial renovation involves generally higher risks, and considerably higher equity commitments from investors (unless they can arrange purchase-money mortgage financing from a seller) than most other types of industrial real estate investment. If the developer already owns the property, he is limited to the use of his own equity funds, or to short-term borrowing from a bank based on his own personal credit. There is virtually no "normal" credit available to finance the conversion or rehabilitation of industrial space. Financing is particularly difficult to obtain if the construction program is entirely speculative. Occasionally, modest financing may be obtained if ten-

---

[39] Seay, *op. cit.,* p. 23.
[40] Balsam, *op. cit.,* p. 3.
[41] Rosen, *op. cit.,* pp. 10–11.
[42] Seay, *op. cit.,* p. 21.

ants are signed in advance, but usually the amount is not substantial because most tenants interested in renovated properties are not high credits.

Relatively large sums are required in industrial renovations, and one of the peculiarities of this type of investment is that the funds tend to be committed for a substantial period of time before a meaningful return is received. This can easily be 24 to 36 months.

Two general types of investors are found in this area of activity. The first is the user firm which is seeking expansion, and which incidentally becomes an investor. Frequently, such purchasers are able to obtain assistance in financing the acquisition of their property from public development corporations. These leaders want to encourage the expansion of employment in the area, and assist in the renovation of industrial space to further that objective.

The second type of investor is a developer seeking a profit on the renovation. It may be a construction firm with sufficient resources to undertake such a project, or it may be the former industrial owner-occupant who has not yet been able to sell it. More frequently, however, it is an investment organization specifically interested in the profits from renovation. Industrial firms owning plants they formerly occupied are generally too impatient or too uneasy to accept with equanimity the risks inherent in rehabilitating and converting their own space. If an owner firm is able to undertake such a project successfully, however, it stands to gain considerably more than it would through sale of the property "as is." Still, most industrial brokers report that they generally advise such clients to sell the property immediately and let someone else worry about conversion or rehabilitation.

Because substantial amounts of equity funds are required, purchasers and developers of industrial properties under renovation programs are often real estate holding companies, investment syndicates, or trusts. These have the advantages of being able to accumulate large quantities of equity funds readily, and of being able to take risks that institutional investors are prohibited from assuming. When they are successful, the returns compensate them well. Because the market is thin on the purchasing side, there are additional pressures on the owners of "problem" properties to sell at relatively low prices, thereby enhancing the chances of success for the large investment company.

The substantial risks, and the need for substantial sums of equity money over relatively long periods, make it vital to have expert technical advice available.

In discussing a highly successful large renovation project on which the new purchaser developed a 20 per cent net annual return, one S.I.R. has stated: "The original major manufacturer just was not oriented to the real estate situation. It was best for him to get out, and he got out almost at book. The people who came in knew what they were doing and knew how to do it, and they, in turn, made a handsome profit within a two-year period." [43]

[43] Frank G. Binswanger, Jr., "Techniques in the Rehabilitation and Marketing of Problem Properties," *Advanced Course in the Techniques of Industrial Real Estate* (Washington, Society of Industrial Realtors, 1964).

THE ROLE OF THE INDUSTRIAL REAL ESTATE BROKER IN RENOVATION PROGRAMS

Because of the complexities and the risks involved in rehabilitation and conversion work, substantial demands are placed on the broker. Indeed, a high degree of specialization is desirable because of the many pitfalls that can overtake anyone participating in rehabilitation or conversion work. Why, then, should the industrial real estate broker even consider becoming involved in such projects? Experienced brokers writing about this field give several reasons:

1. "Older properties can be tremendously profitable; substantial values can be created that did not exist before; good, long-term incomes can be created." [44]
2. "There is a satisfaction, beyond dollars, in taking a building which is a liability to its owner and turning it into an asset to the community job-wise, an excellent investment for the owner, and a good income-producer for the managing broker." [45]
3. There is personal gratification in overcoming a substantial and challenging problem.
4. There is real service to an owner who is otherwise stuck with a "problem" property.
5. Excellent public relations are provided for the industrial broker for future business, which is often highly remunerative.

The task of the broker is to identify an effective means of resolving the particular problem posed by the property in question. This takes experience, imagination, knowledge, and a certain amount of courage. It requires the ability to advise convincingly, as well as knowing when to bring in outside experts and technicians. "Professional experience in finding and analyzing potentialities [of older buildings] can be of invaluable assistance to the investor. Without such know-how, there is greater risk than the prudent investor wishes to incur; with it, there is a good chance of acquiring an investment which will be profitable for years to come." [46] The advice and assistance that the industrial real estate specialist provides the potential investor fall under several major headings.

Construction and Cost Analysis

The broker participating in renovation activities must keep up with contractors and learn the terms and techniques of construction in this particular field. He must know what questions to ask, and he must be able to communicate effectively between the owner and the contractor. Although he does not have to be a construction expert, he must know enough about conversion costs to serve the interests of his client effectively.

Feasibility Analysis

The broker must know enough about manufacturing and distribution pro-

[44] Melnyk, *op. cit.*, p. 91.
[45] Balsam, *op. cit.*, p. 1.
[46] Binswanger, *op. cit.*

cesses to appreciate what kind of space is usable for different types of industry, and to be quite specific in advising his client about the requirements of particular industries. It is then possible to identify the most appropriate type of use for the space which a rehabilitation or conversion project can develop. The broker must recognize that he will probably require the assistance of an experienced appraiser in estimating "before and after" values. The broker is often the best source of information about the rents that can be expected and the costs that will be involved.

Financial Analysis

Although he is not necessarily a financial expert, and may require the advice of an accountant or a mortgage banker, the broker can recognize those improvements and alterations which are most likely to reduce costs for the owner and increase his net operating revenues. In addition, he should be able to identify the types of improvements or changes in the property that will reduce the operating costs of the tenant firms, such as quicker turn-around time for shippers and easier materials handling with better docking facilities.

Leasing and Management

In the final analysis, no rehabilitation, remodeling, modernization, or conversion program is successful until the renovated space has been marketed— either sold or leased. The principles and techniques involved are those considered in Chapter 6. The only difference is that the market to which the broker addresses himself in this instance is more narrowly defined. In order to make the program successful, it is occasionally necessary to plan for one "key" tenant, and then develop the rest of the space more or less on speculation.

Sales

In two types of situations, properties appropriate for renovation represent sales brokerage opportunities for the broker. In the first case, resales or sales subsequent to renovation offer capital gains prospects for the owner-developer of the renovated building. As in all sales transactions, it is the broker's function to advise his client on price and on timing. If the rehabilitation and conversion program has been handled effectively, there is an opportunity for a substantial additional commission for the broker when the property is subsequently sold.

On the other hand, there are situations in which an owner should be advised to sell immediately. It may be that the owner, particularly an industrial firm no longer interested in occupying the space itself, is not willing to wait or to take the risks involved in a rehabilitation or conversion program. Such a situation is illustrated in the following exchange:

Q: What did you advise the manufacturing company to do?
A: Sell. They drove us crazy trying to tell us how to fix it up. Their engineering people were not oriented to this kind of conversion. Unless they would have been willing to say 'Look, you do it and do not bother us

about it. The money is here to finish the job,' it would not work. They were not that type. They wanted to know about every little item, and the ideal situation for everybody in this particular case was for them to sell.[47]

Finally, it may be that rehabilitation or conversion is simply not economically feasible for the property in question. Under these circumstances, it is best for the owner to get rid of the property.

SELECTED REFERENCES

American Institute of Real Estate Appraisers, *The Appraisal of Real Estate,* 4th ed. (Chicago, The Author, 1964).

Balsam, Arthur, "Rehabilitation, Operation and Management of Older Multi-Story Mill Buildings," paper presented at Society of Industrial Realtors Regional Seminar, Atlantic City, New Jersey, October 5, 1962.

Institute of Real Estate Management, *Rehabilitation As a Business* (Washington, The Author, 1952):
   Ewald, L. A., and Ewald, George C., "Dollars and Sense—as Applied to the Conversion of a Loft Building into a Modern Office Building";
   Goodrich, Harold S., "Rehabilitation and the Property Manager";
   Thorpe, Benjamin, "How to Turn a White Elephant into Valuable Property."

Kahn, Sanders A., Case, Frederick E., and Schimmel, Alfred, *Real Estate Appraisal and Investment* (New York, Ronald Press, 1963).

Korb, Irving, "Light Industrial Properties," Ch. 38 of *Training Manual for Real Estate Salesmen,* prepared for Sacramento Metropolitan Real Estate Offices, Inc. (Lafayette, Calif., Duncan B. Campbell, 1957).

Melnyk, Stephen L., "Opportunities in Older Properties," *Real Estate Investment Opportunities* (Los Angeles, California Real Estate Association, 1965).

National Institute of Real Estate Brokers, *New Uses for Old Properties,* Miller, Henry S., Jr., Sponsor (Chicago, The Author, June, 1966):
   Rosen, Harold, "Versatile Adaptations";
   Schlesinger, Frank A., "Variation in Conversion";
   Seay, Thomas F., "New Lives for Old Lofts."

Purling, Alan M., "Modernization of Real Estate," *Real Estate Encyclopedia,* Edith J. Friedman, ed. (Englewood Cliffs, N.J.; Prentice-Hall, 1960).

Shenkel, William M., *A Guide to Appraising Industrial Property* (Chicago, Society of Real Estate Appraisers, 1967).

Shenkel, William M., *Principles and Practices of Industrial Real Estate: A Course Syllabus* (Washington, Society of Industrial Realtors, 1963).

Shenkel, William M., "The Rehabilitation of Industrial Buildings," *Journal of Property Management,* Vol. 28, No. 2, Winter, 1962.

Society of Industrial Realtors, *Advanced Course in the Techniques of Industrial Real Estate* (Washington, Society of Industrial Realtors, 1964):
   Binswanger, Frank G., Jr., "Techniques in the Rehabilitation and Marketing of Problem Properties;"
   Sawyer, J. D., "Industrial Property Investment Opportunities."

[47] *Ibid.*

12 | Industrial Real Estate Valuation: General Principles

WHEN industrial real estate is to be bought or sold, there must be some agreement between buyer and seller on the transaction price or there is no transaction. When industrial space is to be leased, the rental must be agreed upon, and it will often be calculated as a percentage of either cost or value, as the discussion in Chapter 10 indicates. When industrial real estate is to be financed with a mortgage, a lending institution must have an indication of the worth of the property; this establishes the limits on the amount of loan that can be granted. In these and countless other market transactions, the question is continually raised: "What is it worth?"

In all phases of industrial real estate activity, the question of value is fundamental to nearly every action or decision that is taken by any participant in the transaction. Therefore, the broker should be familiar with the forces that combine to influence the value of industrial real estate. If he appreciates the workings of the industrial real estate market as represented by the materials in Chapters 1–11, he comprehends the forces that create value in industrial real estate.

Coupled with this basic understanding, there must also be a working knowledge of the techniques and methods of value estimation utilized by the professional real estate appraiser. Whether the broker engages in value estimation for a fee or not, he should be able to follow the reasoning of the appraiser hired to assist the broker's client in making a final decision.

The major objective in these two chapters (12 and 13) is to enable the industrial real estate specialist to recognize the basic issues involved in industrial real estate appraisal. Secondarily, the distinguishing features of industrial real estate appraisal are presented and analyzed for the enlightenment of the appraiser with little previous exposure to valuation problems concerning industrial real estate. For more detailed analyses of both the rationale and the methodology of real estate appraisal, the reader is referred to the basic texts and professional journals in the field.[1]

VALUE ESTIMATION

An appraisal is an estimate of value. As such, it is always a forecast of what is expected to prevail under a given set of market circumstances. Since anyone can make an estimate of value, however, it is necessary to go further and indicate what characterizes a good or professional appraisal. This is an estimate of value which is convincing to any reader or user, arrived at by an analysis of data developed by the appraiser. In most instances, the findings of the real estate appraiser are presented in written form, although an appraisal report (the physical, written document) should not be confused with either the appraisal (the estimate of value) or the appraisal process (the pattern of data-gathering and reasoning by which the estimate of value is reached). In the industrial real estate field, most appraisal reports are in narrative form. While space does not permit a detailed consideration of the contents of a narrative industrial real estate appraisal report, the recommended elements to be included in such a report are provided in the listing which constitutes Appendix A at the end of this chapter.

Nature of Value Estimated

Since an appraisal is an estimate of value, hopefully convincing to persons other than the appraiser, it is important to identify what value is being estimated. In the great majority of cases, this will be *Market Value*.

1. *Market Value.* If the user of the appraisal report wishes to establish a basis for a market sale transaction, the financing of the real estate, the leasing of industrial space, the exchanging of industrial real estate for some other property, or compensation for a public taking under the right of eminent domain (with or without condemnation proceedings), then market value is the appropriate focus of the appraisal estimate. Since it is so generally used, it is highly desirable for the industrial real estate broker to have a good working knowledge of what is meant by Market Value.

The most widely utilized and accepted definition of Market Value is: "The

---

[1] Throughout the discussion in these two chapters, particular emphasis is placed on the authoritative text of the American Institute of Real Estate Appraisers, *The Appraisal of Real Estate*, 4th ed. (Chicago, The Author, 1964). Special reference is also given to William M. Shenkel, *Principles and Practices of Industrial Real Estate: A Course Syllabus* (Washington, Society of Industrial Realtors, 1963), Chs. 7 & 8; Paul Fullerton, "Appraisal of Industrial Property," Ch. 16 of *Encyclopedia of Real Estate Appraising* (Englewood Cliffs, N.J., Prentice-Hall, 1959); William N. Kinnard, Jr., *A Guide to Appraising Apartments*, 2nd ed. (Chicago, Society of Real Estate Appraisers, 1966); and William M. Shenkel, *A Guide to Appraising Industrial Property* (Chicago, Society of Real Estate Appraisers, 1967). Other sources are indicated in the Selected References at the end of Chapters 12 and 13. To maintain currency both with developments in theory and with applications of techniques to new problem situations, it is recommended that *The Appraisal Journal* (American Institute of Real Estate Appraisers) and *The Real Estate Appraiser* (Society of Real Estate Appraisers) be read regularly. Finally, particular recognition should be given to Max J. Derbes, Jr., MAI, SREA, S.I.R., of New Orleans, for making available the outlines and notes which he developed in preparation for a course on industrial real estate appraisal for the American Institute of Real Estate Appraisers.

highest price estimated in terms of money which a property will bring when exposed for sale in the open market, allowing a reasonable time to find a purchaser who buys with knowledge of all the uses to which it is adapted, and for which it is capable of being used." [2] From this definition, it is clear that *Market Value* and *Market Price* are not synonymous. Market Price is the amount of money which is actually paid or offered or asked for a particular property; it is an historic fact. Market Value, on the other hand, is the price that would most likely occur under given market conditions.

An alternative way of defining Market Value, and also of explaining the meaning of that definition, together with the use of the concept, is as follows:

The highest price which a property will bring in a competitive market under all conditions requisite to a fair sale, which would result from negotiations between a buyer and a seller, each acting prudently, with knowledge, and without undue stimulus.

Regardless of the exact wording of the definition, market value contemplates the consummation of a sale and the passing of full title from seller to buyer by deed, under conditions whereby:

1. Buyer and seller are free of undue stimulus and are motivated by no more than the reactions of typical market participants;
2. Both parties are well-informed and well-advised and act prudently, each in what he considers his own best interest;
3. A reasonable time is allowed to test the market;
4. Payment is made in accordance with financing terms generally available in the community for the property type in its locale, and to the type of purchaser or investor typically involved. [3]

In seeking market value, the appraiser must recognize that the market can be defined in terms of geographic area, rent level, location, type of space, type of user, and type of purchaser. Early in the analysis, the appraiser must identify the precise segment of the market with which he is dealing. This identification helps the appraiser to develop an appropriate data program, and to identify the sources of those data.

Once the appropriate market within which value is to be estimated has been ascertained, "the appraiser must also identify who or what the typical purchaser most probably will be. This is because market value is defined or expressed from the viewpoint of the buyer." [4] The buyer may be an industrial firm seeking space for its own use. If so, the data and analysis may be different from those undertaken when the purchaser is an investor. The type of user or investor most likely to be attracted to the space in question will ultimately influence the value of the property.

The discussions in Chapters 5 and 9 have shown, for example, that life insurance companies and pension funds can and will pay more for certain types of properties because of their peculiar tax status. If the property being appraised is of a type that will normally be attractive as an investment to either or both of these groups of purchasers, the market is different from

[2] AIREA, *op. cit.*, p. 21.
[3] Kinnard, *op. cit.*, pp. 65–66.
[4] *Ibid.*, p. 4.

one in which the most likely purchaser is a manufacturing firm seeking owner-occupancy of the space.

2. *Value in Use.* This is also termed *Use Value,* and refers to the fact that the value of any real estate to its owner-occupant (for a specific use) can always be ascertained by capitalizing the anticipated future benefits to be derived from the occupancy of that real estate to a present worth estimate. This is a particularly important concept in industrial real estate appraisal, because the special-purpose (or even single-use) character of much real estate means that other uses would produce less benefits from such space. Its value, therefore, is best indicated by the present worth or capitalized value of the benefits of occupying and using that space.[5]

For instance, a major bus servicing facility specially constructed for this purpose may have a much lower value for uses other than by an interstate bus company, yet have a high special-use value to the owning bus company. The contribution of the real estate to the bus company and its operation is different from that to an auto repair company, or motor rebuilder or other possible user.

Part of the task of the industrial real estate appraiser is to decide which value is to be estimated. This is the *purpose* of the appraisal. It is not unusual for different value estimates to emerge: one for Market Value and one for Value in Use. Particularly when he is advising a client on an investment decision, the industrial real estate appraiser will find that a comparison of the two value estimates is most useful.

Basic Value Principles

Whatever concept of value is employed or sought in the appraisal analysis, the presumption is that the potential purchaser or investor is informed and will act rationally on the basis of the market and investment information received. This typical, informed purchaser is expected to select the alternative use which, at the time of the appraisal, is anticipated to produce the highest net gain or present worth. This is the highest and best use. The anticipated future net returns based on this use are capitalized into a present worth figure. Thus, the usability of the property is the ultimate determining factor in its value. It is up to the investor-purchaser to discover what the alternative uses of the property may be. The broker and appraiser together can offer him the information necessary to make an appropriate decision. In order to understand the valuation process, it is necessary first to understand a number of basic value principles, the most significant of which are indicated here.[6]

1. *Supply and Demand.* The principle of supply and demand states that

---

[5] This concept is particularly associated with Frederick M. Babcock, and is discussed in AIREA, *op. cit.,* pp. 20–22; and in Kahn, Case, and Schimmel, *Real Estate Appraisal and Investment* (New York, Ronald Press, 1963), pp. 30–32. Note also that the Market Value of general-purpose space can also be estimated by capitalizing expected net income based on market rentals.

[6] See AIREA, *op. cit.,* Ch. 3 for a detailed discussion of the entire range of real estate value principles, their interaction with one another, and their application.

value is the result of the interaction of the basic market forces of supply and demand. Therefore, it is necessary to identify these forces in the particular appraisal problem, examine them, and evaluate their impact on the property being appraised.

One important question to answer is: "The supply of and demand for what?" In the case of industrial real estate, it is the supply of and the demand for industrial space. The supply of and demand for investment properties and investment funds are secondary considerations.

2. *Highest and Best Use.*   Over the long run, urban space tends to be put to its highest and best use if investors and purchasers act rationally on the basis of the information that is provided them. The highest and best use of real estate may be defined as "that reasonably proximate and probable use which will support the highest present value." [7] Highest and best use is the basis for a wide variety of investment decisions as well as appraisal measures.

Land or site value is always estimated as if the site were available to be put to its highest and best use. In the cost approach, the reproduction cost new of those improvements which represent the highest and best use of the land tends to set the upper limit to value. If existing improvements do not represent the highest and best use of the property, then conversion or change of use is indicated. The highest and best use of improved property (land and buildings together) may not necessarily be the same as the highest and best use of the vacant site alone. If the two do not correspond, the structure is an inappropriate improvement on the land as judged by the current market. The property then suffers from functional obsolescence, economic obsolescence, or both.

The selection of highest and best use from among alternative possibilities involves a choice of both the type of use and the intensity of use of the space. Therefore, zoning and other use regulations—which typically control both type and intensity of land building use—must be studied in detail by the appraiser, because they limit this range of alternatives.

Since industrial real estate produces income to its owner, its highest and best use "can be expressed and analyzed in terms of alternative net income flows anticipated from alternative use combinations. So once again, both the type and intensity of use must be ascertained." [8] The type of use depends on the market for industrial space, while the intensity of the use depends primarily on investment considerations.

3. *Substitution.*   Basic to all comparative market analysis, which means all appraisal analysis, is the *Principle of Substitution.* "The upper limit of value of a property tends to be set by the cost of acquisition of an equally desirable substitute, providing there are no costly delays in effecting the substitution. A prudent purchaser would pay no more than the cost of acquiring such a substitute on the open market." [9] The operation of the

---

[7] Kinnard, *op. cit.*, p. 62.
[8] *Ibid.*, p. 4.
[9] *Ibid.*, p. 65.

Principle of Substitution is basic to the application of each of the "Three Approaches" to value estimation available to the appraiser.[10] If the cost of acquiring a substitute property is to be accurately estimated, it is important that truly comparable and competitive items be compared with one another. Moreover, substitute income flows must be found in the market place for an application of the income approach. These should be highly comparable or competitive with the one being appraised, with respect to risk, stability, duration, and other major components.

4. *Contribution.* The *Principle of Contribution* holds that the value of any component of a property "consists of what its addition adds to the value of the whole, or what its absence detracts from the value of the whole." [11] Economists call contribution "marginal productivity." In appraising industrial real estate, the concept of contribution is important because it provides a basis for evaluating alternative investments or alternative development programs. It is basic to a conclusion as to highest and best use. In the Cost Approach, contribution is employed to ascertain whether a physical or functional deficiency is "curable." In the Market Data or Direct Sales Comparison Approach, it provides the basic justification for adjustments between comparable sales properties and the subject property. Contribution is particularly significant in the Income Approach for estimating the value of productive factors, as well as for judging the feasibility of proposed renovation programs. In estimating Value in Use, the contribution of the real estate to the total enterprise is the only logical measure.

Fundamental Appraisal Requirements

From the foregoing principle, it can be seen that the appraisal of industrial real estate is essentially applied economics, and financial or investment analysis. The effective application of the principles to the specific case, however, requires more than economic and financial reasoning. An appropriate framework of analysis must also be developed. Three fundamental considerations are required in every appraisal. Together they represent the important first step in identifying precisely what problem the appraisal is designed to solve. They consist of the answers to three questions:

1. What value is to be estimated? (What purpose?)
2. Under what market conditions is that value to be estimated? (As of what date?)
3. What property rights are being valued?

1. *Purpose.* The purpose of any appraisal is to estimate a value. The identification of purpose in any appraisal report is an indication of which value is to be estimated. While this normally will be Market Value, it may be Value in Use, or some other value. The approach to be taken and the data to be gathered and studied will vary considerably, depending on which value is to be estimated. Therefore, at the outset the appraiser should identify what

---

[10] For a discussion of the applicability of the Principle of Substitution to each of the "Three Approaches," see AIREA, *op. cit.,* pp. 28–29, 43.

[11] Kinnard, *op. cit.,* p. 5.

value is to be estimated. In any written communication with his client, this should be stated unequivocally.

2. *"As Of" Date.* The date as of which an appraisal is made defines the market conditions, in terms of which value is estimated. The forces of supply and demand are subject to continual change. A value estimate valid under one set of market circumstances will not necessarily be appropriate if market conditions change. For example, the introduction of a new fork-lift truck capable of stacking palletized goods higher can lead to a demand for increased ceiling heights for storage space. This may make existing space with lower ceilings less marketable and hence less valuable.

Another example would be a change in mortgage interest rates, based on money market changes. These higher interest charges on mortgage loans would be reflected in increased rates of return required on investments. All things being equal, this would tend to lower values of real estate. Therefore, the date as of which the value estimate pertains should be carefully identified by the appraiser, both in his definition of the problem at the outset of the appraisal process, and in the presentation of his findings in the appraisal report.

3. *Rights Appraised.* In a strict technical sense, one can never "own" real estate. Rather, "ownership of real estate consists of the possession of enforceable rights in realty. These rights are separable, divisible, and transferable, as indicated in the so-called 'Bundle of Rights Theory.' " [12] Under ordinary circumstances, the fee simple estate is appraised, subject to any minor liens or encumbrances (such as utility easements or rights of way) that may exist on the property. In the case of real estate subject to a lease, however, the ownership "bundle" is divided between lessor and lessee. Both lessor and lessee have marketable estates in the realty. Each estate may be valued separately and independently from the value of the unencumbered fee simple estate. The estate of the lessor is called the *Leased Fee,* while that of the lessee is termed the *Leasehold Estate.*

Appraisers often value real estate as if unencumbered, which means that leases and indebtedness are ignored. While it may be interesting to a potential purchaser of industrial real estate to learn what an appraiser believes the property would bring on the open market if it were vacant and available for occupancy, a property is frequently transferred subject to an existing lease or mortgage. Indeed, in many instances a transaction is completed only *because* there is a lease on the property to a tenant whose credit reduces the risk to owner and to lender alike. In appraising industrial real estate, therefore, special attention must be paid to the rights or estates being valued.

USES OF INDUSTRIAL REAL ESTATE APPRAISALS

Value estimates on industrial real estate are sought for a variety of reasons. In understanding appraisal terminology and usage, it is extremely important for the industrial broker to recognize the sharp distinction that is

---

[12] *Ibid.,* p. 6. For a detailed discussion of the importance of rights in appraisal analysis, see AIREA, *op. cit.,* pp. 9–12.

made between the *purpose* of an appraisal and its *function*. The *purpose* of any real estate appraisal is to estimate value. The specific purpose of a particular real estate appraisal is to estimate a particular value: usually Market Value or Value in Use.

On the other hand, the *function* of a real estate appraisal is the use to which it is intended to be put by the client. While the appraiser need not know what the *function* of the appraisal is, he must know its *purpose*. The reasons for seeking industrial real estate appraisals are based on their uses or functions.

A Market Value estimate may be sought for any of the following reasons:

Sale or purchase (assist buyer and/or seller);

Listing (assist owner to set an appropriate asking price);

Leasing (establish the basis for the annual "lease factor");

Lending or financing (establish the basis for the amount of loan which can be granted; establish the amount of equity money that is necessary to be assembled);

Renovation or conversion (estimate "before and after" values);

Exchanging (establish a basis for comparison of properties exchanged);

Merger or consolidation (establish a basis for exchange of corporate securities);

Property tax assessments;

Income tax liability (establish a base for depreciation; establish the basis for capital gains calculations; provide the "reasonable" price for an option-to-purchase under a lease);

Insurance (establish a basis for co-insurance provisions, and for compensation in the event of loss);

Eminent Domain—Condemnation (establish a basis for "Just Compensation" in public takings of private property rights).

While a transaction or exchange of rights is normally contemplated in appraisals involving Market Value estimation, such a transaction is not necessary when Value in Use is estimated for the present user. To a large extent, Value in Use estimates will normally be grouped under the general heading of "investment advice," for which the appraisal provides essential market and financial information.

Investment advice, of course, can be concerned with decisions of whether to sell or lease property already owned; whether to buy or lease property to be used; and whether to hold or sell property which can conceivably be renovated or converted to a new use. In each of these decision situations, it is possible that the value to the client will be the particular value which stems from continued use and occupancy of the property, as opposed to the most probable price it would command on the open market.

In addition, much feasibility or development analysis centers around what the property is expected to be worth when the development is completed, in comparison with what it is worth or would cost now. The comparison may be between two Market Value figures, or between a Market Value and a Value-in-Use figure, depending on the character of the property. Market Value estimation does not permit a consideration of the particular requirements of the individual user or client; Value in Use does.

The industrial real estate specialist must be aware of the difference between these two measures, and the uses to which estimates of each may be put in his practice.

TECHNIQUES OF REAL ESTATE VALUATION

Armed with a working knowledge of the basic principles of real estate value, and with an appreciation of the market data and financial information necessary to complete his inquiry, the real estate appraiser applies a systematic series of logical steps known as "The Appraisal Process" to his valuation problem. This process, which is depicted in outline form in Exhibit 55, represents the framework through which the appraiser will proceed in working toward the solution of *any* valuation problem.

The various steps in the appraisal process can be grouped into three major headings: market and background analysis; application of the three approaches; and development of the final estimate of value. It is not possible in this presentation to examine in detail the various methods and techniques employed by the real estate appraiser. The answers to virtually every question concerning appraisal technique and methodology, together with substantial numbers of illustrative examples, can be found in three basic sources: American Institute of Real Estate Appraisers, *The Appraisal of Real Estate,* 4th edition; Kahn, Case and Schimmel, *Real Estate Appraisal and Investment;* and Ellwood, *Ellwood Tables for Real Estate Appraising and Financing.*[13]

Market and Background Analysis

The appraiser defines his problem by ascertaining the purpose of the appraisal, the rights to be appraised, and the date as of which the value estimate is to be made. Then he examines the market framework within which his analysis is to be undertaken. This helps to identify the data he will need, and the specific forces at work in the market environment that are pertinent to his problem. Preliminary investigation and sifting helps ensure that the attack on the appraisal problem is as efficient as possible.

The market framework is in large part defined when the purpose, date of appraisal, and rights to be appraised are indicated. In the appraisal of income-producing properties such as industrial real estate, market investigation and data-gathering may well occupy the major portion of time and effort expended by the appraiser. The appraisal report that finally emerges is in some respects similar to an iceberg, with the background and market studies representing the sub-surface (but substantially larger) portion. In deciding whether information of a particular type should be assembled or not, the test should always be: What is the impact of this factor or this information on the value of the property being appraised? Moreover, merely listing data or facts and figures which are supposed to influence value is not enough. It is the appraiser's job to show how and why these items influence the value of the property being appraised.

---

[13] Detailed citations for these works may be found in the Selected References at the end of this chapter.

Exhibit 55

THE APPRAISAL PROCESS

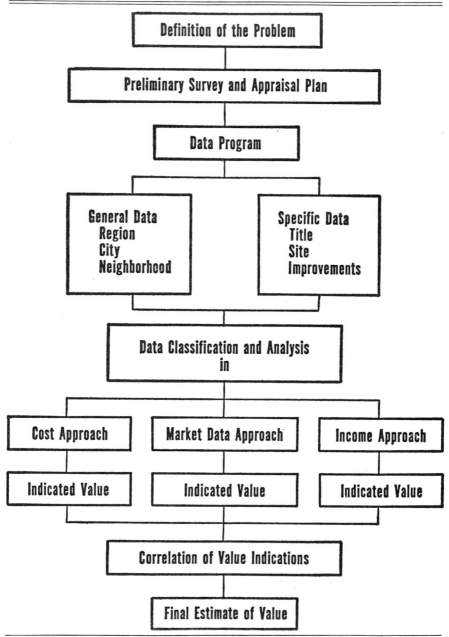

[SOURCE: American Institute of Real Estate Appraisers, *The Appraisal of Real Estate,* 4th edition, (Chicago, The Author, 1964), p. 48.

A market is an area within which properties are competing with the subject property. Therefore, it represents the range of alternatives that confront the typical buyer, tenant, investor, seller, developer, or lender. It is the area within which data must be gathered on rentals, market sales, economics, and financing.

A market area is not necessarily defined geographically. For industrial real estate in particular, competing properties may be located at a substantial distance from the subject of the appraisal. This is particularly true of highly specialized or limited-purpose industrial real estate. Economic function, rather than physical location, is the guiding determinant of what constitutes the significant market to be studied in a given appraisal assignment.

1. *Characteristics of the Real Estate Market.* The basic nature of industrial real estate determines the character of industrial real estate markets. Real estate is an immobile asset which provides services at a fixed location. Therefore, the market for real estate is either highly localized, or it is diffused. Industrial real estate markets are more likely to be widely scattered. The product is highly differentiated; much industrial real estate is custom tailored to the needs of owners or users, and direct comparison among "similar" properties is often extremely difficult. There is also a predominance of custom financing and negotiating, which further differentiates each transaction from others involving essentially similar properties. Moreover, the industrial real estate market may be an uninformed market, primarily because many items of market information are regarded as confidential by the parties to a given transaction, and not generally revealed to others.

Real estate is a relatively high-value product, and it is relatively durable physically. Moreover, industrial real estate generally involves long-term commitments on the part of users. Except for warehousing and distributive users, most industrial firms find moving difficult and expensive. The result is relatively low turnover rates for industrial real estate. The industrial real estate market is generally quite sensitive to changes in money market conditions and in technology. Finally, because most industrial space is relatively highly specialized, it is not easily adapted to new uses. As a consequence, substantial vacancy is often associated with the low turnover that characterizes much of industrial real estate.

2. *Location Analysis.* It has often been said that the three most important determinants of the value of a site are (in order of importance): location, location, and location. However, location cannot be considered in the abstract. It implies access, and the question is: Access to what?

Industrial users place varying degrees of emphasis and importance on access to labor, to markets, and/or to sources of supplies and materials. The appraiser must recognize the uses to which the space being appraised is most appropriately adapted, and then evaluate the location in terms of those qualities of access desired by the most probable users.

The first step in any location study is a detailed (but always pertinent) economic survey of the market environment within which the property is to be acquired, owned, and operated. Then the neighborhood and the site are scrutinized and evaluated so that the physical surroundings can be related properly to the appraisal problem.

The analysis of site location within the context of a metropolitan area or city is precisely the same when working on an appraisal problem as it is in judging a location as to its marketability or attractiveness for a particular use or group of users. Because of limitations of space here, the reader is referred to illustrative examples in other, more specialized presentations.[14]

One authority on the valuation of industrial real estate has indicated that there are general or "standard" factors that should be considered in estimating the value of *any* market area and site. These include: accessibility, neighborhood, restrictions, site layout, subsoil, taxes, utilities, and vacancy (of competitive properties).[15] Reinforcing this position, another argues that the technical demands of appraising industrial property require not only a specialized working knowledge of the three valuation techniques, but "additional data: (1) a knowledge of industrial zoning, construction costs, and land planning; (2) principles of taxation, local economic trends, and principles of industrial location." [16]

Thus, the appraiser must first identify the market area within which the property being appraised is currently competing, and the status of the pertinent forces of supply and demand in that market area at the time of the appraisal. He must also recognize and measure trends in those forces of supply and demand so that an appropriate forecast of market conditions can be made.

3. *Neighborhood Analysis.* A neighborhood is usually more easily identified on a map, or on the ground, than it is defined. One working definition that may be helpful is that a neighborhood is a geographic area within which any change has a direct impact on the value of the property being appraised. This is the physical environment in which the property is located, and from which it cannot move. It embodies the external forces directly bearing on the value of the property. They influence the use to which the property is going to be put, as well as the most probable user.

Some guides have been devised to ascertain the character of a neighborhood. First, there is compatibility of uses and users. This does not mean absolute identity or homogeneity. Rather, it means that greater stability and hence greater enforcement of value result when the various uses in an area do not counteract negatively on one another. For example, blighted residential areas near an industrial plant might well interfere with the attraction of female office workers, as well as requiring increased expenditures for protection against vandalism.

Zoning and land use restrictions can influence the value of any location. They limit what may be done with the property. They also provide potential protection against the intrusion of inharmonious or incompatible uses and users. Similarly, building codes or fire codes can encourage the mainte-

[14] See, for example, AIREA, *op. cit.,* Chs. 5–7; Kahn, Case and Schimmel, *op. cit.,* Chs. 4–6; Shenkel, *Principles and Practices of Industrial Real Estate,* Chs. 7–8; Shenkel, *A Guide to Appraising Industrial Property,* pp. 11–36.
[15] Fullerton, *op. cit.,* pp. 326–331.
[16] Shenkel, *Principles and Practices of Industrial Real Estate,* pp. 66–67.

nance and stability of values in an area; or they can impede growth and development because of excessive costs engendered by unreasonable or outmoded regulations arbitrarily enforced.

The availability of utilities to an area always influences value, particularly for many industrial users. It is not simply a matter of whether electrical service or gas or public water is available, but what the capacities of the adjacent distribution systems are, and what rates are charged. Utilities should be analyzed in terms of their *economic* impact in an industrial appraisal, rather than as physical factors.

Finally, access to and from the neighborhood as well as to and from the site is an important value determinant. If the streets in the vicinity are narrow and congested, it really does not matter how much on-site parking or how much space for loading and unloading is provided. The character of the neighborhood and its development influence significantly the ease or difficulty of access to and from the industrial site. This can have as much influence as any other single factor on the value of the location, by affecting its attractiveness or marketability.

4. *Sources of Information.* There are both general and specific sources of market information to which a real estate appraiser will turn when attempting to evaluate the impact of market forces on the property being appraised. They fall under four major headings. First, there are published sources of information, especially those containing data on costs, mortgage recordings, price levels, employment, operating standards or ratios. These are made available by both public and private agencies, and are cited in standard works on appraising.[17] They are particularly useful when the appraiser is seeking to set standards for "going market" conditions, in terms of which the specifics of the individual property are evaluated.

Public agencies and public records provide the next important source of information. These include deed recordings, mortgage recordings, assessment figures, building permits, subdivision plats, and the like. In addition, market studies require information on population, employment, income, industrial development, and economic base. These are also often available from public agencies, most especially the Bureau of the Census of the U.S. Department of Commerce, and constituent agencies of the U.S. Department of Housing and Urban Development. A considerable amount of extremely useful market information may be found in a public library, or (more significantly) a university or college library.

Community development groups often assemble information that is extremely useful. For example, many chambers of commerce gather reliable economic data on the local community, although the publicity brochures that are based on the data may be biased. Many local banks prepare community analyses, as do local boards of Realtors and local chapters of professional appraisal groups. Colleges and universities are becoming increasingly involved in research studies relating to the growth and development

---

[17] Annotated bibliographies as well as detailed discussions of data sources are found in AIREA, *op. cit.*; Kahn, Case and Schimmel, *op. cit.*; Kinnard, *op. cit.*; and Shenkel, *A Guide to Appraising Industrial Property.*

of individual communities or metropolitan areas. These studies often contain data extremely useful to the appraiser in evaluating the market area—and the neighborhood.

Finally, private sources should not be overlooked, even though they are more likely to represent confidential gatherers and users of such information. Nevertheless, the appraiser or industrial real estate specialist seeking to evaluate a market area would be well advised to seek help from other local brokers or appraisers, as well as from local lending institution files.

Whatever the source of the information, the appraiser is usually not justified in simply taking the word of someone else who has undertaken an investigation of a particular aspect of a local real estate market. The appraiser should always attempt to verify the information, particularly when he is dealing with sales or financing data.

Highest and Best Use

Once the data program has been completed, the first analytical conclusion that the appraiser should reach is the highest and best use, or the optimum use, of the property. This will influence the remainder of his analysis, and determine what additional information may have to be gathered.

Land or site is always valued in terms of its highest and best use. Improved real estate is valued in terms of the most profitable use to which the total property can be put. The market that will be attracted, as well as the utility of the space on that market, is a function of highest and best use. The conclusion as to highest and best use is often the most time-consuming and difficult aspect of the appraisal.

Related to the estimate of highest and best use are two other judgments that the appraiser must make before he can proceed. First, there is the question of who or what the "typical buyer" will be. This is the type of user or investor most likely to be attracted to the property. His market requirements must be ascertained before meaningful analysis can be undertaken through any of the three approaches.

The second related conclusion is the remaining economic life of the improvements. This is basically a function of the use to which the improvements are going to be put. It involves an evaluation of the market acceptability of the improvements, both at the time of the appraisal and in the foreseeable future. Since every appraisal is a forecast to the extent that it must be based upon expectations of future benefits and an estimate of their present worth, this remaining economic life must be carefully considered and evaluated.

Selection of Units of Analysis or Units of Comparison

In studying income-producing real estate in particular, the appraiser often cannot find properties for which information on sales, income, and/or cost is available, and which are otherwise fully comparable with the property being appraised. Moreover, often only generalized standards of performance for a given type of property or in a given market area are available to the appraiser. One important tool in making such data useful in the valuation of industrial real estate is the unit of comparison.

The use of units of comparison involves reducing apparently (or hopefully) competitive properties to what the appraiser concludes are appropriate units or common denominators. This often permits comparisons among properties which are otherwise not directly comparable. These units of comparison (or units of analysis) are the basic building blocks which can then be applied to individual properties to develop value, income, or cost estimates. They should represent typical units in terms of which similar real estate is actually sold, rented, or built in the applicable market. In essence, units of comparison help to convert *similar* properties to truly *comparable* properties.

Almost any unit can be developed for examination purposes by dividing one quantity by another. The appraiser (possibly assisted by the broker in the case of industrial real estate) must discover what units are meaningful in the problem at hand. This requires examining the market to discover what units reflect the ways in which buyers, sellers, tenants, builders, and/or lenders think and act.

A unit of comparison may be a physical unit, such as a square foot, a cubic foot, an acre, a front foot, or a unit-in-place. These are easy to define and to measure, but they are often less meaningful and less useful than "economic" units. The latter frequently come closer to depicting the thinking of participants in the real estate market. A commonly employed "economic" unit of analysis in the valuation of industrial properties is the Gross Rent Multiplier.

The Three Approaches

The potential purchaser of industrial real estate is theoretically confronted with three alternatives when seeking to acquire space for use or investment.

First, he can go into the market and acquire existing property. Through the operation of the Principle of Substitution, if he acts rationally, the informed purchaser will pay no more for a particular unit of real estate than the cost to him of "acquiring an equally desirable substitute property, assuming no costly delay in making the substitution." [18] This is the basis for the Market Data Approach or Direct Sales Comparison Approach. Value is estimated by comparing the sales prices of competitive properties that have sold in the immediate past, and translating them to an indication of value for the property being appraised.

Alternatively, "no man is justified in paying more for a property than that amount by which he can obtain, by purchase of a site and construction of a building, without undue delay, a property of equal desirability and utility." [19] This is the foundation of the Cost Approach to value estimation. It is based on the premise of production cost of a similar property.

Finally, in the Income Approach to value estimation, the informed purchaser would pay no more for a property than "the investment necessary to acquire, without undue delay, a comparable substitute income property of-

[18] AIREA, *op. cit.*, p. 28.
[19] *Ibid.*

fering an equally desirable net income return." [20] In this instance, comparing the present worth of alternative flows of income with that generated by the property in question tends to set its value.

All three approaches to value estimation are comparative approaches, since they utilize information about other properties, and compare them with one another in order to establish market standards. Moreover, all require comparison of data for other properties with the facts of the subject property in order to derive an indication of value. Thus, it is not proper to refer to any of these approaches as *the* "Comparative Approach."

Similarly, all three approaches utilize market information. It is therefore somewhat misleading, although quite common, to call the Direct Sales Comparison Approach the "Market Data Approach." Such usage implies that only one of the three approaches to value estimation utilizes market data, whereas in fact all three are entirely dependent upon good market information. It cannot be emphasized too strongly how critical the availability of verified, reliable market information is to value estimation. Any or all of the alternative means of estimating value are simply logical, analytical frameworks which can do nothing to improve the quality of the information that is fed into them initially. The best appraiser in the world is at a loss without reliable market data. Given such data, he can then develop a defensible estimate of value via one or more of the three approaches.

While it is theoretically and potentially possible that all three approaches may be appropriately applied to a particular appraisal problem, this is not necessarily the case. It depends to a very large extent upon the availability of good data. If information required for one or more of the approaches is not available, then any estimate of value based on that approach, or those approaches, is highly suspect.

In any given situation, moreover, one approach to value estimation may represent more closely the way in which the typical purchaser or investor approaches the problem. It is the task of the appraiser to examine the property through the eyes of the informed, rational purchaser or investor, and not to intrude his own standards or judgments into the consideration. In the case of industrial real estate, greatest reliance will often be placed on the income approach to value estimation—in part because reliable data are often not available for value estimation via the other two approaches, and in part because the capitalization of anticipated future earnings represents the closest approximation to the thinking of the informed investor in industrial real estate.

Direct Sales Comparison Approach

This approach is employed whenever dependable sales data are available for properties that are truly competitive with the subject property. In many instances it is relied on most heavily even though good income and expense information may also exist. Even in an active market for investment properties, however, information about the attitudes and aims of typical purchaser-investors should also be sought. It is not appropriate for the

---

[20] *Ibid.*

appraiser to infer motivations, regardless of the number of *bona fide* transactions available under a given set of market conditions. The appraiser must investigate the terms and conditions of the comparable sales transactions more carefully for industrial property studies than is the case with residential appraisals.

When adequate amounts of reliable data are available, the direct sales comparison approach has the advantage of being the simplest and most readily understood of the three approaches. For this reason, it tends to be favored both by courts and by laymen.

1. *Steps in the Direct Sales Comparison Approach.* In developing an estimate or indication of value via the Direct Sales Comparison Approach, the appraiser has taken five steps:

a. He has discovered similar and competitive properties in the same market for which pertinent information on sales, listings, and rentals can be obtained.
b. He has verified the prices and the rentals as to amount, terms of sale, *bona fide* character and motivating forces; the verification has been provided by the buyer, seller, lessor, lessee, or other reliable and knowledgeable source.
c. After ascertaining what the salient and meaningful elements of comparability are for the type of property in question, he has identified each of those characteristics for every comparable sale property (as well as the subject property) and compared them one with another under the general headings of time (market conditions), terms of sale, location, and physical characteristics. This step is preceded by a field inspection of both the subject property and the comparable or competitive properties.
d. He has adjusted each of the comparable sales properties in accordance with the degree of variation of these properties from the subject, basing his adjustments on observed market reactions to the presence or absence of each of the factors in question. In each instance, he has derived an adjusted sales price for the comparable property, which indicates the price at which it would have sold if it had in fact possessed all of the significant characteristics of the subject property.
e. He has developed an opinion of the value of the subject property as a whole, or the unit value of the subject property, based upon comparison of each of the sales transactions analyzed with the subject property.[21]

2. *Further Considerations.* The required inspection of both the subject property and the comparable sales property includes a physical inspection of the premises, an investigation of the public record, and an analysis of the terms, conditions, and motivation of each transaction.

Because of the difficulty in making direct comparisons among highly differentiated industrial properties, standard units of comparison (or units of analysis) are generally used in the Direct Sales Comparison Approach.

The comparisons are usually reproduced for the client in the appraisal report. In order to show appropriate adjustments, a comparative rating grid is often developed for ease of presentation and analysis. Each adjustment on the grid must be justified, preferably with direct evidence from the market

---

[21] For details and further examples, see AIREA, *op. cit.*, Chs. 20–21; and Kahn, Case and Schimmel, *op. cit.*, Ch. 8.

of how much more difference in sales price is reflected by the presence or absence of the factor in question.

Mechanically, adjustments are always made in the comparables to the subject. For example, if a comparable property has a larger lot than the subject, and this means that the comparable sold for $10,000 more than it would have with a lot the same size as the subject's, the comparable is adjusted downward by $10,000. Similarly, a deficiency in the comparable property vis-à-vis the subject means that the comparable is adjusted upward by an appropriate amount.

The adjustments can be either in dollar amounts or in percentages. Which is used depends on the type and quality of information that is available on the market. If percentage adjustments are made, however, they are usually sequential. This means that each succeeding decimal figure is multiplied by the ones that have preceded it. For example, if there is one plus adjustment of 10 per cent, and one minus adjustment of 10 per cent, the result is not $1.00 + 0.10 - 0.10 = 1.00$. Rather, it is $1.00 \times 1.10 = 1.10$; $1.10 \times 0.90 = 0.99$. In this example, little difference results. It can make a substantial difference in certain instances, however.

Consistency in treatment is imperative. It is not acceptable or correct to mix cumulative percentage adjustments with plus and minus dollar adjustments in the same analysis grid.

When the adjustments have been completed for each comparable property, the resultant figure is its adjusted sales price (not the indicated sales price of the subject property). This is based on the assumption that the analysis has accounted for all the meaningful differences between the comparable sale property and the subject. The several adjusted comparable sales figures are then brought together for the development of an indicated value of the subject property, or an indicated unit value of the subject property.

This approach may be utilized for both site valuation and value estimation of improved properties. The mechanics are precisely the same in either case. The only difference is in the units employed for analysis.

The use of the sales comparison grid in the valuation of an industrial site is illustrated in Exhibit 56. Certain elements were not included in the comparison grid, because all of the sites were identical in these respects. All properties involved were zoned for industrial use; all had utilities available at the property line; and all had rail available.

After analyzing all of the comparables, the appraiser in this case concluded that particular emphasis should be placed on sales 1, 2 and 5 since they were closer in size to the subject site. He concluded that the unit value of the subject property, which contained 36,000 square feet, was $1.00 per square foot. This resulted in a value estimate for the site of $36,000.

3. *Gross Rent Multiplier.* One important unit of comparison widely utilized among income properties in the Direct Sales Comparison Approach is the gross rent multiplier (or gross income multiplier). This is the ratio between the sales price or market value of a property and its annual gross rental or gross income receipts. Usually, an annual gross rent multiplier is utilized for industrial properties, while a monthly gross rent multiplier is

Exhibit 56

ILLUSTRATIVE SALES COMPARISON GRID
(Industrial Site Valuation by Direct Sales Comparison Approach)

Sale No.	Address	Sale Date	Sales Price	Site Size	Square Footage	Price Per Sq. Ft.	Adjustments Time	Adjustments Location	Indicated Price Per Foot
1	AAA	2/64	$ 40,000	237 x 167	39,600	$1.01	—	—	$1.01
2	BBB	7/61	40,000	200 x 235	47,000	.85	1.15	1.05	1.03
3	CCC	12/62	141,000	3.7 acres	160,227	.88	—	1.05	.92
4	DDD	8/60	10,000	100 x 120	12,000	.83	1.20	—	1.00
5	EEE	7/63	27,000	200 x 150	30,000	.90	—	1.05	.95
6	FFF	10/62	198,400	4.4 acres	192,000	1.03	—	.90	.93

more commonly employed in estimating residential values. In some areas, however, monthly multipliers are also used for industrial properties.

The gross rent multiplier has the advantages of simplicity and ease of calculation. It is also understood fairly readily. It is based on the premise that rentals and sales prices tend to move in essentially the same direction and proportion, being subject to essentially the same market forces.

The very ease of calculation is often a pitfall, because easy comparisons sometimes hide elements of noncomparability among the properties. Nevertheless, it is one widely utilized measure, particularly for developing a first approximation in making a value estimate. The "going" relationship between value or sales price and gross annual income can be ascertained in the market. Then, through independent analysis, a conclusion is reached as to the appropriate annual rental for the subject property. In the case of industrial property, this would most likely be based on an annual rental per square foot of floor area.

For example, a 10,000-square-foot, single-story industrial building might command a rental of $.90 per square foot per year. This would represent an annual rental of $9,000. If by market analysis it was concluded that the appropriate multiplier was 8.75, then the estimated value of the property (land and buildings included) would be $78,750 via the gross rent multiplier analysis. This figure might be rounded to $79,000 or even $80,000.

4. *Advantages and Disadvantages of the Direct Sales Comparison Approach.*   The most obvious advantage of the Direct Sales Comparison Approach (market data approach) to value estimation is its simplicity. It is not complex either as an idea or as a mechanical technique. Moreover, its simplicity and directness appeal both to the layman and to the courts. Relying as it does on market sales information, it has the appearance of being the most logical and the most objective of the alternative approaches to value.

Its chief limitation, however, is that it must rely on a substantial volume of accurate and verified data for its validity. If data are insufficient, the reliability of this approach is seriously reduced. Adjustments may be lengthy and complex in many instances, with relatively little available basis for evaluating the differences, even though the sales data themselves are fully verified. Beyond this, it is often difficult to ascertain whether a particular transaction is a *bona fide* sale, or whether peculiar circumstances underlay the transaction.

In estimating the value of industrial real estate, "the direct sales-comparison method is most appropriate for properties frequently sold and highly standardized. But unique, special-purpose properties make comparisons difficult." [22]

Cost Approach

The Cost Approach to value estimation is also often called the summation method, because it involves summing separate estimates of site and building value. It is based on the premise that the informed purchaser would pay no

---

[22] Shenkel, *op. cit.,* p. 74.

more for improved industrial real estate than the cost to him of *producing* a substitute property. The chief limitation of this approach is that it requires direct estimation of accrued depreciation on the improvements. This estimate becomes increasingly subjective as physical deterioration and functional obsolescence are observed. It is generally, but not exclusively, related directly to the age of the improvements.

In making an estimate of value via the Cost Approach, particular emphasis is placed on the *physical* components and characteristics of the real estate. Therefore, particular care must be taken in measuring the building and the site. Unit values are significant, and a variation in the number of units valued can lead to substantial deviation from an appropriate figure. The type of floor-plan sketch and cross section that are particularly useful to the appraiser (as well as his client) in visualizing the building and in calculating both square foot area and cubic foot volume is illustrated in Exhibit 57.

In addition to accurate measurement, special care must be taken in describing the building and other improvements. This includes both the components and features of the building and their condition. These provide the basis for the estimate of reproduction cost new, and of accrued depreciation, respectively. A checklist of the type illustrated in Chapter 6 for listing purposes will also serve as an appropriate appraisal inspection checklist, if it contains enough detail.

1. *Steps in the Cost Approach.* In developing an estimate of value via the Cost Approach, the appraiser will go through the following steps:

    a. Estimate site value as if vacant and available to be put to its highest and best use.
    b. Measure and describe improvements in detail, via inspection checklist.
    c. Estimate reproduction cost new of building(s).
    d. Estimate accrued depreciation of building(s), in terms of physical deterioration, functional obsolescence, and/or economic obsolescence.
    e. Subtract accrued depreciation from estimated reproduction cost new of building(s); the result is estimated present worth of building(s).
    f. Estimate value of site improvements (if any) in present condition.
    g. Add present worth of building(s), present value of site improvements, and site value.
    h. Round sum derived in "g" to indicated value of subject property via cost approach.

2. *Reproduction Cost New.* The starting point for value estimation in the Cost Approach is the reproduction cost new of improvements or buildings, not their replacement cost. "Replacement" involves creation of improvements with the same utility. Unless the improvements are new and represent highest and best use of the land, they will have experienced some accrued depreciation. To provide the same utility, it is necessary to create improvements with the same value as the depreciated improvements being appraised. If it were possible to estimate this directly, the complexities of estimating accrued depreciation could be circumvented entirely. Since it is not possible, reproduction cost new is utilized. This involves the hypothetical

Exhibit 57

ILLUSTRATIVE SKETCH OF FLOOR PLAN AND CROSS SECTION
FIVE-STORY INDUSTRIAL BUILDING

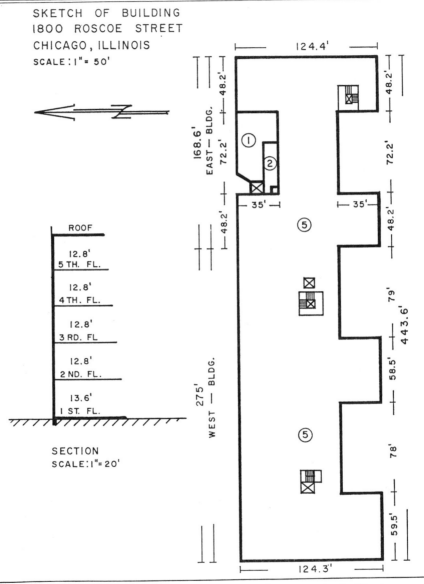

SKETCH OF BUILDING
1800 ROSCOE STREET
CHICAGO, ILLINOIS
SCALE: 1" = 50'

creation of a replica of the improvements being appraised, "in terms of price levels, materials, and construction methods in existence at the time of the appraisal." [23]

---

[23] Kinnard, *op. cit.*, p. 29.

a. *Methods of Cost Estimation.* Essentially three alternative methods are available for estimating reproduction cost new. The most complex, difficult, and expensive—as well as the most nearly accurate—is the Quantity Survey method. This involves reducing the structure to its component raw materials, and estimating the cost of all components in detail. An estimate of value via the cost approach rarely justifies utilizing this method, which is illustrated in Exhibit 58. While the prices shown in Exhibit 58 may be inappropriate for many areas, the method is exactly the same.

Exhibit 58

ILLUSTRATIVE COST ESTIMATE VIA
QUANTITY COST SURVEY: MATERIAL COST AND
LABOR COST INDIVIDUALLY PRICED

The West Wall Frame Framing Members	Wood Construction	Number of Board Feet*			
3 Posts	14" x 14" x 14'	686			
54 Lineal Feet	14" x 14" caps	882			
8 Braces	8" x 10" x 8'	427			
4 "	6" x 8" x 10'	160			
1 Beam	14" x 18" x 12'	252			
1 "	14" x 14" x 12'	196			
1 "	10" x 14" x 12'	140			
120 Lineal Feet	4" x 6" girts	240			
Total Materials Used		2,983	@	$.14	$417.62
Carpenter Labor, 15 days @ $30					450.00
					$867.62
Sheathing					
1" x 12" Sheathing		740			
Storeroom and office siding		1,600			
		2,340	@	$.12	$280.80
Carpenter Labor, 5 days @ $30					150.00
Total Materials and Labor, Wood Frame and Sheathing					$1,298.42

* The number of board feet is calculated by multiplying the width and thickness in inches by the length in feet. The resulting product, divided by 12, gives the number of board feet.

The Unit-in-Place method of cost estimation is less detailed than the Quantity Survey method, and hence less expensive to calculate. It is still time-consuming, however, because it requires an estimate of the cost of installing a standard unit of the structure. For example, the installed price per linear foot or per square foot of exterior wall might be calculated, including all labor and materials. It would also include an allowance for overhead and profit. A total cost estimate utilizing the Unit-in-Place method is illustrated in Exhibit 59.

The Comparative Unit method of cost estimation is most commonly employed, least expensive, easiest to apply, and least accurate. Either cost per

Exhibit 59

ILLUSTRATIVE COST ESTIMATE: UNIT-IN-PLACE, LABOR AND MATERIAL COSTS COMBINED

Building Costs							
Excavation	2,435	Cubic Yards at	$	2.00	....	$	4,870
Footings, Foundation ...	565	” ” ”		35.00	....		19,775
Walls, Front	11,600	Square Feet at		2.50	....		29,000
Side, Rear	42,840	” ” ”		2.30	....		98,532
Enclosure	38,016	” ” ”		1.20	....		45,619
First Floor	33,814	” ” ”		.75	....		25,361
Upper Floors	135,256	” ” ”		1.90	....		256,986
Roof Deck, Roof	33,814	” ” ”		2.00	....		67,628
Office Areas	4,000	” ” ”		1.50	....		6,000
Plant Areas	165,070	” ” ”		.50	....		82,535
Penthouses	1,000	” ” ”		3.00	....		3,000
Stack	100	feet			....		6,500
Heating	Boilers, 250 Horsepower at $90				....		22,500
	Rad. and Vent. 22,000 Square						
	Feet at $2.50				....		55,000
Plumbing	97 fixtures at $150 Average				....		14,550
	Piping, 10,000 Lineal Feet at $2.50				....		25,000
Electric	1600 Fixtures, at $35				....		56,000
	600 Outlets, at $25				....		15,000
Sprinkler	600 Outlets, Power at $50				....		30,000
	Tank 40,000 Gallon and Pump				....		15,000
	1600 Heads at $20				....		32,000
Elevators	2 at $18,000				....		36,000
Alarm, Incinerator,							
Miscellaneous					....		5,000
	Total				....	$	951,856
	Add Overhead and Profit, 20%				....		190,371
	TOTAL BUILDING COST						
	(169,070 Square Feet at $6.76)				....		$1,142,227
Other Site Improvements							
Tracks	330	Lineal Feet at $8.00			....		2,640
Fence	1,750	” ” ”	2.00		....		3,500
Paving	7,860	Square Feet at	.60		....		4,716
Shipping Platforms	2,840	” ” ”	3.50		....		9,940
Yard Grade, Gravel,							
Drainage	80,000	Square Feet			....		9,600
	TOTAL COST, UNIT-IN-PLACE				......		$1,172,623

square foot or cost per cubic foot of building is utilized. This lumps together a variety of characteristics, and requires that the standard building utilized for cost estimation be as nearly similar to the subject property as possible. While the comparative cost method is favored in many areas, the Unit-in-Place method (or a variant called the Contractor's Method) is generally required if the "breakdown method" of estimating accrued depreciation is to be applied.

The estimation of reproduction cost new via a square foot unit cost method is illustrated in Exhibit 60. It should be noted that in some instances

Exhibit 60

ILLUSTRATIVE REPRODUCTION COST ESTIMATE VIA SQUARE FOOT COST
METHOD, PLUS LUMP SUM ADDITIONS FOR SPECIAL BUILDING FEATURES

Item	Number of Square Feet	Cost Per Square Foot	Total Cost New
Office Building	1,890	$10.00	$ 18,900
Steel Frame	11,600	2.11	24,480
Add:			
Foundations and			
Concrete Slabs			$ 3,600
Miscellaneous			
Items			1,500
Temporary			
Buildings			1,370
Plumbing			500
Septic Tank			1,000
Process Piping			2,700
Electrical			11,000
Manifold Slab			230
Traveling Cranes			13,000
Land Improvements			2,500
Estimated Reproduction Cost New of Improvements			$ 80,780

the cost per square foot is based upon the total number of square feet in
the building. In other instances, it is based upon the total square foot area
of the foundation. This can make a substantial difference, and the appraiser
(as well as the broker) should make sure that the proper measure and the
appropriate unit cost are used.

b. *Use of Cost Manuals.* In many areas, it is possible to utilize standardized manuals of building costs, either for whole buildings or for building
components, if they are carefully applied to the property being appraised.
Corrections normally must be made for time and for location, based upon
index number adjustments provided by the publishers of the cost services.
For many problems the use of a cost manual and accompanying cost service
will suffice for estimating reproduction cost new. Such manuals provide
substantial detail on construction standards as well as methods and materials.
Their supplementary cost services provide a means for the appraiser and
the broker to remain current with the requirements and methods employed
in industrial construction.

3. *Accrued Depreciation.* The discussion of the need for industrial renovation contained in Chapter 11 deals with the three basic causes of accrued
depreciation: physical deterioration, functional obsolescence, and economic
obsolescence. All three are significant in the measurement of accrued depreciation for real estate valuation purposes. However, the estimation of functional obsolescence is especially important for industrial real estate valuation.
Physical deterioration is the result of wear and tear, or simple wearing out

of the structural components. Functional obsolescence is the result of reduced capacity on the part of the structure or its components to perform the function for which it is (or was) intended, in accordance with current market standards. Economic obsolescence is the result of changes external to the property itself, which have resulted in a decreased income-producing capability on the part of the property. In all three cases, accrued depreciation is measured by a deduction from reproduction cost new of the improvements.

Space does not permit a detailed consideration of all the techniques and methodology involved in estimating accrued depreciation, with their many nuances. That must be left to lengthier treatises dealing exclusively with real estate valuation.[24] Here only the highlights of technique can be considered.

a. *Curable versus Incurable.* Some accrued depreciation is held to be "curable," while other elements are regarded as "incurable." The market is the ultimate test of curability. If the evidence of the market place indicates that the expenditure of funds to correct a deficiency, an inadequacy, or a worn out item will increase the value of the property at least as much as the amount of the expenditure or "cost to cure," then the element of accrued depreciation is "curable"; otherwise it is "incurable." Therefore, curability is an economic rather than a physical consideration.

b. *Effective Age and Economic Life.* Although the Cost Approach is essentially oriented toward the physical components of the real estate, it emphasizes the economic or productive life of the improvements, rather than their physical life. The years of economic life "used up" at the time of the appraisal, based upon the observed condition of the improvements, is the "Effective Age." The difference between the Effective Age and the original Economic Life is the Remaining Economic Life. Any amortization of investment and improvements must be provided over the Remaining Economic Life. The ratio of Effective Age to Economic Life (the so-called age-life ratio) provides the simplest and most direct method for estimating accrued depreciation beyond that which is "curable." The chief difficulty with this approach is that its simplicity hides a variety of potential pitfalls. Nevertheless, a variant of the age-life method is employed in every recommended technique for estimating incurable physical deterioration.

c. *Rent Loss.* An alternative method for estimating incurable accrued depreciation, particularly functional obsolescence and/or economic obsolescence, is to calculate the present worth of the estimated loss in rental that can be attributed to the deficiency or inadequacy.

In most instances, the rent loss that is attributable to the incurable functional or economic obsolescence is capitalized via the gross rent multiplier developed in the Direct Sales Comparison Approach. Otherwise, the rent loss must somehow be reduced to a net income loss, and then capitalized

---

[24] See, for example, AIREA, *op. cit.,* Ch. 13; Kahn, Case and Schimmel, *op. cit.,* Ch. 14; Boeckh, *op. cit.,* Ch. 31. See also Max J. Derbes, Jr., "Accrued Depreciation—Classical Method," *The Real Estate Appraiser,* August, 1965, Vol. XXXI, No. 8.

at an appropriate rate of capitalization. This is complex and difficult, and rarely attempted.

4. *Site Valuation.* Site, rather than land, is valued in the case of industrial real estate. The important economic consideration is the availability of area that is immediately usable as a location for improvements. To be a site, raw land must have necessary utilities, drainage, grading, access, and zoning. The site is always valued as if available for, and put to, its highest and best use.

a. *Site Analysis.* In establishing a basis for value estimation, the major characteristics of an industrial site that would be analyzed include:

(1) *Physical characteristics:* size, shape, dimensions, topography, drainage, bearing capacity, and permeability of the soil.
(2) *Zoning and other public controls:* use restrictions, structural restrictions, setback requirements, height limitations, on-site parking requirements, safety requirements, fire code requirements.
(3) *Title limitations:* liens, easements, special assessments, covenants.
(4) *Access (location):* transit, highways, visual access; labor, customers, suppliers; ease and speed of access.
(5) *Community services (utilities):* water, sanitary sewer, storm sewer, gas, electricity, fire and police protection, trash and garbage collection, sidewalks, street lights.
(6) *Availability:* price, financing terms.

Most of these factors are items about which precise and specific factual information can be obtained. Some require analysis beyond this. It is in terms of this analysis that standards of what is appropriate, and what is acceptable, must be developed.

b. *Methods of Site Valuation.* There are essentially five methods of site valuation potentially available to the appraiser. Each has its uses and functions, which both the appraiser and the real estate broker should understand. In some instances, one may serve as a check against the other.

(1) *Direct sales comparison (market data method).* This has already been considered earlier in this chapter, and an illustration of its application is shown in Exhibit 56. This is by far the most widely utilized method, particularly when comparable sales data are available.

(2) *Abstraction or allocation.* This technique is often employed when good sales data on vacant sites are not available. The appraiser obtains information on sales of improved properties, and deducts the estimated value or contribution of the improvements from the total sales price. The remainder is the estimated or indicated value of the site. The chief difficulty with this approach, of course, lies in developing the appropriate technique for abstracting the value of the building. There is also a further problem in that the ratio of building value to land value must usually be assumed to be equal for the subject property and all "comparable" properties.

(3) *Anticipated use or development method.* This method is particularly applicable in the valuation of acreage for industrial districts or industrial parks. It consists of estimating first what the completed lots or

units would sell for when acreage is developed for resale in individual sites. From the anticipated receipts, the appraiser deducts the costs of development, including interest and carrying charges on money during the waiting period, as well as a reasonable profit for the developer. The difference between the anticipated receipts and the estimated cost of generating those receipts is the value of the acreage on the date of the appraisal. This is the amount that the developer can afford to pay for the acreage.

Exhibit 61 illustrates the application of the development cost approach to site value estimation. Under the conditions assumed for the 10-acre site in Exhibit 61, the most that a developer could afford to pay for the raw land is $16,200 or $1,620 per acre.

Exhibit 61

ILLUSTRATIVE ESTIMATE OF VALUE OF 10-ACRE INDUSTRIAL SITE VIA
DEVELOPMENT COST APPROACH

Utility Costs		
Sewer Lines		
500 feet of 8″ sewer mains at $6.00	$3,000	
100 feet of 4″ sewer laterals at $4.00	400	
		$3,400
Water Mains		
500 feet of 6″ water mains at $4.00	$2,000	
2 fire hydrants, $250 each	500	
		$2,500
Development Costs		
Engineering Costs		
Land Survey	$ 500	
Soil Survey	1,000	
		$1,500
Land Preparation		
Land clearing and leveling, $200 an acre		$2,000
Total Improvement Costs		$9,400
Estimated Sales Receipts		$40,000
Less: Improvement Costs		9,400
Less: Overhead, Profits, Sales Expense,		
Waiting Cost (36%)		14,400
Net Available for Land Purchase		$16,200

(4) *Land residual technique.* If vacant land is improved with a new building which represents the highest and best use of that land, then the reproduction cost new of that building represents its contribution to the total value of the property. The cost may therefore be taken as the measure of value. If the return on investment necessary to sustain the expenditure in the building is then deducted from the net income to the total property, the remainder or residual income is available for the ownership of the land. This residual income, capitalized at the appropriate interest rate (return on investment) yields an estimate of the present worth of the land, via the land

residual technique. Perhaps the most significant criticism of this approach is that the results are subject to wide variation because of the large number of factors that must be estimated in order to generate a final answer. It is often utilized, however, in cases in which there is literally no market for similar parcels of land, such as reuse sites in urban redevelopment areas.

Despite its serious shortcomings, the land residual technique is employed widely enough for the real estate appraiser and the industrial real estate broker to be familiar with its application. It is illustrated in Exhibit 62, which also shows the derivation of the net before capital recapture, and the application of straight-line capital recapture on a land residual basis.

Exhibit 62

ILLUSTRATIVE INDUSTRIAL SITE VALUE ESTIMATE VIA LAND RESIDUAL TECHNIQUE

Potential Gross Income, 23,500 square feet,		
@ $.65 per square foot	$15,275	
Less: Allowance for Rent Loss	− 375	
Effective Gross Income		$14,900
Less Operating Expenses:		
Real estate taxes	$1,375	
Fire and liability insurance	300	
Exterior and structural maintenance	500	
Management costs	750	
Total Operating Expenses		−2,925
Net Income Before Capital Recapture		$11,975
Less Income Required to Cover Building Investment:		
Return on $115,000 building investment, 8.5%		
(2.0% for capital recapture and 6.5%		
for investment return)		−9,775
Net Income Available to Land		$ 2,200
Land Value Estimate, $2,200 capitalized at 6.5%		
($2,200/.065)		$33,846
	or rounded	$34,000
Land Value per square foot:		
47,000 square feet ($34,000/47,000)		$ .72

(5) *Direct capitalization of net ground rents.* The ground lease is common enough in industrial real estate transactions for both the appraiser and the broker to be aware that a technique exists for estimating the value of the land, based on the net ground rents under a ground lease. If the gross rental is considered by the appraiser to be a fair market rental (economic rent), then he need only deduct what the owner must pay (property tax, insurance, management) and capitalize the net ground rent at the appropriate rate in perpetuity. Sometimes the ground rent (contract rent) represents something other than the economic rent. The rental should then be capitalized over the period of the lease, with a reversion provided at the expiration of the lease. An annuity factor is used in capitalizing a net ground rent. The lease is a contractual arrangement. It usually involves a high

degree of safety for the lessor, particularly since the leasehold improvements normally revert to him at the expiration of the lease.

5. *Final Value Estimate Via Cost Approach.* Once the estimates of site value, present worth of site improvements, and present worth of the structure have been derived, the last step in the Cost Approach is to add all three. The resulting sum is then rounded to an appropriate figure. This figure is the indicated value of the property via the Cost Approach. It does *not* set the upper limit of value, nor does it tend to do so, as is often erroneously thought. It is equally possible to overestimate accrued depreciation, or to underestimate accrued depreciation. If accrued depreciation is overestimated, then the Cost Approach estimate of value may very well be the lowest estimate. The Cost Approach simply provides one estimate of value.

The application of the Cost Approach to value estimation of an industrial warehouse is illustrated in Exhibit 63. In this case, the reproduction cost new was calculated on a square foot (comparative unit) basis. The cost of site improvements was added directly into reproduction cost new of improvements, and depreciated with the building (since together they represent an economic entity), rather than being valued and added separately. Physical incurable deterioration was estimated on an age-life basis, and incurable functional obsolescence was estimated via capitalization of the annual net income loss per square foot, attributable to a low ceiling height. Finally, no economic obsolescence was observed, so none was charged. This presentation represents a professionally acceptable format and defensible reasoning, even though it may vary somewhat from the precise indications of specific text suggestions.

6. *Advantages and Disadvantages of the Cost Approach to Value Estimation.* When new improvements represent the highest and best use of the site, then the reproduction cost new of these improvements tends to set the upper limit of value. This fact has limited applicability, however, beyond its use as the basis for judging the feasibility of proposed development. For proposed new construction, the Cost Approach estimate can be extremely valuable. It is also helpful in situations which require a conclusion of the appropriate intensity of development of a site. That is to say, it can be useful as one ingredient in the analysis of highest and best use of the site.

Cost can also serve as the basis for checking the feasibility of a renovation program. The basic question is: Will it pay? The anticipated increase in value can be checked against the estimated cost of effecting the change.

Moreover, the Cost Approach must be used when a value estimate via either the Income Approach or the Direct Sales Comparison Approach is not possible. It may also be required in instances when the data available to utilize either or both of the other approaches are regarded by the appraiser as unreliable.

A Cost Approach estimate is often used as the basis for establishing the "lease factor" for new structures. It may also be employed to ascertain the amount of financing that can be obtained for new construction.

The most serious limitation of the Cost Approach is that any property on

Exhibit 63

ILLUSTRATION OF VALUE ESTIMATION OF AN INDUSTRIAL WAREHOUSE VIA COST APPROACH

Building Calculations
Square Footage:	160 x 125 = 20,000 sq. ft.	
Cubic Footage:	20,000 x 12.5 = 250,000 cu. ft.	

Reproduction Cost New

Warehouse:	20,000 sq. ft. @ $7 = $140,000	
Asphalt Paving:	2,000	
Total Reproduction Cost:	$142,000	$142,000

Estimated Accrued Depreciation
Physical Incurable:
Remaining Economic life—40 years (85%)
Effective age—7 years (15%)

Total Physical Incurable	$ 21,300	
Physical Curable—Deferred Maintenance		
Repair asphalt paving	50	
Total Physical Deterioration	$ 21,350	

Functional Obsolescence

Curable: Trackage	$ 2,400	

Incurable: Low ceiling height
Annual Rental loss @ 6¢ per sq. ft.

20,000 @ 6¢—$1,200 cap. @ 9%	13,330	
Total Functional Obsolescence	$ 15,730	

Economic Obsolescence
There was no observed economic obsolescence
affecting the property.

Total Accrued Depreciation	$ 37,080
Reproduction Cost Less Depreciation	$104,920
Land Value	36,000
Total Value Indicated by Cost Approach	$140,920
Final Value Estimate by Cost Approach: Rounded	$141,000

which the improvements are not new, and/or do not represent the highest and best use of the site, requires a direct estimation of accrued depreciation. This is both difficult to accept as a concept, and mechanically complicated to produce. Generally speaking, the further an improved property is from the ideal of new improvements representing the highest and best use of the site, the less appropriate the application of the Cost Approach tends to be.

Beyond this, estimating reproduction cost new of industrial buildings is often quite difficult because of the highly specialized nature of many of their components. Quite often, if the Cost Approach is to be utilized in estimating the value of industrial real estate, a cost estimator and/or a specialist in the valuation of industrial equipment will be required. This adds to the expense and the time involved in making the appraisal, which the client is often unwilling to support.

Income Approach

The Income Approach to value estimation, often referred to as the capitalization of income approach, is based on the premise that the value of the real estate is equal to the present worth of the anticipated future benefits to be derived from the ownership rights in that real estate. It can be the basis for estimating either market value or value in use. In either case, the mechanical techniques are precisely the same. Only the values of the components that are inserted into the analytical framework will vary. Because industrial real estate is often investment property, it is widely agreed that this approach to value estimation should be emphasized when industrial real estate is to be valued. Even in the case of owner-occupied industrial property, the Income Approach may be applied although selecting the appropriate rate of capitalization is more difficult.

1. *Capitalization.* The process by which anticipated future net income is converted into a present worth or present value estimate is called capitalization. This lies at the heart of the Income Approach to value estimation. Capitalization merely involves dividing a net income figure (I) by an appropriate rate of capitalization (R) to obtain a value estimate (V). Therefore, $V = I/R$. This process is simple; the complexities arise because it is not easy to develop the figures to substitute for I and R. Since this rarely can be done directly, most of the effort involved in the Income Approach to value estimation consists of finding values for I and R.

There are essentially four decisions to be made before I and R can be ascertained and substituted in the formula to derive V. The four quantities involved are: the amount of annual net income that is to be capitalized (Net Income Before Capital Recapture, or NIBR); the rate of return on investment at which the income is to be capitalized, reflecting risk (Interest Rate); the period of time over which income is expected to be received and investment in improvements is expected to be recaptured (Capital Recapture Period), which determines the annual rate at which capital is to be recaptured (Capital Recapture Rate); and the method by which capital is to be recaptured, reflecting the character of the income flow (Straight-Line versus Annuity). These four determinations must be made before the necessary quantities can be developed for inclusion in the capitalization formula.

a. *Technical Note.* When a rate of capitalization is applied to net income in order to estimate value, the annual income figure is divided by the rate, expressed as a decimal figure. Thus, a net income of $1,000 per month is always expressed as $12,000 per year; and a rate of capitalization of, say, 8 per cent would be expressed as .08. Therefore, with these figures, the estimate of value would be $12,000 divided by .08, or $150,000.

In annuity capitalization, both capital recapture and interest return are included in one figure. For the sake of convenience, annuity capitalization tables have been prepared covering most interest rates and most capital recapture periods. Whole numbers, rather than fractions or decimals, are generally utilized in these annuity capitalization tables. These composite figures are called "Factors," and value is estimated by *multiplying* net income by a factor. Thus $V = I \times F$. A factor is simply the reciprocal of a rate. Any rate may be converted to a factor by dividing that rate into one, i.e., $1/R = F$.

Further, all rates and factors normally utilized in capitalization calculations presume that the net income consists of a series of annual payments made at the end of the year. The techniques for conversion of year-end payments to beginning-of-year payments are simple, and are described in several basic sources.[25] Moreover, adjustments can be made to convert income streams to accommodate payments on a semiannual, quarterly or monthly basis. In addition to the possibility of making adjustments manually, many published sets of tables make these adjustments for the user.[26]

2. *Steps in the Income Approach.* In estimating value via the Income Approach, the appraiser must go through the following steps:

- a. Estimate annual potential gross income: either economic rent of space plus service income, or contract rent plus service income.
- b. Estimate annual effective gross income by deducting an appropriate allowance for rent loss based on market experience.
- c. Estimate annual operating costs of the real estate borne by the owner, under the following headings: fixed expenses, operating expenses, repairs and maintenance, and replacements; estimates are based on appropriate operating standards.
- d. Compute estimated annual net income before capital recapture by subtracting operating costs from effective gross income.
- e. Develop an interest rate based upon evaluation of risk and going market rates, via one of several alternative methods.
- f. Estimate appropriate capital recapture period.
- g. Estimate capitalization rate, based upon interest rate and capital recapture rate; alternatively, select appropriate annuity factor.
- h. Select appropriate method of capital recapture, reflecting character of income flow (straight-line versus annuity).
- i. Select appropriate residual technique in accordance with the characteristics of the problem at hand.
- j. Apply the mechanical techniques accurately and correctly to develop an estimate of value.

3. *Gross Income Estimation.* The first step in the estimation of net income before recapture is to estimate the potential gross income for the property on an annual basis. This is based on the economic rent of the space at 100 per cent occupancy, plus any service income that may be generated from the property. In many industrial properties, particularly multitenant loft properties, the sale of utilities (service income) provides a substantial proportion of total income to the property owner.

Economic rent is the fair market rental or going market rental for space of the type in question at the time of the appraisal. It is ascertained by conducting an analysis of the local rental market. It is utilized in all cases in which there is not a long-term lease. If there is such a lease, however, and the appraisal is conditioned upon this lease, then the rent called for under the lease (Contract Rent) is utilized. It may be capitalized directly, or modi-

[25] See AIREA, *op. cit.,* Ch. 19; Kahn, Case and Schimmel, *op. cit.,* Ch. 11; Alfred A. Ring, *The Valuation of Real Estate* (Englewood Cliffs, N.J., Prentice-Hall, 1963), Ch. 14.
[26] See especially L. W. Ellwood, *Ellwood Tables for Real Estate Appraising and Financing* (Ridgewood, N.J., The Author, 1959).

fied by the present worth of the lease advantage or disadvantage. Lease arrangements are quite common among industrial properties, and contract rent is therefore widely utilized.

Contract rent is utilized in estimating the value of the leased fee (the lessor's interest), while economic rent is the basis for estimating the market value of the unencumbered fee simple estate in the realty. In many instances, particularly when contract rent is less than economic rent, estimates of the value of both the leased fee and the fee simple are made because the difference is usually the value of the leasehold estate. The applications of this point to industrial properties are considered in Chapter 13.

Potential gross income, since it is based on 100 per cent occupancy, is usually adjusted downward on the basis of standard market experience in terms of vacancy, turnover, noncollection of rent, or other rent loss. This allowance for rent loss is usually expressed as a percentage of potential gross, based upon observation of the experience of similar properties in the market. The difference between potential gross income and the allowance for rent loss is effective gross income. This is the figure which represents anticipated annual rent collections.

For industrial properties subject to a long-term lease, there need not necessarily be any allowance for rent loss, if it is expected that the tenant will pay his rent in accordance with the terms of the lease. As much care must be taken not to *underestimate* effective gross income as to *overestimate* it.

4. *Operating Costs.* In order to develop an estimate of annual net income before capital recapture, it is necessary to subtract operating costs of the real estate from effective gross income. These operating costs represent those expenditures or commitments which are normally borne by the owner of the real estate, and which are directly related to the generation of income from that real estate. They must be carefully separated from operating costs of a business enterprise, particularly if the real estate is owner-occupied.

Operating costs are divided for purposes of analysis into four general categories: fixed expenses (property taxes, property insurance); operating expenses (management, heat, power, janitorial service, etc.); repairs and maintenance (but not structural improvements); and replacements (of equipment normally replaced). The appraiser must "stabilize" operating cost statements for two reasons. First, many expenditures will vary substantially from year to year, and it is necessary to average them out over a three- to five-year period to develop a "typical" expenditure pattern for the property in question. Secondly, the real estate is valued as if subject to normal good management: neither exceptionally efficient nor exceptionally bad. As a result, the standards of the market are often utilized in order to check the acceptability of expenditures encountered in a particular set of operating statements for a given property.[27]

There are four types of expenses to the owner which are *not* operating

[27] For a much more detailed discussion of the identification and measurement of operating costs, and of the development of an operating cost statement, see AIREA, *op. cit.*, Ch. 16; and Kahn, Case and Schimmel, *op. cit.*, Ch. 9.

costs of the real estate. The appraiser and the broker must guard against including them as operating costs. They are: depreciation or capital recapture of investment in the improvements; income or business taxes of the owner; financing costs (both mortgage interest and mortgage amortization); and capital improvement expenditure.

The discussion of leases in Chapter 10 indicates clearly that there is no standard pattern of responsibility for particular items of expense by either lessor or lessee. In the valuation of industrial properties in particular, special attention must be paid to the terms of the lease to ascertain precisely what items of operating cost are borne by the lessor, and therefore what operating costs should be deducted from effective gross income in order to estimate net income. At the same time, the appraiser or broker should not be misled by the terminology of "net" leases into thinking that *no* operating costs are borne by the lessor. The terms and conditions of the specific lease(s) must be analyzed, so that the leased fee can be evaluated appropriately. The terms and conditions of typical leases for the same type of property should be ascertained, for the valuation of the fee simple.

5. *Net Income Before Recapture.* The net income figure derived by subtracting operating costs of the real estate from the effective gross is really net operating income for the real estate. It includes a capital recapture payment. It is termed "net income before recapture" because capital recapture has not yet been deducted. It is therefore a composite of return *on* investment (Interest Rate) and return *of* investment (Capital Recapture). Net income before recapture (NIBR) is the "I" in the valuation equation: $V = I/R$.

6. *Interest Rate.* The annual rate of return on the investment in real estate is called the Interest Rate. (This is distinguished from the "rate of interest," which is the term applied to the interest payment on borrowed funds.) The Interest Rate is also called the Market Rate of Interest. This rate applies equally to land and to buildings. The rate of return on the investment is usually no different whether the source of the income is the land or the improvements. Except in the case of certain ground leases or specific industrial park developments, it is impossible to differentiate (other than for purely analytical purposes) the income attributable to the land from the income attributable to the building.

The Interest Rate is expressed as an annual percentage rate of return, and constitutes compensation for the four component parts of any rate of interest: pure or riskless return for having given up liquidity or current command over assets through the ownership of funds; administrative or management costs (the costs of administering the investment or the loan, but not the costs of administering the property); a compensation for nonliquidity (particularly important in the case of industrial real estate, where the asset does not move readily on the market); and compensation for risk. Generally speaking, higher risk calls for a higher rate of return or Interest Rate.[28]

a. *Methods of Rate Selection.* Whatever the precise method employed,

---

[28] For more explanation of these considerations, see AIREA, *op. cit.,* Ch. 17; Kahn, Case and Schimmel, *op. cit.,* Ch. 10; Kinnard, *op. cit.,* pp. 35–36.

the interest rate appropriate in any income property appraisal is derived from market analysis. As a practical matter, little choice among methods usually exists in any given appraisal assignment.

If good market data are available on sales prices and on net income flows of comparable properties that have sold, then the rate indicated from these comparable sales will provide an excellent measure for the subject property by *Direct Comparison*. The difficulty is that such information is rarely available in sufficient quantity on the market at any time to make this a realistic alternative for the investor or the appraiser.

The *Band of Investment Method* is most commonly used by practicing appraisers in one of its variant forms. It involves assuming that the purchaser of income-producing real estate will trade on equity to the extent allowed by lending institutions. Therefore, the maximum mortgage at going rates will be obtained, and the remainder of net income must provide a return adequate enough to attract equity investment. The simpler version of the band of investment method is illustrated in Exhibit 64, in which it is assumed that a 50 per cent first mortgage at 6.5 per cent interest can be obtained on the property in question, and a 25 per cent second mortgage at 8 per cent interest. The remaining 25 per cent of the investment in the property (the equity) requires a 14 per cent return to be attractive to current investors. The weighted rates total 8.75 per cent. This is the indicated interest rate which would represent a rate of return on the total investment sufficient to cover 6.5 per cent on 50 per cent of it, 8 per cent on another 25 per cent of it, and 14 per cent on the remaining 25 per cent.

Exhibit 64

ILLUSTRATION OF BAND OF INVESTMENT METHOD OF INTEREST RATE SELECTION

Property Interest	Per Cent of Total Property Value	Interest Rate	Weighted Interest Rate
First Mortgage (lowest risk)	50%	6.5%	3.25%
Second Mortgage (intermediate risk)	25	8.0	2.00
Equity Interest (higher risk)	25	14.0	3.50
Interest Rate			8.75%

Although it is widely utilized, the foregoing version of the band of investment method does not take into account either the maturity of the mortgage or the fact that mortgages are likely to be direct-reduction loans, in which the equity interest of the investor increases with the passage of time. An adjustment to cover these can be made relatively easily.[29]

Other methods of interest rate selection include the "Built-up" or "Summation" method, the "Banker's Rate Selection" method, the "Market Invest-

---

[29] See especially Ellwood, *op. cit.*, for a discussion of the techniques for making the adjustments.

ment Comparison Quality" method, and the "Abstraction" method. While these are available for use by the appraiser, they have little applicability in practice.[30]

b. *Overall Rate.* The Overall Rate (OAR) is really a capitalization rate rather than an interest rate, since it includes a provision for capital recapture. It is a widely used measure of compensation for risk in real estate investment. The OAR is found by comparing net income before capital recapture to sales prices for comparable properties that have recently sold on the open market. It can also be developed via the Ellwood method, without the necessity of having direct sales comparisons. The development and use of overall rates are increasingly important for the appraiser of investment properties. The appraiser and the broker should familiarize themselves with this approach to value estimation. Several excellent sources exist for further study.[31]

7. *Capital Recapture Period.* The period over which the investor will normally seek to recapture the recoverable or depreciable investment in the improvements is called the Capital Recapture Period (Capital Recovery Period). It may or may not be equal to the economic life of the improvements. The economic life depends on market expectations of the productivity of the real estate; the capital recapture period is a direct function of investment, financial, and income tax considerations.

For owner-occupied properties and for properties owned by institutional investors, such as life insurance companies and pension funds, the remaining economic life of the improvements may well constitute the capital recapture period. On properties subject to a long-term lease, the remaining term of the lease is often the capital recapture period. For investment-type properties owned by private, profit-seeking investors, the capital recapture period may be influenced by the minimum period over which the improvements may be amortized under federal income tax regulations. The significance of these alternatives to the appraiser is that the nature of the market within which the property is most likely to be bought and sold will to a large extent determine what the capital recapture period shall be. It is therefore essential to be able to identify what type of purchaser or investor is most likely to be attracted to the property, and what the character of the user of the space (whether as owner or tenant) is most likely to be.

8. *Provision for Capital Recapture.* There are, for practical purposes, two alternative methods of providing directly for capital recapture: straight-line recovery and annuity recovery. A third theoretical possibility is the sinking-fund (or Hoskold) method. In actual practice, however, it has little applicability, and is not considered further in this discussion.[32]

---

[30] See Ring, *op. cit.,* Ch. 17 for details of these other methods; see also AIREA, *op. cit.,* Ch. 17.

[31] See, for example, Ellwood, *op. cit.;* Kinnard, *op. cit.,* pp. 38–39, 43–44; James E. Gibbons, "Mortgage-Equity Capitalization: Ellwood Method," *The Appraisal Journal,* Vol. 34, No. 2, April, 1966.

[32] Those interested in the rationale and mechanics of Sinking Fund capital recapture should consult AIREA, *op. cit.,* Chs. 18–19; Kahn, Case and Schimmel, *op. cit.,* p. 143; or Ring, *op. cit.,* Ch. 18.

Under straight-line capital recapture, the assumption is made that equal annual installments of the investment in the improvements are returned over the capital recapture period. A simple percentage figure is then calculated, which is known as the Capital Recapture Rate. For example, if the capital recapture period is 40 years, as it is in the illustrative example in Exhibit 65, then the annual payment for capital recapture is 1/40 of the investment in the improvements, or 2.5 per cent. This capital recapture rate, when added to the interest rate, constitutes the Capitalization Rate for the improvements. It is applied to improvements only, because land is presumed not to depreciate or to be recoverable over time. This does not mean that land does not change in value; however, the investment in land may not legally be recaptured for investment or income tax purposes.

The straight-line method of capital recapture carries with it the presumption that net income decreases continuously and predictably over time, because interest income is earned on only that portion of the investment in the improvements not already recovered. This implication in the mechanics of the straight-line method may be overlooked by appraisers. It explains why an apparently identical income will yield a lower value estimate if straight-line capital recapture is applied to it, in comparison with an annuity method of capital recapture. This differential is illustrated in Exhibits 65 and 66.

The straight-line capital recapture method is widely employed because it has the twin virtues of simplicity and ease of understanding. It can also be adjusted by a knowledgeable appraiser to reflect variations in risk. Its chief drawback is that it often does not reflect the way investors really think and act in the market. Moreover, it tends to result in relatively low value estimates. Finally, it is both mechanically and logically inappropriate for properties subject to a long-term lease.

The annuity (Inwood) method of capital recapture presumes that income remains constant and steady throughout the capital recapture period. Varying proportions of interest income and capital recapture are included in each annual income flow, with the segment represented by capital recapture increasing each year. The calculations are relatively complex, but many are performed in advance for the appraiser through the use of tables. The most commonly utilized table is the Inwood Table, which shows the present worth of level annuities at different interest rates over varying periods of time. These tables are typically based on annual payments made at the end of the year.[33]

The figure found in an annuity capitalization table is a "Factor" by which an annual NIBR is multiplied in order to obtain an estimate of value ($V = I \times F$). Annuity capitalization, presuming as it does a level flow of income over time, is particularly appropriate for the valuation of leased fees subject to long-term leases. The contractual character of the lease is especially adapted to annuity treatment. As the level of risk varies, it can be accommodated by altering the interest rate, which will result in a different factor, and hence a different value estimate. There is a trend toward more general use of annuity capitalization in all income property appraisals, with ad-

_____
[33] More detailed tables are provided for other income periods in Ellwood, *op. cit.*

justments in the interest rate reflecting variations in risk, rather than having a different method of capital recapture accomplish essentially the same objective.[34]

The Factor in annuity capitalization is the reciprocal of the Capitalization Rate. Any Factor can be converted into a Capitalization Rate by dividing it into 1.0.

9. *Residual Techniques.* In estimating the value of an investment or income-producing property via the Income Approach, it is usually necessary to make an assumption about one of the two physical components of the property (site or improvements), or to estimate the present worth of one independently. The derivation of the other as a residual then completes the analysis. This is necessary because Direct Capitalization (discussed in the next section) is frequently not feasible. Therefore, the appraiser must often resort to indirection in estimating value via the income approach.

a. *Building Residual Technique.* This is by far the most commonly utilized technique for income property appraisals, unless there is a long-term lease whose term is used as the capital recapture period. The building residual technique begins with the assumption that the site can be valued independently by any of the valuation techniques previously enumerated *except* the land residual technique. If this were the case, it would involve circular reasoning.

Starting from an estimate of site value, the analysis then proceeds to identify the amount of annual income necessary to provide a competitive return on the investment in the site. This is found by multiplying the value of the site by the interest rate. When subtracted from net income before recapture, this leaves the income which is available to cover the investment in buildings, including both interest return and capital recapture. At this point, depending upon whether straight-line capital recapture or annuity capitalization is employed, the income available to the investment in the buildings is either divided by the capitalization rate or multiplied by the appropriate factor. In either event, an estimate of the present worth of the buildings is derived, to which the value of the land is added. The sum is the estimate of value of the property via the Income Approach, utilizing the building residual technique.

Exhibit 65 illustrates the estimation of value of an industrial plant via the building residual technique, with straight-line capital recapture.

A similar approach is employed when an annuity method of capital recapture is combined with the building residual technique, as illustrated in Exhibit 66. The use of the same income figures result in a higher value estimate when an annuity method of capital recapture is employed, as opposed to straight-line recapture. Annuity recapture is valid only when stable income can reasonably be anticipated. The appraiser really has no choice in selecting his capital recapture method, however. The facts of the case will determine

---

[34] This is especially the case among those who subscribe to the basic thesis of L. W. Ellwood. See Ellwood, *op. cit.;* Gibbons, *op. cit.;* William N. Kinnard, Jr., "The Ellwood Approach to Valuation: A Return to Fundamentals," *The Real Estate Appraiser,* Vol. XXXII, No. 5, May, 1966.

Exhibit 65

ILLUSTRATION OF VALUE ESTIMATION OF INDUSTRIAL PLANT VIA
CAPITALIZATION OF NET INCOME, STRAIGHT-LINE CAPITAL RECAPTURE,
BUILDING RESIDUAL TECHNIQUE

Potential Gross Income, 40,762 square feet, @ $1.05			$ 42,800
Less Vacancy Rate, 5%			−2,140
Effective Gross Income			$ 40,660
Less Expenses:			
Fixed Expenses			
Property Taxes	$9,000		
Management Expenses, 3%			
of effective gross income ...	1,220		
Insurance, Fire and			
Liability	838		
Operating Expenses,			
Maintenance Expenses,			
Roof and Walls	500		
Reserve for Equipment			
Replacement	200		11,758
Net Income before Capital Recapture			$ 28,902
Less: Net Income Necessary to cover $60,000			
Investment in Land at 8%			−4,800
Net Income Available to Building			$ 24,102
Capitalization Rate (40-Year Building Life):			
Return on Capital (Interest Rate)		8.0%	
Return of Capital (Capital Recapture Rate)		2.5%	
Capitalization Rate		10.5%	
Present Worth of Building	$24,102/.105	..	$229,543
Add: Land Value			60,000
Indicated Value via Income Approach			$289,543
or rounded			$290,000

which method is the appropriate one; that is the *only* method which can
legitimately be employed in the particular appraisal assignment.

b. *Land Residual Technique.* When new improvements represent the
highest and best use of the site, and their reproduction costs are known, or
when there are similar proposed developments whose construction costs and
anticipated net income can be adequately estimated, the land residual technique is an appropriate device for estimating the value of land. It can also
be used to estimate the value of the entire property. Its application has already been illustrated in Exhibit 62, in which straight-line capital recapture
was utilized for the building. Starting with the estimate of building cost,
interest rate, capital recapture rate, and net income before recapture, the
land residual technique proceeds first to deduct the amount of annual income
necessary to cover the investment in the improvements, both through the
interest rate and through capital recapture. The remaining net income is the
amount available to cover an investment in the land. The present worth of
the land is estimated by capitalizing the net income available to the land at
the interest rate ($V = I/R$). The value of the property is then ascertained

Exhibit 66

ILLUSTRATION OF VALUE ESTIMATION OF INDUSTRIAL PLANT VIA
CAPITALIZATION OF NET INCOME: BUILDING RESIDUAL TECHNIQUE,
INWOOD PREMISE (ANNUITY METHOD)

Net Income before Capital Recapture	$ 28,902
Less Net Income Necessary to Cover $60,000	
Investment in Land at 8%	−4,800
Net Income Available to Building	$ 24,102
Present Worth of Building: 8% Interest Rate,	
Present Worth of One Per Annum (Inwood Premise),	
40-year recovery: 11.925 times $24,102	$287,416
Add: Land Value	60,000
Indicated Value via Income Approach	$347,416
or rounded	$348,000

by adding the estimated value of the land to the known cost of the improvements, and rounding the sum appropriately.

Unless the condition of new improvements representing the highest and best use of the land is met, the estimate resulting from the application of the land residual technique will normally be wide of the mark.

c. *Property Residual Technique.* Particularly when there is a long-term lease on real estate, the property residual technique may be employed. This consists of capitalizing the net income at the appropriate rate of interest, utilizing an annuity factor over the term of the lease. The result represents the present worth of the right to receive income during the term of the lease.

At the expiration of the lease, the lessor will receive full title to the real estate once again. This is termed a "reversion." That reversion may consist of land only (on the assumption that the improvements have been fully depreciated over the term of the lease), or it may consist of a combination of land and buildings. Whatever reverts to the lessor will likely have some market value. That market value must be estimated and then discounted to the present by reference to a Present Worth of One Table. That is to say, an estimate is made of the amount that an investor would pay today for the right to receive the reversion at a specified time in the future; the anticipated value of the reversion at that future date is discounted at the appropriate interest rate.[35]

The property residual technique is illustrated in Exhibit 67, in which the interest rate is 8 per cent, the term of the lease is 25 years, and the value of the reversion at the expiration of the lease is estimated to be $100,000. In estimating the present worth of the reversion, it is not acceptable to select an arbitrary figure for the estimated amount of the reversion at the expiration of the lease. It must be based on the best available evidence of what is likely to occur, as well as the most probable expectations of informed investors.

---

[35] This technique is explained and illustrated in more detail in AIREA, *op. cit.*, Chs. 19, 25; Kahn, Case and Schimmel, *op. cit.*, pp. 121–122; Ring, *op. cit.*, Ch. 20.

Exhibit 67

ILLUSTRATION OF VALUE ESTIMATE VIA PROPERTY RESIDUAL TECHNIQUE,
INCOME APPROACH

Net Income Before Capital Recapture	$ 25,000
Present Worth of Right to Receive $25,000 per year	
for 25 years (term of lease) at 8% interest rate	
(Present worth of one per annum at 8% for 25 years):	
10.675 x $25,000	266,875
Plus: Present Worth of Right to receive $100,000	
Reversion, 25 years deferred (Present worth of one	
at 8% 25 years hence): .1460 x $100,000	14,600
Indicated Value Via Income Approach	$281,475
Rounded	$282,000

10. *Direct Capitalization.* If the information is available from the market, the simplest, most direct, and most defensible technique of capitalization of net income is simply to divide NIBR by the overall rate of capitalization. This OAR is the indicated ratio (expressed as an annual percentage rate) between NIBR and sales price of comparable properties recently sold on the market. The difficulty is that in most instances such market information is not available.

a. *Ellwood Approach.* A related variant of direct capitalization with an overall capitalization rate is the Ellwood Approach, associated with the writings of L. W. Ellwood.[36] Because of the mathematical complexities involved in many of the applications of Ellwood's thinking and writings, it is possible here only to mention the analysis. It represents an important alternative method of investment analysis, and can be effectively employed in estimating the return that may be expected from an investment in income property. It is particularly helpful in testing alternative assumptions about the amount of the reversion at the end of the capital recapture period. Special emphasis is placed on the short-term orientation of the profit-seeking investor, although this is not necessarily required for the application of the Ellwood approach. Being investor-oriented, the Ellwood analysis is particularly compatible with equity-mortgage analysis, and is often regarded as one version of that approach. A critical feature of the Ellwood analysis is the development of an appropriate overall rate based upon financing and investment consideration, and the application of that overall rate directly to the anticipated net income flow.

11. *Equity-Mortgage Analysis.* Rather than dividing improved real estate into its physical components of land and buildings, as the residual techniques do; or into legal estate, as leased fee and leasehold evaluation do, the equity-mortgage analysis divides the real estate into its two major investment components: equity, and mortgage (debt). It is argued with con-

---

[36] For further details, see Ellwood, *op. cit.;* Gibbons, *op. cit.;* Kinnard, "The Ellwood Approach to Valuation," *loc. cit.*

siderable conviction that the debt financing terms available to a particular type of real estate transaction are generally predictable. These terms, as discussed at some length in Chapter 8, include the rate of interest, the mortgage maturity, amortization provisions, and the loan to value ratio. Since both the amount and the terms of mortgage financing can be estimated in advance, the mortgage constant necessary to cover annual debt service can also be predicted with a reasonably high degree of accuracy.

The difference between net income before capital recapture and mortgage debt service represents the cash flow to the investor. This, it is claimed, is the income flow that particularly interests most investors. This cash flow is then capitalized at the appropriate equity rate, obtained from analyses of what similar investors in the market are seeking and obtaining. The present worth of the equity income flow, added to the outstanding principal on the mortgage, equals the present worth of the property on the market.

This approach takes advantage of the financial and investment emphasis of the Ellwood analysis, and leads to the development of an overall rate for direct capitalization of net income. It has particular appeal to private investors in evaluating the attractiveness or feasibility of a particular commitment, in large part because it approximates their thinking with respect to income-producing real estate.

12. *Advantages and Disadvantages of the Income Approach.* The outstanding advantage of the Income Approach is that it approximates the thinking of the typical investor in income-producing real estate. For appraising industrial real estate, this is particularly important. Further, if value in use is to be estimated, then the Income Approach is most logical.

The difficulties and disadvantages of the Income Approach are numerous. They all revolve around the fact that a large number of estimates must be made, and a complex set of relationships must be developed in most cases. The appraiser may have to inject his own analytical judgment and skills into the analysis more than is desirable, in many instances. Moreover, the complexities of the Income Approach tend to leave laymen (including judges and juries) perplexed and confused. Nevertheless, the Income Approach is an important tool in the kit of every professional appraiser, and must be understood by every professional industrial real estate broker.

Correlation and Final Value Estimate

If value has been estimated by more than one approach during the course of the appraisal analysis, the final step confronting the appraiser is to reconsider these various approaches and resolve them into one estimate of value. Although many professional real estate appraisers argue that a more logical and defensible position is to provide a range of values, rather than a single value estimate, it is still necessary in most appraisal assignments to develop one specific figure. The process by which the appraiser resolves a range of estimates into one value estimate is termed "Correlation." Correlation is *not* averaging. It is an analytical process by which the various facts and procedures employed in the estimation of value via alternative ap-

Exhibit 68

THE CAPITALIZATION PROCESS

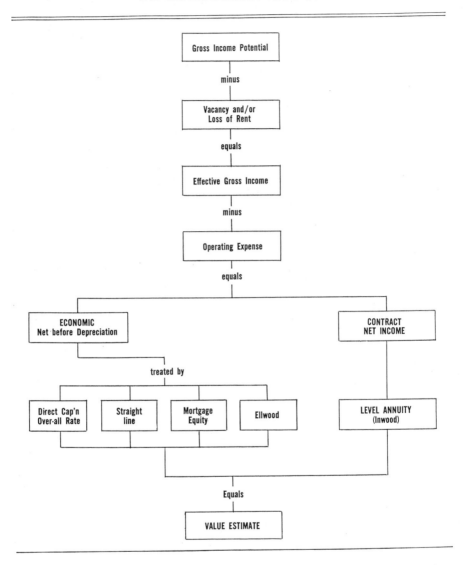

proaches are weighed and evaluated, so that each is given its appropriate emphasis in reaching a final value figure.

In addition to considerations of logic, there are also important questions of data availability. In some instances, the most appropriate method cannot be effectively employed because the data required simply are not available.

If there is no fundamental difference in the availability or quality of data for the alternative approaches, the estimate of value via the Income Approach is often regarded as most appropriate, and most logical, for industrial real estate. This is income-producing property, after all.

The final value estimate, which is derived through the process of correlation, is precisely that: an estimate. The appraiser should always round this figure to an appropriate level, in part to indicate the fact that it is indeed an estimate.

The Appraisal Report

"The appraisal report is the culmination of the appraiser's work and art. It must say clearly and convincingly what he did and why he did it. It should be capable of standing alone. Therefore, it should be a complete and consistent presentation of the materials considered and the logic followed in the appraiser's analysis. The good appraisal report will lead the reader inevitably and inexorably to the same conclusions as those reached by the appraiser." [37]

Narrative reports are commonly prepared in industrial real estate practice. This is partly because relatively large sums of money are involved. The client needs a substantial amount of evidence, in many instances, to reach a decision. Moreover, clients are often geographically distant from the property and from the appraiser. These clients are frequently financial institutions or business corporations which follow formalized procedures (i.e., decision by committee) in making decisions. Finally, the analyses contained in industrial real estate appraisals are often complex and require careful explanation and documentation.

As a guide to the ingredients of a good appraisal report, the outline contained in Appendix A to this chapter indicates what a thorough industrial real estate narrative report should contain. The listing is adapted from the requirements for demonstration appraisal reports established by the American Institute of Real Estate Appraisers, and recommended for the use of candidates for the MAI designation.

APPENDIX A

Recommended Components for a Narrative Appraisal Report on Industrial Real Estate

1. Title Page, including:
    a. Address of the property.
    b. Type of property: e.g., warehouse, multistory loft building, etc.
    c. Name and address of owner.
    d. Name and address of appraiser, and date.

---

[37] Kinnard, *A Guide to Appraising Apartments, loc. cit.,* p. 52.

2. Letter of Transmittal, including:
   a. Identification of the property.
   b. Identification of rights appraised.
   c. Purpose of appraisal and definition of value.
   d. Reference to appraisal report.
   e. Value estimate and "as of" date.
   f. Signature of appraiser.
3. Table of Contents with page references to all components of reports.
4. Summary of Salient Data and Conclusions (no more than one page). This is a brief resume to assist the client or reader, and not a summary of the entire report.
5. Assumptions and Limiting Conditions, indicating particularly items for which the appraiser either cannot or may not accept responsibility.
6. Identification of the Property: both legal description and address. The property must be unequivocally defined and described.
7. Purpose of the Appraisal: value to be estimated.
8. Definition of Value, including source.
9. Property Rights Appraised, including explanations as necessary (e.g., leased fee, leasehold, etc.).
10. Regional and City Analysis. This is a discussion of the market background: the economic, social, political, and physical forces influencing the value of real estate in general, and industrial real estate in particular, in the market area in question. It also contains an identification and explanation of that market area. This is considerably more than a listing of facts which the reader must interpret.
11. Neighborhood Data. This involves both descriptions and analyses of trends in factors directly influencing the subject property. It will include many items from the following:
    a. Delineation of the neighborhood and its relation to community growth pattern.
    b. Age and history.
    c. Per cent built up.
    d. Type of improvements and level of maintenance.
    e. Population characteristics and income level.
    f. Transportation facilities and access.
    g. Special hazards or adverse influences.
    h. Zoning and land use control.
    i. Availability, cost, and adequacy of sewers, water, electrical power, gas, or other utilities.
    j. Room for expansion and parking.
    k. Raw material supply and market.
    l. Taxes and local attitude toward industry.
    m. Labor supply, wage level, and housing.
    n. Trends in significant factors.
12. Site Data. This is an accurate description, including:
    a. Dimensions and shape.
    b. Area (size).

    c. Topography and drainage.
    d. Soil and subsoil conditions.
    e. Availability and capacity of utilities.
    f. Street improvements and access.
    g. Other appropriate data such as trackage.
    h. Parking and on-site loading facilities.
13. Zoning. In addition to an indication of what the zoning designation of the property is, a detailed discussion of the meaning of that designation is required. This will include an indication of permitted (or prohibited) uses; appropriate land and building use codes and regulations should be considered. There should also be a statement indicating any non-conforming use of the subject property.
14. Assessment and Taxes. This will include an indication of the current assessed value, tax rate and taxes, together with an indication of past trends and anticipated future developments.
15. Highest and Best Use. This should include a discussion of the adequacy of existing improvements, and the probable optimum use of the subject site. For existing industrial properties, this also would include a consideration of any pressure or market indications leading to a proposal for conversion of use.
16. Description of Improvements. The buildings and other major improvements should be identified as to character or type, and described in some detail. To assist the reader, a plot plan and floor plan should be included, either at this stage in the report or among the exhibits in the Appendix, with a reference to them. Among the points to be included in the description of improvements are:
    a. Age and condition.
    b. Dimensions: square foot area and/or cubic content.
    c. Design and layout, number of units, number of rooms, number of floors.
    d. Details of construction and finish, including an estimate of quality.
    e. A detailed analysis and discussion of equipment and fixtures. This will include not only a description of the equipment and fixtures and their condition, but commentary on their apparent functional adequacy.
    f. Commentary on deferred maintenance or needed repairs, together with conditions and functional adequacy of structure.
    g. Yard or site improvements, including description of physical condition and functional adequacy.
17. The Cost Approach
    a. Site value estimate.
    b. Reproduction cost new estimate, including accurate measurements and dimensions of the building and justification of the unit costs employed.
    c. Accrued depreciation, including *justification* of adjustments and charges made, preferably on the basis of market evidence.
    d. Estimate of present worth of improvements.

    e. Estimate of value via cost approach, including a summary table of the cost approach for the convenience of the user or reader.

18. The Market Data Approach (Direct Sales Comparison Approach)

    a. Description of Comparable Sales. These data should be presented and carefully related to the subject property in terms of meaningful or salient features. Each property should be described in sufficient detail to permit the reader to follow the appraiser's logic. These descriptions are often included in the Appendix section of the report.

    b. Units of Comparison. For industrial properties in particular, a unit of comparison or unit of analysis should be established and used throughout this approach. This may be a square foot, cubic foot, gross income multiplier, or other appropriate unit.

    c. Summary Analysis Grid. A summary tabulation or sales adjustment grid should be developed for the convenience of the reader or user.

    d. Justification of Adjustments. All adjustments should be justified on the basis of market evidence. Specific commentaries should be included on elements of condition or functional obsolescence in comparable sales properties, when charges for such deficiencies or inadequacies have been made against the subject property in the Cost Approach.

19. The Income Approach

    a. Gross Income Estimate. This should be based on economic rents derived from market analysis and/or rentals included in leases on the subject-property. Service income from the sale of utilities or other sources must be included.

    b. Effective Gross Income. A charge for vacancy or rent loss should be made *only* when it is appropriate. If such a charge is made, it must be based on *market evidence.*

    c. Operating Expenses. The actual history of expenses for the past three to five years for the subject property should be shown, if possible, together with an analysis of going *market standards* for similar properties.

    d. Net Income Estimate. This is based on a summary of the reconstruction operating statement. Net income is net income before capital recapture (NIBR).

    e. Interest Rate Selection. The method chosen must be explained and *justified.*

    f. Select Residual Technique. This requires *justification* in terms of the characteristics of the property, as well as the market.

    g. Select Capitalization Method. This is based on the character of the income flow, and must be *justified.*

    h. Select Capital Recapture Period. This must be distinguished from remaining economic life, if the two are different. The basis for the selection of the capital recapture period must be explained and *justified.*

    i. If any decision is predicated upon the credit strength of a tenant or tenants, the basis for such consideration must be explained and *justified*.

j. Estimate Value of Fee Simple, via capitalization of net income based on economic rents.

k. Estimate Value of Leased Fee, based upon capitalization of contract rent.

l. Estimate Value of Reversion. *Justify* and explain.

m. Develop Estimate of Value via Income Approach, providing summary tabulation for the assistance of user or reader.

20. Correlation and Final Value Estimate
    a. Review all approaches used for logical consistency *and* for arithmetic accuracy.
    b. Select final value estimate via analysis for available materials.
    c. Round final estimate.

21. Certificate of Appraisal. Here the appraiser makes specific claims and statements, including:
    a. He has personally inspected the property, and considered all the factors affecting its value.
    b. He has no present or contemplated future interest in the property.
    c. His estimate of value is in no way contingent upon his fee.
    d. The report has been made in conformity with the standards and rules of professional ethics of appropriate professional appraisal organizations.
    f. The date and signature of the appraiser.

22. Qualifications of the Appraiser

23. Appendix or Exhibits. Many items which add to the presentation do not necessary belong in the body of the report. They are more appropriately included at the end, for the use of anyone interested in pursuing the work beyond the text presentation itself. All exhibits should be professional in appearance. They may include the following:
    a. Photographs of the subject property. These should be dated.
    b. Photographs of the neighborhood to show the environment of the property. These should be dated.
    c. Photographs of comparable sales properties and comparable rental properties. These should be dated.
    d. Maps: city and metropolitan area, neighborhood, comparable sales and comparable rental locations.
    e. Plot plan, showing location of improvements, known easements or encroachments, yard facilities, north arrow, streets, etc.
    f. Floor plans with essential dimensions. In addition, a building cross section is often useful.
    g. Resumes of important leases, party-wall or easement agreements, zoning or other land use regulations, etc.
    h. Detailed description of the improvements, if it is not included in the body of the report.
    i. Detailed descriptions of comparable sales or comparable rental properties, if they are not included in the body of the report.

SELECTED REFERENCES

American Institute of Real Estate Appraisers, *The Appraisal of Real Estate*, 4th ed. (Chicago, The Author, 1964).

Derbes, Max J., Jr., "Industrial Real Estate Appraisal," Unpublished course syllabus and outline, 1965.

Ellwood, L. W., *Ellwood Tables for Real Estate Appraising and Financing* (Ridgewood, N.J., The Author, 1959).

Fullerton, Paul, "Appraisal of Industrial Property," Ch. 16 of *Encyclopedia of Real Estate Appraising*, Edith J. Friedman, ed. (Englewood Cliffs, N.J., Prentice-Hall, 1959).

Kahn, Sanders A., Case, Frederick E., and Schimmel, Alfred, *Real Estate Appraisal and Investment* (New York, Ronald Press, 1963).

Kinnard, William N., Jr., *A Guide to Appraising Apartments*, 2nd ed. (Chicago, Society of Real Estate Appraisers, 1966).

Kinnard, William N., Jr., "Investment and Financing Considerations," *Appraising Apartments: Instructor's Manual* (Chicago, Society of Real Estate Appraisers, 1963).

Kinnard, William N., Jr., "New Thinking in Appraisal Theory," *The Real Estate Appraiser*, Vol. 32, No. 8, August, 1966.

Maisel, Sherman J., *Financing Real Estate: Principles and Practices* (New York, McGraw-Hill, 1965).

Ricks, R. Bruce, *Recent Trends in Institutional Real Estate Investment*, Research Report 23, Center for Real Estate and Urban Economics (Berkeley, University of California, 1964).

Ring, Alfred A., *The Valuation of Real Estate* (Englewood Cliffs, N.J., Prentice-Hall, 1963).

Shenkel, William M., *A Guide to Appraising Industrial Property* (Chicago, Society of Real Estate Appraisers, 1967).

Shenkel, William M., *Principles and Practices of Industrial Real Estate: A Course Syllabus* (Washington, Society of Industrial Realtors, 1963).

13   Industrial Real Estate Appraisal: Applications

THE appraisal of industrial real estate requires a comprehensive working knowledge of its characteristics, both in physical and in economic or market terms.

The appraiser, no less than the industrial real estate broker, must understand the market for the specific type of industrial property being examined. In estimating market value, data on sales, rentals, costs, and income must be analyzed in terms of the market acceptability of the industrial space in question. Otherwise, adaptability and utility of the space must be used as the major guides to value analysis, which then must take the form of investment studies or Value in Use estimation.

DISTINGUISHING FEATURES OF INDUSTRIAL REAL ESTATE APPRAISAL

Valuation Approach

In addition to the standard factors that will normally be considered in the appraisal of any real estate, which are noted in Chapter 12, there are many factors which are applicable primarily to industrial real estate because of its special characteristics. These would include, but not be restricted to: adaptability; accessibility to rail and high-speed highway facilities; proximity to labor and/or raw materials; special-use design; high average annual rate of obsolescence; larger number of locational determinants; greater difficulty of financing; and increased importance of credit rating of the occupant. These have all been noted as determinants of the location, use, and financing of industrial real estate. Their presence also influences the type of value to be sought, and the appropriate approaches to estimating that value.

1. *Specialized Improvements.* Many industrial buildings, particularly those designed for manufacturing purposes, are highly specialized. They are constructed to meet the specific requirements of a particular process, product

441

line, or user. The more specialized the building, the greater the difficulty in adapting it to the requirements of another user. Much appraisal analysis of existing industrial properties, therefore, focuses on fitting or changing the structure to suit a new tenant or tenants. The adaptability of the property must be considered from the point of view of both function and investment feasibility.

Because ready marketability is often lacking, much existing industrial real estate is appraised for Value in Use, or "Going Concern Value," as well as Market Value. The difference between the two estimates helps the current owner-occupant decide whether to vacate a plant or keep it in production.

The appraiser must carefully gauge turnover or market absorption rates because discounts for waiting periods are often required. "Who is to create a market where no buyers are to be found? The marketplace, in the ordinary sense of the term, does not exist for these large or special-use properties. . . . The appraiser must place himself in the position of a potential *user* of the subject property." [1] This analysis brings him very close to a Value in Use approach.

2. *Functional Utility.* Potential users of industrial space emphasize primarily the functional utility of that space. Even site location may be a secondary consideration to the functional utility of the improvements.[2]

It is therefore incumbent on the appraiser to know the space standards of industry, and particularly what the most probable user of the space being appraised needs and wants. To accomplish this, he must know industrial processes and their technical requirements, including the needs of different industrial users as to floor loads, ceiling heights, loading bay sizes, elevator capacities, and the like.

Because of the emphasis on function and efficiency, industrial real estate is particularly susceptible to functional obsolescence as a result of innovation and technological change. For example, "13-foot warehouses [ceiling heights] originally were most functional due to limitations on height imposed by the capacity of the fork-lift truck. The advent of the telescopic fork-lift allowed a third pallet, so that the 21-foot warehouse came into vogue. Then insurance rates and the cost of construction entailed in 21-foot warehouses, particularly with double, dry-head sprinkler systems, came into play in some industries, and made the 21-foot warehouse functionally unattractive (obsolete). Then construction techniques in some areas with pre-cast concrete allowed for 28-foot clearance in 32-foot warehouses with a mezzanine, allowing for both a double sprinkler system and two times two pallet storage." [3] To a large extent, the utility of any industrial property "involves not only the ability of the real estate (and movable equipment) to perform a given function efficiently; utility also depends upon the utility of the end product." [4]

---

[1] Paul Fullerton, "Appraisal of Industrial Property," Edith J. Friedman, ed., *Encyclopedia of Real Estate Appraising* (Englewood Cliffs, N.J., Prentice-Hall, 1959), p. 323
[2] Unpublished manuscript by Max J. Derbes, Jr., S.I.R., MAI, SREA, New Orleans.
[3] *Ibid.*
[4] *Ibid.*

3. *Access.* Transportation facilities influence the value of industrial properties more than is true of most other types of real estate. This includes not only street or highway access, but also rail, barge or air facilities at or near the site. The functional utility of any industrial complex is greatly enhanced for a large volume shipper and receiver if more than one means of transportation is available at the site. For example, many industrial firms have paid premium prices for sites with rail facilities, even though they rarely utilize railroads for shipping and receiving. The rail siding or spur is a form of insurance policy for the firm, in the event of a truckers' strike, for example. Moreover, "the greater the quantity of materials handled and the longer the distances they must travel (either to or from the plant), the more likely the existence of multiple-transportation outlets will increase value. For instance, petro-chemical plants often have truck, rail, waterway, and pipeline outlets in order to assure themselves of a competitive transportation position." [5]

4. *User-Occupant Orientation.* Industrial real estate appraisal is much more user-oriented than is most other real estate valuation. The specialized nature of much industrial real estate and the emphasis placed on functional utility of existing space require the appraiser to attempt to identify who the most probable user, or what the most probable use, may be. This requires more specific analysis than is true in other areas of real estate appraisal, and is complicated by the wide variation in types of uses and users possible in the industrial field.

There is a close relationship between the success of the industrial occupant and the value of industrial real estate. This depends in part on the market acceptability of the occupant's product, and in part on his credit rating. The type of financing, in turn, influences the return on the investment to the owner, and hence the value of the real estate to him. The appraiser, therefore, cannot ignore the economics of the most probable user's industry, nor the financial and economic status of the firm itself when there is a long-term lease on the property.

"In essence, highest and best use involves the function utility of the physical plant, the economic future of the end product or service, and the potential alternative uses of the real estate." [6] Particularly if the transaction is a "paper deal," the real estate appraiser is at least as much a credit and financial analyst as he is an evaluator of real estate.

5. *Market.* The market within which industrial space is traded is often geographically broader than the market for other real estate. At the same time, it can be characterized economically as a thinner, narrower market.

Properties which are competitive with the subject may be much more widely dispersed. This requires the appraiser to consider carefully just how far and how broad that market is. For example, a truck terminal in Hartford, Connecticut, is more likely to be competing with a similar facility in either New Haven, Connecticut, or Springfield, Massachusetts, than it is with

---

[5] *Ibid.*
[6] *Ibid.*

a mill building on the same block. The appraiser must therefore ascertain precisely what type of space is competitive with that being appraised, and where comparable sales or lease transactions might be found.

The market is thin in the sense that there are relatively few participants in it. Because of the specialized nature of industrial real estate, relatively few potential users are available to bid for the space at any time. There are also few potential investors because of the relatively large sums of money involved, especially required equities. In this imperfect market framework, wide variation in the prices of seemingly similar or competitive properties will often result. The market is sensitive to shifts in supply and demand, and price or rental reactions are generally more prompt and more substantial.

6. *Interdependence.* In common with much nonindustrial real estate, the value of industrial properties is substantially influenced by the uses and users in the area surrounding the property in question. The difference, however, lies in the fact that the specific users can have a major impact on the utility of the property in question, and therefore directly on its value. The profitability of many industrial operations is dependent on easy access to and from interrelated uses. This phenomenon has been termed "unity of use." "Truck terminals, bus freight depots, even satellite chemical plants may be worth very little standing alone; however, they may be quite valuable as part of a large-scale operation." [7] A chemical plant in eastern Connecticut, which was designed specifically for the production of dyes for the textile industry, for example, was abandoned when its client firms moved out of the area. It remained unoccupied for several years until the firm owning the plant "gave it away" to a developer, who then proceeded to renovate it for multiple occupancy. Most of the specialized equipment first had to be removed and scrapped at considerable expense to the owner. Under such circumstances, the appraiser must be able to distinguish carefully and convincingly between Market Value and Book Value.

Appraisal Methodology

The characteristics of industrial real estate influence the methods necessary for the appraiser to apply, and the data to be gathered, in estimating whatever value is sought.

1. *Technical Demands.* The specialized nature of industrial real estate, the emphasis on functional utility, the nature of the user of the industrial space, and the peculiar sensitivity of the market for industrial space to shifts in supply and demand all combine to place particular technical burdens on the appraiser. Aside from analyzing the building in the case of improved property appraisals, the appraiser needs a good working knowledge of costs, industrial zoning, land planning, property taxation, area economic trends, industry trends, and industrial location. These must be combined into a market survey that sets the framework within which the value of the particular industrial property is estimated.

---

[7] *Ibid.*

2. *Highest and Best Use.* In estimating highest and best use of the property, the appraiser must first identify the most probable user of the space. Highest and best use is intimately interrelated with the process, the product, and the producer in a way that is rarely encountered in nonindustrial appraisals.

3. *Site Valuation.* The utility of the site for the specific use that is planned or currently applied is a major determinant of which site valuation method is employed. Although it is most widely employed, and most suitable when necessary data are available, the Direct Sales Comparison Approach is often not appropriate for the valuation of industrial sites. There may be no "going market" for that specific use at the time of the appraisal, especially when the site is improved. The appraiser of industrial sites must be able to apply alternative valuation methods, especially the capitalization of net income via either the land residual technique, or the direct capitalization of ground rents. Further, raw acreage values may be estimated by the development cost method for land suitable for planned industrial districts or "industrial parks," when good market sales comparisons are lacking.

4. *Sales Comparisons.* The specialized character of industrial real estate, and the specialized demands of industrial users, combine to render the Direct Sales Comparison Approach difficult to apply in many situations when improved industrial real estate is to be appraised. Industrial properties have an extremely low turnover rate, and the non-liquidity risk is high. Therefore, in assessing the marketability of improved industrial real estate, the appraiser is often confronted with a conversion or rehabilitation study. This requires "Before and After" analysis.

On the other hand, industrial real estate can be effectively appraised via the Direct Sales Comparison Approach *if* the type of property in question is bought and sold frequently enough on the market so that a sufficient quantity of comparable sales data is available. Loft buildings or single-story industrial warehouses are examples of properties which can be appraised fruitfully via the Direct Sales Comparison Approach. Industrial properties which can be appropriately valued as real estate, rather than on the basis of a credit transaction, are usually more susceptible to the Direct Sales Comparison Approach.

Care must be taken in the selection of units of comparison (or units of analysis) for industrial buildings. For example, reducing a 20,000-square-foot warehouse and a 60,000-square-foot warehouse to a "per square foot" value basis may be inappropriate, because they may be competing in different markets. The discussion in Chapter 8 indicates that general-purpose industrial property varies from one market area to another.

It is also highly desirable for the appraiser to recognize that as a result of adaptability or convertibility, industrial real estate may be competing in a nonindustrial market. For example, an effective device in appraising a loft building may be to compare it with older office buildings in the same market.

5. *Functional Obsolescence.* The primary task of the appraiser attempting to apply the Cost Approach to industrial property is to measure accrued functional obsolescence effectively. This represents such a sub-

stantial challenge that the Cost Approach is often avoided by experienced industrial appraisers, or else its contribution to a final value estimate is minimized.

Special-purpose buildings and equipment, together with technological change and innovation (resulting in altered standards of acceptability on the part of industrial users) combine to accelerate the process of functional obsolescence for industrial buildings and sites. An example of the latter is a small, centrally located site which cannot possibly provide off-street parking for employees, or off-street loading and unloading at the shipping docks.

No less important is functional obsolescence of complex and specialized equipment which has been made an integral part of the building. In many instances, cost estimators or engineers are required as advisers to the appraiser. They indicate the probable reproduction cost new of such equipment, its present market value "in place" (if any), and the probable cost of removing it from the premises. As an example of the importance of such costs, a large Connecticut silver hollowware firm with headquarters in one city offered to sell a 22-year-old, three-story, 60,000-square-foot branch plant in another town for the cost of moving the specialized equipment and machinery in the branch plant to the headquarters plant. In effect, it was offering the real estate free, if its equipment were moved to the main plant. After three years, there still were no takers. The branch plant and its site were not worthless; the cost of moving the equipment was simply greater than the value of the real estate to potential users.

6. *Income Capitalization.* In the appraisal of industrial real estate, the capitalization of net income is most frequently employed and defended by professional appraisers. If the emphasis is on improved real estate, a building residual analysis is applied, utilizing either annuity capitalization, or straight-line capital recapture (depending on the character of the income flow likely to be generated). When industrial sites are valued, either a land residual technique or net ground rent capitalization is applied. In such cases, the income stream is usually treated as though it were an annuity.

A large proportion of income capitalization involves the valuation of interests under a long-term lease. Comparisons of contract rent and economic rent are required of the industrial real estate appraiser, in most industrial valuation problems. Because industrial leases are typically long-term, "net" leases, particular care must be taken in reading and interpreting the terms of the lease. Annuity capitalization and overall rate analysis are both common and logical in industrial appraisals.

Because of the widespread use of leases in industrial real estate practice, particular emphasis is placed on the credit of the user of industrial space. Therefore, the appraiser must analyze the credit status of that user. The lessee's credit rating affects both the risk to the lessor-investor (reflected in the interest rate developed for capitalization purposes), and the terms of financing (which also influence the interest rate). The higher the credit rating of the tenant, the lower the interest rate required to satisfy the standards of both lessor and mortgagee. The lower the interest rate, the higher the value of any given income stream.

Units and Standards

Although they may be expressed in physical terms, the units of comparison employed in industrial real estate appraisals are functional units. That is to say, they represent those units which are most related to the use of the site and/or the building.

Industrial sites are usually valued on a square-foot basis, or on a per-acre basis if large areas are involved. As long as there is enough width (even through an easement or right of way) to allow appropriate vehicular access to the site, the amount of frontage required for most industrial activities is negligible. Many operations with retail or service outlets attached do seek frontage, but even their sites are rarely valued on a front-foot basis. Depth is also not usually an important consideration. Rather, the total area and the shape of the site influence most the functions it may perform.

When there is a single occupant for an entire building, the usual base for estimating the number of square feet is the gross area of the building (outside dimensions). Occasionally, truly comparable multistory buildings are meaningfully compared for sale purposes in terms of "per square foot of foundation area," or "per square foot of land area covered."

Industrial rentals are commonly expressed in terms of so much per square foot per year, although in many market areas the unit is the *monthly* rental per square foot. In single-occupant buildings, or in multitenant buildings with one tenant per floor, the unit of measure is usually based on gross area or outside dimensions. When there are two or more tenants per floor, then the rental is expressed in terms of net area occupied, with common space such as air shafts, stairways, and elevators excluded. This distinction is extremely important. The appraiser might make the mistake of comparing unlike rentals simply because they are all expressed as so much "per square foot per year" (or "per month").

Occasionally, measures other than the square foot of floor area are employed. For example, both values and rentals of truck terminals are often expressed on a per dock or per loading platform basis. Parking area is commonly valued at so much per parking space (automobile, truck, or trailer).

When improved property is valued, the square foot of building area measure includes land as well. The presumption is that the relationship or ratio between land and buildings is "appropriate," or at least essentially the same, in each case. If it is not, it may not be possible to value the site independently to develop an appropriate comparable figure for the building area. Therefore, "frequently the gross income multiplier is the only comparative characteristic that can be applied." [8] This ratio between sales price and gross income is actually a measure of the market. It is one means by which seemingly different but still competitive properties can be compared with one another, and is widely used in the valuation of industrial properties.

Finally, percentage rates are important comparative measures. The rent "factor" as a percentage of cost (for new improvements) or as a percentage

---

[8] American Institute of Real Estate Appraisers, *The Appraisal of Real Estate,* 4th ed. (Chicago, The Author, 1964) p. 348.

of the owner's investment (for existing improvements) is a standard which can be applied from one property to another, if they are truly competitive. Similarly, there is a presumption of comparability whenever a mortgage constant, based in part on a standardized loan-to-value ratio, is applied to all properties of the same type in the analysis of a given market. Thus, financial units of measurement or comparison are as important as are those involving sales and rentals.

Data Requirements and Sources

The appraiser will generally utilize a detailed property checklist to make sure that the information he gathers is pertinent and adequate for the requirements of an industrial appraisal. In addition to detailed analysis of the site, the building, and off-site improvements, there are several elements involved in the survey of the market environment. These include considerations of the city or metropolitan area, the neighborhood, and comparable sales properties.

Property taxes, municipal services, and transportation facilities are particularly important elements of community analysis in industrial appraisals. Moreover, the development and enforcement of industrial zoning and land use regulations are a matter of special concern for the appraiser, as are plans for civic improvement programs, especially industrial renewal or redevelopment projects. Manufacturing concerns are keenly interested in technically trained workers, and thus the place of technical schools in the educational system of the area should be studied. The circulation of traffic flow plan for the community is a matter of great concern to most industrial establishments, as are the implementation and enforcement of that plan. The attitude of the local community toward industry can be an important determinant of the attractiveness of that community to industrial space users. This attitude is expressed most eloquently in capital improvement programs calling for utilities, transportation and parking facilities, protection services, and application of zoning regulations. Platitudes, banquets, and expressions of warmth on the part of the mayor during an annual "Industrial Week" are simply not enough.

Neighborhood considerations particularly pertinent to the industrial appraiser include, first and foremost, access and transportation. Beyond this, protection from inharmonious elements, both through land use controls and through effective policing, can make a neighborhood substantially more attractive to a potential industrial occupant. Proximity to employee service facilities is also a major consideration. If, for example, adequate numbers of attractive and diversified eating establishments are available in the area, the pressures to provide cafeteria facilities within the industrial building itself are reduced. This consideration is particularly important for multi-tenant loft buildings not already equipped with eating and food-handling facilities.

In establishing a data program for comparable sales and comparable rental properties, the appraiser will consider such basic factors as sales price, date of sale, land and building area, age of building, and the like. For industrial properties, however, great emphasis must be placed on the utility of the space, as well as on any special-purpose character either the building or the major equipment in the building may have. Moreover, the terms and conditions of any leases on the comparable sales properties require detailed investigation.

In studying comparable sales information, it is also extremely important to know how much and what kind of remodeling or renovation the purchaser undertook, how much it cost, and when it occurred.

Most information required for industrial property analysis is obtainable only through painstaking search in the market. There are some sources of published information, however, and the appraiser should familiarize himself with them. The basic sources are cited in a number of bibliographical listings.[9]

INDUSTRIAL SITE VALUATION

In the estimation of value of industrial sites, the appraiser must pay particular attention to his analysis of highest and best use. In this analysis, he must not be misled by zoning. Considerably more than zoning is necessary before land can realistically be regarded as an industrial site. "Industrial land values are the product of a combination of utility and scarcity of sites for the use intended." [10]

Site Analysis

In developing his conclusion as to the highest and best use of the site, the appraiser must carefully consider a minimum of eight sets of attributes of the site. This will enable him to discover the uses for which it is best suited, and it will serve as an important basis for comparative analysis, whichever method of value estimation he employs. Whatever the precise order of listing, these eight elements cover the major considerations that any appraiser of an industrial site would make.

1. *Location.* "The value of industrial sites is closely related to the advantage of the location." [11] The ingredients of a good industrial location are analyzed in detail in Chapters 2 and 3. Proximity and access to markets, suppliers and/or labor are basic considerations. Because location is fixed, all of the other elements of site analysis must emanate from the presumption of a given location.

2. *Accessibility and Transportation.* Speed and ease of travel to and from the site are critical to its use, financing, development, and value. This point cannot be emphasized too strongly or too often.

3. *Physical Attributes.* In the examination of any industrial site, these

---

[9] See, for example, AIREA, *op. cit.,* pp. 467–470; Fullerton, *op. cit.,* pp. 335–341; Sanders A. Kahn, Frederick E. Case, and Alfred Schimmel, *Real Estate Appraisal and Investment* (New York, Ronald Press, 1963), bibliographies throughout the book; William M. Shenkel, *A Guide to Appraising Industrial Property* (Chicago, Society of Real Estate Appraisers, 1967), pp. 38–44.

[10] Statement by Max J. Derbes, Jr., S.I.R., MAI, SREA.

[11] William M. Shenkel, *Principles and Practices of Industrial Real Estate: A Course Syllabus* (Washington, Society of Industrial Realtors, 1963), p. 67.

determine the use to which the site can be put. Physical attributes to be studied and measured include: size, shape, dimensions, topography, drainage, and subsoil conditions, at the least. Size is especially important in evaluating the prospects of plant expansion.

4. *Site Facilities and Services.* For an industrial site to be usable, it must be served with appropriate utilities in the proper capacities, and at competitive rates. These include electricity, gas, water, and sewer service.

5. *Taxes.* In addition to the usual considerations of tax rates and assessment ratios, industrial real estate appraisal requires that special attention be focused on levies against equipment, fixtures, and manufacturers' or distributors' inventory. These may not appear to be directly related to *site analysis,* but they do represent part of the environment of a particular site, and influence its utility.

6. *Use Restrictions.* Zoning, land use controls, and building or fire codes are the most obvious limitations on the use to which an industrial site can be put. They influence both the feasibility and the expense of a particular use pattern. Both the regulations and their enforcement must be studied. Private deed restrictions and title limitations can often play an equally significant role in development pattern of an industrial site.

7. *Protection.* Fire and police services are important to all industrial users. The neighborhood environment will also influence the type of protection required. In many instances, fencing, flood lighting, alarm systems, and other on-site protective devices may be necessary to safeguard both buildings and site improvements. This increases the cost of developing a given pattern of land use, and will directly affect the value of the site.

8. *Neighborhood Environment.* This involves such intangible factors as reputation, appearance, safety, and availability of supporting facilities.

Direct Sales Comparison Approach

The application of the Direct Sales Comparison Approach to industrial site valuation is illustrated in Exhibit 56. This method is less widely used for industrial sites than it is for the valuation of residential or commercial sites. The appraiser must often go further afield to find comparables.

Moreover, land and site costs are usually a small percentage of the total price or cost of industrial realty. "The larger the industrial land need and the larger the plant, the less a percentage will be represented by land costs, generally." [12] One result of this is that the prices paid for industrial land in many instances tend to vary over a rather broad range. There is often less pressure on the purchasing firm to negotiate or "dicker" quite so hard. This poses problems for the appraiser, if no really consistent pattern of sales prices emerges for certain types of industrial sites.

In the verification of sales data, particular emphasis must be placed on the motivations of participants in the transaction. Moreover, a discount is often necessary for "waiting time." The appraiser must also be careful not to place too much emphasis on purchases of sites adjacent to property of the buyer. Industrial plants often pay premium prices for abutting properties

---

[12] Statement of Max J. Derbes, Jr., S.I.R., MAI, SREA.

because this is the only way they can obtain land for expansion. Such a transaction may not be an appropriate comparison for the subject of the appraisal.

Development Cost Approach

When large tracts of acreage may be acquired for industrial development, the Development Cost method of value estimation is generally applicable. This takes into consideration the value of the land in its new industrial use, the timing of its availability, and the costs that must be incurred in order to bring it to that use. It is exemplified in Exhibit 61 in Chapter 12, as well as in detailed illustrations here. It can take the form of feasibility analysis (Is it worth paying the price required in order to acquire the acreage?), or a version of residual analysis (What can a developer afford to pay for the land, in view of the most likely pattern of receipts and costs?).

Before attempting to estimate how much may be obtained from the sale of individual parcels or sites after development, the appraiser must study carefully the proposed land use restrictions and covenants for the development. The appraiser is then in a position to estimate the probable prices at which the developed sites will sell. Since they will not all be available at the same time, and since they will generally not be sold immediately when they are available, it is usually necessary to estimate a rate of market absorption for the sites. Thus, gross receipts are discounted to the present, at the appropriate interest rate, by the use of the Present Worth of One (Reversion) table.

Next, the appraiser must estimate development costs. These are the expenditures necessary to convert the raw acreage to industrial sites. They would include bringing utilities to the sites, advertising, roads and grading, engineering and legal expenses, and sales commissions. In some instances, the sales commissions are treated as deductions from gross receipts, rather than development costs. In addition, there must be provision for interest and carrying charges on borrowed funds until the property is sold, and for the developer's overhead and profit.

When all of these charges are deducted from the discounted estimated gross receipts, the difference indicates the maximum amount that the developer would be justified in paying for the land.

As an example of the application of this technique, a 100-acre tract of land was developed for industrial purposes in a northeastern state. Exhibit 69 shows the land development costs that were anticipated by the developer's staff. The project was staged in five sections, and sold off accordingly.

It was anticipated that it would take five years to sell the land, and that the finished sites would most probably sell at $10,000 per acre. It was further estimated that roads and other community demands would absorb 20 acres, so that a maximum of 80 acres of lots could be sold. This meant that anticipated gross receipts were $800,000.

In the absence of any other evidence, it was estimated that sales receipts would be spread evenly over a five-year period, making gross receipts $160,000 per year. No adjustment was made for any anticipated "scarcity

Exhibit 69

ILLUSTRATIVE LAND DEVELOPMENT COSTS OF
100-ACRE INDUSTRIAL TRACT

Item	*Section I*	*Section II*	*Section III*	*Section IV*	*Section V*	*Total*
Grading	$	$	$	$	$20,000	$ 20,000
Roads	15,600		15,600	24,000	16,800	72,000
Drainage			2,300	2,400	18,000	22,700
Water System	9,100	11,600	15,300	27,400	4,200	67,600
Sewerage System	5,000	44,500		4,100	8,600	62,200
Electric & Gas						
Turfing					10,000	10,000
Engineering & Legal	13,000	6,000	2,000	2,000	2,000	25,000
Contingencies	2,300	3,500	1,800	3,500	4,400	15,500
Totals	$45,000	$65,600	$37,000	$63,400	$84,000	$295,000

factor." A 10 per cent sales commission reduced anticipated sales receipts
to $144,000 per year. The developer planned to pay less in sales commis-
sions, but his staff insisted on providing for the prevailing commission rate
in the area. It was concluded that an appropriate rate of discount was 8 per
cent. By reference to a Present Worth of One table, appropriate factors for
reversions from one to five years at 8 per cent were derived, and a final
estimate of the present worth of the receipts was developed. This is illustrated in Exhibit 70.

Exhibit 70

ILLUSTRATIVE CALCULATION OF PRESENT WORTH OF GROSS RECEIPTS
OF 100-ACRE INDUSTRIAL TRACT

Estimated Annual Gross Receipts Less Sales Commission:	$144,000
Present Worth of One at 8% Discount:	
1-year (.925926 x $144,000) $133,333	
2-year (.857339 x $144,000) 123,457	
3-year (.793882 x $144,000) 114,319	
4-year (.735030 x $144,000) 105,844	
5-year (.680583 x $144,000) 98,004	
Total Present Worth 5-Year Flow $574,957	
Rounded to $575,000	

The technique illustrated in Exhibit 70 is the longer, more roundabout
way of handling the income flow. Since the amount of income was a "constant annuity," a Present Worth of One per Annum (Inwood) factor could
have been used for five years at 8 per cent. This factor is 3.993. (3.993 ×
$144,000 = $574,992). The more detailed method was employed in this
example because the expected annual receipts may vary each year. Then it
is necessary to use successive Present Worth of One factors.

Total development costs were expected to be $295,000 as indicated in Exhibit 69. It was estimated that mortgage interest charges at 6.5 per cent would equal approximately three years' interest on the $295,000. Total interest charges, therefore, were calculated at $57,525 (.065 × $295,000 = $19,175; 3 × $19,175 = $57,525).

The developer wanted a 30 per cent return for overhead and profit on his $295,000 investment. This amounted to $88,500. The final estimate of the maximum amount that could be paid for the land is indicated in Exhibit 71, where two alternative computations are provided. In some instances, the developer may also require an overhead and profit return on the investment in the land. If this is the case, then the $134,000 (derived by subtracting development costs, interest charges, and overhead and profit on development costs from the present worth of anticipated gross receipts) must itself be adjusted downward to account for a 30 per cent return on the investment in the land. This results in an estimated maximum value of the land $103,000.

Exhibit 71

SUMMARY OF INDUSTRIAL ACREAGE VALUATION VIA LAND DEVELOPMENT COST APPROACH

Total Gross Receipts (80 acres at $10,000 per acre)		$800,000
Less 10% Sales Commission		80,000
		$720,000
Less Discount for 5-Year Sales Program at 8%		145,043
Present Worth of Estimated Gross Receipts		$574,957
Rounded to		$575,000
Less:		
Development Costs	$295,000	
Estimated Interest Carrying Charges	57,525	
Overhead and Profit on Development Costs at 30%	88,500	
Total Expense and Cost	$441,025	
Rounded to		$441,000
Maximum Available for Raw Acreage ($1,340 per acre)		$134,000
If 30% Return for Overhead and Profit is Required on Investment, on Land Deduct $31,000; Maximum Net Available for Purchase of Land ($1,030 per acre)		$103,000

The estimates derived via the Land Development Cost Approach are not necessarily market value estimates. Rather, they represent the value or worth to the developer for a specified use pattern.

Land Residual Technique

The Land Residual Technique, utilizing straight-line capital recapture, is set forth in Exhibit 62 in Chapter 12. There are serious limitations to the applicability of this technique in estimating the value of industrial sites, but there are also circumstances in which no other alternative may be available to the appraiser.

When the conditions of the Land Residual Technique are met, it is a powerful analytical tool, particularly for the estimation of value of sites which are not frequently bought and sold on the open market. The Land Residual Technique has been widely utilized in the valuation of reuse parcels in industrial redevelopment projects. While there is much debate over the effectiveness of this technique in practice, it is based upon fundamentally sound principles.[13]

The weaknesses of the Land Residual Technique are primarily those of data limitations. Because a building is hypothecated on a presumably vacant site, there is difficulty in estimating accurately the gross income that will be generated with the hypothetical improvements. Secondly, estimating projected expenses is equally difficult, and often leads to a high degree of variability in results.

For example, assumptions involved in the estimate of site value via the Land Residual Technique illustrated in Exhibit 62 resulted in an estimated value for the site in question of $34,000. The results of slight variations in either the capital recapture period or the interest rate are shown in the summary tabulation in Exhibit 72. If the capital recapture period is reduced by 40 per cent, from 50 years to 30 years, this results in a 68 per cent reduc-

Exhibit 72

SUMMARY ILLUSTRATIONS OF EFFECTS
OF VARYING TERMS IN LAND RESIDUAL TECHNIQUES

Net Income before Capital Recapture (from Exhibit 62)	$11,975
1. Interest Rate 6.5%; Capital Recapture Period 50 Years; Capital Recapture Rate 2.0%: Land Value Estimate	33,846
2. Interest Rate 6.5%; Capital Recapture Period 40 Years; Capital Recapture Rate 2.5%: Land Value Estimate	25,000
3. Interest Rate 6.5%; Capital Recapture Period 30 Years; Capital Recapture Rate 3.3%: Land Value Estimate	10,769
4. Interest Rate 7%; Capital Recapture Period 50 Years; Capital Recapture Rate 2%: Land Value Estimate	23,214
5. Interest Rate 6%; Capital Recapture Period 50 Years; Capital Recapture Rate 2%: Land Value Estimate	46,250

tion in the estimated value of the site, from approximately $34,000 to $10,800. Similarly, a 17 per cent increase in the interest rate, from 6 to 7 per cent, results in a nearly 50 per cent reduction in the estimate of land

[13] For a discussion of the uses and limitations inherent in the application of the land residual technique to reuse appraisals, see articles by Frederick M. Babcock and James E. McCormack in *Papers and Proceedings: The Wisconsin Colloquium on Appraisal Research,* Richard U. Ratcliff, ed. (Madison, Wisconsin; University of Wisconsin, 1963).

value. These findings underscore the extreme importance of special care and precision in the application of the Land Residual Technique.

Net Ground Lease Capitalization

The Capitalization of a Net Ground Lease is mechanically the simplest method of site appraisal. First, it involves selecting an appropriate interest rate to compensate for the risk involved. Then the present worth of the annual rent payments under the lease is estimated. This involves the use of an annuity factor (present worth of one per annum) over the term of the lease. The present worth of the reversion that will devolve to the lessor at the expiration of the lease is estimated by discounting the expected value of the reversion. This may be simply value of the land, or it may include both land and any buildings that the lessee has erected on the site. In either event, the estimated value of the reversion at the expiration of the lease is discounted to the present via the use of a Present Worth of One factor. The two present worth figures are added to obtain the estimated value of the site.

The mechanics are those of the Property Residual Technique illustrated in Exhibit 67 in Chapter 12. The only difference is that the rental income is on the land only, rather than on the land and buildings. There is no depreciation or capital recapture.

If economic rent rather than contract rent is employed in estimating the value of land via income capitalization, then the value of the "real estate" is estimated in contrast with the value of the leased fee.

An interesting footnote is provided by the fact that lengthening the term of a lease beyond approximately 40 years does not significantly increase either safety or value to the lessor, and "the economic advantage of the tenant is not increased substantially by negotiating for leases beyond 40 years. . . . If the contract rent is discounted at 6 per cent or more, a lease of 40 years or more will account, at least, for 90 per cent of the fee simple estate value." [14]

DIRECT SALES COMPARISONS OF INDUSTRIAL PROPERTIES

The application of the Direct Sales Comparison Approach (or Market Data Approach) to the valuation of improved industrial real estate involves the adjustment of comparable sales data to the subject property. Emphasis is placed on the points of meaningful difference or variation. An indication of what comparable properties would have sold for if they had possessed all of the significant attributes of the subject property is developed. From this, an estimate of market value of the subject property is derived.

Exhibit 73 is a further illustration of the sequential percentage adjustment technique. Dollar amounts can also be used, and are strongly advocated by many professional appraisers. In either approach, "the preferred method of a detailed adjustment is to begin with time, then location, finally physical

---

[14] William M. Shenkel, "The Effective Use of Development Leases," *Ground Leases,* Byron Trerice, Jr., sponsor (Chicago, National Institute of Real Estate Brokers, December, 1965), p. 39.

Exhibit 73

ILLUSTRATION OF PERCENTAGE CORRECTIVE ADJUSTMENTS
APPLIED TO COMPARABLE SALES

| Time between Sale and Date of Valuation | Sale Price | Price per Square Foot* | Sale Correctives | | | | Final Adjust- ments | Adjusted S.P./S.F. |
			Time	Loca- tion	Term of Sale	Mo- tives		
1 One year	$100,000	$5.50	120	105	120	100	151.1	$8.31
2 Six months	60,000	7.00	115	100	105	100	120.7	8.45
3 One month	350,000	4.50	100	110	135	125	185.6	8.35
4 Two years	85,000	3.00	135	130	130	120	273.7	8.21
5 Five years	225,000	6.00	140	100	100	100	140.0	8.40

*Price per square foot includes site area as well.

characteristics." [15] As the adjustments in Exhibit 73 show, it is possible to develop cumulatively large final adjustments through this process.

Many appraisers argue that the Direct Sales Comparison Approach cannot often be applied to industrial property because of the necessity to have highly comparable properties as the basis for the analysis. On the other hand, other appraisers argue equally strongly that the Direct Sales Comparison Approach is the best one to employ because it most nearly represents the views of participants in the market. Actually, these divergent views can be reconciled: there is a substantial difference in emphasis on the *type* of industrial property that is susceptible to comparative sales analysis.

While it is necessary to have adequate volumes of data for the approach to be applied with any degree of accuracy or confidence, the number of sales necessary to support a conclusion depends upon the quality of data. "A few well-documented sales are worth more than a great many sales on which the information is sketchy." [16]

Applications of the Direct Sales Comparison Approach

If industrial buildings are adaptable to more than one use, then the properties may usually be evaluated as if they were on a general market. "The Sales Comparison Method is most appropriate for properties frequently sold and highly standardized. A valuation of industrial property by sales comparisons of *like* properties gives the best indication of current market value." [17]

Moreover, older buildings often cannot meaningfully be divorced from their sites for analytical purposes. This means that neither the Cost Approach nor residual techniques in the Income Approach can be utilized in appraising the property. This leaves only the Direct Sales Comparison Approach.

[15] AIREA, *op. cit.,* p. 357.
[16] Fullerton, *op. cit.,* p. 342.
[17] Shenkel, *Principles and Practices of Industrial Real Estate,* p. 74.

Finally, and perhaps most important, many participants in the industrial real estate market tend to think in terms of "going market" sales, prices, and rentals. The Direct Sales Comparison Approach is often used by such participants, and this use is reinforced by the courts in public takings cases. Since sales comparison analysis is widely understood by many of those dealing in industrial real estate, it follows that this is a desirable approach to utilize when the availability of data makes it possible.

Units of Measurement

The square foot is by far the most commonly utilized basis for reducing industrial properties to a comparable basis. It may be a square foot of gross floor area, a square foot of foundation area, a rental per square foot per year, a rental per square foot per month, a cost per square foot, or a square foot of land area. In Exhibit 74, the development of an appropriate annual square foot rental for an industrial warehouse is depicted. The sequential method of percentage adjustments is also illustrated here.

Exhibit 74

DEVELOPMENT OF ECONOMIC RENTAL FROM COMPARABLE RENTALS

| | | | | | | Adjustments | | | | Indicated |
Sale No.	Loca- tion	Building Area Sq. Ft.	Land Area Sq. Ft.	Gross Income	Rent per Sq. Ft.	Loca- tion	Physical Features	Date of Lease	Rent of Sub- ject by Comparison*
A	AAA	12,000	35,000	$ 9,600	.80	.90	1.10	1.10	$0.87
B	BBB	24,000	70,000	20,000	.83	—	1.05	—	.87
C	CCC	18,500	32,000	16,300	.88	.95	—	1.05	.88
D	DDD	14,750	37,500	12,000	.81	.90	1.05	1.05	.81
E	EEE	25,600	47,000	24,000	.94	.90	1.05	—	.89
F	FFF	18,000	35,000	18,000	1.00	.90	.90	—	.81

* Annual Rental Per Square Foot.

Each comparable was leased by a local tenant. Each rental comparable lease is basically the same with the landlord paying taxes, insurance, and exterior maintenance.

A range of 81¢ to 89¢ per square foot per year is indicated for the subject. Comparables D and F have 12-foot ceilings, whereas the other four have 16-foot ceilings. There is a rental difference in the indicated competitive rents of approximately six- to eight-cents per square foot based on ceiling height. The subject has only a 12-foot ceiling. *Subject Fair Market Rental Value per Square Foot per Year is 81¢.*

Functional units of analysis are also often used in the Direct Sales Comparison Approach, as earlier discussions in Chapters 12 and 13 have indicated. For example, the loading dock is a functional unit for a truck terminal. A warehouse for standardized items can be evaluated in terms of pallet levels. Perhaps the most widely used functional or economic unit of analysis, however, is the gross income multiplier. Sales prices and rent levels for competitive properties are expected to move in the same direction and in the same proportion, since they are subject to essentially the same market influences. Based upon this assumption, information about truly comparable properties may be used for the development of an appropriate ratio between sales price or value, and gross annual rental or gross annual income. For example, the warehouse whose annual square foot rental was derived in Exhibit 74 contained 20,000 square feet. The annual economic rental for the warehouse was therefore taken to be $16,200.

With this information, an appraiser could then proceed to estimate the value of the property by deriving a gross rent multiplier from the sales of similar warehouses which recently sold in the same market area, and which were rented at the time of sale. Such a measure is developed in Exhibit 75. The value estimate of $142,000 for the warehouse is based upon the application of the annual gross rent multiplier of 8.75 to the estimated annual fair market rental of $16,200. In the appraisal of industrial properties, the *annual* gross rent multiplier is generally preferred to a monthly multiplier.

Exhibit 75

ESTIMATE OF MARKET VALUE VIA GROSS RENT MULTIPLIER ANALYSIS

Sale No.	Loca-tion	Age of Sale	Sales Prices	Building Area Sq. Ft.	Land Area Sq. Ft.	Age at Sale	Remain-ing Lease Term	Annual Gross Rent	Gross Rent Multi-plier
A	AAA	14 mos.	$100,000	12,000	35,000	7	3	$ 9,600	9.60
B	BBB	1 mo.	175,000	24,000	70,000	2	8	20,000	8.75
C	CCC	11 mos.	147,500	18,500	32,000	5	5	16,300	9.05
D	DDD	17 mos.	110,000	14,750	37,500	8	2	12,000	9.17
E	EEE	15 mos.	200,000	25,600	47,000	6	10	24,000	8.33
F	FFF	11 mos.	155,000	18,000	35,000	1	9	18,000	8.61

Bracket of Comparison

Subject: $16,200 by 9.60 = $155,520
$16,200 by 8.33 = $134,946

These comparisons bracket the estimate of value within reasonable limits with the use of the gross rent multiplier. By using sales B, C and F as most comparable by reason of size, it is the opinion of the appraiser that the subject's Gross Rent Multiplier should be 8.75.

Multiplier: $16,200 by 8.75 = $141,750
Rounded $142,000

Quantity Breakdown Analysis Method

Because of different site areas, surfaced parking areas, fencing, and even the inclusion of non-real estate items in the sales price, a system of breakdown analysis of the comparables may be undertaken by the appraiser. After an appropriate allowance for those portions of the purchase price allocated for other than the main building and the land, a remainder "price" and price per square foot for this base portion emerges. By deducting the value of the land, the resultant figure can be reduced to indicated depreciated value of improvements, and to value per square foot of building.

This procedure is illustrated in Exhibits 76 and 77, using four of the com-

Exhibit 76

ESTIMATE OF BUILDING UNIT PRICE
VIA PRICE BREAKDOWN ANALYSIS

Sale No.	AAA	BBB	CCC	DDD
Sales Price	$100,000.00	$175,000.00	$147,500.00	$110,000.00
Land Value Per Square Foot	$ 1.00	$ 0.85	$ 1.20	$ 0.90
Less:				
Value Land Not Under Building	$ 23,000.00	$ 39,100.00	$ 16,200.00	$ 20,475.00
Value of Yard Surfacing, Fencing, and Non-Real Estate Machinery	$ 9,900.00	$ 21,400.00	$ 10,000.00	$ 11,125.00
Net Price of Building and Land under Building	$ 67,100.00	$114,500.00	$121,300.00	$ 78,400.00
Area of Building (Sq. Ft.)	12,000 sq. ft.	24,000 sq. ft.	18,500 sq. ft.	14,750 sq. ft.
Square Foot Price of Building and Land Under Building	$ 5.59	$ 4.77	$ 6.56	$ 5.32
Value of Land Under Building	$ 12,000.00	$ 20,400.00	$ 22,200.00	$ 13,275.00
Depreciated Price of Building	$ 55,100.00	$ 94,100.00	$ 99,100.00	$ 65,125.00
Price Per Sq. Ft. Improvements	$ 4.59	$ 3.92	$ 5.36	$ 4.42

parable properties included in Exhibit 75. A unit value estimate is developed for the subject property, as shown in Exhibit 77. The analysis in Exhibit 76 merely studies the various comparables without making adjustments for time, terms of sale, location, condition, etc. It is still necessary to adjust either "Price Per Square Foot Improvements" or "Square Foot Price of Building and Land Under Building" for these various differences.

Exhibit 77

ADJUSTMENT OF SQUARE FOOT PRICE OF
BUILDING AND LAND UNDER BUILDING

	AAA	BBB	CCC	DDD
Indicated Unit Price from Price Breakdown Analysis	$5.59	$4.77	$6.56	$5.32
Time of Sale Adjustment	+.28		+.33	+.32
Terms of Sales Adjustment			−.50	
Land Value Difference		+.15	−.20	+.10
Size of Building		+.20	+.10	
Condition and Age			−.49	
Other (Functional):		+.50		
Net Adjustment	+.28	+.85	−.76	+.42
Value Indicated Per Square Foot	$5.87	$5.62	$5.80	$5.74

NOTE: The property being appraised is about 4 years old with total land area of 34,000 square feet and building area of 14,000 square feet. Sale AAA is adjusted up 5% due to a better market than 14 months ago. Sale BBB is adjusted for land value of 85¢ per square foot as compared with subject's $1.00 per square foot land. This building has 24,000 square feet as compared with subject's 14,000, so subject should sell for 20¢ per square foot more. Sale BBB was special purpose to some extent, so that there is functional loss of 50¢ in the "Other" Column. Sale CCC requires many adjustments because it occurred 11 months ago, on liberal terms, with land worth $1.20 per square foot, and was in much better condition than subject (larger office area, etc.). Sale DDD requires an adjustment for time and for land value of 90¢ per square foot.

CONCLUSION: Sales AAA and DDD are most comparable since they require the least adjustments. Value conclusion $5.80 per square foot.

A value estimate for the subject property is then developed from the indicated unit value derived in Exhibit 77. This is illustrated in Exhibit 78.

Of the total value indicated in Exhibit 78, the main building and the land under the main building account for 75.7 per cent of the total value. Therefore, a minor error in fencing value, parking area surfacing, or even in land value from comparable sales will not produce a very large final value difference. By concentration on the sales price per square foot of building in the analysis of comparable sales, the appraiser can adjust for differences in the land-to-building ratio, differential parking area surfacing, etc.

This system allows a check on the total depreciation and effective depreciated value per square foot of the main improvements found via the Cost Approach.

It is particularly important for the appraiser to appreciate the derivation and application of the multiplier analysis in valuing industrial real estate, because "frequently the Gross Income Multiplier is the only comparative characteristic that can be applied." [18]

Exhibit 78

VALUE ESTIMATION VIA QUANTITY BREAKDOWN ANALYSIS METHOD

Value of Main Building and Land Under Main Building: 14,000 Sq. Ft. x $5.80		$ 81,200.00
Value Land Not Under Building: 34,000 Sq. Ft. Total, Less 14,000 Sq. Ft. Bldg. Area =		
20,000 Sq. Ft. x $1.00 Per Sq. Ft.		$ 20,000.00
Fencing: 800 Ft. @ $1.50		$ 1,200.00
Asphalt Surfacing: 16,000 Sq. Ft. @ $0.30		$ 4,800.00
Total Indicated Value		$107,200.00
Divided as Follows:		
Land 34,000 Sq. Ft. x $1.00 Sq. Ft.	$ 34,000.00	
Improvements	$ 73,200.00	
Total	$107,200.00	

---

[18] AIREA, *op. cit.,* p. 348.

Limitations of Direct Sales Comparison Analysis

The sales prices of industrial property can vary substantially according to the time (market conditions) of the sale. Because of the volatility of the market for industrial space, sales data may become outmoded rapidly. The terms of the sale of industrial properties are also customized and non-standardized. It is therefore often difficult to develop a common pattern that can be applied to a particular property, because the motivations and conditions underlying each individual sale reflect the custom character of the industrial real estate market. These peculiarities in individual transactions may not be uncovered unless there is very penetrating analysis by the appraiser.

Sometimes the difficulties are a bit more obvious, as in the case of the purchase of adjacent property at a premium price by an industrial firm that is landlocked and needs room for expansion.

In brief, the appraiser seeking to apply the Direct Sales Comparison Approach to an industrial real estate valuation problem is confronted with this fundamental issue: Where are the data? If good market data can be found, and the information can be related in truly comparable fashion to the subject property, then the approach is highly valuable and valid.

INDUSTRIAL PROPERTY COST AND DEPRECIATION ANALYSIS

Although the Cost Approach is not the most popular method of estimating the value of industrial property, cost estimates provide an important guide to a variety of industrial real estate decisions. Therefore, care is required in deriving a cost estimate in the Cost Approach to industrial real estate value estimation.

Inspection of the Property

Because of the specialized and custom nature of much industrial real estate, including equipment and fixtures, particular care must be taken by the appraiser in his field inspection of the property to be sure that he notes the contents and components of the building, their physical condition, *and* their functional adequacy. He should recognize, for example, the three basic types of industrial construction, designed to accommodate product layout, process layout, or in-place production. Each has its uses, but each has its problems as well, particularly in terms of adaptation to another pattern of use.

In evaluating physical condition, the appraiser should pay particular heed to signs of settlement of the building because of the critical importance of floor loads in industrial buildings. Moreover, he should check carefully on any play in the floors, which may also be indicative of a relatively low load limit. He should look at the size and the spacing of floor joists and columns, for these influence the bearing capacity of the floors as well. Load limit is not the only utility consideration, by any means, but it illustrates the importance of physical characteristics in providing a basis for judgments about the functional utility or functional obsolescence of the structure.

Highest and Best Use Analysis

The most important single determination that the appraiser must make is his conclusion of the highest and best use of the land, as well as the highest and best use of the property. One alternative that any existing industrial structure presents to the appraiser is conversion to another use, or supercession of use. That alternative may require the demolition of all or part of the existing structure.

Cost Estimates

The complexity of the typical industrial real estate building, with its specialized fixtures and equipment, often requires the industrial real estate appraiser to recruit outside specialists for the valuation of equipment and/or fixtures. This is a highly specialized field of valuation, and often involves the estimation of removal costs for superfluous equipment or fixtures. This can be quite expensive for the owner or developer.[19]

Cost manuals can be effectively utilized in estimating the reproduction cost new of fairly standardized industrial buildings, and of some custom buildings if the cost manual itself is detailed enough.[20] Nevertheless, the application of the information in cost manuals still requires a high degree of technical knowledge and technical skill on the part of the appraiser. The complexities involved in attempting to adjust the relatively standardized figures contained in cost manuals leads one authority to argue that "most appraisers prefer to collect cost data from actual cost experiences in their own locality."[21] In many instances, cost data can be verified from actual construction contracts. This is expensive and time-consuming, however, and is justified only when the estimate of reproduction cost new is to be utilized as a firm basis for value estimation.

When relatively new buildings are being appraised, or when proposed construction is to be valued, cost figures are extremely important. Moreover, cost new is the basis for the rent "factor" in many long-term industrial leases on new buildings. However, the reproduction cost new of an industrial building is simply a guidepost and not necessarily a measure of value. Cost is not necessarily equal to value, and cost itself does not create value.

Depreciation Analysis

The measurement of accrued physical deterioration and of economic obsolescence is not significantly different in industrial appraisals, although it is

---

[19] For a detailed discussion of the problems involved in the valuation of industrial equipment and fixtures, see Samuel M. Dix, "Fixture Qualification and Valuation for Condemnation of the Major Industrial Complex," *The Appraisal Journal,* Vol. 34, No. 2, April, 1966.

[20] Examples of the degree of detail that can be provided by such manuals can be examined in the chapters on "Industrial Buildings," "Warehouses" and "Truck Terminals" in E. H. Boeckh & Associates, *Boeckh's Manual of Appraisals,* 6th ed. (Washington, The Author, 1962).

[21] Shenkel, *Principles and Practices of Industrial Real Estate,* p. 74.

occasionally difficult to ascertain what a "cost to cure" may be, since it may include removal of structural components, equipment or fixtures. However, the real problems in industrial real estate appraisal via the Cost Approach center on the identification and measurement of functional obsolescence. Industrial real estate is valued because of its use, and the highly specialized character of much industrial construction combines with continually changing standards of industrial space requirements to accelerate depreciation via functional obsolescence.

"In appraising industrial property, it is essential to base depreciation on local trends and logical reasons that are fully detailed in the narrative report. . . . Probably the final test of functional obsolescence would be the appraiser's judgment of building usefulness for industrial purposes, an opinion based on knowledge of local industrial trends, existing vacancies, and the quality and volume of new industrial construction." [22] Functional obsolescence and its measurement remain *the* basic problem in the estimation of accrued depreciation in industrial buildings, and their adaptability is the final test of their value.

Applications of the Cost Approach to Industrial Property

The Cost Approach is much more appropriate for the valuation of more nearly standardized industrial buildings, especially when there is enough activity in the market to make the standards of that market perfectly clear. New and proposed construction can be valued via the Cost Approach, and cost estimates provide one important side of the equation in feasibility analysis. In insurance valuations, property tax valuations, and problems involving corporate mergers or exchanges of stock, the Cost Approach estimates are often very helpful. [23]

Limitations of the Cost Approach

Cost standards are difficult to apply. Estimating "typical" construction costs for a highly differentiated product, such as an industrial plant, is extremely hazardous. Standardized units are not particularly applicable in the case of specialized industrial properties. Square foot or cubic foot cost estimates rarely will do the job properly. Therefore, a lengthy and complex cost estimating procedure is often required, without particular assurance that it will result in any better estimate of value at the end.

From the point of view of technique, the most fundamental limitation of the application of the Cost Approach to industrial property lies in the necessity to estimate accrued functional obsolescence.

Conceptually, there is a further objection. Industrial real estate that is subject to a long-term lease is not appropriately valued via the Cost Approach because the credit rating of the tenant and the financing that can be based upon that credit rating are most influential on the market, rather than the physical characteristics of the real estate itself.

---

[22] William M. Shenkel, "Valuation of Industrial Buildings," *The Real Estate Appraiser*, Vol. 31, No. 12, December, 1965, p. 10.

[23] Shenkel, *Principles and Practices of Industrial Real Estate*, p. 66.

CAPITALIZATION OF INCOME ON INDUSTRIAL REAL ESTATE

The income-producing character of industrial real estate is underscored by the fact that among all of the types of real estate that generate some net income, industrial real estate produces the highest ratio of net income to gross income.[24]

In the valuation of industrial real estate via the Income Approach, less emphasis is placed on the real estate itself; more is placed upon the user (and the use), the financing, the terms of any lease, and the terms of sale. The market toward which this analysis is oriented is an investment market.

Three types of division of industrial real estate are utilized in the Income Approach for analytical purposes. The most traditional divison is along physical lines, between land and improvements. This is the basis for that portion of the Income Approach that emphasizes the real estate, and utilizes residual techniques for value estimation.

An alternative method of dividing real estate is to emphasize the legal rights (the "bundle of rights") contained in lessor and lessee estates. These are the leased fee and the leasehold, respectively. This is the foundation for the credit-oriented "paper deal" that is so widespread in industrial real estate appraisal.

A third division can be made in terms of the financial or investment interests in the real estate. This is the equity-mortgage approach. It usually involves an attempt to develop an overall capitalization rate for converting net income into value, thereby avoiding the knotty problem of providing directly and separately for capital recapture.

Each of these alternative methods has its uses and its limitations in industrial real estate appraisal.

Residual Techniques

The examples of net income capitalization provided in Chapter 12 illustrate the application of all three residual techniques to industrial property valuation: land residual, building residual, and property residual. The residual techniques are utilized when value estimates of fee simple estates are made. It is presumed that there will be some debt financing in order to take advantage of leverage. Economic rent is the basis for income estimation.

1. *The Income Estimate.* When gross income estimates are made in terms of economic rent, particular care must be taken to include service income generated in the building. In industrial properties (particularly multi-tenant, converted loft or mill structures), income from the sale of utilities to tenants, and from concessions, is often an extremely important segment of total receipts.

When credit is not the basis for value estimation, gross income is much more likely to be adjusted for vacancy, as well as for operating expenses borne by the lessor. Vacancies are in fact encountered in multitenant industrial buildings. The vacancy and rent loss factor is developed from the

---

[24] AIREA, *op. cit.*, p. 267.

standards and experiences of the local market. The only general guide for the appraiser is the admonition that he search that market carefully.

The appraiser must know what operating expenses are appropriate for the type of property in question, and which ones are normally borne by the lessor. In multitenant structures, the lessor is more likely to assume responsibility for a larger proportion of total building operating expenses. However, the appraiser must be careful to deduct only those expenses paid by the *owner*.

In connection with operating expense estimates, the appraiser should be aware of the fact that use can often affect these operating expenses. The previously cited example of the furniture processing firm raising fire insurance premiums is an appropriate illustration.

2. *Rate of Return.* In developing an interest rate, or rate of return on the investment, the appraiser must turn to the market. This does not mean that he can obtain the information with little or no effort. It may require a considerable amount of analysis, as is illustrated in the development of an interest rate for an industrial warehouse in Exhibit 79. Six sales of comparable industrial warehouses that had sold recently in the market were analyzed in order to derive an estimate of the interest rate operative in each transaction. At the time of the sale, each warehouse was leased for no more than 10 years to a local tenant (as was the subject property), and in each instance the lessor assumed responsibility for real estate taxes, insurance, and exterior maintenance.

Exhibit 79

ILLUSTRATION OF DEVELOPMENT OF MARKET INTEREST RATE FOR
INDUSTRIAL WAREHOUSE

No. Sale	Gross Income	Est. Expenses	Est. Net Income	Sales Price	Land	Impv.	Eco-nomic Life	Recap-ture to Improve-ments	Bal. to Interest	Indi-cated Int. Rate
A	$ 9,600	$1,350	$ 8,250	$100,000	$35,000	$ 65,000	33	$1,950	$ 6,300	6.30%
B	20,000	6,000	14,000	175,000	63,000	112,000	40	2,800	11,200	6.40
C	16,300	3,910	12,390	147,500	32,000	115,500	40	2,890	9,500	6.44
D	12,000	2,500	9,500	110,000	35,000	75,000	33	2,250	7,250	6.59
E	24,000	6,050	17,950	200,000	40,000	160,000	33	4,800	13,150	6.58
F	18,000	4,750	13,250	155,000	35,000	120,000	40	3,000	10,250	6.61

Indicated Interest Rate for Subject Property	6.5 %

From the gross rent figure for each of the six comparable warehouse sales, estimates of operating expenses were deducted, to establish an estimate of net income. This net income figure was a Net Income Before Recapture. Next, straight-line capital recapture was calculated from the estimated remaining economic life of each comparable property. This remaining economic life was estimated independently by the appraiser in each instance. The annual provision for recapture in each comparable was subtracted from net income before recapture. The remaining income was then divided by the sale price to develop an indicated interest rate for each comparable sale. Finally, correlation of the six rate indications led to the conclusion that an appropriate interest rate to use for the subject warehouse was 6.5 per cent.

This illustrates one method for the derivation of an interest rate from the market. Although it may appear complex and slightly cumbersome, it is actually quite straightforward.

3. *Capital Recapture.* The appraiser must decide what the appropriate method of capital recapture shall be, and he must also estimate what the capital recapture period is. In most appraisals involving emphasis on the real estate and the application of residual techniques, straight-line capital recapture is employed. Moreover, the typical investor in property of the type to which this approach is most applicable is most probably a private, profit-seeking individual or organization which is attempting to take maximum advantage of depreciation and long-term capital gains provisions in the federal income tax regulations. Capital recapture periods of relatively short duration are not uncommon. Nevertheless, appraisal custom often calls for the utilization of a capital recapture period equal to the remaining economic life of the improvements. This is one of the serious limitations to the application of the real estate-oriented version of the Capitalization of Income Approach.

An example of a building residual technique combined with *annuity* capital recapture is provided in Exhibit 80. This illustrates the fact that these are mechanically compatible. It requires analysis by the appraiser to ascertain the appropriate capital recapture method for any particular problem.

Appraising Credit and Lease Interests

When there is a long-term lease on the property, and the lessee firm has a high credit standing, the emphasis is placed on the financial aspects of the transaction. It becomes a "paper deal." Real estate considerations are secondary. Financing of the real estate is available on more favorable terms to the lessor, and the lessor in turn also has considerably less risk as far as either vacancy or the receipt of rent is concerned.

Under these circumstances, annuity capitalization is always employed. The net income anticipated under the lease (whether it is a "net" lease or not) is capitalized as an annuity until the expiration of the lease. The present worth of the anticipated reversion is added to derive the estimate of value of the property. This actually produces an estimate of value of the leased fee, which may or may not be equal to the value of the fee simple. The two are equal only when the contract rent under the lease equals the economic rent at the time of the appraisal.

Both build-lease and sale-leaseback transactions are typically credit-

Exhibit 80

ILLUSTRATION OF THE CAPITALIZATION OF INDUSTRIAL PROPERTY BY
CAPITALIZING NET INCOME

(Annuity Capitalization, Building Residual Technique)

(The valuation of a multiple-story building suitable for light manufacturing)		
Gross Income, 12,600 square feet at $.85		$10,710
Less Vacancy rate of 10%		−1,070
Effective Gross Income		$ 9,640
Less Expenses		
Taxes	$1,172	
Maintenance and Repair, 12,996 square		
feet at $0.05	650	
Property insurance, $62,000 at $.003	186	
Management 5% of effective gross		
income	482	−2,490
Net income, land and building before depreciation		$ 7,150
Less income attributable to the land, 6% of		
$11,000 (land value)		−660
Net income to building		$ 6,490
Capitalized Value of Building		
$6,490 times Inwood factor, 10.675 (8%, including		
depreciation, 25 years)		69,281
Estimated Land Value		11,000
Estimated Market value, land and building, rounded		$80,000

SOURCE: William M. Shenkel, *Principles and Practices of Industrial Real Estate: A Course Syllabus* (Washington, Society of Industrial Realtors, 1963), p. 76.

oriented. Financing is generally not available for specialized or custom construction unless there is a high-credit occupant of the real estate.

One major aspect of leased fee versus fee simple valuation is the situation in which the contract rent is different from the economic rent. If the contract rent is greater than the economic rent, the lessor has the right to collect more rent than he would receive if the property were leased on an open market basis at the time of the appraisal. This premium to the lessor means that the leased fee is worth more than the fee simple would be. This is why many writers object to a lease being universally regarded as an "encumbrance," since it often results in enhanced value to the lessor.

When the contract rent is less than economic rent, the leasehold estate also has value. This is because the right to occupy the space in question over the remaining period of the lease, at a rental which is less than the going market rate, is a valuable right. It has market value because it is negotiable unless there is a specific prohibition against subletting in the lease.

The question of the respective values of the leased fee and the leasehold, and of their relationship to the value of the fee simple, is a subject of considerable debate among appraisers. Many argue that the leased fee and the leasehold estate together must always add to the value of the fee simple. This is the position taken by the courts in all condemnation proceedings, and the maximum that will be awarded is the value of the fee simple. The allocation of the award between lessor and lessee is their problem, and not the court's.

On the other hand, others argue that there is no necessary reason that the leased fee and the leasehold estate should add to the value of the fee simple. Some contend that it will be true only when the interest rates appropriate to the leased fee, leasehold, and the fee simple are all identical. This position deserves further comment.

As an example, assume an industrial property with a 20-year, net-net-net lease to a good credit calls for an annual rental of $4,000. The reversion at the expiration of the lease has been carefully estimated to be $50,000. The appropriate rate of discount for a risk of this type is 8 per cent. The economic rent of the property is $5,000 per year. The situation is depicted in Exhibit 81, which shows the effects of mechanical versus analytical handling of this situation.

Exhibit 81

ILLUSTRATIVE EXAMPLE OF LEASED FEE, LEASEHOLD AND FEE SIMPLE VALUATION UNDER LONG-TERM LEASE

Present worth of $50,000 reversion 20 years hence at 8% (.214548 x $50,000)	$10,727
Present worth of $5,000 per annum for 20 years at 8% (9.818147 x $5,000)	$49,091
Present worth of $4,000 per annum for 20 years at 8% (9.818147 x $4,000)	$39,273
Present worth of $4,000 per annum for 20 years at 7% (10.594014 x $4,000)	$42,376
Present worth of leasehold estate by subtraction, using 8% for fee simple and for leased fee	$ 9,816
Indicated interest rate, $9,816 present worth of $1,000 per annum for 20 years: 8%	
Present worth of leasehold estate by subtraction, fee simple at 8%, leased fee at 7%:	$ 6,815
Indicated interest rate, present worth at $6,815, $1,000 per annum 20 years: 13.53%.	

The figures provided in Exhibit 81 illustrate the logical pitfall involved in assuming that the interest rate on a leased fee, which calls for a less-than-market rental, will be the same as the interest rate on the fee simple for the same property under an economic rental. It is difficult to imagine a situation in which a lessee would voluntarily abandon space which can be used for below-market rentals. Therefore, there is a higher degree of safety because of less risk to the lessor that the tenant will default, or that there will be any vacancy. The lessor is virtually assured of receiving his rent, so long as it is less than economic rent, because the tenant can always sublet, at the least.

The lessee, on the other hand, has an estate which, while valuable, is also subject to substantial variation in value. If market conditions change, and the $4,000 per year rental is no longer a favorable one, then the value of the leasehold estate will be substantially reduced, or possibly extinguished. This must be reflected in a rate which includes a provision for the lessee's risk. One author has suggested that the leasehold rate might well be figured at twice the leased fee rate.[25] In the example in Exhibit 81, this relationship is very closely approximated. Further support is given this argument in the basic, authoritative text in real estate appraisal which states that "leasehold rates are the counterpart of equity rates, and it follows that leased fee rates tend to correspond to first mortgage rates." [26] Therefore, the practice of estimating the value of the leasehold by subtracting the value of the leased fee from the capitalized value of economic rent (the fee simple) may be appropriate for industrial real estate valuation, provided it is always properly applied.

Equity-Mortgage Analysis

When the focus of industrial real estate analysis is on the profit-seeking investor who utilizes financing terms to maximize his leverage, the thinking of that investor translates itself to the valuation procedures of the industrial appraiser. Equity-mortgage analysis starts out with the presumption that a long-term lease to a well-rated tenant is an asset rather than an encumbrance on the real estate, at least as far as the financial and money markets are concerned.

The investor will utilize the credit available to him through the lease to maximize the financing that he can obtain. Moreover, the investor is not interested in accounting income as much as cash flow. That is, the actual cash return that comes to the investor is the basis for his evaluation of the attractiveness of the industrial real estate purchase, according to this approach. Cash flow is the difference between net income before recapture and mortgage service charges.

Debt service charges are quite important in the equity-mortgage analysis. The appraiser must engage in a careful and detailed study of mortgage market terms and conditions to ascertain with as high a degree of precision as possible the type of financing that is likely to be obtained. All mortgage loan terms influence the constant, and hence the amount that is deducted from the annual net income before recapture in order to develop a cash flow projection.

The cash flow is then capitalized at an appropriate rate in order to estimate what the investor would be justified or warranted in paying *in cash* for the right to receive the cash flow. Capital recapture is achieved in part through mortgage amortization, and in part through the proceeds of sale or refinancing at the expiration of the capital recapture or turnover period.[27]

---

[25] Bruce R. Ricks, "Valuation of Lessor and Lessee Interests in a Physical Asset," *The Appraisal Journal,* Vol. 34, No. 2, April, 1966.

[26] AIREA, *op. cit.,* p. 410.

[27] A concise statement of this position, together with mathematical examples of its application in appraisal practice, is found in James E. Gibbons, "Mortgage-Equity Capitalization: Ellwood Method," *The Appraisal Journal,* Vol. 34, No. 2, April, 1966.

As an example, assume that an industrial property generates $10,000 per year rental income, and on which the annual operating expenses are $2,400. The net before capital recapture is therefore $7,600. There is a $50,000, 20-year, 6.5 per cent mortgage on the property, calling for full amortization over 20 years on an equal monthly payment basis. The annual debt service on the mortgage is approximately $4,474. Therefore, the cash flow before income tax is $3,126. The mortgage constant, incidentally, is 8.95 per cent.

If the mortgage is presumed to be a 60 per cent loan, then the equity is approximately $33,333. The cash flow return is therefore 9.38 per cent. This ignores the value of any reversion at the end of 20 years.

This approach is most useful in investment decision-making, because it shows the investor or potential purchaser what cash return he will receive on his cash investment. This helps in estimating value for "no market" real estate because the potential investor or purchaser has his own standards of acceptability in a rate of return, regardless of what "the market" thinks. This is very close to Value in Use, which has an important role in industrial real estate value analysis.

1. *The Ellwood Approach.* It is impossible in a brief discourse to do more than hint at the implications of the pattern of real estate investment analysis developed by L. W. Ellwood. Several basic references are available for further investigation, however.[28]

The important additional feature that the Ellwood analysis adds to more standard equity-mortgage analysis is that the Ellwood approach provides for the inclusion of the *anticipated* reversion as part of the overall rate of return to the investor. It is a form of direct capitalization that goes to the investment and financial markets, rather than the real estate sales market for its standards and basic data. It emphasizes the income aspect of industrial real estate, rather than its realty features.

The inclusion of the reversion as one of two important ingredients in the total return that the investor is seeking makes it possible to consider the implications of different reversions on the equity return. For example, within the Ellwood framework, an appraiser can discover with relative ease what difference it would make to the investor's overall rate of return if the property were to decrease by 10 per cent over the capital recapture period, if it were to remain at its present value level, or if it were to appreciate by 5 per cent. Investment real estate, including industrial property, does often appreciate; indeed, investors often buy with that anticipation in mind. The Ellwood analysis makes it possible for the appraiser (and for the industrial real estate broker acting as an adviser) to counsel the potential purchaser not only about the present worth of the property, but about the probabilities that he will realize a particular overall rate of return at the expiration of his

[28] Gibbons, *op. cit.*; L. W. Ellwood, *Ellwood Tables for Real Estate Appraising and Financing* (Ridgewood, N.J., The Author, 1959); William N. Kinnard, Jr., "The Ellwood Approach to Valuation: A Return to Fundamentals," *The Real Estate Appraiser*, Vol. 32, No. 5, May, 1966.

holding period. The Ellwood approach offers application in counseling as well as in appraising problems.

SPECIAL PROBLEMS IN INDUSTRIAL REAL ESTATE APPRAISAL

Single-Use Properties

The highly specialized character of much industrial real estate is a feature which is emphasized again and again in discussions of industrial appraisal. In particular, the single-use property represents a serious challenge to the appraiser. There are no sales data, rarely any rent information and certainly no "going market rentals," and almost no facts for comparative purposes. This is what one authority calls "the practical industrial real estate market." [29]

In such circumstances, there are two courses of action open to the appraiser. First, he can estimate the going concern value of the real estate by measuring the contribution that the plant makes to the success of the business enterprise. The character of the user is reflected in the real estate, which in its turn influences the profitability of the user's operations. This is the estimation of Value in Use.

The other alternative is to analyze carefully and thoroughly the adaptability and possible alternative uses of the property. This is, in effect, highest and best use analysis, with alternate use or conversion in mind.

Perhaps the most difficult aspect of this particular type of assignment is "selling" the conclusions to the client, because usually the market value of the property is substantially below its value in use, or its "going concern value." It is also likely to be only a fraction of the book value. Book value is not meaningful on the market, but it does have significance in the mind of the owner.

Reuse Appraisals

In urban renewal clearance projects, appraisers are always required to estimate the value of the cleared and assembled site as if it were available for its new use. The public agency, utilizing its power of eminent domain with the accompanying right of condemnation, can assemble parcels of a size which are usable and economically marketable. In many instances, the proposed reuse is industrial, and the appraiser then must approach this as an industrial site valuation assignment—but with differences.

The first difference is that reuse sites are usually sold subject to a considerable array of use limitations and restrictions. These go far beyond the usual zoning and building code regulations. In addition to density and setback requirements, usual limitations placed on "light industrial" reuse areas include prohibitions against outside storage, requirements of screening for any parking or rear yard areas, landscaping of frontage setbacks, and pro-

---

[29] Statement from Max J. Derbes, Jr., S.I.R., MAI, SREA.

hibitions against or controls of fencing. It is the experience of many industrial reuse appraisers that these controls, important though they may be to the land use plan of the community and of the renewal project, are serious deterrents to the marketability of much industrial reuse land.[30] Therefore, the valuation of such sites must include a detailed analysis of land use controls which is considerably more than a mere recital of the provisions in the proposed regulations. "To the extent that land-use controls are inconsistent with trends in industrial location, the utility of industrial sites will be lowered and, to be sure, the land value decreased." [31] .

Industrial reuse sites in center-city locations are generally intended for "light manufacturing" or distributive use. The locational amenities of these sites often warrant such use. For example, the Windsor Street Project Area in Hartford, Connecticut, is located at the intersection of two Interstate highways and affords fast, toll-free access to virtually all of the northeastern United States via high-speed highway transportation. As a result, nearly all of its occupants are distributors and service firms rather than manufacturing establishments.

Such land is usually relatively expensive. It normally is offered for sale in the range of $0.90 to $1.25 per square foot, when outlying industrial sites in the same general regions are selling for perhaps $0.25 to $0.40 per square foot. Even space for assembly and fabrication is generally priced fairly high when it is in central-city locations. In New Haven, Connecticut, for example, the "going price" for industrial sites in three reuse areas was $0.60 to $0.90 per square foot, and fabricating plants generally paid the $0.60 figure (based on $25,000 per acre)—industrial sites were selling between $10,000 and $12,000 per acre in nearby towns.

An industrial reuse appraisal calls for an opinion of value for a site which may be unique in its own area, and unlike any other property in the community. In such circumstances, comparisons are extremely difficult. The "market" within which the appraiser estimates the value of the site may be geographically scattered. Moreover, because the sums involved are relatively large, the purchasers and developers of industrial sites in reuse areas are often limited in number in any locality. This makes further market analysis demands on the appraiser. Speculation is also usually prohibited in land disposition contracts under urban renewal; the purchasers of land must usually develop it themselves for use or rental of the space. It is common to find a prohibition against resale or lease of the land within a three to five-year period.

The appraiser is attempting to evaluate land in a new environment and a new market area that is being created. He rarely has similar previous sales to study, except in other industrial project areas in nearby or "competitive" communities.[32]

---

[30] See, for example, William M. Shenkel, "Reuse Appraisals: A Critical View," *The Appraisal Journal,* Vol. 34, No. 2, April, 1966. The experience of the present author in several reuse appraisal assignments in New England substantiates this view.

[31] Shenkel, "Reuse Appraisals: A Critical View," p. 21.

[32] This method was used by the present author in appraising an industrial reuse area in New Haven, Connecticut. Comparable market information was developed from industrial reuse

Finally, the "as of" date is usually three to five years in the future, and the appraiser is required to forecast or project market conditions as they are expected to prevail then. Since unanticipated delay seems to occur in nearly every urban renewal project, the investors' expectations of having their time schedules upset must also be built into the probable pattern of bids for the land. Often, the appraiser must estimate a present worth figure, which requires either a built-in waiting period for the purchaser with funds unproductively committed, or a discount of value from some time in the future (three to five years hence) to the present.

Condemnation and Partial Taking Appraisals

When a public agency acquires industrial real estate under eminent domain, with or without condemnation proceedings, the owner of the real estate is entitled to "just compensation." [33] The courts have consistently held that the payment of market value for the rights in realty that are taken constitutes just compensation. When there is a total taking of the entire "bundle" of rights held by an owner, the appraisal problem is no different from that involved in estimating market value under ordinary sale conditions. The owner of the property may argue that he is an unwilling seller, but by definition, in the eyes of the law, he is a willing seller and entitled to the market value of his rights.

There are circumstances involving industrial real estate in which eminent domain and condemnation proceedings create particular valuation problems, however. The first is a partial taking, in which only a portion of the real estate is acquired. In many jurisdictions, taking authorities are not permitted to acquire more land or real estate than is actually needed for the project. The portion of the real estate actually acquired is the "taking," while that which is left is the "remainder." The usual rule in partial taking appraisals is that two separate and distinct appraisals shall be made: a "before" appraisal of the total property immediately before the taking; and an "after" appraisal of the remainder. The difference between the market value of the entire property before the taking and the market value of the remainder after the taking constitutes the damages, which is the measure of just compensation to the owner.

The "before and after" appraisal approach requires two complete and independent appraisals, with particular emphasis on highest and best use analysis, availability, with financing, rentability, and market acceptance— especially of the remainder. A serious problem often emerges when the damages incurred by the property are considerably more than proportionate to the amount of the taking. For example, a large truck terminal was adjacent to a highway that was widened. The proposed taking for widening

site sales in Bridgeport, Hartford, New Britain and Stamford, which were regarded as the best guides to the value of the sites in question. All were between 25 and 50 miles distant from the subject area. For further discussion of Industrial Reuse Appraising, see William M. Shenkel, *A Guide to Appraising Industrial Property* (Chicago, Society of Real Estate Appraisers, 1967), pp. 112–122.

[33] For a detailed discussion of the appraisal problems involved in condemnation, consult George M. Schmutz and Edwin M. Rams, *Condemnation Appraisal Handbook,* rev. ed. (Englewood Cliffs, N.J., Prentice-Hall, 1963).

purposes "nearly" eliminated the driveway to the rear yard where the loading platforms, parking facilities, and service facilities were located. Without that driveway, it was impossible to gain access to the rear. Even though a very small portion of the real estate was taken, value was reduced by approximately 60 per cent, because a new and less productive (in rental income) use became the highest and best use of the property.

A second problem that often confronts the appraiser of industrial real estate on a condemnation assignment is to recommend the allocation of any award between lessor and lessee, on the basis of the respective values of the leased fee and the leasehold estate. This requires the appropriate and separate valuation of each of these estates, and a further estimation of the proportion that each represents of the total value of the real estate. This may also be necessary when an award for a partial taking is made, since part of the damages will be suffered by the lessee. He may be entitled to a *pro rata* share of the damage award, *unless* he is specifically precluded from this under the terms of the lease.

Still another problem arises in partial taking cases in those jurisdictions which require a separate estimate of the part taken. In such cases, the benefits of a project cannot be offset against the value of the part taken. Therefore, it is necessary for the appraiser to apportion to the land and improvements taken that portion of the total estimated "before" value.

When a portion of a building is taken, some states require payment for the entire building. The practical solution, in many cases, is payment for the portion of the improvements in the right of way plus a "cost to cure" of the remaining improvements. Additionally, payment must be made for the land taken and severance damages to the remainder property. By using the cost to cure, the "after" value estimate is based upon the corrected condition. The property owner is paid not only for the difference between the "before" and "after" value, but also an amount of the cost to cure the "open end" building.

Lastly, a project may result in special benefits to the industrial property by changing the highest and best use of the property. This often occurs when the remainder property becomes a strategic location for a motel or service station at a major interchange. The industrial appraiser should be aware of the particular treatment of special benefits under the law of the jurisdiction of the taking.[34]

Renovation

The detailed discussion of rehabilitation and conversion in Chapter 11 includes a reference to feasibility analysis. This involves making two appraisals, in effect: a "before" value estimate of the property "as is"; and an "after" value estimate of the property "as renovated." These two value estimates are analogous to the "before and after" appraisals required in partial takings under eminent domain.

Complete and separate appraisals must be made, with particular emphasis on highest and best use, income, and market acceptability. In point of fact, it might be argued that a third "appraisal" of sorts is necessary to complete the feasibility analysis. That is because the difference between the "before" value and the "after" value must be compared with expected

[34] Statement from Max J. Derbes, Jr., S.I.R., MAI, SREA.

costs in order to make the decision whether to proceed with the renovation program. This cost estimate must also be carefully developed. It often requires the services of a professional cost estimator, a contractor, an engineer and/or an architect—particularly if the project is a substantial one.

ROLE OF THE INDUSTRIAL REAL ESTATE BROKER

In industrial real estate appraisal, there are three types of activity in which the industrial broker may find himself engaged. First, he is an important source of market information for the appraiser. When both are serving the same client, in particular, the broker is often a basic source to whom the appraiser will turn for much information about both the property and the market within which the real estate is to be valued. The broker, therefore, should have a good working knowledge of the data requirements in industrial property appraisal. Beyond this, the technical knowledge he possesses about user requirements can be invaluable to the appraiser.

The second important function of the broker in industrial appraisal analysis is a direct outgrowth of the first. Because of his knowledge of the market and of the requirements of industrial users, the broker can provide the appraiser with important insights into the standards of the market. In particular, he can be an important source of advice and counsel about what constitutes functional utility (and its counterpart, functional obsolescence) for the type of space being appraised.

Finally, many brokers also appraise industrial real estate. Many authorities argue that the appraisal of industrial real estate requires brokerage experience. Most major firms of S.I.R. members have appraisal departments, and many report that a substantial volume of their brokerage business stems directly from appraisal assignments undertaken for clients. Appraisal is most definitely one integral aspect of the industrial real estate brokerage business.

At the same time, however, brokerage experience alone is not sufficient to provide an individual with the technical skills necessary for professional appraisal work. If he offers his services as an appraiser for a fee, then the industrial real estate broker has an obligation both to himself and to his clients to acquire the necessary technical training and skills to do a truly professional job. Necessary as it is, "knowing the market" is simply not enough. The industrial broker-appraiser must also understand the tools he is employing, their meaning, and their application.

SELECTED REFERENCES

American Association of State Highway Officials, *Acquisition for Right-of-Way* (Washington, The Author, 1962).

American Institute of Real Estate Appraisers, *The Appraisal of Real Estate,* 4th ed. (Chicago, The Author, 1964).

Boeckh, E. H., & Associates, *Boeckh's Manual of Appraisals,* 6th ed. (Washington, The Author, 1963), especially Ch. 21, 25 and 26.

Derbes, Max J., Jr., *Industrial Real Estate Appraisal,* Unpublished Manuscript, 1966.

Ellwood, L. W., *Ellwood Tables for Real Estate Appraising and Financing* (Ridgewood, N.J., The Author, 1959).

Fullerton, Paul, "Appraisal of Industrial Property," Ch. 16 of *Encyclopedia of Real Estate Appraising.* Friedman, Edith J., ed. (Englewood Cliffs, N.J., Prentice-Hall, 1959).

Gibbons, James E., "Mortgage-Equity Capitalization: Ellwood Method," *The Appraisal Journal,* Vol. 34, No. 2, April, 1966.

Hoyt, Homer, "Appraisal of Different Types of Real Property," *The Appraisal Journal,* Vol. 32, No. 3, July, 1964.

Kahn, Sanders A., Case, Frederick E., and Schimmel, Alfred, *Real Estate Appraisal and Investment* (New York, Ronald Press, 1963).

Kinnard, William N., Jr., "Investment and Financing Considerations," *Appraising Apartments: Instructor's Manual* (Chicago, Society of Real Estate Appraisers, 1963).

McMichael, Stanley L., *McMichael's Appraising Manual,* 4th ed. (Englewood Cliffs, N.J., Prentice-Hall, 1951).

Ratcliff, Richard U., ed., *Papers and Proceedings: The Wisconsin Colloquium on Appraisal Research* (Madison, Wisconsin, University of Wisconsin, 1963):
    Babcock, Frederick M., "Re-Use Analysis and Valuation";
    McCormack, James E., "Appraisal Limitations from the Standpoint of the Urban Renewal Agency";
    Smith, Larry, "Problems of Real Estate Investment Analysis of Large Projects."

Ratcliff, Richard U., *Private Investment in Urban Redevelopment,* Research Report No. 17 (Berkeley, California, Center for Real Estate and Urban Economics, University of California-Berkeley, 1961).

Ricks, R. Bruce, "Valuation of Lessor and Lessee Interests in a Physical Asset," *The Appraisal Journal,* Vol. 34, No. 2, April, 1966.

Ring, Alfred A., *The Valuation of Real Estate* (Englewood Cliffs, N.J., Prentice-Hall, 1963).

Schmutz, George L., and Rams, Edwin M., *Condemnation Appraisal Handbook,* rev. ed. (Englewood Cliffs, N.J., Prentice-Hall, 1963).

Shenkel, William M., *A Guide to Appraising Industrial Property* (Chicago, Society of Real Estate Appraisers, 1967).

Shenkel, William M., "The Effective Use of Development Leases," *Ground Leases,* Trerice, Byron, Jr., sponsor (Chicago, National Institute of Real Estate Brokers, December, 1965).

Shenkel, William M., *Principles and Practices of Industrial Real Estate: A Course Syllabus* (Washington, Society of Industrial Realtors, 1963).

PART **IV**

Industrial Real Estate
Development

14

Industrial Property Development and Pioneering

WHEN raw acreage is developed into industrial sites, with or without the construction of new buildings on the sites that have been created, there is a variety of opportunity and challenge for the industrial real estate broker. If the acreage is developed under a comprehensive plan, with development and use controls enforced by the developing and owning group, the resulting concentration of industrial uses is called an Industrial Park or a Planned Industrial District. These are the subject of the discussion in Chapters 15 and 16. In the present chapter, the emphasis is placed on tracts of land typically developed for no more than two or three users— and most frequently for a single user or building—as a speculation by the developer. "Speculation" is used in the technical sense of an investment of time and money in expectation of an increase in property values. To the extent that the speculation is successful, the pioneer-developer of industrial real estate is a creator of value.

NATURE OF INDUSTRIAL DEVELOPMENT AND PIONEERING

Industrial development is essentially the process of producing suitably prepared industrial sites and appropriately constructed industrial buildings to meet the anticipated demands of industrial users. It is often divided between land development and building construction. Industrial land development includes platting, zoning, grading, and the installation of streets, utilities, and rail connections—*all* as necessary "to make the land completely available for industrial use. In some cases, development may also include the construction of buildings for sale or lease." [1]

The developer's profit often results from pioneering in a new area and

---

[1] Stuart P. Walsh, "Industrial Land Development," *Real Estate Encyclopedia,* Edith J. Friedman, ed. (Englewood Cliffs, New Jersey, Prentice-Hall, 1960), p. 1020.

actually creating a market. The private entrepreneur is seeking profit or capital increments. Community-sponsored programs of development, on the other hand, usually seek to expand local employment opportunities. Public utilities and railroads occasionally sponsor industrial development projects as a means of stimulating revenues from the sale of their services. Railroad-sponsored development is usually in planned districts, however.

Speculative industrial development or pioneering is feasible because many firms need new buildings quickly. Very often, the potential user of an industrial site or an industrial plant delays the decision to seek a new location until the last minute. When the need for new space becomes critical, sites and/or buildings that are available quickly have a competitive edge on the market. A standing shell building may be available for occupancy as much as five months sooner than a custom building that must be started from scratch.[2]

Distinction from Planned Districts

The development or pioneering of industrial sites and buildings in small numbers should be distinguished from the formation of a planned industrial district or industrial park. Aside from the obvious difference in the size of the operation, the primary distinction lies in the degree of control that is exercised by the developer in managing the project, and in the selection of compatible occupants.

Acreage or sites developed on an individual basis are often referred to as unorganized industrial areas. These represent the bulk of the acreage used or available for industrial purposes. The development is essentially unplanned, and may or may not be particularly efficient. One function of the industrial real estate broker is to indicate the type of approach that is most likely to produce effective results, in the form of profits for the entrepreneur.

The development of unorganized or unplanned industrial areas is often termed the "natural process" of industrial development. "The individually or incidentally grouped sites generally just happen, and we find in this instance that land is used in the initial stages to its fullest potential. Generally speaking, there is inadequate room for expansion, parking, and satellite services." [3]

Despite these differences, pioneering and development of individual tracts is basically similar in concept to the development of an industrial park. There is little difference between the two as far as principles are concerned. The primary distinctions lie in their scope and method of execution.

Parties and Motivations Involved

1. *Private Developers.* The private, profit-seeking developer predominates in industrial pioneering and development. This may be a private individual who is a contractor or perhaps an industrial real estate broker. More likely, it is a private corporation which combines a number of development skills. If the skills are not available among the principals in the

---

[2] Statement in interview with Peter O. Hanson, S.I.R., Hackensack, New Jersey.
[3] Statement in interview with Thomas J. Daly, S.I.R., New York City.

organization, then they must be hired. They include the talents of the site and land planner, the construction contractor, the engineer, the architect, and the financial broker. Moreover, legal, tax, and economic advice must be sought if they are not represented in the development organization.

Most importantly, there must be a competent and experienced project manager for the development program. Otherwise, the necessary coordination of skills and resources will probably be lacking. The experienced industrial real estate broker can usually serve effectively as project manager.

The developer recognizes that a need exists, and that a parcel of land can be improved to meet this need. The developer's profit is the difference between the value of the completed property and the cost of land and building, less the costs of carrying the investment until the project is successfully sold or leased. The private developer-builder usually pays close attention to accelerated depreciation provisions in the federal income tax regulations because this often offers attractive opportunities for a temporary tax-free cash flow.

Whatever the developer's objectives, they must be defined carefully in advance. They influence the steps he will take to achieve the objectives. Recognizing these steps, in turn, helps to identify the type of customers, or the market, that will most likely bring about the desired results. It will also help to discover the type of building or space that should be provided to meet the requirements of this most likely market.

In order to achieve his objectives, the developer may often grant more favorable price or rental terms to the first purchaser or tenant. Many developers argue that it is important to make a "good deal" initially, to give the development the necessary impetus for success. They claim that this requires making concessions to the strong tenant. Alternatively, however:

a speculator who builds speculative buildings is often willing to take weak tenants on short-term leases at higher rentals than would be the case with prime-risk tenants for longer periods. The risk is greater, and he is entitled to the higher yield. This is a great service to the industry, as it creates an incubator for young firms, many of which go on to healthy expansion, thus leaving behind the original building for another user.[4]

Whatever his decision, however, "the broker must be in business. He must be able to act quickly. This is the difference between a developer and a casual owner of acreage that happens to be available." [5] He must also be prepared to pay appropriate commissions to brokers when tenants or purchasers are obtained. Otherwise, the developer will be very much on his own, and will be without the many services that the industrial real estate broker can provide.

2. *Utility Companies.* In addition to private, profit-seeking developers, public utility companies or railroads are often involved in industrial pioneering or development efforts. This is especially true of power companies. They may acquire, develop, and subdivide land, or they may build specula-

[4] Statement by David Scribner, S.I.R., New York City.
[5] Interview with W. W. Dillard, Great Southwest Corporation, Arlington, Texas.

tive shell buildings. The utility company often deals directly with contractors and engages in site promotional work. The difference in motivation, however, is twofold. First, a sponsoring utility company or railroad is interested in attracting heavy users of their particular service: power, rail, gas. Second, utility companies seek to promote community development as much as they promote industrial development, as such. They try to stimulate expansion of the economic base of a community, an increase in jobs and general economic development of the area. An expanding, prosperous community is also more likely to be a large user of utility services.

3. *Public and Private Community Development Organizations.* Finally, there is the community development group, which is public or quasi-public in character. It is commonly a private nonprofit organization financed with loans or outright gifts from local citizens and businesses. It may also be a public agency, however. These community development groups or industrial development commissions often have sufficient funds to option or buy land for development, and in many instances they construct speculative or shell buildings as well. (See Chapter 17 for further details.) There are particular pressures on local community development groups to provide facilities when a loss of jobs results from the decline or withdrawal of one or more large local employers. This has been particularly noticeable in many New England textile communities, as well as in the coal mining regions of Pennsylvania. It is not merely coincidental, for example, that the so-called New England Plan for underwriting industrial mortgages (discussed in Chapters 9 and 17) is concentrated in the New England states and Pennsylvania.

Most community development groups pay commissions to industrial real estate brokers. They have come to recognize that they need the assistance of the broker in order to merchandise their product effectively. For these groups, industrial development is not merely a matter of profit or loss; it is frequently a matter of economic survival.

BACKGROUND ANALYSIS AND PLANNING

Because it involves a substantial commitment of equity investment on a speculative, risk-taking basis, industrial development requires careful advance planning. To a large extent, this is the job of the project manager or coordinator. The types of analysis required in this background planning, however, are particularly dependent on the kinds of skills and information that the industrial real estate broker possesses.

Market Demand

"The builder-developer must know the area in which he is working, and know it well. It is imperative that the developer investigate the market carefully. . . . Much depends on the activity of the market. The degree of emphasis on investigation and planning depends on how active the market is." [6] Economic base analysis of the area provides insights into the com-

---

[6] Interview with Robert Y. Adams, American Electric Power Service Corporation.

munity's "economic metabolism." Market analysis, in turn, involves a fore-cast of both the magnitude and the character of industrial space that will be most attractive to potential industrial users. These represent the first step in planning the development, and provide a preliminary answer to the question: What type of industry should be sought and accommodated? A survey of the community will lead to a conclusion as to what the area can reasonably be expected to attract. It can also lead to a decision whether site develop-ment will be adequate to attract desired industry, or whether shell buildings will also be necessary.

Location

1. *Community Considerations.* This involves an assessment of the at-tractions of the community and the area to industry. The general factors considered will be community attitude toward industrial expansion (as evidenced by actions rather than words), local zoning ordinances, and the general suitability of the area for industry. An analysis of zoning includes not only a question of what industrial uses may be permitted or prohibited, but what protections industrial users will have against the intrusion of in-harmonious or incompatible uses. It may well reveal the necessity for the developer to establish private covenants. The same is true of building codes and subdivision regulations.

Special attention must be paid to subdivision regulations. It is often dif-ficult in smaller, outlying communities to convince the regulatory authori-ties that an industrial subdivision cannot be rapidly platted in advance, in the same way that a residential subdivision can be, since the size and shape of lots will often depend on the specific character of the user and the use to which the land is put. Industrial developers must also pay particular at-tention to the applicability of subdivision regulations because, in the great majority of jurisdictions, the division of a parcel of land into three or more parcels (which is accomplished as soon as two pieces are sold) constitutes a subdivision. This then requires filing of maps, plans, performance bonds, and the like.

From the point of view of an industrial developer, local air and water pollution control ordinances and *attitudes* are also important. So, too, are regulations and attitudes toward scenic easements. Local emphasis on the negative physical aspects of industrial uses puts many proposed develop-ments in a defensive position from the outset, and may be an active deter-rent to some purchasers or tenants that might otherwise be attracted to the area because of its economic features. The industrial real estate broker can perform an important role by acquainting local officials with the implications of some of their regulations.

Local policy concerning the extension and expansion of street and utility easements is also a particular concern in analyzing an industrial location. Not only available services, but also the community's attitudes and prac-tices in assessing the cost of extensions and expansion, can be critical to a proposed industrial real estate development.

2. *Proximity and Access.* After having considered the general char-

acteristics of the area in relation to its suitability and attractiveness for industrial development, the developer should next evaluate the proximity and
access afforded to labor markets (and the skills resident there); materials
and resource supplies (in terms of type, quantity, and cost of delivery);
and markets (in terms of the types of goods likely to be sold). This is no
less important to the potential developer of a site than it is to the potential
user of that site. The developer will acquire important insights into the
market for his developed space. The location analysis, therefore, includes
all of the ingredients discussed at length in Chapter 13 under "Site Analysis"
for valuation purposes. In this respect, an experienced and knowledgeable
industrial real estate appraiser can be an extremely valuable counselor.

User Requirements

An industrial site, or space in an industrial building, is neither sold nor
leased to the market; it is sold or leased to a specific firm. The developer
seeking to produce sites and/or space that are readily marketable at a
profit to him must particularize in his market analysis. He must identify at
least the range of specific users most likely to be attracted to the kind of
space that he can provide, given the limitations of location, physical characteristics, and available funds.

The first major investigation is made in terms of the site requirements of
specific users. If land development is the only activity to be performed by
the developer, this will be the end of the analysis. However, if buildings are
to be constructed as well, there must be an analysis of the requirements of
potential users for ceiling height, width of space, loading areas, office space,
and the like. One important point that must be remembered is that purchasers or tenants are looking for *value*. Economic and locational considerations almost always prevail over personal preferences. For example, visual
appeal is decidedly a positive factor for potential users of industrial sites or
buildings, but only after the basic value and utility of the space have been
developed.

One important guide to the types of space that might be provided is a
careful record of the space requirements of the most recent clients of the
industrial broker, as well as the most recent occupants of new space in the
area. If the effort is truly a pioneering one, with no "going market" in the
near vicinity, then the space standards and requirements of the developer's
(or broker's) most recent clients provide the only meaningful guide to the
characteristics that the pioneering development should have.

Site Characteristics

The developer and/or the broker advising him must analyze the site carefully and specifically. The ingredients in the checklist of site characteristics
detailed in Chapter 13 under "Site Analysis" and "Site Valuation" will
serve the developer well. It has been said that the ideal site has the following characteristics:

(1) It is a level, solid, well drained piece of land;
(2) There is room for expansion;

(3) There is excellent and varied transportation available immediately adjacent to the site;

(4) There is *large capacity* availability of water, sewer, and electrical power;

(5) The community has good schools, good homes, and good government; the site is near a good supply of necessary materials and labor, and is surrounded by an active and prosperous market.[7]

In his analysis, the developer (and the broker advising him) must consider zoning, access, and physical characteristics. These will include topography, which involves surface and subsurface drainage. Taking care of surface water can be at least as important and as expensive for the industrial developer as providing for sanitary sewage disposal. In addition, soil and subsoil conditions must often be tested extensively. The degree of testing required depends to a large extent on the uses that are proposed or anticipated. If the load-bearing capacity or the permeability of the soil is a critical consideration, the engineering tests can be quite expensive. This is a task for trained soils engineers. It is one further example of the importance of detail in analyzing the suitability of land which is proposed to serve as an industrial site.

Investment Feasibility

Once the market analysis is completed and the requirements of probable users ascertained, the developer then must turn to the economics of the situation. He must discover the price at which he can afford to sell or lease lots in comparison with the price at which he is most likely to be able to sell or lease them. The same considerations enter into the analysis of proposed building construction on the developed sites. What he must attempt to obtain, or what he can afford to accept, depends to a large extent on development costs.

1. *Cost Estimation.* The development cost analysis starts with a careful inventory of all the items of cost that should be considered. Because this is a complex and technical process, it is quite possible to overlook an important segment of costs, and therefore to make a very bad or inappropriate investment decision. The costs analyzed will include, as a minimum: development costs, interest charges, property taxes, holding costs, advertising, and marketing expenses. The least obvious are financing expenses and carrying or holding charges. The latter will include such items as property taxes, insurance, fidelity and performance bonds, and other items that go under the heading of "overhead."

The analyst projecting costs must be coldly analytical, and studiously avoid coloring the projections to make the project appear feasible, simply because "it seems like a nice idea." It is imperative to ascertain development costs fairly precisely, and well in advance. "It is better to spend money in testing, planning, and analysis than to be unpleasantly surprised by large development costs. Planning expenditures are very economical in the long run. In addition, the results provide the developer with sales facts that the client or prospect is going to want to have eventually, anyway." [8] In order

[7] Walsh, *op. cit.*, p. 1023.
[8] Interview with W. W. Dillard.

to engage in appropriate planning, a skilled staff must be available. This means good engineering and financial advice, as well as experienced construction personnel.

Appropriate planning makes staging possible. Staging requires good engineering if it is to be economically successful. This can result in substantial construction savings. Good layout, planning, and engineering also provide the basis for estimating size requirements for utilities, roads, and the like.

2. *Investment Decision-Making.* Cost estimation and projection represent one side of the investment analysis that the industrial developer must undertake in advance of any overt action. Market evaluation and an estimation of sales prices or rentals make up the other side. A comparison of the two indicates what type of a return the investor-developer may expect from his expenditure of capital. Both the level of that return and the risk involved in it can be estimated rather closely. The investment decision is then based on the developer's conclusion about the adequacy of the anticipated return. The final step before deciding whether to proceed is a careful consideration of the availability of equity funds, the need for financing, and the prospects for obtaining that financing.

In brief, the developer must go through essentially the same critical evaluation of all the ingredients of the development proposal that a lending institution would follow if the proposal were presented to it.

SITE DEVELOPMENT

Site development consists of converting raw land to industrial sites which are sold or leased to industrial firms. These firms, in turn, have their own facilities constructed. Site development is, of course, also included within any industrial development activity that involves construction. The focus in this section is solely on the portion of the development process that ends with the disposition of a developed site, either through sale or through lease.

Land or site development requires a creative and sophisticated approach by the broker, both in advising the developer and in merchandising the finished project: the industrial site. This is partly because developers and users are themselves often creative and sophisticated. At the same time, the broker cannot forget that industrial managements are typically impersonal and profit-oriented. In the main, dollars and cents influence buyers or tenants much more than do personal considerations.[9]

Selection and Acquisition

The first overt step after market, location, and investment analyses have been completed is to select the particular parcel or parcels of land that are

---

[9] For one evaluation of the relative importance of personal and non-economic considerations in industrial plant location decision-making, see William N. Kinnard, Jr., and Zenon S. Malinowski, *Personal Factors in Small Manufacturing Plant Locations,* Small Business Management Research Report (Storrs, Connecticut, University of Connecticut, 1961).

to be developed into industrial sites. The ideal site, whose characteristics are enumerated in the preceding section of this chapter, will most probably not be found. Therefore, the developer and his broker then seek the best combination of characteristics from among the available parcels. One serious difficulty is that industrially zoned land is often regarded by its owners as extremely valuable (except when they are talking to the local tax assessors). They do not realize or recognize the large expenditure of time, effort, and money that is necessary to convert potentially suitable land into industrial sites. Nevertheless, realistically priced land must be found or the project is finished before it begins. It must be "available" in an economic sense, as well as being technically "for sale."

Generally speaking, developers and their brokers prefer to deal with a single owner of a large tract. It is sometimes necessary to attempt to assemble a development area from several parcels. However, a major problem in dealing with many owners is the frequent difficulty in obtaining the last parcel or parcels. The result is commonly a much higher asking price by the "holdout," and an aura of ill feeling all around.

1. *Financing Acquisition.* In the acquisition of land for development into industrial sites, "the financing arrangements that the landowner makes available are likely to be crucial." [10] The developer rarely has an unlimited supply of cash available for both equity and development purposes. The more he can economize on his cash for development and/or construction expenditures, the more effective his investment can be. As a result, the purchase-money mortgage is widely used in financing the acquisition of land for development into industrial sites.

An alternative to this is what is called in many areas a Land Contract. This is an installment sale arrangement whereby the seller agrees to release parcels as payment is made. It is, in effect, a long-term option on the entire tract, with periodic payments to be made as the parcels are released. The purchaser-developer often pays interest on the total "sales" price.

A device which is used relatively infrequently, but which offers great promise for effective financing of land for industrial development, is the ground lease. This need not be a long-term arrangement, and an extremely broad range of alternatives is possible for applying it.[11] Land leases allow the developer to conserve on his funds and employ them in the productive conversion of the land to sites.

Relatively few financial institutions will make land loans, as the discussion in Chapter 8 indicates. Even the few which are granted are usually based on the credit of long-term ground lease tenants *when the sites are developed.* Many institutional lenders cannot legally lend on raw land at all.

As another alternative, the developer may be able to convince the landowner to "invest" in the project by taking his payment for the land as a

[10] Sherman J. Maisel, *Financing Real Estate: Principles and Practices* (New York, McGraw-Hill, 1965), p. 373.

[11] For details, see E. F. Phillips, "Proposals Involving Variables," *Ground Leases,* Byron Trerice, Jr., sponsor (Chicago, National Institute of Real Estate Brokers, December, 1965), pp. 9–10.

share of the profits to be earned when the developed sites are sold or leased.[12] Generally speaking, the greater the concessions that the landowner is asked to make in deferring receipt of the sales price, the higher the nominal price that is set on the land for purchase-money mortgages or profit-sharing.

It may be necessary for the developer to invest much of his own cash to acquire the land. Financing devices and techniques are designed primarily to avoid this as much as possible. Yet if the project is an attractive one, investing equity funds may be less undesirable than foregoing the profit prospects entirely.

2. *Form of Ownership.* Title to the land is usually held by the development organization, commonly in corporate form. Whatever the form of organization for ownership, however, there should be clear and careful agreement that only one member of the "team" shall be the negotiator for the acquisition of land. Financing arrangements may be made with the assistance of outside technicians or other members of the group, but one project manager should be in charge of the basic thread of development activities, including site acquisition. This role can be effectively carried out by an experienced industrial real estate broker.

Site Preparation

Once the parcel of land has been acquired, the next stage in the development process is to convert it from raw land to effective industrial sites. Precisely what must be done depends on what is already available, as well as what the requirements of the most likely or most probable users of the sites are expected to be. Major items to be considered, however, include:

(1) Improving topographic and drainage conditions;
(2) Extension of utility lines;
(3) Platting and laying out individual sites (if there are to be more than one);
(4) Improving or extending streets;
(5) Compacting soil or changing soil conditions.

1. *Development Costs.* Development costs vary widely, and the standards and experience of similar developments in the area are often the best guide to what may be expected. Because of the possibility of such variation in costs and cost estimates, particular emphasis must be placed on the accuracy of the development plan and the investment feasibility analysis that precede actual construction work.

Either personal familiarity with development costs, or the retention of an experienced industrial site preparation contractor, is important to the success of the undertaking.

2. *Skills Required.* The industrial site development organization should include personnel with appropriate cost, construction, and financing skills if the proper type of planning and forecasting is to be undertaken. Particularly if he is the project manager, the industrial real estate broker must

---

[12] For a discussion of this possibility, see Walsh, *op. cit.,* pp. 1035–1038.

know construction terminology. He must serve as the communicator between the developer and the contractor.

3. *Financing Site Development.* Unless there is a firm commitment on the part of a well-rated purchaser or ground-lease tenant in advance, site development costs are difficult to finance. Equity money is usually required. While some financial institutions will occasionally make land loans, development loans are extremely difficult to obtain. This is because a substantial amount of the expenditure is for improvements off the site itself. Many lending institutions avoid such loans as a matter of policy, even though economically it is quite clear that there is substantial enhancement in value when the land is made an effective site by bringing roads and/or utilities to it.

One major life insurance company has been reported to make development loans with maturities of 13 to 14 years, with mortgage interest only payable the first three years. The loans are made on 50 per cent of the raw land value plus development costs, at a rate approximately 0.5 per cent above the "going" rate for improved industrial properties.[13] The difficulty, however, is that these loans are generally available only to extremely highly rated borrowers, or to borrowers with purchase or lease commitments from highly rated customers. The more speculative developments find mortgage financing almost impossible to obtain. Short-term speculative development loans are occasionally available from real estate investment trusts, but only if the project is relatively large.

Another possible method for financing industrial site development involves subordination of the fee estate to the mortgagee's claim. This can occur when land is leased by the developer or is acquired under a purchase-money mortgage. In either case, if the original owner will agree to subordinate his interest, equity coverage equal to 100 per cent of raw land value *may* be sufficient to convince a mortgage lending institution to grant a development loan.

Another difficulty in obtaining site development loans is that site development costs do not necessarily add to the liquidity of the project or of the land. The final product is still relatively speculative. Although site preparation costs represent a very high percentage of total development costs, the developer often finds it necessary to use his own equity funds to pay for a substantial portion of them.

One real possibility for conserving the developer's funds is for the municipality to install sewer lines, water lines, streets, and the like at the municipality's own expense; or to defer assessments for these installations until after the services have been connected to buildings. If the developer is required to pay these costs, the payments can often be spread over a relatively long period of time.

Industrial land development projects sponsored by utilities or railroads rarely suffer from a lack of either equity or loan funds. The financial resources and credit rating of such sponsors ensure this, regardless of the use

---

[13] Interview with W. W. Dillard.

to which the funds are to be put. Similarly, when an industrial land development project is publicly owned or sponsored, public funds are commonly employed to finance the improvement program.

It is the private, profit-seeking industrial land developer who most often encounters difficulties in obtaining site development financing.

Disposition

The final test of any land development project is the expeditious and successful disposition of the site or sites created, on terms at least as favorable as those anticipated in the original investment analysis. One of the most effective ingredients in any disposition program is a well-planned development. If the project is well-conceived, properly executed, and appropriately priced, a major portion of the sales program has already been accomplished.

In any speculative development, a high degree of flexibility should be built into the disposition plan and maintained throughout the development as long as possible. This means that holding the land in bulk is an important merchandising device. The ability to suit the needs of a desirable but unanticipated customer will enhance the prospects for profit substantially.

Developed sites may be disposed of by sale or by lease, depending on the objectives of the developer and the inclinations and bargaining power of the industrial customer. An inflexible determination by the developer to sell only or to lease only tends to constrict the potential market substantially.

The primary task of attracting users to the developed sites falls to the industrial real estate broker. This is partly merchandising, and partly negotiating between the developer and the user. Advertising through direct mailings and news releases supplements paid advertisements in newspapers or magazines. Strategically located signs can effectively supplement the advertising program. Major expenditures on advertising are not normally advisable for single-site developments.

The development organization should have the capacity to develop prompt proposals that would include (at the least) a site plan, a plot plan, aerial photographs, and color renderings of proposed buildings. The organization should also be oriented to take prompt advantage of opportunities as they arise—and even to create them.

Finally, one very useful and frequently successful way to open up land is to put a shell or speculative building on it.

CUSTOM CONSTRUCTION

When seeking new locations, many industrial firms do not want to become involved with the bother and possible problems of constructing their own buildings. They do not have the necessary skills or experience on their own staff, and they would prefer to delegate the responsibility to a contractor or a developer, paying a fee for the service. When arrangements are made in advance, this is custom or contract construction. There is a commitment on the part of the purchaser or tenant to accept and occupy the building when it is completed, provided it meets the terms and conditions of the construction contract. On the basis of this commitment, the developer-contractor can often obtain a substantial proportion of necessary financing.

In many cases, the developer of industrial land enters into a construction contract to meet the specific needs of a customer firm already committed to acquisition of the site. Sometimes construction is necessary in order to move the developed site at all. In addition, greater profit is usually expected on construction than on the sale or lease of land. Custom or contract construction is always involved in build-lease or sale-leaseback transactions.

There are also situations when the industrial firm already owns a site and contracts with a construction firm to erect a building to its specifications. This situation is not included in the present discussion, because there is no element of development or pioneering involved. As it is considered here, contract construction is combined with the speculative development of industrial sites in order to produce a "package" that meets the specifications of a particular user. It is distinguished from speculative construction in that the speculative developer has no occupant committed for the structure when he begins construction. Surveys conducted by the American Institute of Architects indicate that most large manufacturing firms, at least, favor the custom or contract construction approach.[14]

User Standards

Custom construction entails meeting the requirements of a particular industrial user. The industrial developer therefore must understand the needs of industrial users if appropriate space is to be provided. If the developer is not a construction firm experienced in industrial buildings, then the necessary skills must be hired before any efforts are made to accommodate the needs of a customer, no matter how valued. The technical details and requirements are too great to warrant leaving them to chance.

The preliminary plans for the buildings must be developed in sufficient detail to allow close cost estimates to be made. These form the basis for a preliminary profit analysis, and for rental terms if the space is to be leased. An initial application for financing is usually filed on the basis of the preliminary plans and cost estimates, as well.

The primary responsibility of the development organization in the planning stage is to recognize that the building must be related to the requirements of the user, or it will not be salable.

Operating performance is the only realistic measurement of building value in any industrial plant or commercial facility. ... Planners have to give just as much consideration to the future outlook for change in manufacturing and distribution techniques as they do to the initial layout. There are several ways to ap-

[14] For details, see American Institute of Architects, Committee on Industrial Architecture, *How Large Manufacturers Handle Facility Construction: An Analysis* (Washington, The Author, December, 1965).

proach almost every problem in plant design and layout. It is the engineer's function to explore the various alternatives before he recommends any design or program to meet specific needs. In this process, the relative benefits of such basic long-term operating advantages as flexibility, convertibility, expandability, and low maintenance cost have to be very carefully appraised.

By strict adherence to the precept of structural simplicity, and by taking advantage of opportunities for use of designs which cut steel and equipment fabricating costs and increase efficiency in the field, engineers and builders can provide the type of facilities which side track obsolescence without adding much— if anything—to overall costs.[15]

This is the objective that the industrial developer has in mind when he enters into a custom construction contract. His success in meeting this objective will determine how profitable his operations are in the long run.

Financing

Both construction financing and long-term mortgage financing of custom buildings are generally possible. This is because a commitment to purchase or to lease the space already exists. The amount of financing and the terms on which it is available, as well as the lenders from which it may come, depend primarily upon the credit rating of the purchaser or tenant.

The availability of construction financing is important because "permanent" financing does not normally become effective until the building is completed and occupied, and rent payments start. The commitment contract between the lender and the developer may even require that a certificate of occupancy be obtained and filed with the lender before the long-term funds are released.

It is important, therefore, that the developer be able to convince the lender that the project is a sound one. The lender will check the plans and specifications, the market analysis, the estimated development and construction costs, and the projected operating costs and income when the package is a build-lease transaction. He will check plans and specifications, market analysis, estimated costs, and "reasonableness" of the sales price even on a commitment to purchase. The degree of scrutiny will generally vary with the credit rating of the purchaser or tenant. Care must be taken in putting the loan proposal together, or the lender may be unwilling to consider it.

The developer usually seeks to limit his cash contribution to 10 per cent, with the remainder of his nominal equity made up from anticipated profit, overhead recovery, and equity in the land. A 90 per cent loan from the point of view of the developer may appear on the books of the lending institution as a 66 per cent loan. The difference is that the lender is basing the loan commitment on the anticipated value of the completed project, while the developer is basing his equity requirements on actual cash outlays.

For properties that are custom built on a build-lease or sale-leaseback arrangement, "the leasing and financial negotiations proceed together. The

---

[15] Laurence E. Cooney, "Key Values in Plant Design and Layout," *Technical Supplement to S.I.R.* (Washington, Society of Industrial Realtors, July, 1953), p. 1.

developer needs to know the general terms under which financing will be available. On the other hand, financing usually will not be available until he can show sufficient leases or indications of demand for the lender to feel safe." [16]

Package Development

The industrial real estate broker plays a major role in the creation or development of "package deals." These involve starting from raw land and working through to a finished building that is sold or leased to the occupant. The package deal, in the hands of an experienced and competent development organization, generally offers substantial cost savings to the user. Much more importantly, however, it generally makes faster construction possible without loss of quality or flexibility. While a survey conducted by the American Institute of Architects in 1965 indicates that a substantial percentage of large manufacturing establishments expressed some dissatisfaction with the services of "design-and-build" firms, those who did favor the use of such organizations for plant construction most frequently cited as their reasons "construction within budget" and "on-time completion." [17] Therefore, firms to which meeting construction timetables and budget restrictions are important (and this would appear to include a large segment of American industry) do find attractions in the package deal approach.

For the developer, the package approach offers the prospect of substantial "profit" on real estate that he already owns. To the occupant, the package deal promises on-time delivery and staying within budget limitations. It also offers a wide variety of tenancy and investment options to the user firm. It may be able to lease the entire package, lease the land and purchase the building, or purchase the entire property.

Custom buildings can contain cost pitfalls for the developer, unless he employs an industrial architect who can check the customer's plan and requirements, as well as a contractor who is thoroughly experienced in this field. This is particularly important where the customer's architect or engineer is not familiar with the latest techniques of plant construction.... Custom buildings are usually leased for longer periods and at higher rates of return than are general-purpose shell buildings.[18]

Disposition

Negotiations for the sale or lease of custom-constructed industrial buildings are basically more complex, more varied, more particularized, and (most especially) more technically oriented than are negotiations involved in the disposition of industrial sites. This is really the distinguishing feature of the disposition problem for custom construction. The *general approach* that the broker will take in analyzing and understanding his market, identifying his prospects, and bringing them into contact with the developer, will be no different; the *knowledge* that he must bring to bear in this process is more complex and demanding.

---

[16] Maisel, *op. cit.*, p. 374.
[17] American Institute of Architects, *op. cit.*, p. 3.
[18] Walsh, *op. cit.*, p. 1039.

Unless the developer's own staff is extremely well oriented toward the technical requirements 'of the customer, and unless there is legal and financial expertise on the staff as well, the best and most logical course of action is to contract with an industrial broker to serve as the project negotiator. The broker is usually charged with the responsibility of hiring and assembling the necessary talents and skills to represent the developer's interests most effectively.

In dealing with custom construction, the broker must have a good working knowledge of costs. "He must be able to make ball park estimates for the different types of construction. He ought to be able to indicate to the prospect what a 20,000-square-foot, masonry construction warehouse with 14-foot ceiling heights would cost in his particular area. This is simply one illustration. He must also know how much it would cost to air condition such a building, or how much it would cost to provide lighting to 50 foot-candles. He must know the comparative costs of the different general types of construction." [19]

The type of organizational structure that one S.I.R. member's firm has developed in order to handle custom construction on a package basis is

Exhibit 82

ORGANIZATIONAL STATEMENT OF CLINTON M. BELL COMPANY

TECHNICRAFT CO.

Division of Electronic Specialties Co. A 50,000 sq. ft. building at Thomaston, Conn. and a 70,000 sq. ft. addition. An outstanding example of Bell Complete Project Management. Two old buildings were purchased for cash.

FROM THE GROUND UP
A Comprehensive Project Management Service for Industrial Building Site Location, Construction and Financing

If your company is planning a plant, warehouse or laboratory, the Clinton M. Bell Company offers valuable services. Bell's wide experience and efficient organization coordinates every factor from the choice of location to financing. Your executives are freed from a vast amount of time-consuming detail. Expert realty, engineering and financing advice solves the many problems and simplifies executive decision making. Bell Project Management carries through the entire project in strict accordance with your wishes. The project flows smoothly to completion without misunderstandings or delays. Financing is arranged to suit your specific needs — often including disposal of old facilities. The result is a clean, efficient operation that satisfies all concerned.

THE F. & M. SCHAEFFER BREWING COMPANY

Prestressed concrete distribution center building of integrated design at Newington, Conn. Design and construction of 22,000 sq. ft. building under the supervision of Clinton M. Bell Co.

HARTFORD STEEL BALL COMPANY

Division of Virginia Industries. 125,000 sq. ft. office and manufacturing facility of prestressed concrete at Rocky Hill, Conn. Entire project including site selection, design, construction and financing provided by Clinton M. Bell Co.

[19] Interview with W. W. Dillard.

illustrated in the excerpt from an advertising brochure of Clinton M. Bell Company, New York, shown as Exhibit 82.

SPECULATIVE CONSTRUCTION

It has already been observed that one very useful and often successful way to open up land is to erect a shell or speculative building on it. The terms "shell building," "speculative building," and "spec building" are synonymous. They refer to an industrial structure that is built on speculation in the hope that it will be sold or rented. As a result, it must be highly adaptable.

A custom building is constructed in order to meet the needs of a specific, committed customer; a speculative building is constructed in the hope or expectation of attracting a customer. Speculative buildings may be constructed for either sale or lease.

Although they are designed to be as flexible and adaptable as possible—and flexibility involves as few partitions or interior impediments as feasible—speculative buildings need not necessarily be designed for use by single occupancy only. They may be multitenant structures, depending on the acceptability of multiple tenancy in the local market. They are rarely multistory buildings, however. The only frequent exception might be office space inserted at two levels in one section of a structure with an 18- or 20-foot ceiling height.

A speculative building is called a "shell building" because it is often unfinished inside. The walls and ceiling are completed, and the rough plumbing and electric service are connected. The floor is not necessarily poured, and interior wall finish, partitions, finish plumbing, electrical distribution lines, and fixtures are not installed. These can still be adapted to the specific needs of the particular tenant or purchaser when one is attracted. In fact, much of a "speculative" building may well be "custom" construction by the time the industrial occupant moves in.

Constructing speculative buildings basically involves trying to create a market and to create value. Shell buildings are usually successful because an industrial firm in need of new space is often under pressure to act quickly. Delay in the location decision means that the industrial user is looking for space that can be occupied as quickly as possible. "Depending on how sophisticated the building is and must be, a shell provides a four to five-month jump over the opposition. In addition, a shell building is a selling tool because it helps the client visualize the form that it will finally take. Many clients are not able to do this from models or drawings." [20]

User Standards

The key words in speculative industrial building construction are flexibility and adaptability. The building really is a multi-purpose, basic structure, more than it is speculative or a shell. For example, the location of the building on the site can be at least as important as its interior adapt-

[20] Statement from Peter O. Hanson, S.I.R.

ability. The siting of the structure determines to a large extent whether there can be easy and economical expansion later.

"Speculative buildings must be designed to meet the probable needs of as wide a range of customers as possible." [21] This means that heavy reliance must be placed on the market and user analyses that precede the decision to proceed with the construction project. Usually, not much more than the four walls and the roof is erected, and then construction stops. This allows the occupant to select the configuration or layout of the interior floor plan, and to choose the facilities. For example, if no floor is poured, then a client who needs floor drains will not have to go through the expensive and time-consuming process of chipping them out. No office space is mapped out because varying office-to-plant floor area ratios are found in different industrial operations. In effect, a speculative or shell building can still have the final appearance and most of the facilities of a custom structure. The significant items of equipment and fixtures may still be adapted to his specific needs. The basic building—the shell—is not distinctive; but even this can be obscured with custom exterior finish.

The type and size of speculative building will often vary from one area to another. For example, shell buildings erected in regions where manufacturing establishments are the most likely occupants will more commonly be one-story, tail-gate loading structures with 12- to 14-foot ceilings. On the other hand, in areas such as northern New Jersey, where distribution and warehousing are particularly active, ceiling heights of 18, 20 or even 22 feet are included in shell buildings because materials handling equipment makes this feasible.

Standards may change from time to time in the same area. For example, in one major market area in the northeastern United States, the typical speculative building constructed prior to 1960 contained between 5,000 and 20,000 square feet of floor area. From 1960 to 1965, it was most likely to have between 10,000 and 25,000 square feet. After 1965, it was most frequently between 20,000 and 50,000 square feet.

One reason for this shift was the growing scarcity of well-located industrial sites and a consequent increase in industrial land prices. When land becomes scarce, larger buildings begin to make sense. Setback and density requirements usually apply to each individual structure, rather than as a percentage of total floor area. As a result, in the market area in question several multitenant, one-story speculative buildings have successfully been promoted. They usually require considerably more merchandising than do single-tenant structures. If they meet the needs of the market, however, they can be marketed.

A shell building always represents risk for the developer. To minimize risk, the developer should build for what the bulk of the market is currently seeking. It is important to conduct a background and market analysis every time a speculative building development is proposed. Last year's market analysis is no more valid today than is last year's value estimate. What the

---

[21] Walsh, *op. cit.*, p. 1038.

market wants and will pay for does vary. The speculative developer must know precisely what that market wants *now*.

Financing

Construction financing of speculative or shell buildings generally involves stricter terms than those applied for contract construction. This, of course, assumes that any construction financing is available. Maturities tend to be shorter and loan ratios lower. The permanent loan is not usually funded until a tenant or purchaser is produced.

There is a considerable amount of variation in the availability of construction financing for speculative industrial buildings from one part of the country to another. The general consensus is that more lenders are entering this field, that there is greater sophistication among lenders, and that such financing is becoming less difficult to arrange.

It still helps for the developer to have enough cash available to buy the land. Then he can more likely obtain a construction loan from a lending institution, most probably a commercial bank. This presumably will carry him to the point at which a purchaser or tenant can be attracted. On the basis of either a sales agreement or a lease, a take-out commitment is usually obtainable. The commitment in turn becomes the basis for final construction financing. In certain market areas, it has even become possible for an experienced and successful speculative industrial building developer to obtain a takeout commitment without a specific tenant or purchaser in view, based on his previous success. The evaluation of the strength of the builder-developer has shifted slightly from his credit rating to his apparent market acumen.

Applications

The speculative industrial developer produces package deals no less than the custom developer does. The difference is that his packages are completed in stages: site development and shell construction proceed without a particular user in mind; the structure is nearly always completed after a tenant or a purchaser has been found. This involves more risk-taking than is true in custom construction.

Private speculative developers have some competition from public or community development organizations. In many instances, communities have erected general-purpose buildings in order to attract new firms to the area. These buildings can usually compete strongly with the space offered by private speculative industrial developers because the public groups offer very attractive rentals or sale prices. Their interest is not in making a profit on the real estate, but in attracting industry, employment, and income to the community (and quite possibly increased tax revenues as well). Ordinarily, however, a private speculative developer will not be attracted to a market area where a community development group is likely to be active.

Community development organizations tend to emphasize speed and ease of entry into a finished building, as well as favorable rentals or sale prices. They are also more likely to produce finished or nearly finished buildings than shells. These finished buildings are called "turnkey" buildings. Moreover, because of the emphasis on jobs rather than real estate, speculative industrial buildings sponsored by community development groups are more likely to be aimed at manufacturing tenants than distributive or warehouse users. As a result, they tend to average slightly larger in size than comparable speculative buildings aimed at the distributive or warehouse user. For example, the first 21 speculative industrial buildings constructed under the sponsorship of community development groups in the five northern New England states averaged approximately 37,000 square feet of original floor area, and the largest contained 48,000 square feet.[22] Sixteen of these buildings were turnkey buildings, and only five were shells.

Disposition

Promotion and merchandising are considerably more important to the speculative industrial developer than they are to the contract developer. Most especially, he must be familiar with the space requirements of the most probable users of the type of space that he is planning to develop. At the same time, an existing speculative building is a very important sales tool. Many firms need a plant in a hurry. Moreover, some savings in cost can be effected in a standardized basic structure. Finally, most industrialists are not experienced in construction and have difficulty visualizing their plant on a vacant site.

Space in a speculative building is a particularly important alternative for the smaller firm that cannot make its wishes felt on the market, because it does not have the funds to back up those wishes effectively. Activity in leasing and tenant occupancy is much more common with speculative industrial development than with contract construction. As a result, the speculative developer should have the ready services of an experienced real estate leasing attorney available to him. As part of the speculative developer's team, the attorney and the industrial broker must work hand-in-hand to produce the most effective lease document between the developer and tenant.

In addition, excellent banking and other financial connections are extremely important for the speculative industrial developer. Many transactions involving shell buildings are made, or broken, because of financing.

ROLE OF THE BROKER

An industrial real estate broker can be a developer or a principal in an industrial development firm. In such a situation, his role as developer encompasses his functions as a broker. Nothing further need be said beyond the admonitions to the developer already offered.

If the broker is working for the developer or the development firm either

---

[22] Federal Reserve Bank of Boston, *Tables Describing Speculative Industrial Buildings Sponsored by Community Development Groups in New England* (Boston, The Author, November, 1959).

on retainer or for a fee, however, he does have several important functions to perform that should be reviewed. The most obvious is attracting and securing occupants, either as purchasers or as tenants, and conducting the negotiations between the developer and the potential occupant. For performing this service, the broker typically is paid by the owner-developer. In serving the owner, he often functions best by meeting the technical and market requirements of users for industrial space. Moreover, he should be an influential participant in merchandising and advertising the development.

Because of his peculiar experience in the industrial real estate market, the broker is often the basic source of information to both developer and potential industrial user. This means that at the very least he must know the going market rates and standards. He must be able to conduct necessary background market and location analyses for the developer, and at least participate in the investment feasibility study. The broker should also be a source of information about construction and construction standards. He should know the alternative methods of development and what construction costs are. He need not be experienced in construction as such, because he will usually hire a contractor to perform the work; but he must know construction terminology in order to facilitate communication between the user and the builder.

Even more importantly, the broker should be the focal point through whom all of the technicians, specialists, and experts function in the development process. He should be able to identify the types and levels of technical skills that are required in order to complete the development and consummate the transaction, and where and how to obtain them.

Every industrial development project should have a project manager. In the great majority of cases, the experienced industrial real estate broker is the most logical choice for this critical role, primarily because his experience as coordinator of previous transactions eminently qualifies him to assume the responsibilities involved.

SELECTED REFERENCES

American Institute of Architects, Committee on Industrial Architecture, "Guide to Better 'Crash' Construction," *AIA Journal,* November, 1964.

American Institute of Architects, Committee on Industrial Architecture, "How Large Manufacturers Handle Facility Construction: An Analysis," *AIA Journal,* December, 1965.

USA Standards Institute, *USA Standard Methods of Determining Areas in Industrial Buildings* (New York, The Author, July, 1962).

Bessire, Howard D., *Techniques of Industrial Development* (El Paso, Texas; Hill Printing, 1965).

Cooney, Laurence E., "Key Values in Plant Design and Layout," *Technical Supplement to S.I.R.* (Washington, Society of Industrial Realtors, July, 1953).

Industrial Development Research Council, "Industrial Land—Terminology: What Is an Industrial Park, Zone, District, Estate, City?" *Industrial Development and Manufacturers Records,* June, 1966.

Miller, Harold V., "Modern Plant Characteristics—and Their Relation to Industrial Zoning," *Technical Supplement to S.I.R.* (Washington, Society of Industrial Realtors, September, 1953).

Phillips, E. F., "Proposals Involving Variables," *Ground Leases* (Chicago, National Institute of Real Estate Brokers, December, 1965).

Shenkel, William M., "The Effective Use of Development Leases," *Ground Leases* (Chicago, National Institute of Real Estate Brokers, December, 1965).

U.S. Department of Commerce, Economic Development Administration, *Characteristics of 63 Modern Industrial Plants* (Washington, U.S. Government Printing Office, 1966).

U.S. Department of Defense, *Industrial Plant Equipment Handbook* (Washington, U.S. Government Printing Office, 1966). Several volumes in series.

Walsh, Stuart P., "Industrial Land Development," *Real Estate Encyclopedia,* Edith J. Friedman, ed. (Englewood Cliffs, N.J.; Prentice-Hall, 1960).

15 Development of Planned Industrial Districts and Parks

SINCE the end of World War II, accelerated industrial growth and decentralization of economic activity throughout the United States have combined to give impetus to the expansion and acceptance of planned industrial developments. These are variously called industrial parks, planned industrial districts, or industrial estates. The important, underlying factor that distinguishes them from unorganized areas or individual sites (discussed in Chapter 14) is that the development is planned for efficiency, integrated and compatible uses, and hence success for the sponsor.

The developer-sponsor also exercises substantial control over uses and occupants of the space within the development. These controls or regulations (occasionally called "protective provisions" for sales promotional purposes) must be continuously enforced by the sponsor or some other responsible group. Continuing management is a feature of the planned industrial development that may be lacking in the unplanned or unorganized industrial area.

The rapidly increasing acceptance of planned districts or parks is evidenced by the fact that in 1966, over 85 per cent of the 1,102 industrial parks and districts throughout the United States and Canada included in the annual *Industrial Development and Manufacturer's Record* survey of industrial parks had been in existence 10 years or less.[1] This reinforces similar impressions developed in earlier studies.[2]

This growth has occurred for a variety of interrelated reasons. Accelerated demand for industrial space accompanying the post-war economic expansion encountered a relative shortage of land in established industrial zones.

---

[1] *Industrial Development and Manufacturer's Record*, February, 1966, pp. 7–36.

[2] For example, Robert E. Boley, *Industrial Districts Restudied*, Technical Bulletin No. 41 (Washington, Urban Land Institute, April, 1961), p. 31; William N. Kinnard, Jr., and Zenon S. Malinowski, *The Place of Small Business in Planned Industrial Districts*, Small Business Management Research Report (Storrs, Connecticut, University of Connecticut, 1963), Appendix Tables.

Assembly costs were high for large sites in urban regions. Traffic congestion became a more pressing problem. Technological changes called for new concepts in industrial design to meet assembly and materials handling requirements.

The presentation here concentrates on what the broker should know in order to understand the role and applications of industrial parks or planned industrial districts in solving industrial real estate problems. There are numerous basic works of broader coverage, many of which also provide details to assist the potential developer in attempting to establish his own project.[3]

"The assembly, development, and marketing of land for exclusive use by industry is a highly specialized field, and an intimate knowledge of industrial requirements and development costs is paramount."[4] The industrial park or planned industrial district represents one phase of the total process of industrial development. Industrial parks and districts may be promoted and developed for real estate purposes: to house industry and earn a profit for the sponsor. They may also be developed for community purposes: to provide jobs and broaden the local tax base. The industrial real estate broker must be aware of the implications of the former, and he should be able to evaluate the role of the latter.

CHARACTERISTICS OF PLANNED INDUSTRIAL DEVELOPMENTS

Development objectives, and the means of achieving those objectives, vary considerably among the many hundreds of planned industrial districts. It is both difficult and potentially misleading to attempt to classify them too neatly. They are highly diversified. The range of services and facilities provided within planned industrial developments is also extremely broad. In general, it can be said that they are usually comprehensive in their objectives and in the facilities made available to potential occupants.

Definitions

"In the language of industrial development today, there is no clear distinction between an industrial 'park,' and an industrial 'district.' In most respects the two are alike, but they have some differences."[5] The only apparently meaningful difference between "planned industrial district" and "industrial park" is that "an industrial park is simply a more highly restricted type of planned industrial district in which special attention and emphasis is given to aesthetics and community compatibility."[6]

---

[3] Consult the *Selected References* at the end of this chapter for an indication of the more recent works. Most of these references themselves contain extensive bibliographies for further study. See particularly the two Urban Land Institute monographs by Robert E. Boley (*Industrial Districts Restudied* and *Industrial Districts: Principles in Practice*) for a comprehensive view of the character of planned industrial districts.

[4] Robert E. Boley, *Industrial Districts: Principles in Practice,* Technical Bulletin No. 44 (Washington, Urban Land Institute, December, 1962), p. 9.

[5] Charles Sargent, "Land for Industry," *Urban Land,* Vol. 23, No. 2, February, 1964, p. 3. Boley makes this same point in *Industrial Districts Restudied.*

[6] Boley, *Industrial Districts Restudied,* p. 10.

Since "industrial park" is most widely utilized in the literature of planned industrial developments, the definition used here is that provided by the California State Chamber of Commerce:

A special or exclusive type of industrial subdivision developed according to a comprehensive plan to provide *serviced* sites for a community of compatible industries. The industrial park, under *continuing management,* provides for adequate *control* of the tract and buildings through restrictive covenants and/or adequate zoning with a view to maintaining aesthetic value throughout the development.[7]

The basic characteristics of the industrial park or planned industrial district are: (1) it is planned, with conscious thought going into the pattern and character of development; (2) there is continuing management by either the developer or a subsequent group such as an occupants' association; (3) there is control over the types and character of uses permitted within the district through effective enforcement of public regulations and private covenants; and (4) compatibility of uses is protected for the benefit of both the industrial occupants and the sponsor.

An industrial park or a planned industrial district is clearly distinguished from a miscellaneous collection of industrial structures on separate parcels of land, which happen to be clustered in a contiguous area as a result of individual investment and locational decisions. Especially in discussing industrial parks, the user must avoid applying the term to an industrial area or a vacant tract of land that "the owner or developer chooses to call by that name. . . . In many instances, the term is nothing more than a semantic gimmick used to gain community acceptance on the one hand and to promote a piece of real estate on the other." [8]

Types of Uses and Occupants

The planned industrial district is generally most efficient when it caters to the space requirements of a limited range of uses or users. As in the case of industrial zoning, however, it is often extremely difficult to categorize industry by product, process, or type of land use. Diversified industrial organizations carry on substantially different functions, often in separate plants, so that even the Standard Industrial Classification in its most refined form may not be entirely helpful. The most successful industrial parks are usually those which are not restrictive in terms of use, but rather in terms of function or activity on the site.

Industrial parks are most attractive to distributive or warehousing activities. Distribution is better suited to the locational amenities of industrial parks, and generally better able to pay premium prices for prime locations. Next in order of attractiveness are industrial service organizations, followed by assembly-distribution. The latter would include such activities as bakeries and candy plants, or the assembly, storage, and distribution of final products. Least appropriate for most industrial parks are fabricating or processing firms with relatively large land requirements and relatively little interest in

[7] Sargent, *op. cit.,* p. 3 [emphasis added].
[8] Boley, *Industrial Districts Restudied,* pp. 10–11.

the speed of delivery that distributive users are seeking. Whatever the activity or function, however, industrial park users are more oriented to their markets than to sources of materials or labor.

For those activities or industrial functions most suited for industrial park occupancy, considerations of access and compatibility must be weighed against the relatively high price or rental that is usually required in planned industrial districts.

1. *Specialized Versus General or "Mixed" Industrial Districts.* Efficiency and economy are fostered when the occupancy of an industrial park is restricted to a certain type of activity or function. The sponsor-developer usually profits because he is assured of compatibility among users. There is near identity in site and service requirements, so that comparatively little land is lost through irregular sites or excess capacity of utilities. The economies of similar uses and large-scale development are expressed in higher returns to the developer. The user, in turn, encounters understanding of his particular space requirements and problems, and he is reasonably certain that he will pay for only what he receives in site services.

On the other hand, there are also diseconomies or problems that result from overspecialization. These stem primarily from competition for the same facilities and the same market. Bearing these two countertendencies in mind, one can examine the general types of industrial district patterns that are commonly found in the United States.

a. *General or Mixed Uses.* The least specialized industrial district is one in which nonindustrial uses are both permitted and encouraged. In some instances, they provide supporting service facilities for the industrial occupants of the district. Such services would include a medical center, retail and eating establishments for employees, gasoline service stations, and motels for visitors to the firms in the district. In other instances, however, developers have sold off sites to nonindustrial users primarily to increase their revenues. Most of these efforts have been self-defeating because the character of the district has been lost in the process.

b. *Exclusively Industrial Districts.* This is the most common type of industrial park, and the one which appears to be most attractive to the general developer. It also has particular appeal to the community development sponsor, because it promises the broadest potential market for the sites being offered. It also offers the broadest potential expansion in the community's economic base, if the district is successful.

c. *Single-Use Districts.* While offering a potential for greater profit to the sponsor through specialization, the single-use district carries the danger that a change in tastes or standards within the industry designed to be served can render the entire park obsolete. Since an industrial park is basically a long-term investment, this hazard is a major one that the developer must weigh carefully.

A very specialized variant of the single-use district is the single industry district, such as the General Electric Company's Electronics Park in Syracuse, New York. "Since these are single company operations and are not occupied by a community of industries, they do not meet the definitions of a planned industrial district, or industrial park . . . They do, however, illustrate the importance modern industry places on aesthetics and compatibility in the location and establishment of new plant facilities." [9]

d. *Science and Technology Parks.* Often called "research parks" or "research and development parks," specialized districts concentrating on nonproduction, science-oriented occupants have emerged as a significant force among industrial districts since 1957. "The idea was an attractive one to communities all over the country. It meant highly educated, highly paid new citizens, without the problems that industrialization brings to town." [10]

Along with the attractions came many problems. Such firms and their employees were interested only in locating close to identifiable university centers or major government centers. Moreover, "firms needing large research installations tend to locate separate and apart from other activities. Rather than fitting into a planned environment of a research park, many firms make their own environment." [11] However, many of the highly restrictive aspects of the research and development park have appeal to the developer, the community, and the potential user alike. As a result, a mixture of research, development, engineering, and light manufacturing uses "has been found to be compatible where high performance standards are enforced. In fact, this type of development offers certain long-range advantages to the facility planner not available in the pure research park." [12]

Use restrictions in science and technology parks must permit some manufacturing of prototype end products. Because technology is constantly undergoing change, there is no guarantee that a firm which today is in the developmental field will not suddenly switch to the production of a particular item that it has developed. Therefore, some flexibility within a framework of relatively rigid use restrictions is a decided attraction to many firms.

e. *Office Parks.* Since the end of World War II, nearly every regional center in the United States has experienced an increase in the demand for office space. In many of these regional centers, such as Dallas, Atlanta, Oklahoma City, and Denver, specialized groupings of office space for middle executives and their staffs have appeared on the outskirts of the major community. The office requirement is often in addition to warehousing and manufacturing requirements. This type of facility can provide both single-occupancy and multiple-occupancy buildings. The selection of a site for a regional office often precedes a warehouse or manufacturing plant location in the same area. The existence of an office facility in the region makes it more sensible to follow with other types of operations, if the market seems capable of supporting it.

Exhibit 83 shows the layout of Wellesley Office Park in Wellesley, Massachusetts. It has provisions for both multiple-occupancy and single-occupancy structures. Building Number Two shown on the plan contains 45,000

---

[9] Boley, *Industrial Districts Restudied,* p. 18.
[10] "Sites for Science," *Industrial Development and Manufacturer's Record,* August, 1965, p. 29.
[11] *Ibid.*
[12] *Ibid.*

square feet of space. Building Number One has a total of 14 tenants, at least seven of which can be rated as "national credits."

Exhibit 83

SITE PLAN OF WELLESLEY OFFICE PARK, WELLESLEY, MASSACHUSETTS

Developer: Beacon Construction Company. Architects: Salsberg and LeBlanc

f. *Transportation Site Developments.* Industrial districts that concentrate on users of a particular transportation facility were originated by railroads. These are almost always restricted to heavy users of rail freight. Rail proximity is also provided in many other districts. A premium frequently is attached to sites that have access to rail use, whether the occupant actually needs rail transportation or not. In the discussions of site value in Chapters 12 and 13, the point was made that marketability is enhanced if there is more than one type of transportation facility available to serve any industrial site.

Airport-oriented industrial parks are also found throughout the United States, attracting users to whom fast delivery to customers is a major consideration. Producers of relatively light-weight, high value-added goods are especially likely to take advantage of airport locations. So are those whose executives or technicians utilize air transport frequently and regularly. One such major development in close proximity to an airport is Centex Industrial Park, adjacent to O'Hare Field in Chicago. Its layout is shown in Exhibit 84. (Note also on-site rail and proximity to Northwest Tollway.)

Water sites for industry are important among major bulk shippers, as attention focuses on the use of waterways for transportation. An illustration of the development of water sites through the efforts of the U.S. Army Corps of Engineers is given in Exhibit 85. This provides aerial views of the President's Island Industrial Park on the Mississippi River in Memphis, Tennessee, before and after dredging. The industrial park site was created from dredge spoil.

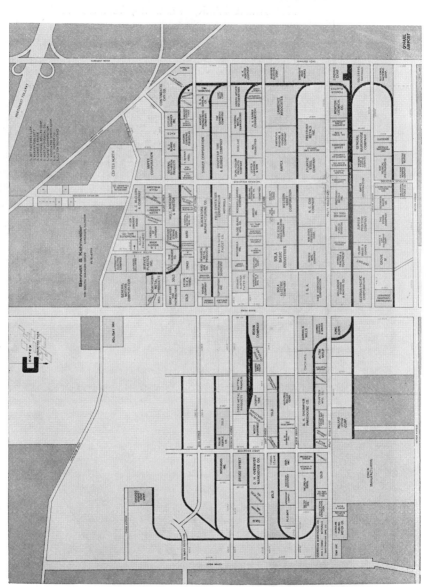

Exhibit 84

LAYOUT PLAN, CENTEX INDUSTRIAL PARK, CHICAGO

Courtesy Bennett & Kahnweiler, Chicago

Exhibit 85

BEFORE AND AFTER VIEWS OF PRESIDENT'S ISLAND
INDUSTRIAL PARK, MEMPHIS, TENNESSEE

U.S. Army Photographs Courtesy Conway Publications, Inc.

2. *Tenancy Status.* Industrial parks may also be classified by the ownership arrangements between developer-sponsor and occupant. In some parks, sites are available for purchase exclusively, while in others it is possible to obtain occupancy only through leasing. A variety of combinations is also found. For example, land may be leased, and the buildings owned by the land lessees. In other districts, there may be a range of different arrangements at the same time: leasing and direct sale; leasing of land only; leasing of land and buildings; sale of land only; sale of complete packages.

The arrangements made depend to a large extent upon the sponsor and his objectives in developing the park. They also depend upon the relative negotiating strength and skill of the sponsor and the potential occupant.

3. *Occupancy and District Characteristics.* "There is a relationship between type of district (manufacturing versus non-manufacturing) and certain land use and employment characteristics. For instance, manufacturing establishments in industrial districts usually require larger sites, utilize a smaller proportion of their total site area for buildings, employ more workers per plant, and exhibit lower employee densities per site acre than do non-manufacturing establishments." [13] Similarly, national credits commonly have smaller plants or buildings in industrial parks than do local firms. The reason is that the establishments of the national firms are most frequently branch plants, branch offices, or branch warehouses; while the local firm usually locates its headquarters operation in the park.

The type of occupancy permitted or sought in a planned industrial district also influences the direction and the character of the sales or promotional efforts of the industrial real estate broker. For example, he will not seek to attract manufacturing establishments to a park that is designed primarily for distributive or wholesaling users, and whose sites are priced accordingly. The customers that may be attracted to a particular facility will vary from one region to another. The broker must advise the developer which types of occupants are most likely to be attracted by a particular proposal or plan. Once the developer has decided the direction his efforts will take, however, this determines to a large extent what the broker can do. He cannot alter the market; he can merely attempt to take advantage of it for his client.

Facilities Offered

In order to compete effectively on the market, the industrial park must provide adequate facilities for the industrial user seeking space. The land must be in the form of serviced sites, and not simply undeveloped acreage. Minimum standards must be established so that the sites will be competitively attractive on the market. This means at least control over the size and shape of lots and the use of the land, for the protection of current and prospective users, the developer, and the community.

1. *Improvements and Services.* The industrial park offers, as a minimum, a site "package" to the potential industrial user, along with protection

---

[13] Boley, *Industrial Districts Restudied*, p. 7.

of the investment in the site. The amenities and site improvements offered will include at least the following:

a. *Good Location.* This means quick and easy access to and from the *critical* mode of transportation. Moreover, it means that the district is located in the line of growth of the metropolitan area, so that the acquisition of a site is a good investment that also provides increasingly improved proximity to labor supplies and markets.

b. *Utilities.* The kinds of utilities available in the industrial park, and their capacities, are important considerations for potential occupants. Once utilities are installed, it is rarely economically feasible to dig them up and expand them, except in exceptionally large industrial districts or for major new users. The utilities available will tend to determine the kinds of occupants that can successfully and appropriately be attracted to the park.

Of particular significance to the broker is the availability of *heavy* power facilities, natural gas supply, water under enough pressure to operate sprinkler systems, and "excess" capacity storm water drains. In many of the larger parks, the developers have installed sewage treatment plants and pumping stations to provide back-up facilities for the municipal system, or to ensure the capacities and the pressures required for industrial use. Exhibit 86 illustrates the type of installation that may be found. It shows the sewage treatment plant installed by the developer of the Crocker Industrial Park in San Francisco.

Exhibit 86

SEWAGE TREATMENT PLANT, CROCKER INDUSTRIAL PARK, SAN FRANCISCO

Photo: Morton-Waters Co.

c. *Transportation.* Nearly every industrial park developed since 1955 has been adjacent to, or in close proximity to, a major arterial highway. Highway access is virtually indispensable. In addition, over 90 per cent of the industrial districts in operation are still served by rail.[14] Air, water and pipeline transportation are also important for specific types of users. To a large extent, their significance depends on the anticipated character of the park. In this respect, the development of the industrial park is no different from the development of unplanned industrial districts. The same basic considerations of proximity and access prevail.

One important issue in relation to highway access is the pattern and character of the streets within the district. Their width and quality of construction have an important bearing on the ease of traffic flow as well as the volume of traffic they can handle effectively. Many developers have learned to their sorrow that skimping on street construction or on the width of rights of way within the district can offset many of the district's locational advantages.

Finally, streets within the park should be well lighted and curbed, regardless of the setbacks or the character of the surrounding area. This is for the safety and protection of users of these streets, as well as for the protection of the developer so long as the streets are not dedicated to the community.

d. *Services.* Services available within the park, particularly for employees, are important determinants of the types of uses that can be attracted to the district. Manufacturing firms with large number of employees, as well as office operations, often encourage the development of compatible retail and restaurant facilities either within or (more preferably) immediately adjacent to the park itself.

Generally speaking, a relatively large district is required before service facilities can be attracted to locate nearby, although appropriate eating establishments may be drawn to a smaller market. Gasoline service stations, medical facilities, and transient quarters (motels) generally depend on large districts or large-scale manufacturing establishments for successful operation.

2. *Level of Development.* The industrial park or planned industrial district may be a large tract of land that is subdivided into usable industrial sites which are then sold or leased to prospective users for construction of their own buildings. It may involve the development of whole "new towns." The land-only type of development is much more common among smaller, community-owned and sponsored districts.

The professional industrial park developer is usually in the construction business. Indeed, much of his profit is derived from construction. He commonly offers a "package plan" for industrial purchasers or tenants. The developer can provide necessary services, and has the staff and experience to resolve economically and efficiently the occupant's new building requirements. "The Comprehensive Package Plan program provides: design, engineering, construction, and financing either on a sale or long-term lease basis." [15]

Large-scale developments of entire new communities are becoming in-

---

[14] See *Ibid.*, p. 6, for the basis of the statements made in this paragraph.
[15] Cabot, Cabot and Forbes, Boston, Massachusetts: *Windsor (Connecticut) Industrial Park,* Undated Promotional Brochure.

creasingly significant in the real estate scene. These are new communities,

designed to accommodate residential, commercial, and industrial uses in harmonious patterns and compatible surroundings. Two notable examples of this trend are found in Don Mills, a community in the Toronto area, and Elk Grove Village in the Chicago area. Although not truly self-contained or self-sufficient, as the term would imply, this type of development has proved that with careful planning and judicious development it is possible to house selected industries, commercial activities, and residences in the same development without detracting in any way from the livability, attractiveness, or efficiency of any of the above land uses.[16]

The Don Mills development is illustrated in the aerial view shown as Exhibit 87. This illustrates the compatibility and harmony of use between the industrial portion in the lower left segment of the photograph, and the surrounding uses.

Larger "self-contained" communities have also been initiated in many

Exhibit 87
AERIAL VIEW, DON MILLS, TORONTO

From *Industrial Districts Restudied,* Technical Bulletin No. 41 (Washington, Urban Land Institute, April, 1961), p. 20.

---

[16] Boley, *Industrial Districts Restudied,* p. 25.

parts of the United States. They provide industrial parks and industrial districts on a planned basis. The districts are consciously designed to develop in harmony with commercial, service, recreational, and residential areas in the community. Laguna Niguel and the Irvine Ranch Development, both in California, are outstanding examples of the planned community with integrated industrial space provided within it. So are Reston, Virginia, and Columbia, Maryland, both in the Washington, D.C., metropolitan area. This type of community offers substantial opportunities for the industrial real estate broker, in serving both the developer and the industrial firm seeking a planned environment.

Sponsorship

Each sponsor-developer of an industrial park has his own style and peculiarities which influence the characteristics of the park. The industrial real estate broker should be able to recognize the differences among the general types of district sponsorship. Most industrial park developers, of whatever stripe, will pay a commission to a broker. The only frequent exceptions are some community development foundations, and a few utility companies. The broker should check with the sponsor in advance before negotiating a transaction in such a park.

The objectives of the several types of sponsors are different, as are the means of accomplishing these objectives. Some will want to sell sites only, while others are interested in producing total packages. Others will insist on leasing space rather than selling it, and still others will restrict occupancy to firms using a particular service or transportation facility. If the broker is to do a professional job in the industrial park market, he must recognize the different types of arrangements that prevail in his market area, and identify the types of occupants most likely to be attracted to them.

There are five major groups of sponsors of industrial districts. "In order of importance they are: private real estate developers; railroads; private local community groups; government sponsored groups; and joint government-local community groups." [17] There are also some minor groups or subgroups, including cooperatives and condominiums. These have been tried with indifferent success thus far, and some authorities argue that they are incompatible with industrial use.[18] They do exist as a possibility, however.

Generally speaking, private developers (whether operating as proprietorships, partnerships, corporations, or joint ventures) are seeking profit. They may be seeking capital gain (whether taxable as long-term capital gains or not) or long-term income, or a combination of both. What they strive for will determine to a large extent the type of tenancy arrangements they seek to establish.

Railroads and utility companies (to the extent that they sponsor districts)

---

[17] *Ibid.*, p. 26. See the Appendix Tables in the cited work for detailed analysis and presentations of industrial district characteristics by type of sponsor.

[18] For a development of this view, see Marshall Bennett, "Techniques in Industrial Development," *Advanced Course in the Techniques of Industrial Real Estate* (Washington, Society of Industrial Realtors, 1964).

are also seeking gain, but they are more interested in expanding the volume of their business. Therefore, the direct returns from the development and sale or lease of industrial sites are secondary to the increases in sales revenues expected from user-occupants. Only relatively heavy users of rail freight are welcome in most railroad-sponsored industrial districts; utility companies seek to attract particularly heavy users of their services.

Public agencies, community groups, and private nonprofit local development organizations generally seek to expand employment, income, and real estate tax revenues in the community. For them, real estate profit is also secondary. Indeed, from a strict accounting basis, many of these developments show a "loss." Their orientation is toward *community* development rather than *industrial* development.

Within this framework, a few other notable characteristics of each group can be identified. Because of his interest in deriving a direct profit by merchandising the industrial land or an industrial "package," the private real estate developer tends to seek out older, well-established firms that are good credit risks. The credit is the basis for financing much of the subsequent development. The firms serve as attractions for further expansion. Generally speaking, solid prosperity characterizes the firms usually found in privately sponsored industrial parks. Moreover, they are more likely to be branches of large, national establishments than the headquarters or home office establishments of local firms. The actual plants or structures may in fact be smaller, simply because they are branch plants. Privately sponsored districts are generally close to major metropolitan centers.

Community development organizations emphasize "the indirect benefits that industrialization may bring to their communities in the form of increased employment, payrolls, business, and tax revenues." [19] Accordingly, they tend to favor manufacturing over distributive or warehousing firms. Manufacturing establishments generally provide higher levels of employment for a given building or land area. Moreover, community-sponsored districts are found predominantly in communities of less than 50,000 population. This is not surprising, since these are not major centers of employment and industrial activity. Inducements are often necessary to attract industrial firms to such areas.

Generally, districts started since 1960 have been smaller in average area than those started during the 1950's.[20] According to sponsorship, the largest districts on the average were found in the Urban Land Institute survey to be those developed by port authorities (including water site developments), and the smallest were those sponsored by redevelopment authorities.[21] While site densities and employee density figures are relatively low for industrial parks, densities are normally quite high in redevelopment authority-sponsored districts.

---

[19] Boley, *Industrial Districts Restudied*, p. 29.
[20] "Seventh Annual Industrial Park Survey," *Industrial Development and Manufacturer's Record*, February, 1966, p. 7.
[21] Boley, *Industrial Districts Restudied*, p. 6.

DEVELOPMENT OF INDUSTRIAL DISTRICTS
AND INDUSTRIAL PARKS

The principles and most of the techniques of development of a planned industrial district are not substantially different from those underlying unplanned or single-parcel industrial development. The emphasis is still on the problems of the private developer, and the functions of the industrial real estate broker in assisting and advising the developer.

One important difference in the development of industrial parks is the obvious fact that larger areas, with more units, are usually involved. Development also covers a considerably longer period of time. A greater financial commitment requires considerably more planning and preparation than is necessary for the isolated or unorganized development.

In addition to being larger, more time-consuming, and more money-consuming, the planned industrial district is also a complex series of combinations of resources. The developer provides the facilities and utilities that convert land into sites. Moreover, the developer creates a controlled environment within which industrial occupants can be attracted because facilities are available, and protection of their use and investment is assured. In this way, the developer is creating a market for his product, and is actually creating value. Many developers of industrial parks contend that they are "manufacturing appreciation."

In providing sites for building space, industrial park developers are improving land on a wholesale basis, and taking advantage of the economies and savings attached to larger-scale operations. By marketing at retail (whether through sale or lease), they generally show a greater profit margin than single-site developers can. Yet there is no quick or easy way to profit in industrial park development. While industrial parks provide many benefits to the developer, the community, and the industrial occupant, these benefits are gained only after long-range planning, extensive development expenditures, and the passage of considerable time.

Industrial park development is a systematic process that involves careful planning and control. These are two of the basic distinctions of the planned district from the single-site development: planning and control. Timing is another important distinction. Timing is critical to the initiation of the development, the subdividing of the land, the installation of site improvements, and the sale or lease of the sites and buildings.

The principal steps in the development of an industrial park include:

(1) preliminary or background analysis;
(2) site selection and acquisition;
(3) preparation of a development plan;
(4) formulation of use restrictions and controls;
(5) preparation of a district layout;
(6) installation of site improvements; and
(7) building construction.[22]

---

[22] This sequence has been adapted from Boley, *Industrial Districts: Principles in Practice,* p. 9; and Sargent, *op. cit.,* p. 3.

Running through the several steps in planned industrial district development is the thorny and recurring problem of financing. When the development phase has been completed, *then* marketing of the sites or building space becomes the next concern.

Industrial park development is based on the general proposition that for the sites to be marketable and attractive on the market, the essential services must be installed in advance of sale or lease.

Preliminary Analysis

The development of an industrial park "should not be undertaken . . . unless considerable research and analysis of the local situation has been obtained." [23] After evaluating the market very carefully, the developer must decide what is going to be sold or leased, where, and for what price. This is necessary for advance planning and detailed examination of long-run prospects.

1. *Identification of the Market.* Market analysis is essential to the success of the industrial park, and it must be carefully and professionally completed before actual development activity begins. Good feasibility studies include highest and best use analysis, identification of the most probable industrial users, and a determination of what those users' site requirements are. In addition, the decision of what type of industry to aim for rests on a detailed knowledge of the assets and liabilities of the community. Finally, there must be an appreciation of how to adapt the resources at the disposal of the developer (the land, his funds, his skills, community facilities) to meet the needs and requirements of the most probable occupants of the developed sites and buildings.

2. *Relation to the Community.* The developer must consider the probable relation of his park to the community and to the market. The district and the community must complement each other rather than competing or conflicting. The developer is in a position to encourage advance planning in the community, often by providing leadership and an example in the district. [24] In evaluating the community, the developer often finds logic in locating in the path of movement and growth. This is what the developer of Centex Industrial Park near O'Hare Airport in Chicago attempted to do. In order to accomplish this, and to ascertain whether an ample supply of good labor was likely to be available for firms attracted to the park, "the first thing we did was to make a market feasibility study." [25]

3. *Investment Feasibility.* In undertaking a market survey and feasibility study, it is also necessary to estimate and project costs: development costs, marketing costs, operating costs. The velocity of sales must also be

---

[23] For details and examples, consult Boley, *Industrial Districts Restudied*, p. 23; Gerald W. Blakeley, Jr., "Techniques in Industrial Development," *Advanced Course in the Techniques of Industrial Real Estate* (Washington, Society of Industrial Realtors, 1964); W. C. Windsor, Jr., "Promotion, Sales and Profits of an Industrial Park," *Industrial Parks, Start to Finish*, Proceedings of First Annual Workshop, Pittsburgh, Pennsylvania (Washington, Society of Industrial Realtors, 1959), p. 15; Paul P. Shepherd, "Developer's Viewpoint," *The Good and the Bad in Industrial Parks, S.I.R. Newsletter*, July, 1966, p. 3.
[24] Boley, *Industrial Districts: Principles in Practice*, p. 9.
[25] Bennett, *op. cit.*

carefully projected and related to costs, since sales (or leases) represent the revenues that the developer anticipates.

Preliminary analysis can be costly and time-consuming, but it can prevent mistakes and save larger costs later. It represents the best form of insurance policy that the developer can obtain, provided the study is conducted professionally and objectively. The task should be performed by an outside organization, rather than the developer's own staff. An industrial brokerage office experienced in feasibility analysis is an obvious and logical choice.

4. *Ingredients of Preliminary Investigations.* The preliminary analysis will also cover a search of title to the land, land surveys, and similar investigations. The greatest economy is achieved when the best talent (legal, engineering, economic) is acquired to undertake these researches.

The kinds of information required in any preliminary analysis include the following: [26]

(1) Analyze the potential market for industrial land in the area.
    (a) Economic conditions and industrial profile of the community.
    (b) Assets and liabilities of the community.
    (c) Types of industrial locations in the community in the recent past.
    (d) Absorption rate for industrial land in the community.
    (e) Supply of adequate, properly zoned and available industrial land in the area.
(2) Check the attitude of residents in the area toward industrial development.
(3) Discover industrial park orientation of industries likely to be attracted to the area.
(4) Analyze labor supply and labor situation in the area.
(5) Determine quantity and quality of public utilities available to serve park.
(6) Measure political and business climate of the area.
    (a) Community development projects likely to attract industry (highways, utilities, etc.).
(7) Consider state and local building and land use controls.
    (a) Zoning, subdivision regulations; enforcement.
    (b) Codes and their enforcement.
(8) Study tax situation in the community.
(9) Analyze financial status of development.
    (a) Anticipated development, marketing, and operating costs.
    (b) Pricing required by cost and profit considerations.
    (c) Pricing dictated by competitive sites.

If it then appears logical to proceed with the development of an industrial park proposal, the next step to be studied is land selection and acquisition.

Land Selection and Acquisition

The general principles of land selection and assembly that apply to single-site developments are equally appropriate for the larger industrial park. The attributes of the "ideal" industrial site listed in Chapter 13 offer the industrial park developer one important set of standards to strive toward

---

[26] This list is adapted from Boley, *Industrial Districts: Principles in Practice*, p. 23; and Sargent, pp. 3–4. Consult these two references for details.

in providing the individual sites for industry within the park. In general, the developer should purchase land that already has as many attributes as possible that industry wants. This helps minimize the elements of site conversion and development. At the least, land should be selected which is level, well drained, well served by transportation facilities (or with excellent access to them), and appropriately zoned.

1. *Selection.* In selecting the land to be developed into an industrial park, the developer must be guided by two sets of basic considerations. First, can the sites to be provided in the park be made attractive to the kinds of industrial occupants the developer is seeking? Second, is it possible to provide the proper kinds of facilities at reasonable costs? In providing these facilities, "flexibility is vital to industrial district development." [27]

Consideration of marketability of the developed sites must be combined with analysis of the costs expected to be associated with the acquisition, development, and conversion of the land into marketable sites. The land to be selected is that which offers the prospect of development into acceptable sites with the least cost.

2. *Acquisition.* In acquiring the land to be developed into industrial district sites, the developer has three major factors to consider: assembly, price, and carrying costs (financial and holding). As far as assembly is concerned, the basic principles applied to single-site developments are still appropriate. It is easier to deal with one owner than with several in assembling a parcel. Moreover, it is usually better to buy "too much" land than not enough. The excess can often be sold off profitably later, and the developer has the added advantage of controlling the growth of at least part of the surrounding area.

Assembly problems constitute one aspect of the acquisition price or cost. One such problem confronting the developer may be convincing owners of land suitable for development into an industrial park (or industrial sites) that it is not especially valuable in its raw state. The addition of improvements converts it into valuable sites.

Acquisition costs include, in addition to the price of the land itself, fees for options, attorneys' fees, commissions, title searches, title insurance, surveys, and the like. Even more important than the price paid for the land are the terms on which it is available to the developer. Conserving on cash is always a major consideration. Financing that economizes on the developer's funds is generally preferred: purchase-money mortgages, options with staged releases, or ground leases with subordination to the primary mortgage lender on development financing. Land is often valued for pricing purposes by the Land Development Cost Method discussed in Chapters 12 and 13. This reveals the "permissible price" that the developer can afford to pay, based on the findings of the study. In the final analysis, the price the developer can and will pay depends more on the financing that can be arranged than on any other single factor.

Although the acquisition cost of the land may not represent a particularly large proportion of total development costs, "a particular site, regardless of

---

[27] Boley, *Industrial Districts: Principles in Practice,* p. 11.

how good its location may be, may simply not be feasible if it cannot be bought right." [28]

Development Plan

As soon as a specific parcel of land has been selected and arrangements made for its acquisition, a firm plan of development of the entire project must be prepared. This involves more than physical layout or design. It includes the financing, construction, marketing, and management phases of the development, as well. It requires that the developer and his staff (with outside assistance where the necessary skills are lacking on the staff) plan well into the future. The development of an industrial park requires that the sponsor take a long-term outlook to make sure that the later stages of the project are not jeopardized or undermined by early development activities. For example, all existing road frontage should not be sold off first. Otherwise, it may be both difficult and expensive to develop the remaining interior area later.

In planning, therefore, the developer considers the conditions under which the sites are to be made available, and then proceeds to create the environment to fulfill those planned conditions.

1. *Size and Shape of Lots.* One major determination to be made by the developer is the physical planning or layout of the lots. This should be based on the requirements of industrial firms likely to be attracted to the park. Maximum flexibility in design will allow for custom plotting for individual customers and provide room for subsequent expansion. The real "solution" to the expansion problem, of course, is to convince industrial purchasers or tenants to acquire plenty of land at the outset for expansion. Failing this, however, a high degree of flexibility in street layout and plot planning is most helpful.

This is not always easy. In some communities, especially more suburban or rural ones, zoning and planning authorities may insist on strict application of subdivision regulations to industrial "subdivisions" as well as to residential developments. The result is rigidity in the recorded development plan, which is both unwelcome and uneconomic. Continual revisions may have to be filed to meet the requirements of new purchasers or tenants.

The size and shape of lots are also limited by the terrain, the availability of utilities, and the location of transportation facilities.

2. *Facilities to Be Installed.* The utilities, streets, and other improvements to be installed (whether by the developer or by the community) depend on the requirements of potential users, and on the present availability of facilities in the area. Moreover, the plan must include specific determinations of *how much* as well as *what*. It is not enough to know that there is a water main running through the property that can be tapped by industrial users. The developer needs to know what the diameter of that main is, what its capacity is, and what the pressure is. If these ingredients are

---

[28] Gerald W. Blakeley, Jr., "Economics of an Industrial Park," *Industrial Parks, Start to Finish,* Proceedings of First Annual Workshop, Pittsburgh, Pennsylvania (Washington, Society of Industrial Realtors, 1959), p. 10.

inadequate, then new water lines of proper proportions must be installed, despite the fact that "water is already in."

The facilities must meet the standards of potential users. These standards will vary from one geographic area to another. Specific studies are necessary to discover the local norms. The criteria must be changed, if necessary, to meet changing needs of industry.

The costs of providing the necessary facilities must also be considered and analyzed as early in the development process as possible. The developer should retain an experienced, qualified engineer early in the planning phase to generate these cost figures.

Finally, in determining what facilities are to be offered, the developer must decide what level of services is to be provided.

3. *Staging.* Land absorption is slower in the larger industrial district or park. Also, considerable sums will usually be expended before any revenues are received by the park developer. Therefore, staging the development process can be a major factor in the success of the entire undertaking. It conserves on cash, and requires less total commitment on the part of the sponsor at any one time. This in turn reduces the developer's risk.

Both engineering and financing considerations may dictate staging in a relatively large undertaking. Land costs and development costs are usually too high to warrant holding developed sites for future growth. It is preferable, both financially and for future flexibility in development, to hold the land in bulk. Then the specific demands of individual customer firms can be met more easily, with little upset to the over-all plan of development. One illustration of a staged development is provided in Exhibit 88, which shows the layout plan for the initial development of the Great Southwest Industrial District, Dallas–Fort Worth, Texas.

Preliminary engineering and design plans may serve subdivision plans in some communities, and therefore make it unnecessary to put all plot plans down in advance. A good planning layout and engineering design provide the basis for estimating the location and size requirements of utilities and roads. By providing a timetable, the staged plan makes it possible to avoid spending money before it is necessary. This constitutes part of the financial plan for district development as well.

Major frontage should be conserved and not sold off first, if early sale can be deferred. The remaining frontage becomes more valuable as the development of the district progresses successfully. There will be greater profits if some of the more desirable locations are conserved for later sale. This is assisted by staging, which also provides greater flexibility in planning, platting, and subsequent development. A hypothetical example of the kind of variation in plot size and shape that is possible with careful planning and staging is provided in Exhibit 89.

Restrictions and Controls

The developer of an industrial park must provide the means of protecting the environment he has created. This protection is generally provided through deed restrictions, covenants in leases, and park standards relating

Exhibit 88

LAYOUT PLAN, INITIAL DEVELOPMENT, GREAT SOUTHWEST INDUSTRIAL DISTRICT

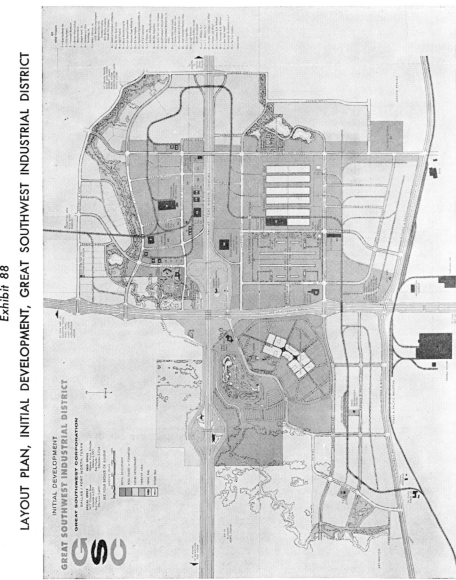

From *Industrial Districts: Principles in Practice,* Technical Bulletin No. 44 (Washington, Urban Land Institute, April, 1961), p. 116.

Exhibit 89

HYPOTHETICAL LAYOUT SHOWING VARIATION IN SITE SIZES AND SHAPES

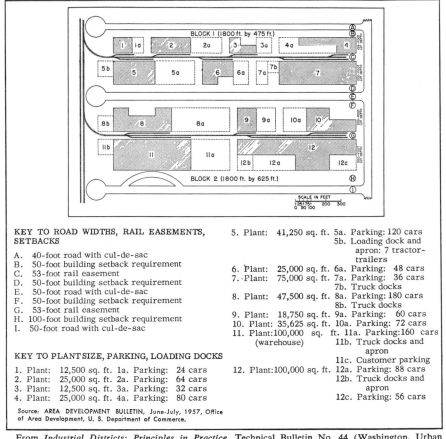

KEY TO ROAD WIDTHS, RAIL EASEMENTS, SETBACKS

A. 40-foot road with cul-de-sac
B. 50-foot building setback requirement
C. 53-foot rail easement
D. 50-foot building setback requirement
E. 50-foot road with cul-de-sac
F. 50-foot building setback requirement
G. 53-foot rail easement
H. 100-foot building setback requirement
I. 50-foot road with cul-de-sac

KEY TO PLANT SIZE, PARKING, LOADING DOCKS

1. Plant: 12,500 sq. ft. 1a. Parking: 24 cars
2. Plant: 25,000 sq. ft. 2a. Parking: 64 cars
3. Plant: 12,500 sq. ft. 3a. Parking: 32 cars
4. Plant: 25,000 sq. ft. 4a. Parking: 80 cars

5. Plant: 41,250 sq. ft. 5a. Parking: 120 cars
                          5b. Loading dock and
                              apron: 7 tractor-
                              trailers
6. Plant: 25,000 sq. ft. 6a. Parking: 48 cars
7. Plant: 75,000 sq. ft. 7a. Parking: 36 cars
                          7b. Truck docks
8. Plant: 47,500 sq. ft. 8a. Parking: 180 cars
                          8b. Truck docks
9. Plant: 18,750 sq. ft. 9a. Parking: 60 cars
10. Plant: 35,625 sq. ft. 10a. Parking: 72 cars
11. Plant:100,000 sq. ft. 11a. Parking:160 cars
    (warehouse)   11b. Truck docks and
                               apron
                          11c. Customer parking
12. Plant:100,000 sq. ft. 12a. Parking: 88 cars
                          12b. Truck docks and
                               apron
                          12c. Parking: 56 cars

Source: AREA DEVELOPMENT BULLETIN, June-July, 1957, Office of Area Development, U. S. Department of Commerce.

From *Industrial Districts: Principles in Practice,* Technical Bulletin No. 44 (Washington, Urban Land Institute, December, 1962), p. 15.

to land and space use. These are in addition to any zoning regulations or other land use controls in effect in the community. District controls may supplement local regulations; in the case of inadequate or improper community regulations, they may supplant them.

Even when they are sugar-coated by being called "protective provisions" for promotional purposes, district controls and standards must be provided. They must be enforced effectively and impartially if the park is to be successful. The establishment of controls is one of the most critical aspects of park planning. Controls set the park's character for the future. Minimum standards and controls tend to insure compatibility among occupants of the district, as well as between the district and the community. Property values are protected for the industrial occupant as well as for the developer.

The developer owes the existing occupants of the park the assurance that the standards of acceptance and of use will not be changed, so that their occupancy can proceed as originally intended. "Developers offer industrial occupants of planned districts the advantage of protection against nuisances created by undesirable neighbors. This helps assure the continued attractiveness of the district and thereby protects the investments of the developer and industry alike." [29]

1. *Types of Controls.* The kinds of controls and protective covenants recommended are not merely prohibitions and limitations of land and building use. Workable industrial park controls emphasize function and performance standards. They are specifically geared to the needs and requirements of the kind of industry that the developer is seeking to attract to the park. "District development standards have evolved to accommodate the expanded space needs of the modern industry, and contemporary protective covenants take cognizance of the increasing attention being given to aesthetics and community compatibility." [30]

Performance standards establish the type of limitations on use and occupancy that are employed. Whatever form the controls take, they must be binding on all occupants of the district in perpetuity, or at least for the same long-term period. While flexibility in planning and design of the district is an important virtue for development purposes, flexibility in the application of restrictive covenants is not. Minimum standards and their universal application to all occupants (potential and existing) are essential to the preservation of property values in the park.

2. *Provisions of Restrictions.* The specific contents of district-wide standards, and the specific covenants included in individual leases or deeds, will vary with the circumstances of the individual park and the objectives of its developer. Moreover, they will vary by geographic region. For example, outdoor storage is much more commonly accepted in California than it is in the New England states. As a result, prohibitions of outdoor storage are frequently found in industrial parks in New England, while the emphasis is much more likely to be on screening outdoor storage in parks in California. Even within this framework of area or individual developer variation, however, certain groups of restrictions and covenants appear most frequently as answers to specific types of problems or to serve particular objectives: [31]

a. *Control of Nuisances.* The diversity of uses found in many successful industrial parks leads to the conclusion that "under controlled conditions, most products can be processed without adversely affecting adjacent operations or land uses." [32] Performance standards based on *measurable external nuisances,* usually measured at the property line, provide the most usual and the most effective means of dealing with nuisances. These would include (not necessarily in the same set of controls) limitations on or pro-

---

[29] Boley, *Industrial Districts: Principles in Practice,* p. 20.

[30] Boley, *Industrial Districts Restudied,* p. 6.

[31] This list is adapted from Boley, *Industrial Districts: Principles in Practice,* pp. 20–23. The reader is also referred to the Appendix in Boley, *Industrial Districts Restudied,* which contains a detailed discussion of one district's standards, controls and covenants.

[32] Boley, *Industrial Districts: Principles in Practice,* p. 20.

hibitions of the emission of noise, light, odor, smoke, vibration, heat, or industrial waste.

b. *Use of the Land.*   The most common limitation on the use of the land in industrial parks is the prohibition of residential uses or structures (except possibly a watchman's shack). Commercial (especially retail) uses are prohibited in many purely "industrial" districts. Other districts, particularly larger ones, include separate commercial "centers" to provide shopping, medical, service station, eating, and other employee-oriented services.

c. *Outdoor Storage.*   As noted above, provisions relating to outdoor storage are either prohibitions or requirements for effective screening from view. This is primarily aimed at preserving the "parklike" aspect of the district. These restrictions must be worded carefully, however, because loopholes may appear unexpectedly. One developer told of a trucking firm that circumvented outdoor "storage" prohibitions by "parking" trailers (often with goods inside) in the parking lot. The neighbors complained, but the trucking firm was within its rights under the park restrictions.

d. *Site Coverage.*   The most common site coverage provisions in industrial parks call for between 30 per cent and 70 per cent as a *maximum.* Higher percentages are usually associated with the most expensive sites. Many authorities argue that a 3 to 1 land/building area ratio should be a minimum standard, but this is not the experience of industrial parks throughout the United States.[33] Moreover, site coverage controls that are too stringent may be self-defeating by discouraging industrial firms from locating in the park. Site coverage requirements should be set with a view toward the uses to be included in the park, the functions of the buildings, other restrictions on use and occupancy, and the price of the land.

Site coverage requirements should *not* be substitutes for adequate expansion planning by the individual industrial occupants. If maximum coverage is permitted when the firm originally acquires its site, every plant expansion will necessarily require a variance of the park's controls. This may soon lead to a breakdown in the enforcement program. It can also discourage firms which are looking for protection from locating in the park.

e. *Building Lines and Setback Lines.*   Front, side and rear setback and building lines often add up to maximum site coverage requirements, although their motivation may be different. In addition to setting coverage maximums, setback requirements also help the developer of the park achieve the following objectives: [34]

(1) Provide ample area for attractive landscaping.
(2) Provide space for off-street parking and loading.
(3) Permit easier building identification.
(4) Encourage better and safer traffic flow.
(5) Provide added margin of fire safety.

f. *Building Construction and Design.*   Many districts require that speci-

---

[33] For development of this point, see Bennett, *op. cit.;* Blakeley, "Techniques in Industrial Development"; and Boley, *Industrial Districts Restudied,* p. 16.
[34] Adapted from Boley, *Industrial Districts: Principles in Practice,* p. 22.

fied building materials be used, or conversely that others be avoided. A common prohibition involves metal buildings. One developer told of denying a major steel producer permission to erect a warehouse and district office building of steel. The building was finally faced in brick, with stainless steel trim, and a stainless steel sculpture of the company's trademark standing on the front lawn. Approval of building plans is often required, particularly in exclusively industrial-use parks. Such control is relatively easy to exercise when the developer builds the buildings himself. When the industrial firms have their own buildings erected, then the approval and materials provisions must be included as covenants in the deed or lease.

g. *Sign and Billboard Control.* Increasing numbers of industrial district developers have come to recognize that the size, shape, character, and location of outdoor signs on the plots occupied by industrial users can dramatically influence the character and attractiveness of the district. As a result, most parks now regulate the location, size, and type of signs. Some even provide them.

h. *Off-Street Parking and Loading.* An industrial park cannot operate efficiently or successfully unless on-street parking is prohibited. The flow of traffic is seriously impeded by curbside parking. The appearance of the district quickly deteriorates. The difficulty is that many types of uses require relatively little parking (e.g., warehousing) while others call for much larger amounts of parking for the same size building (e.g., manufacturing, trucking). This is where maximum site coverage limits, strictly adhered to, are effective. They offer support for the off-street parking requirements.

In some districts, the developer's off-street parking requirements are inserted in the building design specifications, rather than the deed covenants. In this way, the developer is able to exert more control and more protection for adjoining site occupants, when a specific building is planned and constructed for a particular purpose. Off-street parking and loading regulations usually specify that loading docks shall be placed at the rear or the side of the building, and that adequate turnaround and docking facilities shall be designed into the building. Most requirements are expressed as a given number of parking spaces per unit of building floor-area. Many are calculated on the basis of maximum shift employment for manufacturing firms.

i. *Landscaping.* Park occupants are usually required to provide a lawn area in the front of their buildings, as a minimum. If they are not adequately maintained, the developer often has the right to provide landscaping and lawn maintenance service, and bill the occupant.

j. *Other Provisions.* A wide range of additional protective or regulatory controls is found in many parks. One important consideration for the developer is a limitation on the "holding" period of a site by an industrial purchaser before a building must be erected. Undeveloped sites, even if sold, are not a strong advertisement for the district. One district cited in the Urban Land Institute study of planned industrial districts had a clause in all its deeds calling for reacquisition of the site by the developer at the original purchase price if construction were not begun within 12 months of the sale date.[35]

3. *Frequency of Controls.* One study of industrial districts measured the frequency with which specific controls were employed by the developers of some 202 parks throughout the United States.[36] In the order of frequency employed, the most common controls were: setback requirements; off-street parking; preliminary building plan approval; architectural limitations; site coverage restrictions; landscaping control; and a prohibition of outdoor storage.

4. *Enforcement.* Industrial district regulations and controls are meaningless unless they are continuously, rigorously, and impartially enforced. The restrictions must be studied carefully before they are put into effect, because they can be too tight, and therefore discourage development. Once the rules are in effect, however, district occupants are entitled to fair and impartial enforcement. Although restrictions on occasion lead to initial buyer or tenant resistance, they generally improve the quality of the development.

Layout

The layout plan for the industrial district is developed in terms of the objectives of the developer, the physical and other construction considerations involved, and the use controls and restrictions decided upon by the developer and his advisers. Having discovered what the attractions of the park are most likely to be, and having identified the market he is attempting to attract, the developer should proceed to subdivide his land to meet the anticipated requirements of those users.

1. *Flexibility.* "If there is a single cardinal rule for industrial district development, it is to provide as much flexibility as possible in the layout plan." [37] Land absorption in most industrial park developments is slow and erratic (averaging only about 10 acres per year in most cases). Predicting specific space requirements of industrial users can be extremely difficult. For this reason, staging the development, discussed as part of "Development Plan" preparation earlier in this chapter, is an important planning and development tool. To the extent that local planning and zoning authorities allow ambiguity in subdivision plans filed, time and money may be saved because numerous revisions are avoided.

Block planning, rather than lot platting, is one way to provide flexibility while still adhering to an over-all general plan of district development. The application of block planning is illustrated in Exhibit 89, which shows how lot sizes and depths can be varied within a general framework of planned blocks. *Some* aspects of the development plan must be set before streets and utility lines (and rights of way) can be put in place. The basic idea is to maintain as much flexibility and adaptability to varying market conditions as possible, *within* this block pattern.

---

[35] *Ibid.,* p. 23.
[36] Kinnard and Malinowski, *op. cit.*
[37] Boley, *Industrial Districts: Principles in Practice,* p. 14.

2. *Lot Shapes and Sizes.* The developer has a strong interest in the pattern of lot sizes and shapes, because they can influence his costs and his profits. Generally speaking, the shallower the lots or individual sites, the greater the loss of land to street and utility rights of way. Also, the greater will be the development cost involved in installing streets and rights of way.

Despite the actual experience of individual districts reported in the preceding section, many authorities argue that the developer should plan his sites and his lot layout to provide for a 3 to 1 land/building area ratio.[38] This, too, will influence the pattern of block planning and layout that is developed. One successful development plan is illustrated by the aerial view and accompanying layout plan for the Fair Lawn Industrial Park, Fair Lawn, New Jersey, which are provided in Exhibit 90.

3. *Components of a Layout Plan.* The layout plan of the industrial park is essentialy the physical portion of the district development plan. It indicates the location of the major facilities that are to be provided by the developer, and sets the general shape pattern of the blocks of sites. It may often be designed to be executed in stages or phases. These stages must be carefully integrated with one another, so that continuity in development is provided. At the same time, provision for maximum variation must be built into the design. The preparation of the layout plan calls for experienced, highly skilled, and imaginative personnel.

The layout plan of the industrial park should provide for as much adjustment and adaptation to the topography of the land as possible to take full advantage of gravity drainage and flows. Within this general framework, the industrial park layout plan will normally include:

a. *District Streets.* The details of the design must be worked out in advance, and the utilization of district streets for parking or loading should be prohibited.

   (1) Rights of way and pavement widths should be as wide as necessary to accommodate anticipated traffic, but not so wide that traffic flow problems are created.

   (2) Curbs should be provided for all streets, primarily for effective surface water drainage; sidewalks are rarely necessary in modern industrial districts because pedestrian traffic is quite limited.

   (3) Paving materials should be adequate to support the weight of heavy trucks.

   (4) Street grades and intersections should be at less than a 5 per cent slope if possible, so that trailer trucks can negotiate the streets and the turns in the district with ease. Moreover, to the extent possible, the streets should follow the contours of the land longitudinally. Then trailers can be loaded, unloaded, and parked on level land. Finally, there should be no acute angles at intersections; corners should be rounded sufficiently for large trailer trucks to negotiate them easily.

   (5) The ownership of streets is a matter of debate. Some authorities argue they should be owned and maintained by the developer, to provide

---

[38] For example, see Bennett, *op. cit.;* and Blakeley, "Techniques in Industrial Development."

Exhibit 90
AERIAL VIEW AND LAYOUT PLAN—FAIR LAWN INDUSTRIAL PARK
FAIR LAWN, NEW JERSEY

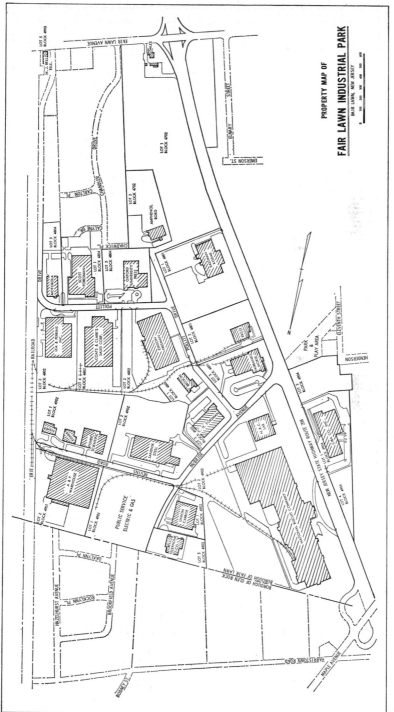

PROPERTY MAP OF
FAIR LAWN INDUSTRIAL PARK
FAIR LAWN, NEW JERSEY

From *Industrial Districts: Principles in Practice*, Technical Bulletin No. 44 (Washington, Urban Land Institute, December, 1962), pp. 70 and 72. Photo: Flite Fotos.

best control over them; others claim they should be owned and maintained by the municipality, to effect the greatest saving in costs to the developer. In either event, it is likely that eventually they will be owned and maintained by the community. Therefore, they should be constructed to meet local community specifications.

b. *Rail Leads and Spurs.* The former are often owned and maintained by the railroad, but the latter are nearly always the responsibility of the user-occupant.

   (1) Rail right of way standards are usually prescribed by the state Public Utilities Commission, or other regulatory authority.
   (2) Curvature standards are set by P.U.C. limits, together with the curve that the longest car to be handled can negotiate without danger of upset.
   (3) Rail gradient standards are similarly set by both P.U.C. regulations and the slopes that rail cars servicing the particular site can negotiate.
   (4) Spur trackage is typically owned and maintained at the expense of the user.

c. *Utilities.* The criteria for district utilities are: adequacy for the user; efficiency of operation for the developer; flexibility for adaptation to unanticipated use demands; and economy for user, developer, and possibly community. In general, utility capacities will be larger than those associated with other types of industrial developments, because of the need for both expansion and flexibility in industrial parks. Development and installation costs are generally quite high, so the developer is anxious to keep his utilities as short and as straight as possible.

   (1) Easements are generally in street or rail rights of way, or else across the rear of the lots in the planned industrial district.
   (2) Water capacity is measured primarily in terms of adequate pressure to operate sprinkler systems and maintain fire rating association acceptance. Pressure should be both high and steady. Pumping stations within the district *may* be required if community systems cannot provide the flow and the pressure necessary.
   (3) Sanitary sewer systems should be designed to serve either "wet" or "dry" industry, depending on what is planned for the park. "Wet" industry includes operations that require water in the manufacturing or fabricating process, and consequently have a considerably greater sewer runoff. To the extent possible, gravity flow of sewage should be incorporated into the district's system. If this is not possible, then pumping stations may be required. Treatment plants, such as illustrated in Exhibit 86, may have to be installed by the developer to accommodate the effluent from the district's occupants, if the district is large and the community system serving it inadequate.
   (4) Storm sewers should be included within the street rights of way to the extent possible, and should be gravity flow systems if possible.
   (5) Electric power service and distribution lines should be located where they are least obvious to view, without loss of efficiency in serving the occupants of the district. Overhead lines provide the greatest flexibility.
   (6) Gas service lines must be provided by the appropriate utility company. It is inappropriate to assume that they will be adequate.
   (7) Telephone service can be a real handicap if it is not adequate. Ad-

vance planning with telephone company representatives is necessary to assure adequacy.

d. *Landscaping.* The basic scheme of a park assumes an attractive, aesthetically pleasing setting. The developer must assure the creation of such a setting through his layout design.

   (1) Grounds maintenance is generally provided by the individual occupant, but may often be supplemented with service provided by the developer and charged to the occupant.[39]

Site Improvements

After development and layout plans have been prepared, land selected and acquired, and park controls decided upon, the developer must begin to follow his development plan by installing necessary facilities. The stages in which site improvements are put in place can affect substantially the success of the initial sales effort of the park. Therefore, both technical and administrative supervision of the improvement process is required. A competent, experienced engineer should be available to handle the technical side. The industrial real estate broker is a logical choice for administrator or project manager.

The guiding principle for the developer is to provide the kind of facilities that will make the sites in the park marketable to the occupants he plans to attract. Market analysis furnishes guidance to what should be provided; engineering studies indicate how the necessary facilities can be provided. Once the facilities plan is set, the engineers and the administrative manager carry it out.

The developer must work closely with the local community in planning and installing streets and utilities, because there may be local minimum requirements preceding their use, regardless of who owns and maintains them. The developer will usually find it advantageous to have the community take over ownership (and maintenance) of streets, water lines, and sewer lines eventually. This will not be possible unless they are built to community specifications.

1. *Facilities Provided.* In the planned industrial district, all utilities, streets, and drainage systems should be available to the individual sites before industry occupies them. The utilities lines, in the proper capacities, pressures, or flows to meet the use requirements of industry, will include: water for human use, water for processing, water for fire protection, sanitary sewer disposal (for both "wet" and "dry" industry), storm water drainage, natural or manufactured gas, electricity, and telephone. Some "excess" capacity or provision for expansion should be built into the lines when they are originally installed because of the difficulty of correcting and enlarging them later.

To the extent possible, utilities systems should be connected with public networks. It is often more economical in the long run to bring in public water and sewer lines from a distance than to attempt to serve the needs

[39] This listing and the explanations of its components are adapted from Boley, *Industrial Districts: Principles in Practice,* pp. 14–20.

of the park's occupants with drilled wells and septic fields or private sewage disposal systems. If the district is large enough, it may pay to construct major facilities within it to serve the needs of the industrial firms, as illustrated by the sewage treatment plant shown in Exhibit 86.

Correcting topography may be both difficult and expensive. Some terracing may be necessary, however, particularly if large trailer trucks are to use the park's streets, load and unload at docks in the park, and be parked in off-street parking areas. The objective is generally to provide level areas for building sites, docking facilities, and parking areas. Even with terracing, street grades should still be kept at less than 5 per cent. The project manager will often have to supervise several heavy equipment crews at one time in a large undertaking.

Streets must be wide enough to meet the requirements of anticipated traffic, especially for high-employment manufacturing uses. In addition, corners must be rounded and intersection angles kept as close to right angles as possible, so that large trailer trucks can negotiate them easily and safely. Otherwise, many potential occupants will be discouraged from locating in the park. The developer can expect to lose between 10 and 25 per cent of total land area to streets and rights of way.[40]

2. *Site Development Costs and Financing.* The discussions in Chapters 13 and 14 have already indicated that site improvement costs constitute the largest segment of total district development costs. The magnitude of site improvement compels the developer to plan and stage site development carefully in order to economize on the funds (especially his own cash) available to him.

One inducement to create larger industrial districts is that many substantial elements of overhead and indirect cost are spread over a larger total development, with the result that unit costs are considerably reduced. These economies are important enough to warrant careful consideration.

Development costs include the obvious expenditures for grading and topographic correction, installation of utilities, preparing and surfacing streets, installing rail spurs (if any), and landscaping. These are obvious because they result in tangible changes in the landscape. Not so obvious, but equally important in the cost calculations and planning of the developer, are the indirect costs that rarely result in tangible physical changes.

One developer has characterized these indirect costs as "extraneous costs that go along with you constantly."[41] In reporting on the development of one major industrial district, he noted that these "extraneous costs" equaled total land acquisition and utility installation costs. An enumeration of these costs include the following:[42]

(1) Engineering.
(2) Surveys.
(3) Real estate taxes (during the development period before sites were sold).

---

[40] Boley, *Industrial Districts Restudied*, p. 7.
[41] Bennett, *op. cit.*
[42] *Ibid.*

(4) Commissions (to industrial brokers).
(5) Promotions and advertising.
(6) Legal fees.
(7) Title charges (searches and insurance).
(8) Office expenses.
(9) Interest (on development expenditures for land and utilities).
(10) Land loss (20 per cent in this instance for streets, rights of way, rail, storm drainage).
(11) Miscellaneous (travel and entertainment, primarily).

The broker should be able to advise the developer about the "reasonableness" of cost estimates. Moreover, he should know how best to finance site development costs. He must understand what alternative methods are available to provide needed facilities if a particular pattern of development appears too costly.

Building Construction

1. *Contract Construction.* Industrial park developers often build plants to the specifications of industrial firms, and then sell (custom contract construction) or lease (build-lease) the finished product to the occupant. They may also purchase and then lease back to the industrial user a plant built to its specifications (sale-leaseback). In many instances, these activities result in greater profits to the developer than are associated with the development and sale or lease of sites alone. It requires a much larger and much more diversified organization to carry out a development *and* construction program, however. If construction is to be undertaken as part of the developer's activities, then experienced construction personnel must be available, together with architectural services.

The principles to be followed in undertaking a contract construction or build-lease program are exactly the same as those discussed in Chapter 14 for single-site developments. The only real difference within the industrial district development program is that a larger volume of activity and expenditure must be carefully coordinated by the development manager.

In some instances, developers have agreed to construct a building in order to attract a particularly desirable industrial firm as an occupant. In other cases, they have turned to custom construction because the added opportunities for financing that it offers means support for installing site improvements.

2. *Speculative Construction.* One of the most effective sales tools for an industrial park is an available building either ready for immediate occupancy (a "turnkey" building) or ready for finishing to the specifications of the occupant (a "shell" building). The developer must decide whether speculative construction is to be undertaken, and what form it is to take.

a. *Types of Speculative Buildings.* The construction of a speculative building requires extremely careful market analysis to identify the type of user most likely to be attracted to a building in the park. The developer must build for the broadest possible market, within the framework established for his planned district by the development plan. The basic advantage of the speculative building, whether it is a shell or a turnkey building, is that it offers usable space quickly. The attraction of fast action is what often sells or leases the speculative building.

The turnkey building is more of a risk than the shell building because it can be adapted to the peculiar needs of the individual user only with expense and difficulty. It is most likely to be built in an area where relatively standardized warehousing or assembly activities are very strong. It can, of course, be adapted to the needs of the specific occupant, but then much of the real advantage of *immediate* occupancy is lost.

b. *Flexibility.*   The speculative building offers much flexibility in final layout and interior design. The possibilities for adjustment and variation are indicated in Exhibit 91, which shows a standard 3,200-square-foot

Exhibit 91

ILLUSTRATIVE FLOOR PLANS OF
STANDARDIZED SPECULATIVE INDUSTRIAL BUILDINGS

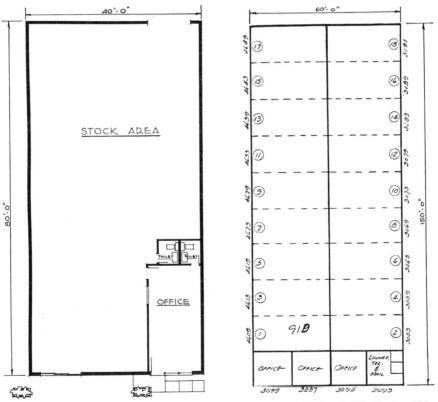

From *Industrial Districts: Principles in Practice,* Technical Bulletin No. 44 (Washington, Urban Land Institute, December, 1962), p. 98.

warehouse which can be expanded readily by increasing its length, and the floor plan of a multiple-occupancy, one-story building which can be divided into expandable 15 x 30-foot modules. If a building is to be expandable, it must be sited properly to accommodate expansion.

c. *Occupancy.* Speculative buildings offer quick occupancy of usable space, and they relieve many managements of the responsibility of planning for new space. If the operation can be accommodated effectively in standardized space, then there is a real saving in time, money, and worry. The existing shell or completed building helps the firm's management decide what they really do want.

d. *Merchandising.* Speculative buildings may be sold or leased, but they are most likely to be leased by the developer. They encourage more rapid occupancy of the park, especially in its initial stages. However, speculative building development ties up a much greater amount of the developer's equity until the building is sold. In addition, financing speculative buildings is not easy, since most institutional lenders do not like to participate in risky undertakings.

3. *Costs.* As with site development, construction involves many sets of costs and expenses about which the developer and the industrial broker should be well informed. All the costs of site preparation must be prorated to the individual site, especially if a sale or lease of the site, independently of the building, is contemplated. If it is part of a total "package," then the developer must have good cost accounting figures to substantiate the allocation of costs and expenses to the site in question.

Actual construction costs include the obvious expenditures on materials, labor, and supervision. These may all be combined into one bill, if an outside contractor is hired to carry out the construction activity. Otherwise, if the developer's staff performs all or some of the construction activities, good cost accounting is again essential. To these direct construction costs must be added: landscaping; engineering (plans and construction supervision); architect's fees; financing costs; commissions and fees for the broker and other specialists; office expenses and other overhead; and miscellaneous items such as legal expenses, title expenses, permits, bonds, and insurance.

4. *Financing.* Arranging for construction financing in industrial parks, whether contract construction or speculative construction, involves more effort and more working knowledge of the financing market than does financing of site development only.

Industrial park construction financing is generally easier to arrange than construction financing of single-site developments. This is partly a function of the greater equities that industrial district developers have in their land and site improvements. Moreover, many institutional lenders are convinced that sites and buildings in industrial parks are generally more marketable (in the unhappy event of default and foreclosure) than are free-standing, individual industrial buildings.[43]

[43] Norman McIntosh, "Lender's Viewpoint," *The Good and the Bad in Industrial Parks,* S.I.R. Newsletter, August, 1966, pp. 3–4.

Financing

Financing the industrial park development is a challenging, often complex and difficult task that requires expert advice and assistance. The specialist in industrial financing usually offers the most effective help the developer can obtain.

The basic objective of the developer's financing plan is to conserve his own cash, and maximize the use of others' funds. This makes his own equity funds go further and last longer for larger development activities.

Industrial parks offer larger commitments for institutional lenders, which means that their overhead costs per dollar loaned are reduced. Servicing is generally lower because a number of loans on individual sites and buildings within the park, as well as development and construction loans on the park itself, can usually be handled by one representative in the area. Institutional lenders also like the stability that park controls afford, and the presumably wider marketability that sites in planned districts have in the event of a forced takeover and resale.[44]

Despite this relatively easier financing through larger institutional lenders, however, financing remains a critical consideration in the success of the planned industrial development.

1. *Land Acquisition.* Many institutional lenders are prohibited by law from making loans on "unimproved" land. Many others avoid such loans as a matter of policy. As a result, the developer often needs a substantial amount of cash to pay for the land.[45] Much more common, however, is some sort of arrangement with the landowner-seller to defer payment of the full purchase price until development is well along. This permits the developer to put more of his cash into development and construction.

Installment sales contracts and purchase-money mortgages are commonly employed to finance acquisition of the land. The purchase-money mortgage from the seller, especially if it can be subordinated to a first mortgage to a lending institution on a development loan, offers the greatest attractions to both developer and landowner. The developer can use the equity in the land to support financing of site development costs, and the landowner usually receives a higher price for the land as a result. Leasing land with options to purchase, usually in stages, represents another alternative that the developer might find attractive in a given situation.

2. *Site Development.* Perhaps the most effective means of financing the installation of streets and utilities in an industrial district is to have the local community assume responsibility for them. To the extent that this is possible, the developer's cash *and* his credit are unimpaired. They are then available for use in other site improvement expenditures, and in building construction. Improvement bond financing is often undertaken by the community for this purpose. This means that the municipality uses its credit and public funds to provide the facilities needed by the industrial park. If the developer must ultimately pay for the installation, he can usually

---

[44] *Ibid.,* pp. 3–4.
[45] Bennett, "Techniques in Industrial Development"; Blakeley, "Economics of an Industrial Park," p. 10.

arrange for deferred payments. These will either be staggered over a relatively long period of years, or else be delayed until service connections with individual buildings are actually made.

Institutional lenders can occasionally be attracted to development lending, especially on a major industrial park. As long as the bulk of the improvement expenditures from the proceeds of the loan are made *within* the confines of the district, lenders are more likely to grant improvement loans. They still tend to shy away from loans for major expenditures *outside* the district, such as those for bringing water or sewer lines a mile or two to the edge of the district. Banks, insurance companies, and real estate investment trusts are all likely sources for development loan financing in an industrial park. Many banks and insurance companies like to see a few sales or commitments first.

In some instances, institutional lenders will want to participate in the success of the park as a condition of granting the development loan. For example, one industrial park in Massachusetts was financed by an insurance company that purchased 10 acres of "sites" at a low price at the same time the development loan was granted. In effect, they took "land as a piece of the equity. This expected profit is part of the lender's rate. It is a 'tail-end takeout.' " [46]

Financing can be obtained in large part because of the credit rating of the developer. Often the credit of firms committed to purchase or lease space in the park is used as well. With good credits as park occupants, many development loans become "paper" deals, with the added attractions to lenders that these imply.

3. *Construction.* Institutional lenders may be induced to finance construction in industrial parks. Contract construction is usually not difficult to finance, because the lender has the credit of both the developer and the occupant to back up the real estate. Although banks and insurance companies still concern themselves with the adaptability and potential marketability of the real estate in the event of default, they are much more likely to emphasize the financial strength of developer and user. This is the case whether the commitment is to buy or to lease the completed building.

Commercial banks are particularly likely sources of construction loans. The added attraction of industrial park construction financing is that the environment is much more subject to control, so that stability in real estate value is often coupled with good credit. As a result, loans on buildings in industrial parks are generally available on more favorable terms to the borrower than are comparable loans on single industrial properties.

Speculative construction is generally more difficult to finance than is contract construction, primarily because there is no credit of the user on the note. Nevertheless, responsible developers of planned districts find construction financing much more readily available for their speculative building than do developers of individual industrial properties.

The financing of completed industrial packages (site and building together) can take several forms. Banks, insurance companies, and real estate

---

[46] Interview with David Scribner, S.I.R., New York City.

investment trusts in particular may make loans available to finance plant acquisition by the industrial firm. They generally prefer locations in industrial parks to free-standing sites. For the same reason, developers report that leasehold financing is generally easier in industrial parks, and on relatively favorable terms. Institutional investors often *purchase* the complete package from the developer, which represents full financing both for him and for the tenant industrial firm.

The developer is often called on to provide financing himself. The developer can usually arrange to hold the property as a long-term lessor, and finance the leased fee. This is particularly true when the tenant is a good credit, and the developer is willing to subordinate the lease and rent payments to the lender. The developer can assist the industrial occupant by offering a leasing arrangement rather than sale, by allowing for deferred payments or by taking back a purchase-money mortgage as partial payment. All of these possibilities require that the developer have funds to support the ownership or the loan, however. This means that the developer must turn once again to institutional lenders or to his own equity funds for financing. Since he wants to avoid the latter as much as possible, loan financing based on the combined credit of the developer and the occupant is a major factor in the financial plant of the park.

Whatever the types of loans that the developer and the industrial broker helping him can arrange, a substantial equity reserve is necessary for successful development of an industrial park. "You should not go into this unless you have a backbone of cash." [47]

SELECTED REFERENCES

American Society of Planning Officials, "Planned Industrial District Zoning," *Planning Advisory Service,* Information Report No. 120, March, 1959.

Boley, Robert E., *Industrial Districts Restudied,* Technical Bulletin No. 41 (Washington, Urban Land Institute, April, 1961).

Boley, Robert E., *Industrial Districts: Principles in Practice,* Technical Bulletin No. 44 (Washington, Urban Land Institute, December, 1962).

Bredo, William, *Industrial Estates: Tool for Industrialization* (Glencoe, Illinois, Free Press, 1960).

Byrnes, Vincent J., "Industrial Park Trends," *The National Real Estate Investor,* May, 1964.

Farr, Newton C., and Kitchen, Lewis, "Urban Renewal," *Real Estate Specializations* (Chicago, National Institute of Real Estate Brokers, 1962).

Industrial Development and Manufacturers Record (Atlanta, Georgia; Conway Research, Inc.):
"Industrial Financing Facts in the 50 States," October, 1965.
"The Office Park," September, 1965.
"Sites for Science," Annual August Study.
"State and Provincial Development Agencies," December, 1965.

---

[47] Bennett, *op. cit.*

"Industrial Parks," Annual February Survey.

"Watersites for Industry," June, 1966.

Industrial Development Research Council, "Industrial Land—Terminology: What Is an Industrial Park, Zone, District, Estate, City?" *Industrial Development and Manufacturers Record,* June, 1966.

Kinnard, William N., Jr., and Malinowski, Zenon S., *The Place of Small Business in Planned Industrial Districts,* Small Business Management Research Report (Storrs, Connecticut, University of Connecticut, 1963).

Sargent, Charles, "Land for Industry," *Urban Land,* Vol. 23, No. 2, February, 1964.

Sheltraw, Howard G., "Urban Renewal in Industrial Development," *The National Real Estate Investor,* May, 1964.

Shenkel, William M., *Principles and Practices of Industrial Real Estate: A Course Syllabus* (Washington, Society of Industrial Realtors, 1963).

Society of Industrial Realtors, *Advanced Course in the Techniques of Industrial Real Estate* (Washington, The Author, 1964):
    Bennett, Marshall, "Techniques in Industrial Development."
    Blakeley, Gerald W., Jr., "Techniques in Industrial Development."

Society of Industrial Realtors, *The Good and Bad in Industrial Parks,* 2 parts, July and August, 1966 issues of *S.I.R. Newsletter* (Washington, Society of Industrial Realtors):
    Shepherd, Paul P., "Developer's Viewpoint," July, 1966.
    Saint, Paul F., "Community's Viewpoint," July, 1966.
    Gibson, Joseph W., "Industry's Viewpoint," August, 1966.
    McIntosh, Norman, "Lender's Viewpoint," August, 1966.

Society of Industrial Realtors, *Industrial Parks, Start to Finish,* Proceedings of First Annual Workshop, Pittsburgh, Pennsylvania (Washington, The Author, 1959):
    Blakeley, Gerald W., Jr., "Economics of an Industrial Park."
    Schmidt, P. J., "Why Industrial Subdivisions?"
    Windsor, W. C., Jr., "Promotion, Sales and Profits of an Industrial Park."

Sawatzky, Jasper J., and Connett, Russell R., *The Broker's Role in Attracting Industrial, Commercial and Recreational Development* (Sacramento, California Division of Real Estate, 1965).

Walsh, Stuart Parry, "The Elite Industrial Investment: A Park," *The National Real Estate Investor,* May, 1964.

Walsh, Stuart Parry, "Industrial Land Development," *Real Estate Encyclopedia,* Friedman, Edith J., ed. (Englewood Cliffs, N.J., Prentice-Hall, 1960).

Windsor, W. C., Jr., "Management of an Industrial Park," *Real Estate Encyclopedia,* Friedman, Edith J., ed. (Englewood Cliffs, N.J., Prentice-Hall, 1960).

16 Marketing and Operating Planned Industrial Districts

ONCE the industrial park development plan has been put into effect, the developer and the industrial real estate broker assisting him must turn to considerations of marketing and continued operations of the park. The broker assisting in park development, marketing, and operation should understand both the benefits and the costs to various parties participating in industrial parks. Finally, he should be aware of the basic responsibilities of the developer, the community, and the broker, respectively.

MARKETING SPACE IN INDUSTRIAL DISTRICTS AND PARKS

In establishing and carrying out his marketing plan, the developer must choose among sale, leasing, or a combination of both. The industrial real estate broker must be in a position to advise the developer on the implications (advantages and disadvantages) of the alternative courses of action open to him.

As a general marketing principle, one leading S.I.R. with extensive experience in the development of industrial parks has stated that once the restrictions and controls within the park have been set, the developer then should accept everyone he can.[1] This requires that the developer adhere to the regulations and standards he sets. Otherwise, this marketing pattern cannot work.

Before effective marketing can begin, the essential services must be ready. Therefore, merchandising requires that at least the first phase of the site development program be nearing completion.

Site Sales

The most common means of disposing of prepared sites in planned in-

---

[1] Interview with R. John Griefen, S.I.R., Boston, Massachusetts.

540

dustrial districts is to sell them, with or without a building on the site.[2] One recent survey of 202 industrial parks throughout the United States and Canada indicated that 71 per cent of the developers would either sell or lease sites; 21 per cent would sell only, and not lease; and 8 per cent had sites available for lease only.[3] Once the decision to sell sites has been made, it is then necessary to consider the appropriate steps in an effective sales program.

1. *Sales Plan.* For prompt and profitable action, the developer must be able to transfer fee title to the sites. Therefore, the developer should have title to the land prior to the time he begins actually offering developed sites for sale. It is not enough at this point to have the land controlled via a lease or options.

Sales provide cash to the developer, and are often particularly important early in the creation of the planned industrial district. Receipts from developed site sales provide the basis for further site improvement and development activities.

In establishing a sales plan, the developer must recognize that his product is a prepared site, which provides essential industrial services for potential site occupants. Site preparation is really the first step in the sales plan. The sales plan must also contain flexibility and adapability. Therefore, phasing or staging in the development plan is an important ingredient in the disposition plan.

One other type of adaptability often offered by industrial parks is space for new, relatively small firms in "incubator" buildings. They may be an important source of additional business for the developer if they thrive in the planned environment of the park. Sites are not commonly sold for this purpose; it is more usual for leased space to be provided by the developer. The sales plan is affected, however, to the extent that some provision is made for later acquisition of sites by new firms attracted to the park.

2. *Sales Program.* The developer's own efforts can very largely determine the success of the industrial park. They begin with effective market analysis and site development. The sales and promotional program for the park (whether sites only are sold, sites and buildings are sold as packages, or space in buildings is leased) cannot be directed at the market haphazardly. The services provided by the park must meet the space and use requirements of those industrial firms most likely to be occupants of the park.

The sales program must go further than this, however. It must be considerably more specific. The efforts of the developer and the sales personnel assisting him must be directed toward attracting the individual firms to which space in the park should make economic sense. Sales are not made to industries or types of firms; they are made to specific, individual business organizations. As a preliminary to this phase of the sales program, a detailed prospect list should be developed.

---

[2] Robert E. Boley, *Industrial Districts Restudied,* Technical Bulletin No. 41 (Washington Urban Land Institute, 1961), pp. 6–7; William N. Kinnard, Jr. and Zenon S. Malinowski, *Planned Industrial Districts and Small Business,* Small Business Management Research Summary (Washington, Small Business Administration, 1963), p. 1.
[3] Kinnard and Malinowski, *op. cit.,* p. 1.

The developer and the broker helping him should not lose sight of the fact that the primary objective is to generate as large and as strong a cash flow as possible. Early dollars are usually more attractive than deferred receipts. An aggressive site sales program helps in managing the cash flow.

The first occupant of an industrial park can set (or at least influence) the tone of the entire development. Providing the proper image requires the sponsor to solicit the kinds of occupants that will be an attraction to further growth and success of the district. This means carefully screening and selecting the few firms that the developer's sales staff will actively solicit at the outset. Then, any prospective occupant meeting the minimum standards and requirements established for the district should be accepted.

In the sales program, the developer still should maintain as much control over the development of the park as possible. In some instances, the decisions will be to lease land or building space rather than to sell it. Most importantly, the use of occupancy standards and restrictions must be rigorously enforced from the outset. Relaxation of the use standards is not a legitimate concession to attract a first occupant. The restrictions may result in the loss of a few early customers. Nevertheless, the experience of most industrial park developers is that the restrictions are actually an important and effective sales tool, and gain more customers than they ever lose.[4]

While a few industrial park developers have their own sales staff and do not particularly encourage sales efforts by outside industrial real estate brokers, most do pay commissions to brokers bringing them purchasers or tenants. The industrial broker would do well to check with the developer in advance, however, to avoid possible misunderstandings. One major industrial park developer says that his organization always pays commissions. He regards the professional industrial broker (particularly the S.I.R.) as the best salesman that his park could have.[5] Surveys and published statements indicate that most other developers seem to agree.

3. *Promotion.* "Promotion of a park transforms plans into reality. A most critical requirement is financing."[6] Even though the sites in the district may offer everything that a reasonable industrial firm's management could possibly expect or hope for, purchasers will not acquire a site in the district unless they are aware of its attractions. The basic principles of promoting and advertising sites or building space in an industrial park are the same as those for promoting the sale or lease of any industrial space.

The distinguishing characteristic of the industrial park that requires special care in a promotion program is the fact that it is a long-term commitment by the developer. What he does in the early phases of the develop-

---

[4] See, for example, Gerald W. Blakeley, Jr., "Techniques in Industrial Development," *Advanced Course in the Techniques of Industrial Real Estate* (Washington, Society of Industrial Realtors, 1964).

[5] Marshall Bennett, "Techniques in Industrial Development," *Advanced Course in the Techniques of Industrial Real Estate* (Washington, Society of Industrial Realtors, 1964)

[6] W. C. Windsor, Jr., "Promotion, Sales and Profits of an Industrial Park," *Industrial Parks, Start to Finish,* Proceedings of First Annual Workshop, Pittsburgh, Pennsylvania (Washington, Society of Industrial Realtors, 1959), p. 16.

ment will influence considerably its later success. "The best way to promote an industrial park is to perform well and look for repeat business."[7]

The basic idea in promoting or advertising industrial parks is to tell the story of the park and its development over and over. This may involve sponsoring luncheons and community promotional activities. It can mean the preparation and distribution of brochures by direct mail to a selective prospect list. It certainly means large numbers of personal contacts with individual industrial managements. It also means preparing sales kits for interested industrial real estate brokers, so that they may be an effective arm of the sales effort of the developer.

Part of the sales plan must include a careful estimate of promotional costs. Moreover, the development of a really useful prospect list can be time-consuming and expensive. Travel expenses are involved in visiting prospects, as well as bringing them to the site. It is necessary to maintain a nucleus of a staff, even when the bulk of the sales effort is undertaken by independent brokers on a commission basis. There are legal expenses and closing costs associated with sales transfers.

4. *Pricing.* One of the important ingredients in the sales effort is the developer's pricing policy. It must be acknowledged to be fair to each of the several occupants, yet flexible enough to offer inducements to particularly attractive prospects, large users, early occupants of the park, and old or "favored" customers offering repeat business. The developer will normally set his prices after studying other districts in the vicinity to ascertain what the competition is charging and receiving, and what industry expects to pay.

The developer may set his prices on the basis of his land acquisition and site development costs, plus a markup for "profit." This markup may take the form of a percentage or a fixed amount per square foot (or per acre). However, prices cannot be set entirely in terms of costs. They must be competitive with surrounding parks' prices. They must also seem fair to potential occupants of the park, relative to the services and facilities that the park provides.

Pricing is a sales tool when concessions are granted to early occupants or to particularly attractive national firms in order to induce them to locate in the park. Early occupancy tends to stimulate further development, and to accelerate the rate of absorption of the sites by the market. A survey of over 200 industrial parks revealed that 40 per cent of the developers made price concessions to the first firm or the first few firms to occupy sites in the park.[8] In addition, size concessions are quite commonplace.

The kinds of occupants that can be attracted to an appropriately developed and properly promoted planned industrial district are illustrated in the pictures that comprise Exhibit 92. These show a number of representative industrial occupants of Bohannon Industrial Park, San Mateo, California.

---

[7] Blakeley, *op. cit.*
[8] Kinnard and Malinowski, *op. cit.*, p. 1.

Exhibit 92

REPRESENTATIVE OCCUPANTS OF
BOHANNON INDUSTRIAL PARK, SAN MATEO, CALIFORNIA

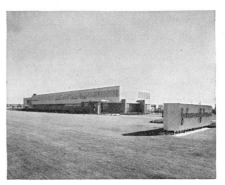

From *Industrial Districts: Principles in Practice,* Technical Bulletin No. 44 (Washington, Urban Land Institute, December, 1962), p. 170. Photos: Norton Pearl Photography and Moulin Studios.

5. *Rate of Market Absorption.* The rate of industrial land absorption is normally quite slow. One major responsibility of the broker is to accelerate the velocity of site sales in order to provide higher profits for the developer. If the broker can stimulate a relatively large volume of early sales, funds expended for site improvements are tied up "unproductively" for a shorter period of time. A 10-year "sellout" or sales program is most common among successful major industrial park developments.[9]

Sales velocity must also be related to a realistic program of price maintenance in order for profits to be realized. Therefore, the industrial real estate broker must emphasize selling sites at the price advertised or anticipated. If concessions are to be made, particular care must be taken that they do not undermine the over-all pricing and profit plan. Rapid turnover,

[9] Bennett, *op. cit.;* Charles Sargent, "Land for Industry," *Urban Land* (Washington, Urban Land Institute), Vol. 23, No. 2, February, 1964, p. 5.

therefore, must not be achieved at the cost of unrealistically reduced prices.

The factors influencing the rate of market absorption of sites include the growth rate of the community, and the availability of competing land. The more nearly the industrial park has a monopoly position in the local market area, the greater the prospect for rapid acceptance of the development. Finally, the quality of the promotional and advertising program is a significant consideration in the rate of market acceptance, and hence of market absorption of the sites.

Industrial Building Space

The marketing of existing or proposed space in industrial buildings in planned industrial districts follows the same general principles as those developed and examined in detail in Chapters 6 and 7. The developer must still pay careful attention to the probable impact of early sales or leases on the marketability of the remaining space in the park. Moreover, because he has sold or leased space to industrial firms with certain promises about the remainder of the industrial district, a developer is limited in the range of potential new customers.

In making industrial building space available, the developer usually engages in contract construction. There may be a subsequent sale-leaseback to an institutional investor, but this is not the direct concern of the developer. As an attraction to tenants, the most effective service that the industrial park developer can provide is the package or "turnkey" plan. The developer may offer custom construction through a build-lease arrangement, or he may offer "customizing" by finishing a shell building to the specifications of the tenant. He may also make generalized or standardized space available in a turnkey building.

If space is to be leased, it may be in a single-occupant building, or there may be multiple occupancy of the building. Multiple-occupancy rental buildings are increasingly used as "incubators" by industrial park developers in order to provide space for new and relatively small firms that can still benefit from the advantages of a location in a planned industrial district.

The industrial developer offers one-stop negotiations and planning services for the industrial firm. "Here the developer provides an integrated service for the location, design, construction, and financing of new facilities on an ownership or long-term net lease basis. Thus, the package plan makes it possible for the client to complete all necessary negotiations (tailored to his needs and specifications) in one office." [10]

1. *Custom Vs. Shell Vs. Turnkey Building.* One important decision that the developer must make is whether to engage exclusively in contract construction, or to speculate with either a shell or a turnkey building. The nature of market demand will indicate what is likely to be marketable in the district. In addition, a careful check should be maintained on what is currently being sold or leased in other planned industrial districts, as well as the apparent acceptance of industrial building space being encountered in the subject district. Finally, the availability of equity funds is an im-

[10] Boley, *Industrial Districts Restudied*, p. 17.

portant determinant of the type of construction program that can be undertaken.

2. *Sale Vs. Lease.* Both sale and lease are effective marketing devices in the experience of successful industrial park developers. A study of some 200 industrial parks throughout the United States and Canada revealed that over 70 per cent of industrial park management did *not* restrict their disposition policies to either sale or lease; both were utilized in these parks.[11] The firm has the use of its plant over a long period either way. The advantage to the developer of a policy which includes both sale and leasing is that it offers one more element of flexibility in the disposition program. By providing a choice for the industrial firm, the developer of the planned industrial district can add considerably to the potential effectiveness of his disposition or marketing program.

3. *Financing.* The ability to attract adequate funds on favorable terms is often critical to the success of the industrial park development. At the same time, the developer may be called upon to offer financing or "terms" to the industrial occupant. This inducement is frequently a very effective sales device. Nearly 80 per cent of industrial park managements included in a major survey reported that they offered some form of financing to oc-

Exhibit 93

AERIAL VIEW—WALTHAM, MASSACHUSETTS, INDUSTRIAL CENTER

Courtesy, Cabot, Cabot & Forbes Co., Boston. Photo: Aerial Photos of New England.

[11] Kinnard and Malinowski, *op. cit.,* pp. 1–2.

cupants or users if necessary.[12] Exhibit 93 is an aerial view of an industrial park in Waltham, Massachusetts, in which extensive financing was made available by the developer. That this park achieved virtually 100 per cent occupancy during its planned development period testifies to the effectiveness of financing as a sales device.

The financing that the developer makes available to industrial occupants may take the form of long-term leasing. The long-term lease permits the industrial firm to acquire the use of industrial space on what amounts to 100 per cent financing. In addition, the developer will often arrange for the sale of leased property to an institutional investor. This represents 100 per cent financing for the developer also.

Purchase-money mortgages, installment sales, and build-lease arrangements are commonly employed by industrial park developers to stimulate sales.

4. *Organization for Sales.* The kind of industrial sales organization appropriate for single-site developments is equally effective for industrial park sales. If the district is large enough, a resident promotional and sales staff or exclusive agent is generally utilized to attract and solicit prospects. The industrial park sponsor should pay full commissions and acknowledge the efforts of industrial real estate brokers in bringing occupants to the district.

Leasing

While over 70 per cent of the industrial parks included in a nationwide survey disclosed that they would either lease or sell sites and space to prospective occupants, 8 per cent of the sample indicated that they would lease only.[13] One such successful development is Stanford Industrial Park in Palo Alto, California. Lying adjacent to the Stanford University campus, the 850-acre park is owned and developed by the University, and all transactions are on a "lease only" basis. This policy has not deterred its acceptance by industrial users.

Because leasing represents a special set of circumstances, a feasibility study must be conducted in the local market to identify the users most likely to be attracted by leasing. Specific recommendations of long-term lease terms and conditions should be provided to the developer by the industrial real estate broker or consultant conducting the feasibility study. Even in parks in which leasing is the only method of marketing space, minimum standards should be clearly stated for the entire district. It is not enough to have individual covenants in each of the leases, because the individual tenants will want to know what restrictions are placed on their neighbors as protections for themselves.

1. *Land Leasing.* Most industrial park developers do not lease sites independently of buildings. This is occasionally undertaken, however, to enable a firm seeking a location in the park to finance construction of its plant. In most instances, a land lease will carry an option to purchase. Al-

---

[12] *Ibid.*
[13] *Ibid.*

ternatively, the building may be purchased by the developer on a sale-leaseback, so that the entire property is subject to lease. Ground leases with the lessee firm owning the building for the period of the lease are much less common within planned industrial districts than they are in single-site developments.

One developer with major parks throughout the United States reports that "we are leasing our expensive land and selling the other." [14] In this way, the sponsor is most likely to receive the benefits of land-value increases over time. However, the park must have a high degree of market attractiveness to make this policy possible.

2. *Total Property Leasing.* The industrial park developer usually leases an entire "package" to the industrial tenant. This may take the form of a build-lease arrangement with custom construction. It may also involve either a shell building with customized finishing, or a turnkey building with standardized space. There are substantial advantages to the developer in leasing, which include control over the development and reasonably assured long-term income.

3. *Subleasing.* Subleasing is generally easier for an occupant in a successful industrial park, if the developer agrees to the sublease, because an established location provides important attractions for industrial occupants. From the point of view of the developer, subletting may be attractive as well. Usually, both the prime tenant and the subtenant will be required to remain on the lease as a protection for the developer.

4. *Financing Lease Interests.* Leasehold financing is feasible in an industrial park, if the developer will subordinate to the lender. Since it is to the developer's advantage to stimulate rapid market absorption and utilization of the space in the park, he usually will agree. In addition, financial institutions will often make such loans because of a general presumption that sites and buildings in industrial parks are more marketable than are free-standing industrial properties.

Sale-leaseback and build-lease transactions can usually be financed through institutional lenders as well. In these circumstances, the credit of the tenant will influence considerably both the availability of loan funds and the terms on which they are available. When reinforced with good credit firms on long-term leases, industrial park properties are often the most readily financed of all industrial real estate.

Management

The necessity to provide continuing management and supervision over the industrial park, during the development and selling phases and after the park has been sold out, sets it apart from single-site industrial development. The basic objective of management during any of these phases is to insure an adequate, stable cash flow to the developer. In seeking to provide this, the developer usually will acquire the services of a broker with special experience in industrial property and industrial park management.

---

[14] Blakeley, *op. cit.*

Because the industrial park is a long-term investment and commitment for the developer, it is necessary to maintain its attractiveness throughout the development phase. Lack of attention to industrial district appearance can undermine the success of later stages. Moreover, if the developer is leasing space in the park on a long-term basis, he wants to protect his investment over the long run. Finally, even if all lots are sold to industrial users, and the development organization moves out, the reputation of the developer for future efforts of a similar nature are in large measure dependent on the reputation of his existing parks. Arrangements for continuing management and control will help to reinforce any favorable reputation created through the development of the park.

Managing an industrial park involves the management of a complex within a larger market environment. Since that complex also influences the nature of the market environment, management personnel must pay particular attention to the interaction between the growth and development of the park and the surrounding community. One authority has likened the management of an industrial park to the management of a high-rise office building, while at the same time underscoring the fact that it is "quite different from the management of single industrial buildings or sites." [15]

The smaller development organization will find it most advantageous to hire a knowledgeable industrial real estate broker to serve as park manager on a long-term contract. The broker must be kept fully informed about development plans for the district. They should be flexible. The broker's efforts and advice are important in maintaining this flexibility. "There is more to managing an industrial park than establishing land use controls and promotion. Industrial park management also includes handling contracts, making lease and sale arrangements, providing for brokers' commissions, and generally taking care of the day-to-day, practical aspects of management." [16]

1. *Occupant Selection.* The management of a planned industrial district requires that continuous attention be paid to the "mix" of occupants in the park, to provide maximum compatibility among them. The appropriate "mix" of industrial users gives it the reputation of being a good location for those types of firms toward which it is aimed. Compatibility is best provided through the establishment and impartial enforcement of appropriate district standards and requirements. The selection of occupants must be worked out carefully within this framework, however, for the benefit of both existing and potential users of the park. Any deviation from the stated practice, to achieve a short-term advantage, will usually result in longer-term difficulties and loss.

2. *Enforcement of Standards.* Existing and potential occupants must be assured that the regulations will be enforced on a continuing basis over time. "Control and supervision must be exercised. Industry wants to know on whom they can depend to control the area and police the covenants. It

[15] Interview with R. John Griefen, S.I.R., Boston.
[16] Statement of Robert E. Boley, Secretary, Industrial Council, Urban Land Institute.

must be a responsible party generating confidence." [17] This responsible party will be the developer, in most instances, especially in parks in which occupancy is based on long-term leases. In the event that the park is entirely sold out, the developer should arrange for a district association that will have both the responsibility and the authority to enforce the standards on *all* occupants, equally and impartially. Such an association is particularly useful in a relatively large development, when it is difficult, if not impossible, for the developer's staff to keep track of all possible infringements or violations. In effect, the occupants of the district become self-policing.

When arrangements have been made for continuing management and enforcement of park standards, most developers find that lenders are more willing to make loans both to the developer and to individual occupants of the park.[18] By making the park and properties within it more attractive to lenders, the enforcement of minimum standards enhances long-term stability of property values.

As with any good and reliable product, an industrial park must be backed by guarantees, and serviced by responsible management. Fair but firm management provides the proper answer to the question, "How tightly will the protective provisions be enforced when the firm across the street moves in?" This helps the developer to maintain the attractions of the park to potential new occupants, and to maintain the quality of the environment that he has created.

3. *Provisions for Continuing Management.* Continuing management of the park also assures existing occupants, whether they are tenants or owners, that their interests are still important to the developer. "You cannot make a deal with a man and then turn your back on him." [19]

Many services and functions can be provided through an owners' or occupants' association. In addition, many larger parks have action groups made up of representatives of the industrial firms in the park, so that appropriate representations may be made to municipal authorities when matters affecting the interests of the occupants of the park come before local boards and commissions. This includes such matters as water and sewer assessments, tax levies, street paving or widening programs, or zoning changes. Such community relations are much better handled by representatives of the actual taxpaying and employing firms in the community than by the developer's organization. A monthly newsletter or other internal communications device is often effective in keeping occupants informed of developments within the district. It also provides them with a means of making their own plans known. It keeps open the door of communication with the developer and his staff.

Ultimately, however, the major responsibility for the day-to-day well-

---

[17] P. J. Schmidt, "Why Industrial Subdivisions?" *Industrial Parks, Start to Finish,* Proceedings of First Annual Workshop, Pittsburgh, Pennsylvania (Washington, Society of Industrial Realtors, 1959), p. 7.

[18] Norman McIntosh, "The Good and Bad in Industrial Parks: Lender's Viewpoint," *S.I.R. Newsletter,* August, 1966, pp. 3–4.

[19] Bennett, *op. cit.*

being of the park rests with the developer—or with the industrial real estate broker hired by the developer to manage the park. As long as he has anything to do with the park, the developer must attempt to resolve problems that may arise with individual occupants, from the selection of grass seed to the expansion of parking space. Landscaping represents another important area of supervision and control (as well as assistance). Physical appearance is an important ingredient in the outward aspect of the success of an industrial park, and most developers provide landscaping service. Some provide it free of charge (by including it in sales prices and leases), while others render the service and then prorate the charges to individual occupants on a periodic billing basis.

4. *Financial Management.* The developer's staff must be able to provide good cost accounting, financing, and pricing information as a supplement to the merchandising activities of the sales force. The basic objective of industrial park management is to maximize the long-term cash flow to the developer. This often calls for an annual projection of costs and revenues, revised quarterly in the light of sales and expenses actually realized. Without effective financial control, the efforts of the sales organization and the construction program can be seriously undermined. There is more to the management of an industrial park than simply real estate considerations; it includes careful financial management as well.

One important aim in the financial management of the district is to control the cost of continuing enforcement of district standards and supervision of occupants. Continuing management and enforcement entail expense, and these expenses must be budgeted carefully.

5. *Reputation.* The sales broker may or may not care about the future of the industrial park. The developer most certainly does. His management program is developed, therefore, with a view toward establishing and maintaining a reputation which will help in disposing of all the space in the current development. In addition, the park developer usually has contingent plans for future districts. Much of the success of these subsequent developments will depend on the reputation of his past efforts.

"The growth of industrial districts will depend on how honest the people who are developing them will be in maintaining their character. The secret of their success will depend on how many of them are maintaining well." [20]

BENEFITS AND LIMITATIONS OF PLANNED INDUSTRIAL DISTRICTS

"The beneficiaries of the planned industrial district are not limited to the developer and district tenants." [21] It is important for the industrial real estate broker to understand who profits, and to what extent, in an industrial park. In addition, he should be equally aware that there are costs and limitations involved for the participating parties.

---

[20] Blakeley, *op. cit.*
[21] Boley, *Industrial Districts Restudied*, p. 28.

The Developer

The attractions and limitations of industrial parks to the developer can be expressed broadly in terms of: money receipts and requirements; planning; marketing; and real estate business considerations. The developer will usually compare the opportunities offered on net balance by the proposed industrial park development with whatever else he might do with his time, talents, and money. In order to analyze the alternatives carefully and properly, he needs a good working knowledge of the prices, costs, and profits of competitors.

1. *Attractions.* The industrial park developer usually is attracted to the park because of anticipated profits and other financial benefits. He has the opportunity for substantial appreciation in the value of the land. In addition, there is value in owning buildings with long-term leases (preferably net leases to good credits). "The developer hopes to realize a higher return in going through the development of an industrial park, as opposed to just selling raw land as required." [22] Even though in many cases "his employer, the customer, makes more money in industrial parks than the developer," [23] he anticipates a high enough return to make the whole undertaking worthwhile. Successful industrial parks bear out this expectation; not all *are* successful, however.

As far as planning is concerned, the industrial park offers the developer the possibility of continued control of a large area. There is generally less land wastage in preparing sites under such circumstances. It allows planning for the maximum yield of both sites and profits from the entire area. Control of the building appearance and setbacks permits the developer to influence the behavior of current occupants, which enhances the attractions to future users.

In terms of marketing, developers usually find much better acceptance of sites and buildings in industrial parks than of single-site developments. The developer is offering the market the reliability of a prequalified product. Further, there is usually more acceptance of this product by financial institutions, as evidenced by the generally more favorable terms that institutional lenders are willing to grant on loans to developers and to occupants of industrial parks.

Finally, "from a real estate business point of view, you can control your own destiny, or at least further the appreciation from your own efforts. Your own efforts on a large property determine to a large extent the appreciation you are going to have . . . You have the long-range dollar return and the cooperation from the government and utility companies." [24]

2. *Limitations.* Despite the expectations of good returns to the developer-sponsor, some authorities contend that industrial park development is not a profitable business. It is certainly not a business for amateurs to enter.

[22] Paul P. Shepherd, "The Good and Bad in Industrial Parks: Developer's Viewpoint," *S.I.R. Newsletter,* July, 1966, p. 1.
[23] *Ibid.*
[24] *Ibid.*

A heavy capital investment is required, and the developer typically needs a substantial amount of working capital. This can be a serious limitation. In particular, initial costs are high. In many instances, landowners must be paid in cash when the land is being assembled for the preparation of sites. Holdout owners of land (when the park area must be assembled) often command very high prices. These costs usually are borne by the developer, at least at the outset.

Costs of improving the sites are high, especially in comparison with single-site developments, which are often served by existing streets and utility lines. There is a much higher "lead-in" investment in streets, utilities, and other improvements. The developer has this money tied up for a considerable period of time before any revenues are realized. For all these reasons, equity funds must be available to the developer in substantial volume.

In planning the industrial district, the preparation of preliminary market and feasibility analyses is usually costly and time-consuming. Even with the most professional and competent studies, a degree of inflexibility is introduced into future development. This is particularly true as soon as site improvements are put in place because of the extremely high cost and technical difficulty involved in expanding sewer lines or water lines, or in widening streets.

Frequently, local communities tend to apply subdivision regulations to industrial park developments. More inflexibility is then introduced in the initial layout plan. This necessitates either costly and time-consuming negotiations with representatives of the municipality, or else costly amendments to adapt the plan to the requirements of prospective new occupants. Municipalities often impose off-site development requirements on industrial districts that are not applied with equal fervor to individual site developments, in the opinion of many industrial park developers. "This matter of determining where the responsibility for off-site improvements begins and ends can be quite delicate." [25]

Municipalities and state agencies cannot always be relied upon to complete improvement programs as scheduled. The developer of an industrial park, depending on public improvements to provide his area with better access or improved facilities, may be embarrassed at the least, and may possibly run the risk of substantial losses. Exhibit 94 is a "Site Access and Utility Map" of an industrial park planned in New Jersey, which illustrates the dependence of the developer on public improvements for the timing of his own developmental efforts and the success of the venture.

Continuing enforcement of district standards and controls can also be expensive, time-consuming, and troublesome. The development of an industrial park requires continuous involvement by the developer and his staff. It is neither a short-term, nor an "in-and-out," investment. The developer has the responsibility of carrying out the plan which is announced and "sold" to early occupants. It is sometimes difficult from either a marketing or a public relations point of view to alter a plan, even when changed

---

[25] Shepherd, *op. cit.*, p. 3.

Exhibit 94

SITE ACCESS AND UTILITY MAP—RUTGERS INDUSTRIAL CENTER, PISCATAWAY, NEW JERSEY

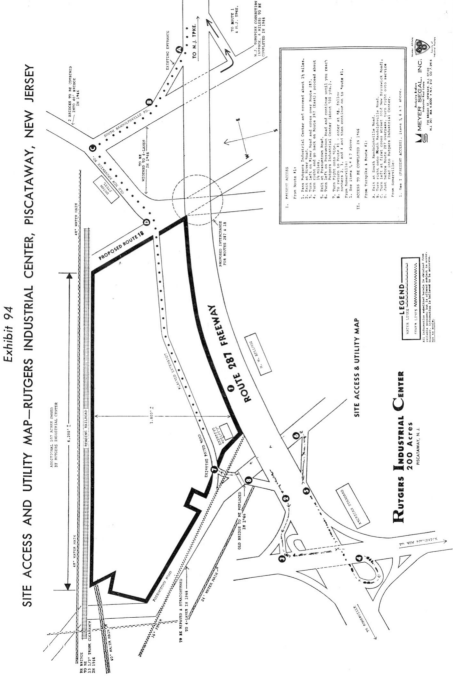

Map provided by Meyer Segal, S.I.R., Newark, N.J.

market conditions would seem to dictate it. Moreover, early customers may often resist restrictions and regulations in the park. Before several sales have been made, potential occupants frequently cannot visualize the character and direction that the development will take.

The developer is largely at the mercy of a changing market, in part because he is committed to a plan and a set of protective regulatory provisions that may be rendered inappropriate as market conditions change. Finally, he has the continuing expense of supervision during the marketing and construction phases, and also when all the space has been occupied.

Industrial Occupant

Although most industrial occupants occupying space in planned industrial districts find that there are attractions and economies in locating in an industrial park, not all industrial users find that a plant in a planned district makes either economic or business sense for them. Industrial parks are particularly well suited for distribution firms and warehouse activities. The real estate manager of one large industrial firm reports that "about 25 per cent of our total space, between two million and three million square feet, is in industrial parks . . . We have a directive to procure warehouses or distribution centers only in recognized negotiable areas or park areas where we could sell a building if we outgrew it." [26]

1. *Attractions.* The appeal of industrial park locations to occupant firms falls under three general headings: financial advantages or monetary savings; availability of necessary facilities; and compatibility of environment. It is occasionally difficult to categorize a particular advantage neatly. For example, there is serious question whether there are direct cost savings to industrial park occupants as opposed to locating in individual, free-standing sites; or whether the industrial firm receives more services for approximately the same expenditure. Such debate is fundamentally fruitless. There *is* an operating advantage to the industrial occupant. Some of the more detailed advantages of park locations to industrial firms include:

a. *Low Unit Site Development Costs.* Because costs are distributed over a large area, the cost per unit is often lower than is the case with single-site developments. This reduced cost is frequently passed on to the user in lower unit site price.

b. *Operating Economies.* Greater efficiency in access and the availability of necessary services in a park location usually result in reduced unit operating costs for the tenant firm.

c. *Availability of Building Space.* This may be provided through a turnkey building, a shell building, contract construction, or existing buildings in an established park. In any of these situations, the industrial firm is able to obtain better located space more quickly than is usually the case outside a planned industrial district.

d. *Site Availability.* For the firm that is a frequent purchaser or lessee of new industrial space, the availability of prepared sites, with all facilities

[26] Joseph W. Gibson, Polaroid Corporation, "The Good and Bad in Industrial Parks: Industry's Viewpoint," *S.I.R. Newsletter,* August 1966, p. 1.

ready to accept a new building, is a very decided attraction. "We have distribution centers and warehouses in nine parks across the nation. We like them because in most cases the zoning, public relations, traffic flow, water supply, sewer, power, and so forth already have been taken care of." [27]

e. *Flexibility of Site Choice.* A variety of different sizes and shapes of sites is generally available within the park, as are different types of locations with the same basic access and locational amenities.

f. *Stability in Location.* The environment is essentially controlled. The occupant firm can rely on stability in its location and the character of its neighbors over a substantial period of time.

g. *Protection of Investment.* Sites and buildings in planned industrial districts generally have higher marketability, and the environment is usually stable. The industrial firm's investment is therefore usually protected against early depreciation.

h. *Profit on Resale or Sublease.* The industrial occupant is assured of a generally more ready market for the space that he purchases or leases, in the event that resale or subletting is necessary later. Some developers even contend the customer firm makes more profit in industrial parks than the developer.

i. *Tax Savings.* These "can be effective in arrangements for tenancy in some instances." [28] They are apparently additional inducements to many industrial firms to locate in industrial parks.

j. *Compatibility.* The industrial firm in a planned district finds itself in a group of compatible industries. This is provided by the controlled environment, not only among the occupants of the park itself but between the park and the community. Among other things, industrial occupants note an absence of hostile residential neighbors, such as are often found in single-site developments or unplanned districts.

k. *Proximity of Industrial and Employee Services.* An efficiently planned industrial complex usually provides nearby necessary services to industrial occupants and their employees. These are sometimes available within the park itself.

l. *Security.* An industrial park usually offers security provisions, so that there is less danger of vandalism, robbery, or fire. There is not complete agreement on this point, however, and some occupants argue that this is actually a limitation of the industrial park. Whether security is an attraction or a deterrent depends largely upon the provisions made by the developer.

m. *Park Services.* In addition to utilities, streets, and other necessary site facilities, planned industrial districts often offer landscaping services, snow plowing, street cleaning, supplementary security protection, and the like. In many instances, these will be made available through an occupant's association. Whatever the source, the cost to the occupant is generally less than it would be to acquire the same services individually and independently.

---

[27] *Ibid.*
[28] Sargent, *op. cit.,* p. 3.

2. *Limitations.* While there are substantial attractions to many industrial firms, particularly national organizations seeking locations for warehousing and distribution facilities, not all industrial operations find a location in a planned industrial district suitable for their purposes. "For example, manufacturing operations with large land and utilities requirements (such as chemical plants, steel plants, etc.) usually prefer to buy and develop their own acreage." [29]

a. *Room for Expansion.* This is by far the most widely noted and acutely felt problem of industrial establishments located in planned districts. "Land costs usually are too high to hold for future growth, which may or may not develop in that particular area. The location of the growth land is a problem in a park . . . If a company does decide to go into a park, it should nail down the future expansion costs as related to land costs, construction fees, mortgage costs, etc. . . . A company can build much larger than it needs and sublet what it doesn't require immediately or use the space for some of the company's operations that can later be relocated . . . However, something must be worked out in industrial parks to handle this problem." [30] It is generally agreed that a 3 to 1 ratio of land area to building area is the most that a developer reasonably can require. Exchanging may be one means to retain valued occupants, provided room for expansion has been reserved by the developer. This is not always possible, however.

b. *High Land Costs.* Although sites in planned industrial districts usually offer all the necessary facilities for efficient industrial operation, not all firms need them in the capacities or at the levels provided by the park. Site costs can be excessively high for particular industrial users. This is especially true of manufacturing operations which generally require large land areas for employee parking.

c. *High Initial Costs.* As a result of the large investment required, many new or relatively small firms cannot afford a location in an industrial park, even though it might be more efficient from an operational point of view.

d. *Labor Market Problems.* "The labor market for companies using semiskilled female help is sometimes hindered in an industrial park. We find the best market for female help seems to be the city. . . . If industrial parks could push for rapid transit nearby, this problem would be solved." [31]

e. *Loss of Freedom.* Restrictions on use and occupancy may be deterrents to many industrial firms whose managements feel constricted or excessively hampered in their decision-making. This loss of freedom may be coupled with a loss of identity because public recognition focuses on the park as an institution, rather than on the individual tenants. From an advertising or public relations point of view, many smaller firms cannot afford to be overshadowed by their environment in this way.

f. *Security.* Although industrial parks may offer group protection from the risks of crime and fire, not all occupants of all parks find this to be the case. One real estate manager of an industrial firm with many warehouses

---

[29] *Ibid.*
[30] Gibson, *op. cit.,* p. 1.
[31] *Ibid.*

and plants in industrial parks reports that "we are concerned about security in industrial parks. We had one case where one of our distribution centers in a park was held up at 8 o'clock in the morning. The employees were tied up, bound, and gagged as they came in. The robbers brought in their own trucks, loaded them with cameras and film, and drove off and nobody in the park knew it." [32]

g. *Unbalanced Services.* Some industrial firms with locations in planned industrial districts find that many parks are not sufficiently "well rounded in what they can supply, including off-street parking, police protection, and better methods of financing." [33]

On balance, it appears that the national organization with good credit, seeking to locate a warehousing or distribution center, finds that an industrial park site is particularly attractive. This is not the only type of organization or operation that can utilize an industrial park location effectively. However, it is the type most likely to be able to do so.

The Community

Successful industrial parks mean income and economic expansion to a community. They often mean an improvement of municipal services and facilities as well. They also generally require some expenditures and cooperative action on the part of the community. Perhaps most significant is the anticipated impact that a new planned industrial development is expected to have on the local area. Commenting on this point, the chief executive officer of a New England town reported the following:

I recently reviewed the minutes for the 1952 and 1953 town meetings, and it is amazing that many of the questions raised so vociferously then about the New England Industrial Center have not materialized. One group was very vocal in its opposition to an industrial park in Needham. They fought it for two years on the basis that the values of the residential property adjacent to the park would depreciate. According to our chief assessor, however, the value of the residential property in the area adjacent to the industrial park has risen just as rapidly in the past 10 years as values in other parts of Needham.

Many people felt such services as fire and police would be prohibitive in taking care of this area, but this has not proven to be true.

In spite of the problems, large and small, caused by the New England Industrial Center, we are fortunate to have it.[34]

1. *Attractions.* From the point of view of the community, the attractions will generally far outweigh the limitations. They include:

a. *Employment.* The planned industrial district generally increases local manufacturing and industrial employment. It also creates a wider base of diversified job opportunity in the area.

b. *Income and Payroll.* Most communities report substantial jumps in

[32] Gibson, *op. cit.,* p. 3.
[33] *Ibid.*
[34] Paul F. Saint, "The Good and Bad in Industrial Parks: Community's Viewpoint," *S.I.R. Newsletter,* July, 1966, p. 5. Mr. Saint is Chairman of the Board of Selectmen of Needham, Massachusetts.

local incomes after an industrial park has been developed in the area. As one example, "in the past 10 years [1956–1966], the payroll in Needham has increased an average of $684,000 a year, whereas in the previous 10-year period it had only increased an average of about $448,000." [35]

c. *Industrial Base.*   The diversification of industry provided by a planned industrial district generally broadens the local economic base and makes it more stable. Moreover, a planned industrial district often offers opportunities for growth through "incubator" rental space for new or small firms.

d. *Attract Related Activities.*   As the industrial park grows and develops, the needs of its occupants (both corporate and human) will be served by service establishments and suppliers which locate in the vicinity in order to attract their business. Moreover, as the community becomes better attuned to the needs and requirements of industry, other industrial firms are attracted to locations outside the park but still within the community. This creates a favorable atmosphere for the community in its efforts to expand further its economic base.

e. *Tax Revenues.*   The successful development of a planned industrial district normally results in substantial increases in the tax revenues of the community. Equitable tax rates are more easily established and administered, since the base for taxes generally rises greatly. The assessment of the area of the industrial park itself usually increases dramatically.

f. *Increased Land Values.*   The development of a planned industrial district usually results in increased values of land in the areas adjacent to the park. This is a net gain to the economy of the community, as well as a further enhancement of its tax base.

g. *Community Services Required.*   The advantage of increased tax revenues is usually *not* accompanied by a proportionate increase in the services required of the community. In most instances, fire and police protection are the only services that must be increased.

h. *Utilities and Streets Provided.*   Even when the community ultimately takes over the maintenance of streets and/or utilities, the initial costs of development are often borne by the developer. As a result, the debt limit and the budget of the community are put under less strain. These facilities are often made available to serve intervening land; bringing streets and utility lines to the park often involves extending them a substantial distance.

i. *Traffic.*   The planned design of the industrial park usually reduces traffic congestion substantially, at least within the park. This is not necessarily true for existing streets that become main arteries to and from the park.

j. *Harmonious Development.*   The industrial park generally offers compatibility between the industrial uses within its confines and the surrounding segments of the local community. This is an important contribution to the harmonious development of the community, especially surrounding residential areas.

k. *Nuisance Control.*   The industrial park generally provides effective control over nuisances, with its stringent regulations and controls. These

---

[35] *Ibid.*

performance standards usually mean that little negative impact is experienced by the remainder of the community.

1. *Control of Blight.* Planned industrial district development may help offset blight associated with older industrial and residential areas. It can serve as the means to alternative new industrial sites within the older, downtown neighborhoods, especially through the use of urban renewal and redevelopment powers. An illustration of the effect of redevelopment is provided in Exhibit 95. This shows Before and After views of the same street in the West Side Industrial No. 1 project in Detroit. The marked improvement in the area was realized through careful planning for reuse on a coordinated basis.

2. *Limitations.* An industrial park is not entirely an unmixed blessing for the local community, however attractive it may appear. There are at least three areas of potential difficulty for the local administration.

a. *Traffic and Parking.* "Traffic is one of the major problems we have in the Needham Industrial Park, with between 3,000 and 3,500 cars entering and leaving the park daily. . . . Parking was not a problem in the park initially because there were parking facilities planned for each building. However, problems arose when buildings were subleased." [36] While the street pattern and layout plan for the industrial park may create more efficient and easier traffic flows within the district, the additional commuting traffic and truck traffic generated by the park may overtax the existing streets and highways in the surrounding community.

b. *Service Demands.* While the park developer in many instances provides for the extension of utility lines, he will always attempt to convince the community to assume this responsibility. Moreover, as the park grows and expands, the trunk lines feeding the area in which the park is located will normally have to be expanded, or auxiliary lines installed. These involve considerable expenditures by the community, many of which have to be financed through bond issues.

c. *Retail Outlet Competition.* In some instances, retail outlet warehouses in industrial parks have competed with existing merchants in the downtown area. This has resulted in vigorous protests from the existing merchants, who usually are found to be among the most vociferous supporters of industrial parks that are exclusively "industrial." In one community, "a retail outlet opened in the industrial park and the Chamber of Commerce and small merchants flooded us with complaints. Four or five small merchants went out of business. . . . A community can control this problem by zoning (not allowing retail stores in an industrial park), which we now do, or by putting such provisions in the basic covenant of the tenant. If this is handled correctly between all parties, it is not too much of a problem." [37]

Others

The developer, the occupant firm, and the community represent the three most directly involved interests in a planned industrial district. Others

---

[36] *Ibid.*
[37] *Ibid.*

Exhibit 95

LAND USES IN WEST SIDE INDUSTRIAL NO. 1 PROJECT—DETROIT BEFORE AND AFTER REDEVELOPMENT

Photos: Courtesy, U.S. Department of Housing and Urban Development

affected include lending institutions, industrial real estate brokers, and service industries.

1. *Lenders.* Industrial park locations are generally favored by institutional lenders. Banks and insurance companies are more prone to finance individual construction projects within the park, however, than to make funds available for site development in advance of commitments by industrial firms to buy or to lease space within the park. To this extent, the banker or the insurance company lender must be "educated" with respect to what they are getting into in industrial park development financing." [38] This is large-scale financing, which requires institutions of substantial size. If the protection afforded lenders by a controlled environment is to be effective, provisions must be made to be sure the restrictions are enforced.

2. *Industrial Real Estate Brokers.* The opportunity to sell or lease space in a planned industrial district generally offers the industrial real estate broker a prospect of greater revenues. At the same time, there are substantial challenges that he must recognize and overcome.

On the positive side, the industrial park offers the broker the opportunity to give much better service to an industrial prospect. He can cover a much wider range of space alternatives in a relatively short period of time. By operating within a concentrated area with a wide variety of choices, "the broker gets a much better insight into his customer's needs." [39] It is also easier for the broker to assemble information on an industrial park. Most developers (and their staffs) cooperate fully with the broker. Comparable sales or comparable rentals are generally readily available among properties within industrial parks.

On the other hand, there is the recurrent problem of the developer and the industrial firm dealing directly with each other. "The more marketable a piece of property, the less it appears to the customer or seller that a broker is needed." [40] Similarly, when a prime industrial tenant is seeking to sublease space, he often gives the broker the strong impression that he believes the location is so good that it is not necessary to pay a commission to the broker.

Despite these minor limitations, however, the industrial broker (and especially the S.I.R.) can do very well in dealing with industrial parks. One major developer has estimated that over 90 per cent of sales in planned industrial districts are handled through brokers. [41]

3. *Service Industries.* Railroads, truck lines, and private utility companies all profit from industrial development. First, there is more demand for their services. Second, because their service requirements are concentrated, they usually anticipate a higher return from a given amount of investment.

---

[38] McIntosh, *op. cit.*, p. 3.

[39] Thomas E. Leggat, "The Good and Bad in Industrial Parks: Broker's Viewpoint," *S.I.R. Newsletter*, August, 1966, p. 4.

[40] *Ibid.*

[41] Windsor, *op. cit.*, p. 15.

INGREDIENTS OF SUCCESS IN
PLANNED INDUSTRIAL DISTRICT DEVELOPMENT

The industrial park is by no means a cure-all for the investor, the industrial firm, or the local community. It is simply one more tool available to industrial developers and brokers in the continuing effort to satisfy the space requirements of industrial firms.

Once a decision has been made to develop a planned industrial district, several points should be noted in formulating the development plan. From the points of view of the developer, the community, and the broker, there are both tips to follow for successful development, and mistakes or pitfalls to avoid.

Role of the Developer

In the process of creating value, the developer of a planned industrial district must be able to perform a variety of operations, including "speaking the language" of his prospects. He is the driving force behind the entire process of industrial park planning, construction, marketing, and management. He is also the focal point of cooperative efforts with local officials to create a harmonious atmosphere within which the park can be developed most effectively. In his efforts to maximize his own net returns, a developer must be guided by the experience of others, both successful and unsuccessful.

1. *Development Tips.* A wide variety of "do's" for industrial park developers can be assembled from a number of authoritative sources.[42] The most important and compelling of these admonitions are:

a. *Define Objectives.* The objectives or goals of the industrial firm and of the community will often be at variance with those of the developer. Moreover, the entire pattern or plan of development will depend on the developer's objectives.

b. *Select a Favorable Location.* This involves finding land which has the closest approximation to all of the amenities that industry is seeking in industrial sites.

c. *Identify the Market.* This involves conducting preliminary surveys and market analyses. Basically, what specific firms would be interested in occupying sites or building space in this location?

d. *Plan a Flexible Layout.* To the extent possible, the developer should avoid detailed subdivision plans within which either no adjustments can be made, or adjustments can be made only with great difficulty and expense.

e. *Determine Development Costs.* This requires a thorough study of engineering problems and site development costs. It involves the use of both engineering and construction skills, often under the organizational supervision of an experienced industrial real estate broker serving as project manager.

---

[42] See especially: Bennett, *op. cit.*; Blakeley, *op. cit.*; Boley, *Industrial Districts: Principles in Practice,* pp. 24–26; Sargent, *op. cit.,* p. 6.

f. *Arrange for Adequate Financing.* An industrial park is an expensive, long-range, and rather speculative undertaking. It requires adequate amounts of cash at all stages of development. If financing is not available, then an otherwise well-conceived plan will probably be doomed to failure.

g. *Secure a Desirable Lead Occupant.* The first purchaser or tenant should be an attraction to subsequent potential occupants. The proper initial tenant or purchaser will stimulate interest and help to develop high standards from the outset. It may be necessary to offer concessions to the lead occupant in order to induce the firm to locate in the park; these concessions should not include relaxation of use standards or occupancy restrictions.

h. *Name the Park Early.* This is important for promotional and public relations purposes. In addition, it is recommended to avoid having an undesirable local colloquial name attached to the project by default.

i. *Create a Distinctive Character.* The use of imaginative layout, landscaping, architecture, or promotional symbols is called for here. Retaining imaginative public relations staff or consultants will help considerably.

j. *Provide All Necessary Services and Protections.* The industrial user comes to a park largely because services and protective provisions are available. A developer, however, should provide only those services and protections which he can perform better and more efficiently than the industrial user can for himself.

k. *Know the Competition.* The developer should learn the advantages and disadvantages of competing districts. The experience of other developers will indicate the pricing, promotional and planning devices most likely to succeed.

l. *Take Care in Timing.* Appropriate timing of subdividing, of installing site improvements, of constructing buildings, and of sales—all require continuing market sensitivity.

m. *Arrange Appropriate Cash.* The industrial developer will need equity funds throughout the development process. Beyond any debt financing that may be available, the developer must turn to his own funds and those of his associates. Undercapitalization is a major hazard to be avoided studiously.

n. *Provide for Flexibility.* "No matter how you plan it, your plans are going to change." [43] The developer and his organizaton must provide adaptability to change at all stages in the creation of the industrial park complex.

o. *Employee and Visitor Services.* "Industrial parks need employee and visitor services, such as gas stations, nearby. Retail stores, drugstores, banks, restaurants, motor inns, etc., are needed to serve the people who work in or visit the park. This will make the park complete." [44]

p. *Provide Incubators.* A very successful device for many industrial park developers has been to provide all-purpose rental space in standardized buildings, such as illustrated in Exhibit 91 in Chapter 15. These serve as

[43] Blakeley, *op. cit.*
[44] Gibson, *op. cit.*, pp. 1–3.

"incubators" for new, small firms that could not otherwise enjoy the advantages of a location in a planned industrial district.

q. *Emphasize Moving the Sites at the Prices Set.*   Price concessions that seriously upset the financial plan should be avoided.

r. *Help Park Occupants in Public Relations.*   Advertising the success of industrial occupants within the park advertises the park itself. One major industrial park developer reports that "from the day a company signs its contract to purchase a site or lease a building, the park's developers work with the firm through a public relations representative to maintain a constant flow of information which often results in increased business for the company. The developers carry out a communications program with a firm's suppliers and customers, keeping them informed of construction progress and helping to maintain relations during the shift of operations from the old plant to the new . . . facility." [45]

s. *Establish an Effective Sales Organization.*   The developer must be able to tell a prospect about the park. More importantly, the sites or building space must be marketed once they have been created.

You should seek, woo, implore, encourage, and appreciate broker cooperation. You should pay him a full commission and encourage his participation, because the broker is the best salesman of any industrial park. When an industrial developer forgets that simple concept, he is going to be out of business because when he antagonizes these brokers, he has lost his whole sales force. The success of our industrial park has been due to the S.I.R. and other industrial brokers in the Chicago area. Eighty per cent of the deals that have been made have been made with the cooperation of these brokers. [46]

2. *Mistakes to Be Avoided.* [47]   Many common mistakes in the development of industrial parks can be avoided, in most instances, through conscious effort on the part of the developer.

a. *Initial Mistakes.*   These occur in the early phases of the planned development undertaking. They include:

(1) Picking the wrong piece of land.
(2) Judging the land for what the owner or his agent represents it to be, rather than selecting it for its marketability.
(3) Failure to obtain firm and specific commitments for essential physical facilities from the community.
(4) Neglecting thorough feasibility analysis.
(5) Underestimating the time and cost involved in site preparation.

b. *Planning Mistakes.*   These are errors commonly made after the site has been acquired and the project is already under way.

(1) Tract design is often unsuitable and impractical. This includes traffic circulation, location of utilities, and lot layout. It must be both functional and marketable.

---

[45] Bennett, *op. cit.*
[46] *Ibid.*
[47] Stuart Parry Walsh, "Twelve Common Mistakes in Industrial Land Development," *Urban Land,* June, 1963.

(2) Tract preparation is made slow and costly by inefficient scheduling of development work. This is where the industrial real estate broker serving as project manager can be particularly useful to the developer.

(3) Zoning and restrictive covenants are often inadequate or unsuitable. The developer must supplement inadequate regulations, always with the assistance of appropriate professional advisers.

c. *Marketing Mistakes.* Errors in marketing can undermine or undo all of the good created during the development process.

(1) A frequent omission in descriptive material is an adequate map of the property. If the prospective purchaser cannot visualize the site and the location, it is difficult to attract him to further consideration of occupancy.

(2) A sales program is often inadequate. Less than professional sales personnel are utilized. Improper or inadequate promotional efforts are made.

(3) Unless the developer can provide a *bona fide* "package deal," either with build-lease, shell or turnkey buildings, the marketing program is neither complete nor well rounded.

(4) Inappropriate concessions made to initial occupants can downgrade an entire project. Concessions must be realistic and financial, not a relaxation of restrictions or use controls.

3. General Warnings. In addition to more specific items, a number of general observations apply to all industrial park developments. In particular, "inadequate working capital, unskilled management, and unsuitable promotion methods are the most frequent causes of failure. . . . It is important to warn against over-optimism, and to remember that there is a lapse of time between desire and accomplishment, as an industrial program is one of continuing effort and intelligent application of sound ideas." [48]

If they are honest and follow all the rules and regulations enumerated above, then "the most successful developers of industrial parks are those who go in as principals, rather than as subordinants or agents of others." [49]

Role of the Community

In many instances, the community or a community-sponsored development foundation may be the industrial park's developer. To the extent that a public or quasi-public agency is the developer, it should follow the same admonitions and suggestions provided in the foregoing section on the role of the developer.

Beyond this, the community has a role to play in fostering and encouraging industrial park development. How much it actually does often depends on how seriously the community wishes to encourage local industrial development.

1. Development Bonds. The local government is often empowered to issue development bonds to finance the extension of utility lines, the extension or widening of streets, or other municipal services for a proposed new industrial park. This involves the use of public funds to sustain and support private development. It is usually justified by the anticipated benefits to the community from industrial park development.

[48] Sargent, *op. cit.*, p. 6.
[49] Interview with R. John Griefen, S.I.R.

Development bond financing of utilities and other facilities represents a recognition by the community that the industrial park developer is not Santa Claus. Developers generally believe that local communities too often regard an industrial park primarily as a source of direct and immediate benefits to the community.

"As an industrial district is no short-term undertaking, there is an incentive for the community to assist in the opening of a tract by the construction of public facilities such as water mains, sewers, and roads. This sphere of operation in planned industrial districts is, in fact, part of the community's contribution." [50]

2. *Land Use Controls.* The locality often provides the framework of zoning regulations and subdivision controls within which the developer plans and creates his park. If it wishes to encourage local industrial growth and development, the municipality must adapt and adjust its controls to provide for the kind of flexibility that is essential to successful industrial park development. A fairly recent addition to modern zoning ordinances is a special zone for "planned industrial district" or "industrial park" use. "Patterned somewhat after the 'shopping center' concept, this highly restricted type of industrial zone is designed to accommodate only those industries meeting standards very similar to those found in covenants contained in deeds and leases of contemporary planned industrial districts. Major emphasis is placed on ensuring greater compatibility among industrial and residential uses than that which has existed heretofore." [51]

3. *Industrial Redevelopment.* Particularly in central city areas, industrial reuse projects sponsored by urban renewal agencies help in fighting urban blight, and in providing sorely needed industrial sites. This is a function which local government can support emphatically, and thereby serve both its own industrial development needs and the objectives of the private developer. In industrial renewal activity, the developer is often called the "redeveloper."

4. *Cooperation with the Developer.* The officials of the community in which a planned industrial district is proposed can encourage good cooperative planning, so that both the district and the area around it grow harmoniously and efficiently. In some instances, local officials may represent firms in the industrial park in their dealings with other governmental bodies. This is simply enlightened self-interest. Cooperation also includes assuming the responsibility which is logically and legitimately that of the community. For example, in most cases, streets in planned industrial districts are ultimately turned over to the municipality for maintenance and continued operation.

5. *Cooperation with the Broker.* Whether the local community is a district developer or simply assisting a privately sponsored park, municipal officials must be continuously and keenly aware of the important role that the industrial real estate broker can play in increasing the chances of success for the undertaking. In particular, local officials should welcome as-

---

[50] Boley, *Industrial Districts Restudied*, p. 28.
[51] *Ibid.*, p. 25. A detailed example of such a zoning ordinance is provided on pages 25–28.

sistance from brokers, and foster a policy of full payment of commissions.

Role of the Industrial Broker

Industrial parks essentially make it possible for the broker to do a better job for his industrial customer. The broker's function is "to understand his client's needs, and to bring his knowledge of the market to bear in order to advise his client and meet his needs. . . . Industrial parks help a broker give a client much better service." [52] The several specific activities of the broker in assisting in the development of a planned industrial district are more numerous, however.

1. *Cooperation with the Developer.* Industrial districts often have their own sales staff, but they usually will pay a commission to brokers bringing in purchasers or tenants. The broker should therefore seek to establish good working relationships with industrial park developers, and settle the important question of commissions early in the relationship.

Cooperation of a different sort is occasionally provided when the broker is a principal in the industrial park development. This is not the rule, however, though it is becoming more common.

2. *Sales and Lease Negotiation.* In serving as a sales or leasing broker, the Realtor seeks to increase the velocity of turnover of the space in the industrial park. This enhances the profits of the developer and the fees of the broker. Most developers agree that the outside industrial broker is especially useful in conducting negotiations once a user has been attracted to the park, and to a site in that park.

3. *Agents of the Developer.* In many instances, the industrial real estate broker is hired on a retainer or continuing basis to serve as agent for the developer. He screens applicants and selects occupants for the park, without necessarily providing the negotiating services that the outside broker offers. It is often useful for the developer to have his own broker on retainer for advice and counsel, as well as to act as his agent.

4. *Management and Control.* Industrial real estate brokers are particularly well suited to serve as industrial park managers, and as project managers during the development phase of the district. When a broker is acting in his capacity as manager, he rarely will serve as a negotiator or sales agent. Management and enforcement of park standards represent full-time activities, which should not be intermingled with sales efforts.

5. *Advising and Counseling.* Because the broker is particularly sensitive to the market for industrial space, and to the needs and requirements of industrial users, he is especially well qualified to advise the developer throughout the several phases of the development of the industrial park. This work naturally entails a fee. Moreover, his experience and ability usually qualify him to conduct the preliminary feasibility and market studies that must precede the planning and development of any industrial park.

6. *Profitability.* Generally speaking, the industrial park makes it possible for the broker to earn considerably larger fees than is possible with the same effort in single-site development. One S.I.R. has devised a "customer

---

[52] Leggat, *op. cit.,* p. 4.

estimate of profitability," by which he measures the return on the time and effort that is expended in selling or leasing industrial space. "Simply stated, the formula is this: dollars divided by the hours times the probability. The dollars and the number of hours a broker puts in are obvious. The probability which one can express percentagewise is the tough part. . . . In this respect, I think industrial parks really help the broker. The dollars are larger because of the need for financing the long-term lease." [53] The general impression from industrial real estate brokers writing or speaking on the subject is that greater returns come to the broker from working with, and through, industrial park developers.

Finally, in order to protect both himself and his customers, the industrial real estate broker must take special care that "when you are taking a customer into an industrial park, make sure that it really is an industrial park and not just a lot of promoter's propaganda." [54]

SELECTED REFERENCES

American Society of Planning Officials, "Planned Industrial District Zoning," *Planning Advisory Service,* Information Report No. 120, March, 1959.

Boley, Robert E., *Industrial Districts Restudied,* Technical Bulletin No. 41 (Washington, Urban Land Institute, April, 1961).

Boley, Robert E., *Industrial Districts: Principles in Practice,* Technical Bulletin No. 44 (Washington, Urban Land Institute, December, 1962).

Bredo, William, *Industrial Estates: Tool for Industrialization* (Glencoe, Illinois, Free Press, 1960).

Byrnes, Vincent J., "Industrial Park Trends," *The National Real Estate Investor,* May, 1964.

Industrial Development and Manufacturers Record (Atlanta, Georgia, Conway Research, Inc.) :
    "Industrial Financing Facts in the 50 States," October, 1965;
    "The Office Park," September, 1965;
    "Sites for Science," Annual August Study;
    "State and Provincial Development Agencies," December, 1965;
    "Industrial Parks," Annual February Survey;
    "Water Sites for Industry," June, 1966.

Industrial Development Research Council, "Industrial Land—Terminology: What Is an Industrial Park, Zone, District, Estate, City?" *Industrial Development and Manufacturers Record,* June, 1966.

Kinnard, William N., Jr., and Malinowski, Zenon S., *The Place of Small Business in Planned Industrial Districts,* Small Business Management Research Report (Storrs, Connecticut, University of Connecticut, 1963).

Sargent, Charles, "Land for Industry," *Urban Land* (Washington, Urban Land Institute), Vol. 23, No. 2, February, 1964.

---

[53] *Ibid.*

[54] Gerald W. Blakeley, Jr., "Economics of an Industrial Park," *Industrial Parks, Start to Finish,* Proceedings, First Annual Workshop, Pittsburgh, Pennsylvania (Washington, Society of Industrial Realtors, 1959), p. 12.

Sheltraw, Howard G., "Urban Renewal in Industrial Development," *The National Real Estate Investor,* May, 1964.

Shenkel, William M., *Principles and Practices of Industrial Real Estate: A Course Syllabus* (Washington, Society of Industrial Realtors, 1963).

Society of Industrial Realtors, *Advanced Course in the Techniques of Industrial Real Estate* (Washington, The Author, 1964):
  Bennett, Marshall, "Techniques in Industrial Development";
  Blakeley, Gerald W., Jr., "Techniques in Industrial Development."

Society of Industrial Realtors, *The Good and Bad in Industrial Parks,* 2 parts, July and August, 1966 issues of *S.I.R. Newsletter* (Washington, The Author):
  Shepherd, Paul P., "Developer's Viewpoint," July, 1966;
  Saint, Paul F., "Community's Viewpoint," July, 1966;
  Gibson, Joseph W., "Industry's Viewpoint," August, 1966;
  McIntosh, Norman, "Lender's Viewpoint," August, 1966.

Society of Industrial Realtors, *Industrial Parks, Start to Finish,* Proceedings of First Annual Workshop, Pittsburgh, Pennsylvania (Washington, The Author, 1959):
  Blakeley, Gerald W., Jr., "Economics of an Industrial Park";
  Schmidt, P. J., "Why Industrial Subdivisions?";
  Windsor, W. C., Jr., "Promotion, Sales and Profits of an Industrial Park."

Sawatzky, Jasper J., and Connett, Russell R., *The Broker's Role in Attracting Industrial, Commercial and Recreational Development* (Sacramento, California Division of Real Estate, 1965).

Walsh, Stuart Parry, "The Elite Industrial Investment: A Park," *The National Real Estate Investor,* May, 1964.

Walsh, Stuart Parry, "Industrial Land Development," *Real Estate Encyclopedia,* Edith J. Friedman, ed. (Englewood, Cliffs, N.J., Prentice-Hall, 1960).

Walsh, Stuart Parry, "Twelve Common Mistakes in Industrial Land Development," *Urban Land,* June, 1963.

Windsor, W. C., Jr., "Management of an Industrial Park," *Real Estate Encyclopedia,* Edith J. Friedman, ed. (Englewood Cliffs, N.J., Prentice-Hall, 1960).

17 Aids to Industrial Development

LARGE volumes of money and personnel are devoted to industrial development. Much of this activity is privately initiated and motivated by profit. In addition, nonprofit assistance groups seek to stimulate industrial development in local communities. Their motives vary, but real estate profit is not usually one of them. They are oriented more toward stimulating employment, increasing incomes, increasing the revenues of the sponsor, or stabilizing the economic base of the area.

Programs of development assistance seek to change the direction of actions by industrial firms and by private industrial real estate developers. They have little to do directly with the economics of investment. They are based upon considerations which are not necessarily measurable in terms of dollars and cents. "For example, the Department of Defense has a very substantial influence on where plants will locate in terms of what contracts will be let. In general, its programs and those of all other public agencies tend to emphasize the community development aspects of industrial location, rather than the investment aspects." [1]

Industrial assistance consists of offering inducements and incentives of various sorts either to influence the final decision of the industrial firm in selecting a location, or to influence the decision of an investor to allocate his resources to a particular area. Aids to industrial development range from providing advice and technical assistance, through direct financial aid, to such special inducements as tax concessions. Assistance groups are usually selective in offering this help to industry. Much of this activity is competitive and unproductive. Instead of adding to the sum total of industrial activity, it can result simply in a shift from one area to another.

A second major consideration is whether industrial location aids can override basic locational factors, or whether they are important only in

---

[1] Interview with Robert Y. Adams, Community Planning Consultant, American Electric Power Service Corporation.

selections between otherwise similarly desirable and efficient sites. There is substantial evidence that for major industrial firms, at least, basic economic considerations of industrial location cannot be offset by "artificial" incentives offered by private or public industrial development groups. In describing the selection of a location for a major aluminum facility, an officer of one national industrial corporation noted that "it should be pointed out that incentives as we normally think of them—tax concessions, etc.—did not play a particularly strong part in the evaluation. The proximity of the market, power availability, transportation facilities, and labor supply were the chief and overwhelming considerations. If, for example, power were not readily available, tax concessions would be academic." [2]

In terms of the three levels of industrial location selection, industrial development assistance programs normally are not effective until the third level —that of actual site selection—is reached. At the same time, incentives, concessions, and other forms of assistance may be critical in the survival of new, growing industrial firms. A stimulus to such firms can lead to a considerable gain in local employment and incomes.

In his professional capacity, the industrial real estate broker can do little to influence the character of industrial assistance programs. It is his responsibility to learn what they contain and what they involve for both the community and the industrial firm. He can then advise clients how best to adjust to them, and how to take advantage of them when appropriate. Beyond this, the propriety of industrial development incentives may be analyzed in terms of the references that appear at the end of this chapter.

Professional industrial real estate organizations, especially the Society of Industrial Realtors, represent the appropriate channel through which industrial brokers can operate if efforts to influence industrial assistance programs are to be undertaken. For the individual broker, however, a knowledge of industrial development incentive programs is important for an appreciation of potential sources of business.

PUBLIC AGENCY AND GOVERNMENT PROGRAMS

Although they will not usually alter the fundamental philosophy of the industrial firm seeking a new location, special inducements can be an added attraction to a particular site or location. "A community can take positive measures to make itself attractive to industry, and these provide the wider field of incentives or inducements." [3]

Public agencies and government corporations can offer inducements and assistance that private organizations simply cannot match. Whatever the level of government, a program of special inducements involves the interjection of artificial factors into industrial development. Basic economic deficiences cannot be offset by such artificial or manufactured items, but the efforts can influence individual industrial location decisions. They also rep-

---

[2] Statement by Fred R. Morrow, Kaiser Aluminum and Chemical Corporation, *Industrial Location Incentives* (Washington, Society of Industrial Realtors, 1956), p. 6.
[3] Statement by Charles L. Bolte, AFC Industries, *Industrial Location Incentives, loc. cit.,* p. 11.

resent an indication of interest on the part of the community, its workers, and its leaders in attracting industry. Proof of such interest can be demonstrated through "funds raised by public subscription to provide capital for leaseback arangements, extension of utility lines, or to assure availability of land at a reasonable price. . . . Hard cash is not lip service. . . . Tax money voted for community planning, utility expansion, or zoning studies shows a progressive community." [4]

An allocation of tax funds or a remission of taxes should not result in poorer service to all the remaining industrial occupants of an area. In addition, tax inducements or easy loan funds may attract the types of industries that could not survive without such inducements. These are neither enhancements to the economic base of the community nor good industrial neighbors for existing firms.

Special inducements are attractive and useful to industry when they are intelligently tailored to meet real needs, rather than the desires of local community sponsors. They are useful when they are designed to attract responsible industry, however small it may be, but to discourage the types of firms that can survive only with special assistance from public agencies. Finally, they are useful when there is a broad base of community participation, and there is an obvious advantage to be gained by all parties involved. Special inducements are often regarded by industrial managers as a good barometer of community interest.

Levels of Public Assistance

Public agencies at all three levels of government provide industrial development programs: federal, state and local. Efforts to influence the location of manufacturing activities date from the early 1930's. Yet concerted programs of influencing industrial location decisions to encourage local industrial development are basically a post-World War II phenomenon. Indeed, the great majority of formal industrial development programs at the state and local level date since 1950. The federal programs described in outline form in Exhibit 96 stem mostly from congressional actions in 1964 and 1965.

Economic and industrial development programs have become accepted adjuncts to efforts to improve the employment, income, and tax status of underdeveloped or economically depressed areas in particular. Because of the acceptance of governmental intrusion into what has historically been a private field, much of the effort is competitive simply to offset any advantages that other areas might otherwise obtain. Whether or not this is socially and economically defensible is beside the point. It is a fact of economic life, and the industrial real estate broker should familiarize himself with the programs that are current.

1. *Federal Programs.* Federal programs of industrial assistance are

[4] Morrow, *op. cit.,* p. 10. For details of the 1965 industrial development programs of both federal agencies and state governments, see American Industrial Development Council, "Guide to Federal Development Legislation—1965," special issue of *A.I.D.C. Journal,* Volume I, No. 2, April, 1966.

summarized in Exhibit 96. The information contained there includes the type of assistance that is available, the type of recipient toward which the assistance program is aimed, and the federal agency through which the assistance is offered. This listing is subject to almost continuing change as new programs are instituted, and existing programs are reinterpreted and redefined. It illustrates the *kinds* of assistance programs available through federal agencies. The industrial real estate broker seeking to obtain detailed information about a particular program for a specific client should consult the sources indicated in Exhibit 96, or the appropriate agencies directly.

Exhibit 96

SUMMARY OF FEDERAL INDUSTRIAL ASSISTANCE PROGRAMS*

I. ASSISTANCE TO INDUSTRY
  A. *Financial*
    1. *Loans*
      a. Economic Development Administration, Department of Commerce: Public Works and Economic Development Program.
        (1) Loans for the purchase or development of land and facilities for industrial use. Available only in eligible areas as designated by EDA, and only if otherwise unavailable. Must be in keeping with formally developed Overall Economic Development Plan.
        (2) Guarantee working capital loans for firms in designated areas.
        Not available for relocation of jobs or business from one area to another. Emphasis on the creation of job and employment opportunities.
      b. Small Business Administration: Small Business Financial Assistance Program.
        (1) Direct loans to small businesses when otherwise unavailable.
        (2) Participations and commitments in loans to small businesses from banks.
        (3) "Special" loans for disaster areas, relocation from public improvement project areas, to small businesses only.
      c. Small Business Administration: Small Business Investment Company Program.
        (1) Loans to Small Business Investment Companies to provide funds to be re-loaned or invested in small businesses.
      d. Small Business Administration: Economic Opportunity Loan Program.
        (1) Loans to small businesses through SBA Regional Offices.
        For low income, "disadvantaged" businessmen; $25,000 maximum.
    2. *Investment Opportunity*
      a. Bureau of Land Management, Department of the Interior: Sale of public lands.
  B. *Technical Assistance, Advice*
    1. Agricultural Research Service, Department of Agriculture: Development of rural areas.
    2. Rural Community Development Service, Department of Agriculture: Development of rural areas.
    3. Rural Electrification Administration, Department of Agriculture: Development of rural areas. Advice and consultation in construction, facilities planning and business operations—either through electric and telephone borrowers, or directly through Rural Area Development staff.
    4. Business and Defense Services Administration, Department of Commerce: Industrial and commodity information. Continuing study of selected industries and dissemination of information about them.

5. Department of Commerce: State Technical Services Program.
   Assist in stimulating economic and industrial growth and development by bringing the latest state of the art (technological especially) into production applications.
6. Office of Economic Adjustment, Department of Defense: Community Economic Adjustment Program.
   Provide assistance and advice in adjusting to potential adverse effects felt in a local area as a result of closing or changing Department of Defense installations.
7. U.S. Employment Service, Department of Labor: Industrial Services.
   Advice and consultation to industrial employers in solving workforce problems.
8. Small Business Administration: Management and Technical Assistance to Small Business.
   a. Management development courses. Cooperation with universities and colleges.
   b. SCORE Program. Advice and consultation free of charge through retired executives.
   c. Direct Advice and Assistance. Technical and management advice through SBA staff.
   d. Publications: Management Aids; Marketing Aids; Management Research Reports.

II. ASSISTANCE TO COMMUNITY DEVELOPMENT ORGANIZATIONS (PRIVATE)
   A. *Financial*
      1. *Loans*
         a. Small Business Administration: Loans to State and Local Development Organizations.
            (1) Loans to local development companies for plant construction, conversion or expansion. To be used solely to assist "an identifiable small business concern for a sound business purpose."
            (2) Loans to state development companies. To provide funds to make long-term loans or equity investments in small businesses.
      2. *Investment Opportunity*
         a. Bureau of Land Management, Department of Interior. Sale of public lands.
      3. *Grants*
         a. Economic Development Administration, Department of Commerce: Public Works and Development Facilities.
            Grants (matching) of 50–80% to private or public nonprofit development organizations within redevelopment areas or economic development centers, for water and sewer systems and access roads, "to encourage industrial development that will result in long-term employment and long-range economic growth."

III. ASSISTANCE TO PUBLIC AGENCIES AND COMMUNITIES
   A. *Financial*
      1. *Loans*
         a. Soil Conservation Service, Department of Agriculture: Water Supply Development. Loans for local water supply development. Low interest and long maturities.
         b. Department of Housing and Urban Development: Public Facility Loans. Long-term loans to small communities under 50,000 population. (Private nonprofit corporations may receive loans in communities under 10,000 population.) 100% loans for 40 years are allowed.
         c. Department of Housing and Urban Development: Advances for Public Works Planning. Interest-free advances for planning public works projects, to be repaid from grants when projects are completed.
         d. Department of Housing and Urban Development: Urban Renewal Loans

and Advances. Loans and advances for planning and execution of urban
renewal (including urban redevelopment) projects, in advance of grant
payments.
  e. Department of Housing and Urban Development: Community Renewal
Program. Loans and advances in anticipation of grants for study and plan
preparation.
  2. *Investment Opportunity*
  a. Bureau of Land Management, Department of Interior: Sale of public
lands.
  3. *Grants*
  a. Economic Development Administration, Department of Commerce: Public Works and Development Facilities.
50% matched grants to communities for provision of needed public
facilities, "to encourage industrial development that will result in long-
term employment and long-range economic growth."
  b. Economic Development Administration, Department of Commerce: Economic Development.
Matching grants for operating expenses of economic development region
staffs.
  c. Federal Aviation Agency: Airport Development Program. 50% matching
grants.
  d. Department of Housing and Urban Development. Grants for Basic Sewer
and Water Facilities.
Up to 50% of cost of constructing or improving basic sewer or water
facilities.
  e. Department of Housing and Urban Development: Advance Acquisition
of Land.
Grants equal to interest on borrowed funds to acquire land for public
facilities not more than five years in advance of construction.
  f. Department of Housing and Urban Development: Urban Renewal Program Grants.
   (1) Grants equal to ⅔ or ¾ of net project cost in urban renewal redevelopment.
   (2) Grants for relocation of businesses within urban renewal project
areas.
   (3) Grants for planning and analysis under community renewal programs.
B. *Technical Assistance, Advice*
  1. Economic Development Administration, Department of Commerce: Technical Assistance to States, Redevelopment Areas and Multi-state Regional
Commissions.
Research assistance and advice, provided either through direct staff assistance, or payment of consultants or agencies by EDA.
  2. Office of Economic Adjustment, Department of Defense: Community Economic Adjustment Program.
Assistance and advice in adjusting to adverse effects of closing or changing
Department of Defense installations.

BASIC SOURCES: Economic Opportunity Act of 1964; Housing Act of 1965; Public
Works and Economic Development Act of 1965.

  * Adapted from information in:
American Industrial Development Council, "Guide to Federal Development
Legislation—1965," Special Issue of *A.I.D.C. Journal,* Vol. I, No. 2, April 1966.

U.S. Department of Commerce, Economic Development Administration, *Handbook of Federal Aids to Communities* (Washington, U.S. Government Printing
Office, 1966).

U.S. Office of Economic Opportunity, *Catalog of Federal Programs for Individual and Community Improvement* (Washington, U.S. Government Printing Office, December 1965).

2. *State and Local Programs.* The types of assistance offered through state agencies and state corporations differ considerably. Within a general framework of broad headings, there is a substantial amount of individual adaptation in each state. As a result, it is extremely difficult to categorize many of the programs. Nevertheless, an effort has been made to indicate both the range of assistance programs provided through state agencies, and the utilization of those programs by the individual states, in Exhibits 97 and 98. Exhibit 97 lists the types of *financial* assistance or incentives offered to industrial firms. Such financial aids are, in some instances, also available to municipalities within the several states. Exhibit 98 shows the major types of *technical* assistance and advice that are offered to both industrial firms and municipalities by state governments.

Exhibit 97

STATE PROGRAMS OF FINANCIAL ASSISTANCE TO INDUSTRY*

State	State-Wide Development Credit Corporation	Local General Obliga- tion Bonds	Local Revenue Bonds	State Industrial Finance Authority (Direct Loans)	State Guaranty of Mortgages	Tax Conces- sions and Incentives
Alabama	No	Yes	Yes	No	No	Yes
Alaska	Yes	Yes	Yes	Yes	No	Yes
Arizona	No	No	Yes	No	No	Yes
Arkansas	Yes	Yes	Yes	No	No	Yes
California	No	No	No	No	No	No
Colorado	No	No	Yes	No	No	No
Connecticut	Yes	No	No	Yes	Yes	No
Delaware	No	No	No	Yes	Yes	Yes
Florida	Yes	No	No	No	No	No
Georgia	No	No	Yes	Yes	No	No
Hawaii	Yes	Yes	Yes	Yes	No	No
Idaho	Yes	No	No	No	No	No
Illinois	No	No	Yes	No	No	No
Indiana	Yes	No	No	No	Yes	No
Iowa	Yes	No	Yes	No	No	No
Kansas	Yes	No	Yes	No	No	Yes
Kentucky	Yes	Yes	Yes	Yes	No	Yes
Louisiana	Yes	Yes	Yes	Yes	No	Yes
Maine	Yes	Yes	Yes	Yes	Yes	Yes
Maryland	Yes	Yes	Yes	No	Yes	Yes
Massachusetts	Yes	No	No	No	No	Yes
Michigan	Yes	No	Yes	No	No	No

State	State-Wide Development Credit Corporation	Local General Obligation Bonds	Local Revenue Bonds	State Industrial Finance Authority (Direct Loans)	State Guaranty of Mortgages	Tax Concessions and Incentives
Minnesota	Yes	No	Yes	No	No	Yes
Mississippi	Yes	Yes	Yes	No	No	Yes
Missouri	Yes	Yes	Yes	No	No	No
Montana	No	No	No	No	No	Yes
Nebraska	No	No	Yes	No	No	Yes
Nevada	No	No	No	No	No	Yes
New Hampshire	Yes	No	No	Yes	Yes	No
New Jersey	Yes	No	No	Yes	No	No
New Mexico	No	No	Yes	No	No	No
New York	Yes	No	No	Yes	No	Yes
North Carolina	Yes	No	No	No	No	No
North Dakota	No	Yes	Yes	No	No	No
Ohio	Yes	No	Yes	Yes	Yes	Yes
Oklahoma	No	Yes	Yes	Yes	No	Yes
Oregon	Yes	Yes	Yes	No	No	No
Pennsylvania	Yes	No	Yes	Yes	Yes	No
Rhode Island	Yes	No	Yes	No	Yes	No
South Carolina	Yes	No	No	No	No	Yes
South Dakota	Yes	No	Yes	No	No	No
Tennessee	Yes	Yes	Yes	No	No	Yes
Texas	No	No	No	No	No	No
Utah	No	No	No	No	No	No
Vermont	Yes	No	Yes	Yes	Yes	Yes
Virginia	Yes	No	Yes	No	No	No
Washington	Yes	No	Yes	No	No	No
West Virginia	Yes	No	Yes	Yes	No	No
Wisconsin	Yes	Yes	Yes	No	No	No
Wyoming	No	Yes	Yes	No	No	No

SOURCES: New York State Department of Commerce, *The Use of Public Funds or Credit in Industrial Location,* October 1963, and June 1964; *Industrial Development and Manufacturers Record,* June 1966; *New England Business Review,* October 1963, December 1963, June 1964, October 1964.

* Includes legislative authorizations not yet activated.

The information contained in Exhibit 97 illustrates clearly the variation among states in the patterns of financial assistance provided to industry. It includes what has been authorized or sanctioned within a state. This does not necessarily mean that there has been any activity in the particular program. For the informed industrial real estate broker, however, the tabulations do show the legal opportunities that exist within each of the states.

There is no identifiable pattern of financial assistance programs among the various geographic regions of the United States. It can be noted, however, that industrial mortgage guaranty is aptly termed the "New England plan," since it is concentrated heavily in the New England states. Similarly, tax concessions or inducements seem to be more common among southern states. Beyond this, however, it is very difficult to generalize.

As of the time Exhibit 97 was developed, a total of 34 states had authorized development credit corporations, and 34 had also passed legislation permitting local communities to issue revenue bonds to finance industrial development programs. Tax concessions or inducements were legal (at either the state or local level, or both) in 22 states. Sixteen states permitted direct state loans through state industrial finance authorities, and 16 also had legalized the use of local general obligation bonds to finance industrial development programs. Ten states (five of them in New England) had provisions for state guaranty of industrial mortgages. Only three states (California, Texas and Utah) had *no* provision for financial assistance of any sort to attract industry. On the other hand, only one state (Maine) appeared to have authorized all six categories of financial assistance to industry summarized in Exhibit 97. These differences underscore the individual and varied programs developed among the 50 states.

In the provision of technical assistance, advice, and information to industrial firms, even wider disparities among the 50 states are noted. Exhibit 98 shows considerable variation in the types of information gathered and made available, and in the types of services offered to potential industrial residents.

Exhibit 98

STATE PROGRAMS OF TECHNICAL ASSISTANCE
FOR INDUSTRIAL DEVELOPMENT

State	Information Assembly *	Report Preparation *	Promotional Activity **	Industrial Directory	Aid and Advice to Communities
Alabama	1,2,3,4,5,6,7,8	1,4,8	A,B	No	Yes
Alaska	No	No	A,B,D	No	Yes
Arizona	1,2,4,8	No	A,B,D	No	Yes
Arkansas	1,2,3,4,5,6,7,8	1,2,3,4,5,6,7,8	A,B,C.D	Yes	Yes
California	N.A.	N.A.	N.A.	N.A.	N.A.
Colorado	1,2,3,4,5,6,7,8	4,5,6,7,8	A,B,C,D	No	Yes
Connecticut	1,2,4,5,6,7,8	4,5,6,7,8	A,B,D	Yes	Yes
Delaware	N.A.	N.A.	N.A.	N.A.	N.A.
Florida	1,2,3,4,5,6,7,8	1,2,3,4,5,6,7,8	A,B,C,D	Yes	Yes
Georgia	7,8	No	A,B,C,D	Yes	Yes
Hawaii	1,2,3,4,5,6,8	3	A,D	No	Yes
Idaho	1,2,3,4,5,6,7,8	1,2,3,4,5,6,7,8	A,B,C,D	Yes	Yes
Illinois	1,2,4,5,6,7,8	2,4,5,6,7,8	A,B,C,D	Yes	Yes
Indiana	1,2,3,4,5,6,7,8	1,2,3,4,5,6,7,8	A,B,D	Yes	Yes

State	Information Assembly *	Report Preparation *	Promotional Activity **	Industrial Directory	Aid and Advice to Communities
Iowa	1,2,3,4,5,7,8	No	B,D	Yes	Yes
Kansas	1,3,4,5,6,7,8	1,3,5,6,7,8	A,B,C,D	Yes	Yes
Kentucky	1,3,4,5,6,8	1,3,4,5,6,8	A,B,C,D	Yes	Yes
Louisiana	1,2,3,4,5,6,7,8	1,2,3,4,5,6,7,8	A,B	Yes	Yes
Maine	3,4,8	No	B,C	No	Yes
Maryland	1,4,5,6,7,8	1,4,5,6,7,8	A,B,D	Yes	Yes
Massachusetts	1,2,4,5,6,7,8	4,5,6,7,8	A,B,D	Yes	Yes
Michigan	1,2.3,4,5,6,7,8	1,2,3,4,5,6,7,8	A,B	No	Yes
Minnesota	1,2,3,4,5,6,7,8	1,2,3,4,5,6,7,8	A,B,C,D	Yes	Yes
Mississippi	1,2,3,4,5,6,7,8	No	A,B,C,D	No	Yes
Missouri	1	4,5,6,7,8	B,C,D	Yes	Yes
Montana	1,2,3,4,5,6,7,8	No	No	Yes	Yes
Nebraska	1,3,4,5,6,7.8	1,3,4,5,6,7,8	A,B,C	Yes	Yes
Nevada	1,2,3,4,5,6,7,8	4,5,6,7,8	A,B,D	Yes	Yes
New Hampshire	1	4,5,6,7,8	A,D	Yes	Yes
New Jersey	1,2,4,5,6,7,8	No	D	No	No
New Mexico	1,2,3,4,5,6,7,8	1,2,3,4,5,6,7,8	A,B,C,D	Yes	Yes
New York	1,2,3,4,5,6,7,8	1,2,3,4,5,6,7,8	A,B,C	Yes	Yes
North Carolina	1,3,4,5	2,3,4,5,6,7,8	A,B,C	No	Yes
North Dakota	1,2,3,4,5,6,7,8	1,2,3,4,5,6,7,8	A,D	Yes	Yes
Ohio	1,2,3,4,5,6,7,8	No	B,D	Yes	Yes
Oklahoma	1,2,3,4,5,6,7,8	1,4,5,7,8	A,B,D	Yes	Yes
Oregon	2,4,5,6,7,8	1,3	A	Yes	Yes
Pennsylvania	1,4,5,6,7,8	1,4,5,8	A,B,C	No	Yes
Rhode Island	1,2,3,4,5,6,7,8	1,2,3,4,5,6,7,8	A,B,C,D	Yes	Yes
South Carolina	1,4,5,6,7,8	2,8	A,B,D	No	Yes
South Dakota	1,3,4,5,6,7.8	1,3	No	Yes	Yes
Tennessee	1,3,4,5,6,7.8	No	B	Yes	Yes
Texas	No	No	A,B	No	Yes
Utah	1,2,3,4,5.6,7,8	1,2,3,4,5,6,7,8	A,B,C,D	No	Yes
Vermont	N.A.	N.A.	N.A.	N.A.	N.A.
Virginia	1,2,3,4,5,6,7,8	1,2,3,4.5,6,7,8	A,B,D	Yes	Yes
Washington	1,2,3,4,5,6,7,8	1,2,3,4,5,6,7,8	A,B,C,D	Yes	Yes
West Virginia	1,3,4,5,6,7,8	1,3,4,5,6,7,8	A,B,C,D	Yes	Yes
Wisconsin	N.A.	N.A.	N.A.	N.A.	N.A.
Wyoming	1	1	A	Yes	Yes

* **Key to Types of Information:**
1. Natural Resources and Water Information
2. Wholesale Trade, Retail Trade, Services
3. Agriculture
4. Transportation
5. Labor Supply
6. Education and Culture

7. Recreation
8. Industrial Sites
** Key to Types of Activity:
A. Direct Mail
B. Advertising
C. Films
D. Tourism
N.A. Not Available

SOURCE: Adapted from "State Development Agencies: Third Annual Report," *Industrial Development and Manufacturers Record,* Vol. 134, No. 12, December 1965, pp. 14–16 (Atlanta, © Conway Research, Inc.)

All 46 of the reporting states indicated essentially the same aid and advice to local communities from state agencies. Beyond this, however, relatively little uniformity was found. Every state that reported had *some* program of technical assistance and advice to both industrial firms and local communities. This is further indication that formal assistance programs are an integral part of the industrial location process in the United States.

All state programs are designed to serve a threefold objective: to attract new industry to the state; to encourage the expansion of existing industry; and to retain existing industry, often in the face of efforts by other states to induce such industry to move. The basic underlying theme is that a broad, strong and growing industrial base is highly desirable for a state, and for the individual communities within that state. The encouragement of industrial growth and development is accepted as a fundamental tool in the economic program of any state government.

Types of Public Assistance and Aids

Public agencies can offer four major types of assistance in their efforts to influence the location of industry.

First, they can provide industrial space directly to the prospective industrial user. This may involve industrial sites, or it may mean the construction of either custom or speculative buildings. Public agencies frequently sponsor planned industrial districts. Urban redevelopment project areas designated for industrial reuse also represent sponsorship of a planned industrial area. The space may be offered at a competitively attractive, or even less than competitive, sale price or rental. This is not often necessary, however, because the mere availability of well-located and appropriate industrial space is the single most effective inducement for industry to locate in a given area.[5] This still will not offset basic locational defects, but it comes closer than any other individual factor. The difficulty, of course, is that it involves the most expense and the most risk for the governmental entity involved.

A second type of assistance commonly provided by *local* governments in particular is the installation of necessary community facilities to convert land areas into effective industrial sites. This most frequently includes the

---

[5] For details, see the discussion in William N. Kinnard, Jr. and Zenon S. Malinowski, *Highways as a Factor in Small Manufacturing Plant Locations,* Small Manufacturers Business Management Research Report (Storrs, Connecticut; University of Connecticut, 1963).

installation of water lines, sewer lines, and roads. It usually involves the use of public funds, through either increased tax levies or bond issues, to finance the development.

The third type of public assistance to industrial firms involves some sort of financial inducement. This may include direct loans from either public agencies or public corporations, or the guaranty by public agencies of loans from private sources to industrial firms. Occasionally, public funds are available for equity investment in industrial real estate. Much more frequently, a tax concession or inducement is granted, either in local property taxes, or in state income or franchise taxes. Local communities often promise (and deliver) low service charges for utilities. Public bodies which provide industrial space or industrial sites often charge rents or prices lower than going market figures.

The fourth general type of assistance offered by public bodies to industrial firms may be characterized under the general heading "encouragement." This includes providing an environment designed to make industry thrive. Appropriate local planning, zoning, and related programs often mean that the firm will be operating in an atmosphere that is conducive to its success. The attitude of the local community is also important. It cannot be quantified, but its influence in industrial locational decisions is emphasized throughout the literature. One indication of an encouraging attitude is the availability of reliable factual information about the area, and about specific individual sites within the area. In addition, public agencies frequently offer advice to individual firms on the selection of a site, the construction or selection of plant space, and the operation of the business itself. Technical assistance from federal and state agencies to encourage more efficient operations, especially in manufacturing, is a growing activity.

In addition to direct aids to industrial firms from government at all levels, there are many assistance programs from one level of government to another in the over-all effort to stimulate industrial growth and development. This is found especially in aid from federal agencies to either state agencies or local communities. In addition, every state has some sort of industrial development assistance and advisory program for local communities.

Beyond this, government at every level offers some sort of assistance to both public and private nonprofit development corporations. Most of these operate at the local community level, and are presumably independent of governmental control or influence. Nevertheless, large proportions of their funds, and a substantial amount of technical advice, come from federal, state, and local governmental sources. Both federal agencies and regional development commissions (under the aegis of the Economic Development Administration, Department of Commerce) offer advice and technical assistance to local development groups for the encouragement and stimulation of industrial expansion.

Public Ownership of Industrial Space

By making sites and/or buildings available to industrial firms, governmental units meet the single most pressing need of those industrial firms:

readily available and suitable locations. It is at the local community level that the sites or the buildings are actually provided. Federal and state (as well as regional) agencies offer both financial assistance and technical advice. Local communities provide the space. This can be seen clearly in the tabulations of federal and state assistance programs found in Exhibits 96 and 97. They show that federal and state agencies do not directly offer sites or building space.

1. *Site Availability.* Over 20 states are identified in Exhibit 97 as permitting the use of either local general obligation bonds or local revenue bonds to finance industrial facilities development. Local communities in these states may acquire land, and resell or lease it for industrial purposes. Although this is relatively unusual in practice, it is legal in nearly half the United States.

Many states which do permit local acquisition and disposal of land (independently of urban renewal programs) often stipulate that the powers may be exercised only in formally designated areas of underemployment or redevelopment. In several states, the legality of this approach has not been tested. Nevertheless, it represents a basis for local communities to attract industry by making sites available, both on highly competitive terms and selectively. The most successful programs of site development by local communities are those which do "discriminate" among potential candidates for the subsidized locations.

Finally, the local community often provides a desired industrial firm with the opportunity to finance its building by making the site available on favorable terms. This frees more credit and more funds for the construction of the building. For the relatively small, growing firm most likely to be attracted to a subsidized site, this can be critical.

2. *Building Availability.* A few states permit local communities to construct buildings for occupancy by industrial firms. This function is more commonly performed by private, local nonprofit corporations in industrial development programs. However, both shell and turnkey buildings have been successfully developed by municipalities. One study indicated that less than 1 per cent of the buildings thus provided remained vacant for any substantial period of time.[6]

Providing building space may take three forms. First, in a few instances, speculative buildings (shell or turnkey) have been constructed. In Vermont, for example, six out of seven such buildings were occupied within six months of their completion.[7] In other states, custom construction has been employed. Finally, in states such as Mississippi, local funds have been made available for expansion of existing plants to retain local employment.[8]

Although it is infrequently employed, the preparation of building space by the locality (usually financed through industrial development bonds) can be a powerful weapon in the competition for industrial growth. Interestingly,

---

[6] Edwin C. Gooding, "New War Between the States: Part III," *New England Business Review,* July, 1964 (Federal Reserve Bank of Boston), p. 3.

[7] Edwin C. Gooding, "New War Between the States: Part I," *New England Business Review,* October, 1963 (Federal Reserve Bank of Boston).

[8] Gooding, "New War Between the States: Part III," p. 5.

the question of whether the use of municipal bond financing results in "pirating" of industry is obscured by the fact that "the most common use of this type of financing is for branch plants. Some of these branches serve entirely new markets while others lead to the phasing out of older plants. . . . Although not sufficiently influential to draw industry to a region, such programs may be responsible for retaining plants in a particular community within a region." [9]

3. *Sponsorship of Planned Industrial Districts.* Governmental units occasionally sponsor planned industrial districts. This is independent of urban renewal projects for industrial reuse purposes.

Exhibit 99 shows the distribution of sponsorship of planned industrial districts in the United States found in two nationwide surveys conducted by the Urban Land Institute and the School of Business Administration of the University of Connecticut. The tabulations in Exhibit 99 indicate clearly that publicly sponsored industrial parks represent a significant portion of total planned districts. Most industrial parks sponsored by public bodies are owned and developed by *local* communities or *local* agencies; relatively few are sponsored by states, regional authorities, or port authorities.

Exhibit 99

INDUSTRIAL DISTRICTS AND PLANNED INDUSTRIAL DISTRICTS IN THE UNITED STATES BY TYPE OF SPONSOR

	Industrial Districts		*Planned Industrial Districts*			
	Number[1]	*Per Cent[1]*	*Number[1]*	*Per Cent[1]*	*Number[2]*	*Per Cent[2]*
Private Real Estate Developers	88	32.4%	70	42.4%	102	39.4%
Government Sponsored Groups	30[3]	11.0	18	10.9	28	10.8
Private Local Community Groups	48	17.6	25	15.2	59	22.8
Joint Government-Private- Local Community Groups	16	5.9	12	7.3	25	9.7
Railroads	82	30.2	33	20.0	33	12.7
Other (Utilities, Misc.)	8	2.9	7	4.2	12	4.6
Totals	272	100.0	165	100.0	259	100.0

SOURCES: Boley, Robert E., *Industrial Districts Restudied,* Technical Bulletin No. 41 (Washington, Urban Land Institute, 1961); Kinnard, William N., Jr., and Malinowski, Zenon S., *The Place of Small Business in Planned Industrial Districts,* Small Business Management Research Reports (Storrs, Connecticut: University of Connecticut, 1963).

[1] Boley, *Industrial Districts Restudied,* p. 30, Tables 1 and 2.

[2] Kinnard and Malinowski, *The Place of Small Business in Planned Industrial Districts,* p. 126.

[3] Distributed as follows: Local Governments   17
                              Federal, State, Regional   8
                              Port Authority   5

_____

[9] *Ibid.,* p. 4.

Industrial park sponsorship gives the sponsoring local community control over the character and future development of an industrial area. It calls for considerably more skill and effort than does encouragement of private development, and a substantially larger amount of money to support it. State authorization to issue industrial development bonds usually is required before the local community can finance a planned industrial district. States, regional authorities, and port authorities already have bonding authorization, so no special action is normally required for them to embark on an industrial park development program. Nevertheless, because this is a relatively risky undertaking, and because it is usually attacked as being highly competitive with private financing and development, it is not a widespread development practice. Yet where it has been employed, it has usually been quite successful.

Publicly sponsored industrial parks tend to be concentrated in smaller communities, are smaller on the average than privately sponsored industrial parks, and generally attract smaller and less well-established local concerns as occupants.[10]

4. *Urban Renewal.* The Housing Acts of 1949, 1954 and 1965, as amended, provide for the renewal and/or redevelopment of blighted areas in urban communities. Actual sponsorship is initiated and controlled by local communities and local agencies, but the bulk of the financing comes from the federal government. In many instances, state assistance is also available to local communities. The general characteristics of urban renewal programs as they apply to industrial development assistance are indicated in Exhibit 96.[11] Nevertheless, the required initiative of the local government or Local Public Agency (LPA) may be regarded as the "equity" position in an urban redevelopment project.

Industrial reuse projects have been undertaken both in downtown areas and outlying sections of cities.[12] Large-scale redevelopment for industrial use has been encouraged by amendments to the Housing Acts that permit the utilization of vacant acreage for industrial purposes. The LPA assists private industry by assembling sites (which would be prohibitive for the private firm to obtain), razing the buildings, and developing new industrial sites that make sense in terms of both location and configuration. The net cost or differential is borne by society, rather than by the industrial firms that use the newly created sites. These sites are typically sold to private industrial users, subject to substantial use restrictions.

5. *Sources of Financing.* Public development of industrial sites and

---

[10] Robert E. Boley, *Industrial Districts Restudied,* Technical Bulletin No. 41 (Washington, Urban Land Institute, 1961), pp. 30–33.

[11] For further details of urban renewal programs as they are applied to industrial development, see Economic Development Administration, U.S. Department of Commerce, *Handbook of Federal Aids to Communities* (Washington, U.S. Government Printing Office, 1966); and U.S. Office of Economic Opportunity, *Catalogue of Federal Programs for Individual and Community Improvement* (Washington, U.S. Government Printing Office, December, 1965).

[12] See Boley, *op. cit.;* and Boley, *Industrial Districts: Principles in Practice,* Technical Bulletin No. 44 (Washington, Urban Land Institute, 1963) for examples of both types. Projects in Norfolk, New Haven and Chicago illustrate close-in development. The vast Eastwick Project in Philadelphia is a dramatic example of the outlying project.

industrial buildings is financed from four basic sources. First, budget appropriations may be utilized if tax revenues can be collected in large enough amounts to support an industrial development program. This is rarely the case, although the possibility does exist. Appropriations from tax collections are more likely to be used either to support an operating development staff, or to supplement the proceeds of revenues from other sources.

Special assessments against existing property owners also rarely provide adequate funds to mount and sustain an effective industrial development program. This is particularly true for local communities.

Most commonly, local communities resort to industrial bond financing when there is authorization permitting them to do so.[13] The geographic range is indicated in Exhibit 97. Bonds are also commonly employed to finance the local share of industrial redevelopment projects. These are always general obligation bonds, whereas industrial development bonds are revenue issues at least as often as they are general obligation bonds.

Local communities, which are most often the developers of publicly created industrial space, also receive substantial amounts of financial assistance from federal and state agencies. These may take the form of loans or outright grants-in-aid. In some instances, federal or state money is utilized to supplement local funds on a participating basis. This, for example, is the case in Pennsylvania with the Pennsylvania Industrial Development Authority. The general range of federal and state aids to local communities to assist in financing local industrial development programs is indicated in Exhibits 96 and 97.

Providing Community Facilities

Modern industry cannot function effectively without adequate utilities (especially sewer and water facilities), streets and highways, and ancillary community services. Indeed, nearly 10 per cent of the 1,000 largest manufacturing firms in the United States reported that they regard the availability of facilities in advance as a decided attraction for industrial location.[14] Making necessary utilities and related community facilities available in advance is a fundamental aspect of governmental activity that can significantly affect plant location decisions.[15] Moreover, it makes the sites and buildings that are made available considerably more productive.

Most of the actual responsibility for utilities, streets, and related facilities is at the local governmental level—the local sewer authority actually lays the sewer line; the municipality extends the street. Much of the money that finances these development programs, however, comes from state and federal sources. The general outlines of the major types of financial assistance to local communities for necessary community facilities to assist in industrial

---

[13] Gooding, "New War Between the States: Part III," pp. 2–7; Advisory Commission on Intergovernmental Relations, *Industrial Development Bond Financing* (Washington, U.S. Government Printing Office, June, 1963), pp. 53–57.

[14] Gooding, "New War Between the States: Part III," pp. 4–5.

[15] This is confirmed by the findings in Kinnard and Malinowski, *op. cit.* See also Robert A. Will, "Federal Influences on Industrial Location: How Expensive?" *Land Economics*, February, 1964.

development programs are given in Exhibits 96 and 97. Both planning and construction of sewer, water, and highway facilities are usually heavily financed with federal and state assistance.

Many programs offer financing on particularly favorable terms to areas which are designated as being underdeveloped, or as having chronic unemployment problems.

At both the state and local level—but most especially locally—tax-exempt bonds are issued to finance the installation of utilities, streets, and other community facilities to support industrial development. There is widespread controversy over the propriety of using the tax-exempt status of municipal bonds in this way, especially when industrial expansion efforts are competitive among many localities within the same state or region. It is argued that this is an improper use of public funds, and discriminates among beneficiaries unfairly. In addition, it is contended that communities may overextend their credit facilities, but that firms not in need of any assistance will still take advantage of it. Finally, it is deplored as a means of "pirating" industry from one area to another.[16]

As a partial remedy against the charge of "pirating," at least, many federal programs carry a stipulation that no federal funds may be expended to provide facilities that will result in the transfer of employment or incomes from one area to another. In addition, many states and a few federal agencies require that facilities bonding be restricted to underdeveloped or chronically depressed areas. These conditions are partially explained in Exhibits 96 and 97.

Federal agencies in particular, and some state agencies as well, offer technical advice and assistance to local communities for the preparation of plans and specifications for utilities, highway, and community facility developments. By making the planned developments as efficient and effective as possible, this type of assistance can be even more useful than a simple outlay of money.

Whatever the merits or propriety of financing community facilities to support industrial expansion programs through the use of tax-exempt development bonds, its use is expanding.

Financial Assistance

An almost endless variety of financing devices and techniques is available to assist both industrial firms and local communities in publicly initiated industrial development efforts. A detailed listing of the various alternatives is essentially meaningless on two counts. First, it would require a volume many times the size of the present book. Second, and even more important, there is such continuing change in this dynamic and competitive field that any listing would be outmoded before it could be published.

Therefore, in the presentation here, emphasis is placed on the general kinds of financial assistance provided, the sources, the recipients, and the funding of the programs.

---

[16] Advisory Commission on Intergovernmental Relations, *op. cit.*, pp. 3–17; Gooding, "New War Between the States: Part III," pp. 3–5.

1. *Types of Financial Assistance.* As indicated in Exhibits 96 and 97, there are four major types of direct financial assistance to industrial firms, local governments, or development corporations from public agencies: direct lending; loan guaranty or underwriting; equity investments and grants; and tax inducements or concessions. In addition, a fifth type of concession which represents a financial advantage is the charging of low rents or low prices for industrial space, or the levying of low charges for community services. In this context, "low" means lower than going market rates. The objective is to provide a competitive advantage for the governmental agency granting the concession, and an attraction to the industrial firm receiving it.

a. *Lending.* Direct loans from public agencies or public supported organizations are often available to finance the acquisition or construction of industrial plants. This is especially true for manufacturing establishments, since they are more likely to increase employment in a given area. State Development Credit Corporations, as noted in Exhibit 97, are usually quasi-independent corporations established by state charter. They combine funds from both public and private sources to *supplement* private lending programs. Direct lending by state governments or state agencies, on the other hand, is usually accomplished through State Industrial Finance Authorities. The industrial real estate broker should investigate carefully the details of any program in the state in which he is operating.[17]

Federal loan funds are available both to specified types of industrial firms, especially small businesses, and to industrial development corporations. The latter in turn may make funds available directly to industrial firms. The basic outlines of these federal loan programs are provided in Exhibit 96.

Because they are often aimed at special groups of industrial firms, or seek to encourage development in certain designated areas, direct loans commonly require lower than market rates of interest and offer more favorable loan terms than are found on "regular" industrial loans. The difficulty lies in qualifying. Moreover, favorable loan terms cannot entirely offset otherwise unfavorable locational factors. For example, California has experienced a boom in industrial development without any public aids or incentives, while on the other hand, New Hampshire and Pennsylvania have experienced major declines in industrial employment and income despite the fact that they offer a wide range of financial inducements to industry. Although the pattern is very mixed, it appears that lending either directly by a state agency or indirectly through a state development credit corporation is more typical in northern states, as is the guaranty or underwriting of private loans (primarily mortgage loans) to industrial firms.[18]

b. *Loan Guaranty or Underwriting.* The so-called "New England Plan" for providing financial assistance to industrial firms as an inducement to locate within a state involves the guaranty or underwriting of a

---

[17] For a detailed discussion, see Gooding, "New War Between the States: Part I and Part II"; and American Industrial Development Council, *op. cit.*

[18] See Gooding, "New War Between the States: Part I and Part II."

private loan to an industrial firm. This is usually achieved through an Industrial Building Authority, which adds its credit to that of the industrial firm.

This process is based on loan insurance, and has been called an "industrial FHA." "An industrial building authority is essentially a state-sponsored loan insurance program for industrial buildings. In principle it is quite similar to the FHA. . . . The state authority insures a loan ranging up to 90 per cent of the land and building costs. . . . To back the loan, the state pledges its full faith and credit and usually provides a reserve fund for claims in the case of a default." [19]

As Exhibit 97 indicates, industrial loan guaranty programs are not widespread. They are concentrated in the New England states. The experience of industrial loan insurance programs has been quite good since their inception. Loan insurance premiums are charged to the borrower, usually equal to 0.5 to 1.0 per cent of the outstanding balance of the loan.

To be effective, a loan insurance program must have the cooperation of local private lending institutions. State officials in those areas in which industrial loan insurance is operative are unanimous in their support of the principle and its effectiveness. By making the loan more marketable, insurance makes it more attractive to the private lender in the first instance. In brief, "a state program for industrial mortgage insurance makes risk credit available to some capital-shy firms with good income prospects." [20] Industrial loan insurance or guaranty is an activity of state government exclusively.

c. *Equity Investments and Grants.* Local communities rarely make equity investments or direct grants in manufacturing firms. If equity investment funds *are* made available, they are placed in the real estate by the local community.

On the other hand, federal and state programs exist to provide funds to local communities and to community development corporations as either grants or investments. As indicated in Exhibit 96, for example, grants may be obtained through the Economic Development Administration (EDA) and the Department of Housing and Urban Development (HUD), both for planning and for constructing local water and sewer facilities. Grants are also available to local communities from HUD to finance urban redevelopment projects, including those with industrial reuse plans. Equity investment funds are offered by the Small Business Administration to Small Business Investment Corporations to provide these SBIC's with operating funds. SBIC's in turn may invest in equities, or make loans to small industrial firms. [21]

d. *Tax Inducements and Concessions.* Tax inducements are more widely applied in southern states, and represent the major portion of the program of industrial inducement offered in the South. Tax concessions may be

---

[19] See Gooding, "New War Between the States: Part II," p. 2.

[20] *Ibid.*

[21] For further details on these and other grant programs, see American Industrial Development Council, *op. cit.;* Economic Development Administration, *op. cit.;* and U.S. Office of Economic Opportunity, *op. cit.*

granted by either local governments or state governments, or both. Local governments generally allow property tax exemptions or reductions. Exemptions may be permanent, or limited to a specified period of time. They may also be granted for the initial plant, but not for additions. Certain states allow local property tax exemptions to specified industries only, while others permit local concessions in depressed areas only.

Tax reductions or "tax understandings" (the former legal and open; the latter extra-legal and negotiated) often substitute for full exemption from property taxes. Whether it takes the form of an exemption, a reduction, an abatement, or a remission of property taxes, the inducement results in reduced operating costs to the affected industry. Despite arguments that property tax reductions or concessions place existing local firms at a competitive disadvantage, as well as reducing the effective local tax base, the practice continues in at least 20 states.

Over 35 states provide some form of free-port exemption for goods earmarked for interstate shipment. "These laws have already yielded substantial tax savings for industry and have led to the establishment of some large distribution centers in free-port states to the disadvantage of their neighbors." [22] Free-port treatment of goods may apply to all items in interstate transit, or to specified products only. Several states allow accelerated depreciation, which reduces state income tax liability during the period of rapid write-off. Other states grant exemptions from excise taxes or reductions in the state income tax for a specified period for new industries.

Although it is argued in some quarters that competitive tax concessions lead only to a re-allocation of industry on a less than efficient basis, many officials of major industrial firms regard tax concessions as significant factors in industrial plant location decisions.[23] Yet tax concessions are basically contrary to the rationale of industrial development programs, because they reduce the tax base of a community. For this and other reasons, "it appears unlikely that traditional property tax concessions will gain the widespread acceptance of other forms of industrial development promotion. Nevertheless, it seems probable that such concessions will continue to be part of the industrial development programs of more rural and less prosperous areas." [24]

A final consideration of importance is that the purchasers of local or state bonds do not have to pay federal income taxes on the interest received from those bonds. This tax-exempt feature of "municipals" means that lower-than-market interest rates can be used to finance private occupancy of industrial space in projects supported with local or state industrial bond proceeds. Whatever the moral arguments against the use of such bond financing, it can give a competitive advantage to a firm by reducing its occupancy costs.

[22] Edwin C. Gooding, "New War Between the States: Part IV," *New England Business Review*, October, 1964 (Federal Reserve Bank of Boston), p. 2.
[23] Gooding, "New War Between the States: Part III," p. 6.
[24] Gooding, "New War Between the States: Part IV," p. 6. See also William M. Shenkel, *Principles and Practices of Industrial Real Estate: A Course Syllabus* (Washington, Society of Industrial Realtors, 1963), Chapter 4.

e. *Low Rents, Prices or Service Charges.* Local communities offer a substantial inducement to industrial firms that are sought as local "residents," when sites or buildings are available at less-than-market rates. Concessions in water and sewer charges can be equally effective. They have essentially the same effect as tax concessions, and have the advantage of not upsetting a community-wide pattern of assessment and taxation. They may not be quite as apparent to industrial firms already located in the community. Not all industries occupy land or buildings owned by the community or by a local development corporation; all do pay taxes, however. As a public relations device, concessions in charges, rather than concessions in levies, are often more palatable to the general public.

2. *Sources of Financial Assistance.* Federal and state agencies make loans to industrial firms. State agencies insure private loans to industrial firms. Property tax concessions are made by local governments; income and excise tax concessions, as well as free-port arrangements, are made by state governments. Rent and price concessions, and reductions in service charges, are granted by local governments.

The industrial real estate broker should familiarize himself with the different types of financial incentives that are available from government, and he should maintain current knowledge about changes in policies and programs. A working library of references, providing detailed information of the types summarized in Exhibits 96 and 97, is a necessary tool for the broker seeking to work effectively with industrial firms or community development groups.

Federal, state, and local governments all provide assistance to local nonprofit community development organizations. The Small Business Administration, for example, makes loans to state and local development companies. This allows them to make long-term loans or equity investments to small business. State development corporations and other financial agencies often provide local development corporations with initial working capital. They also occasionally guarantee loans from banks to development corporations; in such cases as the Pennsylvania Industrial Development Authority, they also participate in loans made by local development groups. This enhances the effectiveness of the funds from the local industrial development corporations themselves. Finally, local governments are often major investors in, or lenders to, their own local development corporations, particularly to provide "seed money" to initiate a development program.

Federal funds are available to both state and local governments for grants, loans, and planning advances. States often supply funds to local communities to supplement federal grants. For example, eligible redevelopment projects in the state of Connecticut may receive a state grant equal to one-half the local community's share of total net project costs.

Confronted with an array of alternative opportunities potentially available to finance local industrial development efforts, the broker must familiarize himself with the specifics of locally pertinent programs, so that every opportunity for any client can be effectively and meaningfully exploited.

3. *Funding of Public Financial Assistance.* Local communities can

and do receive loans, grants, and advances from both federal and state sources to assist in financing many aspects of their industrial development programs. The federal programs themselves are financed by regular budget appropriations from tax revenues. Similarly, both state and local governments may raise taxes to meet appropriations of financial assistance to industries that are hopefully being attracted to the locality. In limited circumstances, special assessments have also been effectively employed. The most powerful and the most widely employed method of funding public financial assistance to industrial development, however, is the use of tax-exempt bonds.

Despite the reservations, voiced by federal authorities in particular, about the propriety of using the tax-exempt status of municipal bonds to finance selective programs of assistance to industrial firms, municipal bonding remains the most frequent and the most vigorously supported method of funding public financial assistance to industry.

The relative strength of municipal bonding presents a dilemma for regions where it has not been used. This powerful device provides an industrial property with tax exemption plus a low-interest, long-term supply of capital. . . . The use of municipal bonding for industrial building has served a useful function in southern rural areas in financing small-scale industries which lack access to a capital market. In effect, these industries may have brought employment to previously unemployed and low skilled farm laborers who were displaced by farm mechanization, but tied to the community by family, limited skills, or inertia. . . . Municipal bonding, however, entails two important drawbacks. From the point of view of the locality, this device deeply involves local governments in the ownership of industrial property. From the federal viewpoint, widespread use of municipal bonds would result in further erosion of the federal tax base.[25]

Other Public Assistance

Public agencies and local communities offer non-financial as well as financial assistance to encourage industrial development. These aids fall under three general headings: the provision of an appropriate environment for the growth and development of industry; the provision of both technical and business counsel; and promotional, advertising, and public relations efforts.

1. *Environment.* Creating an atmosphere of encouragement to industry, particularly by a local government, cannot be overemphasized. The local community can do a great deal about its own image in its efforts to attract desirable industry. In seeking a location which will serve its needs, industry considers a number of intangible factors that indicate community interest. As far as human relations and employee relations are concerned, the industrial firm is attracted to a community whose cultural, recreational, and educational facilities will promote employee satisfaction. A community that is stable and has a reputation for good, honest government has a decided advantage in competing for most industrial firms. The attitude of existing local industry toward newcomers, and the desirability of these existing local firms as neighbors for newcomers are further considerations.

[25] Gooding, "New War Between the States: Part IV," pp. 6–7.

Finally, the prestige of the "mailing address" is often a public relations factor.

The local community can also provide an appropriate environment for industry through its community improvement program. Sound community planning, supplemented with appropriate zoning and subdivision regulations, can forestall many of the conflicts that inharmonious uses and unsuitable neighbors produce. Moreover, a fair but firm and continuing program of code enforcement, that is applied equally to all industrial establishments in the community, can generate a park-like atmosphere for the entire town. If there are still spots of blight or substandard development that require surgical treatment, urban redevelopment is a tool at the disposal of the local community.

These measures are not entirely non-financial because they require the expenditure of public funds and the allocation of public resources. At the same time, the inducements to industrial firms seeking a location are environmental rather than monetary.

Federal programs and state laws can provide both the funding and the legal opportunity for local communities to act. Local action is necessary, however, if this encouragement to industrial development is to be generated. The broker advising a local community in its industrial development program can render a significant service by insisting that professionals be brought in to develop the necessary controls within which industry can be attracted and can be expected to thrive.

2. *Business and Technical Advice.* Programs of advice and counsel to industrial firms are rarely available from local governments. Instead, state and federal assistance must be channeled appropriately by local authorities.

At the federal level, as the summary tabulation in Exhibit 96 indicates, several advisory programs are available. The Small Business Administration provides management and technical assistance to small businesses. This includes both training courses and counseling (possibly through the SCORE program) to individual small industrial firms. On occasion, local community groups may also be counseled on the appropriate way to attempt to attract industry. The U.S. Department of Commerce has a State Technical Services Program which permits states to establish centers for the dissemination of technological information. This effort is designed to stimulate economic and industrial growth and development within the area in question. The basic idea is to bring the most current production and management information to the attention of the industrial firms, and to put technological developments to work on the production line. The program is aimed particularly at manufacturing industry, although modern materials handling and office management methods are also included in technical services programs.

State agencies frequently offer assistance to municipalities by conducting or sponsoring local community analyses that can be presented to industrial prospects. They also provide technical help to local planning and zoning boards, and advise community industrial financing organizations on the most effective techniques. As the tabulation in Exhibit 98 shows, every state which responded to a national questionnaire survey indicated that these services were actually provided to local community groups.

3. *Advertising and Public Relations.* By publicizing their programs and the firms that have benefited from them, both municipalities and states perform a joint service to industrial prospects and industrial real estate brokers. Industrial managements are informed about what their competition is doing, and what alternatives are available to them. The broker has an opportunity to discover what is current in industrial development. He learns what actions public agencies are taking in their efforts to offset the influence of open market forces. In this way, he is much better equipped to advise his clients on the most appropriate course of action. He is also better equipped through this same knowledge to advise local communities which efforts appear effective, and which ones do not particularly influence industrial decision-makers.

Marketing Publicly Sponsored Development Projects

Experience in industrial development programs indicates that local governmental groups in particular need an appreciation of the role that can be played by professional advisers in stimulating industrial development. For the objectives of both industrial firms and local communities to be met, there should be effective cooperation between brokers and local industrial development officials.

Brokers' fees must be paid if appropriate industry is to be attracted to the locality. This means gaining the type of industry that the community is seeking to attract. It also means expeditious marketing of available space.

In many instances, the community or public agency will also retain a real estate consultant. He is not a sales agent, but serves as an adviser to the community. Exclusive sales agencies are sometimes bad politics, even though the arrangement may make good sense economically. The reason is that favoritism or discrimination may be claimed, whether founded in fact or not. The result can be confusion and undermining of the sales campaign to the detriment of all concerned.

When a community hires a consultant on retainer, he should not be involved in any way with the sale or leasing of land or buildings. Any broker bringing in an industrial firm that buys or locates in the area still receives his appropriate commission.

The most common decision that must be made about disposition is whether to sell or to lease land or buildings. In most instances, the choice is to lease. The reason is that the local community retains control over the land. In addition, community development programs are particularly attractive to newer and smaller industrial firms. Economizing on the amount of their capital that must be invested in real estate is a decided financial advantage.

Depending upon the objectives of the community industrial development program, there may be restrictions on the types of users permitted in certain areas. Discrimination among industrial prospects will generally favor manufacturing establishments because they offer the prospect of greater increases in employment and in the tax base. The broker must bear in mind throughout all his dealings with public industrial development organizations that their major objective is to enhance the economic base and the employment base of the area. Serving the specific needs of industry is a secondary consideration for public development groups.

LOCAL INDUSTRIAL DEVELOPMENT CORPORATIONS

Local industrial development corporations are usually private, nonprofit organizations organized to stimulate industrial growth in a particular locality. They are not chartered by the state, although they may require legal authorization through state legislation in the same way that any private corporation requires an enabling legislative base. A local industrial development corporation is *not* a public agency, even though its objectives are basically consistent with those of the community that it seeks to serve. It may be called a community improvement corporation, or an industrial development corporation, or simply a development corporation. Its detailed characteristics will vary widely; its basic character is essentially the same, however.

Organization and Financing of Local Development Corporations

Depending in part upon prevailing state and local law, and in part upon the original impetus for a local industrial development program, the industrial development corporation may be a separately organized private corporation, or it may be an adjunct to the local Chamber of Commerce. It may also have quasi-governmental status within the local community. Other nonprofit community service groups may be the original sponsors.[26]

Whatever the initial source of funds and organization, the industrial development corporation must have a broad base of community participation and representation if it is to be successful. It must, in effect, truly represent the viewpoint of the community.

Although there are variations from state to state in the specific authority given to industrial development corporations, they typically have the power to buy, own (or hold), sell, and rent both land and buildings. In most states, they are also empowered to lend money to industrial firms for the purchase or construction of industrial plants. Unlike Small Business Investment Corporations, however, local industrial development corporations usually cannot invest directly in industrial firms. Their purpose is community development, rather than profit as such. Indeed, most are chartered and operated as nonprofit organizations.

1. *Sources of Funds.* Industrial development corporations obtain funds from a broad range of sources. The actual donors effectively exploited in any given situation will depend in part upon the character and organization of the individual development corporation, and in part upon applicable state law.

---

[26] For details of the organization of industrial development corporations, see Howard D. Bessire, *Techniques of Industrial Development* (El Paso, Texas; Hill Printing Co., 1965), Chapters 11–12.

The most common method for raising money for industrial development corporations is by public subscription. These are private contributions or "investments" which are rarely, if ever, repaid. They provide the "seed money" for a revolving fund that is the basis of the initial operations of the organization. Donations or subscriptions are solicited from private individuals, community organizations such as the Chamber of Commerce or the local board of trade, and local business establishments. Utility companies and railroads often contribute both funds and advice to help initiate the local development corporation.

Local government funds are often made available as an initial contribution to the development corporation. In addition, some states permit local communities to levy a limited tax specifically earmarked for the support of a local industrial development corporation. This is the case in Connecticut, for example.

If sufficient pledges are received, local financial institutions will often advance funds to the development corporation. These usually have to be secured either with a pledge of any property that the corporation may own or with the endorsements of a number of substantial citizens who lend their credit as well as their money to the undertaking.

State loan and grant programs are operative in many areas, making funds available to local development groups. More significantly, the Small Business Administration has a program of loans to state and local development companies to provide them with funds that may in turn be loaned to, or invested in, small industrial firms. Since most local industrial development programs are aimed at the smaller, newer, riskier firm, this SBA program has a broader appeal than might appear at first glance. Local private nonprofit development organizations are also eligible for matching grants from the Economic Development Administration for the construction of public works facilities to encourage industrial development.

Within this spectrum of sources of funds, the organizers of a local nonprofit industrial development corporation *must* generate enough money to mount and sustain an effective program of industrial development and expansion. The most serious handicap is undercapitalization at the start. This becomes a chronic problem which is often difficult, if not impossible, to cure.

One method of reducing the continuing need for funds is for the nonprofit corporation to achieve tax-exempt status. For example, the Philadelphia Industrial Development Corporation is organized so that, under a ruling from the Internal Revenue Service, interest paid to holders of PIDC's mortgage obligations is exempt from federal income tax. Thus, PIDC is able to borrow long-term money at interest rates lower than going competitive market rates.

Types of Assistance to Industry

The services performed by local industrial development corporations depend to a large extent on what is permitted by state legislation, as well as the specific economic needs of the community involved. In general, however, four types of assistance or service to industry can be identified.

1. *Provision of Sites and Plants.* As with local governments, local industrial development corporations can and do acquire land, and then make sites available to individual industrial firms. They also construct buildings on either a custom or a speculative basis. If the construction is speculative, the building may be either a shell or a turnkey structure. A survey in New England revealed that of the first 21 speculative industrial buildings sponsored by community development groups, 16 were turnkey buildings and five were shell structures.[27]

Whether the development corporation makes sites or buildings available, it usually leases space. It thereby maintains control over the area for future development. Leasing also helps economize on the funds of the industrial firm. Since the relatively new or small firm is particularly attracted to communties offering financial assistance, this is a further inducement.

One development organization which has operated successfully over a relatively long period of time is the Philadelphia Industrial Development Corporation. PIDC takes advantages of tax exemption of the interest that it pays to borrow at low rates, and then enters into a build-lease agreement with any company whose credit is strong enough to support the following kind of project:

"A. PIDC will acquire and fully develop an industrial site selected by your company in Philadelphia.

"B. In cooperation with your company, PIDC will arrange for construction of a new plant built to your specifications.

"C. PIDC will lease this plant to your company at a low rental reflecting its lower financing costs.

OR

"D. PIDC will purchase any existing available building, renovate it to your specifications, finance it against your lease, and rent it to you on the same advantageous terms.

"PIDC becomes the owner, mortgagor, and lessor of the property. Your company becomes a tenant. An option to purchase can be negotiated." [28]

In addition to individual site or building development, local industrial development corporations are frequent sponsors of industrial parks. The information in Exhibit 99 shows that private local community groups are the third most frequent sponsors of planned industrial districts throughout the United States. If joint sponsorship by local community groups and private developers is included, local industrial development organizations are overshadowed only by the private real estate developers in the number of planned districts sponsored and operated throughout the United States. These are, as might be expected, concentrated in smaller communities. They also generally have smaller firms as occupants, and are not usually as large as districts sponsored by railroads or private developers. Never-

---

[27] Federal Reserve Bank of Boston, "Speculative Industrial Building," *New England Business Review,* November, 1959.

[28] Philadelphia Industrial Development Corporation, *Help for Industry "On the Grow" in Philadelphia,* undated promotional brochure, p. 2.

theless, collectively they represent an important force in the industrial development field. The Committee of 100 of Tampa, Florida, is one example
of a community-sponsored group that manages a successful industrial park.

2. *Provision of Facilities.* When necessary, and when possible by virtue
of sufficient funds and legal authorization, local industrial development
groups also install utilities and streets to open up new areas for industrial
use. This is a saving both to the local community and to the industrial firm
seeking a suitable location. The Economic Development Administration
makes grants available to local industrial development groups to finance
such developments in "eligible areas." Public facilities loans equal to 100
per cent of the project cost are also available from the Department of Housing and Urban Development to private nonprofit development corporations
in communities of less than 10,000 population. If it can take advantage of
these programs, the local development corporation can enhance the community's appeal to industrial users, with no direct or immediate cost to
either the municipality or the individual industrial firm.

3. *Financial Assistance.* Local industrial development corporations are
sometimes empowered to make loans, although these are much less common than are loans and financial aids from public bodies. The most common
form of financial assistance offered by development corporations is a sub-
sidy through low rents or below-market prices for land and buildings. As
already noted, the Philadelphia Industrial Development Corporation passes
on the advantage of its tax exempt status to participating industrial firms
in the form of reduced rents. Lower rents are a decided operating advantage
to the industrial firm, and can have a significant influence on its location
decision.

4. *Non-Financial Assistance.* The local industrial development corporation can assist the industrial firm in advertising and public relations
activities, and may represent it before local zoning boards, utilities companies, tax boards, or financial institutions. Thus, the development corporation, in effect, often serves as the local agent for the incoming industrial
firm, bargaining for concessions or the most favorable treatment possible.
To the extent that their staff skills permit, industrial development corporations also offer management advice and technical assistance for new firms
moving into the area.

Marketing Policy

Many local industrial development corporations are less likely to pay
commissions to brokers as a matter of course than are other types of developers or sponsors. Part of the reason is that they are operating on relatively
tight budgets and narrow margins. In addition, the staff and its advisory
committee often feel that their efforts are most instrumental in creating the
proper atmosphere and attracting an industrial prospect. As a result, many
development corporations expect the broker to seek his commission from
the industrial prospect.

This attitude prompts many industrial brokers not to seek business with
industrial development corporations in small communities. Substantial edu-

cation of local development officials is required with respect to broker co-operation and the payment of fees. The industrial real estate broker working with such an organization should make sure that his fee is protected in advance of any substantial effort, so as to avoid difficulty and even possible litigation later.

In the words of one S.I.R.:

"The industrial broker is needed most *after* the research is done, assuming that the research is done well. In other words, many can perform the research functions, but it takes a real professional to perform the basic industrial brokerage function. Aside from 'incubator cities,' such as New York, Philadelphia and Cleveland, the community *must* hire men who have local knowledge of the industries involved and local knowledge of the area. The community group *must* pay brokers, or it will not attract the services of competent brokers. In other words, the broker should be paid by the industrial development group, rather than the industrial firm he brings to the community. Industrial brokers are busy, valuable men. To get the job of industrial development done properly, professionals are needed. The only way to attract professionals is to pay them." [29]

UTILITY COMPANIES

Electric utilities, gas utilities, and railroads often cooperate with local communities and with industrial firms in efforts to find appropriate locations for industry. The motivation is twofold. In the first place, an appropriately located industrial customer within the franchise or service area will increase business. A utility company will sell more gas or electricity to the firm; a railroad will receive more freight revenues. Secondly, continued economic and industrial growth of local communities within the franchise or service area also increases the total volume of business generated for the utility company or the railroad.

To this end, most utility companies and railroads maintain industrial development staffs of skilled, experienced personnel who work with both industrial prospects and community development groups. Because their profits or returns are dependent more on the continued operation of industrial firms in the area rather than on the sale or leasing of the real estate itself, utilities and railroads are closer to community development groups than to private investors in their motivations and in their mode of behavior.

Railroads are frequently major sponsors of planned industrial districts, as the data in Exhibit 99 clearly show. When they are industrial district sponsors, railroad companies often make space available at 20–40 per cent below going market prices (or rents).[30] Their basic profit orientation is reflected in the fact that most railroad-sponsored industrial districts are limited to heavy users of rail freight.

Utility companies are not frequent sponsors of industrial parks. In the few cases in which an electric utility has developed a planned industrial district, no restrictions on the type of occupant based on electrical power usage have been imposed. The utility company counts on total new business

[29] Statement of James E. Hanson, S.I.R., Hackensack, New Jersey.
[30] Interview with Irving Korb, S.I.R., Oakland, California.

generated to produce profits, as well as any gains from the development and sale of sites. Neither railroads nor utilities concentrate on either sale or lease. They simply make space available on the best terms they can, to users that seem most attractive from the developer's point of view.

Although utility companies often subscribe funds to help start local development corporations, neither utilities nor railroads are significant lenders in the industrial development field. Their primary role is non-financial. The industrial development staff of the railroad or utility company will provide technical advice and assistance to both industrial prospects and local community development groups. They advise local groups on advertising and public relations campaigns. More and more, they offer advice and assistance in the creation of a proper environment for the encouragement of industry through planning, zoning, and subdivision regulation. They offer advice on the kinds and locations of sewer and water lines necessary to serve the type of industry that is being sought. They provide counsel on the extension and location of access roads to new areas. They help in circularizing industrial firms seeking new (or branch) locations, and in attracting them to communities within their franchise or service areas.

In addition to cooperating with the leadership of the local community, the industrial development staff of the typical utility company or railroad also works closely with state and regional development commission staff personnel. Most importantly, they seek out suitable sites for industrial firms that come to them for help.

Because their interest is in attracting industry to their franchise area rather than making a profit on real estate transactions, most utility companies and railroads will protect the interests of the industrial real estate broker. Nevertheless, the broker dealing with a utility company or railroad should reach a clear agreement in advance of negotiations and final settlement, so that there will be no difficulty about the payment of fees at a later date. When a client is looking at sites in several different utilities' franchise areas, there *is* a conflict between the interest of the utility or railroad industrial development staff, and that of the broker. If this conflict can be overcome, however, there is a substantial advantage in having professionals on both sides of the transaction working together for a common cause.

SELECTED REFERENCES

American Industrial Development Council, "Guide to Federal Development Legislation—1965," Special Issue of *A.I.D.C. Journal,* Vol. I, No. 2, April, 1966:
    Foley, Eugene: "Public Works and Economic Development Act";
    Hollomon, J. H.: "Technology for New and Existing Industry";
    Lindley, Jonathan: "Regional Action for Economic Development";
    McAuliff, Joseph: "State Economic Development Programs";
    Roterus, Victor: "Legislation and Industrial Development in 1965";
    Schussheim, Morton: "Housing and Urban Development Act of 1965."

Bessire, Howard D., *Techniques of Industrial Development* (El Paso, Texas; Hill Printing, 1965).

Federal Reserve Bank of Boston, "New War Between the States," Parts I–IV, *New England Business Review,* October, 1963, December, 1963, July, 1964, October, 1964.

New York State Department of Commerce, Division of Economic Research and Statistics, *The Use of Public Funds or Credit in Industrial Location,* Research Bulletin No. 6 (Albany, N.Y.; The Author, October, 1963).

Roterus, Victor, "Reservation of Land for Industry," Speech before the Southeastern Virginia Regional Planning Commission, Norfolk, Virginia, November 10, 1961.

Shenkel, William M., *Principles and Practices of Industrial Real Estate: A Course Syllabus* (Washington, Society of Industrial Realtors, 1963).

Society of Industrial Realtors, *Advanced Course in the Techniques of Industrial Real Estate,* Northwestern University, August 1964 (Washington, The Author, 1964):
    Binswanger, Frank G., Jr., "Techniques in the Rehabilitation and Marketing of Problem Properties."

Society of Industrial Realtors, *Industrial Location Incentives* (Washington, The Author, 1956).

Society of Industrial Realtors, *Urban Renewal and the Real Estate Market* (Washington, The Author, 1964).

U.S. Advisory Commission of Intergovernmental Relations, *Industrial Development Bond Financing* (Washington, The Author, 1963).

U.S. Department of Commerce, Economic Development Administration, *Handbook of Federal Aids to Communities* (Washington, U.S. Government Printing Office, 1966).

U.S. Office of Economic Opportunity, *Catalog of Federal Programs for Individual and Community Improvement* (Washington, U.S. Government Printing Office, December, 1965).

U.S. Small Business Administration, *Loan Sources in the Federal Government,* Bulletin No. 52 (Washington, U.S. Government Printing Office).

U.S. Small Business Administration, *SBIC Financing for Small Business,* Bulletin No. OPI-13 (Washington, U.S. Government Printing Office).

Will, Robert A., "Federal Influences on Industrial Location: How Extensive?" *Land Economics,* February, 1964.

Index